PRENTICE HALL
Realidades

Guided Practice
Activities

PEARSON
Prentice
Hall

Boston, Massachusetts
Upper Saddle River, New Jersey

ISBN 0-13-166023-3

11 12 13 14 15 16 V004 13 12 11 10 09

Table of Contents

Dear Parents and Guardians:

Learning a second language can be both exciting and fun. As your child studies Spanish, he or she will not only learn to communicate with Spanish speakers, but will also learn about their cultures and daily lives. Language learning is a building process that requires considerable time and practice, but it is one of the most rewarding things your child can learn in school.

Language learning calls on all of the senses and on many skills that are not necessarily used in other kinds of learning. Students will find their Spanish class different from other classes in a variety of ways. For instance, lectures generally play only a small role in the language classroom. Because the goal is to learn to communicate, students interact with each other and with their teacher as they learn to express themselves about things they like to do (and things they don't), their personalities, the world around them, foods, celebrations, pastimes, technology, and much more. Rather than primarily listening to the teacher, reading the text, and memorizing information as they might in a social studies class, language learners will share ideas; discuss similarities and differences between cultures; ask and answer questions; and work with others to practice new words, sounds, and sentence structures. Your child will be given a variety of tasks to do in preparation for such an interactive class. He or she will complete written activities, perform listening tasks, watch and listen to videos, and go on the Internet. In addition, to help solidify command of words and structures, time will need to be spent on learning vocabulary and practicing the language until it starts to become second nature. Many students will find that using flash cards and doing written practice will help them become confident using the building blocks of language.

To help you help your child in this endeavor, we offer the following insights into the textbook your child will be using, along with suggestions for ways that you can help build your child's motivation and confidence—and as a result, their success with learning Spanish.

Textbook Organization

Your child will be learning Spanish using **REALIDADES**, which means "realities." The emphasis throughout the text is on learning to use the language in authentic, real ways. Chapters are organized by themes such as school life, food and health, family and celebrations, etc. At the beginning of each **Tema** (*theme*) is a section called **A ver si recuerdas**, which reviews key vocabulary and grammar from first-year Spanish as it relates to the individual theme of the upcoming chapter. Each chapter begins with a section called **A primera vista** (*At First Glance*), which gives an initial presentation of new grammar and vocabulary in the form of pictures, short dialogues, audio recordings, and video. Once students have been exposed to the new language, the **Manos a la obra** (*Let's Get to Work*) section offers lots of practice with the language as well as explanations of how the language works. The third section, **¡Adelante!** (*Moving Ahead!*), provides activities for your child to use the language by understanding readings, giving oral or written presentations, and learning more about the cultural perspectives of Spanish speakers. Finally, all chapters conclude with an at-a-glance review of the chapter material called **Repaso del capítulo** (*Chapter Review*), with summary lists and charts, and practice activities like those on the chapter test. If students have trouble with a given task, the **Repaso del capítulo** tells them where in the chapter they can go to review.

Here are some suggestions that will help your child become a successful language learner.

Routine:
Provide a special, quiet place for study, equipped with a Spanish-English dictionary, pens or pencils, paper, computer, and any other items your child's teacher suggests.

- Encourage your child to study Spanish at a regular time every day. A study routine will greatly facilitate the learning process.

Strategy:

- Remind your child that class participation and memorization are very important in a foreign language course.
- Tell your child that in reading or listening activities, as well as in the classroom, it is not necessary to understand every word. Suggest that they listen or look for key words to get the gist of what's being communicated.
- Encourage your child to ask questions in class if he or she is confused. Remind the child that other students may have the same question. This will minimize frustration and help your child succeed.

Real-life connection:

- Outside of the regular study time, encourage your child to review words in their proper context as they relate to the chapter themes. For example, when studying the chapter about community places, Capítulo 3B, have your child bring flash cards for place names on a trip into town and review words for the places you pass along the way. Similarly, while studying Capítulo 4A vocabulary, bring out family photos and remind your child of the toys he or she used to have and the activities that he or she liked. Ask your child to name the toys and activities in Spanish. If your child can include multiple senses while studying (see the school and say *escuela*, or taste ice cream and say *helado*), it will help reinforce study and will aid in vocabulary retention.
- Motivate your child with praise for small jobs well done, not just for big exams and final grades. A memorized vocabulary list is something to be proud of!

Review:

- Encourage your child to review previously learned material frequently, and not just before a test. Remember, learning a language is a building process, and it is important to keep using what you've already learned.
- To aid vocabulary memorization, suggest that your child try several different methods, such as saying words aloud while looking at a picture of the items, writing the words, acting them out while saying them, and so on.
- Suggest that your child organize new material using charts, graphs, pictures with labels, or other visuals that can be posted in the study area. A daily review of those visuals will help keep the material fresh.
- Help your child drill new vocabulary and grammar by using the charts and lists in the **Manos a la obra** and **Repaso del capítulo** sections.

Resources:

- Offer to help frequently! Your child may have great ideas for how you can facilitate his or her learning experience.
- Ask your child's teacher, or encourage your child to ask, about how to best prepare for and what to expect on tests and quizzes.
- Ask your child's teacher about the availability of audio recordings and videos that support the text. The more your child sees and hears the language, the greater the retention. There are also on-line and CD-ROM based versions of the textbook that may be useful for your child.
- Visit www.PHSchool.com with your child for more helpful tips and practice opportunities, including downloadable audio files that your child can play at home to practice Spanish. Enter the appropriate Web Code from the list on the next page for

Capítulo	A primera vista	Manos a la obra	Repaso
Para empezar			jdd-0099
Capítulo 1A	jdd-0187	jdd-0188	jdd-0189
Capítulo 1B	jdd-0197	jdd-0198	jdd-0199
Capítulo 2A	jdd-0287	jdd-0288	jdd-0289
Capítulo 2B	jdd-0297	jdd-0298	jdd-0299
Capítulo 3A	jdd-0387	jdd-0388	jdd-0389
Capítulo 3B	jdd-0397	jdd-0398	jdd-0399
Capítulo 4A	jdd-0487	jdd-0488	jdd-0489
Capítulo 4B	jdd-0497	jdd-0498	jdd-0499
Capítulo 5A	jdd-0587	jdd-0588	jdd-0589
Capítulo 5B	jdd-0597	jdd-0598	jdd-0599
Capítulo 6A	jdd-0687	jdd-0688	jdd-0689
Capítulo 6B	jdd-0697	jdd-0698	jdd-0699
Capítulo 7A	jdd-0787	jdd-0788	jdd-0789
Capítulo 7B	jdd-0797	jdd-0798	jdd-0799
Capítulo 8A	jdd-0887	jdd-0888	jdd-0889
Capítulo 8B	jdd-0897	jdd-0898	jdd-0899
Capítulo 9A	jdd-0987	jdd-0988	jdd-0989
Capítulo 9B	jdd-0997	jdd-0998	jdd-0999

the section of the chapter that the class is working on and you will see a menu that lists the available audio files. They can be listened to on a computer or on a personal audio player.

Above all, help your child understand that a language is not acquired overnight. Just as for a first language, there is a gradual process for learning a second one. It takes time and patience, and it is important to know that mistakes are a completely natural part of the process. Remind your child that it took years to become proficient in his or her first language, and that the second one will also take time. Praise your child for even small progress in the ability to communicate in Spanish, and provide opportunities for your child to hear and use the language.

Don't hesitate to ask your child's teacher for ideas. You will find the teacher eager to help you. You may also be able to help the teacher understand special needs that your child may have, and work together with him or her to find the best techniques for helping your child learn.

Learning to speak another language is one of the most gratifying experiences a person can have. We know that your child will benefit from the effort, and will acquire a skill that will serve to enrich his or her life.

Realidades 2

Para empezar

Nombre _____

Hora _____

Fecha _____

Vocabulary Flash Cards, Sheet 1

Copy the word or phrase in the space provided.

¿Quién(es)? _____	**¿Cómo?** _____	**¿De dónde?** _____
viejo, vieja _____ , _____	**atrevido, atrevida** _____ , _____	**desordenado, desordenada** _____ ; _____
reservado, reservada _____ , _____	**gracioso, graciosa** _____ , _____	**sociable** _____

Realidades ②

Para empezar

Nombre _____

Hora _____

Fecha _____

Vocabulary Flash Cards, Sheet 2

These blank cards can be used to write and practice other Spanish vocabulary for the chapter.

_____	_____	_____
_____	_____	_____
_____	_____	_____

Nombre _____ Hora _____

Fecha _____ **Vocabulary Check, Sheet 1**

Tear out this page. Write the English words on the lines. Fold the paper along the dotted line to see the correct answers so you can check your work.

¿Cómo eres tú?   _____

alto, alta   _____

atrevido, atrevida   _____

bajo, baja   _____

desordenado,   _____
desordenada

estudioso,   _____
estudiosa

gracioso, graciosa   _____

guapo, guapa   _____

impaciente   _____

inteligente   _____

ordenado,   _____
ordenada

reservado,   _____
reservada

sociable   _____

trabajador,   _____
trabajadora

Fold In →

Tear out this page. Write the Spanish words on the lines. Fold the paper along the dotted line to see the correct answers so you can check your work.

What are you like? _____

tall _____

daring _____

short _____

messy _____

studious _____

funny _____

good-looking _____

impatient _____

intelligent _____

neat _____

reserved, shy _____

sociable _____

hard-working _____

Fold In →

Adjectives (p. 3)

- Remember that adjectives describe nouns: people, places, and things. The following is a list of some common adjectives in Spanish.

Masculine		Feminine	
Singular	**Plural**	**Singular**	**Plural**
serio	serios	seria	serias
deportista	deportistas	deportista	deportistas
trabajador	trabajadores	trabajadora	trabajadoras
paciente	pacientes	paciente	pacientes
joven	jóvenes	joven	jóvenes

A. Read each sentence. Circle the adjective and underline the noun. Follow the model.

Modelo Enrique es un <u>joven</u> (serio.)

1. Mi primo es joven.

2. Mis hermanas son chicas jóvenes.

3. Carlos y Pedro son chicos deportistas.

4. Tú eres una persona paciente.

5. Yo soy una chica trabajadora.

6. Nosotras somos estudiantes serias.

- In Spanish, if a person, place, or thing is masculine, the adjective that describes it must be masculine: **El** *chico* **es muy** *serio*.
- If it's feminine, then the adjective must be feminine: *María* **es muy** *alta*.

B. Find the noun in each sentence below. Determine whether each noun is masculine or feminine and write **M** for masculine and **F** for feminine in the first blank. Then, fill in the missing letter in each adjective: **-o** for masculine nouns and **-a** for feminine nouns. Follow the model.

Modelo <u>M</u> Ricardo es muy seri _o_ .

1. ___ Mi amiga Karla es alt___.

2. ___ Mi tía es una mujer ordenad___.

3. ___ Mi abuelo es un hombre desordenad___.

4. ___ Ese chico es muy gracios___.

WEB CODE jdd-0001
PHSchool.com

Adjectives (*continued*)

- In Spanish, if the person, place, or thing is singular, the adjective that describes it must be singular.

    Mi hermano es paciente. *My brother is patient.*

- If the person, place, or thing is plural, then the adjective is also plural.

    Mis abuelos son pacientes. *My grandparents are patient.*

C. Circle the adjective that best completes the sentence. Use the underlined word to help you. Follow the model.

| Modelo | Mi <u>abuela</u> es | **(a.)** graciosa. | **b.** graciosas. |

1. Mis <u>hermanas</u> son   **a.** joven.   **b.** jóvenes.

2. <u>Pedro</u> es   **a.** guapo.   **b.** guapos.

3. Los <u>niños</u> son   **a.** serios.   **b.** serio.

4. <u>Marta</u> es   **a.** trabajadoras.   **b.** trabajadora.

5. <u>Eduardo</u> es   **a.** altos.   **b.** alto.

6. <u>Nosotras</u> somos   **a.** desordenadas.   **b.** desordenada.

D. Look at each sentence below and write the correct ending in the space provided. Follow the model.

| Modelo | María y Anita son chicas muy simpátic_*as*_.

1. Tú no eres una chica ordenad_____.

2. Mis primos son chicos gracios_____.

3. Nosotros somos personas estudios_____.

4. Tú y Pancho son estudiantes reservad_____.

5. Mi padre es un hombre baj_____.

6. Mis hermanos no son niños atrevid_____.

7. Nacho es un chico sociabl_____.

Go Online WEB CODE jdd-0001
PHSchool.com

Realidades ②

Para empezar

Nombre _____

Hora _____

Fecha _____

Guided Practice Activities PE-3

The verb *ser* (p. 5)

- **Ser** is an irregular verb and it means "to be." These are its present-tense forms:

yo	**soy**	I am	nosotros(as)	**somos**	We are
tú	**eres**	You are (*fam.*)	vosotros(as)	**sois**	You are (*fam., pl.*)
Ud./él/ella	**es**	He, she is; You are (*form.*)	Uds./ellos/ellas	**son**	They are; You are (*form.*)

- Remember that you can use **ser** with adjectives to tell what someone is like:

  Esas chicas son altas. *Those girls are tall.*

A. Choose the correct form of the verb **ser** in the word bank to complete the sentences. Follow the model.

eres	somos	soy	son	es

Modelo Tú ____*eres*____ reservado.

1. Yo _____ sociable.

2. Nosotros _____ deportistas.

3. Elena _____ alta.

4. Tú _____ inteligente.

5. Ustedes _____ trabajadores.

- To tell where someone is from, use **ser** + **de** + place:

  Ricardo es de México. *Ricardo is from Mexico.*

B. Say where each of the people is from below based on their nationality. Follow the model.

Modelo Linda: venezolana   ___*Linda*___ ___*es*___ ___*de*___ Venezuela.

1. Juan Carlos y Sofía: españoles _____ _____ _____ España.

2. Rosa: guatemalteca _____ _____ _____ Guatemala.

3. tú: mexicano _____ _____ _____ México.

4. Orlando: cubano _____ _____ _____ Cuba.

5. Luz y Marisol: colombianas _____ _____ _____ Colombia.

6. Mercedes y yo: panameñas _____ _____ _____ Panamá.

Realidades ②

Para empezar

Nombre _____

Hora _____

Fecha _____

Vocabulary Flash Cards, Sheet 3

Copy the word or phrase in the space provided. Be sure to include the article for each noun.

bailar	**cantar**	**caminar**
_____	_____	_____
comer	**correr**	**dibujar**
_____	_____	_____
escuchar música	**usar la computadora**	**practicar deportes**
_____	_____	_____

Realidades 2

Para empezar

Nombre _____

Hora _____ ⟋

Fecha _____

Vocabulary Check, Sheet 3

Tear out this page. Write the English words on the lines. Fold the paper along the dotted line to see the correct answers so you can check your work.

practicar deportes _____

bailar _____

caminar _____

cantar _____

comer _____

dibujar _____

nadar _____

usar la computadora _____

música _____

a menudo _____

a veces _____

nunca _____

siempre _____

después (de) _____

Fold In

Realidades 2

Para empezar

Nombre _____

Hora _____

Fecha _____

Vocabulary Check, Sheet 4

Tear out this page. Write the Spanish words on the lines. Fold the paper along the dotted line to see the correct answers so you can check your work.

to play sports _____

to dance _____

to walk _____

to sing _____

to eat _____

to draw _____

to swim _____

to use the computer _____

music _____

often _____

sometimes _____

never _____

always _____

afterwards, after _____

Fold In

To hear a complete list of the vocabulary for this chapter, go to www.phschool.com and type in the Web Code jdd-0099. Then click on **Repaso del capítulo**.

Realidades 2

Para empezar

Nombre _____

Fecha _____

Hora _____

Guided Practice Activities PE-4

Present tense of regular verbs (p. 9)

- **Hablar** (*to talk*), **comer** (*to eat*), and **vivir** (*to live*) are regular verbs. To form the present tense, drop the **-ar**, **-er**, or **-ir** endings and add the present-tense endings.

	hablar	*comer*	*vivir*
yo	**hablo**	**como**	**vivo**
tú	**hablas**	**comes**	**vives**
usted/él/ella	**habla**	**come**	**vive**
nosotros/nosotras	**hablamos**	**comemos**	**vivimos**
vosotros/vosotras	**habláis**	**coméis**	**vivís**
ustedes/ellos/ellas	**hablan**	**comen**	**viven**

A. Circle the present-tense verb form in each sentence.

Modelo Nosotros (corremos) en el parque.

1. Mis amigas viven en Nueva York.

2. Carlos come en casa a las seis.

3. Yo escribo mi tarea en el cuaderno.

4. Ustedes hablan inglés y español.

B. Look at the drawings below. Complete each description by circling the correct form of the verb using the subject pronouns given.

Modelo Él (escuchan / (escucha)) la radio.

1. Andrea (**escribimos** / **escribe**) cuentos.

2. Tú (**usa** / **usas**) la computadora. ⟶

Realidades 2

Para empezar

Nombre _____

Hora _____

Fecha _____

Guided Practice Activities PE-4a

Present tense of regular verbs (*continued*)

3.   Nosotras (**comes** / **comemos**).

4.   Marta (**toca** / **tocamos**) la guitarra.

5.   Ustedes (**cantan** / **canto**) muy bien.

C. Choose the correct ending for each incomplete verb and draw a line beneath your choice. Follow the model.

Modelo   Ana camin(**-a** / **-e**) a la escuela.

1. Tomás escrib(**-a** / **-e**) cuentos fantásticos.

2. Nosotros practic(**-amos** / **-emos**) muchos deportes.

3. Yo escuch(**-a** / **-o**) la música clásica.

4. Juan y Lola le(**-en** / **-an**) novelas de horror.

D. Write the correct form of each verb in the space provided.

Modelo   Luis _____*nada*_____ (**nadar**) en la piscina.

1. Lolis _____ (**correr**) en el parque todos los días.

2. ¿Tú _____ (**montar**) en monopatín?

3. Vicente y yo _____ (**comer**) en el restaurante mexicano.

4. Tú y Rodrigo _____ (**vivir**) en el mismo pueblo.

5. Yo _____ (**sacar**) la basura.

Presentación escrita (p. 13)

Task: Write a poem in the shape of a diamond. The poem is going to describe you.

A. Look at the poem Linda has written about herself. Circle all the words she uses to say what she is or is not like (adjectives). Then, underline all the words that tell what Linda does or does not do (verbs). The first ones have been done for you.

Me <u>llamo</u> Linda.

No soy ni (seria) ni vieja.

Soy alta, sociable, estudiosa.

Todos los días yo escucho música, leo, corro, uso la computadora.

En el verano mis amigos y yo nadamos, cantamos, bailamos.

Nunca patino ni monto en bicicleta.

¡Así soy yo!

B. Look at the word list below and complete the sentence with two words from the list that do *not* describe you. Remember to use the **-o** ending if you are a boy and **-a** if you are a girl. And remember that **sociable** and **impaciente** don't change gender. Follow the model.

| alto, -a | atrevido, -a | desordenado, -a | estudioso, -a | gracioso, -a |
| ordenado, -a | reservado, -a | sociable | impaciente | |

Modelo No soy ni ___*ordenada*___ ni ___*sociable*___ .

No soy ni _____ ni _____ .

C. Now, choose three words from the list in **part A** that describe you. Complete the sentence with those words. Be sure to use the appropriate endings on words you choose.

Soy _____, _____ y _____ .

Presentación escrita (*continued*)

D. Circle the activities in the box that you like to do and complete the sentence below with those activities.

bailo	canto	camino	dibujo
leo revistas	monto en bicicleta	uso la computadora	escucho música

Todos los días yo _____, _____, _____ y

_____.

E. Which of the activities in **part D** do you like to do with friends? Complete the sentence below using three of those activities.

En el verano, mis amigos y yo _____, _____ y

_____.

F. Complete the sentence below with two activities you never do.

Nunca _____ ni _____.

G. Finally, use your answers from **parts B** through **F** to complete this poem in the shape of a diamond.

Me llamo _____.

No soy ni _____ ni _____.

Soy _____, _____ y _____.

Todos los días yo _____, _____,

y _____.

Mis amigos y yo _____, _____ y _____.

Nunca _____ ni _____.

¡Así soy yo!

Go Online WEB CODE jdd-0001
PHSchool.com

Realidades 2

Capítulo 1A

Nombre _____

Fecha _____

Hora _____

AVSR 1A-1

The verb *tener* (p. 15)

- Remember that **tener** means "to have." It is also used to tell how old you are (**tener años**), or to say that you're hungry (**tener hambre**), sleepy (**tener sueño**), or thirsty (**tener sed**).
- Here are the present-tense forms of **tener**:

yo	tengo	nosotros/nosotras	tenemos
tú	tienes	vosotros/vosotras	tenéis
usted/él/ella	tiene	ustedes/ellos/ellas	tienen

A. Circle the correct form of **tener** to complete each sentence.

Modelo   Alicia ((tiene) / tenemos) un reloj nuevo.

1. Yo no (tienes / tengo) los carteles.

2. Paco y Lulú (tenemos / tienen) hambre.

3. Nosotros (tenemos / tienen) los bolígrafos.

4. Marco (tiene / tienes) 14 años.

5. ¿Cuántos diccionarios (tiene / tienes) tú?

6. Alicia y tú no (tienen / tienes) calculadoras, ¿verdad?

- To say that someone has to do something, use **tener** + **que** + infinitive.
  Marta tiene que estudiar. *Marta has to study.*

B. Write the correct form of **tener** + **que** to tell what these people have to do.

Modelo   Susana ___*tiene*___ ___*que*___ esquiar.

1. Yo _____ _____ practicar deportes.

2. Nosotros _____ _____ comer a las 6.

3. Juana y Julio _____ _____ ir a clase.

4. Los estudiantes _____ _____ hacer la tarea.

5. Tú _____ _____ traer el libro a clase.

Realidades ②

Capítulo 1A

Nombre _____

Hora _____

Fecha _____

AVSR **1A-2**

Verbs with irregular *yo* forms

- The **yo** form of **tener** in the present tense is irregular. It ends in **-go** (Yo ten**go**).
- Other verbs that are irregular in the **yo** form are:

hacer *(to do, to make)*	poner *(to put)*	traer *(to bring)*
hago	**pongo**	**traigo**

C. Write the **yo** form of each verb in parentheses.

1. Yo (**tener**) _____ un asiento.

2. Yo (**poner**) _____ los cuadernos en la mesa.

3. Yo (**hacer**) _____ la tarea.

4. Yo (**traer**) _____ la papelera.

D. Complete the sentences with forms of **traer, tener, poner,** or **hacer.** Follow the model.

Modelo   (**traer**) Alejandro _____*trae*_____ su mochila a clase.

1. (**tener**)   Raúl y yo _____ que estudiar.

2. (**hacer**)   Yo _____ la tarea.

3. (**poner**)   Juliana _____ sus libros en su mochila.

4. (**hacer**)   Tú _____ un experimento en la clase de ciencias naturales.

5. (**traer**)   Los estudiantes no _____ un sacapuntas a clase.

6. (**poner**)   Yo _____ una manzana en el escritorio del profesor.

Go Online WEB CODE jdd-0101
PHSchool.com

Realidades 2

Capítulo 1A

Nombre _____

Fecha _____

Hora _____

Vocabulary Flash Cards, Sheet 1

Write the Spanish vocabulary word or phrase below each picture. Be sure to include the article for each noun.

_____

_____

_____

_____

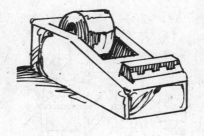

_____

_____

_____

_____

_____

Realidades 2

Capítulo 1A

Nombre _____

Fecha _____

Hora _____

Vocabulary Flash Cards, Sheet 2

Write the Spanish vocabulary word or phrase below each picture. Be sure to include the article for each noun.

_____

_____

_____

_____

_____

_____

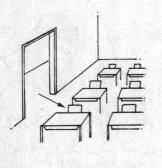

_____

_____

_____

Write the Spanish vocabulary word below each picture. If there is a word or phrase, copy it in the space provided. Be sure to include the article for each noun.

_____	_____	_____
el proyecto _____	**conocer** _____	**lo que** _____
la palabra _____	**la regla** _____	**respetar** _____

Nombre _____   Hora _____

Fecha _____   **Vocabulary Flash Cards, Sheet 4**

Copy the word or phrase in the space provided. Be sure to include the article for each noun.

se prohíbe... _____ _____	**alguien** _____	**algún, alguna, algunos, algunas** _____, _____, _____, _____
nadie _____	**ningún, ninguno, ninguna** _____, _____, _____	**almorzar** _____
empezar _____	**entender** _____	**repetir** _____

Realidades 2

Capítulo 1A

Nombre _____

Hora _____

Fecha _____

Vocabulary Flash Cards, Sheet 5

Copy the word or phrase in the space provided. These blank cards can be used to write and practice other Spanish vocabulary for the chapter.

sobre

_____

_____

_____

_____

_____

_____

_____

_____

_____

Realidades 2

Capítulo 1A

Nombre _____

Hora _____

Fecha _____

Vocabulary Flash Cards, Sheet 6

These blank cards can be used to write and practice other Spanish vocabulary for the chapter.

_____	_____	_____
_____	_____	_____
_____	_____	_____

Realidades ②

Capítulo 1A

Nombre _____

Hora _____

Fecha _____

Vocabulary Check, Sheet 1

Tear out this page. Write the English words on the lines. Fold the paper along the dotted line to see the correct answers so you can check your work.

prestar atención _____

se prohíbe... _____

la regla _____

respetar _____

entregar _____

explicar _____

pedir ayuda _____

el informe _____

el proyecto _____

alguien _____

nadie _____

contestar _____

discutir _____

hacer una pregunta _____

llegar tarde _____

Fold In →

Nombre ______________________ Hora ________

Fecha ______________________

Vocabulary Check, Sheet 2

Tear out this page. Write the Spanish words on the lines. Fold the paper along the dotted line to see the correct answers so you can check your work.

to pay attention ______________

it's forbidden... ______________

rule ______________

to respect ______________

to turn in ______________

to explain ______________

to ask for help ______________

report ______________

project ______________

someone, anyone ______________

no one, nobody ______________

to answer ______________

to discuss ______________

to ask a question ______________

to arrive late ______________

Fold In ←

Realidades 2

Capítulo 1A

Nombre _____

Hora _____

Fecha _____

Vocabulary Check, Sheet 3

Tear out this page. Write the English words on the lines. Fold the paper along the dotted line to see the correct answers so you can check your work.

aprender de
memoria   _____

el laboratorio   _____

la palabra   _____

sacar una buena
nota   _____

a tiempo   _____

el armario   _____

el asiento   _____

el carnet de
identidad   _____

la cinta adhesiva   _____

la grapadora   _____

los materiales   _____

las tijeras   _____

Fold In

Nombre _____

Hora _____

Fecha _____

Vocabulary Check, Sheet 4

Tear out this page. Write the Spanish words on the lines. Fold the paper along the dotted line to see the correct answers so you can check your work.

to memorize _____

laboratory _____

word _____

to get a good grade _____

on time _____

locker _____

seat _____

I.D. card _____

transparent tape _____

stapler _____

supplies, materials _____

scissors _____

Fold In

To hear a complete list of the vocabulary for this chapter, go to Disc 1, Track 1 on the guided Practice Audio CD or go to www.phschool.com and type in the Web Code jdd-0189. Then click on **Repaso del capítulo.**

Realidades ②

Capítulo 1A

Nombre

Hora

Fecha

Guided Practice Activities 1A-1

Stem-changing verbs (p. 27)

- Stem-changing verbs have one spelling change in their stem in the present tense:
  alm**o**rzar → Yo alm**ue**rzo en la escuela.

- The stem change, as seen in the verb chart below, resembles a shoe because the
  nosotros(as) and **vosotros(as)** forms do not change.

yo	**duermo**	nosotros/ nosotras	**dormimos**
tú	**duermes**	vosotros/ vosotras	**dormís**
usted/él/ella	**duerme**	ustedes/ellos/ellas	**duermen**

- Look at the **yo** form of the verbs in the chart below.

e → ie	o → ue	e → i	u → ue
empezar → emp**ie**zo	poder → p**ue**do	pedir → p**i**do	jugar → j**ue**go
entender → ent**ie**ndo	almorzar → alm**ue**rzo	repetir → rep**i**to	
		servir → s**i**rvo	

A. Look at the verbs below and connect the letter in each stem with the letters it changes to in the conjugated form. Follow the model.

Modelo empezar ───→ empiezo

1. poder   puede
2. pedir   pides
3. servir   sirven

4. almorzar   almuerzo
5. jugar   juega
6. entender   entienden

B. Fill in the blanks with the correct stem-change letters for each verb in the sentences below. Follow the model.

Modelo Miguel alm__u__ __e__rza en la cafetería.

1. Los chicos j____ ____gan al fútbol americano.
2. El camarero s_____rve la comida a tiempo.
3. Yo p_____do café con leche en el bar.
4. La clase emp____ ____za a las cuatro y media.
5. La manzana c____ ____sta veinticinco centavos.
6. Los estudiantes rep_____ten lo que dice la profesora.

Stem-changing verbs (*continued*)

● Remember that the **nosotros** and **vosotros** forms do not change their stem.

C. Look at each pair of sentences below. In the space provided in the second sentence, write the **nosotros** form of the underlined verb from the first sentence to say that we don't do what the persons in the first sentence do. Follow the model.

| Modelo | Claudia empieza a hablar. Nosotros no ___*empezamos*___ a hablar. |

1. Tú juegas al fútbol. Nosotros no _____ al fútbol.

2. Jorge entiende la clase. Nosotros no _____ la clase.

3. Yo almuerzo con Juan y Rebeca. Nosotros no _____ con Juan y Rebeca.

4. Rebeca pide una cinta adhesiva y una grapadora.

   Nosotros no _____ una cinta adhesiva y una grapadora.

D. Answer the following questions choosing the stem-changing verb that makes the most sense in the sentence. Once you have chosen a verb, write the correct form in the space provided. Follow the model.

| Modelo | Es el mediodía y tú tienes hambre. ¿Qué haces tú? |
| | Yo ____*almuerzo*____ (almorzar / entender) en la cafetería. |

1. Son las diez de la noche y nosotras estamos cansadas. ¿Qué hacemos?

   Nosotras _____ (querer / dormir).

2. Juan y Felipe son camareros en un restaurante. ¿Qué hacen todos los días?

   Ellos _____ (repetir / servir) la comida.

3. Tú sacas buenas notas en la clase de ciencias naturales. ¿Por qué?

   Porque yo _____ (entender / dormir) la información.

4. Nosotros estamos en el equipo de voléibol. ¿Qué hacemos?

   Nosotros _____ (jugar / almorzar) al voléibol.

Go Online WEB CODE jdd-0104
PHSchool.com

Affirmative and negative words (p. 31)

- Affirmative and negative words are opposites.
- Affirmative words are used to say that something does exist, or that it does happen. Negative words are used to say that something doesn't exist, or that it doesn't happen.
- **Yo siempre hago preguntas** is an affirmative sentence. It means "I always ask questions."
- **Yo nunca hago preguntas** is a negative sentence. It means "I never ask questions."

Affirmative	Negative
alguien *someone, anyone*	**nadie** *no one, nobody*
algo *something*	**nada** *nothing*
algún *some, any* ⌈ **alguno(s)** ⌊ **alguna(s)**	**ningún** *no, none, not any* ⌈ **ninguno** ⌊ **ninguna**
siempre *always*	**nunca** *never*
también *also, too*	**tampoco** *neither, either*

A. Rubén and Nora are talking about a class. Look at the underlined affirmative or negative words in each sentence. Then, write + next to the sentence if the word is affirmative and − if the word is negative. The first one is done for you.

1. RUBÉN: ¿Por qué tú <u>siempre</u> haces preguntas en esa clase? _____

   NORA: Porque yo <u>nunca</u> entiendo y me gusta entender. _____

2. RUBÉN: ¿Conoces a Marina? A ella <u>también</u> le gusta hacer preguntas. _____

   NORA: ¡Sí! Ella <u>tampoco</u> entiende la clase. _____

3. RUBÉN: Yo <u>siempre</u> te quiero ayudar. _____

   NORA: Yo <u>también</u> quiero ayudar a Marina. _____

B. Each sentence below has an affirmative or negative word from the above chart. Find the word and circle it. Then, write its opposite in the blank. Follow the model.

| Modelo | Yo ⟨siempre⟩ respeto las reglas. | _____*nunca*_____ |

1. Alguien contesta la pregunta. _____

2. Lucía siempre llega tarde. _____

3. Mis padres nunca dan un discurso. _____

Affirmative and negative words (*continued*)

4. Tú también haces tu proyecto. _____

5. Marta y María tampoco piden ayuda. _____

6. Yo no tengo ninguna clase aburrida. _____

- When you want to say "some," change the ending of **alguno** so it matches what you're describing in gender (masculine or feminine) and number (singular or plural): **alguna chica, algunos libros, algunas chicas.** The same is true for **ninguno: ninguna clase.**
- Before a masculine singular noun, **alguno** and **ninguno** change to **algún** and **ningún.**

C. Look at the list of school supplies below. Is the word (or words) masculine or feminine, singular or plural? Circle the correct form of **alguno** or **ninguno** in parentheses.

1. (algunas / algunos) asientos   **4.** (ningún / ninguna) libro

2. (alguna / algunos) cinta adhesiva   **5.** (algunos / alguna) materiales

3. (algunos / algún) armario   **6.** (ninguna / ningún) grapadora

D. Circle the letter of the answer that best completes each sentence.

1. —¿Conoces a alguien en el laboratorio?
—No, yo no conozco a
  a. algúien.   **b.** nadie.

2. —¿Va a comer algo Anita?
—No, no va a comer
  a. algo.   **b.** nada.

3. —¿Conoce Sandra a alguien en el laboratorio?
—Sí, ella conoce a
  a. alguien.   **b.** nadie.

4. —¿Conoce el maestro a alguien en el laboratorio?
—No, el maestro no conoce a
  a. alguien.   **b.** nadie.

5. —¿Alfonso siempre llega a clase a tiempo?
—Sí, él ___ llega a tiempo.
  a. siempre   **b.** nunca

Go Online WEB CODE jdd-0105
PHSchool.com

Realidades 2

Capítulo 1A

Nombre _____

Fecha _____

Hora _____

Guided Practice Activities 1A-5

Lectura: Para estudiar mejor... (pp. 34–35)

A. The reading in your textbook is an article about good study habits. First, look at the heads and subheads in the article. They can help you understand what the material will be about before you begin reading. Then, based on the information you read in the heads and subheads, list three things you would expect to find in this article.

1. _____

2. _____

3. _____

B. The following words are cognates from the reading. Remember that cognates are words that have similar spellings and meanings in English and Spanish. Write the letter of the English word that matches the Spanish word.

1. _____ comprender   **a.** comprehend   **b.** communicate

2. _____ clases   **a.** cases   **b.** classes

3. _____ atención   **a.** attitude   **b.** attention

4. _____ hábitos   **a.** habits   **b.** abilities

C. Read the following excerpt from the first section of the article in your textbook. Then, complete the chart below based on the excerpt. Write the answers in the space provided. The first one has been done for you.

¿Qué debes hacer a la hora de estudiar?

Para estudiar mejor necesitas una buena organización del trabajo y unos hábitos saludables. Siempre debes ser positivo. Repite frases como "yo puedo hacerlo" o "soy capaz (capable)". Cuida (Take care of) tus libros y otros materiales.

Para estudiar mejor, necesitas...	Debes ser positivo(a) y usar frases como...	Debes cuidar...
una buena organización del trabajo		

Realidades 2

Capítulo 1A

Nombre _____

Fecha _____

Hora _____

Guided Practice Activities 1A-6

Presentación oral (p. 37)

Task: You have been invited to be a school principal for a day. As principal, you will make new school rules and display them on a poster. Then, you will present your poster to a partner.

A. Think about what students will and will not be allowed to do in your school. Then list some phrases to describe these rules. A few phrases have been provided to get you started.

llegar a tiempo, hacer la tarea, conocer al director, _____,

_____, _____, _____

B. Using the phrases from **part A**, complete the columns. In the **Hay que...** column, write three phrases to describe what students should do at your school. In the **Se prohíbe...** column, write three phrases to describe what should not be done at your school. One has been done for you.

Hay que...

1. _hacer la tarea_____

2. _____

3. _____

Se prohíbe...

1. _____

2. _____

3. _____

C. On a piece of posterboard, write out *complete* sentences using your answers from **part B**. Leave space between each for your drawings. Follow the models.

Modelos Hay que _____hacer la tarea_____.

Se prohíbe _llegar tarde a la clase_____.

D. Now, illustrate each of your school rules on the poster.

E. Tell a partner about your school rules. Refer to the illustrations on your poster as you speak. Be sure to:

- include three things that students are allowed and three things that are not allowed
- use complete sentences
- speak clearly

Realidades 2

Capítulo 1B

Nombre _____

Hora _____

Fecha _____

AVSR **1B-1**

The verb *ir* (p. 43)

- The verb **ir** is used to say where someone goes or is going.
  Voy a casa.   *I'm going home.*
  Vamos al café.   *We're going to the café.*
- Look at the forms of **ir** below:

yo	**voy**	nosotros/nosotras	**vamos**
tú	**vas**	vosotros/vosotras	**vais**
usted/él/ella	**va**	ustedes/ellos/ellas	**van**

A. Circle the correct form of the verb **ir** in each sentence. Follow the model.

Modelo   Amalia (voy /(va)) al gimnasio.

1. ¡Nosotros (van / vamos) al parque!

2. ¿A qué hora (vas / voy) tú a la biblioteca?

3. Mis padres (van / vas) a la piscina.

4. Yo (voy / van) al trabajo.

5. ¿Cuándo (voy / va) la familia al restaurante mexicano?

- To tell what someone is going to do, use **ir** + **a** + infinitive.
  Voy a ver una película.   *I'm going to see a movie.*
  Vamos a estudiar esta tarde.   *We are going to study this afternoon.*

B. Write the correct form of **ir** + **a** to tell what these people are going to do. Follow the model.

Modelo   Jorge _____*va*_____ ____*a*____ salir.

1. Ellas _____ _____ estudiar.

2. Yo _____ _____ leer.

3. Marta _____ _____ nadar.

4. Tulio y Ana _____ _____ comer en un restaurante.

5. Chucho y yo _____ _____ comer.

Write the Spanish vocabulary word or phrase below each picture. Be sure to include the article for each noun.

_____

_____

_____

_____

_____

_____

_____

_____

_____

_____

_____

_____

_____

_____

_____

_____

_____

_____

Write the Spanish vocabulary word or phrase below each picture. Be sure to include the article for each noun.

Realidades 2

Capítulo 1B

Nombre _____

Hora _____

Fecha _____

Vocabulary Flash Cards, Sheet 3

Write the Spanish vocabulary word or phrase below each picture. Be sure to include the article for each noun.

_____

_____

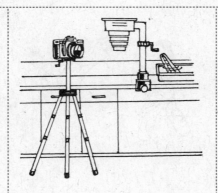

_____

_____

_____

_____

_____

_____

_____

_____

_____

_____

_____

_____

_____

_____

_____

_____

Nombre _____

Hora _____

Fecha _____

Vocabulary Flash Cards, Sheet 4

Copy the word or phrase in the space provided. Be sure to include the article for each noun.

la canción _____ _____	**las actividades extracurriculares** _____ _____ _____	**navegar en la Red** _____ ___ ___
el club _____ _____	**el club atlético** _____ _____ 	**el equipo** _____ _____
ser miembro _____ _____	**el pasatiempo** _____ _____	**la reunión** _____ _____

Copy the word or phrase in the space provided. Be sure to include the article for each noun.

el coro _____ _____	**ensayar** _____	**el ensayo** _____ _____
asistir a _____ _____	**ganar** _____	**participar (en)** _____ _____
tomar lecciones _____ _____	**volver** _____	**entre** _____

Copy the word or phrase in the space provided. Be sure to include the article for each noun.

el interés _____ _____	**la oportunidad** _____ _____	**¿Cuánto tiempo hace que...?** _____ _____ _____ _____
saber _____	**conocer** _____	**el miembro** _____ _____
Hace + _time_ + que... _____ _____ _____ _____ _____	**tantos, tantas + _noun_ + como** _____ , _____ _____ _____ _____	**tan + _adj_. + como** _____ _____ _____

Realidades 2

Capítulo 1B

Nombre _____

Hora _____

Fecha _____

Vocabulary Flash Cards, Sheet 7

These blank cards can be used to write and practice other Spanish vocabulary for the chapter.

_____   _____   _____

_____   _____   _____

_____   _____   _____

Realidades 2

Capítulo 1B

Nombre _____

Hora _____

Fecha _____

Vocabulary Check, Sheet 1

Tear out this page. Write the English words on the lines. Fold the paper along the dotted line to see the correct answers so you can check your work.

el músico, la música _____

la orquesta _____

el equipo _____

la natación _____

el ajedrez _____

la fotografía _____

hacer una búsqueda _____

ser miembro _____

ganar _____

el pasatiempo _____

participar (en) _____

la reunión _____

volver _____

asistir a _____

Fold In

Realidades 2

Capítulo 1B

Nombre _____

Fecha _____

Hora _____

Vocabulary Check, Sheet 2

Tear out this page. Write the Spanish words on the lines. Fold the paper along the dotted line to see the correct answers so you can check your work.

musician _____

orchestra _____

team _____

swimming _____

chess _____

photography _____

to do a search _____

to be a member _____

to win, to earn _____

pastime _____

to participate (in) _____

meeting _____

to return _____

to attend _____

Fold In

Realidades 2

Capítulo 1B

Nombre _____

Hora _____

Fecha _____

Vocabulary Check, Sheet 3

Tear out this page. Write the English words on the lines. Fold the paper along the dotted line to see the correct answers so you can check your work.

el hockey _____

jugar a los bolos _____

hacer gimnasia _____

las artes marciales _____

el animador,
la animadora _____

la práctica _____

los jóvenes _____

el club _____

la banda _____

el bailarín,
la bailarina _____

el coro _____

ensayar _____

tomar lecciones _____

entre _____

el interés _____

Fold In

Tear out this page. Write the Spanish words on the lines. Fold the paper along the dotted line to see the correct answers so you can check your work.

hockey _____

to bowl _____

to do gymnastics _____

martial arts _____

cheerleader _____

practice _____

young people _____

club _____

band _____

dancer _____

chorus, choir _____

to rehearse _____

to take lessons _____

among, between _____

interest _____

To hear a complete list of the vocabulary for this chapter, go to Disc 1, Track 2 on the guided Practice Audio CD or go to www.phschool.com and type in the Web Code jdd-0199. Then click on **Repaso del capítulo**.

Fold In

Realidades 2

Capítulo 1B

Nombre _____

Hora _____

Fecha _____

Guided Practice Activities 1B-1

Making comparisons (p. 53)

- To say that people or things are equal to each other, use **tan** + *adjective* + **como**.

  El hockey es tan popular como la natación.
  Hockey is as popular as swimming.

- To say that people or things are not equal, use the negative verb form.

  El hockey no es tan popular como la natación.
  Hockey is not as popular as swimming.

A. Fill in the blank with **tan**, **como**, or **es** to correctly complete the sentences. Follow the model.

Modelo   El hockey es tan popular ____*como*____ la fotografía.

1. La banda es _____ popular como la orquesta.

2. Jugar a los bolos no es tan popular _____ el ajedrez.

3. Hacer gimnasia _____ tan popular como las artes marciales.

4. Las animadoras no son _____ populares como los miembros del equipo.

5. El bailarín no es tan popular _____ el cantante.

B. Each person thinks the activities below are equal. Complete their thoughts by filling in the correct form of **ser**, the comparative expression **tan...como**, and the adjective in parentheses. Follow the model.

Modelo   Yo creo que cantar __*es*__ __*tan*__ __*divertido*__ __*como*__ (**divertido**) bailar.

1. Creo que el ajedrez _____ _____ _____ _____ (**interesante**) jugar a los bolos.

2. Yo creo que las dos actividades _____ _____ _____ _____ (**aburridas**) la fotografía.

3. Para mí el hockey _____ _____ _____ _____ (**emocionante**) bailar.

4. ¡Ay! Para mí, las actividades _____ _____ _____ _____ (**difíciles**) las clases de la escuela.

Making comparisons (*continued*)

- Use **tanto, -a** + *noun* + **como** to say "as much as":
  tanto interés como, *as much interest as*
- Use **tantos, -as** + *noun* + **como** to say "as many as":
  tantos jóvenes como, *as many young people as*
- Note that **tanto** also agrees in gender and number with the item that is being compared.
  Elena no hace tantas actividades extracurriculares como Juan.
  Elena doesn't do as many extracurricular activities as Juan.

C. Look at the following sentences and decide if the underlined word is masculine or feminine, singular or plural. Then, circle the correct form of **tanto** in parentheses. Follow the model.

Modelo   Yo asisto a ((tantas) / tanta) <u>reuniones</u> como Elena.

1. Yo tengo (tantos / tantas) <u>prácticas</u> como mi hermano.

2. Juan toma (tantas / tanta) <u>lecciones</u> de artes marciales como Carlos.

3. Elena tiene (tantas / tantos) <u>pasatiempos</u> como Angélica.

4. Camilo tiene (tanto / tantos) <u>interés</u> en el hockey como Juan.

5. Hay (tantas / tantos) <u>bailarinas</u> como bailarines.

D. Write the correct form of **tanto (tanta/tantos/tantas)** in the following phrases. Remember that **tanto** agrees in gender and number with the noun. Follow the model.

Modelo   Hay _____*tantos*_____ chicos como chicas en el coro.

1. Hay _____ personas mayores como personas menores.

2. En la escuela hay _____ equipos de deportes como clubes.

3. Hay _____ profesores simpáticos como antipáticos.

4. Hago _____ trabajo como Javier.

5. La clase crea _____ páginas Web como los técnicos.

6. El hombre rico tiene _____ cuadros como un museo.

Realidades 2

Capítulo 1B

Nombre _____

Fecha _____

Hora _____

Guided Practice Activities 1B-3

The verbs *saber* and *conocer* (p. 56)

• These are the present tense forms of **saber** and **conocer**.

yo	**sé**	nosotros/ nosotras	**sabemos**	yo	**conozco**	nosotros/ nosotras	**conocemos**
tú	**sabes**	vosotros/ vosotras	**sabéis**	tú	**conoces**	vosotros/ vosotras	**conocéis**
usted/ él/ella	**sabe**	ustedes/ ellos/ellas	**saben**	usted/ él/ella	**conoce**	ustedes/ ellos/ellas	**conocen**

A. Circle the correct form of the verb **saber** or **conocer**.

1. Mi amiga (sabe / sabes) mucho del hockey.

2. Yo no (conoces / conozco) al cantante nuevo.

3. ¿Tú (conoces / conozco) a Juan?

4. ¿(Sabemos / Saben) ustedes cuándo son las reuniones del club?

5. Mi madre y yo (conocemos / conocen) a un músico.

6. ¿(Sabes / Sabemos) tú mi número de teléfono?

• **Saber** means to know information and facts.

   ¿Sabes si tenemos una reunión mañana? *Do you know if we have a meeting tomorrow?*

• **Conocer** means to know a person or to be familiar with a place or thing. Use the **a** *personal* with **conocer** to say you know a person:

   ¿Conocen Uds. la música de Gloria Estefan? *Do you know/Are you familiar with the music of Gloria Estefan?*

   ¿Conoces a María? *Do you know María?*

B. Look at the following sentences. Decide if you would use the form of **conocer** or **saber** in parentheses. Circle your choice. Follow the model.

Modelo Julián _____ la orquesta de San Francisco.   **a.** conoce   **b.** sabe

1. ¿_____ tú el equipo profesional de fútbol en tu ciudad?   **a.** Sabes   **b.** Conoces

2. La abuela _____ navegar en la Red.   **a.** sabe   **b.** conoce

3. Nosotros _____ la ciudad de Boston.   **a.** sabemos   **b.** conocemos

4. ¿_____ Uds. que el equipo ganó el partido?   **a.** Saben   **b.** Conocen

5. Mis amigos y yo _____ jugar a los bolos.   **a.** conocemos   **b.** sabemos

The verbs *saber* and *conocer* (continued)

- Use the verb **saber** + *infinitive of another verb* to say that you know how to do something:

  Sabemos hacer gimnasia.   *We know how to do gymnastics.*

C. Look at the pictures below. Complete the answers with the verb form of **saber** and the infinitive of another verb. Follow the model.

Modelo   Kiko y Roberto _saben_ _patinar_.

1.   Andrés _____ _____ a los bolos.

2.   Sara y Rebeca _____ _____ gimnasia.

3.   Yo _____ _____ la guitarra.

4.   ¿Tú no _____ _____ un disco?

D. Read the following sentences and decide whether **saber** or **conocer** should be used. Write an **S** for **saber** and a **C** for **conocer** in the first space. Then, write the form of the verb you chose to complete the sentence. The first one is done for you.

1. _S_ Yo _____sé_____ jugar a los bolos.

2. _____ Ellos no _____ al profesor de música.

3. _____ Él no _____ visitar salones de chat.

4. _____ Mis amigos y yo _____ hacer una búsqueda en la Red.

5. _____ Nosotros no _____ el club de ajedrez.

Go Online WEB CODE jdd-0115
PHSchool.com

Hace + time expressions (p. 58)

- When you want to ask how long something has been going on, you use **¿Cuánto tiempo + hace que +** *present-tense verb*? For example,

    ¿Cuánto tiempo hace que eres miembro del coro?
    How long have you been a member of the choir?

A. Look at the sentences using **¿Cuánto tiempo + hace que...?** and write in the word that is missing from the sentence. Follow the model.

Modelo ¿Cuánto tiempo hace ____*que*____ ustedes ensayan con el club de música?

1. ¿Cuánto _____ hace que tú no asistes a las reuniones del club?

2. ¿Cuánto tiempo _____ que Juana toma lecciones de fotografía?

3. ¿Cuánto _____ hace que tus padres no vuelven a casa?

4. ¿_____ tiempo hace que nosotros no hacemos gimnasia?

5. ¿Cuánto tiempo hace _____ Paco no toca el saxofón?

- When you want to tell how long something has been going on, you use **hace +** *period of time* **+ que +** *present-tense verb*. For example,

    Hace cuatro meses que soy miembro del club atlético.
    I have been a member of the athletic team for four months.

B. Complete the following answers using the present tense of the verb in parentheses. Follow the model.

Modelo Hace tres días que nosotros ____*ensayamos*____ (**ensayar**) con el club de música.

1. Hace un mes que ustedes no _____ (**volver**) al club atlético.

2. Hace dos años que Juana _____ (**tomar**) lecciones de fotografía.

3. Hace ocho semanas que tú no _____ (**asistir**) a las reuniones del club.

4. Hace cinco años que Elena y yo no _____ (**bailar**).

5. Hace diez meses que Tomás no _____ (**ir**) a Cancún.

Realidades 2

Capítulo 1B

Nombre _____

Fecha _____

Hora _____

Guided Practice Activities 1B-4a

Hace + time expressions (*continued*)

C. Read the following questions and answer with the information provided in parentheses and the present tense of the verb. Follow the model.

Modelo ¿Cuánto tiempo hace que tú participas en la natación? (dos meses)

Hace ___*dos*___ ___*meses*___ que yo ___*participo*___ en la natación.

1. ¿Cuánto tiempo hace que Carlos juega en el equipo? (un año)

   Hace _____ _____ que Carlos _____ en el equipo.

2. ¿Cuánto tiempo hace que ustedes navegan en la Red? (cinco semanas)

   Hace _____ _____ que nosotros _____ en la Red.

3. ¿Cuánto tiempo hace que tú grabas música? (cuatro horas)

   Hace _____ _____ que yo _____ música.

4. ¿Cuánto tiempo hace que tu hermana visita salones de chat? (diez días)

   Hace _____ _____ que mi hermana _____ salones de chat.

5. ¿Cuánto tiempo hace que tú y Mariana trabajan en el café? (seis meses)

   Hace _____ _____ que nosotras _____ en el café.

6. ¿Cuánto tiempo hace que Jorge y Ana hablan por teléfono? (cuarenta minutos)

   Hace _____ _____ que ellos _____ por teléfono.

Realidades ②

Capítulo 1B

Nombre _____

Hora _____

Fecha _____

Guided Practice Activities 1B-5

Lectura: ¡A bailar! (pp. 62–63)

A. The reading in your textbook is about a dance school. Here you will find information about the many dance classes at this school. What kind of information do you expect to find about each class? Some information has already been provided.

1. Tango: _____the cost of each class_____ _____

2. Merengue: _____ _____

3. Flamenco: _____ _____

4. Swing: _____ _____

B. Read the following schedule from the reading in your textbook. Then, answer the questions that follow.

Cursos	Día y hora
Tango	lunes 17.30h a 18.30h
Merengue	martes 17.00h a 18.00h

1. What course does the school teach on Tuesdays? _____

2. At what time does the tango course begin? _____

C. Read the following class descriptions from the schedule in the reading. Then, look at the sentences that follow and write **L** (for **Lectura**) if the sentence tells about something you read. Write **N** (for **No**) if the sentence tells something you didn't read.

Swing
Baila toda la noche con tu pareja este baile muy popular de los Estados Unidos.

Tango
Ven a aprender este baile romántico de Argentina que se hizo famoso por las composiciones musicales de Gardel y de Piazzolla.

1. El tango es el baile tradicional de Argentina. ____

2. El swing es un baile popular en los Estados Unidos. ____

3. El tango es un baile romántico de Andalucía. ____

4. El swing se baila con una pareja. ____

Presentación escrita (p. 65)

Task: Your school offers many extracurricular activities. Your teacher wants you to write about the activities you like and why you like them.

❶ Prewrite. Look at the following activities and circle the ones that you like to do.

jugar al béisbol	usar una computadora	jugar al ajedrez
sacar fotos	jugar a los bolos	tocar la guitarra
leer libros	hacer gimnasia	cantar en el coro

❷ Draft. Complete the sentences below using some of your answers from **part 1**. Tell why you like those activities, and how long you have been doing them.

1. Me llamo _____ y tengo _____ años.

2. Me gustaría _____ y _____.

3. Me gustan estas actividades porque _____

_____.

4. Hace _____ que _____.

❸ Revise. Use the completed sentences from part 2 to help you write a paragraph. Then, read and check your paragraph by asking the following questions:

- Does my paragraph list two activities?
- Does my paragraph describe the activities?
- Does my paragraph explain why I like these activities?

❹ Evaluation. Your teacher may give you a rubric for how the paragraph will be graded. You will probably be graded on:

- how much information you provide about yourself
- use of vocabulary
- accuracy and use of the writing process

Realidades 2

Capítulo 2A

Nombre _____

Hora _____

Fecha _____

AVSR **2A-1**

Verbs and expressions that use the infinitive (p. 71)

- Many verbs are often followed by the infinitive. Some of the most common verbs of this type are:

me gusta/gustaría	I like/would like	querer (e→ie)	to want
me encanta	I love	pensar (e→ie)	to plan to
poder (o→ue)	to be able to	necesitar	to need
preferir (e→ie)	to prefer	tener que	to have to
deber	ought to, should	ir a	to be going to

A. The sentences below each contain two verbs. Circle the conjugated verb in each sentence and underline the verb in the infinitive. Follow the model.

Modelo   Sara (necesita) salir temprano.

1. Rafael y Jorge van a trabajar por la noche.

2. Yo prefiero jugar al fútbol.

3. Tú debes poner la mesa.

4. Oscar piensa hacer una búsqueda en la Red.

5. Nosotros queremos estar de vacaciones.

6. El camarero puede servir ocho bebidas a la vez (*at the same time*).

B. Write in the missing word or phrase for each sentence using the cues given in English. Follow the model.

Modelo   ___Me___ ___encanta___ bailar la rumba.
                              (I love)

1. _____ jugar a los bolos.
    (I prefer)

2. _____ _____ sacar buenas notas en la escuela.
                    (I have to)

3. _____ _____ cantar en el coro.
        (I like)

4. _____ ir de compras.
        (I want)

5. _____ decir la verdad.
        (I should)

Realidades **2**

Capítulo 2A

Nombre _____

Hora _____

Fecha _____

AVSR **2A-2**

Verbs and expressions that use the infinitive (*continued*)

- The verb **acabar** + **de** + *infinitive* is used to say what someone just finished doing.
  Alicia acaba de volver.   *Alicia has just come back.*

C. Tell what the people just finished doing by writing forms of **acabar** + **de** + *infinitive* in the blanks. Use the pictures to help you. The first one is done for you.

1. María _____*acaba*_____ _____*de*_____
   _____*leer*_____ una revista.

2. Javier _____ _____ _____.

3. Yo _____ _____
   la guitarra.

4. Los Rodríguez _____ _____
   _____ en la Red.

D. Use the sentence parts to create a complete sentence. Follow the model.

Modelo   Yo / tener que / estudiar / esta noche
   Yo tengo que estudiar esta noche .

1. Tú / acabar de / almorzar

   _____

2. Me gustaría / pasar tiempo con mis amigos / mañana

   _____

3. Alejandro / pensar / visitar a sus primos / durante las vacaciones

   _____

4. Los buenos estudiantes / deber / practicar el español

   _____

5. Nosotros / no poder / hacer mucho ruido / en la biblioteca

   _____

Realidades **2**

Capítulo 2A

Nombre _____

Hora _____

Fecha _____

Vocabulary Flash Cards, Sheet 1

Write the Spanish vocabulary word below each picture. Be sure to include the article for each noun.

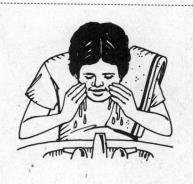

_____

_____

_____

_____

_____

_____

_____

_____

_____

_____

Realidades 2

Capítulo 2A

Nombre _____

Fecha _____

Hora _____

Vocabulary Flash Cards, Sheet 2

Write the Spanish vocabulary word or phrase below each picture. Be sure to include the article for each noun.

_____

_____

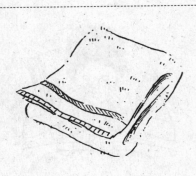

_____

_____

_____

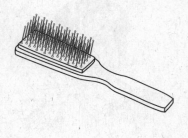

_____

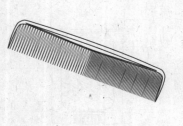

_____

_____

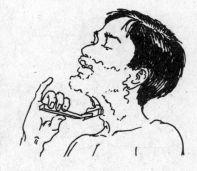

_____

Write the Spanish vocabulary word or phrase below each picture. Be sure to include the article for each noun.

_____

_____

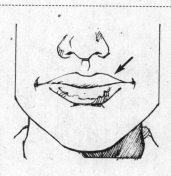

_____

_____

_____

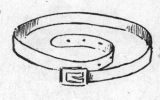

_____

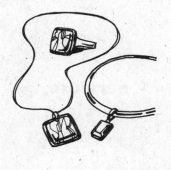

_____

_____

_____

Write the Spanish vocabulary word below each picture. If there is a word or phrase, copy it in the space provided. Be sure to include the article for each noun.

pedir prestado,
prestada (a)

_____,
_____

el
pelo

_____

levantarse

entusiasmado,
entusiasmada

_____,
_____

nervioso,
nerviosa

_____,

Copy the word or phrase in the space provided. Be sure to include the article for each noun.

tranquilo, tranquila _____ , _____	**las uñas** _____	**la cita** _____
ponerse _____	**prepararse** _____	**antes de** _____
depende _____	**elegante** _____	**lentamente** _____

Copy the word or phrase in the space provided. Be sure to include the article for each noun. These blank cards can be used to write and practice other Spanish vocabulary for the chapter.

luego	**por ejemplo**	**rápidamente**
_____	_____	_____
te ves (bien)	**ser**	**estar**
_____	_____	_____
_____	_____	_____

Nombre _____

Hora _____

Fecha _____

Vocabulary Check, Sheet 1

Tear out this page. Write the English words on the lines. Fold the paper along the dotted line to see the correct answers so you can check your work.

acostarse _____

afeitarse _____

arreglarse (el pelo) _____

bañarse _____

cepillarse
(los dientes) _____

cortarse el pelo _____

despertarse _____

ducharse _____

levantarse _____

lavarse (la cara) _____

pintarse
(las uñas) _____

ponerse _____

prepararse _____

secarse _____

Fold In

Realidades 2

Nombre _____

Hora _____

Capítulo 2A

Fecha _____

Vocabulary Check, Sheet 2

Tear out this page. Write the Spanish words on the lines. Fold the paper along the dotted line to see the correct answers so you can check your work.

to go to bed _____

to shave _____

to fix (one's hair) _____

to take a bath _____

to brush
(one's teeth) _____

to cut one's hair _____

to wake up _____

to take a shower _____

to get up _____

to wash (one's face) _____

to paint, to polish
(one's nails) _____

to put on _____

to get ready _____

to dry _____

Fold In →

Realidades 2

Capítulo 2A

Nombre

Hora

Fecha

Vocabulary Check, Sheet 3

Tear out this page. Write the English words on the lines. Fold the paper along the dotted line to see the correct answers so you can check your work.

el agua de colonia _____

el cepillo _____

el cinturón _____

el desodorante _____

la ducha _____

el gel _____

las joyas (de oro, de plata) _____

el maquillaje _____

el peine _____

el pelo _____

el salón de belleza _____

el secador _____

la toalla _____

las uñas _____

Fold In

Tear out this page. Write the Spanish words on the lines. Fold the paper along the dotted line to see the correct answers so you can check your work.

cologne _____

brush _____

belt _____

deodorant _____

shower _____

gel _____

(gold, silver) jewelry _____

make-up _____

comb _____

hair _____

beauty salon _____

blow dryer _____

towel _____

nails _____

Fold In

To hear a complete list of the vocabulary for this chapter, go to Disc 1, Track 3 on the guided Practice Audio CD or go to www.phschool.com and type in the Web Code jdd-0289. Then click on **Repaso del capítulo**.

Reflexive verbs (p. 80)

- You use reflexive verbs to say that people do something to or for themselves. All reflexive verbs in the infinitive form end with **-se.** For example, **secarse el pelo** means "to dry one's hair."
- The reflexive pronouns are **me, te, se, os,** and **nos.** Here is the present-tense form of the reflexive verb **secarse:**

yo	**me seco**	nosotros/nosotras	**nos secamos**
tú	**te secas**	vosotros/vosotras	**os secáis**
usted/él/ella	**se seca**	ustedes/ellos/ellas	**se secan**

A. Look at the underlined word(s) and circle the correct reflexive pronoun for each sentence.

1. <u>Ellos</u> **(nos / se)** lavan el pelo.

2. <u>Tú</u> **(te / se)** pintas las uñas.

3. <u>Javier y yo</u> **(nos / se)** preparamos.

4. <u>Roberto</u> **(nos / se)** viste.

5. <u>Yo</u> **(me / se)** baño.

6. <u>Lola y Rita</u> **(se / nos)** arreglan.

7. <u>Maya</u> **(te / se)** acuesta tarde.

8. <u>Tú</u> **(te / me)** secas el pelo.

B. Write the correct reflexive pronoun and form of the verb in parentheses to complete each sentence. Follow the model.

Modelo (**despertarse**) Yo siempre _me_ _despierto_ a las 6:30.

1. (**ducharse**) Nosotras _____ _____ a las 7:00 de la mañana.

2. (**arreglarse**) Yo _____ _____ el pelo a las 7:30 de la mañana.

3. (**cepillarse**) Tú _____ _____ los dientes todos los días.

4. (**acostarse**) Sandra _____ _____ temprano durante la semana.

5. (**secarse**) Uds. _____ _____ después de ducharse.

Reflexive verbs (*continued*)

- Some verbs can be used in reflexive and non-reflexive forms.

  Me lavo el pelo todos los días. *I wash my hair every day.*
  Lavo el coche. *I wash the car.*

C. Read these sentences. First, circle the whole verb (for example, **lavo** or **me despierto**). Then, write if it is reflexive [**R**] or non-reflexive [**N**]. Follow the model.

| Modelo | El ruido (despierta) el perro.   _N_ |

1. Me despierto a las seis. _____   **4.** Yo me lavo la cara. _____

2. El chico pinta las paredes. _____   **5.** Yo lavo el carro de mis padres. _____

3. La chica se pinta las uñas. _____

- Reflexive pronouns can be placed before the conjugated verb or attached to the infinitive. These two sentences have the same meaning:

  Me voy a duchar. *or* **Voy a ducharme.** *I am going to take a shower.*

D. In each sentence, the reflexive pronoun is placed either before the conjugated verb or attached to the infinitive. Rewrite the sentence you are given using the other order without changing the meaning of the sentence. The first one is done for you.

1. Elena se tiene que maquillar. _____*Elena tiene que maquillarse.*_____

2. José se va a duchar. _____

3. Yo voy a arreglarme el pelo. _____

4. Elena e Isabel siempre se tienen que preparar lentamente.

_____

5. Tú acabas de vestirte. _____

Go Online WEB CODE jdd-0204
PHSchool.com

The verbs *ser* and *estar* (p. 86)

- Remember that the verb **ser** means "to be." Use **ser** to:
  1. describe what a person or thing is or is like (*María es simpática.*)
  2. tell where someone or someting is from (*Soy de Argentina.*)
  3. tell what something is made of (*El anillo es de plata.*)
- Remember that the verb **estar** also means "to be." Use **estar** to:
  1. tell how a person is or feels at the moment (*Elena está entusiasmada hoy.*)
  2. tell where a person or thing is located (*Yo estoy en el baño.*)

A. A student is telling others about the exchange students at school. If the statements tell where the students are from, circle the correct form of **ser**. If the statements tell where the students are, circle the correct form of **estar**.

1. Los estudiantes japoneses (**son** / **están**) en la clase.

2. Ellos (**son** / **están**) interesantes.

3. Arnaldo (**es** / **está**) muy alto y guapo.

4. Arnaldo (**es** / **está**) preocupado hoy.

5. Tatiana (**es** / **está**) en la cafetería.

B. A teacher describes people and things in the school. If the teacher is describing what the things and people are like or what they are made of, then write **son** in the blank. If the teacher describes how the things are or how the people feel, then write **están** in the blank. Follow the model.

Modelo   Sara y Jenny _____*están*_____ entusiasmadas hoy.

1. Las joyas _____ de oro.

2. Los anillos _____ elegantes.

3. Ana y Jorge _____ muy nerviosos.

4. Los padres de Mateo _____ inteligentes.

C. Complete the conversation using the verbs from the word bank. The first one has been done for you.

soy	estoy	estás	es	está

1. CARMEN: Yo ___*soy*___ de México. ¿De dónde ___*es*___ él?

   ELENA: Él _____ de Honduras.

2. CARMEN: Yo _____ nerviosa hoy porque tengo una audición. Y tú, ¿cómo _____ hoy?

   ELENA: Yo _____ muy contenta porque tengo una cita con Rafael.

3. CARMEN: ¿Sí? Yo conozco a Rafael. Él _____ muy simpático. ¿Dónde _____ él?

   ELENA: Rafael _____ en el laboratorio.

Possessive adjectives (p. 88)

- Spanish possessive adjectives have a long form that comes after the noun:

  ¿Tienes un peine mío? *Do you have a comb of mine?*
  El secador es nuestro. *The dryer is ours.*

- These forms are often used for emphasis:

mío/mía	míos/mías	nuestro/nuestra	nuestros/nuestras
tuyo/tuya	tuyos/tuyas	vuestro/vuestra	vuestros/vuestras
suyo/suya	suyos/suyas	suyo/suya	suyos/suyas

- Possessive adjectives agree in gender and number with the noun they describe:

  El peine es mío. *The comb is mine.*
  Sara, las tijeras son tuyas, ¿no? *Sara, the scissors are yours, right?*

A. Circle the correct form of the possessive adjectives in parentheses. Follow the model.

Modelo   El jabón es ((suyo) / suyos).

1. Los peines son (mía / míos).

2. Las toallas son (nuestras / nuestro).

3. El cinturón es (tuyas / tuyo).

4. Los cepillos son (mío / míos).

5. El maquillaje es (nuestro / nuestra).

6. La corbata es (suyo / suya).

B. Read the conversations about who owns various objects. Then, complete each answer with the correct form of the Spanish possessive adjective, using the cues given in English. Follow the model.

Modelo   —¿Es tu secador? *(mine)*
—Sí, el secador es _____*mío*_____.

1. —¿Es tu toalla? *(mine)*

   —Sí, la toalla es _____.

2. —¿Son estas joyas de tu madre? *(hers)*

   —Sí, las joyas son _____.

3. —¿Son nuestros cepillos? *(ours)*

   —No, los cepillos no son _____.

4. —¿Tienes un cinturón mío? *(yours)*

   —No, no tengo ningún cinturón _____.

Realidades 2

Capítulo 2A

Nombre _____

Fecha _____

Hora _____

Guided Practice Activities 2A-5

Lectura: El Teatro Colón: Entre bambalinas (pp. 90–91)

A. The reading in your textbook is about a theater in Argentina called **El Teatro Colón**. Look at the word below that describes how you feel before giving a performance in such a theater. Then, write four more descriptive words in English.

nervous, _____, _____, _____

B. How do you think the author of the reading feels about singing and acting in a theater? Look at the following reading selection and underline the words that describe how the author feels.

> *Pasar una noche en el Teatro Colón de Buenos Aires siempre es un evento especial y hoy es muy especial para mí. Vamos a presentar la ópera "La traviata" y voy a cantar en el coro por primera vez. ¡Estoy muy nervioso! ... "La traviata" fue la ópera que se presentó en la inauguración del teatro el 27 de abril de 1857. Por eso estamos muy entusiasmados.*

C. Now, read the following advertisement about student auditions from your textbook reading. Then, use the information to decide if the following students are qualified to audition. Circle **Sí** if they are qualified or **No** if they are not qualified.

> ## AUDICIONES
> *para jóvenes de 15 a 25 años de edad.*
> *Si quieres ser músico, cantante o bailarín, tienes talento, eres joven y vives en Buenos Aires, tienes la oportunidad de hacer tus sueños realidad.*

1. José Luis es músico y tiene mucho talento. Él tiene 15 años.
   (Sí / No)

2. A Isabel no le gusta bailar ni cantar. Le interesa la tecnología y el arte. Ella tiene 18 años.
   (Sí / No)

3. Elena quiere ser bailarina. Ella tiene 13 años.
   (Sí / No)

4. Enrique toca la guitarra. Él tiene 30 años y vive en Los Ángeles.
   (Sí / No)

5. A Juan le gusta cantar. También sabe tocar el piano. Tiene 25 años.
   (Sí / No)

Realidades **2**

Capítulo 2A

Nombre _____

Fecha _____

Hora _____

Guided Practice Activities 2A-6

Presentación oral (p. 93)

Task: Pretend you are an exchange student in Mexico. Your host family wants to know how you celebrate special events in the United States. Bring in a photo from home or from a magazine that shows a special event.

A. Look at your photo and use it to answer the following questions.

1. What is the special event? _____

_____

2. What clothing are people wearing? _____

_____

3. How do you think the people feel? _____

_____

B. Look again at your photo and your answers from **part A.** Imagine you are going to attend the special event in the photo. How do you get ready? How do you feel before, during, and after the special event? Complete the sentences below in Spanish using your chapter vocabulary.

Me gusta prepararme antes de un evento especial. Primero, yo **1.** _____.

Después, yo **2.** _____. Antes de salir, yo **3.** _____.

Antes de un evento especial yo estoy **4.** _____. En un evento especial,

me gusta estar **5.** _____. Después de un evento, yo estoy

6. _____.

C. Write your answers in complete sentences from **part B** on index cards. Make sure you describe the event, how you prepare for the event, and how you feel before, during, and after the event.

D. Then, practice giving an oral presentation using your completed index cards and your photo. Go through your presentation several times. Try to:

- provide as much information as you can about each point
- use complete sentences
- speak clearly

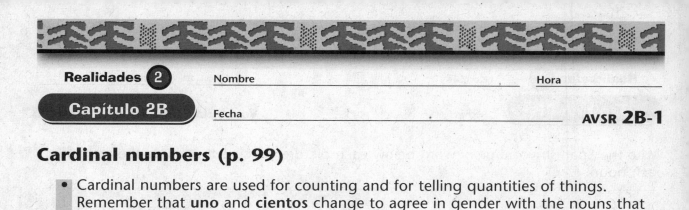

Cardinal numbers (p. 99)

• Cardinal numbers are used for counting and for telling quantities of things.
Remember that **uno** and **cientos** change to agree in gender with the nouns that
follow them.

treinta y un perros	thirty-one dogs
seiscientas personas	six hundred people

A. Match the series of numbers on the left with the numerals on the right.

1. _____ mil ochocientos setenta y tres   **a.** 2104

2. _____ cinco mil quinientos   **b.** 1707

3. _____ mil setecientos siete   **c.** 1873

4. _____ mil cuatrocientos noventa y dos   **d.** 5500

5. _____ dos mil ciento cuatro   **e.** 1928

6. _____ mil novecientos veintiocho   **f.** 1492

B. Write the numbers indicated numerically. Follow the model.

Modelo   ciento cuarenta y seis   ___146___

1. trescientos treinta y tres   _____

2. mil ochenta y cinco   _____

3. dos mil novecientos   _____

4. quinientos setenta y seis   _____

5. ciento cuarenta y cuatro mil   _____

6. doscientos noventa y ocho   _____

7. cincuenta mil veinticinco   _____

8. nueve mil seiscientos treinta   _____

Realidades 2

Capítulo 2B

Nombre _____

Fecha _____

Hora _____

Vocabulary Flash Cards, Sheet 1

Write the Spanish vocabulary word below each picture. Be sure to include the article for each noun.

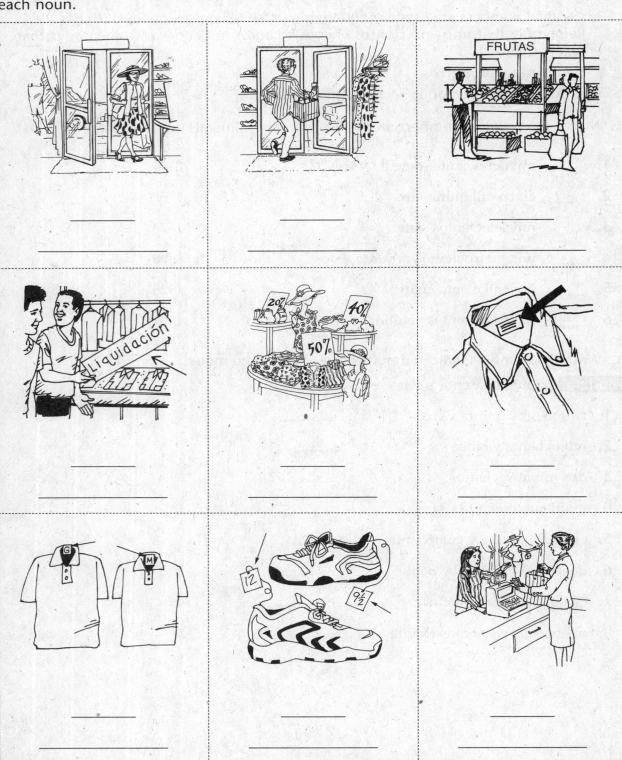

_____

_____

_____

_____

_____

_____

_____

_____

_____

Realidades 2

Capítulo 2B

Nombre _____

Hora _____

Fecha _____

Vocabulary Flash Cards, Sheet 2

Write the Spanish vocabulary word below each picture. If there is a word or phrase, copy it in the space provided. Be sure to include the article for each noun.

flojo, floja

_____,
_____

apretado, apretada

_____,
_____

vivo, viva

_____,
_____

Realidades ②

Capítulo 2B

Nombre _____

Hora _____

Fecha _____

Vocabulary Flash Cards, Sheet 3

Copy the word or phrase in the space provided. Be sure to include the article for each noun.

la liquidación _____	**tan + _adjective_** _____ _____	**me/te importa(n)** _____
claro, clara _____, _____	**de sólo un color** _____ _____ _____ _____ _____	**oscuro, oscura** _____, _____
pastel _____	**¿De qué está hecho, hecha?** _____ _____ _____ _____, _____	**Está hecho, hecha de...** _____ _____ _____ _____, _____

Realidades 2

Capítulo 2B

Nombre _____

Hora _____

Fecha _____

Vocabulary Flash Cards, Sheet 4

Copy the word or phrase in the space provided. Be sure to include the article for each noun.

algodón _____	**cuero** _____	**lana** _____
seda _____	**tela sintética** _____	**alto, alta** _____, _____
bajo, baja _____, _____	**gastar** _____	**el precio** _____

Realidades 2

Nombre _____

Hora _____

Capítulo 2B

Fecha _____

Vocabulary Flash Cards, Sheet 5

Copy the word or phrase in the space provided. Be sure to include the article for each noun.

escoger	**estar de moda**	**el estilo**
_____	_____ _____	_____
exagerado, exagerada	**mediano, mediana**	**probarse**
_____ , _____	_____ , _____	_____
anunciar	**encontrar**	**en realidad**
_____	_____	_____

Realidades **2**

Capítulo 2B

Nombre _____

Fecha _____

Hora _____

Vocabulary Flash Cards, Sheet 6

Copy the word or phrase in the space provided. Be sure to include the article for each noun. These blank cards can be used to write and practice other Spanish vocabulary for the chapter.

inmediatamente _____	**me parece que** _____ _____ _____	**¿Qué te parece?** _____ _____ _____
recientemente _____	**el cheque de viajero** _____ _____ _____ _____	 _____
    _____	 _____	 _____

Realidades ❷

Nombre _____

Hora _____

Capítulo 2B

Fecha _____

Vocabulary Flash Cards, Sheet 7

These blank cards can be used to write and practice other Spanish vocabulary for the chapter.

_____	_____	_____
_____	_____	_____
_____	_____	_____

Realidades **2**

Capítulo 2B

Nombre _____

Hora _____

Fecha _____

Vocabulary Check, Sheet 1

Tear out this page. Write the English words on the lines. Fold the paper along the dotted line to see the correct answers so you can check your work.

la entrada _____

la ganga _____

el letrero _____

la liquidación _____

el mercado _____

la salida _____

el cajero, la cajera _____

el cheque (personal) _____

el cheque de viajero _____

el cupón de regalo _____

en efectivo _____

el precio _____

la marca _____

la talla _____

Fold In

Nombre ____________ Hora ____________

Fecha ____________

Vocabulary Check, Sheet 2

Tear out this page. Write the Spanish words on the lines. Fold the paper along the dotted line to see the correct answers so you can check your work.

entrance ____________

bargain ____________

sign ____________

sale ____________

market ____________

exit ____________

cashier ____________

(personal) check ____________

traveler's check ____________

gift certificate ____________

cash ____________

price ____________

brand ____________

size ____________

Fold In ←

Realidades 2

Capítulo 2B

Nombre

Hora

Fecha

Vocabulary Check, Sheet 3

Tear out this page. Write the English words on the lines. Fold the paper along the dotted line to see the correct answers so you can check your work.

algodón   _____

cuero   _____

lana   _____

seda   _____

tela sintética   _____

apretado, apretada   _____

flojo, floja   _____

mediano, mediana   _____

estar de moda   _____

encontrar   _____

anunciar   _____

escoger   _____

probarse   _____

comprar   _____

Fold In

Realidades 2

Capítulo 2B

Nombre _____

Fecha _____

Hora _____

Vocabulary Check, Sheet 4

Tear out this page. Write the Spanish words on the lines. Fold the paper along the dotted line to see the correct answers so you can check your work.

cotton _____

leather _____

wool _____

silk _____

synthetic fabric _____

tight _____

loose _____

medium _____

to be in fashion _____

to find _____

to announce _____

to choose _____

to try on _____

to buy _____

Fold In

To hear a complete list of the vocabulary for this chapter, go to Disc 1, Track 4 on the guided Practice Audio CD or go to www.phschool.com and type in the Web Code jdd-0299. Then click on **Repaso del capítulo**.

Preterite of regular verbs (p. 110)

- Use the preterite tense to talk about actions that were completed in the past. To form the preterite tense of a regular verb, add the preterite endings to the stem of the verb.

- Here are the preterite forms for the verbs **mirar** (*to look*), **aprender** (*to learn*), and **escribir** (*to write*):

yo	**miré** **aprendí** **escribí**	*I looked* *I learned* *I wrote*	nosotros/ nosotras	**miramos** **aprendimos** **escribimos**	*we looked* *we learned* *we wrote*
tú	**miraste** **aprendiste** **escribiste**	*you looked* *you learned* *you wrote*	vosotros/ vosotras	**mirasteis** **aprendisteis** **escribisteis**	*you looked* *you learned* *you wrote*
usted/ él/ella	**miró** **aprendió** **escribió**	*you/he/she looked* *you/he/she learned* *you/he/she wrote*	ustedes/ ellos/ellas	**miraron** **aprendieron** **escribieron**	*you/they looked* *you/they learned* *you/they wrote*

A. Read the sentences below. If they tell what happens regularly in the present (using the present tense), write a **1**. If they tell what happened in the past (using the preterite tense), write a **2**. Follow the model.

Modelo	Yo aprendí a leer.	2

1. Tú miraste el letrero. _____

2. Mi papá escribió un cheque. _____

3. Las chicas estudian mucho en la clase. _____

4. Uds. escriben el libro. _____

5. Yo miré la tele anoche. _____

B. Write the appropriate ending to complete each verb stem. Follow the model.

Modelo (**comer**) Nosotros com*imos* en la cafetería.

1. (**aprender**) Uds. aprend_____ a leer en la escuela.

2. (**escribir**) Yo no escrib_____ la carta.

3. (**aprender**) Carlos y yo aprend_____ el inglés.

4. (**mirar**) Rafael no mir_____ el precio de la camisa.

5. (**enviar**) Mis abuelos me envi_____ una carta.

6. (**comer**) Tú com_____ con Antonio anoche, ¿verdad?

7. (**preparar**) Mi padre prepar_____ la comida.

Realidades 2

Capítulo 2B

Nombre

Hora

Fecha

Guided Practice Activities 2B-2

Preterite of regular verbs (*continued*)

- Note that **-ar** and **-er** verbs that have a stem change in the present tense do not have a stem change in the preterite.

  Present tense: **Siempre encuentro gangas en el mercado.**
  I always find bargains at the market.

  Preterite tense: **Ayer no encontraste gangas en el mercado.**
  Yesterday you didn't find bargains at the market.

C. Complete the following paragraph by filling in each blank with the correct preterite form of the verb in parentheses. The first one is done for you.

La semana pasada yo _____*fui*_____ (**ir**) al centro comercial, pero yo no _____

(**encontrar**) una camiseta de mi talla porque soy grande. Mi mamá también buscó la

camiseta ayer pero _____ (**costar**) mucho dinero. Recientemente, me

_____ (**probar**) una camiseta apretada y no me gustó. Esta mañana nosotros

_____ _____ (**despertarse**) temprano para ir de compras. ¡Qué bien, porque

yo _____ (**volver**) a la tienda y compré mi camiseta!

- Verbs that end in **-car, -gar,** and **-zar** have a spelling change in the **yo** form of the preterite.
- Other preterite forms of these verbs are regular.

buscar	c→qu	yo busqué	él/ella	buscó	ellos/ellas	buscaron
pagar	g→gu	yo pagué	él/ella	pagó	ellos/ellas	pagaron
almorzar	z→c	yo almorcé	él/ella	almorzó	ellos/ellas	almorzaron

D. Read the following conversation. Circle the verb in each question. Then, write the appropriate form of that same verb in the blank. The first one has been done for you.

1. JUAN: ¿(Buscaste) una camisa nueva?

EMILIO: Sí, yo ___*busqué*___ una camisa nueva. Tere _____ zapatos.

2. JUAN: ¿Pagaste la camisa en efectivo?

EMILIO: Sí, yo _____ en efectivo. Miguel _____ con tarjeta de crédito.

3. JUAN: ¿Almorzaste con Elena en el restaurante?

EMILIO: Sí, yo _____ con Elena. Nosotros _____ a las dos.

4. Juan: ¿Llegaste temprano a la tienda?

Emilio: Sí, yo _____ a las nueve. Emilia y Víctor _____ tarde.

Demonstrative adjectives (p. 114)

- Demonstrative adjectives show how close something is to the speaker. Here's a chart that compares the demonstrative adjectives:

Singular		Plural	
este/esta	*this*	**estos/estas**	*these*
ese/esa	*that*	**esos/esas**	*those*
aquel/aquella	*that (over there)*	**aquellos/aquellas**	*those (over there)*

A. Write the equivalent word(s) in English for each underlined demonstrative adjective. Follow the model.

Modelo Me gustan <u>aquellas</u> camisas blancas. *English:* <u>those (over there)</u>

1. Yo prefiero <u>estas</u> camisas rojas. *English:* _____

2. A mí me gusta <u>esta</u> gorra roja. *English:* _____

3. Yo quiero comprar <u>esos</u> zapatos. *English:* _____

4. A mi madre le gusta <u>aquella</u> blusa elegante. *English:* _____

5. Ella compró <u>ese</u> bolso cuando fue a París. *English:* _____

B. Circle the correct demonstrative adjective in parentheses to complete the dialogue. Remember adjectives must agree in gender and number with the noun they describe.

LUPE: Mamá, ¡mira **(este / esta)** suéter de lana! Es perfecto para papá.

MADRE: Sí, pero él prefiere **(esos / esas)** pantalones azules allí. Son más prácticos.

LUPE: ¡Oh! Quiero comprar **(aquellos / aquellas)** faldas bonitas cerca de la ventana.

MADRE: Me gustan, pero **(este / esta)** falda es tu número, el dos.

LUPE: Pero no va bien con **(ese / esa)** camisa que me gusta, la roja.

MADRE: Entonces, prueba las dos.

LUPE: Bien. Gracias, mamá.

Demonstrative adjectives (*continued*)

C. Look at the pictures of clothing below. Then, answer the question by writing in the correct demonstrative adjective for each article of clothing. The smallest article of clothing is the farthest away. Follow the model.

Modelo  —¿Qué falda prefieres?
—Prefiero ___*aquella*___ falda.

1.  —¿Qué camisa vas a comprar?
—Voy a comprar _____ camisa.

2. —¿Qué pantalones te gustan?
—Me gustan _____ pantalones.

3. —¿Qué traje prefieres?
—Prefiero _____ traje.

4. 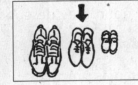 —¿Qué zapatos piensas comprar?
—Pienso comprar _____ zapatos.

D. Write the correct demonstrative adjectives based on the English cues you are given.

1. (*this*)   Debes leer _____ libro. Es muy interesante.

2. (*those over there*)   ¿Quiénes son _____ señoritas?

3. (*that*)   ¿Leíste _____ novela antes?

4. (*these*)   ¿De quiénes son _____ cheques de viajero?

5. (*this*)   No me gusta _____ lápiz. Prefiero uno azul.

Go Online WEB CODE jdd-0215
PHSchool.com

Realidades 2

Capítulo 2B

Nombre _____

Fecha _____

Hora _____

Guided Practice Activities 2B-4

Using adjectives as nouns (p. 116)

• When you compare two similar things, you can avoid repetition by dropping the noun and using the *article* + the *adjective* for the second thing.

¿Cuál prefieres, el vestido apretado o el flojo? *Which do you prefer, the tight dress or the loose one?*

Prefiero el flojo. *I prefer the loose one.*

A. Read the questions below. Circle the noun in each question. Then, answer the questions using the appropriate article and adjective as a noun.

Modelo —¿Pagaste el (precio) alto o el bajo?

—Pagué __el__ __bajo__ .

1. —¿Compraste la blusa clara o la oscura?

—Compré _____ _____ .

2. —¿Probaste los zapatos caros o los baratos?

—Probé _____ _____ .

3. —¿Encontraste el vestido grande o el mediano?

—Encontré _____ _____ .

4. —¿Te gustan los jeans apretados o los flojos?

—Me gustan _____ _____ .

B. Read the sentences below. Complete the second sentence in each pair using an article and the opposite adjective as a noun. Choose from the word bank. Follow the model.

antipáticos	~~blanca~~	claro	floja	largas	pequeñas

Modelo A Juan le encanta la ropa negra. No le encanta __la__ __blanca__ .

1. Nosotros preferimos las tiendas grandes. No preferimos _____ _____ .

2. A ellas les gustan los cajeros simpáticos. No les gustan _____ _____ .

3. Yo no me pruebo la ropa apretada. Me pruebo _____ _____ .

4. Emily no prefiere las faldas cortas. Prefiere _____ _____ .

5. No compraste el traje oscuro. Compraste _____ _____ .

Lectura: Los jeans (pp. 118–119)

A. The reading in your textbook is about the history of jeans. Before you read the selection, think about and answer the following questions.

1. Do you like to wear jeans? Why? _____

2. Why are jeans popular with many students? _____

B. The second section from your textbook reading is about one of the inventors of jeans. Read the selection and answer the questions. Use the *Hints* below to help you answer the questions.

> *Un poco de historia*
> *Levi Strauss, un joven alemán, llegó a los Estados Unidos con su familia en 1847 a la edad de 18 años. Después de trabajar algunos años con su familia, Strauss viajó a California para abrir una tienda de ropa y accesorios. Esta tienda se convirtió en un negocio próspero durante los siguientes 20 años, y Strauss se hizo rico.*

1. What type of store did Levi Strauss open in California? *Hint:* Look for the words **una tienda de.**

   _____

2. What happened over the next 20 years? *Hint:* Look for the words **próspero** and **rico.**

   _____

C. Now, look at the dates and events from the life of Levi Strauss and answer the following questions.

1847: Levi Strauss llegó a los Estados Unidos.
1872: Recibió una carta de Jacob Davis que le explicó un proceso para hacer más fuertes los pantalones. Ellos pidieron la patente de este proceso.
1873: Recibieron la patente y empezaron a fabricar *waist overalls*.

1. When did Levi Strauss arrive in the United States?

   a. 1873   **b.** 1847

2. Before Levi Strauss and Jacob Davis began to make waist overalls, they needed a

   a. patent.   **b.** letter.

3. When Strauss and Davis received the patent, they began to

   a. make waist overalls.   **b.** explain the process.

Go Online   WEB CODE jdd-0217
PHSchool.com

Realidades 2

Capítulo 2B

Nombre _____

Fecha _____

Hora _____

Guided Practice Activities 2B-6

Presentación escrita (p. 121)

Task: You received $200 for your birthday and have just purchased some articles of clothing. Write an e-mail to your friend describing your shopping trip.

A. Before you write the e-mail, it would be helpful to organize the information about your purchases. Fill in the table below. The first line is done for you.

	¿Qué compraste?	¿Dónde...?	¿Cuánto pagaste?
1.	*camiseta*	*en el centro comercial*	*$20*
2.			
3.			

B. Answer the following questions about your shopping trip. You can look back at your answers in **part A** to help you.

1. ¿Qué compraste?

   Yo _____.

2. ¿Dónde compraste la ropa?

   Yo _____.

3. ¿Cuánto pagaste?

   Yo _____.

4. ¿Por qué compraste esta ropa?

   Yo _____.

C. Use the answers to the questions in **parts A** and **B** to write an e-mail to your friend below. You may use the following model.

¡Hola _____! Yo recibí _____ en mi cumpleaños. Yo compré ropa en el _____. Compré _____. Yo pagué _____. Luego, compré _____. Pagué _____ por _____. _____ está de moda y me gusta mucho. ¿Qué te parece mi ropa? Adiós, _____

D. Check your e-mail for spelling, forms of the preterite, and agreement. Then, send it to your teacher or a classmate.

Realidades 2

Capítulo 3A

Nombre _____

Hora _____

Fecha _____

AVSR **3A-1**

Telling time

- Remember that to tell time, you use **es** or **son** + numbers and time expressions. Some common time-telling expressions are:

y	Son las cinco **y** veinte.	*It's twenty after five (5:20).*
cuarto	Son las dos y **cuarto**.	*It's quarter after two (2:15).*
media	Es la una y **media**.	*It's one thirty (1:30).*
menos	Son las doce **menos** cuarto.	*It's quarter of twelve (11:45).*
faltan...para	**Faltan** diez **para** las tres.	*It's ten of three (2:50).*

A. Fill in the blanks with the words necessary to complete the times shown in the drawings. The first one is done for you.

1. `3:05` Son ___*las*___ tres ___*y*___ cinco.

2. `5:15` Son las cinco _____ _____.

3. `4:10` Son _____ cuatro _____ diez.

4. `8:52` Faltan ocho _____ _____ nueve.

5. `6:30` Son _____ seis y _____.

- Use *a* in order to tell at what time you do something or something takes place. Use *de* to tell what part of the day it is.

  ¿A qué hora es la clase de español?   *At what time is Spanish class?*

  A **las nueve y media** *de* **la mañana.**   *At nine thirty in the morning (AM).*

  A **la una** *de* **la tarde.**   *At one o'clock in the afternoon (PM).*

B. Look at the television listings below and answer the questions that follow.

6:30 AM	Las noticias	12:00 PM	Plaza Sésamo	6:55 PM Concierto
7:15 AM	El tiempo	1:30 PM	Telenovelas	

Modelo ¿A qué hora es Plaza Sésamo?   *A las doce de la tarde* .

1. ¿A qué hora es el concierto? _____.

2. ¿A qué hora son las noticias? _____.

3. ¿A qué hora son las telenovelas? _____.

4. ¿A qué hora es el tiempo? _____.

Go **O**nline   WEB CODE jdd-0301
PHSchool.com

Realidades 2

Capítulo 3A

Nombre _____

Fecha _____

Hora _____

Vocabulary Flash Cards, Sheet 1

Write the Spanish vocabulary word or phrase below each picture. Be sure to include the article for each noun.

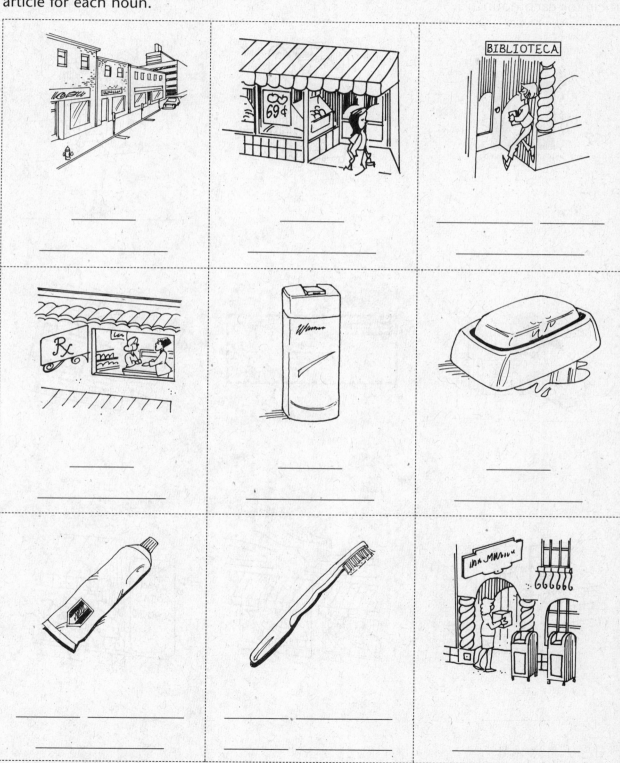

Nombre _____

Hora _____

Fecha _____

Vocabulary Flash Cards, Sheet 2

Write the Spanish vocabulary word or phrase below each picture. Be sure to include the article for each noun.

_____

_____

_____

_____

_____

_____

_____

_____

_____

Realidades 2

Capítulo 3A

Nombre _____

Fecha _____

Hora _____

Vocabulary Flash Cards, Sheet 3

Write the Spanish vocabulary word or phrase below each picture. Be sure to include the article for each noun.

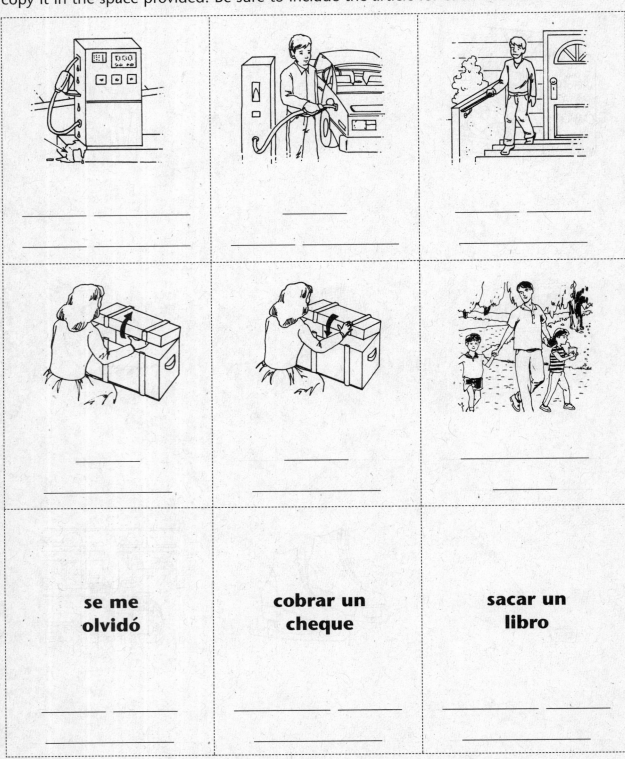

Realidades 2

Capítulo 3A

Nombre _____

Fecha _____

Hora _____

Vocabulary Flash Cards, Sheet 4

Write the Spanish vocabulary word below each picture. If there is a word or phrase, copy it in the space provided. Be sure to include the article for each noun.

se me olvidó

cobrar un cheque

sacar un libro

Copy the word or phrase in the space provided. Be sure to include the article for each noun.

caramba	**casi**	**¡Cómo no!**
_____	_____	_____
en seguida	**hasta**	**por**
_____	_____	_____
pronto	**Hasta pronto.**	**quedarse**
_____	_____	_____

Copy the word or phrase in the space provided. Be sure to include the article for each noun. These blank cards can be used to write and practice other Spanish vocabulary for the chapter.

todavía	**varios, varias**	**cerrar**
	_____ ,	
_____	_____	_____
la gasolina		
_____		
_____	_____	_____
_____	_____	_____

Realidades 2

Capítulo 3A

Nombre _____

Hora _____

Fecha _____

Vocabulary Check, Sheet 1

Tear out this page. Write the English words on the lines. Fold the paper along the dotted line to see the correct answers so you can check your work.

la farmacia _____

el supermercado _____

el banco _____

el centro _____

la estación
de servicio _____

enviar _____

el sello _____

la tarjeta _____

el buzón _____

todavía _____

cerrar _____

cuidar a _____

devolver (un libro) _____

Hasta pronto. _____

ir a pie _____

Fold In

Tear out this page. Write the Spanish words on the lines. Fold the paper along the dotted line to see the correct answers so you can check your work.

pharmacy _____

supermarket _____

bank _____

downtown _____

service station _____

to send _____

stamp _____

card _____

mailbox _____

still _____

to close _____

to take care of _____

to return (a book) _____

See you soon. _____

to go on foot _____

Fold In

Tear out this page. Write the English words on the lines. Fold the paper along the dotted line to see the correct answers so you can check your work.

la carta _____

echar una carta _____

el correo _____

el equipo deportivo _____

el palo de golf _____

los patines _____

la pelota _____

la raqueta de tenis _____

el cepillo de dientes _____

el champú _____

el jabón _____

la pasta dental _____

caramba _____

casi _____

Fold In

Realidades 2

Capítulo 3A

Nombre _____

Hora _____

Fecha _____

Vocabulary Check, Sheet 4

Tear out this page. Write the Spanish words on the lines. Fold the paper along the dotted line to see the correct answers so you can check your work.

letter _____

to mail a letter _____

post office _____

sports equipment _____

golf club _____

skates _____

ball _____

tennis racket _____

toothbrush _____

shampoo _____

soap _____

toothpaste _____

good gracious _____

almost _____

Fold In

To hear a complete list of the vocabulary for this chapter, go to Disc 1, Track 5 on the guided Practice Audio CD or go to www.phschool.com and type in the Web Code jdd-0389. Then click on **Repaso del capítulo**.

Realidades 2

Capítulo 3A

Nombre _____

Hora _____

Fecha _____

Guided Practice Activities 3A-1

Direct object pronouns (p. 138)

- A direct object tells who or what receives the action of the verb. Direct objects may represent people or things.
- To avoid repeating a direct object noun, you can replace it with a direct object pronoun.

  ¿Martín echó la carta ayer? (**Carta** is the direct object noun.)
  No, la echó hoy. (**La** is the direct object pronoun. It replaces the word **carta**.)

- Here are the direct object pronouns you have already used:

Singular	Plural
lo it, him, you *(masculine formal)*	**los** them, you *(masculine formal)*
la it, her, you *(feminine formal)*	**las** them, you *(feminine formal)*

A. Circle the direct object noun in each sentence. Then, write the direct object pronoun that replaces the circled words. Follow the model.

Modelo   Margarita cobró el (cheque) _____*lo*_____

1. Paquito pasó la aspiradora ayer. _____

2. Juanucho buscó los patines. _____

3. Tú llenaste el tanque del coche. _____

4. Yo envié las tarjetas a la tía. _____

5. Uds. sacaron los libros de la biblioteca. _____

6. Ella cerró la estación de servicio. _____

B. Look at the sentences from exercise A. Replace the direct object noun you circled with the pronoun that corresponds to it. Follow the model.

Modelo   Margarita _____*lo*_____ cobró.

1. Paquito _____ pasó ayer.

2. Juanucho _____ buscó.

3. Tú _____ llenaste.

4. Yo _____ envié a la tía.

5. Uds. _____ sacaron de la biblioteca.

6. Ella _____ cerró.

Direct object pronouns (*continued*)

C. Circle the direct object noun in each question. Then, answer each question by using a direct object pronoun in your answer. Use the verbs given. Follow the model.

Modelo   ¿Él cobró el (cheque) el martes pasado?

Sí, ____*lo*____ _____*cobró*_____ el martes pasado.

1. ¿Ella pasó la aspiradora ayer? Sí, _____ _____ ayer.

2. ¿Ellos arreglaron el cuarto esta semana? No, no _____ _____ esta semana.

3. ¿Quién echó la carta en el buzón? Anita _____ _____ en el buzón.

4. ¿Quién envió las tarjetas de cumpleaños? Billy _____ _____ .

5. ¿Ellas sacaron los libros de la biblioteca? Sí, _____ _____ de la bilbioteca.

6. ¿Jenny y Miguel cerraron la estación de servicio? No, no _____ _____ .

7. ¿Él lavó los platos anoche? Sí, _____ _____ anoche.

- The direct object pronoun is placed before conjugated verbs. When an infinitive is present, the pronoun may come before the conjugated verb *or* attached to the infinitive.

   Lo tengo que hacer.   *or*   Tengo que hacerlo.

D. Rewrite the following sentences to show a second possibility for where the direct object pronouns can be placed. Follow the model.

Modelo   ¿La raqueta? La voy a comprar mañana.   _____*Voy a comprarla mañana*_____ .

1. ¿Las cartas? Las vamos a echar hoy.   _____ .

2. ¿El palo de golf? Lo tengo que comprar.   _____ .

3. ¿Los patines? Los vas a usar esta tarde.   _____ .

4. ¿La mesa? La voy a poner hoy.   _____ .

5. ¿Los periódicos? Los voy a separar esta noche.   _____ .

6. ¿El dentista? Lo tengo que visitar hoy.   _____ .

Go Online WEB CODE jdd-0304
PHSchool.com

Realidades ②

Capítulo 3A

Nombre _____

Fecha _____

Hora _____

Guided Practice Activities 3A-2

Irregular preterite verbs: *ir, ser* (p. 140)

- The preterite forms of **ser** (*to be*) and **ir** (*to go*) are the same.

yo	**fui**	nosotros/nosotras	**fuimos**
tú	**fuiste**	vosotros/vosotras	**fuisteis**
usted/él/ella	**fue**	ustedes/ellos/ellas	**fueron**

- Usually the context of the verb is what makes the meaning clear:

     Mi doctora fue la Dra. Serrano. *My doctor was Dr. Serrano.*
     El año pasado fue muy difícil. *Last year was very difficult.*
     Yo fui a la farmacia. *I went to the pharmacy.*

     (If you see the preposition "**a**" following one of these verb forms, the verb is **ir** and the meaning is "*went*".)

A. Circle the correct conjugated verb in parentheses.

```
¡Hola Margarita!

Ayer ( fuimos / fue ) un día muy interesante. Primero, mi

familia y yo ( fuimos / fue ) al parque zoológico. Mis padres

( fueron / fue ) a ver los monos y mis hermanos y yo

( fueron / fuimos ) a comer un helado. ¡( Fuimos / Fue )

delicioso! A las cinco todos nosotros ( fueron / fuimos )

a comer en un restaurante argentino. La comida ( fui / fue )

fantástica y yo ( fuiste / fui ) a la casa muy contenta.

¿Y tú? ¿Adónde ( fue / fuiste ) ayer?

Un abrazo

—Victoria
```

Realidades 2

Capítulo 3A

Nombre _____

Fecha _____

Hora _____

Guided Practice Activities 3A-3

Irregular preterite verbs: *ir, ser* (*continued*)

B. Write the correct form of the verb within parentheses. Follow the model.

| Modelo | Rafael y Hernando no __*fueron*__ (**ir**) al consultorio ayer.

1. Anoche yo _____ (**ir**) al centro.

2. Luego, Marcela y yo _____ (**ir**) a cobrar un cheque.

3. La noche _____ (**ser**) divertida.

4. Y tú ¿adónde _____ (**ir**)?

5. La tarde _____ (**ser**) aburrida.

6. Ellos _____ (**ir**) a un concierto en el parque.

7. El plato principal _____ (**ser**) bistec y papas.

8. Nosotras _____ (**ir**) a la playa.

Irregular preterite verbs: *hacer, tener, estar, poder* (p. 142)

- The preterite of the irregular verbs **hacer** (*to do*) and **tener** (*to have*) follow a similar pattern.

yo	hice tuve	nosotros/nosotras	hicimos tuvimos
tú	hiciste tuviste	vosotros/vosotras	hicisteis tuvisteis
usted/él/ella	hizo tuvo	ustedes/ellos/ellas	hicieron tuvieron

A. Complete the dialogue by circling the correct form of the verb within parentheses. The first one is done for you.

1. LAURA: ¿Qué (**hicieron** / **hizo**) tú y tu familia ayer?

   DANIEL: Nosotros (**tuvimos** / **tuvieron**) que ir al centro.

2. LAURA: ¿Qué (**hizo** / **hice**) tu papá?

   DANIEL: Él (**tuve** / **tuvo**) que enviar una carta.

3. LAURA: ¿Qué (**hiciste** / **hizo**) tu mamá?

   DANIEL: Ella (**tuvo** / **tuve**) que devolver un libro.

4. DANIEL: Y tú Laura, ¿qué (**hizo** / **hiciste**) en la noche?

   LAURA: Yo (**tuve** / **tuviste**) que cuidar a mi hermanito.

WEB CODE jdd-0306
PHSchool.com

Irregular preterite verbs: *hacer, tener, estar, poder* (continued)

- Like the verbs **hacer** and **tener**, the verbs **estar** (*to be*) and **poder** (*to be able*) are also irregular in the preterite.
- Unlike regular preterite verbs, **hacer**, **tener**, **estar**, and **poder** do not have accent marks on their preterite forms.
- Here are the preterite forms of **estar** and **poder**:

yo	**estuve**	nosotros/nosotras	**estuvimos**
tú	**estuviste**	vosotros/vosotras	**estuvisteis**
usted/él/ella	**estuvo**	ustedes/ellos/ellas	**estuvieron**

yo	**pude**	nosotros/nosotras	**pudimos**
tú	**pudiste**	vosotros/vosotras	**pudisteis**
usted/él/ella	**pudo**	ustedes/ellos/ellas	**pudieron**

B. Write the missing endings of the preterite forms of **estar** and **poder** in the sentences below.

1. Ayer yo estuv_____ en el parque por una hora.

2. Mi amigo Pablo no pud_____ venir.

3. Pablo y su papá estuv_____ en la oficina del doctor.

4. Después, Pablo no pud_____ ir a la escuela.

5. Él estuv_____ enfermo por tres días.

6. Tú estuv_____ enfermo también, ¿no?

C. Complete the sentences below with the correct preterite form of the verb in parentheses. Follow the model.

Modelo Yo _____*hice*_____ (**hacer**) mucha tarea anoche.

1. El fin de semana pasado, yo _____ (**estar**) en casa.

2. Mi hermano Tito _____ (**tener**) que hacer una tarjeta para nuestro tío, Julio.

3. Tito casi no _____ (**poder**) terminarla a tiempo.

4. Después, echó la tarjeta al buzón y por la noche, nosotros _____ (**hacer**) la cena.

5. ¿Dónde _____ (**estar**) Uds. el fin de semana?

Lectura: La unidad en la comunidad internacional (pp. 146–147)

A. The reading in your textbook is about **Ciudades Hermanas Internacional** or the Sister Cities program. As you look at the reading, you will notice several headings. Headings are a way of organizing ideas in a reading. Look at the headings below from the reading to help you complete the following activity.

> *Ciudades Hermanas Internacional*
> *¡Quiero tener una ciudad hermana!*
> *Intercambio económico*
> *Intercambio cultural*
> *Intercambio educativo*

Now, write **L** (for **Lectura**) next to the sentence below if it is something you might find in the reading. Write **N** (for **No**) next to the sentence if it is something you might not find in the reading.

1. The Sister Cities International program is for sports teams. _____

2. The mission of the Sister Cities International program is exchange and cooperation. _____

3. The sister cities can have educational, economic, and cultural exchanges. _____

4. How to have a sister city. _____

5. Sister cities cannot be from different countries. _____

B. Read the following excerpt from the reading in your textbook. Then, determine the important ideas of the excerpt and place a ✓ next to them.

> *¡Quiero tener una ciudad hermana!*
> *Cualquier (Any) ciudad en los Estados Unidos puede tener una ciudad hermana. Primero es necesario encontrar otra ciudad extranjera (foreign). Esta ciudad puede tener alguna relación con la ciudad original. Por ejemplo, ciudades que tienen el mismo nombre, como Toledo, Ohio y Toledo, España, pueden asociarse. También, las ciudades que celebran el mismo festival pueden formar relaciones de hermandad.*

1. It is difficult for people in the United States to find a sister city. _____

2. People in the United States can easily find a sister city. _____

3. Cities with the same names can become sister cities. _____

4. Cities that don't celebrate the same festivals can become sister cities. _____

Go Online WEB CODE jdd-0307
PHSchool.com

Realidades **2**

Capítulo 3A

Nombre _____

Hora _____

Fecha _____

Guided Practice Activities 3A-6

Presentación oral (p. 149)

Task: Pretend you need to prepare for a trip to Mérida, Mexico. You will visit some Mayan ruins and the beach in Cancún. Remember that it will be very hot and humid.

A. Complete the following chart. Write **Sí** in the middle column, **¿Lo necesitas?**, if you need the item, or **No** if you do not need the item. Then, place a ✓ in the right column, **¿Lo tienes?**, if you already have the item.

Ropa	¿Lo necesitas?	¿Lo tienes?
pantalones cortos		
camisetas		
abrigo		
traje de baño		
sombrero para el sol		
botas		
cepillo de dientes		

B. Review your answers in **part A**. List three items that you need but that you already have at home.

1. _____ 2. _____ 3. _____

C. Pretend you already went shopping for the items you did not have. In the left column, list those items you had to buy for your trip. In the right column, write down where you bought them. The first one is done for you.

Tuve que comprar...	¿Dónde?
pantalones cortos	*el almacén*

D. Use the information in **parts B** and **C** to talk about your trip preparation. Tell what you need and what you have or don't have. You may also bring in and show articles of clothing as props. You can use the following as a model.

Para mi viaje a México necesito camisetas, pero ya las tengo.
Tuve que comprar unos pantalones cortos en el almacén...

Realidades 2

Capítulo 3B

Nombre _____

Fecha _____

Hora _____

AVSR 3B-1

The verbs *salir*, *decir*, and *venir* (p. 155)

- **Salir, decir,** and **venir** are three **-ir** verbs that have irregular **yo** forms in the present tense (**salgo, digo,** and **vengo**). **Decir** and **venir** follow stem-changing patterns **e→i** and **e→ie**.

yo	**salgo** **digo** **vengo**	*I left* *I said, I told* *I came*	nosotros/ nosotras	**salimos** **decimos** **venimos**	*we left* *we said, we told* *we came*
tú	**sales** **dices** **vienes**	*you left* *you said, you told* *you came*	vosotros/ vosotras	**salís** **decís** **venís**	*you left* *you said; you told* *you came*
usted/ él/ella	**sale** **dice** **viene**	*you/he/she left* *you/he/she said; told* *you/he/she came*	ustedes/ ellos/ellas	**salen** **dicen** **vienen**	*you/they left* *you/they said; told* *you/they came*

A. Circle the correct form of the verb in parentheses. Follow the model.

Modelo   Yo ((salgo) / sale) de la casa.

1. Nosotros (**decimos** / **dicen**) la verdad.

2. Las hermanas (**vienes** / **vienen**) tarde.

3. Yo (**viene** / **vengo**) a tiempo.

4. Mis padres (**sales** / **salen**) del trabajo a las cinco.

5. Tú (**dices** / **digo**) que sabes más que yo.

B. Write the correct verb form to complete each sentence.

1. Mi profesor _____ (**decir**) que soy buen estudiante.

2. Yo _____ (**salir**) de casa muy temprano por la mañana.

3. Mis tíos _____ (**venir**) a mi casa esta noche.

4. Yo siempre _____ (**decir**) la verdad.

5. Nosotros _____ (**salir**) de la escuela a las tres y media.

6. La profesora está enferma y no _____ (**venir**) a clase hoy.

Go Online
PHSchool.com
WEB CODE jdd-0311

Realidades 2

Capítulo 3B

Nombre _____

Hora _____

Fecha _____

Vocabulary Flash Cards, Sheet 1

Write the Spanish vocabulary word below each picture. Be sure to include the article for each noun.

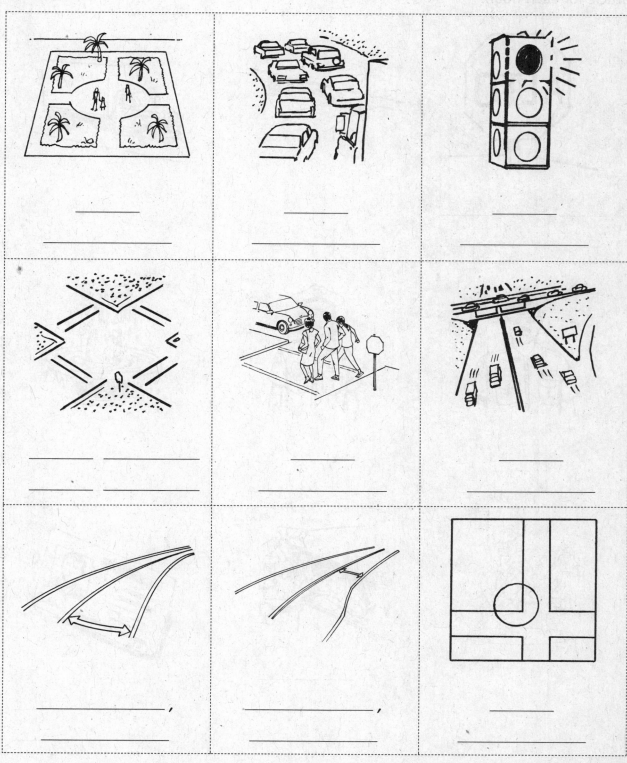

Realidades 2

Nombre _____

Hora _____

Capítulo 3B

Fecha _____

Vocabulary Flash Cards, Sheet 2

Write the Spanish vocabulary word or phrase below each picture. Be sure to include the article for each noun.

Realidades 2

Capítulo 3B

Nombre _____

Hora _____

Fecha _____

Vocabulary Flash Cards, Sheet 3

Write the Spanish vocabulary word below each picture. If there is a word or phrase, copy it in the space provided. Be sure to include the article for each noun.

_____

_____

¡Basta!

_____

De acuerdo.

_____

dejar

_____

Déjame en paz.

_____

despacio

_____

estar seguro, segura

_____ , _____

Me estás poniendo nervioso, nerviosa.

_____

_____ , _____

Realidades 2

Capítulo 3B

Nombre _____

Fecha _____

Hora _____

Vocabulary Flash Cards, Sheet 4

Copy the word or phrase in the space provided. Be sure to include the article for each noun.

peligroso, peligrosa _____ , _____	**quitar** _____	**tener cuidado** _____
ya _____	**aproximadamente** _____	**¿Cómo se va...?** _____ _____ _____
complicado, complicada _____ , _____	**cruzar** _____	**desde** _____

Copy the word or phrase in the space provided. Be sure to include the article for each noun.

hasta _____	**por** _____	**quedar** _____
seguir _____	**tener prisa** _____	**la avenida** _____
la cuadra _____	**en medio de** _____	**parar** _____

Realidades 2

Capítulo 3B

Nombre _____

Hora _____

Fecha _____

Vocabulary Flash Cards, Sheet 6

Copy the word or phrase in the space provided. Be sure to include the article for each noun. These blank cards can be used to write and practice other Spanish vocabulary for the chapter.

pasar	**el conductor, la conductora**	**esperar**
_____	_____ _____ , _____ _____	_____ _____
manejar	**el metro**	
_____	_____	_____
_____	_____	_____

Realidades 2

Capítulo 3B

Nombre _____

Hora _____

Fecha _____

Vocabulary Check, Sheet 1

Tear out this page. Write the English words on the lines. Fold the paper along the dotted line to see the correct answers so you can check your work.

la avenida   _____

el camión   _____

la carretera   _____

el conductor,   _____
la conductora

el tráfico   _____

el cruce de calles _____

la cuadra   _____

la esquina   _____

la estatua   _____

la fuente   _____

el peatón   _____

el permiso   _____
de manejar

la plaza   _____

el policía, la policía _____

el puente   _____

Fold In

Realidades **2**

Capítulo 3B

Nombre

Hora

Fecha

Vocabulary Check, Sheet 2

Tear out this page. Write the Spanish words on the lines. Fold the paper along the dotted line to see the correct answers so you can check your work.

avenue _____

truck _____

highway _____

driver _____

traffic _____

intersection _____

block _____

corner _____

statue _____

fountain _____

pedestrian _____

driver's license _____

plaza _____

police officer _____

bridge _____

Fold In

Realidades **2**

Capítulo 3B

Nombre _____

Fecha _____

Hora _____

Vocabulary Check, Sheet 3

Tear out this page. Write the English words on the lines. Fold the paper along the dotted line to see the correct answers so you can check your work.

ancho, ancha _____

¡Basta! _____

De acuerdo. _____

dejar _____

Déjame en paz. _____

despacio _____

esperar _____

peligroso, peligrosa _____

tener cuidado _____

ya _____

cruzar _____

parar _____

pasar _____

quedar _____

Fold In

Realidades 2

Capítulo 3B

Nombre _____

Fecha _____

Hora _____

Vocabulary Check, Sheet 4

Tear out this page. Write the Spanish words on the lines. Fold the paper along the dotted line to see the correct answers so you can check your work.

wide _____

Enough! _____

OK. Agreed. _____

to leave, to let _____

Leave me alone. _____

slowly _____

to wait _____

dangerous _____

to be careful _____

already _____

to cross _____

stop _____

to pass, to go _____

to be located _____

Fold In →

To hear a complete list of the vocabulary for this chapter, go to Disc 1, Track 6 on the guided Practice Audio CD or go to www.phschool.com and type in the Web Code jdd-0399. Then click on **Repaso del capítulo**.

Realidades ②

Capítulo 3B

Nombre _____

Fecha _____

Hora _____

Guided Practice Activities 3B-1

Direct object pronouns: *me, te, nos* (p. 166)

- Remember that you can replace a direct object noun with a direct object pronoun.
- The pronouns **lo, la, los,** and **las** can refer to people, places, or things. The pronouns **me, te, nos,** and **os** refer only to people, not to places or things.
- Here are all the direct object pronouns.

Singular		Plural	
me	me	**nos**	us
te	me *(familiar)*	**os**	you *(familiar)*
lo	it, him, you *(masculine formal)*	**los**	them, you *(masculine formal)*
la	it, her, you *(feminine formal)*	**las**	them, you *(feminine formal)*

- Remember that in Spanish the subject and the verb ending tell who does the action. The direct object pronoun indicates who receives the action:
  ¿Me escuchas, por favor?   *Can you listen to me please?*

A. Read the following sentences. In each sentence, circle the subject of the verb and underline the verb ending that matches the subject. Follow the model.

Modelo   (Lucas) te habló por teléfono anoche.

1. Lola me lleva a mí a la ciudad.

2. Nuestros amigos nos esperan allí.

3. Yo los busqué a Ricardo y a Enrique ayer.

4. Tú nos dices la verdad, pero tu hermano no.

5. Elena me ayuda a ir hasta la plaza.

6. La banda te sigue porque eres conductora.

B. Now, look again at the sentences from exercise A. This time, draw an arrow pointing to the direct object pronoun. Follow the model.

Modelo   Lucas te habló por teléfono anoche.

1. Lola me lleva a mí a la ciudad.

2. Nuestros amigos nos esperan allí.

3. Yo los busqué a Ricardo y a Enrique ayer.

Realidades 2

Nombre _____

Hora _____

Capítulo 3B

Fecha _____

Guided Practice Activities 3B-2

Direct object pronouns (*continued*)

4. Tú nos dices la verdad, pero tu hermano no.

5. Elena me ayuda a ir hasta la plaza.

6. La banda te sigue porque eres conductora.

C. Read the questions below and circle the letter of the correct answer for each. Follow the model.

| Modelo | Julio te ayuda a veces, ¿no? |

　　　a. Sí, me ayuda mucho.　　　**b.** Sí, te ayuda mucho.

1. ¿Me esperas en la esquina cerca del museo?

　　a. Sí, nos espera en la esquina.　　**b.** Sí, te espero allí.

2. El policía siempre nos deja pasar, ¿verdad?

　　a. No, a veces no nos deja pasar.　　**b.** No, no nos dice la verdad.

3. ¿Te pongo nerviosa?

　　a. Sí, me pones nerviosa.　　**b.** Sí, me pongo nervioso.

4. ¿El policía me va a dejar en paz?

　　a. No, no me pones una multa.　　**b.** No, te va a poner una multa.

5. Señor policía, ¿me puede quitar la multa, por favor?

　　a. Sí, me puede quitar la multa.　　**b.** Sí, le puedo quitar la multa.

Realidades 2

Capítulo 3B

Nombre _____

Hora _____

Fecha _____

Guided Practice Activities 3B-3

Irregular affirmative *tú* commands (p. 168)

• Remember that to form an affirmative command in the **tú** form, use the **él/ella/Ud.** form of the verb.

Habla con la policía.   *Talk to the police.*

A. Write the affirmative **tú** command of the regular verbs in parentheses. Follow the model.

Modelo   (**manejar**) Patricia, ___*maneja*___ con cuidado, por favor.

1. (**esperar**) Tere, _____ un minuto, por favor.

2. (**escribir**) Ramón, _____ tu nombre aquí, por favor.

3. (**dejar**) Esteban, _____ el coche aquí, por favor.

4. (**leer**) Lisa, _____ el párrafo, por favor.

5. (**doblar**) Raúl, _____ a la derecha aquí.

• Some verbs have irregular forms for the affirmative **tú** commands. To form the command, take the **yo** form of the present tense and drop the ending **-go**.

infinitive	*yo* form	command form	example
poner	pon**go**	**pon**	**Pon la mesa.**
tener	ten**go**	**ten**	**¡Ten cuidado!**
decir	di**go**	**di**	**¡Di la verdad!**
salir	sal**go**	**sal**	**Sal de la casa.**
venir	ven**go**	**ven**	**Ven acá, por favor.**

B. Complete the following sentences with the **tú** command of the verb in parentheses. Follow the model.

Modelo   (**Salir**) ___*Sal*___ del coche sucio.

1. (**Tener**) _____ tu nuevo permiso de manejar.

2. ¡Miguel, (**venir**) _____ rápido; el tren va a salir!

3. (**Decir**) _____ tu nombre al policía.

4. (**Poner**) _____ el libro en la mesa.

5. (**Salir**) _____ a las doce para llegar a tiempo.

Irregular affirmative *tú* commands (*continued*)

- The verbs **hacer, ser,** and **ir** also have irregular **tú** commands:

hacer: **haz**	ser: **sé**	ir: **ve**

C. Complete the following exchanges with the **tú** command of the verb in parentheses. Follow the model.

Modelo ELISA: ¿Cómo llego a la fiesta, Mamá?

MAMÁ: ¡(**Ir**) ____*Ve*____ en un coche!

1. CARLOS: No sé dónde queda la plaza. ¿Qué hago?

   MAMÁ: ¡(**Hacer**) _____ una pregunta!

2. PATTY: ¿Qué debo hacer para no recibir multas de la policía?

   RUTH: (**Ser**) _____ una buena conductora.

3. ALBERTO: ¿Cómo llego a la Avenida Juárez?

   LOLA: ¡(**Ir**) _____ en el metro!

4. JUANJO: Tengo miedo de hablar con la policía sobre la multa que recibí.

   RAÚL: (**Ser**) _____ cortés y todo va a estar bien.

- If you need to use an affirmative command with a direct object pronoun, the pronoun is attached to the end of the command. Remember to add a written accent over the stressed vowel if the command had two or more syllables.

   Ponlo aquí.   *Put it here.*

   Búscame en el parque.   *Look for me in the park.*

D. Read the sentences below. Complete the second sentence in each pair by writing the appropriate direct object pronoun in the space provided. Don't forget to add any necessary written accents.

Modelo Manda la carta.   Mánda_*la*___.

1. Haz la pregunta.   Haz_____.

2. Pide las direcciones.   Pide_____.

3. Visita el Parque de las Palomas.   Visita_____.

4. Pon el permiso de manejar en tu mochila. Pon_____ en tu mochila.

5. Mira las señales cuando manejas.   Mira_____.

6. Invita a tu amigo y a mí a la fiesta.   Invita_____ a la fiesta.

Go Online WEB CODE jdd-0315
PHSchool.com

Present progressive: irregular forms (p. 171)

- Remember that you form the present progressive by using **estar** + the present participle:

   Estoy hablando con Lucía.   *I am talking to Lucía.*

A. Fill in the blanks using **estar** + the present participle of the verbs in parentheses. The first one is done for you.

1. (**hablar**) Mis padres ___*están*___ ___*hablando*___ con la policía.

2. (**compartir**) Juanita y Pepito _____ _____ la comida.

3. (**quedar**) Yo me _____ _____ en el hotel.

4. (**poner**) Tú me _____ _____ nerviosa.

5. (**doblar**) El coche _____ _____ en la esquina.

- Some verbs have irregular present participle forms. To form the present participle of -**ir** stem-changing verbs, the **e** in the stem of the infinitive changes to **i**, and then the **o** in the stem changes to **u**:

decir → **diciendo**	pedir → **pidiendo**	repetir → **repitiendo**
servir → **sirviendo**	seguir → **siguiendo**	dormir → **durmiendo**

B. Fill in the missing vowels to form the present participle of the verbs that have been started in each sentence below. Follow the model.

Modelo   La camarera está s_*i*_rv_*i*_ _*e*_ndo a las chicas primero.

1. El perro está d__rm__ __ndo en el piso.

2. Mi mamá me está s__gu__ __ndo en su coche.

3. La profesora está rep__t__ __ndo la tarea.

- To form the present participle of the following -**er** verbs, add -**yendo** instead of -**iendo**:

creer → **creyendo**	leer → **leyendo**	traer → **trayendo**

C. Write the present participle of each verb in parentheses to complete the sentence. The first one has been done for you.

1. Yo estoy ___*creyendo*___ en mi equipo. (**creer**)

2. Los estudiantes están _____ sus tareas. (**traer**)

3. Nosotras estamos _____ un libro. (**leer**)

4. Mario está _____ la comida. (**traer**)

Present progressive: irregular forms (*continued*)

D. Change the underlined verb in the following sentences from the present tense to the present progressive tense. Follow the model.

Modelo	Adriana <u>dice</u> la verdad.	_está_	_diciendo_

1. Tú <u>pides</u> ayuda. _____ _____

2. Mi padre <u>lee</u> el periódico. _____ _____

3. La profesora <u>repite</u> la pregunta. _____ _____

4. Ana y yo <u>traemos</u> las bebidas. _____ _____

5. El camarero <u>sirve</u> la comida. _____ _____

6. Paulo y Javier <u>duermen</u> en clase. _____ _____

7. Los estudintes <u>siguen</u> al profesor. _____ _____

8. Yo no te <u>creo</u>. _____ _____

• When you use a direct object pronoun with a present progressive verb, the pronoun can either come before **estar** or attached to the present participle. It is necessary to add a written accent if the pronoun is attached to the present participle.

  Lara lo está trayendo.   *or*   **Lara está trayéndolo.**

E. Rewrite the sentences adding the direct object pronoun to the end of the present progressive form. Remember to write an accent on the stressed **a** or **e**. Follow the model.

Modelo	Felipe nos está llevando.	_Felipe está llevándonos_ .

1. Nosotros lo estamos esperando. _____.

2. Ella me está siguiendo. _____.

3. Tú las estás leyendo. _____.

4. Sancho me está diciendo la verdad. _____.

5. El profesor nos está enseñando. _____.

Go Online WEB CODE jdd-0316
PHSchool.com

Lectura: ¿Qué es manejar a la defensiva? (pp. 174–175)

A. The reading in your textbook is about developing safe driving habits. You may not understand the meaning of some important words in the reading. Sometimes you can use context clues to guess the meaning of these unknown words. Read the following sentences and answer the questions.

> *Manejar bien requiere muchos años de práctica. Si puedes practicar todos los días después de obtener tu permiso de manejar de estudiante, es mejor porque así vas adquiriendo experiencia.*

1. In the first sentence, what words tell you what **requiere** means?

_____

2. What do you think **vas adquiriendo experiencia** means? How do you know? (Hint: Do any of these words look or sound like English?)

_____

B. This excerpt is taken from the first section of your textbook reading. Read the excerpt and find the meaning of the underlined words below by using context clues. Circle the choice that best describes the meaning of each word.

> *¿Qué es manejar a la defensiva?*
> *Manejar a la defensiva quiere decir practicar buenos hábitos para no tener <u>colisiones</u> u otra clase de accidentes.*
>
> *Distracciones al manejar*
> *Un buen conductor siempre maneja con atención y <u>se concentra</u> en la carretera, sin pensar en otras cosas que pueden ser distracciones.*

1. colisiones:

   a. clase de accidentes

   b. clase de coches

2. se concentra:

   a. se ponen libros en la mochila

   b. se pone atención

C. Imagine that you are driving a car. You want to reassure your passenger that you have safe driving habits. Circle the word in parentheses that best completes each sentence.

1. Estoy (**manejando** / **vistiendo**) con atención.

2. La carretera es estrecha, por eso estoy (**siguiendo** / **poniendo**) mucha atención.

3. No estoy (**diciendo** / **leyendo**) en el coche.

4. No estoy (**manejando** / **durmiendo**).

5. Estoy (**siguiendo** / **durmiendo**) las señales de tráfico.

Presentación escrita (p. 177)

Task: Pretend that you have received your first driver's license. Make a poster that reminds your classmates of safe driving practices and important traffic signs.

A. Look at the traffic signs below. Then, write the meaning of each sign in English in the middle column and in Spanish in the right column.

	English	Spanish
1. ALTO		
2.		
3.		

B. From the following list, circle the word describing the meaning of each traffic light color.

rojo (**seguir / parar**)

amarillo (**parar / manejar**)

verde (**seguir / parar**)

C. The following are two actions a driver should take to drive safely. Think about two other actions for safe driving which you have read about in the chapter. Then write them below.

1. manejar despacio por calles estrechas

2. tener cuidado cerca de las señales de tráfico

3. _____

4. _____

D. Read through your answers in **parts A, B,** and **C**. Decide which information to use to make a poster about safe driving practices. Be sure to include drawings or photos of traffic signs and some of the safe driving practices.

E. Share your poster with a partner who will check the following:

_____ Does the poster present important and accurate information?

_____ Is the visual representation clear and easy to understand?

_____ Is there anything to add, change, or correct?

A ver si recuerdas: Suffixes (p. 183)

- To say that something is *small* or *little* or to add a feeling of affection to a noun, use the suffix **-ito (-a, -os, -as)**. This is called the diminutive. Generally, you drop the **-o, -a, -os,** or **-as** from the end of the noun and add the suffix.

    perro → perrito   novela → novelita

A. Change these nouns to the diminutive. First, drop the underlined part of the noun. Then, add the appropriate suffix: **-ito, -ita, -itos, -itas.** Follow the model.

Modelo libro _____*librito*_____

1. escuela _____
2. hermanos _____
3. gato _____
4. abuelo _____
5. zapatos _____
6. vaso _____
7. galletas _____
8. regalo _____

- To add emphasis to an adjective (as if adding *really* in English), use the suffix **-ísimo (-a, -os, -as)**. Remember the written accent over the first "i" of the suffix.

    Mi amiga es divertida.   *My friend is fun.*
    Mi amiga es divertidísima.   *My friend is really fun.*

B. Rewrite the descriptions of the people and things in these sentences, using the **-ísimo** form of the adjective. Follow the model.

Modelo Julia es muy inteligente. _____*Es inteligentísima*_____.

1. La fiesta fue muy buena. _____.
2. Estas piñatas son muy lindas. _____.
3. Los globos son preciosos. _____.
4. Mi mamá estuvo muy ocupada hoy. _____.
5. Las fotos son muy graciosas. _____.

Realidades ②

Capítulo 4A

Nombre _____ Hora _____

Fecha _____ **Vocabulary Flash Cards, Sheet 1**

Write the Spanish vocabulary word or phrase below each picture. Be sure to include the article for each noun.

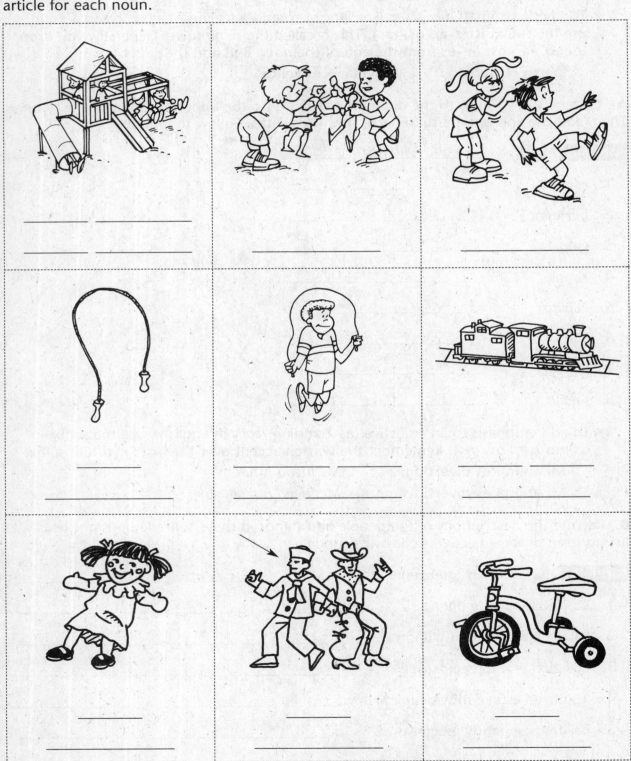

Write the Spanish vocabulary word below each picture. If there is a word or phrase, copy it in the space provided. Be sure to include the article for each noun.

de niño,
de niña

Realidades ②

Capítulo 4A

Nombre _____

Hora _____

Fecha _____

Vocabulary Flash Cards, Sheet 3

Copy the word or phrase in the space provided. Be sure to include the article for each noun.

de vez en cuando _____ _____	**mentir** _____	**obedecer** _____
ofrecer _____	**permitir** _____	**por lo general** _____ _____ _____
todo el mundo _____ _____	**de pequeño, de pequeña** _____ _____, _____ _____	**la verdad** _____ _____

Realidades 2

Capítulo 4A

Nombre _____

Hora _____

Fecha _____

Vocabulary Flash Cards, Sheet 4

Copy the word or phrase in the space provided. Be sure to include the article for each noun.

consentido, consentida _____, _____	**desobediente** _____	**generoso, generosa** _____, _____
obediente _____	**tímido, tímida** _____, _____	**travieso, traviesa** _____, _____
coleccionar _____	**el mundo** _____	**portarse bien/mal** _____

These blank cards can be used to write and practice other Spanish vocabulary for the chapter.

_____

_____

_____

_____

_____

_____

_____

_____

_____

Tear out this page. Write the English words on the lines. Fold the paper along the dotted line to see the correct answers so you can check your work.

los bloques _____

la colección _____

la cuerda _____

el dinosaurio _____

la muñeca _____

el muñeco _____

el oso de peluche _____

el tren eléctrico _____

el triciclo _____

el pez _____

la tortuga _____

la guardería infantil _____

el patio de recreo _____

el vecino, la vecina _____

Fold In ←

Realidades 2

Capítulo 4A

Nombre _____

Hora _____

Fecha _____

Vocabulary Check, Sheet 2

Tear out this page. Write the Spanish words on the lines. Fold the paper along the dotted line to see the correct answers so you can check your work.

blocks _____

collection _____

rope _____

dinosaur _____

doll _____

action figure _____

teddy bear _____

electric train _____

tricycle _____

fish _____

turtle _____

daycare center _____

playground _____

neighbor _____

Fold In

Tear out this page. Write the English words on the lines. Fold the paper along the dotted line to see the correct answers so you can check your work.

coleccionar _____

molestar _____

pelearse _____

saltar (a la cuerda) _____

mentir _____

obedecer _____

permitir _____

portarse
bien/mal _____

de niño, de niña _____

de vez en cuando _____

Fold In ←

Realidades 2

Capítulo 4A

Nombre

Hora

Fecha

Vocabulary Check, Sheet 4

Tear out this page. Write the Spanish words on the lines. Fold the paper along the dotted line to see the correct answers so you can check your work.

to collect _____

to bother _____

to fight _____

to jump (rope) _____

to lie _____

to obey _____

to permit, to allow _____

to behave
well/badly _____

as a child _____

once in a while _____

Fold In

To hear a complete list of the vocabulary for this chapter, go to Disc 1, Track 7 on the guided Practice Audio CD or go to www.phschool.com and type in the Web Code jdd-0489. Then click on **Repaso del capítulo**.

Realidades 2

Capítulo 4A

Nombre _____

Fecha _____

Hora _____

Guided Practice Activities 4A-1

The imperfect tense: Regular verbs (p. 194)

- The imperfect tense is used to talk about actions that happened repeatedly in the past.

  Rafael caminaba y Ramiro corría en el parque.
  Rafael used to walk and Ramiro used to run in the park.

- Here are the regular forms of **-ar**, **-er**, and **-ir** verbs in the imperfect tense:

	jugar	hacer	vivir
yo	jugaba	hacía	vivía
tú	jugabas	hacías	vivías
usted/él/ella	jugaba	hacía	vivía
nosotros/nosotras	jugábamos	hacíamos	vivíamos
vosotros/vosotras	jugabais	hacíais	vivíais
ustedes/ellos/ellas	jugaban	hacían	vivían

- Note the accents on **jugábamos** and throughout the conjugations of the **-er** and **-ir** verbs.

- These expressions can cue you to use the imperfect: **generalmente, por lo general, a menudo, muchas veces, de vez en cuando, todos los días, nunca.**

A. Write the infinitive form of each conjugated verb. The first one is done for you.

1. jugaba _____*jugar*_____

2. molestaba _____

3. coleccionaban _____

4. obedecías _____

5. ofrecía _____

6. permitían _____

7. corríamos _____

8. vivíamos _____

B. Fill in the blanks with the correct form of the **-ar** verbs in the imperfect tense. Follow the model.

Modelo Tú habl_*abas*_ con mucha gente.

1. Alicia siempre molest_____ a su hermana.

2. Mis tíos nunca nos regal_____ nada a nosotros.

3. Pedro le d_____ agua al perro muchas veces.

4. Yo siempre me port_____ bien enfrente de mis padres.

5. A menudo nosotros jug_____ en el parque.

Realidades 2

Capítulo 4A

Nombre _____

Fecha _____

Hora _____

Guided Practice Activities 4A-2

The imperfect tense: regular verbs (*continued*)

C. Write the correct endings for the **-er** and **-ir** verbs below. Follow the model.

Modelo   Por lo general, yo obedec *ía*_____ a mis padres.

1. Mis primos me ofrec_____ sus bloques de vez en cuando.

2. A menudo mis tíos me permit_____ comer una galletas.

3. Generalmente, mamá pon_____ la mesa.

4. Mis hermanos y yo hac_____ la cama todos los días.

5. Tú viv_____ en la misma ciudad que yo.

D. Complete the sentences below to describe what people *used to do*. Use the drawings and the verbs in parentheses as clues. Follow the model.

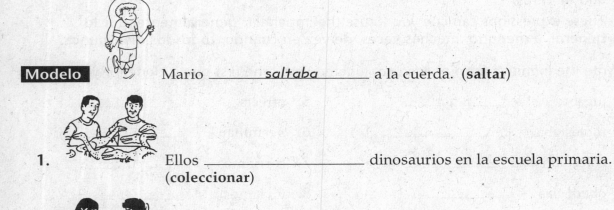

Modelo   Mario _____ *saltaba* _____ a la cuerda. (**saltar**)

1. Ellos _____ dinosaurios en la escuela primaria. (**coleccionar**)

2. Ellas _____ _____ todos los días. (**pelearse**)

3. Nosotros _____ al tenis los domingos. (**jugar**)

4. Tú _____ en la biblioteca los fines de semana. (**leer**)

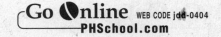

Go Online WEB CODE jdd-0404
PHSchool.com

Realidades ②

Capítulo 4A

Nombre _____

Fecha _____

Hora _____

Guided Practice Activities 4A-3

The imperfect tense: irregular verbs (p. 196)

- There are only three irregular verbs in the imperfect tense: **ir**, **ser**, and **ver**. Here are their forms:

	ir	**ser**	**ver**
yo	iba	era	veía
tú	ibas	eras	veías
usted/él/ella	iba	era	veía
nosotros/nosotras	íbamos	éramos	veíamos
vosotros/vosotras	ibais	erais	veíais
ustedes/ellos/ellas	iban	eran	veían

- Note that only the **nosotros** forms of **ir** and **ser** carry accents.
- **Ver** uses the exact same endings as regular **-er** verbs, and is only irregular because of the added "**e**".

A. Choose the correct verb in parentheses to complete each sentence. Circle your choice. Use the chart above to help you. Follow the model.

Modelo   Clara y Nubia ((eran)/ **iban**) mis amigas.

1. Por lo general, yo (**era** / **veía**) a mis primas.

2. Mis primos nunca (**veían** / **iban**) conmigo al mercado.

3. Mis hermanos y yo (**éramos** / **íbamos**) muy traviesos.

4. ¿Tú (**ibas** / **veías**) muchas películas?

B. Complete the following sentences using the imperfect form of the verb in parentheses. Follow the model.

Modelo   Nosotros (**ir**) _____*íbamos*_____ a la escuela todos los días.

1. ¡Mi mamá (**ser**) _____ muy traviesa de niña!

2. Nosotros generalmente (**ver**) _____ la tele en casa.

3. De niña, yo (**ir**) _____ a la casa de mis tíos de vez en cuando.

4. La familia de mi mamá (**ver**) _____ a la abuela durante las vacaciones.

5. Juana y yo (**ser**) _____ muy buenas amigas.

Realidades **2**

Capítulo 4A

Nombre _____

Hora _____

Fecha _____

Guided Practice Activities 4A-3a

The imperfect tense: review

A. Below are two paragraphs about Christopher Columbus. As you read, fill in the blanks with the appropriate imperfect form of the verbs given. The first one has been done for you.

Cuando Cristóbal Colón _____*tenía*_____ **(tener)** diez años, le

_____ **(gustar)** mucho navegar *(to sail)* con su papá. Cristóbal y

sus amigos _____ **(imaginar)** lugares distantes y exóticos que

ellos _____ **(ir)** a visitar algún día. Sus padres siempre

_____ **(decir)**: "Es importante imaginar y descubrir *(discover)*".

Cristóbal _____ **(pensar)** mucho y realmente

_____ **(querer)** buscar un lugar nuevo.

Cuando _____ **(ser)** mayor, él _____ **(hablar)** de

vez en cuando con los reyes *(kings, rulers)* de España para pedirles dinero

para sus exploraciones. Los reyes _____ **(decir)**: " Cristóbal, tú

_____ **(ser)** un buen explorador de niño con tu padre. Tú

_____ **(ver)** muchos lugares nuevos. Es importante ahora

descubrir una nueva ruta a la India". Cristóbal siempre _____

(explorar) y _____ **(ver)** muchos lugares nuevos, pero nunca

encontró la ruta a la India.

Go Online WEB CODE jdd-0405
PHSchool.com

Realidades 2

Capítulo 4A

Nombre _____

Fecha _____

Hora _____

Guided Practice Activities 4A-4

Indirect object pronouns (p. 199)

- An indirect object tells *to whom* or *for whom* something is done.

   Julio escribió una carta <u>a Susana</u>.   *Julio wrote a letter to Susana.*
- Indirect object pronouns can replace an indirect object.

   Julio <u>le</u> escribió una carta.   *Julio wrote her a letter.*
- Indirect object pronouns, especially **le** and **les,** can also be used with an indirect object.

   Julio <u>le</u> escribió una carta <u>a Susana</u>.   *Julio wrote a letter to Susana (to her).*
- Here are the forms of the indirect object pronouns:

Singular	Plural
me (to/for) me	**nos** (to/for) us
te (to/for) you *(familiar)*	**os** (to/for) you *(familiar)*
le (to/for) him, her, you *(formal)*	**les** (to/for) them, you *(formal)*

A. Circle the indirect object pronoun in each sentence. Follow the model.

Modelo   Tú (le) escribías cartas a tu amigo boliviano Carlos.

1. Yo le pedía a mamá una muñeca.

2. Mi abuela me daba muchos besos.

3. Carlos y yo le ofrecíamos unos chocolates.

4. Claudia nos iba a comprar ropa.

5. Roberto les ofrecía el triciclo a sus hermanas.

B. Circle the appropriate indirect object pronoun in parentheses to complete each sentence. Then, underline the part of the sentence that indicates *to whom* the pronoun refers. The first one is done for you.

1. Generalmente mi abuela ((nos) / me) compraba muchos juguetes a <u>nosotros</u>.

2. Mamá y yo siempre (le / nos) dábamos tarjetas bonitas a la tía.

3. Yo (te / le) ofrecía dulces a ti en la escuela primaria.

4. Tú siempre (les / te) dabas osos de peluche a mis hermanas.

5. Mis padres no (me / les) permitían a mí llevar gorra a la iglesia.

Indirect object pronouns (*continued*)

C. Look at each of the following sentences. First, underline the indirect object noun. Then, in the space provided, put the indirect object pronoun that corresponds to the noun you underlined. Follow the model.

Modelo   Nuestros padres siempre ___*nos*___ decían la verdad a <u>nosotros</u>.

1. Por lo general, mis amigos _____ prestaban a mí sus juguetes.

2. Los abuelos de Alicia siempre _____ querían dar a ella buenas cosas.

3. La profesora _____ permitía a los estudiantes jugar en el patio de recreo.

4. Yo no _____ daba dinero a ti para ver las películas.

5. Tío Leo _____ compraba a mi hermano las vías (*tracks*) para su tren eléctrico.

- Indirect object pronouns can be placed before the verb or attached to the infinitive.

  Mi abuela nunca *me* quería dar dinero en mi cumpleaños.
  Mi abuela nunca quería dar*me* dinero en mi cumpleaños.

D. Look at the sentences below and write a new sentence with the same meaning, placing the indirect object pronoun differently. Follow the model.

Modelo   Tía Lisa me quería llevar a la guardería infantil.

    Tía Lisa quería llevarme a la guardería infantil _____.

1. Yo no les podía mentir a mis padres.

   _____

2. Los tíos siempre nos tenían que decir que éramos niños traviesos.

   _____

3. Mis primos malos siempre me querían molestar.

   _____

4. A veces mis hermanos y yo no les queríamos obedecer a nuestros padres.

   _____

Realidades 2

Capítulo 4A

Nombre _____

Fecha _____

Hora _____

Guided Practice Activities 4A-5

Lectura: El grillo y el jaguar (pp. 202–203)

Making predictions is a useful strategy to help prepare you for a reading.

A. The reading in your textbook is a fable from Mexico. Look at the title of the reading and the pictures. Then, using the fables you know as guides, like *Aesop's Fables,* list three things that you think might happen in this fable.

1. _____

2. _____

3. _____

B. In the following paragraph from the reading, the jaguar challenges the cricket to a race. Read the paragraph and then circle the option below that describes what you think will happen.

—Vamos a hacer una carrera (race) hasta aquella roca enorme que está por donde empiezan las montañas. Si llegas primero, te perdono todo y puedes seguir cantando, pero si llego primero yo, te prohíbo cantar.

1. The cricket wins the race and can continue singing.
2. The jaguar wins the race and the cricket can't sing.

C. After you have read *El grillo y el jaguar,* write the letter of the answer that best completes each sentence.

1. Los personajes principales (*main characters*) de esta fábula son: _____
   a. el grillo y el jaguar
   b. el jaguar y el jardín
   c. el grillo y el lago

2. El problema de esta fábula es: _____
   a. El grillo quiere correr tan rápidamente como el jaguar.
   b. El jaguar quiere cantar.
   c. Al jaguar no le gusta la canción del grillo.

3. La moraleja (*moral*) de esta fábula es: _____
   a. El grillo gana porque corre más rápidamente.
   b. El grillo gana porque el jaguar es simpático.
   c. El grillo gana porque es más inteligente.

Realidades 2

Capítulo 4A

Nombre _____

Hora _____

Fecha _____

Guided Practice Activities 4A-6

Presentación oral (p. 205)

Task: Describe what you were like when you were a small child and draw a series of pictures that illustrate your sentences.

A. Think about what you were like when you were a small child, what things you used to do, and what things you weren't allowed to do. Then, complete the following sentences.

1. Cuando era niño(a), era _____ y _____.

2. Yo jugaba con _____.

3. Me gustaba jugar _____.

4. Yo tenía que _____.

5. Mis padres no me permitían _____.

B. On a separate sheet of paper, make a drawing or cut out pictures from a magazine to illustrate each of your sentences from **part A**. Number your pictures 1 to 5.

C. Use your sentences from **part A** and your drawings from **part B** to prepare your presentation. You can practice your presentation with a partner. Make sure that:

- your sentences describe the pictures in order
- you use complete sentences
- you speak clearly so that you can be understood

D. Now, talk about what you were like when you were a child. Hold up your pictures in order during the presentation as you say your sentences to describe them. You can follow the model.

Cuando era niño(a), yo era obediente. Yo jugaba con mis amigos. Me gustaba jugar con mi triciclo. Yo tenía que portarme bien. Mis padres no me permitían saltar en la cama.

E. Your teacher will probably grade you on the following:

- the amount of information you communicate
- how easy it is to understand you
- the quality of visuals

Realidades 2

Capítulo 4B

Nombre _____

Fecha _____

Hora _____

Vocabulary Flash Cards, Sheet 1

Write the Spanish vocabulary word or phrase below each picture. Be sure to include the article for each noun.

_____

_____

_____

_____

_____

_____

_____

_____

_____

Realidades ②

Capítulo 4B

Nombre _____

Hora _____

Fecha _____

Vocabulary Flash Cards, Sheet 2

Write the Spanish vocabulary word or phrase below each picture. Be sure to include the article for each noun.

_____

_____

_____
_____

_____

_____

_____

_____
_____

_____
_____

_____

Realidades 2

Capítulo 4B

Nombre _____

Fecha _____

Hora _____

Vocabulary Flash Cards, Sheet 3

Write the Spanish vocabulary word below each picture. If there is a word or phrase, copy it in the space provided. Be sure to include the article for each noun.

_____	_____	_____
llevarse bien, llevarse mal _____ _____ , _____ _____	**felicitar** _____	**los parientes** _____
alrededor de _____	**la costumbre** _____	**divertirse** _____

Realidades 2

Capítulo 4B

Nombre _____

Hora _____

Fecha _____

Vocabulary Flash Cards, Sheet 4

Copy the word or phrase in the space provided. Be sure to include the article for each noun.

nacer _____	**la reunión** _____	**antiguo, antigua** _____ , _____
frecuentemente _____	**había** _____	**mientras (que)** _____ _____
recordar _____	**el día festivo** _____ _____	**¡Felicidades!** _____

Realidades **2**

Capítulo 4B

Nombre _____

Hora _____

Fecha _____

Vocabulary Check, Sheet 1

Tear out this page. Write the English words on the lines. Fold the paper along the dotted line to see the correct answers so you can check your work.

el bebé, la bebé _____

el aniversario _____

la costumbre _____

el desfile _____

el día festivo _____

la fiesta de
sorpresa _____

los fuegos
artificiales _____

la reunión _____

los mayores _____

los modales _____

abrazar(se) _____

besar(se) _____

dar(se) la mano _____

Fold In

Realidades 2

Capítulo 4B

Nombre _____

Hora _____

Fecha _____

Vocabulary Check, Sheet 2

Tear out this page. Write the Spanish words on the lines. Fold the paper along the dotted line to see the correct answers so you can check your work.

baby _____

anniversary _____

custom _____

parade _____

holiday _____

surprise party _____

fireworks _____

gathering _____

grown-ups _____

manners _____

to hug _____

to kiss _____

to shake hands _____

Fold In

Tear out this page. Write the English words on the lines. Fold the paper along the dotted line to see the correct answers so you can check your work.

despedirse (de) _____

saludar(se) _____

sonreír _____

contar (chistes) _____

llorar _____

reírse _____

reunirse _____

casarse (con) _____

charlar _____

cumplir años _____

hacer un picnic _____

nacer _____

regalar _____

recordar _____

Fold In

Realidades **2**

Capítulo 4B

Nombre _____

Hora _____

Fecha _____

Vocabulary Check, Sheet 4

Tear out this page. Write the Spanish words on the lines. Fold the paper along the dotted line to see the correct answers so you can check your work.

to say goodbye (to) _____

to greet _____

to smile _____

to tell (jokes) _____

to cry _____

to laugh _____

to meet _____

to get married (to) _____

to chat _____

to have a birthday _____

to have a picnic _____

to be born _____

to give (a gift) _____

to remember _____

Fold In

To hear a complete list of the vocabulary for this chapter, go to Disc 1, Track 8 on the guided Practice Audio CD or go to www.phschool.com and type in the Web Code jdd-0499. Then click on **Repaso del capítulo**.

The imperfect tense: describing a situation (p. 219)

- The imperfect tense is also used to describe people, places, and situations in the past:

> **La casa de mis abuelos era pequeña. Tenía dos dormitorios.**
> *My grandparents' house was small. It had two bedrooms.*

> **Mi abuelo era muy generoso.**
> *My grandfather was very generous.*

> **Las fiestas en la casa de mis abuelos eran muy divertidas.**
> *The parties at my grandparents' house were a lot of fun.*

A. Read the following paragraph and draw a line underneath all the verbs used to describe the situation. The first one has been done for you.

Cuando <u>era</u> niño, mi familia y yo siempre íbamos al lago. Mis abuelos tenían una

casa de verano que estaba cerca del lago. El lago era muy grande y bonito. Había

árboles alrededor del lago. Generalmente hacía mucho calor y por eso nos gustaba

nadar en el lago porque era más fresco *(cool)*.

B. Read the following sentences about the paragraph in exercise A. Write **cierto** if they are true or **falso** if they are false. The first one is done for you.

1. La familia siempre iba al océano durante el verano. _____*falso*_____

2. Los tíos tenían una casa de verano cerca del lago. _____

3. Era un lago grande con árboles alrededor. _____

4. Hacía mucho calor en el verano. _____

5. No podían nadar en el lago. _____

The imperfect tense (*continued*)

C. Complete the following sentences by writing the correct form of the verbs in parentheses using the imperfect tense. Use the the pictures to help you with the meaning of the sentences. Follow the model.

Modelo   El tío Pepe (**contar**) _____*contaba*_____ chistes.

1. Nosotros (**charlar**) _____ con los parientes.

2. Mis padres (**hacer**) _____ picnics.

3. Yo (**pasar**) _____ tiempo con mis amigos.

4. Mis hermanos (**jugar**) _____ al fútbol.

5. Andréa (**tener**) _____ buenos modales.

6. Tú (**divertirse**) _____ _____ en las fiestas.

Go Online WEB CODE jdd-0413
PHSchool.com

The imperfect tense (*continued*)

- The imperfect is also used to talk about a past action or situation when no beginning or ending time is mentioned.

  Había mucha gente en la fiesta para el aniversario de mis padres.
  There were many people at the party for my parents' anniversary.

D. Look at the scene to start thinking about what is happening. Then, read the paragraph below it and fill in the missing form of the verbs in parentheses that describe the situation in the past. The first one is done for you.

Cuando yo __era__ (**ser**) niña, mis parientes _____ _____ (**reunirse**)

los domingos en casa de mi abuela. Mi abuela _____ (**preparar**) mucha

comida y mi madre y mis tías la _____ (**ayudar**). Yo

_____ (**jugar**) con mis primos. Todos nosotros (**llevarse**) _____

_____ muy bien, y _____ _____ (**divertirse**) mucho.

Nosotros _____ (**almorzar**) juntos (*together*) y _____

_____ (**reírse**) mucho contando chistes todo el tiempo.

The imperfect tense (*continued*)

- The imperfect tense is also used to tell what someone was doing when something else happened (preterite):

    Mis parientes *charlaban* cuando mi mamá *entró*.
    My relatives were chatting when my mother came in.

E. Read the sentences below about a party. Circle the action that was taking place in the description. Then, underline the action that stopped it. The first one is done for you.

1. Yo (hablaba por teléfono) cuando <u>la fiesta empezó</u>.

2. Mis parientes y yo charlábamos cuando la fiesta empezó.

3. Cuando llegaron sus padres Luz contaba chistes.

4. Marta comía un pastel cuando le dieron los regalos.

5. La bebé jugaba cuando su abuela entró.

6. Cuando llegó Ana los primos bebían refrescos.

7. Luisa y Mariana bailaban cuando la fiesta terminó.

8. Cuando se fueron todos yo escribía sobre la fiesta.

9. Tú sacabas la basura cuando volvieron tus primos para celebrar más.

10. Cuando los primos y yo nos reunimos en el sótano, tú llamabas a la policía.

Go Online WEB CODE jdd-0413
PHSchool.com

The imperfect tense (*continued*)

F. Look at the drawing below of a surprise 50th anniversary party. Then, read the paragraph and fill in the blanks with the correct form of the verbs in parentheses using the imperfect tense. The first one is done for you.

La semana pasada __*era*__ (**ser**) el aniversario de mis abuelos. Todos nuestros

parientes _____ (**estar**) en la casa de mis tíos. Las mujeres

_____ (**charlar**) y los hombres _____ (**contar**) chistes.

_____ (**Haber**) un pastel muy grande en la mesa. El pastel

_____ (**tener**) flores muy bonitas. Nosotros _____ _____

(**divertirse**) mucho.

G. Now, read the paragraph that tells what happened when the couple entered in the room. Fill in the blanks with the correct form of the verbs in parentheses using the preterite tense. The first one is done for you.

Cuando mis abuelos ____*llegaron*____ (**llegar**) todos les _____

(**felicitar**) a ellos. Las personas que charlaban antes, ahora _____

(**saludar**) a los abuelos, y algunas personas los _____ (**besar**).

Mamá _____ (**sacar**) los regalos de otro cuarto. Mis abuelos

_____ (**entrar**) y luego la fiesta _____ (**empezar**).

Realidades 2

Capítulo 4B

Nombre _____

Fecha _____

Hora _____

Guided Practice Activities 4B-4

Reciprocal actions (p. 224)

- You can use **se** and **nos** to express the idea "(to) each other":

    Luis y Jorge se veían con frecuencia.
    Luis and Jorge used to see each other frequently.

    Mis primos y yo nos escribíamos a menudo.
    My cousins and I used to write each other often.

A. Choose the correct reciprocal verb to describe each picture. Then, write the correct form of the verb using the imperfect tense in the blank. Follow the model.

Modelo   Elena y María ___se___ ___pelean___. (pelearse / besarse)

1. Alicia y yo _____ _____. (saludarse / besarse)

2. Gregorio y Andrés _____ _____.
(darse la mano / abrazarse)

3. Daniel y Susi _____ _____ de Tomás.
(pelearse / despedirse)

4. Gloria y yo _____ _____. (saludarse / darse la mano)

5. Antonio y Clara _____ _____. (abrazarse / verse)

Go Online WEB CODE jdd-0414
PHSchool.com

Lectura: El seis de enero (pp. 228–229)

A. *El seis de enero,* or Three King's Day, is one of the most beloved holidays for children in the Hispanic world. Before this holiday arrives, children write letters to the **Reyes Magos** (Three Kings or Wise Men), just as many children in the U.S. write to Santa Claus before Christmas. Put an X next to the things you would expect to find in a letter to the **Reyes Magos.**

1. Los niños dicen sus nombres. _____

2. Los niños dicen que se portan bien. _____

3. Los niños dicen que se portan mal. _____

4. Los niños dicen qué juguetes quieren. _____

B. Now, read the following letter to the **Reyes Magos.** Answer the questions that follow.

> 4 de enero
>
> Queridos Reyes:
>
> Yo soy Carolina y quiero decirles que me porto bien con mami, papi y la maestra. Les escribo para pedirles una bicicleta rosada. Muchas gracias. Feliz año nuevo.
>
> Les quiere,
>
> Carolina

1. See if you can find in the letter any of the things that you marked in **part A.** List three of them in English.

   _____, _____, _____

2. ¿Qué regalo pide Carolina? _____

3. ¿De qué color es la bicicleta? _____

C. Imagine that you are writing a letter to the **Reyes Magos** or to Santa Claus. Write about two gifts that you would like to have and tell why you want each one. You may follow the model.

Yo quiero _____ y _____.

Yo quiero _____ porque _____.

Yo quiero _____ porque _____.

Realidades 2

Capítulo 4B

Nombre _____

Hora _____

Fecha _____

Guided Practice Activities 4B-6

Presentación escrita (p. 231)

Task: Some friends want to learn more about your favorite celebration or holiday. Write a brief paragraph describing such an event from your childhood.

A. Read the names of the following celebrations. Then, circle three of your favorite celebrations.

¿Qué celebrabas con tu familia?			
El Día de San Valentín	El Día de la Madre	La Navidad (Christmas)	La Semana Santa (Easter week)
El Año Nuevo	Halloween	El Día del Padre	El Día de Acción de Gracias

B. Which of the celebrations or holidays from **part A** was your favorite when you were younger? Why was this your favorite celebration or holiday? Name the celebration and then give two reasons below.

_____ era mi celebración favorita porque _____

y _____.

C. Use the chart below to think about what happened during your favorite celebration. What did you use to do? Where did you get together? Who was there? Circle all the expressions that describe the celebration.

¿Qué hacían?	¿Dónde se reunían?	¿Quiénes estaban?
bailábamos había muchos regalos comíamos mucho	en nuestra casa en casa de los abuelos en casa de mis tíos	mis primos y parientes los amigos muchos niños

D. Now, write a brief paragraph about your favorite celebration or holiday. Use your answers from **parts B** and **C**. You may also follow the model below. Remember to use the imperfect in your description.

El Día de los Reyes Magos era mi celebración favorita porque lo celebraba con mi familia. Nosotros íbamos a la casa de los abuelos. Me gustaba mucho porque había muchos regalos. Siempre jugaba con mis primos.

E. Read your paragraph and check for correct spelling and vocabulary use. Share your paragraph with a partner, who should check the following:

_____ Is the paragraph easy to understand?

_____ Is there anything you should add?

_____ Are there any errors?

Realidades 2

Capítulo 5A

Nombre _____

Fecha _____

Hora _____

AVSR **5A-1**

A ver si recuerdas: Expressions using *tener* (p. 237)

- Remember that **tener** is used in many expressions when English uses "to be."

Marta tiene prisa. *Marta is in a hurry.*	**Tengo hambre.** *I am hungry.*
Luisito tiene ocho años. *Luisito is eight years old.*	**Tengo sed.** *I am thirsty.*
Tenemos razón. *We are right.*	**Tienes cuidado.** *You are careful.*
Ellos tienen miedo. *They are afraid.*	**Tengo calor.** *I am warm/hot.*
Los estudiantes tienen sueño. *The students are tired.*	**Tengo frío.** *I am cold.*

A. Read each statement and choose the appropriate phrase within the parentheses. Follow the model.

> **Modelo** Necesito beber algo. Yo (**tengo hambre** / (**tengo sed**)).

1. Juana quiere dormir ahora. Ella (**tiene sueño** / **tiene prisa**).

2. Nosotros sabemos mucho. Creemos que (**tenemos razón** / **tenemos miedo**).

3. Los niños miran en todas las direcciones antes de cruzar la calle. Ellos
   (**tienen frío** / **tienen cuidado**).

4. La temperatura está a ochenta y cinco grados. Tú (**tienes razón** / **tienes calor**).

5. Yo veo un oso en las montañas. Yo (**tengo miedo** / **tengo hambre**).

B. Write the correct **tener** expression according to each picture. Remember to conjugate **tener**. Follow the model.

> **Modelo** Ellos _____ *tienen* _____ _____ *hambre* _____.

1. Jorge _____ _____.

2. Yo _____ _____.

3. ¡Nosotros _____ _____!

4. Tú _____ _____.

Realidades ❷

Capítulo 5A

Nombre _____

Fecha _____

Hora _____

AVSR 5A-2

A ver si recuerdas: The use of ¡Qué...! in exclamations (p. 237)

- As you know, ¡Qué...! is used with adverbs and adjectives to exclaim "How . . . !"

¡Qué buenos son mis estudiantes! *How good my students are!*

¡Qué pronto llegaron! *How quickly they arrived!*

A. Read the following statements and circle the appropriate reaction. The first one is done for you.

1. El gato de Juan está enfermo. (¡Qué triste! / ¡Qué feo!)

2. Llegamos a Boston en sólo cuarenta y cinco minutos. (¡Qué rápido! / ¡Qué sabroso!)

3. Mmmmm. Me encantan las galletas de mi mamá. (¡Qué graciosas! / ¡Qué sabrosas!)

4. Me gustan las flores de tu jardín. (¡Qué lentas! / ¡Qué bonitas!)

5. Mi hijo saca buenas notas en todas sus clases. (¡Qué inteligente! / ¡Qué guapo!)

- As you know ¡Qué ...! is used with nouns to say "What (a) . . . !"

¡Qué bailarina es tu novia! *What a dancer your girlfriend is!*

B. Read the statements below and complete the exclamations with the appropriate nouns. Follow the model.

Modelo Tu hijo es un estudiante muy bueno. ¡Qué ___estudiante___ es tu hijo!

1. María es una cocinera fantástica. ¡Qué _____ es María!

2. Los hermanos Rulfo son increíbles jugadores de fútbol. ¡Qué _____ son los hermanos Rulfo!

3. Yo soy un buen músico. ¡Qué _____ soy yo!

4. Nosotros somos doctores fantásticos. ¡Qué _____ somos nosotros!

Go Online PHSchool.com WEB CODE jdd-0501

Write the Spanish vocabulary word below each picture. Be sure to include the article for each noun.

Realidades ②

Capítulo 5A

Nombre _____

Hora _____

Fecha _____

Vocabulary Flash Cards, Sheet 2

Write the Spanish vocabulary word below each picture. Be sure to include the article for each noun.

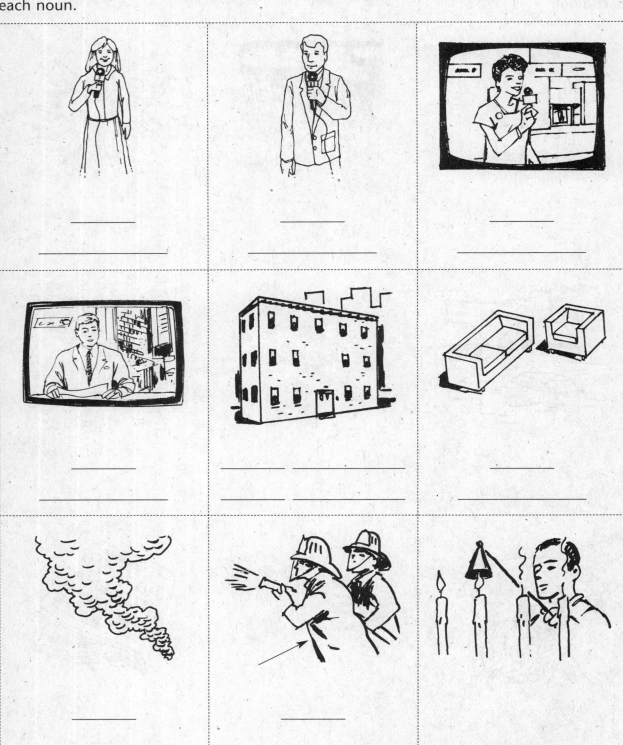

Realidades 2

Capítulo 5A

Nombre _____

Hora _____

Fecha _____

Vocabulary Flash Cards, Sheet 3

Write the Spanish vocabulary word below each picture. Be sure to include the article for each noun.

_____

_____

_____

_____

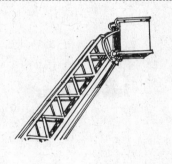

_____

_____

_____

_____

_____

Realidades ②

Capítulo 5A

Nombre _____

Hora _____

Fecha _____

Vocabulary Flash Cards, Sheet 4

Write the Spanish vocabulary word below each picture. If there is a word or phrase, copy it in the space provided. Be sure to include the article for each noun.

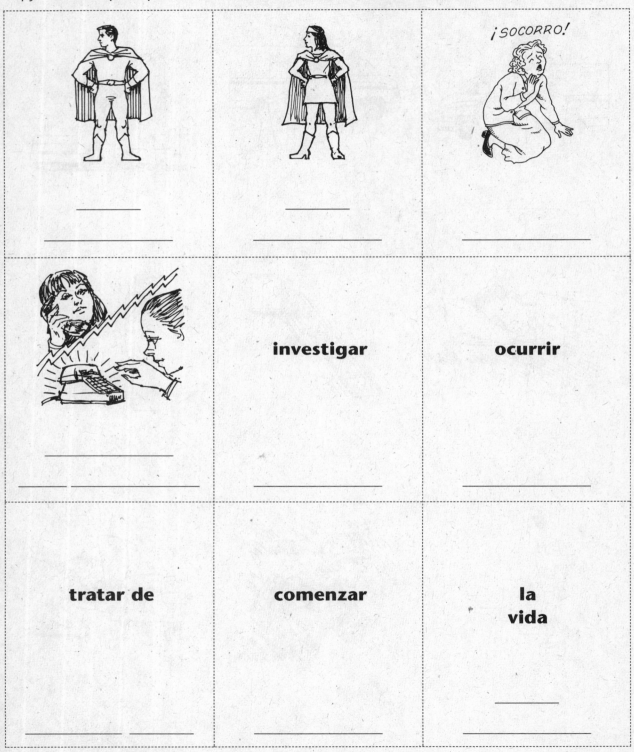

¡SOCORRO!

_____

_____

_____

investigar

ocurrir

tratar de

comenzar

la vida

Copy the word or phrase in the space provided. Be sure to include the article for each noun.

escaparse	**muerto, muerta**	**herido, herida**
_____	_____, _____	_____, _____
el herido, la herida	**salvar**	**valiente**
_____ _____, _____ _____	_____	_____
vivo, viva	**a causa de**	**asustado, asustada**
_____, _____	_____ _____	_____, _____

Guided Practice Activities — *Vocabulary Flash Cards 5A* **167**

Realidades 2

Capítulo 5A

Nombre _____

Hora _____

Fecha _____

Vocabulary Flash Cards, Sheet 6

Copy the word or phrase in the space provided. Be sure to include the article for each noun.

la causa	de prisa	de repente
_____	_____	_____
_____	_____	_____

gritar	hubo	se murieron
		_____
_____	_____	

oír	sin duda	el noticiero
	_____	_____
_____		

Realidades 2

Capítulo 5A

Nombre

Hora

Fecha

Vocabulary Flash Cards, Sheet 7

Copy the word or phrase in the space provided. Be sure to include the article for each noun. The blank cards can be used to write and practice other Spanish vocabulary for the chapter.

afortunadamente	la tormenta	quemar(se)

Realidades 2

Capítulo 5A

Nombre _____

Hora _____

Fecha _____

Vocabulary Flash Cards, Sheet 8

These blank cards can be used to write and practice other Spanish vocabulary for the chapter.

_____ _____ _____

_____ _____ _____

_____ _____ _____

Realidades 2

Capítulo 5A

Nombre

Hora

Fecha

Vocabulary Check, Sheet 1

Tear out this page. Write the English words on the lines. Fold the paper along the dotted line to see the correct answers so you can check your work.

llover _____

nevar _____

el terremoto _____

la tormenta _____

el artículo _____

el locutor,
la locutora _____

el noticiero _____

ocurrir _____

el reportero,
la reportera _____

apagar _____

el bombero,
la bombera _____

la escalera _____

escaparse _____

esconderse _____

Fold In

Nombre ____________________ Hora ____________

Fecha ____________________

Vocabulary Check, Sheet 2

Tear out this page. Write the Spanish words on the lines. Fold the paper along the dotted line to see the correct answers so you can check your work.

to rain	____________
to snow	____________
earthquake	____________
storm	____________
article	____________
announcer	____________
newscast	____________
to occur	____________
reporter	____________
to put out (fire)	____________
firefighter	____________
ladder	____________
to escape	____________
to hide (oneself)	____________

Fold In ←

Realidades 2

Capítulo 5A

Nombre _____

Hora _____

Fecha _____

Vocabulary Check, Sheet 3

Tear out this page. Write the English words on the lines. Fold the paper along the dotted line to see the correct answers so you can check your work.

el humo _____

el incendio _____

el paramédico,
la paramédica _____

quemar(se) _____

el herido, la herida _____

rescatar _____

salvar _____

la vida _____

vivo, viva _____

afortunadamente _____

asustado, asustada _____

la causa _____

gritar _____

¡Socorro! _____

Fold In ←

Realidades 2

Capítulo 5A

Nombre _____

Hora _____

Fecha _____

Vocabulary Check, Sheet 4

Tear out this page. Write the Spanish words on the lines. Fold the paper along the dotted line to see the correct answers so you can check your work.

smoke _____

fire _____

paramedic _____

to burn (oneself), _____
to burn up

injured person _____

to rescue _____

to save _____

life _____

living, alive _____

fortunately _____

frightened _____

cause _____

to scream _____

Help! _____

To hear a complete list of the vocabulary for this chapter, go to Disc 2, Track 1 on the guided Practice Audio CD or go to www.phschool.com and type in the Web Code jdd-0589. Then click on **Repaso del capítulo**.

Fold In

The imperfect tense: other uses (p. 248)

- You can use the imperfect tense to tell what time it was **(qué hora era),** or what the weather was like **(qué tiempo hacía)** when something happened.

  Eran las cinco de la mañana cuando el huracán comenzó.

  It was five in the morning when the hurricane began.

A. Read the following statements and circle the verb that tells what time it was or what the weather was like (the imperfect tense). Then, underline the verb that gives the action (the preterite tense).

Modelo ((Eran)/ Fueron) las diez de la noche cuando <u>terminó</u> el noticiero.

1. (Llovía / Llovió) mucho cuando me levanté.

2. (Nevó / Nevaba) cuando salí de casa.

3. (Eran / Fueron) las tres de la tarde cuando comenzó el huracán.

4. (Hubo / Había) una tormenta de lluvia cuando comenzó la inundación.

5. (Era / Eran) la una de la tarde cuando vi el incendio.

6. (Eran / Era) las nueve cuando me acosté.

7. (Hacía / Hacían) mal tiempo cuando llegué a casa.

B. Write the imperfect form of the verb in parentheses to complete the weather description or time expression in each sentence below. Follow the model.

Modelo (Ser) _____*Eran*_____ las cuatro cuando la explosión ocurrió.

1. (Hacer) _____ mucho viento cuando los paramédicos llegaron.

2. Cuando la locutora comenzó a hablar, (ser) _____ las seis de la noche.

3. Cuando chocaron esos tres coches, (hacer) _____ mal tiempo.

4. (Llover) _____ mucho cuando ocurrió el accidente.

5. (Ser) _____ las doce cuando mi hermano volvió a casa.

The imperfect tense: other uses (*continued*)

• The imperfect tense is also used to tell how a person was feeling when something happened.

Anoche me acosté temprano porque *tenía* sueño.

Last night I went to bed early because I was sleepy.

C. In each sentence, underline the preterite verb, which tells what action took place. Then, complete the sentence with the imperfect form of the verb in parentheses to tell how the people were feeling. The first one is done for you.

1. <u>Fuimos</u> a comer algo porque nosotros ___*teníamos*___ hambre. (**tener**)

2. La reportera habló con muchas personas porque ella _____ (**querer**) saber qué ocurrió.

3. Los paramédicos _____ (**tener**) prisa, y por eso salieron pronto.

4. Cuando apagaron el incendio, los bomberos _____ (**querer**) descansar.

5. Cuando llegamos al edificio, nosotros _____ (**estar**) nerviosos.

6. Juanita gritó porque ella _____ (**estar**) asustada.

D. You have learned three ways to tell about events in the past using the imperfect and preterite tenses in this chapter. Use the graphic below to create three sentences in the past. Remember to conjugate the verbs! Follow the model.

Telling Time		**Action**
Ser las siete de la tarde	cuando >	nosotros ver el noticiero

Modelo

Eran las siete de la tarde cuando nosotros vimos el noticiero.

1.

How they feel		**Action**
Los paramédicos estar cansados	porque >	subir las escaleras de prisa

_____

2.

The weather		**Action**
Hacer mucho viento	cuando >	el huracán llegar a la ciudad

_____

3.

Telling time		**Action**
Ser las cinco y media de la tarde	cuando >	los bomberos apagar el incendio

_____

Go Online WEB CODE jdd-0504
PHSchool.com

Realidades 2

Capítulo 5A

Nombre _____

Hora _____

Fecha _____

Guided Practice Activities 5A-3

The imperfect tense: other uses (*continued*)

- Remember that **hubo** and **había** are forms of **haber**. Both words mean "there was" or "there were." Look at these rules:
- Use **hubo** to say that an event (such as a fire) took place.
  Hubo un incendio ayer.   *There was a fire. = it took place*
- Use **había** to describe a situation in the past.
  Había mucho humo en el edificio.   *There was smoke in the building. = the condition existed*

E. Below there are two sentences in the past for each drawing: one tells about an action and the other gives a description. If the sentence tells that an action took place, write **hubo**. If the sentence describes a situation or condition that existed, write **había**. Follow the models.

Modelos

_____*Hubo*_____ una tormenta muy mala.

_____*Había*_____ muchos árboles en la calle.

1. _____ un terremoto en esta ciudad.

2. _____ poca gente en las calles.

3. _____ muchos heridos.

4. _____ un incendio a las siete de la mañana.

5. _____ una inundación en la ciudad.

6. _____ muchas casas destruidas.

Realidades 2

Capítulo 5A

Nombre _____

Fecha _____

Hora _____

Guided Practice Activities 5A-4

The preterite of the verbs *oír*, *creer*, *leer*, and *destruir* (p. 250)

- The verbs **oír**, **creer**, **leer**, and **destruir** are irregular in the preterite.
- These verbs are irregular in the **Ud./él/ella** and **Uds./ellos/ellas** forms. Instead of an "i" on the endings there is a "y".
- The verbs **oír**, **leer**, and **creer** have accent marks on the **tú**, **nosotros/nosotras** and **vosotros/vosotras** forms, whereas **destruir** does not.

yo	oí	leí	creí	destruí
tú	oíste	leíste	creíste	destruiste
usted/él/ella	oyó	leyó	creyó	destruyó
nosotros/nosotras	oímos	leímos	creímos	destruimos
vosotros/vosotras	oísteis	leísteis	creísteis	destruisteis
ustedes/ellos/ellas	oyeron	leyeron	creyeron	destruyeron

A. Read the sentences below and look at the underlined verbs. Write an **X** in either the **Present** or the **Preterite** column, according to the tense of the underlined verb. The first one is done for you.

	Present	Preterite
1. Anoche <u>oí</u> un grito en la casa.	_____	___X___
2. Ella <u>oye</u> al locutor por la radio.	_____	_____
3. ¿Tú <u>crees</u> que la gente se escapó?	_____	_____
4. Nosotros <u>creímos</u> al reportero.	_____	_____
5. El incendio <u>destruyó</u> el edificio de apartamentos.	_____	_____
6. Anoche Amalia <u>leyó</u> el artículo del terremoto.	_____	_____

B. Complete the following sentences with the correct form of the verb in parentheses.

1. Ayer tú _____ (**oír**) el noticiero en la radio.

2. Mis padres _____ (**creer**) las noticias.

3. El huracán _____ (**destruir**) las casas.

4. Los bomberos _____ (**oír**) la explosión.

5. El incendio _____ (**destruir**) los muebles.

6. Los estudiantes _____ (**leer**) las noticias en la biblioteca.

Go Online WEB CODE jdd-0505
PHSchool.com

Realidades 2

Capítulo 5A

Nombre _____

Hora _____

Fecha _____

Guided Practice Activities 5A-5

Lectura: Desastre en Valdivia, Chile (pp. 256–257)

A. The reading in your textbook is about natural disasters that occurred in Valdivia, Chile. Think of four things that you already know about earthquakes and tsunamis, and write them below.

1. _____   3. _____

2. _____   4. _____

B. Cognates are words that are similar in spelling and pronunciation. Here are some sentences from your textbook reading, in which some of the Spanish words have been circled. Write the English cognates beneath each set of sentences.

1. A las seis y dos (minutos) de la mañana, el 21 de (mayo) 1960, una gran (parte) del país sintió el primer terremoto.

   a. _____   b. _____   c. _____

2. Unos minutos después del (desastroso) terremoto, llegó un (tsunami) que destruyó lo poco que quedaba en la ciudad y en las pequeñas (comunidades.)

   a. _____   b. _____   c. _____

3. La gran ola de agua se levantó (destruyendo) a su paso casas, (animales,) botes y, por supuesto, muchas vidas (humanas.)

   a. _____   b. _____   c. _____

C. Read the following rules from your textbook reading about what to do and what not to do during an earthquake. Place an **X** next to the things you should do, in the **Sí** column, and should not do, in the **No** column.

Si estás en un edificio durante un terremoto:	Sí	No
1. Debes mantener la calma.	_____	_____
2. Debes mantenerte cerca de las ventanas.	_____	_____
3. Debes utilizar los elevadores.	_____	_____
Si estás fuera de un edificio durante un terremoto:		
4. Debes estar lejos de los postes de energía eléctrica.	_____	_____
5. Debes ir a un edificio alto.	_____	_____

Realidades 2

Capítulo 5A

Nombre _____

Hora _____

Fecha _____

Guided Practice Activities 5A-6

Presentación oral (p. 259)

Task: You and a partner will role-play an interview about an imaginary fire that happened in your town or city. You will need to create a list of questions and answers for the interview. Use your lists during the interview.

A. Read the following phrases. Write **dónde** if the phrase describes *where* the fire happened. Write **cuándo** if it describes *when* it happened. Write **quién** if it names people *who* were involved. Write **por qué** if it describes *why* it happened. Follow the model.

Modelo   problema eléctrico ___*por qué*___

1. en una escuela _____

2. ayer por la noche _____

3. una explosión _____

4. muchos niños _____

5. a las cinco de la mañana _____

6. un cable eléctrico _____

7. en un edificio _____

8. algunas personas _____

B. Use the information from **part A** or make up your own to answer the following questions about the fire. The first one is done for you.

1. ¿Dónde fue el incendio? *El incendio fue en un edificio.* _____

2. ¿Cuándo ocurrió? _____

3. ¿Quiénes estaban allí? _____

4. ¿Por qué ocurrió? _____

C. Use the questions and your answers from **part B** to practice for the interview.

D. Your teacher will tell you which role to play. Listen to your partner's questions or answers and keep the interview going. Remember that you should ask or tell "when," "where," and "why" the imaginary fire occurred, and "who" was involved. Complete the paragraph below to start the interview.

Anoche hubo un incendio en _____. Los bomberos estuvieron

allí _____. _____ se salvaron.

El incendio ocurrió porque _____.

Realidades ②

Capítulo 5B

Nombre _____

Hora _____

Fecha _____

Vocabulary Flash Cards, Sheet 1

Write the Spanish vocabulary word or phrase below each picture. Be sure to include the article for each noun.

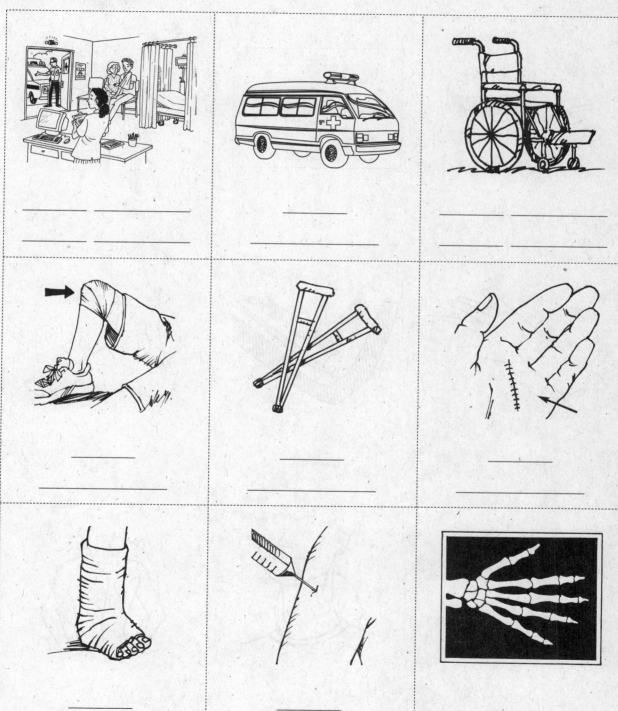

_____

_____

_____

_____

_____

_____

_____

_____

_____

_____

_____

_____

_____

_____

_____

Write the Spanish vocabulary word below each picture. Be sure to include the article for each noun.

_____   _____   _____

_____   _____   _____

_____   _____   _____

Realidades

Capítulo 5B

Nombre _____

Hora _____

Fecha _____

Vocabulary Flash Cards, Sheet 3

Write the Spanish vocabulary word or phrase below each picture. Be sure to include the article for each noun.

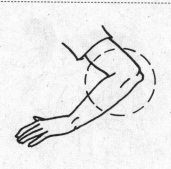

_____

_____

_____

_____

_____

_____

_____

_____

_____

_____

_____

_____

_____

_____

_____

_____

_____

_____

Realidades ②

Capítulo 5B

Nombre _____

Hora _____

Fecha _____

Vocabulary Flash Cards, Sheet 4

Write the Spanish vocabulary word below each picture. If there is a word or phrase, copy it in the space provided. Be sure to include the article for each noun.

_____	_____	_____
	_____	_____
_____	_____	_____
_____	_____	_____
 _____ _____	**doler** _____	**pobrecito, pobrecita** _____,

Realidades 2

Capítulo 5B

Nombre _____

Hora _____

Fecha _____

Vocabulary Flash Cards, Sheet 5

Copy the word or phrase in the space provided. Be sure to include the article for each noun.

la sangre _____ _____	**recetar** _____	**roto, rota** _____ , _____
me caigo _____ _____	**el accidente** _____	**te caes** _____
se cayeron _____ _____	**cortarse** _____	**¿Qué te pasó?** _____ _____

Copy the word or phrase in the space provided. The blank cards can be used to write and practice other Spanish vocabulary for the chapter.

torcerse	**sentirse**	**moverse**
_____	_____	_____
¡Qué lástima!		
_____	_____	_____
_____	_____	_____

Realidades 2

Capítulo 5B

Nombre _____

Fecha _____

Hora _____

Vocabulary Check, Sheet 1

Tear out this page. Write the English words on the lines. Fold the paper along the dotted line to see the correct answers so you can check your work.

el enfermero,
la enfermera _____

la inyección _____

la medicina _____

las pastillas _____

las puntadas _____

la radiografía _____

la receta _____

la sala de
emergencia _____

la sangre _____

la venda _____

el yeso _____

el accidente _____

la ambulancia _____

cortarse _____

lastimarse _____

Fold In

Realidades 2

Capítulo 5B

Nombre _____

Hora _____

Fecha _____

Vocabulary Check, Sheet 2

Tear out this page. Write the Spanish words on the lines. Fold the paper along the dotted line to see the correct answers so you can check your work.

nurse _____

injection, shot _____

medicine _____

pills _____

stitches _____

X-ray _____

prescription _____

emergency room _____

blood _____

bandage _____

cast _____

accident _____

ambulance _____

to cut oneself _____

to hurt oneself _____

Fold In

Nombre ______________________ Hora ______________

Fecha ______________________

Vocabulary Check, Sheet 3

Tear out this page. Write the English words on the lines. Fold the paper along the dotted line to see the correct answers so you can check your work.

romperse ______________

torcerse ______________

tropezar (con) ______________

el codo ______________

el cuello ______________

la espalda ______________

el hombro ______________

el hueso ______________

la muñeca ______________

el músculo ______________

la rodilla ______________

el tobillo ______________

pobrecito, pobrecita ______________

Fold In

Realidades ②

Capítulo 5B

Nombre _____

Fecha _____

Hora _____

Vocabulary Check, Sheet 4

Tear out this page. Write the Spanish words on the lines. Fold the paper along the dotted line to see the correct answers so you can check your work.

to break, to tear _____

to twist, to sprain _____

to trip (over) _____

elbow _____

neck _____

back _____

shoulder _____

bone _____

wrist _____

muscle _____

knee _____

ankle _____

poor thing _____

Fold In

To hear a complete list of the vocabulary for this chapter, go to Disc 2, Track 2 on the guided Practice Audio CD or go to www.phschool.com and type in the Web Code jdd-0599. Then click on **Repaso del capítulo**.

Irregular preterites: *venir, poner, decir,* and *traer* (p. 274)

- The verbs **venir, poner, decir,** and **traer** have a similar pattern in the preterite as that of **estar, poder,** and **tener.** They have irregular stems. Remember that the endings do not have any accent marks.

Infinitive	Stem
decir	dij-
estar	estuv-
poder	pud-
poner	pus-
tener	tuv-
traer	traj-
venir	vin-

Irregular Preterite Endings	
-e	-imos
-iste	-isteis
-o	-ieron, -eron

Preterite of *venir*	
vine	vinimos
viniste	vinisteis
vino	vinieron

A. Look at the drawings showing what happened to Diego. Then, read the paragraph and circle the correct irregular preterite form of the verb in parentheses. The first one has been done for you.

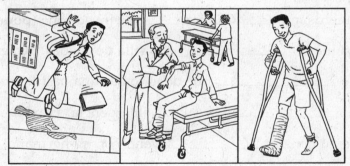

Ayer Diego (**tuve** /(**tuvo**)) un accidente. Sus padres (**vino / vinieron**) a la escuela

porque Diego (**tuvo / tuve**) que ir a la sala de emergencia. Yo fui con ellos.

Nosotros (**estuvieron / estuvimos**) con él en el hospital por seis horas. Diego no

(**pudo / pudiste**) moverse por dos horas. Después, el enfermero le

(**trajo / trajimos**) una venda y le (**puso / pusieron**) la venda en el brazo.

El enfermero (**dije / dijo**) que su brazo no estaba roto pero ellos le

(**pusimos / pusieron**) un yeso en el tobillo. Luego, Diego (**tuvo / tuvieron**) que

caminar con muletas. Yo le (**dijiste / dije**) a Diego que quería escribir mi nombre

en el yeso.

Realidades 2

Capítulo 5B

Nombre _____

Hora _____

Fecha _____

Guided Practice Activities 5B-2

Irregular preterites: *venir, poner, decir*, and *traer* (*continued*)

B. Look at the sentences below and fill in the missing stem of the verb in parentheses for each ending that is given. Follow the model.

Modelo (**traer**) La enfermera me _____*traj*o una silla de ruedas.

1. (**venir**) Todos _____ieron a la sala de emergencia conmigo.

2. (**decir**) Tú _____iste "¡Ay!" cuando te lastimaste.

3. (**traer**) Nosotros le _____imos una venda y medicina.

4. (**poner**) La enfermera me _____o una inyección.

5. (**estar**) La familia _____o en el hospital por cuatro horas.

6. (**tener**) El coche _____o un accidente anoche.

7. (**poder**) Yo no _____e ver lo que pasó.

C. The following actions happened in the past. Write in the correct form of the verb in parentheses to complete each sentence. Follow the model.

Modelo Los enfermeros me _____*pusieron*_____ una inyección. (**poner**)

1. Mi mamá y papá me _____ una silla de ruedas. (**traer**)

2. El enfermero me _____ que debo tomar una pastilla para el dolor. (**decir**)

3. Mi hermano _____ a la sala de emergencia. (**venir**)

4. ¡Qué lástima que tú no _____ venir con mi hermano! (**poder**)

5. Yo no _____ en la sala de emergencia anoche. (**estar**)

6. Nosotros _____ que salir del edificio porque un incendio comenzó. (**tener**)

7. Por desgracia, nadie _____ botellas de agua. (**traer**)

Go Online WEB CODE jdd-0513
PHSchool.com

Imperfect progressive and preterite (p. 277)

- Remember that the present progressive is used to tell what someone is doing. It is formed by the present tense of the verb **estar** + present participle (**-ando** or **-iendo**):

  La doctora está hablando.　　　　*The doctor is talking.*

  Laura y Juan están corriendo.　　*Laura and Juan are running.*

- As shown above, the present progressive is used to tell what *is* happening. The imperfect progressive is used to tell what *was* happening. It uses the imperfect tense of **estar** + present participle:

  La doctora estaba hablando.　　　*The doctor was talking.*

  Laura y Juan estaban corriendo.　*Laura and Juan were running.*

A. First, circle the present progressive in each sentence. Then, change each sentence from the present progressive to the *imperfect* progressive. Follow the model.

| Modelo | Eliana (está caminando) con muletas. | *estaba* | *caminando* |

1. Juana está hablando con el doctor.　　　　　　＿＿＿＿＿　＿＿＿＿＿

2. Nosotros estamos bebiendo bastante agua.　　＿＿＿＿＿　＿＿＿＿＿

3. Yo estoy examinando las puntadas.　　　　　　＿＿＿＿＿　＿＿＿＿＿

4. Tú estás sacando una radiografía.　　　　　　＿＿＿＿＿　＿＿＿＿＿

5. La enfermera está poniendo una inyección.　　＿＿＿＿＿　＿＿＿＿＿

6. El doctor me está dando puntadas.　　　　　　＿＿＿＿＿　＿＿＿＿＿

7. Los paramédicos le están moviendo a otro piso.　＿＿＿＿＿　＿＿＿＿＿

- You can use the imperfect progressive tense to describe something that was happening over a period of time. The imperfect progressive uses the imperfect tense of **estar** + the present participle:

  Teresa estaba escribiendo un cuento.　　*Teresa was writing a story.*

B. The following sentences tell what people were doing yesterday in the hospital when the storm began. Complete each sentence by writing in the correct form of **estar** and the participle of the verb in parentheses. Follow the model.

Cuando la tormenta comenzó…

| Modelo | Mario ＿＿＿＿＿ ＿＿＿＿＿ con muletas. (**caminar**) |

1. mi hermano ＿＿＿＿＿ ＿＿＿＿＿ una radiografía. (**sacar**)

2. mis amigos y yo ＿＿＿＿＿ ＿＿＿＿＿ la ambulancia. (**esperar**)

Realidades **2**

Nombre _____

Hora _____

Capítulo 5B

Fecha _____

Guided Practice Activities 5B-3a

Imperfect progressive and preterite (*continued*)

3. la Dra. Carrillo _____ _____ una receta. (**escribir**)

4. usted _____ _____ a Javier. (**ayudar**)

5. tú _____ _____ una inyección. (**poner**)

- Remember that some present participles have changes in their spelling.
- **-ir** stem-changing verbs have a vowel change to "i" or "u":
  pedir → pidiendo   **vestir → vistiendo**   **dormir → durmiendo**
- **leer, caer, creer**, and **traer** have a "y":
  leer → leyendo   **caer → cayendo**   **creer → creyendo**   **traer → trayendo**

C. A paramedic has to report to his boss about what different patients were doing when they got hurt. Complete his statements. Follow the model.

Modelo   Los niños / seguir / a sus hermanos mayores
_Los niños estaban siguiendo a sus hermanos mayores_____.

1. Los camareros / servir / sopa muy caliente

_____.

2. Felipe Sánchez / leer / una novela muy interesante

_____.

3 Adelita Romero / vestir / a su perro

_____.

4. Nosotros / subir / las escaleras

_____.

5. El señor Peña / dormir / en el sofá

_____.

Realidades ②

Capítulo 5B

Nombre _____

Fecha _____

Hora _____

Guided Practice Activities 5B-4

Imperfect progressive and preterite (*continued*)

- The imperfect progressive and the preterite tenses can be used in the same sentence. The imperfect progressive describes what was happening while the preterite tells about something specific that happened or that interrupted an action.

  Ella estaba corriendo cuando se lastimó el tobillo.
  She was running when she hurt her ankle.

D. For each sentence below, draw a line beneath the verb in the imperfect progressive tense that identifies what was happening. Then, identify the interrupted action by circling the verb in the preterite tense. The first one is done for you.

1. Yo <u>estaba corriendo</u> cuando (tropecé.)

2. Cuando Miguel se lastimó, él estaba jugando al fútbol.

3. Tú estabas sirviendo la comida cuando te lastimaste.

4. Las hermanas Paulatino estaban usando la silla de ruedas cuando tuvieron el accidente.

5. Cuando Teresa llegó a la sala de emergencia le estaba doliendo mucho el brazo.

E. The sentences below describe what different people were doing when something bad happened to them. Read the sentences and circle the verb that completes each sentence in the most logical way. Follow the model.

Modelo Antonio (**estaba jugando** / **jugó**) al tenis cuando se lastimó la rodilla.

1. María y Fernando estaban esquiando cuando (**se estaban cayendo** / **se cayeron**).

2. Nosotros estábamos peleándonos cuando yo (**me estaba rompiendo** / **me rompí**) el dedo.

3. MaríaTeresa (**estaba caminando** / **caminó**) a casa sin chaqueta cuando comenzó a nevar.

4. Cuando yo me lastimé, (**estaba corriendo** / **corrí**) un maratón.

F. Look at the information in the boxes below. Use the imperfect progressive and the preterite to fill in the blanks with the phrases contained in the boxes. Follow the model.

Modelo

What was happening	Specific occurrence that took place
levantar pesas	lastimarse

Marcos *estaba levantando pesas* cuando *se lastimó* el hombro.

1.

What was happening	Specific occurrence that took place
usar tijeras	cortarse

Tú _____ cuando _____ el dedo.

Imperfect progressive and preterite (*continued*)

2.

What was happening	Specific occurrence that took place
leer el periódico	ver

Maricarmen _____ cuando _____ del accidente.

3.

What was happening	Specific occurrence that took place
pedir una silla de ruedas	caerse

Yo _____ cuando _____ .

4.

What was happening	Specific occurrence that took place
vestirse	sentir dolor

Tú _____ cuando _____ en la espalda.

- When you use pronouns with the imperfect progressive, you can put them before **estar** or attach them to the participle. Remember to add an accent over the "e" or "a" of the participle ending.

  Yo me estaba sirviendo. *or:* **Yo estaba sirviéndome.**

G. Rewrite the sentences below by putting the underlined object pronoun after the conjugated present partciple. Follow the model.

Modelo   Javier se estaba cepillando los dientes.

Javier estaba cepillándose los dientes _____ .

1. Tía Luisa me estaba trayendo un sándwich.

_____ .

2. Cristina y Julia nos estaban pidiendo ayuda.

_____ .

3. Tú te estabas duchando.

_____ .

4. Nosotros nos estábamos levantando.

_____ .

Go Online WEB CODE jdd-0514
PHSchool.com

Lectura: Mejorar la salud para todos (pp. 282–283)

A. The articles in your textbook reading are about health campaigns. A good strategy for understanding these articles is to look for cognates. The following words are cognates from the reading. Say each word in Spanish aloud and then write the letter of the English word that matches it.

1. _____ internacional   **a.** international   **b.** internal

2. _____ institución   **a.** institution   **b.** inspiration

3. _____ promover   **a.** protect   **b.** promote

4. _____ prevención   **a.** prevention   **b.** preview

5. _____ voluntarios   **a.** volume   **b.** volunteers

B. Look at this title from one of the health articles in your textbook. Then, read the sentences that follow and write **L** (for **Lectura**) if it's something you read in the title. Write **N** (for **No**) if it's something you didn't read in the title.

> *Cuerpo de la Paz* (*Peace Corps*) *y Medical Aid for Children of Latin America* (*MACLA*) *ayudan a niños que requieren cirugía plástica* (*plastic surgery*).

1. MACLA significa *Medical Aid for Children of Latin America*. _____

2. Cuerpo de la Paz y MACLA ayudan a niños que requieren cirugía plástica. _____

3. Los niños son de Europa. _____

C. The following are quotes from the reading in your textbook. Read what was said by the singers Luis Enrique and Mercedes Sosa. Then, circle the option that best completes each sentence.

> *"La vida nos pone a prueba* (*test*) *día a día, con momentos buenos y malos. Es nuestra responsabilidad tomar las decisiones correctas. ¡Dile no a las drogas y dile sí a la vida, siempre!"* –Luis Enrique

> *"No les falles* (*fail*) *a tus chicos, llévalos a vacunar* (*to be vaccinated*). *Así pueden estar completamente protegidos y darle ¡gracias a la vida!"* –Mercedes Sosa

1. Luis Enrique speaks about
   a. the prevention of drug abuse.
   b. vaccinations.

2. Mercedes Sosa speaks about
   a. donating blood.
   b. vaccinations.

Presentación escrita (p. 285)

Task: Imagine you have to report an accident you saw near school. Organize your ideas before you write the report for your school.

A. First, you need to describe what you were doing when the accident occurred. Choose an activity from the list below. Then, circle the activity.

¿Qué estabas haciendo?

1. Estaba saliendo de la escuela.
2. Estaba jugando con mis amigos.
3. Estaba hablando con la profesora.
4. Estaba entrando en la escuela.
5. Estaba caminando con mi hermano.

B. Next, the chart below can help you organize information about the accident. You need to determine: What happened? When did it happen? Who was hurt? Who helped? Circle one option in each column.

¿Qué pasó?	¿Cuándo ocurrió?	¿Quién se lastimó?	¿Quiénes ayudaron?
un árbol se cayó	por la mañana	un estudiante una estudiante	los estudiantes
un coche chocó con algo	por la tarde	un profesor una profesora	los bomberos
una ventana se rompió	por la noche	una señora un hombre	una enfermera la policía

C. Now, use your answers from **parts A** and **B** to complete a report of the accident. You can follow the model below.

Yo _____ cuando vi un accidente. _____

_____ y _____ se lastimó.

_____ lo/la ayudó.

D. Read through your accident report to check for spelling, correct verb usage, vocabulary, and clarity.

E. Share the report with a partner who should check the following:

_____ Is the report easy to understand?

_____ Is the information in a clear, logical order?

_____ Is there anything to add to give more information?

_____ Are there any errors?

A ver si recuerdas: Verbs like *gustar* (p. 291)

- You are already familiar with the verb **gustar** and other verbs that function like it (**encantar, disgustar, importar, interesar**). Remember that the verb agrees in number with the item or action that follows it. The indirect object pronoun agrees with the person whose preferences are geing discussed.

    A Juan → le encantan los deportes.
    Juan loves sports.

    A nosotros → nos importa el partido de tenis.
    The tennis match is important to us.

A. Write the indirect object pronoun that corresponds to the person listed below. The indirect object pronouns are in the box below to help you.

me	*to me*	**nos**	*to us*
te	*to you (sing.)*	**os**	*to you (pl.)*
le	*to him/her*	**les**	*to them*

Modelo Al profesor Rodríguez ___*le*___

1. A Juliana _____

2. A nosotros _____

3. A mí _____

4. A los doctores _____

5. A ti _____

6. A Juan y a Ramón _____

7. A mi hermano y a mí _____

8. A la profesora _____

Realidades 2

Capítulo 6A

Nombre _____

Hora _____

Fecha _____

AVSR 6A-2

Verbs like *gustar* (*continued*)

B. Look at the picture and corresponding noun for each number. Circle the correct form of the verb that could be used in a sentence about the noun.

 Modelo (encanta /(encantan)) las películas de horror

 **1.** (disgusta / **disgustan**) las telenovelas

 **2.** (gusta / gustan) el cine

 **3.** (interesa / interesan) los programas deportivos

 **4.** (importa / importan) la televisión

 5. (encanta / encantan) los programas musicales

C. Now complete these sentences, which are combined from exercises A and B. Write the appropriate indirect object pronoun in the first blank, and the correct form of the verb given in the second blank. Follow the model.

Modelo A mí __me__ __encantan__ (**encantar**) los programas musicales.

1. A Juan y a Ramón _____ _____ (**interesar**) los programas deportivos.

2. A mi hermano y a mí _____ _____ (**importar**) la televisión.

3. A Juliana _____ _____ (**gustar**) el cine.

4. A nosotros _____ _____ (**encantar**) las películas de horror.

5. A los doctores _____ _____ (**disgustar**) las telenovelas.

6. A ti _____ _____ (**encantar**) los programas musicales.

Go Online WEB CODE jdd-0601
PHSchool.com

Nombre _____

Hora _____

Fecha _____

Vocabulary Flash Cards, Sheet 1

Write the Spanish vocabulary word below each picture. Be sure to include the article for each noun.

_____

_____

_____

_____

_____

_____

_____

_____

_____

Write the Spanish vocabulary word below each picture. Be sure to include the article for each noun.

_____

_____

_____

_____

_____

_____

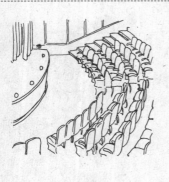

_____

_____

_____

Realidades ❷

Capítulo 6A

Nombre _____

Hora _____

Fecha _____

Vocabulary Flash Cards, Sheet 3

Write the Spanish vocabulary word or phrase below each picture. Be sure to include the article for each noun.

_____

_____

_____

_____

_____

_____

_____

_____

_____

_____

_____

_____ /

_____

Realidades 2

Capítulo 6A

Nombre _____

Hora _____

Fecha _____

Vocabulary Flash Cards, Sheet 4

Copy the word or phrase in the space provided. Be sure to include the article for each noun.

enojado, enojada	**furioso, furiosa**	**agitado, agitada**
_____ , _____	_____ , _____	_____ , _____
al final	**la competencia**	**fenomenal**
_____ _____	_____	_____
la liga	**por ... vez**	**resultar**
_____ _____	_____ _____	_____

Copy the word or phrase in the space provided. Be sure to include the article for
each noun.

último, **última** _____ , _____	**aburrirse** _____	**enojarse** _____
volverse loco, **loca** _____ _____ , _____	**dormirse** _____	**morirse** _____
los **campeones** _____ _____	**competir** _____	**entrevistar** _____

Realidades 2

Capítulo 6A

Nombre _____

Hora _____

Fecha _____

Vocabulary Flash Cards, Sheet 6

Copy the word or phrase in the space provided. These blank cards can be used to write and practice other Spanish vocabulary for the chapter.

ponerse + adjective

_____ _____

_____

_____

_____

_____

_____

_____

_____

_____

_____

Realidades 2

Capítulo 6A

Nombre _____

Hora _____

Fecha _____

Vocabulary Check, Sheet 1

Tear out this page. Write the English words on the lines. Fold the paper along the dotted line to see the correct answers so you can check your work.

aplaudir _____

competir _____

la competencia _____

al final _____

fenomenal _____

resultar _____

último, última _____

el auditorio _____

el comentario _____

entrevistar _____

el público _____

aburrirse _____

alegre _____

emocionado, emocionada _____

enojado, enojada _____

Fold In ←

Realidades **2**

Capítulo 6A

Nombre _____

Fecha _____

Hora _____

Vocabulary Check, Sheet 2

Tear out this page. Write the Spanish words on the lines. Fold the paper along the dotted line to see the correct answers so you can check your work.

to applaud _____

to compete _____

competition _____

at the end _____

phenomenal _____

to result, to turn out _____

last, final _____

auditorium _____

commentary _____

to interview _____

audience _____

to get bored _____

happy _____

excited, emotional _____

angry _____

Fold In

Realidades 2

Capítulo 6A

Nombre _____

Hora _____

Fecha _____

Vocabulary Check, Sheet 3

Tear out this page. Write the English words on the lines. Fold the paper along the dotted line to see the correct answers so you can check your work.

el aficionado,
la aficionada   _____

el atleta, la atleta   _____

el campeonato   _____

el empate   _____

el jugador,
la jugadora   _____

perder   _____

el tanteo   _____

el concurso
de belleza   _____

el premio   _____

la reina   _____

el presentador,
la presentadora   _____

agitado, agitada   _____

furioso, furiosa   _____

dormirse   _____

Fold In

Tear out this page. Write the Spanish words on the lines. Fold the paper along the dotted line to see the correct answers so you can check your work.

fan   _____

athlete   _____

championship   _____

tie   _____

player   _____

to lose   _____

score   _____

beauty contest   _____

prize   _____

queen   _____

presenter   _____

agitated   _____

furious   _____

to fall asleep   _____

Fold In

To hear a complete list of the vocabulary for this chapter, go to Disc 2, Track 3 on the guided Practice Audio CD or go to www.phschool.com and type in the Web Code jdd-0689. Then click on **Repaso del capítulo**.

Preterite of *-ir* stem-changing verbs (p. 302)

- In the preterite, verbs ending in **-ir**, like **preferir**, **pedir**, and **dormir**, have stem changes but only in the **usted/él/ella** and **ustedes/ellos/ellas** forms. The **e** changes to **i**, and the **o** to **u**.

  > Mi mamá se d*u*rmió durante la película.
  > Mis padres pref*i*rieron ver el concurso de belleza.
  > En la liga comp*i*tieron los mejores equipos de México.

- Here are the preterite forms of **preferir**, **pedir**, and **dormir**.

preferir (e → i)		pedir (e → i)		dormir (o → u)	
preferí	preferimos	pedí	pedimos	dormí	dormimos
preferiste	preferisteis	pediste	pedisteis	dormiste	dormisteis
pref_i_rió	**pref_i_rieron**	**p_i_dió**	**p_i_dieron**	**d_u_rmió**	**d_u_rmieron**

A. Complete the following sentences by circling the correct form of the verb in parentheses. Then, draw a line beneath the vowel that represents the stem change. The first one is done for you:

1. Carlos (**prefirió** / prefirieron) asistir al partido el sábado.

2. Las niñas se (**durmió** / **durmieron**) en el auditorio.

3. Usted (**pidió** / **pedimos**) una entrevista al entrenador.

4. Ustedes (**preferiste** / **prefirieron**) ver este partido.

5. Las presentadoras (**pidió** / **pidieron**) a los voluntarios al final del programa.

6. Tomás se (**durmió** / **dormí**) antes de la competencia.

7. El campeón (**pidió** / **pedí**) un millón de dólares.

8. Lucía (**preferimos** / **prefirió**) entrevistar al público.

9. Mis hermanos (**dormiste** / **durmieron**) bien anoche.

10. Yo (**pidieron** / **pedí**) un café ayer en el café.

Preterite of -ir stem-changing verbs (continued)

- Note the special spelling of the preterite forms of **reír**:

  reí, reíste, rió, reímos, reísteis, rieron

- Here are other **-ir** verbs with stem changes in the preterite tense:

  Verbs like **preferir: divertirse, mentir, sentirse**

  Verbs like **pedir: competir, despedirse, repetir, seguir, servir, vestirse**

  Verbs like **dormir: morir**

  Verbs like **reír: sonreír**

B. Sergio and Patricia went out on a Saturday night. Look at the pictures and fill in the blanks with the correct vowel that represents the stem change. Follow the model.

Modelo   Sergio y Patricia se div _i_ rtieron mucho.

1.   Una tarde, Sergio y Patricia salieron a comer. Ellos s___guieron por la calle Miraflores.

2.   Sergio y Patricia p___dieron espaguetis.

3.   El camarero les s___rvió una comida muy buena.

4.   Después de la cena, Sergio y Patricia pref___rieron ir al cine.

5.   Sergio y Patricia se r___eron mucho.

Go Online WEB CODE jdd-0604
PHSchool.com

Realidades 2

Capítulo 6A

Nombre _____

Hora _____

Fecha _____

Guided Practice Activities 6A-3

Preterite of *-ir* stem-changing verbs (*continued*)

C. Use the correct form of the verb in parentheses to complete each sentence. The first one is done for you.

1. Millones de aficionados ____*siguieron*____ al jugador. (**seguir**)

2. La reina _____ mucho cuando ganó el concurso de belleza. (**sonreír**)

3. Pilar y yo nos _____ de los chistes que contó el presentador. (**reír**)

4. Al final, la reina de belleza se _____ del público. (**despedirse**)

5. El entrenador y su equipo se _____ de rojo y blanco. (**vestirse**)

6. La presentadora _____ el tanteo para el público. (**repetir**)

7. Ustedes se _____ alegres al final del partido. (**sentirse**)

8. Yo me _____ mucho en el campeonato. (**divertirse**)

9. La reportera dice que el jugador _____; él no rescató a la señora. (**mentir**)

10. Tú no _____ en el campeonato del año pasado. (**competir**)

11. Nosotros _____ una comida fantástica a los jugadores. (**servir**)

12. Ustedes _____ ver el partido en la tele. (**preferir**)

13. Eugenio y tú _____ durante los comentarios. (**dormir**)

14. Yo _____ bebidas para los aficionados sentados cerca de mí. (**pedir**)

15. Resultó que nadie se _____ en el accidente después del partido. (**morir**)

Realidades 2

Capítulo 6A

Nombre _____

Fecha _____

Hora _____

Guided Practice Activities 6A-4

Other reflexive verbs (p. 305)

- Some reflexive verbs do not have the meaning of a person doing an action to or for himself or herself. These reflexive verbs describe a change. We say that someone "gets" or "becomes" something. Examples of these verbs are:

aburrirse	to get bored	enojarse	to become angry
casarse	to get married	ponerse (furioso, -a; alegre;...)	to become (furious, happy, . . .)
divertirse	to have fun	volverse loco, -a	to go crazy
dormirse	to fall asleep		

Ramiro se aburrió durante la película. *Ramiro got bored during the movie.*
Lalo se enojó al final del partido. *Lalo became angry at the end of the game.*

- Remember that reflexive verbs are used to say that people do something to or for themselves, and they use the reflexive pronouns **me, te, se, os,** and **nos**. Look at the conjugation of the verb **lavarse**:

yo	**me lavo**	nosotros/nosotras	**nos lavamos**
tú	**te lavas**	vosotros/vosotras	**os laváis**
usted/él/ella	**se lava**	ustedes/ellos/ellas	**se lavan**

A. Read the following sentences and write the correct reflexive pronoun in the blank. Then, match the meaning of the Spanish verb in the sentences with the English meanings on the right. Follow the model.

Modelo María __*se*__ casó el domingo. __*c*__

1. Yo _____ puse alegre con las noticias. ____

2. Mis hermanos _____ enojaron cuando su equipo perdió. ____

3. Nosotros _____ divertimos durante el campeonato. ____

4. Juan _____ durmió durante el partido de ayer. ____

5. Yo _____ aburrí mucho en el ballet. ____

6. Tú _____ volviste loco cuando ganaste. ____

a. went crazy

b. had fun

c. got married

d. got bored

e. got mad

f. became happy

g. fell asleep

Go Online WEB CODE jdd-0605
PHSchool.com

Other reflexive verbs (*continued*)

B. Circle the verb in parentheses that completes the paragraph. Use the drawings to help you choose which verb to circle. The first one is done for you.

Ayer mi hermano y yo vimos un partido de fútbol en la televisión. Yo

(**me aburrí** / **me volví loco**) mucho porque no me gusta nada el fútbol y mi hermanito

(**se casó** / **se enojó**) conmigo. Entonces yo

(**me puse furioso** / **me divertí**) y mi hermanito pensó que era muy cómico y

(**se aburrió** / **se rió**). El partido de fútbol era muy aburrido y yo

(**me puse alegre** / **me dormí**). Cuando me desperté mi hermano no estaba en la sala y

comencé a buscarlo. (**Me volví loco** / **Me divertí**) porque estaba muy

preocupado. Al fin encontré a mi hermanito ¡dormido debajo de su cama! No fue un día

bueno para nosotros y no (**nos divertimos** / **nos casamos**) mucho.

C. Complete the sentences telling the changes that took place in the different people. Write the preterite form of the reflexive verb in each sentence.

Modelo (**volverse loco**) Felipe __se__ __volvió__ __loco__ cuando su equipo ganó el campeonato.

1. (**casarse**) Mis tíos _____ _____ al final de la estación.

2. (**ponerse furiosos**) Nosotros _____ _____ _____ cuando el equipo perdió por tercera vez contra el mismo equipo.

3. (**divertirse**) Yo _____ _____ en el partido de ayer.

4. (**aburrirse**) Mis primos _____ _____ porque su equipo nunca ganaba.

5. (**ponerse agitada**) Marina _____ _____ _____ con la reina del concurso.

Lectura: Los Juegos Panamericanos (pp. 310–311)

A. The reading in your textbook is about the **Juegos Panamericanos** or Pan-American Games, a sports event similar to the Summer Olympics. Using what you already know about the Summer Olympics can help you understand the reading. See if you can answer the questions below.

1. What are the Summer Olympics? _____

_____

2. Who can participate in these Olympics? _____

3. What are five sports often featured in the Summer Olympics? _____,

_____, _____, _____, _____

B. Read the following excerpts from your textbook reading. They contain many cognates (words that look and sound like English words) that will help you understand the excerpts. Write what you think some of these words mean in English in the spaces below.

> Los Juegos Panamericanos se establecieron para promover la comprensión entre las naciones del continente americano. Los primeros Juegos se inauguraron el 25 de febrero en 1951 de Buenos Aires, con 2.513 atletas de 22 países.
>
> Todos los países de las Américas pueden mandar atletas a competir. Aproximadamente el 80 por ciento de los deportes de los Juegos Panamericanos se juegan en las Olimpíadas.

1. Panamericanos _____   5. atletas _____

2. se establecieron _____   6. Américas _____

3. naciones _____   7. competir _____

4. febrero _____   8. Olimpíadas _____

C. Now read the sentences below. Based on the excerpts in **part B**, write **Sí** if the sentence tells something that happens during the Pan-American Games. Write **No** if it doesn't happen during these Games.

1. Todos los países del mundo pueden participar en estos Juegos. _____

2. Las personas que participan en estos Juegos son atletas. _____

3. Todos los deportes de los Juegos Panamericanos también se juegan en las

Olimpíadas. _____

Go Online   WEB CODE jdd-0606
PHSchool.com

Realidades 2

Capítulo 6A

Nombre _____

Hora _____

Fecha _____

Guided Practice Activities 6A-6

Presentación oral (p. 313)

Task: Prepare a review of your favorite television program and present it to your class.

A. Complete the following sentences about your favorite television program. Circle one option from the word lists for each sentence and write it in the blank.

una comedia	la telenovela
un programa deportivo	una película de detectives
un programa de concursos	un programa de dibujos animados

1. Mi programa favorito es _____.

niños	mayores	niños y mayores

2. Este programa es para _____.

me río mucho	me enojo mucho
me siento emocionado(a)	me vuelvo loco(a)

3. Cuando veo este programa _____.

interesante	divertido	fenomenal	alegre

4. Este programa es _____.

B. Now use the information from **part A** to complete the following sentences.

1. Mi programa favorito se llama _____ y es _____.

2. Este programa es para _____.

3. Cuando veo este programa _____.

4. Este programa es _____.

C. Use the sentences from **parts A** and **B** to practice your oral presentation. Go through the presentation several times. Try to:

• include all the information in the sentences
• use complete sentences and speak clearly

Realidades 2

Capítulo 6B

Nombre _____

Hora _____

Fecha _____

Vocabulary Flash Cards, Sheet 1

Write the Spanish vocabulary word or phrase below each picture. Be sure to include the article for each noun.

_____

_____

_____

_____

_____

_____

_____

_____

_____

_____

_____

_____

_____

_____

_____

_____

_____

_____

Realidades ②

Capítulo 6B

Nombre _____

Hora _____

Fecha _____

Vocabulary Flash Cards, Sheet 2

Write the Spanish vocabulary word below each picture. If there is a word or phrase, copy it in the space provided. Be sure to include the article for each noun.

el crítico,
la crítica

_____ _____,

Realidades **2**

Capítulo 6B

Nombre

Hora

Fecha

Vocabulary Flash Cards, Sheet 3

Copy the word or phrase in the space provided. Be sure to include the article for each noun.

fascinar	**el fracaso**	**he visto**
has visto	**matar**	**¿Qué tal es...?**
recomendar	**será**	**tener éxito**

Realidades 2

Capítulo 6B

Nombre _____

Hora _____

Fecha _____

Vocabulary Flash Cards, Sheet 4

Copy the word or phrase in the space provided. Be sure to include the article for each noun.

tratarse de _____ _____	**la violencia** _____	**la actuación** _____
el argumento _____	**la dirección** _____	**alquilar** _____
hacer el papel de _____ _____	**el personaje principal** _____	**no... todavía** _____ _____

Realidades 2

Capítulo 6B

Nombre _____

Hora _____

Fecha _____

Vocabulary Flash Cards, Sheet 5

Copy the word or phrase in the space provided. Be sure to include the article for each noun. These blank cards can be used to write and practice other Spanish vocabulary for the chapter.

enamorarse (de)	**(estar) enamorado, enamorada de**	**el crimen**
la ladrona	**la escena**	**estar basado, basada en**
el papel		

Realidades 2

Capítulo 6B

Nombre _____

Hora _____

Fecha _____

Vocabulary Check, Sheet 1

Tear out this page. Write the English words on the lines. Fold the paper along the dotted line to see the correct answers so you can check your work.

alquilar _____

el amor _____

arrestar _____

capturar _____

el (la) criminal _____

enamorarse (de) _____

robar _____

tener éxito _____

el fracaso _____

tratarse de _____

he visto _____

el director, la directora _____

la escena _____

el papel _____

la víctima _____

Fold In

Realidades 2

Capítulo 6B

Nombre _____

Hora _____

Fecha _____

Vocabulary Check, Sheet 2

Tear out this page. Write the Spanish words on the lines. Fold the paper along the dotted line to see the correct answers so you can check your work.

to rent _____

love _____

to arrest _____

to capture _____

the criminal _____

to fall in love (with) _____

to rob, to steal _____

to succeed, to be successful _____

failure _____

to be about _____

I have seen _____

director _____

scene _____

role _____

victim _____

Fold In

Realidades 2

Nombre _____

Hora _____

Capítulo 6B

Fecha _____

Vocabulary Check, Sheet 3

Tear out this page. Write the English words on the lines. Fold the paper along the dotted line to see the correct answers so you can check your work.

la estrella (del cine) _____

el (la) detective _____

el galán _____

el ladrón,
la ladrona _____

la película de
acción _____

los efectos
especiales _____

el (la) extraterrestre _____

la actuación _____

el argumento _____

el crimen _____

matar _____

el crítico, la crítica _____

fascinar _____

¿Qué tal es...? _____

Fold In

Tear out this page. Write the Spanish words on the lines. Fold the paper along the dotted line to see the correct answers so you can check your work.

(movie) star _____

detective _____

leading man _____

thief _____

action film _____

special effects _____

alien _____

acting _____

plot _____

crime _____

to kill _____

critic _____

to fascinate _____

How is (it)…? _____

To hear a complete list of the vocabulary for this chapter, go to Disc 2, Track 4 on the guided Practice Audio CD or go to www.phschool.com and type in the Web Code jdd-0699. Then click on **Repaso del capítulo**.

Fold In

Verbs that use indirect object pronouns (p. 328)

- Many verbs that use indirect object pronouns, such as **aburrir, doler, encantar, fascinar, gustar,** and **importar,** use a similar construction:

    indirect object pronoun + verb + subject

    Le + encantan + las películas de acción.
    He likes action movies.

- You can use **a +** a noun or a pronoun with these verbs for emphasis or to make something clear:

    A Rodrigo le gustan las flores.
    Rodrigo likes flowers.

    or:

    A él le gustan las flores.
    He likes flowers.

- Here are the indirect object pronouns:

(A mí)	**me**	(A nosotros/a nosotras)	**nos**
(A ti)	**te**	(A vosotros/a vosotras)	**os**
(A usted/A él/A ella)	**le**	(A ustedes/A ellos/A ellas)	**les**

A. Circle the correct indirect object pronoun to complete each sentence. Follow the model.

Modelo A María (**le** / **les**) encantan las películas románticas.

1. A mí (**te** / **me**) aburre este programa.

2. A nosotros (**nos** / **les**) molestan los videojuegos.

3. A mi padre y a mí (**nos** / **te**) importan los actores de Hollywood.

4. A Pablo y a Ramón (**le** / **les**) fascina el cine.

5. A los directores (**les** / **le**) encanta trabajar con actores famosos.

6. ¡A ti (**me** / **te**) duele la cabeza después de ver tantas películas!

Verbs that use indirect object pronouns (*continued*)

B. In the sentences below, fill in the first blank with the correct indirect object pronoun. Then, write the correct ending for each verb using the words that come after it as clues. Use the pictures to help you guess the correct indirect object pronouns. The first one is done for you.

1. A Maricarmen __*le*__ interes _an_ las comedias.

2. A ellos _____ molest_____ esperar mucho tiempo.

3. ¿A Ud. _____ parec_____ interesantes los efectos especiales?

4. A mí _____ import_____ el campeón de la liga.

5. A Sara y a Pilar _____ qued_____ bien las camisas.

C. Write questions using the elements given and indirect object pronouns to ask the various people about their entertainment preferences. Follow the model.

Modelo A ti / gustar / ir al cine

¿_A ti te gusta ir al cine_____?

1. A Juan / molestar / las películas de horror

¿_____?

2. A Uds. / interesar / los actores

¿_____?

3. A Steven Spielberg / importar / la ciencia ficción

¿_____?

4. A los criminales / fascinar / las películas de acción

¿_____?

5. A mí / parecer / tristes / los dramas

¿_____?

Go Online WEB CODE jdd-0613 PHSchool.com

The present perfect (p. 331)

Use the present perfect tense to tell what a person has done.

- To form this tense, use present-tense forms of **haber** + the past participle:

    Hemos alquilado dos películas.
    We have rented two movies.

- To form the past participle of a verb, drop the ending of the infinitive and add -**ado** for -**ar** verbs and -**ido** for -**er** and -**ir** verbs.

	alquilar	vivir		alquilar	vivir
he	alquilado	vivido	**hemos**	alquilado	vivido
has	alquilado	vivido	**habéis**	alquilado	vivido
ha	alquilado	vivido	**han**	alquilado	vivido

A. Complete the sentences below with the correct form of the verb **haber**.

Modelo Tú _____*has*_____ vivido en Atlanta, ¿verdad?

1. Mis amigos _____ ido al cine todos los viernes por dos años.

2. Yo nunca _____ alquilado una película de horror.

3. Los directores _____ trabajado mucho en esta película.

4. El actor _____ practicado mucho para este papel.

5. Nosotros _____ oído que es una película muy buena.

- Most verbs that have two vowels together in the infinitive have a written accent on the **í** of the past participle:

    caer → caído   **oír → oído**   **leer → leído**

B. Write the past participle form of the following verbs. Follow the model.

Modelo robar _____*robado*_____

1. matar _____

2. hablar _____

3. perder _____

4. traer _____

5. leer _____

6. aprender _____

7. caer _____

8. oír _____

The present perfect (*continued*)

C. Write the present perfect form of the verb in parentheses in each sentence to tell what things have happened in a recent action movie. Note that in the forms of the present perfect, the past participle does not change; the ending will always be -*o*. Follow the model.

Modelo (**filmar**) El director Mario Fernández ___ha___ ___filmado___ una nueva película.

1. (**matar**) En la película, unos criminales _____ _____ a algunas personas.

2. (**robar**) Ellos _____ _____ su dinero también.

3. (**esconder**) Un criminal _____ _____ el dinero en el campo.

4. (**capturar**) Los detectives _____ _____ a todos los criminales.

5. (**ir**) Mis amigos y yo _____ _____ al cine a ver la película tres veces.

6. (**leer**) Yo _____ _____ los artículos de los críticos en el periódico.

7. (**crear**) Según los críticos, Fernández _____ _____ efectos especiales fantásticos.

8. (**tener**) Las películas del director Fernández siempre _____ _____ éxito.

9. (**oír**) Y tú, ¿ _____ _____ decir algo bueno sobre esta película?

• These verbs have irregular past participles:

decir → *dicho*	poner → *puesto*
escribir → *escrito*	romper → *roto*
hacer → *hecho*	ver → *visto*
morir → *muerto*	volver → *vuelto*

D. Look at the following verbs. Write **I** (for Irregular) if the verb has an irregular past participle form. If not, write **R** (for Regular). Then, in the second blank, write in the past participle form for each verb, paying close attention to spelling. Follow the model.

Modelo alquilar __R__ __alquilado__

1. volver ____ _____   5. decir ____ _____

2. hacer ____ _____   6. vivir ____ _____

3. escribir ____ _____   7. ver ____ _____

4. comer ____ _____   8. morir ____ _____

WEB CODE jdd-0614
PHSchool.com

Realidades 2

Capítulo 6B

Nombre _____

Fecha _____

Hora _____

Guided Practice Activities 6B-4

The present perfect (*continued*)

E. The following sentences describe a movie. Use the correct form of **haber** plus the past participle of the verb in parentheses to complete the sentences. Follow the model.

Modelo   Yo _____ _____ (**ver**) una película policíaca.

1. El director _____ _____ (**decir**) que el argumento es malo.

2. Nadie _____ _____ (**morir**) en esta escena.

3. Luis y Damián _____ _____ (**hacer**) los papeles de las víctimas.

4. Nosotras _____ _____ (**escribir**) el argumento para la película.

5. ¿Tú _____ _____ (**poner**) el coche en la última escena?

6. La estrella _____ _____ (**romper**) el vaso otra vez.

F. Marta is talking about movies. Rewrite her statements by replacing the underlined words with the pronoun in parentheses and placing it before the form of **haber** for each sentence. Follow the model.

Modelo   Yo he alquilado **la película.** (la)

Yo _____ *la he alquilado* _____ .

1. Los detectives han arrestado **a las ladronas.** (las)

Los detectives _____ .

2. Los actores han leído la escena **al director.** (le)

Los actores _____ la escena.

3. El galán ha capturado **a los extraterrestres.** (los)

El galán _____ .

4. El director ha pedido ayuda **a nosotros.** (nos)

El director _____ ayuda.

5. La directora ha escrito **el argumento.** (lo)

La directora _____ .

6. El crítico ha dicho su opinión **a mí.** (me)

El crítico _____ su opinión.

The present perfect (*continued*)

- When you use object or reflexive pronouns with the present perfect, the pronoun goes right before the form of **haber**:

    ¿Has visto la película? Sí, la he visto. *Have you seen the movie? Yes, I have seen it.*

G. Complete the following sentences by writing the correct reflexive pronoun and the present perfect form of the verbs in parentheses. Use the pictures to help you with meaning. Follow the model. *Note: Some verbs have regular past participles, some require accent marks, and some have irregular past participles.*

Modelo   (caerse) La actriz __se__ __ha__ __caído__ .

1. (volverse) ¡El director _____ _____ _____ loco!

2. (enojarse) Yo _____ _____ _____ muchas veces
   cuando veo películas de horror.

3. (casarse) ¡Qué romántico! Los dos actores famosos _____
   _____ _____ .

4. (dormirse) ¿Tú _____ _____ _____ viendo una
   película de acción?

5. (divertirse) Nosotros _____ _____ _____ viendo las
   comedias mexicanas.

6. (vestirse) Los críticos _____ _____ _____ con
   elegancia para estos premios.

Go Online WEB CODE jdd-0614
PHSchool.com

Realidades 2

Capítulo 6B

Nombre _____

Hora _____

Fecha _____

Guided Practice Activities 6B-5

Lectura: La cartelera del cine (pp. 336–337)

A. First, read the title and subtitles and look at the pictures in the textbook reading. These can give you an idea of what the reading is about or what is the "big picture." Then, circle the best option for the choices below.

1. This reading is about
   a. movies.   **b.** sports.   **c.** politics.

2. Each section has a summary and a
   a. comedy.   **b.** review.   **c.** drama.

B. You will notice that each movie review begins with some basic facts. Read the following fact excerpt from your textbook reading. Then answer the questions below.

> *El señor de los anillos 2: Las dos torres*
> *EE. UU., Nueva Zelandia 2002 / Clasificación: B / Director: Peter Jackson /*
> *Actores: Elijah Wood, Ian McKellen, Viggo Mortensen, Liv Tyler, Cate Blanchett*

1. What is the second part of the movie called? _____

2. Who is the director of *Lord of the Rings*? _____

3. In what year was the movie made? _____

4. What is the classification of the movie? _____

C. Read the following *Crítica* or review section for *El ataque de los clones*. Circle the answer that best completes each of the statements below.

> *Esta película es muy comercial. Lo más interesante es el uso de los efectos especiales. El argumento es horrible. Es muy difícil de entender y no es muy lógico. Por los efectos especiales, le doy 10/10. Por el argumento, sólo le doy 5/10.*

1. El crítico de *El ataque de los clones* piensa que la película es
   a. espectacular.   **b.** comercial.

2. Al crítico le gustan
   a. los efectos especiales.   **b.** los actores.

3. El crítico dice que la película es
   a. difícil de entender.   **b.** fenomenal.

Realidades 2

Capítulo 6B

Nombre _____

Hora _____

Fecha _____

Guided Practice Activities 6B-6

Presentación escrita (p. 339)

Task: Think about and write a good movie idea for a class contest. Describe the main characters, the plot, and the scenes. Then draw a few scenes from the movie.

A. Fill in the blanks with information about the kind of movie you would like to write. You can choose an option from the list, or make up your own.

1. Me gustaría escribir _____.

una película de acción	una película romántica	un drama
una película de ciencia ficción	una película policíaca	una comedia
una película de horror		

2. Los personajes principales de mi película pueden ser _____.

ladrones y policías	una familia y sus amigos
extraterrestres	criminales

B. Read the following plot descriptions to get ideas for your movie. You can use these descriptions or make up your own. Then write a brief outline of your plot below.

- Los personajes desean encontrar algo que alguien escondió hace muchos años.
- Los extraterrestres vienen a visitarnos.
- Unos ladrones roban una pintura *(painting)* de un museo y la policía los busca.

_____

_____

_____

_____

C. In the following boxes, sketch four scenes from the movie plot you described in **part B**.

Realidades 2

Capítulo 7A

Nombre _____

Fecha _____

Hora _____

AVSR **7A-1**

A ver si recuerdas: Verbs with irregular *yo* forms (p. 345)

- As you know, some verbs have irregular **yo** forms in the present tense. These fall into two categories:

  Verbs with irregular **-go** forms:

salir → yo salgo	poner → yo pongo	hacer → yo hago
caer → yo caigo	decir → yo digo	venir → yo vengo

  Verbs with irregular **-zco** forms:

conocer → yo conozco	parecer → yo parezco
obedecer → yo obedezco	ofrecer → yo ofrezco

A. Change the following verbs from the **tú** form to the **yo** form. Follow the model.

Modelo pones _____*pongo*_____

1. sales _____

2. conoces _____

3. dices _____

4. ofreces _____

5. obedeces _____

6. caes _____

7. haces _____

8. vienes _____

B. Elena is living with her aunt and uncle for the summer. Complete her e-mail by writing the **yo** form of the verbs given. The first one is done for you.

Estimada Mónica:

¿Cómo estás? Yo estoy muy bien aquí con mis tíos, pero yo _____*tengo*_____ (**tener**) mucho trabajo. Yo me levanto

y _____ (**ponerse**) la ropa muy temprano.

Después, yo _____ (**salir**) de la casa para

trabajar con mi tío. Yo siempre _____ (**hacer**)

lo que él necesita y yo nunca le _____ (**decir**)

que estoy cansada. ¡Es trabajo divertido!

Realidades 2

Capítulo 7A

Nombre _____

Fecha _____

Hora _____

AVSR **7A-2**

A ver si recuerdas: Verbs with irregular *yo* forms (*continued*)

Bueno, yo ya _____ (**conocer**) a muchas personas

del pueblo. ¡Todos dicen que yo _____ _____

(**parecerse**) mucho a mi tío! Al final del día, cuando

_____ (**venir**) a la casa, siempre le

_____ (**ofrecer**) un poco de ayuda a mi tía, que

está preparando la cena. En total, yo _____

(**tener**) una vida muy interesante aquí.

Un abrazo,

Elena

C. Answer the following questions in complete sentences, paying special attention to the verbs with irregular **yo** forms.

| Modelo | ¿Siempre dices la verdad? |

Sí, yo siempre _____ *digo la verdad* _____.

1. ¿Te pareces a alguien de tu familia?

Sí, yo _____ a mi _____.

2. ¿Siempre obedeces a tus padres?

No, yo no _____ siempre.

3. ¿A veces sales por la noche con tus amigos?

Sí, yo _____ a veces _____.

4. ¿Conoces a alguna persona famosa?

No, no _____

5. ¿Tienes mucha tarea esta noche?

Sí, yo _____

6. ¿Haces la tarea por la tarde o por la noche?

Yo _____

Go Online WEB CODE jdd-0701
PHSchool.com

Realidades ②

Capítulo 7A

Nombre _____

Hora _____

Fecha _____

Vocabulary Flash Cards, Sheet 1

Write the Spanish vocabulary word below each picture. Be sure to include the article for each noun.

Realidades 2

Capítulo 7A

Nombre _____

Fecha _____

Hora _____

Vocabulary Flash Cards, Sheet 2

Write the Spanish vocabulary word below each picture. Be sure to include the article for each noun.

Write the Spanish vocabulary word below each picture. Be sure to include the article for each noun.

Write the Spanish vocabulary word below each picture. If there is a word or phrase, copy it in the space provided.

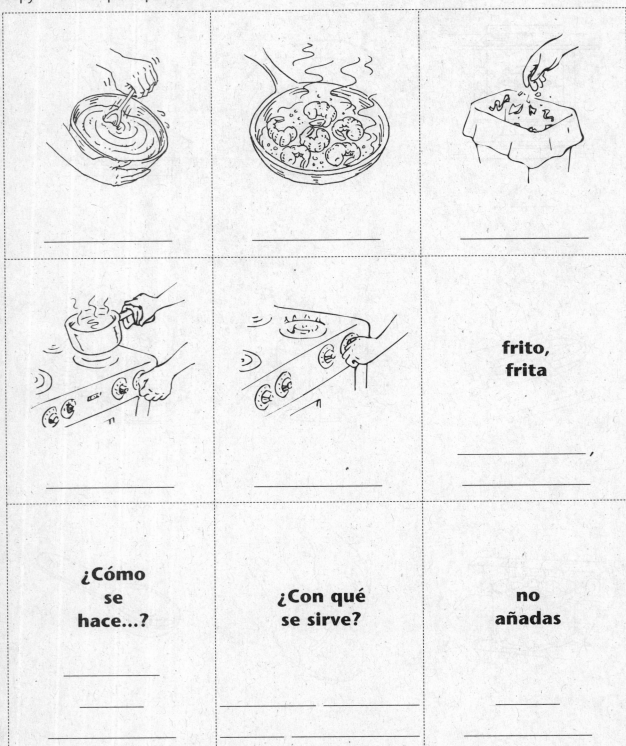

_____ _____ _____

_____ _____ **frito, frita**

_____ ,

¿Cómo se hace...? **¿Con qué se sirve?** **no añadas**

_____ _____ _____

_____ _____ _____

Realidades ②

Capítulo 7A

Nombre _____

Hora _____

Fecha _____

Vocabulary Flash Cards, Sheet 5

Copy the word or phrase in the space provided. Be sure to include the article for each noun.

dejar _____	**no dejes** _____	**olvidarse de** _____
no te olvides de _____ _____	**no tires** _____	**se puede** _____
No hables. _____	**No comas.** _____	**No escribas.** _____

Realidades 2

Nombre _____

Hora _____

Capítulo 7A

Fecha _____

Vocabulary Flash Cards, Sheet 6

Copy the word or phrase in the space provided. These blank cards can be used to write and practice other Spanish vocabulary for the chapter.

congelado, congelada	**enlatado, enlatada**	**fresco, fresca**
_____, _____	_____, _____	_____, _____
_____	_____	_____
_____	_____	_____

Realidades 2

Capítulo 7A

Nombre _____

Hora _____

Fecha _____

Vocabulary Check, Sheet 1

Tear out this page. Write the English words on the lines. Fold the paper along the dotted line to see the correct answers so you can check your work.

la salsa _____

el aceite _____

el ajo _____

la olla _____

el refrigerador _____

el fuego _____

caliente _____

el horno _____

añadir _____

tirar _____

freír _____

mezclar _____

probar _____

la receta _____

olvidarse de _____

Fold In

Realidades 2

Capítulo 7A

Nombre _____

Fecha _____

Hora _____

Vocabulary Check, Sheet 2

Tear out this page. Write the Spanish words on the lines. Fold the paper along the dotted line to see the correct answers so you can check your work.

salsa, sauce   _____

cooking oil   _____

garlic   _____

pot   _____

refrigerator   _____

fire, heat   _____

hot   _____

oven   _____

to add   _____

to spill, to throw away   _____

to fry   _____

to mix   _____

to taste, to try   _____

recipe   _____

to forget about/to   _____

Fold In →

Realidades 2

Capítulo 7A

Nombre _____

Fecha _____

Hora _____

Vocabulary Check, Sheet 3

Tear out this page. Write the English words on the lines. Fold the paper along the dotted line to see the correct answers so you can check your work.

el caldo _____

la estufa _____

el fregadero _____

el pedazo _____

la sartén _____

calentar _____

hervir _____

el ingrediente _____

picar _____

apagar _____

dejar _____

encender _____

fresco, fresca _____

Fold In

Tear out this page. Write the Spanish words on the lines. Fold the paper along the dotted line to see the correct answers so you can check your work.

broth _____

stove _____

sink _____

piece, slice _____

frying pan _____

to heat _____

to boil _____

ingredient _____

to chop _____

to turn off _____

to leave, to let _____

to turn on, to light _____

fresh _____

Fold In

To hear a complete list of the vocabulary for this chapter, go to Disc 2, Track 5 on the guided Practice Audio CD or go to www.phschool.com and type in the Web Code jdd-0789. Then click on **Repaso del capítulo**.

Negative *tú* commands (p. 356)

- Negative commands are used to tell someone what *not* to do.
- To form negative **tú** commands, drop the **-o** of the present-tense **yo** form and add:
  -es for **-ar** verbs
      usar → uso: **No uses el microondas.** *Don't use the microwave.*
  -as for **-er** and **-ir** verbs
      encender → enciendo: **No enciendas el horno.** *Don't turn on the oven.*

A. Look at the following sentences and add the correct endings to the verbs to make negative **tú** commands. Use the verbs in parentheses for reference. Follow the model.

Modelo   Jaime, no com *as* todas las frutas. (**comer**)

1. Raquel, no tir_____ el pollo en el aceite caliente. (**tirar**)

2. Tadeo, no cort_____ el ajo en pedazos tan pequeños. (**cortar**)

3. Susana, no beb_____ el café si está muy caliente. (**beber**)

4. Mario, no us_____ tanto aceite en el sartén. (**usar**)

5. Julia, no añad_____ el ajo ahora. (**añadir**)

- Remember that some verbs have irregular **yo** forms, which are used to form the negative commands.
      salir → salgo   **No salga de la casa.**   *Don't leave the house.*

B. Complete the statements below by writing the correct negative **tú** commands of the verbs given. Follow the model.

Modelo   (**poner**) _____ *No pongas* _____ las manos en la masa.

1. (**salir**) _____ sin comer algo.

2. (**decir**) _____ mentiras (*lies*).

3. (**hacer**) _____ eso, por favor.

4. (**obedecer**) _____ a tus amigos malos.

Negative *tú* commands (*continued*)

- Remember that stem-changing verbs will still have the same stem changes to form the negative commands. Also, if the verb is reflexive, the reflexive pronoun will be placed the same way.

   dormirse → te duermas

   ¡No te duermas en la clase!   *Don't fall asleep in class!*

C. Look at the following verbs in the infinitive. Write the negative command form for each. Follow the model.

Modelo divertirse ___No te diviertas.___

1. encender _____   5. caerse _____

2. calentar _____   6. parecerse _____

3. probar _____   7. olvidarse _____

4. hervir _____   8. dormirse _____

- With negative **tú** commands, some verbs such as **picar** (*to chop*), **pagar** (*to pay*), and **empezar** (*to start*) have spelling changes: **c** changes to **qu**, **g** changes to **gu**, and **z** changes to **c**.

   picar → no pi*qu*es   **pagar → no pa*gu*es**   **empezar → no empieces**

D. Your parents have given you a list of things not to do on the weekend. Complete their list by writing the correct negative **tú** commands of the verbs given. Follow the model.

Modelo ___No___ ___empieces___ la tarea a las nueve de la noche los domingos.
    (**empezar**)

1. _____ _____ en restaurantes caros. (**almorzar**)

2. _____ _____ problemas en la calle. (**buscar**)

3. _____ _____ con las personas malas. (**jugar**)

4. _____ _____ a casa después de las diez de la noche. (**llegar**)

5. _____ _____ cosas de la casa de otra persona sin pedirlas. (**sacar**)

Go Online WEB CODE jdd-0704
PHSchool.com

Realidades 2

Capítulo 7A

Nombre _____

Hora _____

Fecha _____

Guided Practice Activities 7A-2a

Negative *tú* commands (*continued*)

- Some verbs have irregular negative **tú** commands:

  dar → no des   estar → no estés

  ir → no vayas   ser → no seas

E. For each of the following sentences, write the appropriate negative **tú** command of the verb in parentheses.

1. No _____ (**dar**) dulces a tu hermano antes del almuerzo.

2. No _____ (**estar**) en la cocina antes de la cena.

3. No _____ (**ir**) al mercado hoy.

4. No _____ (**ser**) tan desordenada.

- Remember that pronouns are attached to the verb when they are added to the affirmative command form. Note: An accent mark is written on the verb when the added pronoun makes three or more syllables.

  —**¿Añado la sal?**   *Do I add the salt?*

  —**Sí, añádela.**   *Yes, add it.*

F. Read the following questions and unfinished answers. Place the correct pronoun in the spaces provided to finish the answers. Remember to add an accent, if necessary, to the affirmative command in each answer. Follow the model.

Modelo   —¿Mezclo los ingredientes en la taza?

          —Sí, mézcla *los* en la taza.

1. —¿Añado el aceite a la sartén?

   —Sí, añade_____ a la sartén.

2. —¿Tiro los huesos del pollo?

   —Sí, tira_____.

3. —¿Apago el fuego de la estufa?

   —Sí, apaga_____.

4. —¿Pongo la mesa antes de la cena?

   —Sí, pon_____ antes de la cena.

5. —¿Saco los platos después de la comida?

   —Sí, saca_____ después de la comida.

Realidades ②

Capítulo 7A

Nombre _____

Hora _____

Fecha _____

Guided Practice Activities 7A-2b

Negative *tú* commands (*continued*)

• Pronouns always go right before the verb when writing negative commands.

> —¿**Pongo los platos en la mesa?**
> *Should I put the plates on the table?*

> —**No, no** *los pongas* **en la mesa en este momento.**
> *No, don't put them on the table right now.*

G. Señor Báez is giving a class on cooking. Nacho is having trouble with many of the tasks. Follow the conversation below by writing in señor Báez' responses using negative **tú** commands. Remember to correctly place the pronouns in each. The first one is done for you.

1. NACHO: ¿Debo apagar el horno?

   SEÑOR BÁEZ: No, _____*no lo apagues*_____ .

2. NACHO: ¿Debo hacer el arroz?

   SEÑOR BÁEZ: No, _____ .

3. NACHO: ¿Debo pelar los tomates?

   SEÑOR BÁEZ: No, _____ .

4. NACHO: ¿Debo picar los huevos?

   SEÑOR BÁEZ: No, _____ .

5. NACHO: ¿Debo freír la ensalada?

   SEÑOR BÁEZ: No, _____ .

6. NACHO: ¿Debo poner el pan en el microondas?

   SEÑOR BÁEZ: No, _____ allí.

7. NACHO: ¿Debo mezclar la leche con los tomates?

   SEÑOR BÁEZ: No, _____ con los tomates.

8. NACHO: ¿Debo hervir los huevos en la sartén?

   SEÑOR BÁEZ: No, _____ en la sartén.

Go Online WEB CODE jdd-0704
PHSchool.com

Realidades ❷

Capítulo 7A

Nombre _____

Hora _____

Fecha _____

Guided Practice Activities 7A-3

The impersonal *se* (p. 360)

- In Spanish, to say that people in general do a certain thing, you use **se** + the **usted/él/ella** or **ustedes/ellos/ellas** form of the verb. This is called the impersonal **se**.

    Aquí se sirve el pan tostado con mantequilla. *Here they serve the toast with butter.*
    Se comen tortillas frecuentemente. *Tortillas are eaten frequently.*

A. Look at the pictures and read the sentences that describe what people do in general when they prepare food. Circle the appropriate impersonal **se** expression in parentheses to complete each sentence.

1. En mi casa el pollo (**se hace / se tira**) con sal y ajo.

2. Para preparar la salsa (**se calienta / se pica**) el ajo.

3. El plato principal (**se sirve / se hierve**) con ensalada.

4. En mi casa (**se come / se bebe**) mucha fruta.

5. La comida (**se pica / se calienta**) en el microondas.

The impersonal *se* (*continued*)

- Note: The **usted/él/ella form** of the verb is used when the thing following it is singular and the **ustedes/ellos/ellas** form is used when the thing following it is plural.

Se pela la papa.	*The potato is pealed.*
Se pelan las papas.	*The potatoes are pealed.*

B. Complete the following rules by circling the appropriate impersonal **se** expression to tell what is done or not done. Follow the model.

Modelo No ((se fríen)/ se fríe) los camarones.

1. (Se sirven / Se sirve) pan con mariscos.

2. (Se calienta / Se calientan) el pan en el horno.

3. No (se añade / se añaden) sal a la sopa.

4. (Se dejan / Se deja) el ajo en la cocina.

5. No (se hierve / se hierven) los mariscos.

C. Complete the following recipe to prepare **arroz con mariscos**. Use the impersonal **se** form of the verb in parentheses to complete each instruction. The first one is done for you. Be careful to choose between the singular and plural verb forms.

Arroz con mariscos

1. *Se calienta* (**calentar**) el aceite en la sartén.

2. _____ (**preparar**) los mariscos con sal.

3. _____ (**pelar**) el ajo y

4. _____ (**cortar**) en pedazos.

5. _____ (**mezclar**) los mariscos y el ajo.

6. _____ (**hervir**) agua en una olla.

7. _____ (**añadir**) arroz y sal al caldo.

8. _____ (**mezclar**) los mariscos con el arroz.

Realidades 2

Capítulo 7A

Nombre _____

Fecha _____

Hora _____

Guided Practice Activities 7A-5

Lectura: Oda al tomate y Oda a la cebolla (pp. 364–365)

A. The two poems in your textbook reading are about tomatoes and onions. What words would you use to describe a tomato or an onion? Write them below.

tomato: _____, _____, _____, _____

onion: _____, _____, _____, _____

B. These poems use many descriptive words to tell us about tomatoes and onions. Some of these words are listed below. Circle the letter of the English meaning of each word.

1. **redonda**   **a.** small   **b.** round

2. **clara**   **a.** clear   **b.** dark

3. **pobres**   **a.** rich   **b.** poor

4. **constelación**   **a.** condition   **b.** constellation

5. **planeta**   **a.** planet   **b.** plantation

C. Look at the excerpt of **"Oda a la cebolla"** below. Read it aloud and look back at your answers from **part B** if you need help with the meaning of certain words. Then, write **C (cierto)** or **F (falso)** for each sentence below.

> (...) cebolla,
> clara como un planeta,
> y destinada
> a relucir (shine),
> constelación constante,
> redonda (round) rosa
> de agua sobre la mesa
> de las pobres gentes.

1. According to the poet, the onion is like a planet. _____

2. An onion is also like a tomato. _____

3. *Redonda rosa de agua* means that it is like a white flower. _____

4. The poet says that everyone has an onion on their table. _____

Realidades ②

Capítulo 7A

Nombre _____

Hora _____

Fecha _____

Guided Practice Activities 7A-6

Presentación oral (p. 367)

Task: Imagine you are a guest on a television cooking show. You will be telling the audience how to prepare your favorite main dish.

A. Write the name of your favorite dish below. Then place an *X* next to the ingredients in the chart that you need to prepare that dish.

Mi plato favorito es _____.

Ingredientes			
_____ huevos	_____ caldo	_____ carne	_____ tomate
_____ agua	_____ pollo	_____ lechuga	_____ ajo
_____ leche	_____ sal	_____ cebolla	_____ pimienta
_____ camarones	_____ queso	_____ aceite	_____ mariscos

B. Use the ingredients you chose in **part A.** Think about the steps you would follow to prepare your dish. You can use the verbs for food preparation from the list or others you have learned in this chapter.

se mezcla	**se corta**	**se sirve**	**se pone**	**se añade**

Now, complete the recipe card below. Include the name of the dish, the ingredients you need, and the steps to prepare this dish.

Nombre del plato: _____

Ingredientes: _____

Preparación:

1. Primero, _____

2. Luego, _____

3. Después, _____

4. Al final, _____

C. Use your recipe card to practice your presentation. Remember to include the ingredients, describe the steps to prepare the dish, and to speak clearly.

Realidades 2

Capítulo 7B

Nombre _____

Fecha _____

Hora _____

Vocabulary Flash Cards, Sheet 1

Write the Spanish vocabulary word or phrase below each picture. Be sure to include the article for each noun.

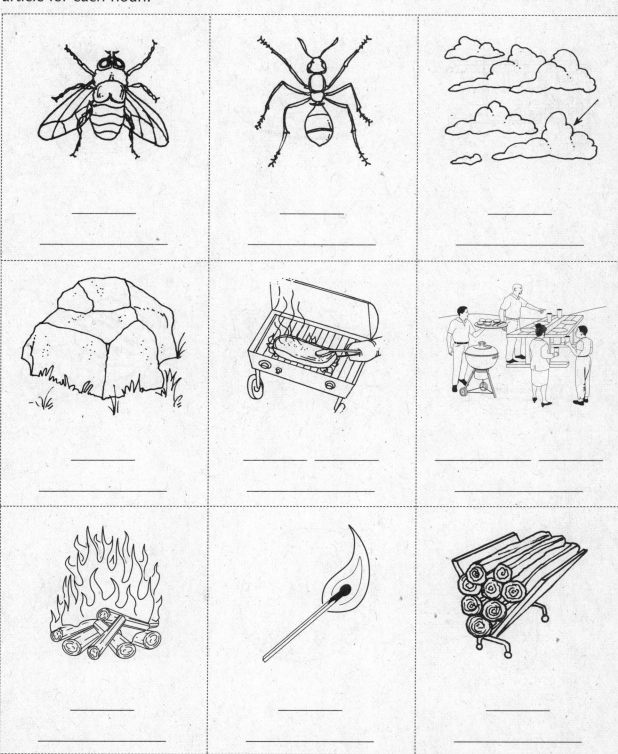

_____

_____

_____

_____

_____

_____

_____

_____

_____

_____

_____

_____

_____

_____

Realidades 2

Capítulo 7B

Nombre _____

Fecha _____

Hora _____

Vocabulary Flash Cards, Sheet 2

Write the Spanish vocabulary word or phrase below each picture. Be sure to include the article for each noun.

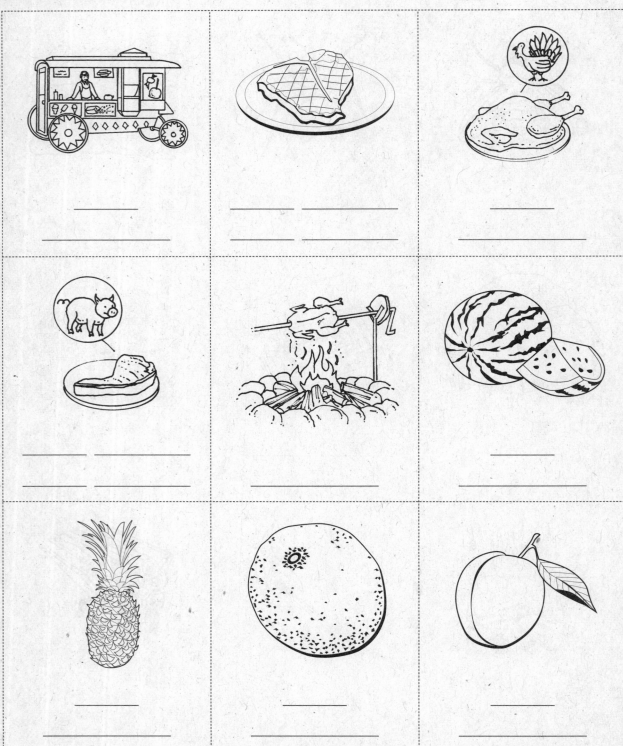

Write the Spanish vocabulary word or phrase below each picture. Be sure to include the article for each noun.

Nombre _____ Hora _____

Fecha _____ **Vocabulary Flash Cards, Sheet 4**

Write the Spanish vocabulary word below each picture. If there is a word or phrase, copy it in the space provided. Be sure to include the article for each noun.

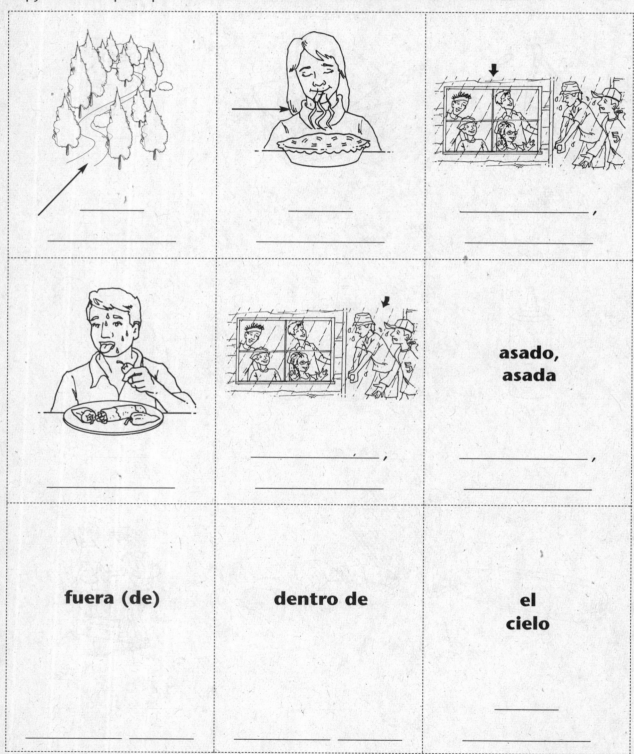

_____	_____	_____ , _____
_____	_____ , _____	**asado, asada** _____ , _____
fuera (de) _____	**dentro de** _____	**el cielo** _____

Copy the word or phrase in the space provided. Be sure to include the article for each noun. These blank cards can be used to write and practice other Spanish vocabulary for the chapter.

la harina	dulce	grasoso, grasosa
_____ _____	_____	_____ , _____

acompañar	al aire libre	el suelo
_____	_____ _____	_____ _____

el sabor		
_____		_____

Realidades 2

Capítulo 7B

Nombre _____

Fecha _____

Hora _____

Vocabulary Flash Cards, Sheet 6

These blank cards can be used to write and practice other Spanish vocabulary for the chapter.

_____   _____   _____

_____   _____   _____

_____   _____   _____

Tear out this page. Write the English words on the lines. Fold the paper along the dotted line to see the correct answers so you can check your work.

al aire libre _____

el cielo _____

dentro de _____

fuera (de) _____

la nube _____

la piedra _____

el aguacate _____

la chuleta de cerdo _____

los frijoles _____

la harina _____

el maíz _____

el sabor _____

dulce _____

picante _____

acompañar _____

Fold In

Vocabulary Check, Sheet 2

Tear out this page. Write the Spanish words on the lines. Fold the paper along the dotted line to see the correct answers so you can check your work.

outdoors ____________________

sky ____________________

inside ____________________

outside ____________________

cloud ____________________

rock ____________________

avocado ____________________

pork chop ____________________

beans ____________________

flour ____________________

corn ____________________

taste ____________________

sweet ____________________

spicy ____________________

to accompany ____________________

Fold In ←

Tear out this page. Write the English words on the lines. Fold the paper along the dotted line to see the correct answers so you can check your work.

el sendero _____

el suelo _____

la fogata _____

el fósforo _____

la leña _____

a la parrilla _____

el puesto _____

asado, asada _____

asar _____

la carne de res _____

la cereza _____

la cesta _____

la mayonesa _____

la mostaza _____

Fold In
←

Tear out this page. Write the Spanish words on the lines. Fold the paper along the dotted line to see the correct answers so you can check your work.

trail _____

ground, floor _____

bonfire _____

match _____

firewood _____

on the grill _____

(food) stand _____

grilled _____

to grill, to roast _____

steak _____

cherry _____

basket _____

mayonnaise _____

mustard _____

Fold In

To hear a complete list of the vocabulary for this chapter, go to Disc 2, Track 6 on the guided Practice Audio CD or go to www.phschool.com and type in the Web Code jdd-0799. Then click on **Repaso del capítulo**.

Usted and ustedes commands (p. 382)

- Use the **usted** command form to tell someone older than you what to do or what *not* to do. Use the **ustedes** form to tell a group of people what to do or what *not* to do.

    Coma Ud. el arroz.   **Beban Uds. la leche.**

- **-ar** verbs use **-e** for **Ud.** commands, and **-en** for **Uds.** commands; **-er** and **-ir** verbs use **-a** for **Ud.** commands, and **-an** for **Uds.** commands.

- The commands for **viajar**, **comer**, and **servir** are shown below.

verbs ending in -*ar*			verbs ending in -*er*			verbs ending in -*ir*		
viajar	usted	ustedes	**comer**	usted	ustedes	**servir**	usted	ustedes
yo viaj**o**	viaj**e**	viaj**en**	yo com**o**	com**a**	com**an**	yo sirv**o**	sirv**a**	sirv**an**

A. Write the correct ending for the **usted** or **ustedes** command form for each of the infinitives below. The first one is done for you.

1. abrir   abr _*an*_ Uds.

2. batir   bat_____ Ud.

3. calentar   calient_____ Ud.

4. entrar   entr_____ Uds.

5. añadir   añad_____ Uds.

6. tirar   tir_____ Ud.

7. hervir   hierv_____ Uds.

8. pelar   pel_____ Ud.

B. Write the correct **usted** or **ustedes** command form for each sentence using the verbs in parentheses. Follow the model.

Modelo (hervir) No _____*hierva*_____ Ud. el agua.

1. (cortar)   No _____ Ud. los huevos.

2. (preparar)   No _____ Uds. el desayuno.

3. (freír)   No _____ Uds. el pescado.

4. (probar)   No _____ Ud. el tocino.

5. (encender)   No _____ Ud. el horno.

Usted and ustedes commands (continued)

- Affirmative and negative **usted** and **ustedes** commands have the same spelling changes and irregular forms as the negative **tú** commands:

(hacer)	Haga Ud.	Hagan Uds.
(buscar)	Busque Ud.	Busquen Uds.
(almorzar)	Almuerce Ud.	Almuercen Uds.

C. Write the correct **usted/ustedes** command for each verb in parentheses. Follow the model.

Modelo (poner) _____*Pongan*_____ Uds. los platos en el fregadero.

1. (hacer) _____ Uds. un picnic para sus amigos.

2. (picar) No _____ Ud. el durazno.

3. (buscar) No _____ Ud. la fogata sin leña.

4. (tener) _____ Ud. cuidado con las hormigas.

5. (almorzar) No _____ Uds. sin vasos.

- If you want to use a pronoun such as **lo, la, los,** or **las** with an affirmative command, attach it to the end of the command. You will need to add a written accent mark in the commands.

—**¿Dónde ponemos la leña?** *Where do we put the firewood?*

—**Pónganla en un lugar seco.** *Put it in a dry place.*

D. Rewrite the following commands, replacing the underlined words with pronouns (**lo, la, los,** or **las**). Remember to add written accents where necessary. Follow the model.

Modelo Preparen <u>la comida</u>. _____*Prepárenla*_____.

1. Compre <u>las hamburguesas</u>. _____.

2. Traigan <u>los frijoles</u>. _____.

3. Busque <u>la leña</u>. _____.

4. Asen <u>el pollo</u>. _____.

5. Piquen <u>los tomates</u>. _____.

6. Coma <u>las galletas</u>. _____.

Go Online WEB CODE jdd-0713
PHSchool.com

Realidades 2

Capítulo 7B

Nombre _____

Hora _____

Fecha _____

Guided Practice Activities 7B-3

Usted and *ustedes* commands (*continued*)

- If you want to use a pronoun with a negative command, put it right before the command.

  —**¿Encendemos la fogata?** *Should we light the fire?*

  —**No, no la enciendan.** *No, don't light it.*

E. Eugenia and señora López are discussing some things students shouldn't do when camping. Fill in señora López's responses with the correct **usted/ustedes** command forms of the verbs in parentheses. The first one is done for you.

1. EUGENIA: ¿Lavamos las ollas aquí? (**lavar**)

   SEÑORA LÓPEZ: No, _____*no los laven*_____ allí.

2. EUGENIA: ¿Traemos la mostaza para encender el fuego? (**traer**)

   SEÑORA LÓPEZ: No, _____ para encender el fuego.

3. EUGENIA: ¿Sacamos los fósforos ahora? (**sacar**)

   SEÑORA LÓPEZ: No, _____ ahora.

4. EUGENIA: ¿Buscamos un parque en la ciudad para la fogata? (**buscar**)

   SEÑORA LÓPEZ: No, _____ en la ciudad.

5. EUGENIA: ¿Servimos las chuletas luego? (**servir**)

   SEÑORA LÓPEZ: No, _____ luego.

6. EUGENIA: ¿Dejamos los fósforos en el bosque? (**dejar**)

   SEÑORA LÓPEZ: No, _____ en el bosque.

Realidades 2

Capítulo 7B

Nombre _____

Hora _____

Fecha _____

Guided Practice Activities 7B-4

Uses of *por* (p. 386)

The preposition **por** is used in many ways.

- To tell about time or distance: **Yo dormí por ocho horas.** *I slept for eight hours.*
- To tell about movement: **Vamos a caminar por el sendero.** *Let's walk along the path.*
- To tell about exchanging one thing for another: **No pagué mucho por la piña.** *I didn't pay much for the pineapple.*
- To tell about a reason: **Yo fui al mercado por unas cerezas.** *I went to the market for some cherries.*
- To tell about an action on someone's behalf: **Encendí la parrilla por Luisa.** *I lit the grill for Luisa.*
- To tell about a way of communication or transportation: **¿Vas a viajar por avión?** *Are you going to travel by plane?*

A. Choose the best ending from the word bank to complete each sentence below. Use the context clues given to help you decide. Follow the model.

| por avión | ~~por tres horas~~ | por la leche | por el sendero | por mis padres |

Modelo Nosotros preparamos la cena _____ *por tres horas* _____.
(how much time?)

1. Vamos a viajar _____.
   (what form of transportation?)

2. Voy a cocinar _____.
   (on whose behalf?)

3. Tú vas a caminar _____.
   (how did you move?)

4. Voy a la tienda _____.
   (for what?)

B. Each of these sentences below ends with an expression that uses **por**. Write the letter of the best ending for each sentence.

1. Yo dormí _____.
   a. por la camisa   **b.** por dos horas

2. Lupe va a la tienda _____.
   a. por avión   **b.** por el periódico

3. Me gusta viajar _____.
   a. por dos tomates   **b.** por avión

4. ¿Cuánto dinero pagaste _____?
   a. por el sendero   **b.** por esa piña

5. Voy a preparar la carne _____.
   a. por mi hermano   **b.** por teléfono

Go **O**nline WEB CODE jdd-0714
PHSchool.com

Lectura: El Yunque (pp. 390–391)

A. Your textbook reading is about a national park called **El Yunque.** What kind of things do you think you'll read about in the reading? Add two more questions to the list about things you think the reading may describe.

¿Dónde está el parque? ¿Qué hay en el parque? ¿Qué tipos de plantas hay?

_____, _____

B. Read the following selections from the reading about **El Yunque.** As you read, find answers to some of the questions in **part A** and write them below.

> El Yunque es una de las atracciones más visitadas de Puerto Rico.... Más de 240 especies de árboles coexisten con animales exóticos, como el coquí y la boa de Puerto Rico.
>
> La mejor forma de explorar este parque es caminando por las varias veredas (paths) que pasan por el bosque.

1. ¿Dónde está el parque? El parque ésta en _____.

2. ¿Qué hay en el parque? Hay _____

_____

3. ¿Qué tipos de plantas hay? Hay _____

C. Look at the following advice from the reading about walking in **El Yunque.** After you read the selection, place a ✓ next to those sentences that are true.

> Consejos para el caminante
> 1 Nunca camine solo. Siempre vaya acompañado.
> 2 Traiga agua y algo para comer.
> 3 Use repelente para insectos.
> 4 No abandone las veredas para no perderse (to get lost).
> 5 No toque (touch) las plantas del bosque.

1. Never walk alone in the park. _____

2. Don't take food or water with you. _____

3. Use insect repellent. _____

4. Don't walk along the paths. _____

5. Touch the plants in the forest. _____

WEB CODE jdd-0716
PHSchool.com

Realidades 2

Capítulo 7B

Nombre _____

Hora _____

Fecha _____

Guided Practice Activities 7B-6

Presentación escrita (p. 393)

Task: You will write and illustrate a poster on safety and fun at an outdoor cookout.

A. Read and circle the sentences below that tell about something you need for an outdoor cookout.

1. Se necesitan fósforos.

2. Se debe comprar carne.

3. Se debe buscar un lugar mojado.

4. Se necesita leña.

5. Se debe llevar regla y lápiz.

6. Se debe comprar agua o refrescos.

7. Se debe mirar una película.

B. Now, read and circle the commands below that provide good advice before, during, and after a cookout.

1. Tengan cuidado con la parrilla caliente.

2. Lleven sus videojuegos.

3. Compren carne para asar.

4. Busquen un lugar seco para hacer la fogata.

5. Lleven repelente para mosquitos.

6. No jueguen cerca de un lago.

7. No tiren nada en el parque.

8. No apaguen la fogata antes de salir.

C. Using your answers from **parts A** and **B,** write a short paragraph. Mention how to stay safe and have fun before, during, and after the cookout. You may use the sentence starters below.

Antes de hacer una parrillada, ustedes necesitan _____.

El lugar debe _____.

Para hacer la fogata deben _____.

No jueguen ustedes con _____.

Antes de salir, _____.

D. Review the spelling and vocabulary on your poster. Check that your paragraph includes the appropriate commands and is easy to understand.

E. Use artwork to illustrate your sentences on the poster.

Realidades 2

Capítulo 8A

Nombre _____

Fecha _____

Hora _____

AVSR **8A-1**

A ver si recuerdas: The infinitive in verbal expressions (p. 399)

- Many verbal expressions contain infinitives. These include:

    Expressing plans, desires, and wishes:

    > **Mi hermana *piensa nadar* pero yo *quiero pasear* en bote.**
    > *My sister is thinking of swimming but I want to take a boat ride.*

    Expressing obligation:

    > **¿*Tienes que descansar* ahora?**
    > *Do you have to rest now?*

- In these expressions, only the first verb is conjugated. The second verb remains in the infinitive. Consider these sentences:

    > **Mi hermana nada y pasea en bote.**
    > *My sister swims and takes boat rides.*

    > **Mi hermana *piensa nadar* y *quiere pasear* en bote también.**
    > *My sister is thinking of swimming and wants to take a boat ride, too.*

A. Read the following sentences. Circle the correct verb from the parentheses. Follow the models.

Modelo 1 Julia y Ramón ((van) / ir) de pesca a menudo.

Modelo 2 Mi tía y yo queremos (vamos / (ir)) al cine.

1. A nosotros nos gustaría (tomamos / tomar) el sol.

2. Mi padre prefiere (esquiar / esquía).

3. Todas las tardes, yo (monto / montar) a caballo.

4. ¿Piensas tú (vas / ir) de cámping?

5. Yo debo (comprar / compro) recuerdos para mi familia.

6. Mis amigos (toman / tomar) muchas fotos.

7. ¿Quieres (ir / vas) a las montañas con nosotros?

8. Juan y yo tenemos que (regresar / regresamos) al hotel ahora.

Realidades 2

Capítulo 8A

Nombre _____

Hora _____

Fecha _____

AVSR 8A-2

A ver si recuerdas: The infinitive in verbal expressions (*continued*)

- The infinitive is also used after impersonal verbal expressions:

  Es necesario tener **mucho cuidado cuando buceas.**
  It is necessary to be very careful when you scuba dive.

  Hay que regresar **antes de las cinco y media.**
  One must (You should) return before 5:30.

B. Circle the most appropriate impersonal expression from the parentheses to complete the sentences below. The first one is done for you.

1. (**Hay que** / **Es divertido**) montar a caballo en la playa.

2. (**Es interesante** / **Es necesario**) hacer planes antes de salir de vacaciones.

3. (**Es malo** / **Es interesante**) visitar el zoológico.

4. (**Hay que** / **Es divertido**) hacer las reservaciones del hotel un mes antes de salir.

5. (**Es necesario** / **Es malo**) descansar mucho durante las vacaciones.

C. Using the words given as clues, write full sentences. Remember to use the infinitive after the verbs expressing plans, desires, wishes, and obligations.

Modelo Ramiro / querer / viajar al campo

Ramiro quiere viajar al campo _____.

1. Jorge y Sara / necesitar / regresar a casa

_____

2. A Marieli / le / encantar / bucear

_____

3. Hay que / calentar el caldo

_____

4. Luz y yo / pensar / pasear en bote

_____

5. Yo / tener que / pasar tiempo con mis tíos

_____

6. Es divertido / hacer una fogata

_____

7. Tú y Bruni / desear / montar en bicicleta

_____

Go Online WEB CODE jdd-0801
PHSchool.com

Realidades ②

Capítulo 8A

Nombre _____

Fecha _____

Hora _____

Vocabulary Flash Cards, Sheet 1

Write the Spanish vocabulary word or phrase below each picture. Be sure to include the article for each noun.

_____

_____

_____

_____

_____

_____

_____

_____

_____

_____

_____

_____

_____

_____

_____

Realidades 2

Capítulo 8A

Nombre _____

Fecha _____

Hora _____

Vocabulary Flash Cards, Sheet 2

Write the Spanish vocabulary word or phrase below each picture. Be sure to include the article for each noun.

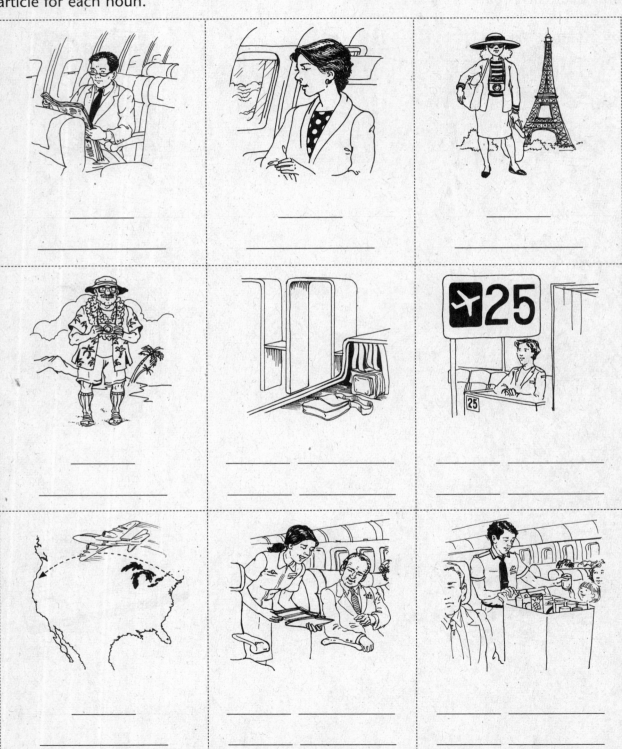

Realidades 2

Capítulo 8A

Nombre _____

Hora _____

Fecha _____

Vocabulary Flash Cards, Sheet 3

Write the Spanish vocabulary word below each picture. If there is a word or phrase, copy it in the space provided. Be sure to include the article for each noun.

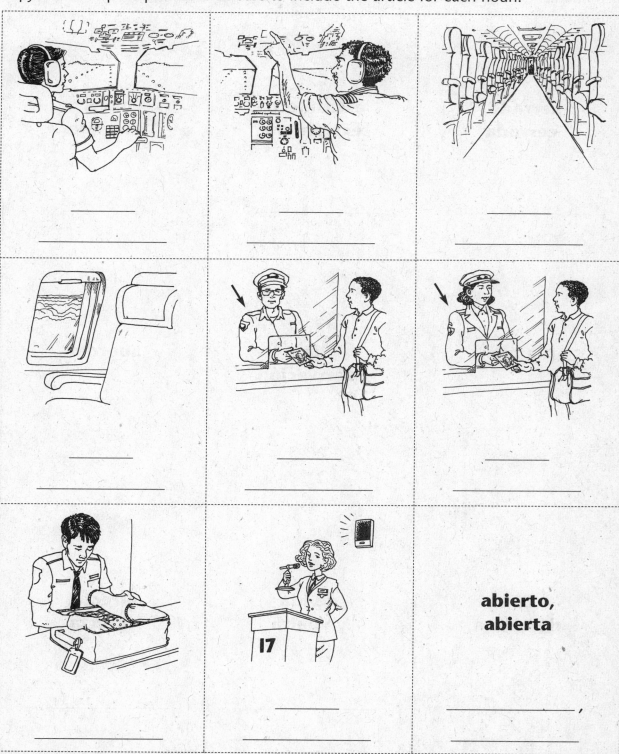

abierto, abierta

_____ ,

Copy the word or phrase in the space provided. Be sure to include the article for each noun.

cerrado, cerrada _____ , _____	**extranjero, extranjera** _____ , _____	**hacer un viaje** ___ ___ ___ ___
planear _____	**la reservación** _____ _____	**abordar** _____
con destino a _____ ___ ___ ___	**de ida y vuelta** ___ ___ ___ ___	**directo, directa** _____ , _____

Realidades 2

Capítulo 8A

Nombre _____

Hora _____

Fecha _____

Vocabulary Flash Cards, Sheet 5

Copy the word or phrase in the space provided. Be sure to include the article for each noun.

durar	**hacer escala**	**la línea aérea**
_____	_____ _____	_____ _____
la llegada	**el retraso**	**la salida**
_____ _____	_____	_____
bienvenido, bienvenida	**insistir en**	**listo, lista**
_____ , _____	_____ _____	_____ , _____

Realidades 2

Capítulo 8A

Nombre _____

Fecha _____

Hora _____

Vocabulary Flash Cards, Sheet 6

Copy the word or phrase in the space provided. Be sure to include the article for each noun. The blank cards can be used to write and practice other Spanish vocabulary in the chapter.

sugerir	**tendremos**	**tener paciencia**
_____	_____	_____
la aduana	**el empleado, la empleada**	**facturar**
_____	_____ , _____	_____
_____	_____	_____

Realidades **2**

Capítulo 8A

Nombre _____

Hora _____

Fecha _____

Vocabulary Check, Sheet 1

Tear out this page. Write the English words on the lines. Fold the paper along the dotted line to see the correct answers so you can check your work.

la agencia de viajes _____

el equipaje _____

extranjero, extranjera _____

hacer un viaje _____

la maleta _____

planear _____

abordar _____

la aduana _____

el aeropuerto _____

el anuncio _____

de ida y vuelta _____

la salida _____

el vuelo _____

abierto, abierta _____

Fold In

Realidades 2

Capítulo 8A

Nombre _____

Fecha _____

Hora _____

Vocabulary Check, Sheet 2

Tear out this page. Write the Spanish words on the lines. Fold the paper along the dotted line to see the correct answers so you can check your work.

travel agency _____

luggage _____

foreign _____

to take a trip _____

suitcase _____

to plan _____

to board _____

customs _____

airport _____

announcement _____

round-trip _____

departure _____

flight _____

open _____

Fold In →

Tear out this page. Write the English words on the lines. Fold the paper along the dotted line to see the correct answers so you can check your work.

el pasaporte _____

la reservación _____

el turista,
la turista _____

directo, directa _____

durar _____

el empleado,
la empleada _____

la línea aérea _____

el pasajero,
la pasajera _____

registrar _____

bienvenido,
bienvenida _____

necesitar _____

permitir _____

preferir _____

cerrado, cerrada _____

Fold In

Tear out this page. Write the Spanish words on the lines. Fold the paper along the dotted line to see the correct answers so you can check your work.

passport _____

reservation _____

tourist _____

direct _____

to last _____

employee _____

airline _____

passenger _____

to inspect, to search (*luggage*) _____

welcome _____

to need _____

to allow, to permit _____

to prefer _____

closed _____

Fold In

To hear a complete list of the vocabulary for this chapter, go to Disc 2, Track 7 on the guided Practice Audio CD or go to www.phschool.com and type in the Web Code jdd-0889. Then click on **Repaso del capítulo**.

The present subjunctive (p. 410)

- You form the present subjunctive in the same way as you form negative **tú** commands and **usted/ustedes** commands. You drop the **-o** of the present-tense indicative **yo** form and add the present subjunctive endings. See the chart below:

hablar		aprender		escribir	
hable	hablemos	aprenda	aprendamos	escriba	escribamos
hables	habléis	aprendas	aprendáis	escribas	escribáis
hable	hablen	aprenda	aprendan	escriba	escriban

A. Write the subjunctive ending for each of the verbs below. Follow the model.

Modelo   yo / asistir   asist_a_____

1. los pasajeros / abordar   abord_____

2. tú / beber   beb_____

3. nosotros / viajar   viaj_____

4. el vuelo / durar   dur_____

5. tú / desear   dese_____

6. yo / vivir   viv_____

7. la familia / planear   plane_____

8. nosotros / llevar   llev_____

- The present subjunctive has the same spelling changes that you used with the negative **tú** commands and **usted/ustedes** commands.
- Here are the present subjunctive forms of **llegar** and **sacar**:

llegar		sacar	
llegue	lleguemos	saque	saquemos
llegues	lleguéis	saques	saquéis
llegue	lleguen	saque	saquen

Realidades 2

Capítulo 8A

Nombre _____

Fecha _____

Hora _____

Guided Practice Activities 8A-2

The present subjunctive (*continued*)

B. Look at the sentences using the present subjunctive below. Underline the second verb in each and then circle the spelling change in each verb that you underlined. The first one has been done for you.

1. La profesora recomienda que nosotros saquemos más libros de la biblioteca.

2. Yo necesito que ustedes paguen por los boletos hoy.

3. Se recomienda que los empleados busquen cosas prohibidas.

4. El niño desea que la mamá no apague la luz.

5. Prefiero que tú llegues a tiempo.

6. El entrenador quiere que los jugadores jueguen todos los días de esta semana.

7. El Sr. Vega prohíbe que nosotros toquemos las exposiciones.

8. Papá recomienda que yo me seque las manos.

- The same verbs that have irregular **yo** forms in the present indicative are also irregular in the present subjunctive.
- Here are the conjugations of two verbs that have this irregular pattern:

tener		conocer	
tenga	tengamos	conozca	conozcamos
tengas	tengáis	conozcas	conozcáis
tenga	tengan	conozca	conozcan

C. Write the irregular **yo** form of the present indicative for the first part of each example below. Then, write the correct present subjunctive form using the cues given in the second part. The first one is done for you.

Present Indicative — **Present Subjunctive**

1. traer yo _____*traigo*_____ Andrés y Toni _____*traigan*_____
2. decir yo _____ tú _____
3. conducir yo _____ Diego _____
4. salir yo _____ yo _____
5. ofrecer yo _____ Ana y Javier _____
6. venir yo _____ tú _____
7. hacer yo _____ María y yo _____
8. oír yo _____ Ud. _____

Go Online WEB CODE jdd-0804
PHSchool.com

Realidades 2

Capítulo 8A

Nombre _____

Hora _____

Fecha _____

Guided Practice Activities 8A-3

The present subjunctive (*continued*)

D. Write the correct present subjunctive forms of the verbs given. The first one is done for you.

> **El agente de viajes sugiere que...**

1. ...nosotros ___*hablemos*___ (**hablar**) con el piloto antes de salir.

2. ...yo _____ (**buscar**) un asiento cerca de la ventanilla.

3. ...mis padres _____ (**llegar**) temprano al aeropuerto.

4. ...nosotros _____ (**hacer**) las reservaciones con el hotel.

5. ...tú _____ (**traer**) el bloqueador solar.

6. ...yo no _____ (**salir**) sin mi pasaporte.

7. ...mis hermanos y yo _____ (**obedecer**) las reglas del viajero.

8. ...Pedro _____ (**pasar**) a la salida.

• The present subjunctive is used when one person is influencing the actions of another, by advising, prohibiting, or suggesting. Some verbs that often introduce the subjunctive mood are:

decir	to say; to tell	preferir	to prefer	querer	to want
insistir en	to insist upon	permitir	to permit	prohibir	to prohibit
necesitar	to need	recomendar	to recommend	sugerir	to suggest

• These verbs are used in the indicative, but the verbs that follow them are used in the subjunctive. The word **que** connects the two parts of the sentence.

> Indicative   Subjunctive
> Su madre le <u>prohíbe</u> *que* Agustina <u>salga</u> de la casa después de las nueve.
> El profesor <u>recomienda</u> *que* nosotros <u>visitemos</u> el zoológico.

Realidades 2

Capítulo 8A

Nombre _____

Hora _____

Fecha _____

Guided Practice Activities 8A-3a

The present subjunctive (*continued*)

- Subjunctive sentences have two parts, each part with its own subject. Notice that the first part uses the present indicative to recommend, suggest, prohibit, and so on:

  El agente de viajes quiere...

- The second part uses the present subjunctive to say what the other subject should or should not do:

  ...nosotros visitemos el zoológico.

  El agente de viajes quiere que nosotros visitemos el zoológico.
  The travel agent wants us to visit the zoo.

E. Read the following sentences. In each sentence, underline the verb that shows that one person is trying to influence the action of another (present indicative) and circle the verb that indicates what the other person should do (present subjunctive). Follow the model.

Modelo Mi maestro <u>permite</u> que nosotros (trabajemos) en grupos.

1. La agente de viajes sugiere que ellos visiten La Paz.

2. El aduanero insiste en que tú tengas el pasaporte en la mano.

3. Los hermanos necesitan que los padres aborden con ellos.

4. El piloto les dice a los pasajeros que apaguen los teléfonos celulares.

5. El tío recomienda que nosotros facturemos el equipaje temprano.

F. In each sentence below, underline the verb that shows that one person is trying to influence the action of another. Then, write the subjunctive form of the verb in parentheses. Follow the model.

Modelo Carlos <u>sugiere</u> que nosotros ___*pasemos*___ a la casa de cambios. (**pasar**)

1. Pancho sugiere que Julián y Lolis _____ los pasaportes a la aduana. (**traer**)

2. Los auxiliares de vuelo recomiendan que yo _____ jugo de manzana. (**beber**)

3. Yo quiero que los auxiliares de vuelo me _____. (**ayudar**)

4. La profesora le dice a Sofía que ella _____ sobre los lugares que visita. (**aprender**)

5. La aduanera permite que tú _____ la maleta ahora. (**hacer**)

Go Online WEB CODE jdd-0804
PHSchool.com

The present subjunctive (*continued*)

G. Fill in the blank in the first part of each sentence below with the present indicative form of the verb to show that someone wants to influence another person's actions. In the second part of the sentence fill in the blanks with the subjunctive form of the verb to say what someone should do. The first one is done for you.

1. Óscar (**sugerir**) _____*sugiere*_____ que nosotros (**visitar**) _____*visitemos*_____ la casa de cambio antes de salir.

2. Nosotros (**recomendar**) _____ que Uds. (**comprar**) _____ una guía de la ciudad.

3. La empleada (**necesitar**) _____ que tú le _____ (**escribir**) tu número de pasaporte.

4. Esa agente de vuelos (**prohibir**) _____ que los pasajeros (**llegar**) _____ tarde.

5. Mis padres (**preferir**) _____ que yo (**comer**) _____ con ellos.

6. Los auxiliares de vuelo (**insistir**) _____ en que nosotros (**obedecer**) _____ a los señales (*signs*).

H. Use the words given to write complete sentences in the order in which the words appear. Follow the model.

Remember: The verb that shows that one person is trying to influence the action of another uses the present indicative while the verb that tells what the other person should do uses the present subjunctive.

> **Modelo**   Felipe / insistir en / que / Amelia / tener paciencia
> *Felipe insiste en que Amelia tenga paciencia* _____.

1. Los profesores / sugerir / que / los estudiantes / estudiar más horas

   _____.

2. Nosotros / recomendar / que / Uds. / llegar temprano a los exámenes

   _____.

3. Mis padres / querer / que / yo / asistir a una buena universidad

   _____.

4. Mamá / necesitar / que / nosotros / poner la mesa

   _____.

5. Yo / preferir / que / tú / buscar otro trabajo

   _____.

Realidades ❷

Capítulo 8A

Nombre _____

Fecha _____

Hora _____

Guided Practice Activities 8A-4

Irregular verbs in the subjunctive (p. 413)

- Verbs with irregular **tú** and **usted/ustedes** commands also have irregular subjunctive forms.

dar		estar		ir		saber		ser	
dé	demos	esté	estemos	vaya	vayamos	sepa	sepamos	sea	seamos
des	deis	estés	estéis	vayas	vayáis	sepas	sepáis	seas	seáis
dé	den	esté	estén	vaya	vayan	sepa	sepan	sea	sean

A. Read each sentence below and circle the verb in its subjunctive form. Then, write the infinitive of the circled verb in the blank. Follow the model.

Modelo   Recomiendo que Ana te (dé) la tarjeta de embarque. _____dar_____

1. Sugiero que el pasajero esté aquí a las cuatro. _____

2. Quiero que vayas a la agencia de viajes. _____

3. Deseo que sepas la hora de llegada. _____

4. Insisto en que sean responsables. _____

5. Necesito que el vuelo sea de ida y vuelta. _____

B. Circle the second subject in each sentence. Then, write the correct form of the verb in parentheses using the present subjunctive. The first one is done for you.

1. Deseo que (ustedes) _____estén_____ en el aeropuerto muy temprano. (**estar**)

2. Recomiendo que ustedes _____ sus maletas a los empleados. (**dar**)

3. Sugiero que tú _____ a la agencia de viajes. (**ir**)

4. Quiero que ella _____ dónde está la puerta de embarque. (**saber**)

5. Necesito que la maleta _____ grande. (**ser**)

6. La empleada de la aerolínea quiere que yo le _____ mi tarjeta de embarque. (**dar**)

Go Online WEB CODE jdd-0804
PHSchool.com

Lectura: Ecuador, país de maravillas (pp. 418–419)

A. The reading in your textbook is about the South American country of Ecuador. Write three things that you would expect to find in your reading about its tourist attractions.

1. _____.

2. _____.

3. _____.

B. You can often predict what a reading is about by looking at the title, subheads, and photo captions. Look at the photos and read the captions on pages 418–419 of your textbook. Place an *X* next to the attractions you can find in Ecuador.

Las atracciones turísticas del Ecuador

_____ woven cloth   _____ la Mitad del Mundo

_____ the island of Puerto Rico   _____ snow-covered mountains

_____ the Galapagos Islands   _____ the church of La Compañía de Jesús

---

C. Read the excerpt from your reading and circle the letter of the answers to the questions that follow.

> *Es un país pequeño, pero tiene paisajes para todos los gustos* (tastes)*: desde playas tropicales hasta montañas nevadas, desde ciudades coloniales hasta parques naturales. Ecuador es una joya.*

1. ¿Qué clase de país es Ecuador?
   a. Es un país pequeño.
   b. Es un país grande.

2. ¿Dónde nieva en Ecuador?
   a. Nieva en las playas tropicales.
   b. Nieva en las montañas.

3. ¿Hay ciudades coloniales en Ecuador?
   a. Sí, hay ciudades coloniales en Ecuador.
   b. No, no hay ciudades coloniales en Ecuador.

4. ¿Qué clase de parques hay en Ecuador?
   a. Hay parques artificiales en Ecuador.
   b. Hay parques naturales en Ecuador.

Realidades 2

Capítulo 8A

Nombre _____

Hora _____

Fecha _____

Guided Practice Activities 8A-6

Presentación oral (p. 421)

Task: Imagine that you work at a travel agency. You need to provide travel information to a client who would like to travel to a Spanish-speaking country.

A. Choose one of the following Spanish-speaking countries: Mexico or Ecuador.

B. Read the following travel information about each country. Then, circle one or two recommendations you would offer based on what you read.

1. La ciudad de Quito en Ecuador está en las montañas y hace mucho frío. Hay una iglesia muy importante.
   a. Recomiendo que lleven poca ropa.
   b. Sugiero que vayan a la iglesia La Compañía de Jesús.
   c. Recomiendo que lleven suéteres o chaquetas.

2. Cancún está en México. En Cancún hay una playa tropical de 14 millas y muchos hoteles elegantes.
   a. Si desean ir a una playa grande, yo recomiendo que vayan a Cancún.
   b. Si buscan un hotel elegante, vayan a Cancún.
   c. Recomiendo que lleven trajes de baño.

C. Use your recommendations in **part B** as a model for your oral presentation. You may use the sentence starters below. Don't forget to use the subjunctive when you are advising, prohibiting, or suggesting something to your client.

Recomiendo que Uds. viajen a _____. *Allí pueden ver*

_____. *Deben llevar* _____

porque _____.

D. Now, practice your presentation using the information you have gathered. Try to present the information in a logical sequence and speak clearly.

E. Present the trip you have planned to your partner. Your teacher will grade you on the following:

- how much information you communicate
- how easy it is to understand you

Realidades 2

Capítulo 8B

Nombre _____

Hora _____

Fecha _____

Vocabulary Flash Cards, Sheet 1

Write the Spanish vocabulary word or phrase below each picture. Be sure to include the article for each noun.

_____

_____

_____

_____

_____

_____

_____

_____

_____

_____

_____

_____

_____

_____

_____

_____

_____

_____

Write the Spanish vocabulary word or phrase below each picture. Be sure to include the article for each noun.

_____

_____

_____

_____

_____

_____

_____

_____

_____

Realidades ②

Capítulo 8B

Nombre _____

Hora _____

Fecha _____

Vocabulary Flash Cards, Sheet 3

Write the Spanish vocabulary word or phrase below each picture. Be sure to include the article for each noun.

_____

_____

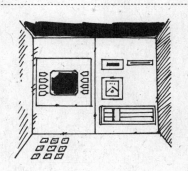

_____

_____

_____

_____

_____

_____

_____

Realidades 2

Capítulo 8B

Nombre _____

Hora _____

Fecha _____

Vocabulary Flash Cards, Sheet 4

Write the Spanish vocabulary word below each picture. If there is a word or phrase, copy it in the space provided. Be sure to include the article for each noun.

_____	POR FAVOR / GRACIAS _____	_____
histórico, histórica _____ , _____	**atento, atenta** _____ , _____	**ofender** _____
puntual _____	**disfrutar de** _____	**la excursión** _____

Realidades 2

Capítulo 8B

Nombre _____

Hora _____

Fecha _____

Vocabulary Flash Cards, Sheet 5

Copy the word or phrase in the space provided.

regatear	**bello, bella**	**en punto**
_____	_____, _____	_____
estupendo, estupenda	**famoso, famosa**	**siguiente**
_____, _____	_____, _____	_____
tal vez	**típico, típica**	**hacer ruido**
_____ _____	_____, _____	_____

Copy the word or phrase in the space provided. Be sure to include the article for each noun. The blank cards can be used to write and practice other Spanish vocabulary in the chapter.

conseguir _____	**observar** _____	_____
_____	_____	_____
_____	_____	_____

Nombre _____ Hora _____

Fecha _____ **Vocabulary Check, Sheet 1**

Tear out this page. Write the English words on the lines. Fold the paper along the dotted line to see the correct answers so you can check your work.

la casa de cambio _____

el palacio _____

el quiosco _____

el ascensor _____

la llave _____

la recepción _____

la artesanía _____

el bote de vela _____

el guía, la guía _____

bello, bella _____

en punto _____

famoso, famosa _____

siguiente _____

tal vez _____

Fold In

Tear out this page. Write the Spanish words on the lines. Fold the paper along the dotted line to see the correct answers so you can check your work.

currency exchange _____

palace _____

newsstand _____

elevator _____

key _____

reception desk _____

handicrafts _____

sailboat _____

guide _____

beautiful _____

exactly (time) _____

famous _____

next, following _____

maybe, perhaps _____

Fold In →

Tear out this page. Write the English words on the lines. Fold the paper along the dotted line to see the correct answers so you can check your work.

el cajero automático _____

la catedral _____

histórico, histórica _____

conseguir _____

la habitación _____

cortés _____

hacer ruido _____

ofender _____

la propina _____

cambiar _____

disfrutar de _____

navegar _____

el vendedor,
la vendedora _____

típico, típica _____

Fold In

Tear out this page. Write the Spanish words on the lines. Fold the paper along the dotted line to see the correct answers so you can check your work.

ATM _____

cathedral _____

historical _____

to obtain _____

room _____

polite _____

to make noise _____

to offend _____

tip _____

to change,
to exchange _____

to enjoy _____

to sail, to navigate _____

vendor _____

typical _____

Fold In

To hear a complete list of the vocabulary for this chapter, go to Disc 2, Track 8 on the guided Practice Audio CD or go to www.phschool.com and type in the Web Code jdd-0899. Then click on **Repaso del capítulo.**

Present subjunctive with impersonal expressions (p. 434)

- You can use impersonal expressions, such as **es importante, es necesario, es mejor,** and **es bueno,** to tell people what they should do. Sentences with these impersonal expressions are often followed by **que** + subjunctive:

    Es necesario que nosotros le demos una propina al empleado.
    It's necessary that we give a tip to the employee.

    Es mejor que tú observes las reglas para el viaje.
    It's better that you observe the rules for the trip.

A. Choose the correct verb form in parentheses to complete each sentence. Follow the model.

Modelo   Es importante que nosotros (⟨llevemos⟩/ llevamos) la llave.

1. Es mejor que nosotros (visitamos / visitemos) la catedral.

2. Es necesario que ustedes (van / vayan) a la recepción.

3. Es bueno que tú (tomas / tomes) el ascensor.

4. Es importante que yo (cambie / cambia) dinero.

5. Es mejor que el grupo (haga / hace) una gira de la capital.

B. Read the sentences below. Fill in the blanks with the correct form of the verbs in parentheses. The first one is done for you.

1. Es importante que ustedes ____*visiten*____ el castillo. (**visitar**)

2. Es necesario que tú _____ la guía. (**llevar**)

3. Es bueno que nosotros _____ en un bote de vela. (**navegar**)

4. Es mejor que yo _____ una gira. (**hacer**)

5. Es importante que Mateo _____ los lugares históricos. (**conocer**)

6. Es necesario que usted _____ dinero en la casa de cambio. (**cambiar**)

7. Es mejor que nosotros _____ un lugar para comer ahora. (**buscar**)

8. Es bueno que Ignacio y Javier _____ con nosotros. (**ir**)

Present subjunctive with impersonal expressions (*continued*)

- To speak generally about things that should or should not be done, use an impersonal expression plus an infinitive. Note that **que** is not used. Compare the following sentences:

  Subjunctive
  Es importante que tú *seas* **cortés.** *It is important that you be polite.* (specific)

  Infinitive
  Es importante *ser* **cortés.** *It is important to be polite.* (general)

C. Read the following sentences. Write **S** (for specific) if the sentence mentions specific people. Write **G** (for general) if it does not mention specific people. Follow the models.

Modelo 1   __*G*__   Es necesario ser puntual.

Modelo 2   __*S*__   Es necesario que ustedes sean puntuales.

1. _____ Es necesario estar atento en el bote de vela.

2. _____ No es bueno que nosotros hagamos ruido en las habitaciones.

3. _____ Es importante que tú observes al guía.

4. _____ Es mejor no ofender a los reyes.

5. _____ Es bueno dar propinas.

6. _____ Es importante que usted sea cortés con los vendedores.

D. Read each sentence and decide if it needs the subjunctive (*specific*) or the infinitive (*general*). Then, fill in the blank with the correct form of the verb given. Follow the models.

Modelo 1 Es esencial _____*dar*_____ (**dar**) propinas.

Modelo 2 Es necesario que la abuela _____*suba*_____ (**subir**) en el ascensor.

1. Es necesario _____ (**cambiar**) dinero en el banco.

2. Es importante _____ (**llevar**) las llaves del hotel.

3. Es bueno que tú _____ (**sacar**) muchas fotos en la ciudad.

4. Es mejor _____ (**llegar**) temprano al aeropuerto.

5. Es importante que nosotros _____ (**ser**) corteses.

Go Online WEB CODE jdd-0813
PHSchool.com

Realidades 2

Capítulo 8B

Nombre _____

Hora _____

Fecha _____

Guided Practice Activities 8B-3

Present subjunctive of stem-changing verbs (p. 437)

- Stem-changing verbs ending in **-ar** and **-er** have the same stem changes in the subjunctive as in the indicative. Just like the present indicative, the **nosotros** and **vosotros** forms do not have a stem change.
- Here are the conjugations for **cerrar** and **volver**:

cerrar (e → ie)		volver (o → ue)	
cierre	cerremos	vuelva	volvamos
cierres	cerréis	vuelvas	volváis
cierre	cierren	vuelva	vuelvan

A. Read each sentence and complete the verb with the correct stem-changing vowels. Follow the model.

Modelo (**recordar**) Es necesario que usted rec_ue_rde la dirección.

1. (**encender**) Es importante que tú enc_____ndas las luces antes de entrar.

2. (**empezar**) La profesora quiere que Simón emp_____ce con el examen ahora.

3. (**contar**) Es mejor que tú c_____ntes el dinero fuera de la tienda.

4. (**poder**) Es bueno que ustedes p_____dan visitar tantos lugares.

5. (**llover**) Hace mal tiempo, pero es mejor que no ll_____va durante el partido de béisbol.

B. Complete the following sentences with the subjunctive form of the verb in parentheses. The first one is done for you.

1. Es mejor que nosotros _almorcemos_ bien antes de ir de excursión. (**almorzar**)

2. Es importante que tú _____ lo que el guía dice. (**entender**)

3. Rosa no tiene dinero. Es necesario que ella _____ un cajero automático. (**encontrar**)

4. Es bueno que ustedes se _____ temprano para visitar el castillo. (**despertar**)

5. Marta no conoce la ciudad. Es mejor que yo le _____ un buen hotel. (**recomendar**)

6. Antes de salir del hotel, es importante que ellos _____ la llave. (**devolver**)

7. El camarero sugiere que nosotros _____ la cena ahora. (**comenzar**)

Present subjunctive of stem-changing verbs (*continued*)

- Stem-changing verbs ending in **-ir** have changes in all forms of the present subjunctive:
- Here are the conjugations for **pedir**, **dormir**, and **divertirse**:

pedir (e → i)		dormir (o → ue), (o → u)		divertirse (e → ie), (e → i)	
pida	pidamos	duerma	durmamos	me divierta	nos divirtamos
pidas	pidáis	duermas	durmáis	te diviertas	os divirtáis
pida	pidan	duerma	duerman	se divierta	se diviertan

C. Complete the following sentences using the present subjunctive of the **-ir** stem-changing verbs in parentheses. Follow the model.

Modelo   (**pedir**) Es necesario que ustedes _____*pidan*_____ ayuda.

1. (**repetir**) Los turistas quieren que la guía _____ la explicación.

2. (**sentirse**) Deseamos que nuestros parientes _____ _____ bien.

3. (**divertirse**) Nuestros padres quieren que nosotros _____ _____ mucho.

4. (**seguir**) Es importante que nosotros _____ las instrucciones.

5. (**dormir**) Es mejor que Felipe y Ana _____ en el avión.

D. Use the words given to write complete sentences in the order in which the words appear. Follow the model.

Modelo   Es bueno / que / ustedes / divertirse / en las vacaciones
_____*Es bueno que ustedes se diviertan en las vacaciones*_____.

1. Es necesario / que / tú / conseguir / una llave para la habitación

_____.

2. Yo no / querer / que / mi hermano / reírse / de mí

_____.

3. Es importante / que / yo / hervir / los huevos primero

_____.

4. Es mejor / que / el camarero / servir / la comida ahora

_____.

5. El jefe / recomendar / que / nosotros / pedir / una propina

_____.

Realidades 2

Capítulo 8B

Nombre _____

Fecha _____

Hora _____

Guided Practice Activities 8B-5

Lectura: Antigua, una ciudad colonial (pp. 442–443)

A. The reading in your textbook is a travel brochure about Antigua, Guatemala. Look at the photos, the heads, and the subheads in this brochure to get an idea of what the reading will be about. What are three things this brochure might mention?

1. _____, 2. _____, 3. _____

B. Read the following excerpt from the reading in your textbook and complete the sentences below.

> ¿Qué hay que ver en la ciudad de Antigua?
>
> La ciudad de Antigua tiene muchos sitios de interés. Se puede apreciar toda la historia de esta ciudad mirando sus casas y monumentos coloniales. En el centro de la ciudad está la Plaza Mayor. Los edificios principales son el Ayuntamiento (City Hall), la Catedral y el Palacio de los Capitanes.

1. In the city of Antigua, you can see _____.
   a. interesting places   **b.** hotels

2. The Plaza Mayor is in _____.
   a. the center of the city   **b.** Tikal

3. The Palacio de los Capitanes is _____.
   a. a sailboat   **b.** one of the important buildings

C. The name **Antigua** means *antique*, or *old* in Spanish. Read this introduction from the reading. Then, write some of the words or phrases that indicate the city is old. One example is provided for you.

> Situada a 45 minutos de la Ciudad de Guatemala, Antigua le fascina al turista por sus calles de piedras, su arquitectura colonial y sus ruinas de iglesias y monasterios. El español Francisco de la Cueva fundó la ciudad el 10 de marzo de 1543. La "Ciudad de las Perpetuas Rosas," nombrada así por sus jardines con flores, tiene un clima muy agradable y preserva un sabor colonial único. Caminar por sus calles es como visitar el pasado y descubrir una ciudad típica española del siglo (century) XVII.

calle de piedras _____

_____

_____

Presentación escrita (p. 445)

Task: Imagine you are going to visit a Spanish-speaking country with a group. Prepare an illustrated brochure so you can share your experience with others.

A. Think about the preparations you must make before you go on your trip. Answer the questions below to help you organize your brochure.

1. ¿Qué país vas a visitar? _____

2. ¿Cómo vas a viajar? _____

3. ¿Qué vas a llevar? _____

4. ¿Qué lugares vas a visitar? _____

_____

5. ¿Qué actividades vas a hacer? _____

_____

B. Use the information from **part A** to complete the sentences below. You can use the following paragraph as a model.

> *Voy a viajar a México. Voy a viajar por avión. Es importante que yo lleve una guía porque voy a visitar el centro histórico y el famoso castillo. También es bueno que yo haga excursiones y navegue en el océano.*

Voy a viajar a _____. Voy a viajar por _____. Es importante

que yo lleve _____ porque voy a visitar _____ y

_____. También es bueno que yo _____ y

_____.

C. Choose some illustrations for your brochure. You can use photos from home or from magazines, or you can draw pictures to illustrate what you will see and do on your trip.

D. Reread your draft and check the spelling, vocabulary, and verb usage. Share your draft with a classmate, who will check for clarity, organization, and errors.

E. Make a new version of the brochure with changes and corrections. Don't forget to attach your illustrations for the brochure where they will be most appropriate.

Realidades 2

Capítulo 9A

Nombre _____

Hora _____

Fecha _____

AVSR 9A-1

A ver si recuerdas: Verbs with spelling changes in the present tense (p. 449)

- As you know, some verbs have spelling changes in the present tense for reasons of pronunciation. Some verbs, such as **escoger, recoger, seguir,** and **conseguir,** change spelling only in the *yo* form.

  Mi hermano *escoge* **unas vacaciones en las montañas mientras que yo** *escojo* **la playa.**
  My brother chooses a vacation in the mountains while I choose the beach.

  Los turistas no siempre *siguen* **las reglas; yo sí las** *sigo*.
  The tourists do not always follow the rules; I do follow them.

- Other verbs, such as **enviar** and **esquiar,** simply add accent marks on the **i** in all persons except **nosotros** and **vosotros.**

  Mi hermano *esquía* **mucho. Nosotros** *esquiamos* **juntos a veces.**
  My brother skis a lot. We ski together sometimes.

A. Write the present tense **yo** form of the infinitives below. Then write the second form in the present tense using the cue provided. Follow the model.

Modelo	escoger	yo _*escojo*_	usted _*escoge*_
1.	conseguir	yo _____	tú _____
2.	enviar	yo _____	nosotros _____
3.	recoger	yo _____	ellas _____
4.	seguir	yo _____	ella _____
5.	escoger	yo _____	nosotras _____
6.	esquiar	yo _____	tú _____

Realidades ②

Capítulo 9A

Nombre _____

Hora _____

Fecha _____

AVSR **9A-2**

A ver si recuerdas: Verbs with spelling changes in the present tense (*continued*)

B. Pablo is working at a summer camp. Complete his letter home by writing the **yo** form of the verbs given. The first one is done for you.

Queridos padres:

¿Cómo están? Yo estoy muy bien aquí en las montañas, y estoy trabajando mucho. Todos los días yo ____sigo____ (**seguir**) las instrucciones de mi jefe. Siempre _____ (**recoger**) la basura de la cafetería y _____ (**enviar**) las cartas de los niños. Después, yo _____ (**conseguir**) el horario del día del director del campamento. Lo _____ (**seguir**) con cuidado, y por la tarde tengo dos horas libres. A veces _____ (**esquiar**) en agua—¡mi actividad favorita! Por la noche, yo _____ (**escoger**) un juego para jugar con los niños. Siempre me acuesto muy cansado.

Un abrazo,

Pablo

C. Complete the following answers, paying special attention to the verbs with spelling changes. Follow the model.

Modelo ¿Les envías muchas cartas a tus parientes?

Sí, yo siempre les ____envío cartas____.

1. ¿Quién recoge la basura en tu casa?

Yo _____ en mi casa.

2. ¿Esquías todos los inviernos?

Sí, yo _____.

3. ¿Siempre sigues las reglas de tus padres?

Sí, yo siempre _____.

4. ¿Dónde consigues regalos para tus parientes?

Yo _____.

Go Online WEB CODE jdd-0901
PHSchool.com

Realidades ②

Capítulo 9A

Nombre _____

Hora _____

Fecha _____

Vocabulary Flash Cards, Sheet 1

Write the Spanish vocabulary word below each picture. Be sure to include the article for each noun.

_____

_____

_____

_____

_____

_____

_____

_____

_____

Realidades ②

Capítulo 9A

Nombre _____

Fecha _____

Hora _____

Vocabulary Flash Cards, Sheet 2

Write the Spanish vocabulary word below each picture. Be sure to include the article for each noun.

_____

_____

_____

_____

_____

_____

_____

_____

_____

_____

_____

_____

_____

_____

_____

_____

_____

_____

Realidades ②

Capítulo 9A

Nombre _____

Fecha _____

Hora _____

Vocabulary Flash Cards, Sheet 3

Write the Spanish vocabulary word below each picture. Be sure to include the article for each noun.

Realidades ②

Capítulo 9A

Nombre _____

Fecha _____

Hora _____

Vocabulary Flash Cards, Sheet 4

Write the Spanish vocabulary word below each picture. Be sure to include the article for each noun.

_____

_____

_____

_____

_____

_____

_____

_____

_____

Realidades 2

Capítulo 9A

Nombre _____

Hora _____

Fecha _____

Vocabulary Flash Cards, Sheet 5

Write the Spanish vocabulary word below each picture. If there is a word or phrase, copy it in the space provided. Be sure to include the article for each noun.

_____

_____

_____

_____

_____

la ley

_____

la política

_____

algún día

_____

los beneficios

_____

Copy the word or phrase in the space provided. Be sure to include the article for each noun.

bilingüe _____	**la carrera** _____ _____	**la escuela técnica** ___ _____ _____
el futuro _____ _____	**ganarse la vida** _____ _____	**habrá** _____
el idioma _____ _____	**militar** _____	**el programa de estudios** _____ _____

Copy the word or phrase in the space provided. Be sure to include the article for each noun. The blank cards can be used to write and practice other Spanish vocabulary for the chapter.

el salario _____ _____	**seguir (una carrera)** _____	**el dueño, la dueña** _____ _____, _____ _____
el gerente, la gerente _____ _____, _____ _____	**las artes** _____ _____	**el derecho** _____ _____
la profesión _____ _____		

Realidades 2

Capítulo 9A

Nombre _____

Hora _____

Fecha _____

Vocabulary Flash Cards, Sheet 8

These blank cards can be used to write and practice other Spanish vocabulary for the chapter.

_____	_____	_____
_____	_____	_____
_____	_____	_____

Realidades 2

Capítulo 9A

Nombre _____

Fecha _____

Hora _____

Vocabulary Check, Sheet 1

Tear out this page. Write the English words on the lines. Fold the paper along the dotted line to see the correct answers so you can check your work.

el científico, la científica _____

el ingeniero, la ingeniera _____

el veterinario, la veterinaria _____

el contador, la contadora _____

el dueño, la dueña _____

el gerente, la gerente _____

los negocios _____

el hombre de negocios, la mujer de negocios _____

el secretario, la secretaria _____

el artista, la artista _____

el abogado, la abogada _____

el derecho _____

el colegio _____

la universidad _____

Fold In

Tear out this page. Write the Spanish words on the lines. Fold the paper along the dotted line to see the correct answers so you can check your work.

scientist _____

engineer _____

veterinarian _____

accountant _____

owner _____

manager _____

business _____

businessman, _____

businesswoman _____

secretary _____

artist _____

lawyer _____

(study of) law _____

high school _____

university _____

Fold In

Tear out this page. Write the English words on the lines. Fold the paper along the dotted line to see the correct answers so you can check your work.

el agricultor, la agricultora _____

el arquitecto, la arquitecta _____

el diseñador, la diseñadora _____

el mecánico, la mecánica _____

el cartero, la cartera _____

el escritor, la escritora _____

el pintor, la pintora _____

la ley _____

la política _____

el político, la política _____

bilingüe _____

la carrera _____

el salario _____

la profesión _____

Fold In

Realidades 2

Capítulo 9A

Nombre _____

Hora _____

Fecha _____

Vocabulary Check, Sheet 4

Tear out this page. Write the Spanish words on the lines. Fold the paper along the dotted line to see the correct answers so you can check your work.

farmer _____

architect _____

designer _____

mechanic _____

mail carrier _____

writer _____

painter _____

law _____

politics _____

politician _____

bilingual _____

career _____

salary _____

profession _____

To hear a complete list of the vocabulary for this chapter, go to Disc 2, Track 9 on the guided Practice Audio CD or go to www.phschool.com and type in the Web Code jdd-0989. Then click on **Repaso del capítulo**.

Fold In

Realidades 2

Capítulo 9A

Nombre _____

Hora _____

Fecha _____

Guided Practice Activities 9A-1

The future tense (p. 460)

- The future tense tells what will happen. To form the future tense of regular verbs ending in **-ar**, **-er**, and **-ir**, add these endings to the infinitive: **-é, -ás, -á, -emos, -éis, -án**.

  En unos años *seré* un abogado.

  In a few years, I will be a lawyer.

- Here are the future forms for **trabajar**, **ser**, and **vivir**:

yo	trabajar**é** ser**é** vivir**é**	nosotros/nosotras	trabajar**emos** ser**emos** vivir**emos**
tú	trabajar**ás** ser**ás** vivir**ás**	vosotros/vosotras	trabajar**éis** ser**éis** vivir**éis**
usted/él/ella	trabajar**á** ser**á** vivir**á**	ustedes/ellos/ellas	trabajar**án** ser**án** vivir**án**

A. Fill in the blanks with the correct future tense ending of each verb using the cues provided. Follow the model.

Modelo   los estudiantes conseguir*án*____

1. yo viajar_____

2. nosotros vivir_____

3. Beto se graduar_____

4. tú ir_____

5. ustedes ser_____

6. Lisa pintar_____

7. yo trabajar_____

8. nosotros comer_____

B. Write the future tense of the verbs in parentheses. Follow the model.

Modelo   (trabajar) Tú ___*trabajarás*___ como gerente en una tienda grande.

1. (asistir) Uds. _____ a la universidad del estado.

2. (ser) Yo _____ el mejor científico de esta región.

3. (hablar) Nosotros _____ con gente famosa.

4. (esquiar) Pablo _____ en las montañas altas del mundo.

5. (graduarse) Tú te _____ el año que viene.

Realidades 2

Capítulo 9A

Nombre _____ Hora _____

Fecha _____

Guided Practice Activities 9A-2

The future tense (*continued*)

C. Look at the underlined verbs in the sentences. Complete each sentence by using the future tense to tell what people will do, according to the picture. The first one is done for you.

1.  Jaime y Victoria <u>son</u> abogados, pero algún día

   _____*serán*_____ jueces.

2.  Mario <u>trabaja</u> de cartero, pero el año que viene él

   _____ de mecánico.

3.  La familia Pérez <u>vive</u> en un apartamento, pero algún día

   la familia _____ en una casa.

4.  Generalmente Pilar y Mateo no <u>ven</u> videos, pero mañana

   ellos _____ la tele.

5.  Isabel <u>es</u> estudiante, pero algún día

   ella _____ política.

6. Yo no <u>escribo</u> muchas cartas, pero más tarde le

   _____ a mi primo.

Go Online WEB CODE jdd-0904
PHSchool.com

Realidades 2

Capítulo 9A

Nombre

Fecha

Hora

Guided Practice Activities 9A-3

The future tense: irregular verbs (p. 462)

- Some verb stems are irregular in the future tense: **hacer → har-; poder → podr-; saber → sabr-; tener → tendr-; haber → habr-.**
- Though the stems are irregular, the endings for these verbs are the same as regular future tense verbs. Look at the verb **hacer.**

HACER			
yo	**haré**	nosotros/nosotras	**haremos**
tú	**harás**	vosotros/vosotras	**haréis**
usted/él/ella	**hará**	ustedes/ellos/ellas	**harán**

A. Write the correct future tense ending of the verb in parentheses for each sentence. Follow the model.

Modelo (**hacer**) Yo har _é_____ la tarea esta tarde.

1. (**poder**) Ricardo podr_____ contarnos unos chistes.

2. (**tener**) Mis primos tendr_____ muchas oportunidades en ese trabajo.

3. (**saber**) Nosotros sabr_____ la verdad después de unos minutos.

4. (**haber**) Habr_____ mucha gente en las tiendas.

B. Read what these people will do in the future. Write the irregular future tense stem to complete the verb in each sentence. Follow the model.

Modelo (**poder**) Mis primos no __*podr*__án venir a la fiesta.

1. (**hacer**) Nosotros _____emos ejercicio este fin de semana.

2. (**poder**) Yo _____é ayudarte con la tarea.

3. (**Saber**) ¿ _____á Juan llegar a tu casa?

4. (**Haber**) _____á una graduación el fin de semana.

5. (**tener**) Tú _____ás tiempo el viernes por la tarde.

6. (**poder**) Ustedes _____án terminar con la tarea esta noche.

7. (**tener**) Nosotros _____emos que ir a la escuela temprano.

The future tense: irregular verbs (*continued*)

C. Complete each sentence in the future tense with the correct form of the verb in parentheses. The first one is done for you.

1. (**poder**) Francisco _____*podrá*_____ usar la computadora.

2. (**saber**) Tú _____ de ciencias.

3. (**hacer**) La veterinaria le _____ un examen a mi perro.

4. (**poder**) Marta _____ ser contadora.

5. (**tener**) Mis amigos y yo _____ clases en la universidad.

6. (**haber**) En junio _____ una graduación.

D. Follow Isidro's list of things that he wants to do after graduation. Use the future tense of the verbs in parentheses. The first one is done for you.

Después de graduarme...

1. ...yo _____*podré*_____ hacer un viaje con mis amigos. (**poder**)

2. ...nosotros _____ a Europa. (**ir**)

3. ...mis amigos y yo _____ mucho dinero. (**gastar**)

4. ...mis padres no _____ qué hago cada minuto de cada día. (**saber**)

5. ...mi hermano _____ un trabajo, pero yo no. (**buscar**)

6. ...yo _____ a una universidad. (**asistir**)

7. ..._____ muchas oportunidades para mí. (**haber**)

Realidades **2**

Capítulo 9A

Nombre _____

Hora _____

Fecha _____

Guided Practice Activities 9A-5

Lectura: ¡Bienvenidos al Centro de Carreras! (pp. 468–469)

A. The reading in your textbook is about a career center in a Spanish-speaking country. Read the heads and subheads to find out some basic information. Then, place an *X* next to the information you may find in this reading.

_____ an aptitude test   _____ career choices

_____ movie listings   _____ a personal information record

B. Read the following selection from the reading and the questions below. Circle the letter of the correct answer for each question.

En nuestro centro, pueden...
* *buscar carreras*
* *buscar y conectar con más de 100 universidades*
* *crear y asegurar un expediente (record) privado para mantenerse informado(a) de las notas y actividades*

1. What can a student do at the Career Center?
a. find out about careers and universities
b. find out about restaurants

2. About how many universities can students find information?
a. less than 100 universities
b. more than 100 universities

3. What is the purpose of an **expediente privado?**
a. to keep information on grades and activities up-to-date
b. to keep information on your daily routine

C. Fill out the following **expediente personal** by using either your own information or made-up information.

Nombre: _____

Dirección: _____

Grado: _____ Intereses extracurriculares: _____

_____

Universidades que me interesan: _____

_____

Presentación oral (p. 471)

Task: Prepare a presentation to a partner about a job you might expect to have in the future. Explain why you would choose that job.

A. Charts can help you organize information for a presentation. Think about classes you like and, in the first column, fill in the two subjects you prefer. In the second column, list two activities that you enjoy doing. The first line is done for you as an example.

Cursos favoritos	Diversiones
la literatura	leer libros

B. Use your answers from **part A** and the list of professions below, or choose another profession you have learned about in this chapter to complete the sentences.

contador, -a	veterinario, -a	abogado, -a	gerente
arquitecto, -a	ingeniero, -a	profesor, -a	pintor, -a

Mis clases favoritas son _____ y _____.

Las actividades que más me gustan son _____ y _____.

Estudiaré para ser _____ porque me gusta _____.

C. Read your statements from **part B** to practice for the oral presentation. Practice your presentation several times. Try to:

- provide as much information as you can
- speak clearly

D. Tell your partner about your interests and what you plan to do in the future.

Realidades 2

Capítulo 9B

Nombre _____

Fecha _____

Hora _____

Vocabulary Flash Cards, Sheet 1

Write the Spanish vocabulary word below each picture. Be sure to include the article for each noun.

Realidades 2

Capítulo 9B

Nombre _____

Hora _____

Fecha _____

Vocabulary Flash Cards, Sheet 2

Write the Spanish vocabulary word below each picture. If there is a word or phrase, copy it in the space provided. Be sure to include the article for each noun.

la calefacción

_____

económico, económica

_____

eficiente

_____

Realidades 2

Capítulo 9B

Nombre _____

Hora _____

Fecha _____

Vocabulary Flash Cards, Sheet 3

Copy the word or phrase in the space provided. Be sure to include the article for each noun.

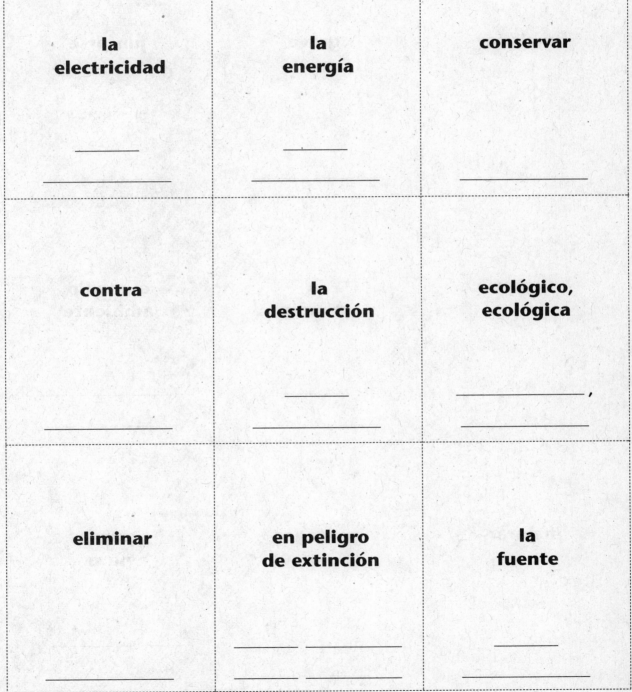

la electricidad

_____

_____

la energía

_____

_____

conservar

_____

contra

_____

la destrucción

_____

_____

ecológico, ecológica

_____ ,

_____

eliminar

_____

en peligro de extinción

_____ _____

_____

la fuente

_____

Realidades ❷

Capítulo 9B

Nombre _____

Hora _____

Fecha _____

Vocabulary Flash Cards, Sheet 4

Copy the word or phrase in the space provided. Be sure to include the article for each noun.

funcionar	**grave**	**juntarse**
_____	_____	_____
luchar	**la manera**	**el medio ambiente**
_____	_____	_____
mejorar	**proteger**	**puro, pura**
_____	_____	_____, _____

Realidades ②

Capítulo 9B

Nombre _____

Hora _____

Fecha _____

Vocabulary Flash Cards, Sheet 5

Copy the word or phrase in the space provided. Be sure to include the article for each noun.

reducir _____	**resolver** _____	**además (de)** _____ _____
dudar _____	**es cierto** _____	**haya** _____
ahorrar _____	**la naturaleza** _____ _____	**contaminado, contaminada** _____ , _____

These blank cards can be used to write and practice other Spanish vocabulary for the chapter.

_____	_____	_____
_____	_____	_____
_____	_____	_____

Realidades 2

Capítulo 9B

Nombre _____

Hora _____

Fecha _____

Vocabulary Check, Sheet 1

Tear out this page. Write the English words on the lines. Fold the paper along the dotted line to see the correct answers so you can check your work.

la naturaleza _____

el bosque _____

el desierto _____

la selva tropical _____

el aire
acondicionado _____

la calefacción _____

la electricidad _____

la energía _____

conservar _____

la contaminación _____

contaminado,
contaminada _____

la destrucción _____

ecológico, ecológica _____

el medio ambiente _____

Fold In

Realidades 2

Capítulo 9B

Nombre _____

Hora _____

Fecha _____

Vocabulary Check, Sheet 2

Tear out this page. Write the Spanish words on the lines. Fold the paper along the dotted line to see the correct answers so you can check your work.

nature _____

forest _____

desert _____

rain forest _____

air conditioning _____

heat _____

electricity _____

energy _____

to conserve _____

pollution _____

polluted _____

destruction _____

ecological _____

environment _____

Fold In →

Tear out this page. Write the English words on the lines. Fold the paper along the dotted line to see the correct answers so you can check your work.

el espacio _____

la Luna _____

la Tierra _____

económico, económica _____

eficiente _____

contra _____

en peligro de extinción _____

funcionar _____

luchar _____

mejorar _____

reducir _____

además (de) _____

dudar _____

proteger _____

Fold In

Tear out this page. Write the Spanish words on the lines. Fold the paper along the dotted line to see the correct answers so you can check your work.

(outer) space _____

the moon _____

Earth _____

economical _____

efficient _____

against _____

endangered, in danger of extinction _____

to function, to work _____

to fight _____

to improve _____

to reduce _____

in addition (to), besides _____

to doubt _____

to protect _____

To hear a complete list of the vocabulary for this chapter, go to Disc 2, Track 10 on the guided Practice Audio CD or go to www.phschool.com and type in the Web Code jdd-0999. Then click on **Repaso del capítulo.**

Fold In

The future tense: other irregular verbs (p. 484)

- Other verbs that have irregular stems in the future tense are:

  decir → dir-   querer → querr-   salir → saldr-
  poner → pondr-   venir → vendr-

- Here is the future tense of the verb **querer**:

QUERER			
yo	**querré**	nosotros/nosotras	**querremos**
tú	**querrás**	vosotros/vosotras	**querréis**
usted/él/ella	**querrá**	ustedes/ellos/ellas	**querrán**

A. Look at each sentence and write the infinitive form of the underlined verb.

Modelo   Ellos <u>dirán</u> que nuestro valle es bonito. *Infinitive:* __*decir*__

1. Nosotros <u>pondremos</u> plantas en las salas de clases. *Infinitive:* _____

2. Yo <u>querré</u> conservar la naturaleza. *Infinitive:* _____

3. Los turistas no <u>vendrán</u> a nuestro pueblo. *Infinitive:* _____

4. Tú <u>saldrás</u> a luchar contra la contaminación. *Infinitive:* _____

5. Ustedes <u>dirán</u> que el agua está contaminada. *Infinitive:* _____

B. Complete the following exchanges by writing the correct future form of the verb in parentheses. Follow the model.

Modelo   PEDRO: ¿Qué _____*dirán*_____ ustedes del medio ambiente? (**decir**)

ILIANA: Nosotros _____*diremos*_____ que está muy contaminado. (**decir**)

1. PEDRO: ¿Cuándo _____ ustedes al bosque? (**salir**)

   ILIANA: Nosotros _____ por la mañana. (**salir**)

2. PEDRO: ¿Qué _____ hacer tú para proteger el medio ambiente? (**querer**)

   ILIANA: Yo _____ usar la energía solar. (**querer**)

3. PEDRO: ¿Tu hermana _____ más plantas en la casa? (**poner**)

   ILIANA: Sí, y ella también _____ flores. (**poner**)

4. PEDRO: ¿Ella _____ con nosotros a proteger la selva tropical? (**venir**)

   ILIANA: Sí, ella y mis hermanos _____. (**venir**)

The future tense: other irregular verbs (*continued*)

C. Look at the pictures and read the sentences. Then, look at the verb choices in parentheses and complete each sentence with the appropriate future form of the verb you choose. Follow the model.

Modelo   Tú _____*querrás*_____ reducir la contaminación. **(querer / salir)**

1.   Ellos no _____ destruir el bosque. **(querer / venir)**

2.   Nosotros _____ que debemos conservar energía en nuestra casa. **(querer / decir)**

3.   Todos los estudiantes _____ en bicicleta para reducir la contaminación del aire. **(venir / poner)**

4.   Nosotros _____ energía solar en nuestras casas. **(salir / poner)**

5.   Si hay demasiada contaminación en la Tierra, Federico

_____ al espacio. **(salir / venir)**

Go Online WEB CODE jdd-0913
PHSchool.com

Realidades 2

Capítulo 9B

Nombre _____

Hora _____

Fecha _____

Guided Practice Activities 9B-3

The present subjunctive with expressions of doubt (p. 487)

- In the same way that the subjunctive is used with impersonal expressions and to communicate a desire to influence someone else's actions, it is also used after verbs and expressions of doubt or uncertainty. Some expressions of doubt or uncertainty are:

dudar que	*to doubt that*
no es cierto que	*it is not certain that*
no creer que	*to not believe that*
no estar seguro, -a de que	*to be unsure that*
es imposible que	*it is impossible that*
es posible que	*it is possible that*

No es cierto que puedan proteger el medio ambiente.
It is not certain that they can protect the environment.

A. In the sentences below, underline the expressions that indicate uncertainty or doubt. Then, circle the verbs in the subjunctive form. The first one is done for you.

1. <u>Es imposible que</u> nosotros no (cuidemos) la Tierra.

2. Dudo que nosotros no luchemos contra la contaminación.

3. Es posible que muchos animales estén en peligro de extinción.

4. No es cierto que en nuestra casa usemos mucha energía.

5. Nosotros no creemos que ellos no cuiden la colina.

6. No estoy seguro de que los bosques se conserven bien.

7. Es imposible que nosotros no protejamos la naturaleza.

Realidades 2

Capítulo 9B

Nombre _____

Hora _____

Fecha _____

Guided Practice Activities 9B-4

The present subjunctive with expressions of doubt (*continued*)

- While the subjunctive is used to show uncertainty, the indicative is used to show certainty. Compare these sentences:

    No es cierto que ellas ahorren energía. *It is not certain that they will save energy.*
    Es cierto que ellos ahorran energía. *It is certain that they are saving energy.*

B. Read the following sentences and underline the expressions of doubt or certainty. If the expression indicates certainty, write **C**. If it indicates doubt or uncertainty, write **D**. Follow the models.

Modelo 1 <u>Es verdad que</u> tenemos que reducir la contaminación. _C_

Modelo 2 <u>No es verdad que</u> tengamos que reciclar. _D_

1. No creemos que el aire esté contaminado. _____

2. Estamos seguros de que muchos animales están en peligro de extinción. _____

3. Creo que la energía solar es muy eficiente. _____

4. No estoy seguro de que sea económico usar la calefacción. _____

5. Es cierto que los problemas ecológicos se resuelven. _____

6. Creo que debemos conservar energía. _____

C. Circle the correct form of the verbs in parentheses to complete each sentence. Use the expression of doubt or certainty in each sentence to choose whether you circle the present subjunctive or the present indicative.

1. Yo estoy seguro de que nosotros **(podamos / podemos)** cuidar la Tierra.

2. Mis profesores creen que los niños de hoy **(trabajan / trabajen)** mucho para conservar energía.

3. Es imposible que los Estados Unidos **(usa / use)** menos energía que otros países.

4. Dudamos que tú **(estés / estás)** preocupado por la conservación de los bosques.

5. Es cierto que Uds. **(quieren / quieran)** resolver los problemas ecológicos.

6. No es cierto que los norteamericanos **(destruyan / destruyen)** los bosques.

Go Online WEB CODE jdd-0914
PHSchool.com

Realidades 2

Capítulo 9B

Nombre _____

Hora _____

Fecha _____

Guided Practice Activities 9B-4a

The present subjunctive with expressions of doubt (*continued*)

- The subjunctive form of **hay** is **haya,** from the verb **haber:**
  Es posible que haya suficiente electricidad.
  *It is possible that **there is** enough electricity.*

D. Complete the sentences by writing either the indicative form **hay** or the subjunctive form **haya.** Follow the model.

Modelo   ¿No crees que ____*haya*____ un problema grave?

1. Dudamos que _____ una fuente de energía nueva.

2. Es cierto que _____ mucha destrucción en las selvas tropicales.

3. Él está seguro de que _____ una manera de reducir la contaminación.

4. Es imposible que _____ vida en el espacio.

5. Es posible que _____ desiertos en la Luna.

E. Complete the following advertisement with the subjunctive or the indicative form of the verbs given. The first one is done for you.

¿Dudas que tu ayuda _____*sea*_____ (**ser**) importante para la Tierra? ¿No estás

seguro de que los humanos _____ (**poder**) hacer cambios importantes para

la naturaleza? Debes visitar el parque zoológico Las Palmas. Aquí sabrás que ¡es cierto

que nosotros _____ (**trabajar**) para los animales que están en peligro de

extinción! ¡Es posible que una corporación grande _____ (**conservar**) agua

y energía! ¡Es imposible que tú no _____ (**ayudar**) a la causa! En el

zoológico Las Palmas, sabemos que tú _____ (**ir**) a divertirte. Creemos que

tú y tu familia _____ (**proteger**) la naturaleza mientras observan los

animales. Juntos, es posible que nosotros _____ (**luchar**) contra la

extinción.

Lectura: Protegemos la Antártida (pp. 492–493)

A. When you read an article, you should be aware that the writer may have strong opinions about the issues. Identify and circle the words below that indicate an opinion.

Dudo...   Hay...   Sabemos...

Es peligroso...   Es importante...   Se llama...

B. Read the following paragraph from the article in your textbook. You may not know some of the words and phrases below from the article. Try to determine the meaning of them from their context in the paragraph and from what you already know about the Antarctic.

¡Estamos en peligro!

Las regiones polares son muy importantes para la supervivencia de la Tierra entera. Los casquetes de hielo en las zonas polares reflejan luz solar y así regularizan la temperatura de la Tierra. Cuando se destruyen estos casquetes, hay menos luz solar que se refleja y la Tierra se convierte en un receptor termal. Esto se llama el efecto de invernadero. Es en la Antártida que en 1985 se reportaron por primera vez los hoyos en la capa del ozono y aquí es donde hoy día se trata de encontrar una solución.

1. casquetes de hielo   **a.** holes   **b.** ice caps

2. efecto de invernadero   **a.** greenhouse effect **b.** point of departure

3. supervivencia   **a.** abundance   **b.** survival

4. hoyos   **a.** holes   **b.** scientific teams

5. capa del ozono   **a.** rules   **b.** ozone layer

C. Determine the author's point of view in the paragraph in **part B** by circling the letter of the correct ending for each sentence.

1. Según el título, el autor cree que _____
   a. todo va bien.
   b. todo no va bien.

2. El autor cree que las regiones polares _____
   a. son importantes para la Tierra.
   b. no sirven para nada.

3. Es posible que el autor piense que _____
   a. es necesario resolver el problema de los hoyos en la capa del ozono.
   b. los hoyos en la capa del ozono son buenos para la Tierra.

Realidades 2

Capítulo 9B

Nombre _____

Hora _____

Fecha _____

Guided Practice Activities 9B-6

Presentación escrita (p. 495)

Task: Write an article for the daily paper explaining your volunteer project to improve your community.

A. Choose a volunteer project from the box or write one that you would like to do in your community.

> • recoger basura en un parque
>
> • comenzar un programa para reciclar periódicos viejos
>
> • ahorrar dinero para proteger a los animales en peligro de extinción
>
> • _____

B. Based on the project you chose in **part A,** complete the following sentences by circling one of the options listed.

1. Para este proyecto trabajaré

    a. todos los días.   **b.** los fines de semana.

2. Pueden participar

    a. personas mayores.   **b.** todas las personas.

3. Es importante porque

    a. protegemos el medio ambiente.   **b.** ayudamos a las personas.

C. Use your answers from **part B** to answer the following questions about your volunteer project. You may use the model to help you.

Modelo	¿Qué ...?	*Me gustaría recoger basura en un parque.*
	¿Quién(es)...?	*Mis amigos y yo vamos a trabajar juntos.*
	¿Por qué...?	*Queremos tener un medio ambiente limpio y sano.*
	¿Dónde...?	*Vamos a trabajar en el parque del centro de la ciudad.*
	¿Cuándo...?	*Trabajaremos todos los fines de semana durante el verano.*

1. ¿Qué...? _____

2. ¿Quién(es)...? _____

3. ¿Por qué...? _____

4. ¿Dónde...? _____

5. ¿Cuándo...? _____

D. Use your answers in **part C** to write your article. Check for correct spelling, verb forms, and vocabulary, and rewrite your article if necessary.

Notes

MACROECONOMICS

Concise Edition

84

Concise Edition

MACROECONOMICS

Roger A. Arnold

California State University
San Marcos

THOMSON

™

SOUTH-WESTERN

Australia · Canada · Mexico · Singapore · Spain · United Kingdom · United States

To
Sheila, Daniel,
and David

Macroeconomics: Concise Edition
Roger A. Arnold

VP/Editorial Director:
Jack W. Calhoun

VP/Editor-in-Chief:
Alex von Rosenberg

Publisher:
Steve Momper

Sr. Acquisitions Editor:
Michael W. Worls

Developmental Editor:
Jennifer E. Baker

Sr. Marketing Manager:
Brian Joyner

Production Project Manager:
Heather Mann

Manager of Technology, Editorial:
Vicky True

Technology Project Editor:
Dana Cowden

Web Coordinator:
Karen L. Schaffer

Sr. Manufacturing Coordinator:
Sandee Milewski

Production House:
Pre-Press Company, Inc.

Printer:
C&C Offset Printing Co., Ltd

Art Director:
Michelle Kunkler

Cover and Internal Designer:
Beckmeyer Design, Cincinnati

Cover Images:
© Getty Images, Inc.

Photography Manager:
Deanna Ettinger

Photo Researcher:
Susan van Etten

For permission to use material from this text or product, submit a request online at http://www.thomsonrights.com.

For more information about our products, contact us at:
Thomson Learning Academic Resource Center
1-800-423-0563

Thomson Higher Education
5191 Natorp Boulevard
Mason, OH 45040
USA

Brief Contents

Contents

FEATURES

Economics in Everyday Life:
Blogging 8
Economics in Popular Culture:
Why LeBron James Isn't in College 9

chapter**2**

FEATURES

Economics in Everyday Life:
Liberals, Conservatives, and the PPF 46
Economics in Popular Culture:
Elvis, Comparative Advantage, and Specialization 53
Economics in Popular Culture:
Jerry Seinfeld, the Doorman, and Adam Smith 54

chapter**3**

FEATURES

Economics in the World:
U4E (((H))) ^5
Yours Forever, Big Hug, High Five 67
Economics in Everyday Life:
Getting to Class on Time 73
Economics in Everyday Life:
Supply and Demand on a Freeway 89

Macroeconomics

chapter 4

chapter 5

FEATURES

Economics in Technology:
The Natural Unemployment Rate, Technology, and Policy Errors 158

FEATURES

Economics in Popular Culture:
The Multiplier Goes on Spring Break 175

chapter 8

FEATURES

Economics in Everyday Life:
English and Money 193
Economics in the World:
Is Money the Best Gift? 194
Economics in Popular Culture:
Economics on the Yellow Brick Road 196

chapter 9

FEATURES

Economics in the World:
Money and Inflation 217
Economics in Popular Culture:
The California Gold Rush, or an Apple for
$72 219

chapter 10

chapter **11**

chapter **12**

chapter 13

The World Economy

Note to Instructors

What do instructors want from an introductory economics textbook? Well, many of them say that they want a solid text that covers all the basics of economics, a text that applies economic thinking to the real world, and a text that gets their students to begin to understand how economists think.

To this list, I would add one more thing. I would say that a good introductory text should also make one's students smarter. What do I mean by this? To explain, let me go back to a time, long ago, when I first studied economics.

I entered my first economics class not knowing much about economics at all. In a matter of weeks, I was learning about opportunity cost, supply and demand, the role prices play in a market economy, and much more. I liked what I was learning, not only because I thought it was relevant to the world I lived in, but because it made me feel smarter.

It seemed (to me) that before I learned economics, I was a person with faulty vision, unable to make sense of much of the world I inhabited. But with economics, things that were once unclear became clear, things that I couldn't understand before I now could, and things that were invisible to me were now visible. Economics opened a new world to me and it gave me the tools to understand it.

If economics is presented the right way, I think it has the power to do for others what it did for me. But what is the right way?

First, I think a first course in economics should focus on the basics—the "meat and potatoes" of economics, the key principles and concepts.

Second, it has to—without a doubt—give students an understanding of what it means to think like an economist.

Third, it has to convince students that the tools they acquire in economics can be used outside the classroom—and for all the days of their lives.

I have organized and written this book with these three objectives in mind. It sticks to the basics, it stresses the key principles, it applies key economic concepts to enough material from the real world to convince students that economics is useful. And finally, it stresses the economic way of thinking.

In short, what I have attempted in *Economics, Concise Edition* is to give to students a good, hearty dose of economics—in its purest form—so that they can first understand what it is, and then learn to appreciate what it can do for them.

Economists look around at the world and see people buying and selling goods in markets in Tokyo, London, and New York. They notice ships filled with goods from Europe and Asia arriving in Los Angeles. They note that the stock market has just had its worst day in 20 years. They observe a young man graduating college, a couple trading wedding vows, and a small grocery store at the corner of 5th and Main just now being robbed.

Economists scratch their heads and wonder what explains the things they see in the world.

Observations and questions—this is how the science of economics begins. All the rest of economics is simply economists' best attempts at answering their questions.

If you were to ask the man on the street what economics is, he'd probably say it has something to do with money, interest rates, the stock market, and things like that. Many people define economics by listing three or four topics.

But defining economics in terms of the topics that economists study and discuss is a little unsatisfying. It doesn't consider whether or not economists use a common approach to studying and discussing all the topics.

The essence of what economics is and what economists do is really seen most clearly when you understand the *economic approach*. Economics is not so much a course of study or a list of topics, but more a way of looking at the world.

To give you a picture of the way the world looks to an economist, imagine the following cartoon: An economist is standing and looking at a globe. He's wearing an odd pair of glasses, unlike any eyeglasses you've seen. The caption reads: These economic eyeglasses sure let you see things in the world that you couldn't see without them.

What exactly does the economist see? Well, that's largely what this book is about. You're going to have an opportunity to look through those economic eyeglasses.

You'll need to keep in mind that learning a new subject sometimes requires unlearning some things that you previously thought were true. In this regard, physics students are often different than economics students. Few physics students enter a college physics class with an intimate knowledge of protons, electrons, quarks, or black holes. When the professor says that electrons do this or that, the student never thinks to himself that what the professor has just said doesn't correspond with his experience with electrons. He has no experience with electrons. He has no way to judge what the professor says. This situation is similar to an alien from some distant planet coming to Earth and telling you what his planet is like. Are you going to tell the alien that he's wrong because you've been to his planet and you know what it's like?

Students have never been to the planet Physics, and so they are ready and willing to accept what the physics professor tells them about that particular planet.

Not so with economics. Most people believe they are well acquainted with the planet Economics. The words economists use—price, costs, firms, competition, monopoly, interest rates, inflation, unemployment, and so on—are some of the same words non-economists use. People use the language of economics on a daily basis; they live and work in the economic world. So when an economics student hears an economics professor say something about firms, costs, or competition, she compares what the professor has said with her experiences and sometimes thinks to herself that what the professor said seems wrong. In fact, what the professor said may be wrong, but that's not really the point. The point is that no matter what the professor says—right or wrong—when you have access to the world the professor is discussing, you will judge what the professor says based on what you know or think you know.

So, an economics professor is in a somewhat more difficult position than is a physics professor. Specifically, an economics professor sometimes not only has to teach what he or she thinks is right but also has to prove that many of the things that the student thinks are true are not. In a way, some of things that the student believes are true (but aren't) have to be unlearned.

To illustrate, many people believe that when the government places a tax on a company, the tax will matter very little to the company. It will simply pass along the tax to the consumer. In other words, if the tax is \$1 per unit, and the consumer is currently paying \$4 a unit, the price after the government imposes the tax will be \$5 a unit.

But things don't usually turn out this way. You will see why later in this book.

Key Content Changes

Loaded with new content, data, and learning opportunities

The groundbreaking new Concise edition of *Economics* will change the way your students think about economics. In addition to completely current examples and exercises, the new edition retains the innovative features you've come to expect in the Arnold product family, while focusing on the basics or "bread and butter" of economics . Extremely student friendly, the book's lively presentation of real-world economic theory and applications doesn't just teach students the definition of economic topics. It equips them with the skills to think like an economist—which gives them a valuable new perspective of the world around them.

Here is just a sampling of the cutting-edge new features in the Concise edition:

NEW! THOMSONNOW FOR ARNOLD CONCISE (Available for purchase separately) ThomsonNOW ties together five fundamental learning activities for use with Arnold's Concise edition: diagnostics, tutorials, homework, quizzing, and testing. The assigned material and unlimited practice improve both retention and remediation. In addition, self-paced tutorials support students with explanations, examples, step-by-step problem solving, and unlimited practice. Students also have access to the Arnold Concise edition Graphing Workshop, Ask the Instructor Video lessons, and access to EconNews, EconDebate, EconLinks and EconData.

Students work at their own pace and reinforce chapter concepts by completing assignments via the Internet. Instructors can make assignments as frequently as desired—the program grades the exercises and tracks student progress in an integrated gradebook. Instructors can easily assess how adequately students prepared for class, identify potential problem areas, and—with students well grounded in the basics—devote more class time to advanced concepts.

For Arnold Concise edition instructors, ThomsonNOW provides a powerful gradebook and course management tools, compatible with both WebCT and Blackboard. Instructors can quickly create their own assignments and tests, drawing from the wealth of exercises provided or authoring their own questions. The variety of problem types allows instructors to assess the way they teach. Customized assignments can be copied easily for use in additional sections or future terms, making class management progressively easier. Some of the key benefits of *ThomsonNOW* include:

> **Assignments/Online Grading**—Instructors pick and choose the assignments from a rich array of resources

http://now.swlearning.com/arnold

for student completion. Student results are automatically recorded in the online gradebook.

> **Graphing Tools and Tutorials**—The program includes assignable questions using graphing tools as well as the proven suite of graphing tutorials, The Graphing Workshop.
> **Customized Learning Path**—Students can begin study of each chapter by completing a pre-test in ThomsonNOW. The results of the pre-test will generate a learning path for students to follow in order to reinforce their understanding of concepts that were not fully grasped according to the pre-test results. Resources referenced in the learning path are drawn from a multimedia library of book-specific and general economics content.
> **ABC Videos**—ThomsonNOW includes access to video segments carefully chosen from ABC's vast library of news and documentary video to correlate with compelling current events and demonstrate economics connections and consequences in those events.
> **Text-Specific**— *ThomsonNOW* is customized specifically for Arnold, *Economics,* Concise Edition 1/e.

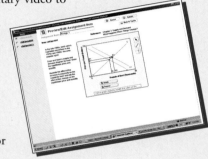

Visit the *ThomsonNOW* demo at http://now.swlearing.com/arnold.

EXPANDED! The beautiful color graphs, photos, and illustrations that distinguish Arnold as one of the most visually striking principles texts are retained in the new Concise edition. Exhibits and graphs strategically use color and cause/effect diagrams for maximum student accessibility and understanding, while *A Closer Look* explanatory flow charts summarize and explain complex material in a highly visual, easy-to-follow format.

CURRENT! Boxed features include abundant examples of economics in everyday life and popular culture, illustrating that almost anything can be analyzed from an economic perspective.

UNIQUE! Thinking Like an Economist features directly show students how economists actually look at the world and conceptually think about the technical material being presented.

STUDENT-FRIENDLY! A unique **active learning format** integrates questions that students would likely ask if they had the opportunity, providing a more active reading experience and clarifying potential problem areas before progressing. In addition, **Self-Check** questions throughout each chapter help students monitor their comprehension.

Customizing content for your classroom has never been easier. And with Thomson Higher Education's powerful resources, the options are virtually limitless.

MarketSim, an online tool comprised of two simulations, helps students better understand how markets work by placing them in the roles of consumers and producers in a simulated economy. (Available as a bundle option.)

Gale Business & Company Resource Center

http://access.gale.com/thomsonlearning

Another expansive resource available is our Gale Business & Company Resource Center. Our exclusive and robust online resource center allows students to conduct detailed business research and analysis from their own desks—anytime and anywhere they have an Internet connection. Through the BCRC, students gain access to a vast assortment of global business information, including competitive intelligence, career and investment opportunities, business rankings, company histories, and much more. (Available as a bundle option.)

Thomson Custom Publishing

http://www.thomsoncustom.com

With Thomson Custom Publishing, it's never been easier to create the perfect learning materials. And with Thomson's vast resources and proven expertise, the possibilities are limitless.

Organization of the Concise Edition

Section I: An Introduction to Economics

Section I presents the "economic way of thinking." Specifically, it introduces key concepts in economics (opportunity cost, efficiency, costs and benefits, decisions at the margin, unintended effects, and more), explains the uses and abuses of theory and theorizing, focuses on two key economic activities—producing and trading—and develops one of the key economic frameworks of analysis in economics—supply and demand.

Section II: Macroeconomics

This section begins with macroeconomic measurements, then discusses various schools of macroeconomic thought (classical, Keynesian, new classical, monetarist, new Keynesian) within the context of key economic phenomena—business cycles, inflation, deflation, economic growth, and more. Both fiscal and monetary policy are extensively discussed, as well as expectations theory.

Section III: Microeconomics

The consistent theme of the microeconomics section of the book is that microeconomics is about objectives, constraints, and choices. What is the objective of the individual consumer? What constraints does she face? How does she make her choices? What is the objective of the firm? What constraints does it face? How does it make its choices?

Specifically, this section begins with marginal utility analysis and elasticity, proceeds to a discussion of the firm and various market structures, and then turns to a thorough discussion of resource markets and microeconomic policies.

Section IV: The World Economy

This section of the book presents international trade theory and international finance theory. It discusses why countries trade, how exchange rates are established, the effects of tariffs and quotas, and more.

The Structure of Each Chapter

Each chapter contains the following features and strategies to help you understand economics:

> Setting the Scene
> Margin Definitions
> Thinking Like an Economist
> Applications Features (*Economics In Everyday Life, Economics In Popular Culture, Economics In The World,* and *Economics In Technology*)
> Analyzing the Scene
> Self-Tests
> A Reader Asks
> Chapter Summary
> Questions and Problems
> Working With Numbers and Graphs
> Key Terms and Concepts

Each of these features and learning strategies is described in words and visually in the *Student Learning Guide* that follows this preface.

Economics, Concise Edition *offers a powerful collection of innovative instructor and student resources.*

For Students:
Learning Resources

Study Guide, by Roger A. Arnold: Helping students gain a solid understanding of chapter material, the Study Guide explains, reviews, and tests for the key facts, concepts, and diagrams in every chapter. Available in micro/macro splits. (0-324-31586-4) (Macroeconomics Study Guide, ISBN 0-324-31594-5), (Micro-economics Study Guide, ISBN 0-324-31590-2)

For Students and Instructors:

Arnold Support Web Site:
http://arnold.swlearning.com
Instructors can access Word files for the Instructor's Manual and Test Bank, as well as PowerPoint slides, from the Instructor's Resource area on the Arnold Support Web Site. Students can access Internet Activities by chapter to encourage interactive learning. Students can also access free quizzes for each chapter to test their understanding of basic concepts.

How to Think Like an Economist (0-324-01575-5)
Most economics instructors believe that a primary goal of this course is to teach you how economists think. There's more to thinking like an economist than knowing the concepts and technical tools of analysis. Pay attention to this feature—it will give you unique insight into the economist's mind, allowing you to see how interesting issues are approached from an economic perspective. This soft-cover guide can be bundled free with new copies of *Economics, Concise Edition.*

InfoTrac College Edition: An InfoTrac College Edition 4-month subscription card is automatically packaged free with new copies of this text. With InfoTrac College Edition, journals like *Business Week*, *Fortune*, and *Forbes* are just a click away! InfoTrac College Edition provides students with anytime, anywhere access to 20 years' worth of full-text articles (more than 10 million!) from nearly 4,000 scholarly and popular sources. Visit http:// infotrac.thomsonlearning.com.

The Wall Street Journal Subscription: *Economics,* Concise Edition makes it easy for students to apply economic concepts to this authoritative publication, and for you to bring the most up-to-date, real-world events into your classroom. For a nominal additional cost, *Economics,* Concise Edition can be packaged with a card entitling students to a 15-week subscription to both the print and online versions of *The Wall Street Journal.*

For a detailed explanation of these supplements, please visit the product snapshot online by going to http://economics .swlearning.comg clicking on the author's name, and selecting the Concise edition.

In Appreciation

Economics, Concise Edition could not have been written and published without the generous expert assistance of many people, particularly those who reviewed the first through seventh editions of my comprehensive text. A deep debt of gratitude is owed to these instructors.

First Edition Reviewers

William Askwig
University of Southern Colorado

Michael Babcock
Kansas State University

Dan Barszcz
College of DuPage, Illinois

Robert Berry
Miami University, Ohio

George Bohler
Florida Junior College

Tom Bonsor
Eastern Washington University

Michael D. Brendler
Louisiana State University

Baird Brock
Central Missouri State University

Kathleen Bromley
Monroe Community College, New York

Douglas Brown
Georgetown University

Ernest Buchholz
Santa Monica Community College, California

Gary Burbridge
Grand Rapids Junior College, Michigan

Maureen Burton
California Polytechnic University, Pomona

Carol Carnes
Kansas State University

Paul Coomes
University of Louisville, Kentucky

Eleanor Craig
University of Delaware

Wilford Cummings
Grosmont College, California

Diane Cunningham
Glendale Community College, California

Douglas C. Darran
University of South Carolina

Edward Day
University of Southern Florida

Johan Deprez
University of Tennessee

James Dietz
California State University, Fullerton

Stuart Dorsey
University of West Virginia

Natalia Drury
Northern Virginia Community College

Lu Ann Duffus
California State University, Hayward

John Eckalbar
California State University, Chico

John Elliot
University of Southern California

Charles Fischer
Pittsburg State University, Kansas

John Gemello
San Francisco State University

Carl Guelzo
Cantonsville Community College, Maryland

Jan Hansen
University of Wisconsin, Eau Claire

John Henderson
Georgia State University

Ken Howard
East Texas Baptist University

Mark Karscig
Central Missouri State University

Stanley Keil
Ball State University, Indiana

Richard Kieffer
State University of New York, Buffalo

Gene Kimmett
William Rainey Harper College, Illinois

Luther Lawson
University of North Carolina

Frank Leori
College of San Mateo, California

Kenneth Long
New River Community College, Virginia

Michael Magura
University of Toledo, Ohio

Bruce McCrea
Lansing Community College, Michigan

Gerald McDougall
Wichita State University, Kansas

Kevin McGee
University of Wisconsin, Oshkosh

Francois Melese
Auburn University, Alabama

Herbert Miliken
American River College, California

Richard Miller
Pennsylvania State University

Ernest Moser
Northeast Louisiana University

Farhang Niroomand
University of Southern Mississippi

Eliot Orton
New Mexico State University

Marty Perline
Wichita State University, Kansas

Harold Petersen
Boston College

Douglas Poe
University of Texas, Austin

Joseph Rezney
St. Louis Community College, Missouri

Terry Ridgway
University of Nevada, Las Vegas

Thomas Romans
State University of New York, Buffalo

Robert Ross
Bloomsburg State College, Pennsylvania

Keith A. Rowley
Baylor University, Texas

Anandi Sahu
Oakland University, Michigan

Richard Scoggins
California State University, Long Beach

Paul Seidenstat
Temple University, Pennsylvania

Shahram Shafiee
North Harris County College, Texas

Alan Sleeman
Western Washington University

John Sondey
University of Idaho

Robert W. Thomas
Iowa State University

Richard L. Tontz
California State University, Northridge

Roger Trenary
Kansas State University

Bruce Vanderporten
Loyola University, Illinois

Thomas Weiss
University of Kansas

Richard O. Welch
University of Texas at San Antonio

Donald A. Wells
University of Arizona

John Wight
University of Richmond, Virginia

Thomas Wyrick
Southwest Missouri State University

Second Edition Reviewers

Scott Bloom
North Dakota State University

Thomas Carroll
University of Nevada, Las Vegas

Larry Cox
Southwest Missouri State University

Diane Cunningham
Los Angeles Valley College

Emit Deal
Macon College

Michael Fabritius
University of Mary Hardin Baylor

Frederick Fagal
Marywood College

Ralph Fowler
Diablo Valley College

Bob Gilette
Texas A&M University

Lynn Gillette
Indiana University, Indianapolis

Simon Hakim
Temple University

Lewis Karstensson
University of Nevada, Las Vegas

Abraham Kidane
California State University, Dominguez Hills

W. Barbara Killen
University of Minnesota

J. David Lages
Southwest Missouri State University

Anthony Lee
Austin Community College

Marjory Mabery
Delaware County Community College

Bernard Malamud
University of Nevada, Las Vegas

Michael Marlow
California Polytechnic State University, San Luis Obispo

Phil J. McLewin
Ramapo College of New Jersey

Tina Quinn
Arkansas State University

Terry Ridgway
University of Nevada, Las Vegas

Paul Snoonian
University of Lowell

Paul Taube
Pan American University

Roger Trenary
Kansas State University

Charles Van Eaton
Hillsdale College

Mark Wheeler
Bowling Green State University

Thomas Wyrick
Southwest Missouri State University

Third Edition Reviewers

Carlos Aguilar
University of Texas, El Paso

Rebecca Ann Benakis
New Mexico State University

Scott Bloom
North Dakota State University

Howard Erdman
Southwest Texas Junior College

Arthur Friedberg
Mohawk Valley Community College

Nancy A. Jianakoplos
Colorado State University

Lewis Karstensson
University of Nevada, Las Vegas

Rose Kilburn
Modesto Junior College

Ruby P. Kishan
Southeastern Community College

Duane Kline
Southeastern Community College

Charles A. Roberts
Western Kentucky University

Bill Robinson
University of Nevada, Las Vegas

Susan C. Stephenson
Drake University

Charles Van Eaton
Hillsdale College

Richard O. Welch
The University of Texas at San Antonio

Calla Wiemer
University of Hawaii at Manoa

Fourth Edition Reviewers

Uzo Agulefo
North Lake College

Kari Battaglia
University of North Texas

Scott Bloom
North Dakota State University

Harry Ellis, Jr.
University of North Texas

Mary Ann Hendryson
Western Washington University

Eugene Jones
Ohio State University

Ki Hoon Him
Central Connecticut State University

James McBrearty
University of Arizona

John A. Panagakis
Onondaga Community College

Bill Robinson
University of Nevada, Las Vegas

George E. Samuels
Sam Houston State University

Ed Scahill
University of Scranton

Charles Van Eaton
Hillsdale College

Thomas Wyrick
Southwest Missouri State University

Fifth Edition Reviewers

Kari Battaglia
University of North Texas

Douglas A. Conway
Mesa Community College

Lee A. Craig
North Carolina State University

Harry Ellis, Jr.
University of North Texas

Joe W. Essuman
University of Wisconsin, Waukesha

Dipak Ghosh
Emporia State University

Shirley J. Gideon
The University of Vermont

Mary Ann Hendryson
Western Washington University

Calvin A. Hoerneman
Delta College

George H. Jones
University of Wisconsin, Rock County

Donald R. Morgan
Monterey Peninsula College

John A. Panagakis
Onondaga Community College

Bill Robinson
University of Nevada, Las Vegas

Steve Robinson
The University of North Carolina at Wilmington

David W. Yoskowitz
Texas Tech University

Sixth Edition Reviewers

Hendrikus J.E.M. Brand
Albion College

Curtis Clarke
Dallas County Community College

Andrea Gorospe
Kent State University, Trumbull

Mehrdad Madresehee
Lycoming College

L. Wayne Plumly
Valdosta State University

Craig Rogers
Canisius College

Uri Simonsohn
Carnegie Mellon University

Philip Sprunger
Lycoming College

Lea Templer
College of the Canyons

Soumya Tohamy
Berry College

Lee Van Scyoc
University of Wisconsin, Oshkosh

Seventh Edition Reviewers

Pam Coates
San Diego Mesa College

Peggy F. Crane
Southwestern College

Richard Croxdale
Austin Community College

Harry Ellis, Jr.
University of North Texas

Craig Gallet
California State University, Sacramento

Kelly George
Embry-Riddle Aeronautical University

Anne-Marie Gilliam
Central Piedmont Community College

Richard C. Schiming
Minnesota State University, Mankato

Lea Templer
College of the Canyons

Jennifer VanGilder
California State University, Bakersfield

William W. Wilkes
Athens State University

Janice Yee
Wartburg College

I would like to thank Peggy Crane of Southwestern College, who wrote the test bank, and Jane Himarios of the University of Texas at Arlington, who wrote the Instructor's Manual.

I owe a deep debt of gratitude to all the fine and creative people I worked with at Thomson South-Western. These persons include Jack Calhoun, Alex von Rosenberg, Mike Worls, Senior Acquisitions Editor; Jennifer "Hurricane" Baker, Developmental Editor; Heather Mann, Production Project Manager, Brian Joyner, Senior Marketing Manager for Economics; Michelle Kunkler, Senior Design Project Manager, and Sandee Milewski, Senior Frontlist Buyer. I would also like to thank Barbara Sheridan, copyeditor, of Sheridan Publications Services, who not only did a masterful job of copyediting the book, but made numerous suggestions on how to improve the presentation.

My deepest debt of gratitude goes to my wife, Sheila, and to my two sons, David, fifteen years old, and Daniel, eighteen years old. They continue to make all my days happy ones.

Roger A. Arnold

Before you begin your study of economics, you will find it helpful to know something about the road you are about to travel. That's what this learning guide is about. Let me suggest how you should read and study this book to get the most out of it. Knowing something about the structure of each chapter and about the learning strategies used throughout will help you understand and appreciate your economics journey.

Chapter Structure

In every chapter, you will find the following features:

Setting the Scene

Each chapter opens with one to four scenarios depicting everyday life. The events and conversations in these scenarios always have something to do with the economic content of the chapter. Read each scenario and the questions at the bottom of the page. Each question will be answered in the chapter.

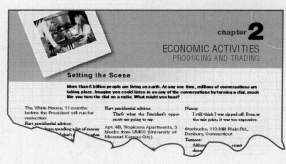

Analyzing the Scene

In this feature, economic analysis is applied to help you understand the economics behind the everyday events and conversations in the scenarios in *Setting the Scene*. These discussions of the questions in the chapter opening allow you to look through economic eyeglasses to see how economists look at the world.

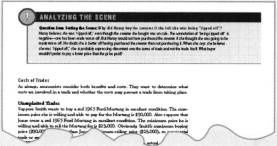

Self-Tests

Frequent feedback plays an important role in learning new material, so a Self-Test is included at the end of each section of each chapter. The answers to the Self-Tests are at the end of the book. Don't skip over the Self-Test because you are in a hurry. Stop, take the test, and then check your answers. If you don't answer a question correctly, go back and reread the sectional material so that you can answer it correctly.

Margin Definitions

The first time you study economics, you have a lot to learn: language, concepts, theories, ways of thinking. This feature helps you to learn the language of economics. All key economics terms are in bold type in the margins of the text. To more effectively learn and understand these definitions, it is very useful to first read them and then state in your own words what you just read.

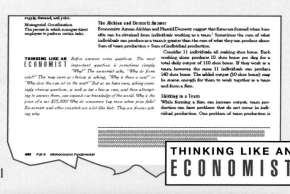

Thinking Like an Economist

Most economics instructors believe that a primary goal of this course is to teach you how economists think. There's more to thinking like an economist than knowing the concepts and technical tools of analysis. There's a special way of looking at situations, events, decisions, and behavior. Pay attention to this feature in each chapter—it will give you unique insight into the economist's mind, allowing you to see how interesting issues are approached from an economic perspective.

Applications Features

Read the boxed features (*Economics In Everyday Life*, *Economics In Popular Culture*, *Economics In the World*, and *Economics In Technology*) in each chapter. Often students will gloss over these features because they think they are irrelevant to the discussion in the main body of the text. Nothing could be further from the truth. These features apply the tools, concepts, and theories discussed in the main body of the text. Without these applications, economics may initially seem dry and abstract. To dispel the notion that economics is simply about inflation, unemployment, costs of production, profit,

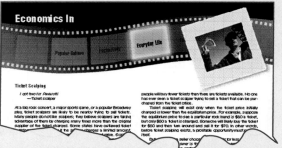

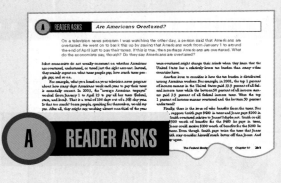

economic growth, monetary and fiscal policy, and so on, I have included these applications features to show you some of the interesting, everyday things that economics is about. Economics, as I hope you will soon learn, is about many more things than you have ever imagined.

A Reader Asks

Do you ever want to ask an instructor a question you thought you might get into trouble for asking? You're learning about supply and demand in economics, and you really want to ask, "How will supply and demand help me?" but you don't ask the question because you think the professor might be offended.

Or suppose you want to ask a very practical question, such as, "How much do economists earn?" or "Is an economics degree respected in the marketplace?" Here, you may not ask the question because you think it isn't quite academic enough.

The feature *A Reader Asks* answers some of the pointed and basic questions that real readers have on their minds.

Graphs and Exhibits

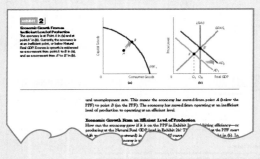

Take your time with the diagrams. An introductory course in economics is full of diagrams, and they are central to communicating economic material. The sooner you learn to "think diagrammatically," the more quickly and thoroughly you will learn economics. The way you learn to think in diagrams is to work with them. Read the caption, identify the curves that are mentioned in the text, explain to yourself what they mean when they shift right and left, and so on. Every diagram tells a story; learn what the story is.

Graphs

I've carefully used consistent colors, shaded arrows to show movement, multistep formats, and boxed explanations to make it easy for you to visually interpret important economic concepts at a glance.

A Closer Look

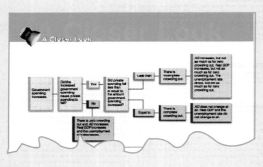

For many students, the difficulty of economics is seeing how it all fits together. Use these special diagrams to more easily understand how the separate pieces of the puzzle fit together to form a cohesive picture of complex interrelationships. Flow diagrams and other unifying devices are used to help you identify cause-effect relationships and clarify the connections between concepts.

End-of-Chapter Material

Chapter Summary

Each chapter ends with a detailed and categorized summary of the main topics in the chapter. It's a useful refresher before class and a good starting point for studying.

Questions and Problems

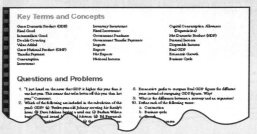

Each chapter ends with numerous questions and problems. Be sure to answer all the questions at the end of each chapter. You never really know how well you have learned economics until someone calls upon you to answer a question. If we can't use what we have read and studied to answer a question, we have to wonder if we learned anything in the first place.

Working With Numbers and Graphs

Each chapter ends with a few numerical and graphical problems. Being able to numerically and graphically analyze economic ideas really helps solidify conceptual understanding.

Key Terms and Concepts

A list of key terms concludes each chapter. If you can define all these terms, you have a good head start on studying.

chapter 1

WHAT ECONOMICS IS ABOUT

© David Young-Wolff/PhotoEdit

Setting the Scene

Jackie and Stephanie share an apartment about a mile from the University of Virginia. Both are juniors at the university; Jackie is a history major and Stephanie is an economics major. The following events occurred one day not too long ago.

7:15 A.M.

Jackie's alarm clock buzzes. She reaches over to the small table next to her bed and turns it off. As she pulls the covers back up, Jackie thinks about her 8:30 American History class. Should she go to class today or sleep a little longer? She worked late last night and really hasn't had enough sleep. Besides, she's fairly sure her professor will be discussing a subject she already knows well. Maybe it would be okay to miss class today.

11:37 A.M.

Stephanie is in the campus bookstore browsing through two economics books. She ends up buying both books. As she leaves the bookstore, she glances over at a blue jacket with the University of Virginia emblem on it. She knows that her brother, who is a junior in high school, would like to have a UVa jacket. Stephanie tells herself that she might buy the jacket for him for his birthday next month.

1:27 P.M.

Jackie, who did skip her 8:30 American History class, is in her European history professor's office talking to him about obtaining a master's degree in history. Getting a master's degree is something that

mildly interests her, but she's not sure whether she wants it enough or not.

9:00 P.M.

Stephanie has been studying for the past three hours for tomorrow's midterm exam in her International Economics course. She says to herself, I think it's better if I stop studying instead of studying some more. Stephanie quits studying, turns on the television, and watches a movie.

? **How would an economist look at these events? Later in the chapter, discussions based on the following questions will help you analyze the scene the way an economist would.**

- Is Jackie more likely to miss some classes than she is to miss other classes? What determines which classes Jackie will attend and which classes she won't attend?
- What does a basic economic fact have to do with Stephanie buying two books at her campus bookstore?
- Does whether or not Jackie will go on to get a master's degree have anything to do with economics?
- What is the likely reason that Stephanie stopped studying?

DEFINITIONS OF ECONOMICS

Although economics has been defined in various ways in its more than 200 year history, some definitions of economics are familiar to almost all economists. We identify three of these definitions in this section, and then give the definition of economics that we use in this text.

The economist Alfred Marshall (1824–1924) was Professor of Political Economy at the University of Cambridge (in England) from 1885 to 1908. Marshall's major work, *Principles of Economics* (first published in 1890), was the most influential economics treatise of its time and has been called the "Bible of British Economics." In the first few lines of the book, Marshall wrote, "Political economy or economics is a study of mankind in the ordinary business of life; it examines that part of individual and social action which is most closely connected with the attainment and with the use of the material requisites of well being." He then said that economics is "on the one side a study of wealth; and on the other, and more important side, a part of the study of man." In short, according to Marshall, economics is the study of mankind in the ordinary business of life; it is the study of wealth and of man.

Lionel Robbins (1898–1984), who taught economics at both Oxford University and the London School of Economics, put forth one of the most widely cited definitions of economics. In his book *The Nature and Significance of Economic Science,* Robbins wrote, "Economics is the science which studies human behavior as a relationship between ends and scarce means which have alternative uses."

Milton Friedman (b. 1912), the 1976 winner of the Nobel Prize in Economics, proposed a similar definition of economics in his work *Price Theory.* Friedman wrote, "Economics is the science of how a particular society solves its economic problems." He then said, "an economic problem exists whenever scarce means are used to satisfy alternative ends."

Ask a noneconomist what economics is and he or she will probably answer that it has something to do with business and wealth. So Marshall's definition of economics accords most closely with the noneconomist's concept of economics. The Robbins and Friedman definitions both stress the relationship between *ends* and *means.* This relationship naturally leads to a discussion of scarcity.

Scarcity is the condition in which our wants are greater than the limited resources available to satisfy them. Our wants are *infinite;* our resources are *finite.* That's scarcity. To define scarcity in terms of ends and means, we can say that our ends are *infinite* and the means available to satisfy those ends are *finite.*

Many economists say that if scarcity didn't exist, neither would economics. In other words, if our wants weren't greater than the limited resources available to satisfy them, there would be no field of study called economics. This is similar to saying that if matter and motion didn't exist, neither would physics, or that if living things didn't exist, neither would biology. For this reason, we define **economics** in this text as the *science of scarcity.* More completely, *economics is the science of how individuals and societies deal with the fact that wants (or ends) are greater than the limited resources (or means) available to satisfy those wants.*

Scarcity
The condition in which our wants are greater than the limited resources available to satisfy those wants.

Economics
The science of scarcity; the science of how individuals and societies deal with the fact that wants are greater than the limited resources available to satisfy those wants.

ECONOMIC CATEGORIES

Economics is sometimes broken down into different categories, according to the type of questions economists ask. Four common economic categories are positive economics, normative economics, microeconomics, and macroeconomics.

Positive and Normative Economics

Positive economics attempts to determine *what is.* **Normative economics** addresses *what should be.* Essentially, positive economics deals with cause-effect relationships that can be tested. Normative economics deals with value judgments and opinions that cannot be tested.

Many topics in economics can be discussed within both a positive framework and a normative framework. Consider a proposed cut in federal income taxes. An economist practicing positive economics would want to know the *effect* of a cut in income taxes. For example, she may want to know how a tax cut will affect the unemployment rate, economic growth, inflation, and so on. An economist practicing normative economics would address issues that directly or indirectly relate to whether the federal income tax *should* be cut. For example, she may say that federal income taxes should be cut because the income tax burden on many taxpayers is currently high.

This book mainly deals with positive economics. For the most part, we discuss the economic world as it is, not the way someone might think it should be. As you read, you should keep two points in mind. First, although we have taken pains to keep our discussion within the boundaries of positive economics, at times we may operate perilously close to the normative border. If, here and there, we drop a value judgment into the discussion, recognize it for what it is. You should not accept as true something that we simply state as an opinion.

Second, keep in mind that no matter what your normative objectives are, positive economics can shed some light on how they might be accomplished. For example, suppose you believe that absolute poverty should be eliminated and the unemployment rate should be lowered. No doubt you have ideas as to how these goals can be accomplished. But will your ideas work? For example, will a greater redistribution of income eliminate absolute poverty? Will lowering taxes lower the unemployment rate? There is no guarantee that the means you think will bring about certain ends will do so. This is where sound positive economics can help. It helps us see what is. As someone once said, It is not enough to want to do good, it is important also to know how to do good.

Positive Economics
The study of "what is" in economic matters.

Normative Economics
The study of "what should be" in economic matters.

Microeconomics and Macroeconomics

It has been said that the tools of microeconomics are microscopes and the tools of macroeconomics are telescopes. Macroeconomics stands back from the trees in order to see the forest. Microeconomics gets up close and examines the tree itself, its bark, its limbs, and the soil in which it grows. **Microeconomics** is the branch of economics that deals with human behavior and choices as they relate to relatively small units—an individual, a firm, an industry, a single market. **Macroeconomics** is the branch of economics that deals with human behavior and choices as they relate to an entire economy. In microeconomics, economists discuss a single price; in macroeconomics, they discuss the price level. Microeconomics deals with the demand for a particular good or service; macroeconomics deals with aggregate, or total, demand for goods and services. Microeconomics examines how a tax change affects a single firm's output; macroeconomics looks at how a tax change affects an entire economy's output.

Microeconomists and macroeconomists ask different types of questions. A microeconomist might be interested in answering such questions as:

- How does a market work?
- What level of output does a firm produce?
- What price does a firm charge for the good it produces?
- How does a consumer determine how much of a good he will buy?

Microeconomics
The branch of economics that deals with human behavior and choices as they relate to relatively small units—an individual, a firm, an industry, a single market.

Macroeconomics
The branch of economics that deals with human behavior and choices as they relate to highly aggregate markets (such as the goods and services market) or the entire economy.

- Can government policy affect business behavior?
- Can government policy affect consumer behavior?

On the other hand, a macroeconomist might be interested in answering such questions as:

- How does the economy work?
- Why is the unemployment rate sometimes high and sometimes low?
- What causes inflation?
- Why do some national economies grow faster than other national economies?
- What might cause interest rates to be low one year and high the next?
- How do changes in the money supply affect the economy?
- How do changes in government spending and taxes affect the economy?

SELF-TEST *(Answers to Self-Test questions are in the Self-Test Appendix.)*

1. Scarcity is the condition of finite resources. True or false? Explain your answer.
2. How are the Friedman and Robbins definitions of economics similar?
3. What is the difference between positive and normative economics? What is the difference between macroeconomics and microeconomics?

KEY CONCEPTS IN ECONOMICS

You can think of the key concepts in economics as tools that the economist keeps in a tool bag. Just as a carpenter uses tools (saw, hammer, screwdriver) to build a house, an economist uses tools to analyze or discuss something of interest. Most of the tools in the economist's tool bag are unique to economics—you won't find them in the sociologist's, historian's, or psychologist's tool bags. A few tools, though, are not unique to economics. The first five concepts we discuss in this section are used principally by economists; the last three concepts are used by both economists and others.

Thinking in Terms of Scarcity and Its Effects

Recall that *scarcity* is the condition in which our wants are greater than the limited resources available to satisfy them. But what are our wants? Our wants include anything that provides utility or satisfaction. In economics, something that provides **utility** or satisfaction is called a **good.** Something that provides **disutility** or dissatisfaction is called a **bad.** For example, for most people pollution is a bad. Basically, people want goods and they don't want bads.

A good can be either tangible or intangible. For example, a car is a tangible good; friendship is an intangible good. Goods do not just appear before us when we snap our fingers. It takes resources to produce goods. (Sometimes resources are referred to as *inputs* or *factors of production.*)

Generally, economists divide resources into four broad categories: land, labor, capital, and entrepreneurship. **Land** includes natural resources, such as minerals, forests, water, and unimproved land. For example, oil, wood, and animals fall into this category. (Sometimes economists refer to this category simply as *natural resources.*)

Labor consists of the physical and mental talents people contribute to the production process. For example, a person building a house is using his or her own labor.

Capital consists of produced goods that can be used as inputs for further production. Factories, machinery, tools, computers, and buildings are examples of capital. One

---

Utility
The satisfaction one receives from a good.

Good
Anything from which individuals receive utility or satisfaction.

Disutility
The dissatisfaction one receives from a bad.

Bad
Anything from which individuals receive disutility or dissatisfaction.

Land
All natural resources, such as minerals, forests, water, and unimproved land.

Labor
The physical and mental talents people contribute to the production process.

Capital
Produced goods that can be used as inputs for further production, such as factories, machinery, tools, computers, and buildings.

country might have more capital than another. This means that it has more factories, machinery, tools, and so on.

Entrepreneurship refers to the particular talent that some people have for organizing the resources of land, labor, and capital to produce goods, seek new business opportunities, and develop new ways of doing things.

Entrepreneurship
The particular talent that some people have for organizing the resources of land, labor, and capital to produce goods, seek new business opportunities, and develop new ways of doing things.

Scarcity and the Need for a Rationing Device

How does scarcity affect your life? Imagine you are considering buying a T-shirt for $10 at the university bookstore. The T-shirt has a price of $10 because of scarcity. There is a scarcity of T-shirts because people want more T-shirts than there are T-shirts available. And as long as there is a scarcity of anything, there is a need for a rationing device. Dollar price is a **rationing device.** If you are willing and able to pay the price, the T-shirt is yours. If you are either unwilling or unable to pay the price, the T-shirt will not become yours.

Rationing Device
A means for deciding who gets what of available resources and goods.

If scarcity didn't exist, there would be no need for a rationing device and people wouldn't pay dollar prices for resources and goods. In every transaction—buying a T-shirt at the university bookstore, buying food in a grocery store, or buying a new computer—scarcity plays a role.

ANALYZING THE SCENE

Question from Setting the Scene: What does a basic economic fact have to do with Stephanie buying two books at her campus bookstore?

Stephanie uses money to buy the two books. She pays the dollar price of each book. But what is dollar price? It is a rationing device. And why do we need rationing devices in society? Because scarcity—a basic economic fact—exists. Both Stephanie *and* the long shadow of scarcity are together in the campus bookstore.

If Not Dollar Price, Then What?

As we stated earlier, dollar price is one rationing device. Some people say that the use of dollar price as a rationing device discriminates against the poor. After all, the poor have fewer dollars than the rich, so the rich can get more of what they want than can the poor. True, dollar price does discriminate against the poor. But then, as the economist knows, every rationing device discriminates against someone.

Suppose that tomorrow, dollar price could not be used as a rationing device. Some rationing device would still be necessary because scarcity would still exist. How would we ration gas at the gasoline station, food in the grocery store, or tickets for the Super Bowl? Let's consider some alternatives to dollar price as a rationing device.

Suppose first-come-first-served is the rationing device. For example, suppose there are only 40,000 Super Bowl tickets. If you are one of the first 40,000 in line for a Super Bowl ticket, then you get a ticket. If you are the 40,001st person in line, you don't. Such a method discriminates against those who can't get in line quickly. What about slow walkers or disabled people? What about people without cars who can't drive to where the tickets are being distributed?

Or suppose brute force is the rationing device. For example, if there are 40,000 Super Bowl tickets, then as long as you can take a ticket away from someone who has a ticket, the ticket is yours. Who does this rationing method discriminate against? Obviously, it discriminates against the weak.

Or suppose beauty is the rationing device. The more beautiful you are, the better your chance of getting a Super Bowl ticket. Again, the rationing device discriminates against someone.

These and many other alternatives to dollar price could be used as a rationing device. However, each discriminates against someone, and none is clearly superior to dollar price.

In addition, if first-come-first-served, brute force, beauty, or another alternative to dollar price is the rationing device, what incentive would the producer of a good or service have to produce the good or service? With dollar price as a rationing device, a person produces computers and sells them for money. With the money, he then buys what he wants—houses, cars, jewelry, vacations in Barbados, and so on. How does a person benefit if the goods he produces are rationed by first-come-first-served, brute force, or beauty? Actually, he doesn't benefit at all. But, if he doesn't benefit by the rationing device, why would he produce anything?

In a world where dollar price isn't the rationing device, people are likely to produce much less than in a world where dollar price is the rationing device.

Scarcity and Competition

Do you see much competition in the world today? Are people competing for jobs? Are states and cities competing for businesses? Are students competing for grades? The answer to all these questions is yes. The economist wants to know why this competition exists and what form it takes. First, the economist concludes, *competition exists because of scarcity*. If there were enough resources to satisfy all our seemingly unlimited wants, people would not have to compete for the available but limited resources.

Second, the economist sees that competition takes the form of people trying to get more of the rationing device. If dollar price is the rationing device, people will compete to earn dollars. Look at your own case. You are a college student working for a degree. One reason (but perhaps not the only reason) you are attending college is to earn a higher income after graduation. But why do you want a higher income? You want it because it will allow you to satisfy more of your wants.

Suppose muscular strength (measured by lifting weights) were the rationing device instead of dollar price. People with more muscular strength would receive more resources and goods than people with less muscular strength would receive. In this situation, people would compete for muscular strength. The lesson is simple: *Whatever the rationing device, people will compete for it.*

Thinking in Terms of Opportunity Cost

As noted earlier, people have to make choices because scarcity exists. Because our seemingly unlimited wants push up against limited resources, some wants must go unsatisfied. We must therefore choose which wants we will satisfy and which we will not. The most highly valued opportunity or alternative forfeited when a choice is made is known as **opportunity cost.** Every time you make a choice, you incur an opportunity cost. For example, you have chosen to read this chapter. In making this choice, you denied yourself the benefits of doing something else. You could have watched television, e-mailed a friend, taken a nap, eaten a pizza, read a novel, shopped for a new computer, and so on. Whatever you would have chosen to do had you decided not to read this chapter is the opportunity cost of your reading this chapter. For example, if

Opportunity Cost
The most highly valued opportunity or alternative forfeited when a choice is made.

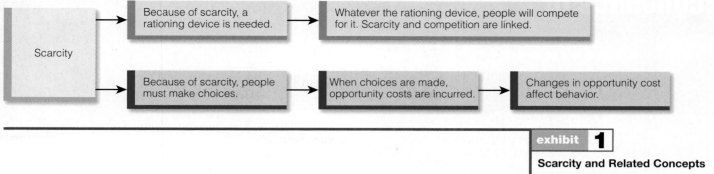

exhibit 1

Scarcity and Related Concepts

you would have watched television had you chosen not to read this chapter—if this was your next best alternative—then the opportunity cost of reading this chapter is watching television.

Opportunity Cost and Behavior

Economists think about people's behavior in terms of opportunity cost. Specifically, they believe that a change in opportunity cost will change a person's behavior. For example, consider Bill, who is a sophomore at the University of Kansas. He attends classes Monday through Thursday of every week. Every time he chooses to go to class he gives up the opportunity to do something else, such as the opportunity to earn $8 an hour working at a job. The opportunity cost of Bill spending an hour in class is $8.

Now let's raise the opportunity cost of attending class. On Tuesday, we offer Bill $70 to cut his economics class. He knows that if he attends his economics class he will forfeit $70. What will Bill do? An economist would predict that as the opportunity cost of attending class increases relative to the benefits of attending class, Bill is less likely to attend class.

This is how economists think about behavior, whether it is Bill's or your own. *The higher the opportunity cost of doing something, the less likely it will be done.* This is part of the economic way of thinking.

Before you continue, look at Exhibit 1, which summarizes some of the things about scarcity, choice, and opportunity cost up to this point.

ANALYZING THE SCENE

Questions from Setting the Scene: Is Jackie more likely to miss some classes than she is to miss other classes? What determines which classes Jackie will attend and which classes she won't attend?

The lower the cost of not attending class, the more likely Jackie will not attend class. On this particular day, Jackie is fairly sure that "her professor will be discussing a subject she already knows well." Therefore, the cost of missing this class is probably lower than missing, say, a class where the professor will be discussing an unfamiliar subject or a class in which a midterm exam will be given. Not all classes are alike for Jackie because the cost of attending each class isn't the same.

There Is No Such Thing as a Free Lunch

Economists are fond of saying that *there is no such thing as a free lunch.* This catchy phrase expresses the idea that opportunity costs are incurred when choices are made. Perhaps this

Blogging

Not too many years ago, people could get the news and opinions of the day only from network television, radio, newspapers, and magazines. Then came cable, followed by the Internet. Today, news and opinions abound. No longer are news and opinions available only from those who have degrees in journalism. Today, anyone with access to the Internet can instantly post his or her opinion about the issues of the day on a blog.

A weblog, or blog, is a web page made up of usually short, updated posts that are arranged chronologically—much like a journal or diary. Some blogs are personal, "what's on my mind" types of musings. Some blogs help members of a small group communicate with each other. Some people post photos and poetry on their blogs.

Many blogs consist of various commentaries on the news of the day. Three examples of this type of blog are:

- Oxblog at http://oxblog.blogspot.com
- Instapundit.com at http://www.instapundit.com
- andrewsullivan.com at http://www.andrewsullivan.com

Why are so many people today so quick to express their opinions on these blogs? At times it seems like almost everyone has become an op-ed writer. Why? The explanation is based on the cost of being an op-ed writer. As noted earlier in this chapter, the lower the (opportunity) cost of doing something, the more likely a person will do it. Because of the Internet, the cost of being an op-ed writer has fallen dramatically. You don't have to go to college, get a degree in journalism, and work for a newspaper for years before you have the privilege of writing a daily opinion column. Now all you need to do is go online to Blogger at www.blogger.com, set up a blog of your own in a matter of a few minutes, and start tapping on the keyboard. Price tag: $0.

Of course, having your own blog doesn't guarantee that anyone will read what you write. People have to find your blog, read what you have written, link to it, and tell others about it. The cost of being a writer that people read probably hasn't changed.

---

is an obvious point, but consider how often people mistakenly assume there *is* a free lunch. For example, some parents think education is free because they do not pay tuition for their children to attend public elementary school. Sorry, but there is no such thing as a free lunch. Free implies no sacrifice, no opportunities forfeited, which is not true in regard to elementary school education. Resources that could be used for other things are used to provide elementary school education.

Consider the people who speak about free medical care, free housing, free bridges ("there is no charge to cross it"), and free parks. None of these are actually free. The resources that provide medical care, housing, bridges, and parks could have been used in other ways.

Thinking in Terms of Costs and Benefits

If it were possible to eliminate air pollution completely, should all air pollution be eliminated? If your answer is yes, then you are probably focusing on the *benefits* of eliminating air pollution. For example, one benefit might be healthier individuals. Certainly individuals who do not breathe polluted air have fewer lung disorders than people who do breathe polluted air.

Why LeBron James Isn't in College

LeBron James was born on December 30, 1984. So, he is currently the age of many people attending college. But LeBron James is not attending college. He went directly from high school into the NBA. He is currently playing professional basketball.

Why isn't LeBron James in college? It's not because he cannot afford the tuition charged at most colleges. Also, it's not because he wouldn't be admitted to any college. LeBron James is not in college because it is more expensive for him to attend college than it is for most 18 to 25 year olds to attend college.

To understand, think of what it costs you to attend college. If you pay $1,000 tuition a semester for eight semesters, the full tuition amounts to $8,000. However, $8,000 is not the full cost of your attending college because if you were not a student, you could be earning income working at a job. For example, you could be working at a full-time job earning $25,000 annually. Certainly this $25,000, or at least part of it if you are currently working part-time, is forfeited because you attend college. It is part of the cost of your attending college.

Thus, the *tuition cost* may be the same for everyone who attends your college, but the *opportunity cost* is not. Some people have higher opportunity costs of attending college than others do.

LeBron James has extremely high opportunity costs of attending college. He would have to give up the millions of dollars he earns playing professional basketball and endorsing products if he were to attend college on a full-time basis.

This discussion illustrates two related points made in this chapter. First, *the higher the opportunity cost of doing something, the less likely it will be done.* The opportunity cost of attending college is higher for LeBron than it (probably) is for you, and that is why you are in college and LeBron James is not.

Second, according to economists, *individuals think and act in terms of costs and benefits and only undertake actions if they expect the benefits to outweigh the costs.* LeBron James is likely to see certain benefits to attending college—just as you see certain benefits to attending college. However, those benefits are insufficient for him to attend college because benefits are not all that matter. Costs matter too. For LeBron James, the costs of attending college are much higher than the benefits, and so he chooses not to attend college. In your case, the benefits are higher than the costs, and so you have decided to attend college.

But benefits rarely come without costs. The economist reminds us that while there are benefits to eliminating pollution, there are costs too. To illustrate, one way to eliminate all car pollution tomorrow is to pass a law stating that anyone caught driving a car will go to prison for 40 years. With such a law in place, and enforced, very few people would drive cars and all car pollution would be a thing of the past. Presto! Cleaner air! However, many people would think that the cost of obtaining that cleaner air is too high. Someone might say, "I want cleaner air, but not if I have to completely give up driving my car. How will I get to work?"

What distinguishes the economist from the noneconomist is that the economist thinks in terms of *both* costs and benefits. Often, the noneconomist thinks in terms of either one or the other. There are benefits from studying, but there are costs too. There are benefits to coming to class, but there are costs too. There are costs to getting up early each morning and exercising, but let's not forget that there are benefits too.

Question from Setting the Scene: Does whether or not Jackie will go on to get a master's degree have anything to do with economics?

Jackie is undecided about whether or not she will pursue a master's degree. When she says she is not sure she wants it enough, she is really thinking about the costs and benefits of getting a master's degree. The benefits of getting the degree relate to (1) how much higher her annual income will be with a master's degree than without it, (2) how much she enjoys studying history, and so on. The costs relate to (1) the income she will lose while she is at graduate school working on a master's degree, (2) the less leisure time she will enjoy during the time she is studying, writing papers, and attending classes, (3) the tuition costs of the program, and so on. Are the benefits greater than the costs, or are the costs greater than the benefits? Jackie is thinking through an economic calculation, although she may know nothing about economics.

Thinking in Terms of Decisions Made at the Margin

It is late at night and you have already studied three hours for your biology test tomorrow. You look at the clock and wonder if you should study another hour. How would you summarize your thinking process? What question or questions do you ask yourself to decide whether or not to study another hour?

Perhaps without knowing it, you think in terms of the costs and benefits of further study. You probably realize that there are certain benefits from studying an additional hour (you may be able to raise your grade a few points), but that there are costs too (you will get less sleep or have less time to watch television or talk on the phone with a friend). Thinking in terms of costs and benefits, though, doesn't tell us *how* you think in terms of costs and benefits. For example, when deciding what to do, do you look at the total costs and total benefits of the proposed action or do you look at something less than the total costs and benefits? According to economists, for most decisions you think in terms of *additional,* or *marginal,* costs and benefits, not *total* costs and benefits. That's because most decisions deal with making a small, or additional, change.

To illustrate, suppose you just finished eating a hamburger and drinking a soda for lunch. You are still a little hungry and are considering whether or not to order another hamburger. An economist would say that in deciding whether or not to order another hamburger, you will compare the additional benefits of the additional hamburger to the additional costs of the additional hamburger. In economics, the word "marginal" is a synonym for "additional." So we say that you will compare the **marginal benefits** of the (next) hamburger to the **marginal costs** of the (next) hamburger. If the marginal benefits are greater than the marginal costs, you obviously expect a net benefit to ordering the next hamburger, and therefore you order the next hamburger. If, however, the marginal costs of the hamburger are greater than the marginal benefits, you obviously expect a net cost to ordering the next hamburger, and therefore you do not order the next hamburger.

What you don't consider when making this decision are the total benefits and total costs of hamburgers. That's because the benefits and costs connected with the first hamburger (the one you have already eaten) are no longer relevant to the current decision. You are not deciding between eating two hamburgers and eating no hamburgers; your decision is whether to eat a second hamburger after you have already eaten a first hamburger.

Marginal Benefits
Additional benefits. The benefits connected to consuming an additional unit of a good or undertaking one more unit of an activity.

Marginal Costs
Additional costs. The costs connected to consuming an additional unit of a good or undertaking one more unit of an activity.

According to economists, when individuals make decisions by comparing marginal benefits to marginal costs, they are making **decisions at the margin.** The President of the United States makes a decision at the margin when deciding whether or not to talk another 10 minutes with the Speaker of the House of Representatives, the employee makes a decision at the margin when deciding whether or not to work two hours over-time, and the college professor makes a decision at the margin when deciding whether or not to add an additional question to the final exam.

Decisions at the Margin
Decision making characterized by weighing the additional (marginal) benefits of a change against the additional (marginal) costs of a change with respect to current conditions.

ANALYZING THE SCENE

Question from Setting the Scene: What is the likely reason that Stephanie stopped studying?
Stephanie likely assumed that the marginal costs of continuing to study were greater than the marginal benefits of continuing to study, so she felt it was no longer worthwhile to continue studying. Remember, individuals undertake those actions for which the marginal benefits are greater than the marginal costs, and they do not undertake those actions for which the marginal costs are greater than the marginal benefits.

Thinking in Terms of Equilibrium

People sometimes think in terms of natural resting places. For example, suppose you call up a friend and ask him how he is doing today. He tells you he is sick. "Do you have a fever?" you ask. He says that he has a fever; his temperature is 103.4 degrees.

Now suppose someone asks you to assign a probability to your friend's body temperature staying at 103.4 degrees for the next two weeks. Would you assign a 100 percent probability, a 75 percent probability, or some much smaller probability? Most people would assign a very tiny probability of your friend's temperature remaining at 103.4 degrees for the next two weeks. Most people would think one of the following two options is more likely: (1) The temperature will rise so high that it kills the person (and therefore it no longer makes much sense to speak of a body temperature) or (2) the temperature will fall until it is close to the normal body temperature of 98.6 degrees.

The normal body temperature of 98.6 degrees is often thought of as a natural resting place in that for living human beings, any temperature higher or lower than 98.6 degrees is a temporary temperature. A person's temperature always seems to settle back down or back up to 98.6 degrees.

Economists tend to think that many economic phenomena have natural resting places. These natural resting places are often called **equilibrium.** One way to think of equilibrium is as a place where economic forces are driving things. To illustrate, let's consider an example.

Equilibrium
Equilibrium means "at rest"; it is descriptive of a natural resting place.

Suppose Smith has a single painting that he wants to sell. He suggests a price of $5,000 for the painting, and at that price, three people say they are willing to buy it. How does he decide to whom he will sell the painting? Will he draw names out of a hat? Will he have the three people draw straws? Most likely he will ask the three people to offer him a higher price for the painting. At $6,000, two people still want to buy the painting, but at $6,500, only one person wants to buy the painting. In other words, the bidding activity of the buyers has moved the price of the painting to its natural resting place or to an equilibrium price of $6,500.

Economists are well known for analyzing economic phenomena in terms of equilibrium. First, they will try to identify whether or not equilibrium exists. Second, if equilibrium exists, they will then proceed to determine how that equilibrium should be specified. They then sometimes proceed to ask, What can change equilibrium? We will have much more to say about this question in Chapter 3.

Thinking in Terms of the *Ceteris Paribus* Assumption

Wilson has eaten regular ice cream for years, and for years his weight has been 170 pounds. One day, Wilson decides he wants to lose some weight. With this in mind, he buys a new fat-free ice cream at the grocery store. The fat-free ice cream has half the calories of regular ice cream.

Wilson eats the fat-free ice cream for the next few months. He then weighs himself and finds that he has gained two pounds. Does this mean that fat-free ice cream causes people to gain weight and regular ice cream does not? The answer is no. But why, then, did Wilson gain weight when he substituted fat-free ice cream for regular ice cream? Perhaps Wilson ate three times as much fat-free ice cream as regular ice cream. Or perhaps during the time he was eating fat-free ice cream, he wasn't exercising, and during the time he was eating regular ice cream, he was exercising. In other words, a number of factors—such as eating more ice cream or exercising less—may have offset the weight loss that Wilson would have experienced had these factors not changed.

Now suppose you want to make the point that Wilson would have lost weight by substituting fat-free ice cream for regular ice cream had these other factors not changed. What would you say? A scientist would say, "If Wilson has been eating regular ice cream and his weight has stabilized at 170 pounds, then substituting fat-free ice cream for regular ice cream will lead to a decline in weight, *ceteris paribus.*"

The term **ceteris paribus** means *all other things held constant* or *nothing else changes.* In our ice cream example, if nothing else changes—such as how much ice cream Wilson eats, how much exercise he gets, and so on—then substituting fat-free ice cream for regular ice cream will result in weight loss. This is based on the theory that a reduction in calorie consumption will result in weight loss and an increase in calorie consumption will result in weight gain.

Using the *ceteris paribus* assumption is important because, with it, we can clearly designate what we believe is the correct relationship between two variables. In the ice cream example, we can designate the correct relationship between calorie intake and weight gain.

Economists don't often talk about ice cream, but they will often make use of the *ceteris paribus* assumption. An economist might say, "If the price of a good decreases, the quantity demanded or consumed of that good increases, *ceteris paribus.*" For example, if the price of Pepsi-Cola decreases, people will buy more Pepsi-Cola, assuming that nothing else changes.

But some people ask, "Why would economists want to assume that when the price of Pepsi-Cola falls, nothing else changes? Don't other things change in the real world? Why assume things that we know are not true?"

Of course, economists do not specify *ceteris paribus* because they want to say something false about the world. They specify it because they want to clearly define what they believe to be the real-world relationship between two variables. Look at it this way. If you drop a ball off the roof of a house, it will fall to the ground unless someone catches it. This statement is true, and probably everyone would willingly accept it as true. But here is another true statement: If you drop a ball off the roof of a house, it will fall to the ground, *ceteris paribus*. In fact, the two statements are identical in meaning. This is

Ceteris Paribus
A Latin term meaning "all other things constant," or "nothing else changes."

because adding the phrase "unless someone catches it" in the first sentence is the same as saying *"ceteris paribus"* in the second sentence. If one statement is acceptable to us, the other should be too.

Thinking in Terms of the Difference Between Association and Causation

Association is one thing, causation is another. A problem arises when we confuse the two. Two events are associated if they are linked or connected in some way. For example, suppose you wash your car at 10:00 A.M. and at 10:30 A.M. it starts to rain. Because it rains shortly after you wash your car, the two events are associated (linked, connected) in time. Does it follow that the first event (your washing the car) caused the second event (the rain)? The answer is no. Association is not causation. If *A* occurs before *B*, it does not necessarily follow that *A* is the cause and *B* the effect.

In the car-rain example, it is obvious that association was not causation. But consider a case where this is not so apparent. Suppose Jones tells you that the U.S. trade deficit grew larger in January and 11 months later economic activity had turned down. She then states that the first event (the growing trade deficit) caused the second event (the downturn in economic activity). You may be tempted to accept this as truth. But, of course, a simple statement of cause and effect is not enough to establish cause and effect. Without any evidence, we can't be certain that we haven't stumbled onto a disguised version of the car-rain example.

Thinking in Terms of the Difference Between the Group and the Individual

Some people will say that what is good or true for the individual is necessarily good or true for the group. Fact is, what is good for the individual may be good for the group, but not necessarily. For example, John stands up at a soccer game and sees the game better. Does it follow that if everyone stands up at the soccer game, everyone will see better? No. Mary moves to the suburbs because she dislikes crowds in the city. Does it follow that if everyone moves from the city to the suburbs for the same reason as Mary, everyone will be better off? No. Andres does his holiday shopping early so he can beat the crowds. Does it follow that if everyone does his holiday shopping early, everyone can beat the crowds? No.

People who believe that what is good for the individual is also good for the group are said to believe in the **fallacy of composition.** Economists do not believe in the fallacy of composition.

Consider two economic examples where the fallacy may appear. Some people argue that tariffs benefit certain industries by protecting them from foreign competition. They then conclude that because tariffs benefit some industries, the economy as a whole benefits from tariffs. This is not true though.

Or consider the fact that some people have limited wants for particular goods. Does it follow that society has limited wants for all goods? Not at all. To argue otherwise is to commit the fallacy of composition.

Fallacy of Composition
The erroneous view that what is good or true for the individual is necessarily good or true for the group.

SELF-TEST

1. How does competition arise out of scarcity?
2. Give an example to illustrate how a change in opportunity cost can affect behavior.
3. Give an example to illustrate how a politician running for office can mislead the electorate by implying that association is causation.

4. Your economics instructor says, "If the price of going to the movies goes down, people will go to the movies more often." A student in class says, "Not if the quality of the movies goes down." Who is right, the economics instructor or the student?

ECONOMISTS BUILD AND TEST THEORIES

An important component of the economic way of thinking is theorizing or building theories or models to explain and predict real-world events. This section discusses the nature and uses of theory.

What Is a Theory?

Almost everyone, including you, builds and tests theories or models on a regular basis. (In this text, the words *theory* and *model* are used interchangeably.) Perhaps you thought only scientists and other people who have high-level mathematics at their fingertips built and tested theories. However, theory building and testing is not the domain of only the highly educated and mathematically proficient. Almost everyone builds and tests theories.

People build theories any time they do not know the answer to a question. Someone asks, "Why is the crime rate higher in the United States than in Belgium?" Or, "Why did Aaron's girlfriend break up with him?" Or, "Why does Professor Avalos give easier final exams than Professor Shaw even though they teach the same subject?" If you don't know the answer to a question, you are likely to build a theory so you can provide an answer.

What exactly is a theory? To an economist, a **theory** is an abstract representation of the world. In this context, **abstract** means to omit certain variables or factors when trying to explain or understand something. For example, suppose you were to draw a map for a friend, showing him how to get from his house to your house. Would you draw a map that showed every single thing your friend would see on the trip from his house to yours, or would you simply draw the main roads and one or two landmarks? If you'd do the latter, you would be abstracting from reality; you would be omitting certain things.

You would abstract for two reasons. First, to get your friend from his house to yours, you don't need to include everything on your map. Simply noting main roads may be enough. Second, if you did note everything on your map, your friend might get confused. Giving too much detail could be as bad as giving too little.

When economists build a theory or model, they do the same thing you do when you draw a map. They abstract from reality; they leave out certain things. They focus on the major factors or variables that they believe will explain the phenomenon they are trying to understand.

Suppose a criminologist's objective is to explain why some people turn to crime. Before actually building the theory, he considers a number of variables that may explain why some people become criminals. These variables include (1) the ease of getting a gun, (2) parental childrearing practices, (3) the neighborhood a person grew up in, (4) whether a person was abused as a child, (5) family education, (6) the type of friends a person has, (7) a person's IQ, (8) climate, and (9) a person's diet.

The criminologist may think that some of these variables greatly affect the chance that a person will become a criminal, some affect it only slightly, and others do not affect it at all. For example, a person's diet may have only a 0.0001 percent effect on the person becoming a criminal. But whether or not a person was abused as a child may have a 30 percent effect.

Theory
An abstract representation of the real world designed with the intent to better understand that world.

Abstract
The process (used in building a theory) of focusing on a limited number of variables to explain or predict an event.

A theory emphasizes only those variables that the theorist believes are the main or critical variables that explain an activity or event. Thus, if the criminologist in our example thinks that parental childrearing practices and family education are likely to explain much more about criminal behavior than the other variables, then his (abstract) theory will focus on these two variables and will ignore the other variables.

All theories are abstractions from reality. But it doesn't follow that (abstract) theories cannot explain reality. The objective in theory building is to ignore those variables that are essentially irrelevant to the case at hand, so that it becomes easier to isolate the important variables that the untrained observer would probably miss.

In the course of reading this text, you will come across numerous theories. Some of these theories are explained in words, and others are graphically represented. For example, Chapter 3 presents the theory of supply and demand. First, the parts of the theory are explained. Then the theory is represented graphically in terms of a supply curve and a demand curve.

Building and Testing a Theory

The same basic procedure for building and testing a theory is used in all scientific work, whether the discipline is biology, chemistry, or economics. Exhibit 2 summarizes the approach outlined next.

1. **Decide what it is you want to explain or predict.** For example, you may want to explain or predict interest rates, the exchange rate between the U.S. dollar and the Japanese yen, or another concept.
2. **Identify the variables that you believe are important to what you want to explain or predict.** Variables are magnitudes that can change. For example, price is a variable. One day the price of a good may be $10, and a week later it may be $12.

exhibit **2**

Building and Testing a Theory

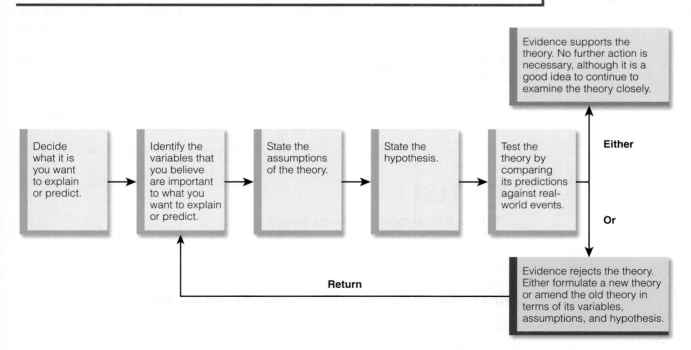

An economist who wants to explain or predict the buying behavior of consumers may build his "theory of buying behavior" on the variable price.

3. **State the assumptions of the theory.** An assumption is a critical or key element of a theory. It is a statement that one supposes to be true. The difference between an assumption and a fact is that a fact represents objective truth. It is a fact that you are reading this book at this moment; no one doubts this. With an assumption, objective truth does not necessarily exist; there is room for doubt. An economist may make the assumption that the owners of business firms have only one motive—to earn as much profit as possible. But, of course, this may not be the truth. The owners of business firms may not be motivated only by profits, or they may not be motivated by profits at all.

4. **State the hypothesis.** A hypothesis is a conditional statement specifying how two variables are related. Typically, hypotheses follow the "if-then" form. For example, if you smoke cigarettes, then you will increase your probability of getting lung cancer. In effect, the hypothesis is a prediction of what will happen to one thing (e.g., to your lungs) when something else changes (you smoke cigarettes).

5. **Test the theory by comparing its predictions against real-world events.** Suppose an economist's theory predicts that as taxes are raised, there will be less saving in the economy. To test this theory, we look at the data on saving to see if the evidence *supports* the theory that produced that specific prediction.

6. **If the evidence supports the theory, then no further action is necessary, although it is a good idea to continue to examine the theory closely.** Suppose a theory predicts that orange prices will rise within two weeks of a cold snap in Florida. If this actually happens, then the evidence supports the theory. Notice that we say "supports the theory" rather than "proves the theory." To explain why, consider a theory that predicts that all swans are white. Researchers go out into the field and record the color of all the swans they see. Every swan they see is white. The evidence does not prove the theory is correct because there may be swans that are not white that the researchers did not see. How can the researchers be certain they saw all the swans? Thus, it is more accurate to say that the evidence supports the theory than to say it proves the theory.

7. **If the evidence rejects the theory, then either formulate a new theory or amend the old theory in terms of its variables, assumptions, and hypothesis.** For example, suppose a theory predicts that interest rates will rise within two months of an increase in the amount of money in circulation. If this does not happen, then it is time to either formulate a new theory or amend the old theory.

SELF-TEST

1. What is the purpose of building a theory?
2. How might a theory of the economy differ from a description of the economy?
3. Why is it important to test a theory?

THREE MAJOR QUESTIONS IN MACROECONOMICS

Almost every macroeconomist, indirectly or directly, tries to answer three key questions. These questions are:

- How does the economy work?
- What causes the ups and downs in the economy?
- What causes economic growth?

Let's consider each of these questions.

How Does the Economy Work?

Medical doctors want to know how the human body works. Physicists want to know how the physical world works. And macroeconomists want to know how the economy works. In fact, figuring out how the economy works is the principal task of the macroeconomist.

To understand how the economy works, macroeconomists look at *connections*. For example, consider the total dollar amount that individuals spend each year on goods and services—called *consumption spending*. How might a rise or fall in consumption spending affect the unemployment rate or economic growth? In other words, what is the *connection* between a change in consumption spending and other economic factors?

Cause and effect is also important to understanding how the economy works. For example, macroeconomists want to know what might cause a change in consumption spending. Do people spend more for no reason at all? Or does their changed consumption spending have a cause? If the latter, what is the cause?

So, to understand how the economy works, macroeconomists first have to understand how the different parts of the economy work, in much the same way that to understand how the human body works, medical doctors first have to understand how the liver, kidney, and heart work. This is why macroeconomists devote years of study to a particular part of the economy, such as consumption spending, investment spending, the interaction between two markets in the economy, and so on.

What Causes the Ups and Downs in the Economy?

An economy often goes on a roller coaster ride: up and down, then up and down again. Specifically, economic activity (buying, selling, producing, borrowing, lending) can be booming or busting. Macroeconomists want to know why the economy behaves this way. Is this behavior simply the inherent nature of an economy? Or is some intervening force outside the economy causing it to behave this way?

What Causes Economic Growth?

For more than two centuries, macroeconomists have tried to determine why some countries are richer than other countries. Today, the United States is a much richer country than, say, Egypt. Why? Trying to answer this question leads macroeconomists to the topic of economic growth. Why do some countries grow faster than other countries? Specifically, what causes economic growth?

THREE MACROECONOMIC ORGANIZATIONAL CATEGORIES

As noted earlier, macroeconomics is the branch of economics that deals with the entire economy. The subject matter in macroeconomics includes (1) macroeconomic problems, (2) macroeconomic theories, (3) macroeconomic policies, and (4) different views of how the economy works. Three macroeconomic categories can help you organize what you learn in macroeconomics and give you a better idea of what macroeconomics is about. These categories are:

- The *P–Q* category
- The self-regulating–economic-instability category
- The effective–ineffective category

This section describes each of these organizational categories.

The *P–Q* Category

Macroeconomics deals with many variables, but two major variables are the price level and Real GDP. The *price level* is the weighted average of the prices of all goods and services. *Real GDP* is the value of the entire output produced annually within a country's borders, adjusted for price changes. Chapter 4 discusses both the price level and Real GDP in depth, but for now, you may simply view the price level as an average price and Real GDP as the quantity of output produced.

We use the symbol *P* for the price level, and we use the symbol *Q* for Real GDP. Thus, we can talk about the *P–Q* category.

Macroeconomics includes numerous topics, such as inflation, deflation, unemployment, and so on. Many of these topics relate directly or indirectly to *P*, to *Q*, or to both *P* and *Q*. The following list of macroeconomic topics notes how each topic relates to *P* and/or *Q*.

- **Gross Domestic Product (GDP).** *P* multiplied times *Q*.
- **Unemployment.** Changes in unemployment are related to changes in *Q*.
- **Inflation.** *P* is rising.
- **Deflation.** *P* is falling.
- **Economic growth.** Related to increasing *Q*.
- **Stagflation.** Both *P* and unemployment are rising.
- **Business cycle.** Recurrent swings up and down in *Q*.
- **Inflationary gap.** The condition of the economy when *Q* is above its natural level.
- **Recessionary gap.** The condition of the economy when *Q* is below its natural level.
- **Fiscal policy.** Concerned with stabilizing *P* and increasing *Q*.
- **Monetary policy.** Concerned with stabilizing *P* and increasing *Q*.

The Self-Regulating–Economic Instability Category

Consider the Great Depression of 1929–1933. During this period in U.S. history, unemployment skyrocketed, the production of goods and services plummeted (*Q* fell), prices fell (*P* fell), banks closed, savings were lost, and companies went bankrupt. What does this period indicate about the inherent properties of a market economy?

Some observers argue that the Great Depression is proof of the inherent instability of a market (or capitalist) economy. They say this time period demonstrates that natural economic forces, if left to themselves, may bring about human suffering.

Other observes see thing differently. They argue that left to itself, the economy would never have nosedived into the Great Depression. They argue that the economy is inherently stable or self-regulating. The Great Depression, they believe, was largely caused and made worse by government tampering with the self-regulating and wealth-producing properties of a market economy.

Which came first? Did the market economy turn down under the weight of its own forces, producing massive unemployment, with government later stepping in to restrain the destructive market forces? Or was the market economy pushed into depression, and held there, by government economic tampering? The answer largely depends on how the inherent properties of a market economy are viewed. As economist Axel Leijonhfvud notes:

The central issue in macroeconomic theory is—once again—the extent to which the economy, or at least its market sectors, may properly be regarded as a self-regulating system. . . . How well or badly, do its "automatic" mechanisms perform?[1]

The Effective–Ineffective Category

Here, the words *effective* and *ineffective* describe fiscal policy and monetary policy. *Fiscal policy* refers to changes in government expenditures and/or decreases in taxes to achieve particular macroeconomic goals (such as low unemployment, stable prices, and so on). *Monetary policy* refers to changes in the money supply, or the rate of growth of the money supply, to achieve particular macroeconomic goals.

Macroeconomists can take one of several positions within the effective–ineffective category. A macroeconomist can believe that both fiscal and monetary policy are always effective (at meeting their goals), or that both fiscal and monetary policy are ineffective, or that fiscal policy is effective and monetary policy is ineffective, and so on. Often, a macroeconomist's position on the effectiveness–ineffectiveness of a policy is implicit in his or her view of how the economy works.

A **READER ASKS** *What's in Store for an Economics Major?*

This is my first course in economics. The material is interesting and I have given some thought to majoring in economics. Please tell me something about the major and about job prospects for an economics graduate. What courses do economics majors take? What is the starting salary of economics majors? Do the people who run large companies think highly of people who have majored in economics?

If you major in economics, you will certainly not be alone. Economics is one of the top three majors at Harvard, Brown, Yale, University of California at Berkeley, Princeton, Columbia, Cornell, Dartmouth, and Stanford. U.S. colleges and universities awarded 16,141 degrees to economics majors in the 2003–2004 academic year, which was up nearly 40 percent from five years earlier. The popularity of economics is probably based on two major reasons. First, many people find economics an interesting course of study. Second, what you learn in an economics course is relevant and applicable to the real world.

Do executives who run successful companies think highly of economics majors? Well, a *BusinessWeek* survey found that economics was the second favorite undergraduate major of chief executive officers (CEOs) of major corporations. Engineering was their favorite undergraduate major.

An economics major usually takes a wide variety of economics courses, starting with introductory courses—principles of microeconomics and principles of macroeconomics—and then studying

intermediate microeconomics and intermediate macroeconomics. Upper-division electives usually include such courses as public finance, international economics, law and economics, managerial economics, labor economics, health economics, money and banking, environmental economics, and more.

According to the National Association of Colleges and Employers Salary Survey in Spring 2004, the average starting salary for a college graduate in economics was $43,000. For a college graduate in business administration, the average starting salary was $36,515, and for a college graduate in computer science, the average starting salary was $46,536. Also, according to the Economics and Statistics Administration of the U.S. Department of Justice, economics undergraduates have relatively higher average annual salaries than students who have majored in other fields. Specifically, of 14 different majors, economics majors ranked third. Only persons with bachelor's degrees in engineering or agriculture/forestry had higher average annual salaries.

---

1. Axel Leijonhufvud, "Effective Demand Failures," *Swedish Journal of Economics* 75 (1973): 28.

Chapter Summary

Definitions of Economics

> Alfred Marshall said, "Political economy or economics is a study of mankind in the ordinary business of life."

> Lionel Robbins said, "Economics is the science which studies human behavior as a relationship between ends and scarce means which have alternative uses."

> Milton Friedman said, "Economics is the science of how a particular society solves its economic problems." He added, "an economic problem exists whenever scarce means are used to satisfy alternative ends."

> In this book, economics is defined as the science of scarcity. More completely, economics is the science of how individuals and societies deal with the fact that wants are greater than the limited resources available to satisfy those wants.

Economic Categories

> Positive economics attempts to determine what is; normative economics addresses what should be.

> Microeconomics deals with human behavior and choices as they relate to relatively small units—an individual, a firm, an industry, a single market. Macroeconomics deals with human behavior and choices as they relate to an entire economy.

Goods, Bads, and Resources

> A good is anything that gives a person utility or satisfaction.
> A bad is anything that gives a person disutility or dissatisfaction.
> Economists divide resources into four categories: land, labor, capital, and entrepreneurship.
> Land includes natural resources, such as minerals, forests, water, and unimproved land.
> Labor refers to the physical and mental talents that people contribute to the production process.
> Capital consists of produced goods that can be used as inputs for further production, such as machinery, tools, computers, trucks, buildings, and factories.
> Entrepreneurship refers to the particular talent that some people have for organizing the resources of land, labor, and capital to produce goods, seek new business opportunities, and develop new ways of doing things.

Scarcity

> Scarcity is the condition in which our wants are greater than the limited resources available to satisfy them. Scarcity implies choice. In a world of limited resources, we must choose which wants will be satisfied and which will go unsatisfied.

> Because of scarcity, there is a need for a rationing device. A rationing device is a means of deciding who gets what quantities of the available resources and goods.

> Scarcity implies competition. If there were enough resources to satisfy all our seemingly unlimited wants, people would not have to compete for the available but limited resources.

Opportunity Cost

> Every time a person makes a choice, he or she incurs an opportunity cost. Opportunity cost is the most highly valued opportunity or alternative forfeited when a choice is made. The higher the opportunity cost of doing something, the less likely it will be done.

Costs and Benefits

> What distinguishes the economist from the noneconomist is that the economist thinks in terms of *both* costs and benefits. Asked what the benefits of taking a walk may be, an economist will also mention the costs of taking a walk. Asked what the costs of studying are, an economist will also point out the benefits of studying.

Decisions Made at the Margin

> Marginal benefits and costs are not the same as total benefits and costs. When deciding whether to talk on the phone one more minute, an individual would not consider the total benefits and total costs of speaking on the phone. Instead, the individual would compare only the marginal benefits (additional benefits) of talking on the phone one more minute to the marginal costs (additional costs) of talking on the phone one more minute.

Equilibrium

> Equilibrium means "at rest." Many natural and economic phenomena move toward equilibrium. Economists will often ask if equilibrium exists for a given phenomenon. If equilibrium does not exist, then the economist will try to identify the condition that must exist before equilibrium ("at rest") is achieved.

Ceteris Paribus

> *Ceteris paribus* is a Latin term that means "all other things held constant." *Ceteris paribus* is used to designate what we believe is the correct relationship between two variables.

Association and Causation

> Association is one thing, causation is another. Simply because two events are associated (in time, for example), it does not necessarily follow that one is the cause and the other is the effect.

The Fallacy of Composition

> The fallacy of composition is the erroneous view that what is good or true for the individual is necessarily good or true for the group.

Theory

> Economists build theories in order to explain and predict real-world events. Theories are necessarily abstractions from, as opposed to descriptions of, the real world.
> All theories abstract from reality; they focus on the critical variables that the theorist believes explain and predict the phenomenon at hand.
> The steps in building and testing a theory are:
> 1. Decide what it is you want to explain or predict.
> 2. Identify the variables that you believe are important to what you want to explain or predict.
> 3. State the assumptions of the theory.
> 4. State the hypothesis.
> 5. Test the theory by comparing its predictions against real-world events.

6. If the evidence supports the theory, then no further action is necessary, although it is a good idea to continue to examine the theory closely.
7. If the evidence rejects the theory, then either formulate an entirely new theory or amend the old theory in terms of its variables, assumptions, and hypothesis.

Major Macroeconomic Questions

> Almost every macroeconomist tries to answer three key questions: How does the economy work? What causes the ups and downs in the economy? What causes economic growth?

Macroeconomic Organizational Categories

> Three categories can help you organize what you learn in macroeconomics and give you a better idea of what macroeconomics is about: (1) the *P–Q* category, which involves the price level and Real GDP; (2) the self-regulating–economic-instability category, which concerns how the inherent properties of a market economy are viewed; and (3) the effective–ineffective category, which is related to fiscal policy and monetary policy.

Key Terms and Concepts

Scarcity	Disutility	Marginal Benefits
Economics	Bad	Marginal Costs
Positive Economics	Land	Decisions at the Margin
Normative Economics	Labor	Equilibrium
Microeconomics	Capital	*Ceteris Paribus*
Macroeconomics	Entrepreneurship	Fallacy of Composition
Utility	Rationing Device	Theory
Good	Opportunity Cost	Abstract

Questions and Problems

1. What is the similarity between the Robbins and Friedman definitions of economics?
2. The United States is considered a rich country because Americans can choose from an abundance of goods and services. How can there be scarcity in a land of abundance?
3. Give two examples for each of the following: (a) an intangible good, (b) a tangible good, (c) a bad.
4. What is the difference between the resource labor and the resource entrepreneurship?
5. Explain the link between scarcity and each of the following: (a) choice, (b) opportunity cost, (c) the need for a rationing device, (d) competition.
6. Is it possible for a person to incur an opportunity cost without spending any money? Explain.

7. Discuss the opportunity costs of attending college for four years. Is college more or less costly than you thought it was? Explain.
8. Explain the relationship between changes in opportunity cost and changes in behavior.
9. Smith says that we should eliminate all pollution in the world. Jones disagrees. Who is more likely to be an economist, Smith or Jones? Explain your answer.
10. A layperson says that a proposed government project simply costs too much and therefore shouldn't be undertaken. How might an economist's evaluation be different?
11. Economists say that individuals make decisions at the margin. What does this mean?

12. Smith lives in country A and earns $40,000 a year; Jones lives in country B and earns $50,000 a year. Will Jones be able to buy more goods and services than Smith?

13. Suppose the price of an ounce of gold is $300 in New York and $375 in London. Do you think the difference in gold prices is indicative of equilibrium? Explain your answer.

14. Why would economists assume "all other things are constant," or "nothing else changes," when, in reality, some other things may change?

15. Give three examples that illustrate that association is not causation.

16. Give three examples that illustrate the fallacy of composition.

17. Why do economists prefer to say that the evidence supports the theory instead of that the evidence proves the theory is correct?

18. Theories are abstractions from reality. What does this mean?

A picture is worth a thousand words. With this familiar saying in mind, economists construct their diagrams or graphs. With a few lines and a few points, much can be conveyed.

TWO-VARIABLE DIAGRAMS

Most of the diagrams in this book represent the relationship between two variables. Economists compare two variables to see how a change in one variable affects the other variable.

Suppose our two variables of interest are *consumption* and *income.* We want to show how consumption changes as income changes. Suppose we collect the data in Table 1. By simply looking at the data in the first two columns, we can see that as income rises (column 1), consumption rises (column 2). Suppose we want to show the relationship between income and consumption on a graph. We could place *income* on the horizontal axis, as in Exhibit 1, and *consumption* on the vertical axis. Point *A* represents income of $0 and consumption of $60, point *B* represents income of $100 and consumption of $120, and so on. If we draw a straight line through the various points we have plotted, we have a picture of the relationship between income and consumption, based on the data we collected.

Notice that our line in Exhibit 1 slopes upward from left to right. Thus, as income rises, so does consumption. For example, as you move from point *A* to point *B,* income rises from $0 to $100 and consumption rises from $60 to $120. The line in Exhibit 1 also shows that as income falls, so does consumption. For example, as you move from point *C* to point *B,* income falls from $200 to $100 and consumption falls from $180 to $120. When two variables—such as consumption and income—change in the same way, they are said to be **directly related.**

Now let's take a look at the data in Table 2. Our two variables are *price of compact discs (CDs)* and *quantity demanded of CDs.* By simply looking at the data in the first two columns, we see that as price falls (column 1), quantity demanded rises (column 2). Suppose we want to plot these data. We could place *price* (of CDs) on the vertical axis, as in Exhibit 2, and *quantity demanded* (of CDs) on the horizontal axis. Point *A* represents a price of $20 and a quantity demanded of 100, point *B* represents a price of $18 and a

Directly Related
Two variables are directly related if they change in the same way.

A Two-Variable Diagram Representing a Direct Relationship
In this exhibit, we have plotted the data in Table 1 and then connected the points with a straight line. The data represent a direct relationship: as one variable (say, income) rises, the other variable (consumption) rises too.

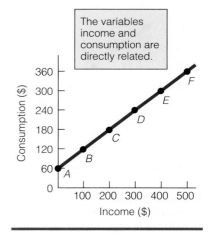

The variables income and consumption are directly related.

(1) When Income Is:	(2) Consumption Is:	(3) Point
$ 0	$ 60	A
100	120	B
200	180	C
300	240	D
400	300	E
500	360	F

table **1**

table **2**

(1) When Price of CDs Is:	(2) Quantity Demanded of CDs Is:	(3) Point
$20	100	A
18	120	B
16	140	C
14	160	D
12	180	E

exhibit **2**

A Two-Variable Diagram Representing an Inverse Relationship
In this exhibit, we have plotted the data in Table 2 and then connected the points with a straight line. The data represent an inverse relationship: as one variable (price) falls, the other variable (quantity demanded) rises.

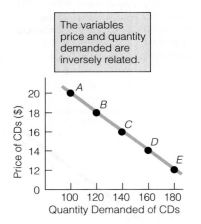

The variables price and quantity demanded are inversely related.

Inversely Related
Two variables are inversely related if they change in opposite ways.

Independent
Two variables are independent if as one changes, the other does not.

Slope
The ratio of the change in the variable on the vertical axis to the change in the variable on the horizontal axis.

quantity demanded of 120, and so on. If we draw a straight line through the various points we have plotted, we have a picture of the relationship between price and quantity demanded, based on the data in Table 2.

Notice that as price falls, quantity demanded rises. For example, as price falls from $20 to $18, quantity demanded rises from 100 to 120. Also as price rises, quantity demanded falls. For example, when price rises from $12 to $14, quantity demanded falls from 180 to 160.

When two variables—such as price and quantity demanded—change in opposite ways, they are said to be **inversely related.**

As you have seen so far, variables may be directly related (when one increases, the other also increases), or they may be inversely related (when one increases, the other decreases). Variables can also be **independent** of each other. This condition exists if as one variable changes, the other does not.

In Exhibit 3a, as the X variable rises, the Y variable remains the same (at 20). Obviously, the X and Y variables are independent of each other: as one changes, the other does not.

In Exhibit 3b, as the Y variable rises, the X variable remains the same (at 30). Again, we conclude that the X and Y variables are independent of each other: as one changes, the other does not.

SLOPE OF A LINE

It is often important not only to know *how* two variables are related but also to know *how much* one variable changes as the other variables change. To find out, we need only calculate the slope of the line. The **slope** is the ratio of the change in the variable on the vertical axis to the change in the variable on the horizontal axis. For example, if Y is on the vertical axis and X on the horizontal axis, the slope is equal to $\Delta Y/\Delta X$. (The symbol "Δ" means "change in.")

$$\text{Slope} = \frac{\Delta Y}{\Delta X}$$

Exhibit 4 shows four lines. In each case, we have calculated the slope. After studying (a)–(d), see if you can calculate the slope in each case.

SLOPE OF A LINE IS CONSTANT

Look again at the line in Exhibit 4a. We computed the slope between points A and B and found it to be -1. Suppose that instead of computing the slope between points A and B,

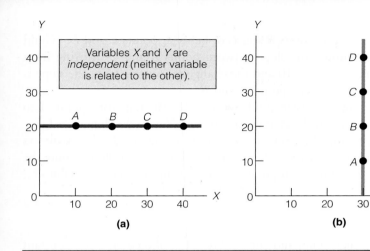

exhibit 3

Two Diagrams Representing Independence between Two Variables

In (a) and (b), the variables X and Y are independent: as one changes, the other does not.

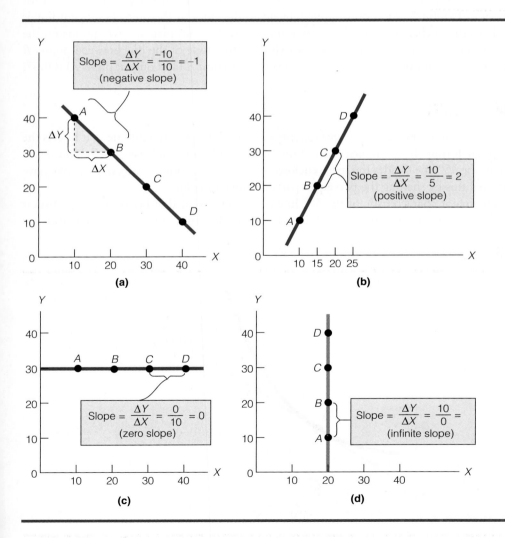

exhibit 4

Calculating Slopes

The slope of a line is the ratio of the change in the variable on the vertical axis to the change in the variable on the horizontal axis. In (a)–(d), we have calculated the slope.

we had computed the slope between points B and C or between points C and D. Would the slope still be -1? Let's compute the slope between points B and C. Moving from point B to point C, the change in Y is -10 and the change in X is $+10$. So, the slope is -1, which is what the slope was between points A and B.

Now let's compute the slope between points A and D. Moving from point A to point D, the change in Y is -30 and the change in X is $+30$. Again the slope is -1.

Our conclusion is that the slope between any two points on a (straight) line is always the same as the slope between any other two points. To see this for yourself, compute the slope between points A and B and between points A and C using the line in Exhibit 4b.

SLOPE OF A CURVE

Economic graphs use both straight lines and curves. The slope of a curve is not constant throughout as it is for a straight line. The slope of a curve varies from one point to another.

Calculating the slope of a curve at a given point requires two steps, as illustrated for point A in Exhibit 5. First, draw a line tangent to the curve at the point (a tangent line is one that just touches the curve but does not cross it). Second, pick any two points on the tangent line and determine the slope. In Exhibit 5 the slope of the line between points B and C is 0.67. It follows that the slope of the curve at point A (and only at point A) is 0.67.

THE 45° LINE

Economists sometimes use a *45° line* to represent data. This is a straight line that bisects the right angle formed by the intersection of the vertical and horizontal axes (see Exhibit 6). As a result, the 45° line divides the space enclosed by the two axes into *two equal parts*. We have illustrated this by shading the two equal parts in different colors.

The major characteristic of the 45° line is that any point that lies on it is equidistant from both the horizontal and vertical axes. For example, point A is exactly as far from the

---

Calculating the Slope of a Curve at a Particular Point
The slope of the curve at point A is 0.67. This is calculated by drawing a line tangent to the curve at point A and then determining the slope of the line.

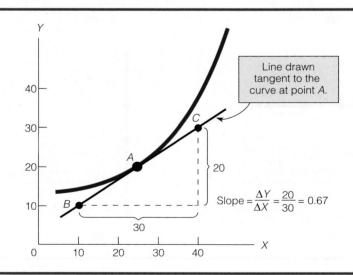

Line drawn tangent to the curve at point A.

$$\text{Slope} = \frac{\Delta Y}{\Delta X} = \frac{20}{30} = 0.67$$

horizontal axis as it is from the vertical axis. It follows that point *A* represents as much *X* as it does *Y*. Specifically, in the exhibit, point *A* represents 20 units of *X* and 20 units of *Y*.

PIE CHARTS

In numerous places in this text, you will come across a *pie chart*. A pie chart is a convenient way to represent the different parts of something that when added together equal the whole.

Let's consider a typical 24-hour weekday for Charles Myers. On a typical weekday, Charles spends 8 hours sleeping, 4 hours taking classes at the university, 4 hours working at his part-time job, 2 hours doing homework, 1 hour eating, 2 hours watching television, and 3 hours doing nothing in particular (we'll call it "hanging around"). Exhibit 7 shows the breakdown of a typical weekday for Charles in pie chart form.

Pie charts give a quick visual message as to rough percentage breakdowns and relative relationships. For example, it is easy to see in Exhibit 7 that Charles spends twice as much time working as doing homework.

BAR GRAPHS

The *bar graph* is another visual aid that economists use to convey relative relationships. Suppose we wanted to represent the gross domestic product for the United States in different years. The **gross domestic product (GDP)** is the value of the entire output produced annually within a country's borders. A bar graph can show the actual GDP for each year and can also provide a quick picture of the relative relationships between the

Gross Domestic Product (GDP)
The value of the entire output produced annually within a country's borders.

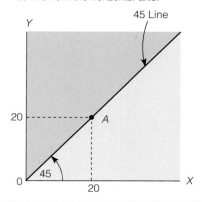

exhibit 6

The 45° Line
Any point on the 45° line is equidistant from both axes. For example, point *A* is the same distance from the vertical axis as it is from the horizontal axis.

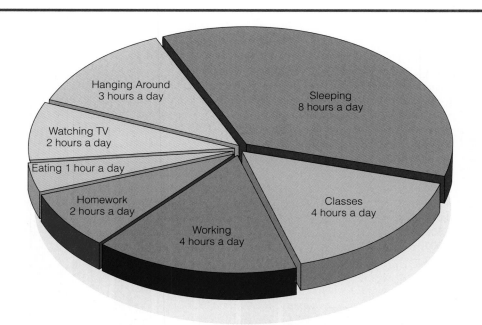

exhibit 7

A Pie Chart
The breakdown of activities for Charles Myers during a typical 24-hour weekday is represented in pie chart form.

GDP in different years. For example, it is easy to see in Exhibit 8 that the GDP in 1990 was more than double what it was in 1980.

LINE GRAPHS

Sometimes information is best and most easily displayed in a *line graph.* Line graphs are particularly useful for illustrating changes in a variable over some time period.

Suppose we want to illustrate the variations in average points per game for a college basketball team in different years. As you can see from Exhibit 9a, the basketball team has been on a roller coaster during the years 1992–2005. Perhaps the message transmitted here is that the team's performance has not been consistent from one year to the next.

Suppose we plot the data in Exhibit 9a again, except this time we use a different measurement scale on the vertical axis. As you can see in part (b), the variation in the performance of the basketball team appears much less pronounced than in part (a). In fact, we could choose some scale such that if we were to plot the data, we would end up with close to a straight line. Our point is simple: Data plotted in line graph form may convey different messages depending on the measurement scale used.

Sometimes economists show two line graphs on the same axes. Usually, they do this to draw attention to either (1) the *relationship* between the two variables or (2) the *difference* between the two variables. In Exhibit 10, the line graphs show the variation and trend in federal government outlays and tax receipts for the years 1994–2004 and draw attention to what has been happening to the "gap" between the two.

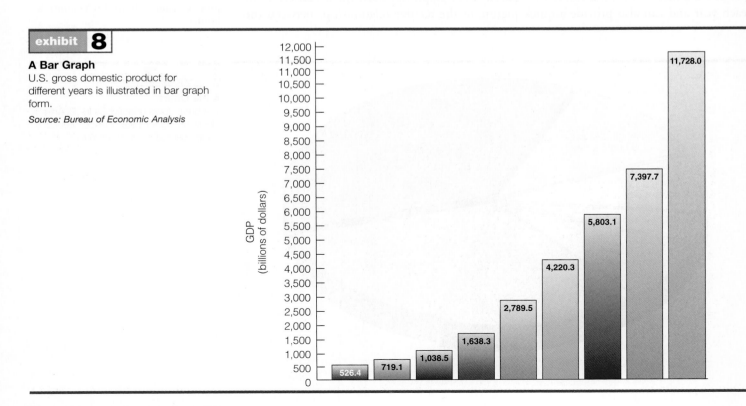

exhibit 8

A Bar Graph
U.S. gross domestic product for different years is illustrated in bar graph form.

Source: Bureau of Economic Analysis

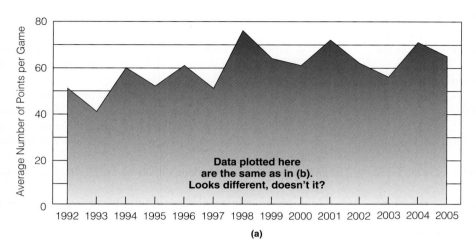

Data plotted here
are the same as in (b).
Looks different, doesn't it?

(a)

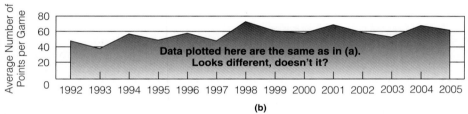

Data plotted here are the same as in (a).
Looks different, doesn't it?

(b)

exhibit 9

The Two Line Graphs Plot the Same Data

In (a) we plotted the average number of points per game for a college basketball team in different years. The variation between the years is pronounced. In (b) we plotted the same data as in (a), but the variation in the performance of the team appears much less pronounced than in (a).

Year	Average Number of Points per Game
1992	50
1993	40
1994	59
1995	51
1996	60
1997	50
1998	75
1999	63
2000	60
2001	71
2002	61
2003	55
2004	70
2005	64

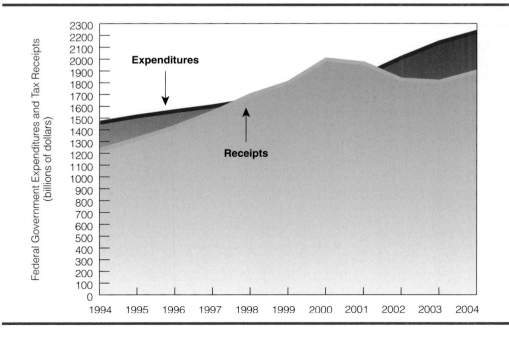

exhibit 10

Federal Government Expenditures and Tax Receipts, 1994–2004

Federal government expenditures and tax receipts are shown in line graph form for the period 1994–2004.

Source: Bureau of Economic Analysis

Appendix Summary

> Two variables are directly related if one variable rises as the other rises.
> An upward-sloping line (left to right) represents two variables that are directly related.
> Two variables are inversely related if one variable rises as the other falls.
> A downward-sloping line (left to right) represents two variables that are inversely related.
> Two variables are independent if one variable rises as the other remains constant.
> The slope of a line is the ratio of the change in the variable on the vertical axis to the change in the variable on the horizontal axis. The slope of a (straight) line is the same between every two points on the line.

> To determine the slope of a curve at a point, draw a line tangent to the curve at the point and then determine the slope of the tangent line.
> Any point on a 45° line is equidistant from the two axes.
> A pie chart is a convenient way to represent the different parts of something that when added together equal the whole. A pie chart visually shows rough percentage breakdowns and relative relationships.
> A bar graph is a convenient way to represent relative relationships.
> Line graphs are particularly useful for illustrating changes in a variable over some time period.

Questions and Problems

1. What type of relationship would you expect between the following: (a) sales of hot dogs and sales of hot dog buns, (b) the price of winter coats and sales of winter coats, (c) the price of personal computers and the production of personal computers, (d) sales of toothbrushes and sales of cat food, (e) the number of children in a family and the number of toys in a family.
2. Represent the following data in bar graph form.

Year	U.S. Money Supply (billions of dollars)
1999	1,124
2000	1,088
2001	1,179
2002	1,217
2003	1,293
2004	1,363

3. Plot the following data and specify the type of relationship between the two variables. (Place "price" on the vertical axis and "quantity demanded" on the horizontal axis.)

Price of Apples ($)	Quantity Demanded of Apples
0.25	1,000
0.50	800
0.70	700
0.95	500
1.00	400
1.10	350

4. In Exhibit 4a, determine the slope between points *C* and *D*.
5. In Exhibit 4b, determine the slope between points *A* and *D*.
6. What is the special characteristic of a 45° line?
7. What is the slope of a 45° line?
8. When would it be preferable to illustrate data using a pie chart instead of a bar graph?

9. Plot the following data and specify the type of relationship between the two variables. (Place "price" on the vertical axis and "quantity supplied" on the horizontal axis.)

Price of Apples ($)	Quantity Supplied of Apples
0.25	350
0.50	400
0.70	500
0.95	700
1.00	800
1.10	1,000

You are probably reading this textbook as part of your first college course in economics. You may be taking this course because you need it to satisfy the requirements in your major. Economics courses are sometimes required for students who plan to major in business, history, liberal studies, social science, or computer science. Of course, you may also be taking this course because you plan to major in economics.

If you are like many college students, you may complain that not enough information is available to students about the various majors at your college or university. For example, students who major in business sometimes say they are not quite certain what a business major is all about, but then they go on to add that majoring in business is a safe bet. "After all," they comment, "you are pretty sure of getting a job if you have a business degree. That's not always the case with other degrees."

Many college students choose their majors based on their high school courses. History majors sometimes say that they decided to major in history because they "liked history in high school." Similarly, chemistry, biology, and math majors say they chose chemistry, biology, or math as a college major because they liked studying chemistry, biology, or math in high school. In addition, if a student had a hard time with chemistry in high school and found it boring, then he doesn't usually want to major in chemistry in college. If a student found both math and economics easy and interesting in high school, then she is likely to major in math or economics.

Students also often look to the dollars at the end of the college degree. A student may enjoy history and want to learn more history in college but tell herself that she will earn a higher starting salary after graduation if she majors in computer science or engineering.

Thus, when choosing a major, students often consider (1) how much they enjoy studying a particular subject, (2) what they would like to see themselves doing in the future, and (3) income prospects.

Different people may weight these three factors differently. But no matter what weights you put on each of the factors, it is always better to have more information than less information, *ceteris paribus*. (We note *"ceteris paribus"* because it is not necessarily better having more information than less information if you have to pay more for the additional information than the additional information is worth. Who wants to pay $10 for a piece of information that only provides $1 in benefits?)

We believe this appendix is a fairly low-cost way of providing you with more information about an economics major than you currently have. We start by dispelling some of the misinformation you might possess about an economics major. Stated bluntly, some things that people think about an economics major and about a career in economics are just not true. For example, some people think that economics majors almost never study social relationships; instead, they only study such things as inflation, interest rates, and unemployment. Not true. Economics majors study some of the same things that sociologists, historians, psychologists, and political scientists study. We also provide you with some information about the major that you may not have.

Next, we tell you the specifics of the economics major—what courses you study if you are an economics major, how many courses you are likely to have to take, and more.

Finally, we tell you something about a career in economics. Okay, so you have opted to become an economics major. But the day will come when you have your degree in hand. What's next? What is your starting salary likely to be? What will you be doing? Are you going to be happy doing what economists do? (If you never thought economics was about happiness, you already have some misinformation about economics. Contrary to what most laypeople think, economics is not just about money. It is about happiness too.)

FIVE MYTHS ABOUT ECONOMICS AND AN ECONOMICS MAJOR

Myth 1: Economics is all mathematics and statistics. Some students choose not to major in economics because they think economics is all mathematics and statistics. Math and statistics are used in economics, but at the undergraduate degree level, the math and statistics are certainly not overwhelming. Economics majors are usually required to take one statistics course and one math course (usually an introductory calculus course). Even students who say, "Math isn't my subject" are sometimes happy with the amount of math they need in economics. Fact is, at the undergraduate level at many colleges and universities, economics is not a very math-intensive course of study. There are many diagrams in economics, but there is not a large amount of math.

A proviso: The amount of math in the economics curriculum varies across colleges and universities. Some economics departments do not require their students to learn much math or statistics, but others do. Speaking for the majority of departments, we still hold to our original point that there isn't really that much math or statistics in economics at the undergraduate level. The graduate level is a different story.

Myth 2: Economics is only about inflation, interest rates, unemployment, and other such things. If you study economics at college and then go on to become a practicing economist, no doubt people will ask you certain questions when they learn your chosen profession. Here are some of the questions they ask:

- Do you think the economy is going to pick up?
- Do you think the economy is going to slow down?
- What stocks would you recommend?
- Do you think interest rates are going to fall?
- Do you think interest rates are going to rise?
- What do you think about buying bonds right now? Is it a good idea?

People ask these kinds of questions because most people believe that economists only study stocks, bonds, interest rates, inflation, unemployment, and so on. Well, economists do study these things. But these topics are only a tiny part of what economists study. It is not hard to find many economists today, both inside and outside academia, who spend most of their time studying anything but inflation, unemployment, stocks, bonds, and so on.

As we hinted earlier, much of what economists study may surprise you. There are economists who use their economic tools and methods to study crime, marriage, divorce, sex, obesity, addiction, sports, voting behavior, bureaucracies, Presidential elections, and much more. In short, today's economics is not your grandfather's economics. Many more topics are studied today in economics than were studied in your grandfather's time.

Myth 3: People become economists only if they want to "make money." Awhile back we asked a few well-respected and well-known economists what got them interested in economics. Here is what some of them had to say:[1]

Gary Becker, the 1992 winner of the Nobel Prize in Economics, said: "I got interested [in economics] when I was an undergraduate in college. I came into college with a strong interest in mathematics, and at the same time with a strong commitment to do something to help society. I learned in the first economics course I took that economics could deal rigorously, à la mathematics, with social problems. That stimulated me because in economics I saw that I could combine both the mathematics and my desire to do something to help society."

Vernon Smith, the 2002 winner of the Nobel Prize in Economics, said: "My father's influence started me in science and engineering at Cal Tech, but my mother, who was active in socialist politics, probably accounts for the great interest I found in economics when I took my first introductory course."

Alice Rivlin, an economist and former member of the Federal Reserve Board, said: "My interest in economics grew out of concern for improving public policy, both domestic and international. I was a teenager in the tremendously idealistic period after World War II when it seemed terribly important to get nations working together to solve the world's problems peacefully."

Allan Meltzer said: "Economics is a social science. At its best it is concerned with ways (1) to improve well being by allowing individuals the freedom to achieve their personal aims or goals and (2) to harmonize their individual interests. I find working on such issues challenging, and progress is personally rewarding."

Robert Solow, the 1987 winner of the Nobel Prize in Economics, said: "I grew up in the 1930s and it was very hard not to be interested in economics. If you were a high school student in the 1930s, you were conscious of the fact that our economy was in deep trouble and no one knew what to do about it."

Charles Plosser said: "I was an engineer as an undergraduate with little knowledge of economics. I went to the University of Chicago Graduate School of Business to get an MBA and there became fascinated with economics. I was impressed with the seriousness with which economics was viewed as a way of organizing one's thoughts about the world to address interesting questions and problems."

Walter Williams said: "I was a major in sociology in 1963 and I concluded that it was not very rigorous. Over the summer I was reading a book by W.E.B. DuBois, *Black Reconstruction,* and somewhere in the book it said something along the lines that blacks could not melt into the mainstream of American society until they understood economics, and that was something that got me interested in economics."

Murray Weidenbaum said: "A specific professor got me interested in economics. He was very prescient: He correctly noted that while lawyers dominated the policy-making

---

1. See various interviews in Roger A. Arnold, *Economics, 2nd edition* (St. Paul, Minnesota: West Publishing Company, 1992).

process up until then (the 1940s), in the future economics would be an important tool for developing public policy. And he was right."

Irma Adelman said: "I hesitate to say because it sounds arrogant. My reason [for getting into economics] was that I wanted to benefit humanity. And my perception at the time was that economic problems were the most important problems that humanity has to face. That is what got me into economics and into economic development."

Lester Thurow said: "[I got interested in economics because of] the belief, some would see it as naïve belief, that economics was a profession where it would be possible to help make the world better."

Myth 4: Economics wasn't very interesting in high school, so it's not going to be very interesting in college. A typical high school economics course emphasizes consumer economics and spends much time discussing this topic. Students learn about credit cards, mortgage loans, budgets, buying insurance, renting an apartment, and other such things. These are important topics because not knowing the "ins and outs" of such things can make your life much harder. Still, many students come away from a high school economics course thinking that economics is always and everywhere about consumer topics.

However, a high school economics course and a college economics course are usually as different as day and night. Simply leaf through this book and look at the variety of topics covered compared to the topics you might have covered in your high school economics course. Go on to look at texts used in other economics courses—courses that range from law and economics to history of economic thought to international economics to sports economics—and you will see what we mean.

Myth 5: Economics is a lot like business, but business is more marketable. Although business and economics have some common topics, much that one learns in economics is not taught in business and much that one learns in business is not taught in economics. The area of intersection between business and economics is not large.

Still, many people think otherwise. And so thinking that business and economics are "pretty much the same thing," they often choose to major in the subject they believe has greater marketability—which they believe is business.

Well, consider the following:

1. A few years ago *BusinessWeek* magazine asked the chief executive officers (CEOs) of major companies what they thought was the best undergraduate degree. Their first choice was engineering. Their second choice was economics. Economics scored higher than business administration.
2. The National Association of Colleges and Employers undertook a survey in the spring of 2004 in which they identified the starting salary offers in different disciplines. The starting salary in economics/finance was $43,000. The starting salary in business administration was 15 percent lower at $36,515.

WHAT AWAITS YOU AS AN ECONOMICS MAJOR?

If you become an economics major, what courses will you take? What are you going to study?

At the lower-division level, economics majors must take both the principles of macroeconomics course and the principles of microeconomics course. They usually also take a statistics course and a math course (usually calculus).

At the upper-division level, they must take intermediate microeconomics and intermediate macroeconomics, along with a certain number of electives. Some of the elective courses include: (1) money and banking, (2) law and economics, (3) history of economic thought, (4) public finance, (5) labor economics, (6) international economics, (7) antitrust and regulation, (8) health economics, (9) economics of development, (10) urban and regional economics, (11) econometrics, (12) mathematical economics, (13) environmental economics, (14) public choice, (15) global managerial economics, (16) economic approach to politics and sociology, (17) sports economics, and many more courses. Most economics majors take between 12 and 15 economics courses.

One of the attractive things about studying economics is that you will acquire many of the skills employers highly value. First, you will have the quantitative skills that are important in many business and government positions. Second, you will acquire the writing skills necessary in almost all lines of work. Third, and perhaps most importantly, you will develop the thinking skills that almost all employers agree are critical to success.

A study published in the 1998 edition of the *Journal of Economic Education* ranked economics majors as having the highest average scores on the Law School Admission Test (LSAT). Also, consider the words of the Royal Economic Society: "One of the things that makes economics graduates so employable is that the subject teaches you to think in a careful and precise way. The fundamental economic issue is how society decides to allocate its resources: how the costs and benefits of a course of action can be evaluated and compared, and how appropriate choices can be made. A degree in economics gives a training in decision making principles, providing a skill applicable in a very wide range of careers."

Keep in mind, too, that economics is one of the most popular majors at some of the most respected universities in the country. Since the mid-1990s, the number of students majoring in economics has been rising. Economics is the most popular major at Harvard University, where 964 students majored in the subject in 2005. The number of economics majors at Columbia University has risen 67 percent since 1995.

WHAT DO ECONOMISTS DO?

Employment for economists is projected to grow between 21 and 35 percent between 2000 and 2010. According to the *Occupational Outlook Handbook:*

> Opportunities for economists should be best in private industry, especially in research, testing, and consulting firms, as more companies contract out for economic research services. The growing complexity of the global economy, competition, and increased reliance on quantitative methods for analyzing the current value of future funds, business trends, sales, and purchasing should spur demand for economists. The growing need for economic analyses in virtually every industry should result in additional jobs for economists.

Today, economists work in many varied fields. Here are some of the fields and some of the positions economists hold in those fields:

Education
College Professor
Researcher
High School Teacher

Journalism
Researcher
Industry Analyst
Economic Analyst

Accounting
Analyst
Auditor
Researcher
Consultant

General Business
Chief Executive Officer
Business Analyst
Marketing Analyst
Business Forecaster
Competitive Analyst

Government
Researcher
Analyst
Speechwriter
Forecaster

Financial Services
Business Journalist
International Analyst

Newsletter Editor
Broker
Investment Banker

Banking
Credit Analyst
Loan Officer
Investment Analyst
Financial Manager

Other
Business Consultant
Independent Forecaster
Freelance Analyst
Think Tank Analyst
Entrepreneur

Economists do a myriad of things. For example, in business, economists often analyze economic conditions, make forecasts, offer strategic planning initiatives, collect and analyze data, predict exchange rate movements, and review regulatory policies, among other things. In government, economists collect and analyze data, analyze international economic situations, research monetary conditions, advise on policy, and much more. As private consultants, economists work with accountants, business executives, government officials, educators, financial firms, labor unions, state and local governments, and others.

Median annual earnings of economists were $64,830 in 2000. The middle 50 percent earned between $47,370 and $87,890. The lowest 10 percent earned less than $35,690, and the highest 10 percent earned more than $114,580.

PLACES TO FIND MORE INFORMATION

If you are interested in an economics major and perhaps a career in economics, here are some places where you can go and some people you can speak with to acquire more information:

- To learn about the economics curriculum, we urge you to speak with the economics professors at your college or university. Ask them what courses you would have to take as an economics major. Ask them what elective courses are available. In addition, ask them why they chose to study economics. What is it about economics that interested them?
- For more information about salaries and what economists do, you may want to visit the *Occupational Outlook Handbook* Web site at http://www.bls.gov/oco/.
- For starting salary information, you may want to visit the National Association of Colleges and Employers Web site at http://www.naceweb.org/.
- To see a list of famous people who have majored in economics, go to http://www.marietta.edu/~ema/econ/famous.html.

CONCLUDING REMARKS

Choosing a major is a big decision and therefore should not be made too quickly and without much thought. In this short appendix, we have provided you with some information about an economics major and a career in economics. Economics may not be for everyone (in fact, economists would say that if it were, many of the benefits of specialization would be lost), but it may be right for you. Economics is a major where many of today's most marketable skills are acquired—the skills of good writing, quantitative analysis, and thinking. It is a major in which professors and students daily ask and answer some very interesting and relevant questions. It is a major that is highly regarded by employers. It may just be the right major for you. Give it some thought.

© Photograhper's Choice/Getty Images

Setting the Scene

More than six billion people are living on earth. At any one time, millions of conversations are taking place. Imagine you could listen in on any of the conversations by turning a dial, much like you turn the dial on a radio. What might you hear?

The White House, 11 months before the President will run for reelection

First presidential advisor:

We've been spending a lot of money on defense, and that's probably what the American people want, but I can't help but think about what Eduard Shevardnadze said in 1990. You remember, he was the Soviet foreign minister. He said the Soviet Union collapsed because of the conflict between the Kremlin and the people. The Kremlin wanted "more guns," and the people wanted "more butter," but it was impossible to get more of both. Something had to give, and so it did: the Soviet Union imploded.

Second presidential advisor:

You think we increased defense spending too much, too fast?

First presidential advisor:

That's what the president's opponents are going to say.

Apt. 4B, Tropicana Apartments, three blocks from UMKC (University of Missouri Kansas City)

Bob:

I have two final exams tomorrow—biology at 9 and calculus at 2. I think it's come down to choosing where I want to get an A. I don't have enough study time tonight to get A's in both courses.

Jim (Bob's roommate, who is also studying for finals):

If we could only produce "more time" the same way people produce more watches or more cars. I bet we could sell *that* for a pretty penny.

Outside of Macy's, Mall of America, Bloomington, Minnesota

Winona:

It was a good thing that sweater was on sale.

Nancy:

I still think I was ripped off. Even at the sale price, it was too expensive.

Starbucks, 113 Mill Plain Rd., Danbury, Connecticut

Terrence:

Although Mark's a smart guy, he doesn't even know how to change the oil in his car. I mean, you'd think a person with a Ph.D. would be smart enough to know how to change the oil in his car.

Karen:

I see that kind of thing all the time. Some of the smartest people are just plain stupid.

eBay, Inc., San Jose, California

Jayant (who works at eBay):

What eBay did really wasn't that hard.

Helena (who also works at eBay):

I just wish I had done it.

? **How would an economist look at these events? Later in the chapter, discussions based on the following questions will help you analyze the scene the way an economist would.**

- What do scarcity and choice have to do with the collapse of the Soviet Union and the reelection prospects of the President of the United States?
- Why can't Bob get A's in both biology and calculus, and what does Jim's desire to produce "more time" tell us about life?

- Why did Nancy buy the sweater if she felt she was being "ripped off"?
- Why doesn't a smart guy with a Ph.D. know how to change the oil in his car?
- What did eBay do that really wasn't that hard?

THE PRODUCTION POSSIBILITIES FRONTIER

In order to analyze the various aspects of production, economists find it helpful to define a model or framework in which to examine production. This section introduces and discusses such a framework—the production possibilities frontier (PPF).

The Straight-Line PPF: Constant Opportunity Costs

Assume the following: (1) Only two goods can be produced in an economy, computers and television sets. (2) The opportunity cost of 1 television set is 1 computer. (3) As more of one good is produced, the opportunity cost between television sets and computers is constant.

In Exhibit 1a, we have identified six combinations of computers and television sets that can be produced in our economy. For example, combination *A* is 50,000 computers and 0 television sets, combination *B* is 40,000 computers and 10,000 television sets, and so on. We plotted these six combinations of computers and television sets in Exhibit 1b. Each combination represents a different point. For example, the combination of 50,000 computers and 0 television sets is represented by point *A*. The line that connects points *A*–*F* is the production possibilities frontier (PPF). A **production possibilities frontier** represents the combination of two goods that can be produced in a certain period of time, under the conditions of a given state of technology and fully employed resources.

Production Possibilities Frontier (PPF)
Represents the possible combinations of the two goods that can be produced in a certain period of time, under the conditions of a given state of technology and fully employed resources.

The production possibilities frontier is a *straight line* in this instance because the opportunity cost of producing computers and television sets is *constant.*

Straight line PPF = Constant opportunity costs

exhibit 1

Production Possibilities Frontier (Constant Opportunity Costs)
The economy can produce any of the six combinations of computers and television sets in part (a). We have plotted these combinations in part (b). The production possibilities frontier in part (b) is a straight line because the opportunity cost of producing either good is constant: for *every* 1 computer not produced, 1 television set is produced.

Combination	Computers	and (number of units per year)	Television Sets	Point in Part (b)
A	50,000	and	0	*A*
B	40,000	and	10,000	*B*
C	30,000	and	20,000	*C*
D	20,000	and	30,000	*D*
E	10,000	and	40,000	*E*
F	0	and	50,000	*F*

(a)

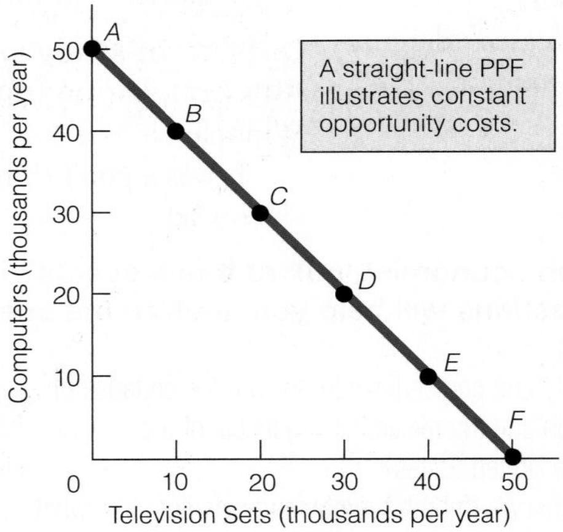

(b)

For example, if the economy were to move from point *A* to point *B*, or from *B* to *C*, and so on, the opportunity cost of each good would remain constant at 1 for 1. To illustrate, at point *A*, 50,000 computers and 0 television sets are produced. At point *B*, 40,000 computers and 10,000 television sets are produced.

> Point *A*: 50,000 computers, 0 television sets
> Point *B*: 40,000 computers, 10,000 television sets

We conclude that for every 10,000 computers not produced, 10,000 television sets are produced—a ratio of 1 to 1. The opportunity cost—1 computer for 1 television set—that exists between points *A* and *B* also exists between points *B* and *C*, *C* and *D*, *D* and *E*, and *E* and *F*. In other words, opportunity cost is constant at 1 computer for 1 television set.

The Bowed-Outward (Concave-Downward) PPF: Increasing Opportunity Costs

Assume two things: (1) Only two goods can be produced in an economy, computers and television sets. (2) As more of one good is produced, the opportunity cost between computers and television sets changes.

In Exhibit 2a, we have identified four combinations of computers and television sets that can be produced in our economy. For example, combination *A* is 50,000 computers and 0 television sets, combination *B* is 40,000 computers and 20,000 television sets, and so on. We plotted these four combinations of computers and television sets in Exhibit 2b. Each combination represents a different point. The curved line that connects points *A–D* is the production possibilities frontier.

Combination	Computers	and	Television Sets	Point in Part (b)
		(number of units per year)		
A	50,000	and	0	*A*
B	40,000	and	20,000	*B*
C	25,000	and	40,000	*C*
D	0	and	60,000	*D*

(a)

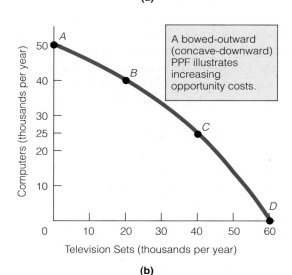

> A bowed-outward (concave-downward) PPF illustrates increasing opportunity costs.

(b)

exhibit 2

Production Possibilities Frontier (Changing Opportunity Costs)
The economy can produce any of the four combinations of computers and television sets in part (a). We have plotted these combinations in part (b). The production possibilities frontier in part (b) is bowed outward because the opportunity cost of producing television sets increases as more television sets are produced.

In this case, the production possibilities frontier is *bowed outward* (concave downward) because the opportunity cost of television sets *increases* as more sets are produced.

Bowed outward PPF = Increasing opportunity costs

To illustrate, let's start at point *A,* where the economy is producing 50,000 computers and 0 television sets, and move to point *B,* where the economy is producing 40,000 computers and 20,000 television sets.

Point *A:* 50,000 computers, 0 television sets
Point *B:* 40,000 computers, 20,000 television sets

What is the opportunity cost of a television set over this range? We see that 20,000 more television sets are produced by moving from point *A* to point *B but at the cost of only 10,000 computers.* This means for every 1 television set produced, 1/2 computer is forfeited. Thus, the opportunity cost of 1 television set is 1/2 computer.

Now let's move from point *B,* where the economy is producing 40,000 computers and 20,000 television sets, to point *C,* where the economy is producing 25,000 computers and 40,000 television sets.

Point *B:* 40,000 computers, 20,000 television sets
Point *C:* 25,000 computers, 40,000 television sets

What is the opportunity cost of a television set over this range? In this case, 20,000 more television sets are produced by moving from point *B* to point *C but at the cost of 15,000 computers.* This means for every 1 television set produced, 3/4 computer is forfeited. Thus, the opportunity cost of 1 television set is 3/4 computer.

What statement can we make about the opportunity costs of producing television sets? Obviously, as the economy produces more television sets, the opportunity cost of producing television sets increases. This gives us the bowed-outward production possibilities frontier in Exhibit 2b.

Law of Increasing Opportunity Costs

We know that the shape of the production possibilities frontier depends on whether opportunity costs (1) are constant or (2) increase as more of a good is produced. In Exhibit 1b, the production possibilities frontier is a straight line; in Exhibit 2b, it is bowed outward (curved). In the real world, most production possibilities frontiers are bowed outward. This means that for most goods, the opportunity costs increase as more of the good is produced. This is referred to as the **law of increasing opportunity costs.**

Law of Increasing Opportunity Costs
As more of a good is produced, the opportunity costs of producing that good increase.

But why (for most goods) do the opportunity costs increase as more of the good is produced? The answer is because people have varying abilities. For example, some people are better suited to building houses than other people are. When a construction company first starts building houses, it employs the people who are most skilled at house building. The most skilled persons can build houses at lower opportunity costs than others can. But as the construction company builds more houses, it finds that it has already employed the most skilled builders, so it must employ those who are less skilled at house building. These people build houses at higher opportunity costs. Where three skilled house builders could build a house in a month, as many as seven unskilled builders may be required to build it in the same length of time. Exhibit 3 summarizes the points in this section.

We start with the assumption that not all people can build houses at the same opportunity cost.

When houses are first built, only the people who *can* build them at (relatively) low opportunity costs *will* build them.

As increasingly more houses are built, people with higher opportunity costs of building houses will start building houses.

This is the same as saying that as more houses are built, the opportunity cost of building houses increases.

And this is why the PPF for houses and good *X* is bowed outward (concave downward). See diagram at left.

Notice that when we go from building 60 to 70 houses (10 more houses), we forfeit 5 units of good *X*; but when we go from building 110 to 120 houses (again, 10 more houses), we forfeit 20 units of good *X*.

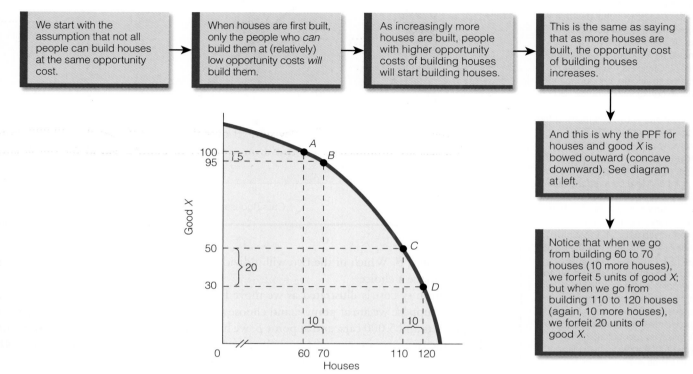

exhibit 3

A Summary Statement About Increasing Opportunity Costs and a Production Possibilities Frontier That Is Bowed Outward (Concave Downward)
Many of the points about increasing opportunity costs and a production possibilities frontier that is bowed outward are summarized here.

Economic Concepts Within a PPF Framework
The PPF framework is useful for illustrating and working with economic concepts. This section discusses numerous economic concepts in terms of the PPF framework.

Scarcity
Recall that scarcity is the condition where wants (for goods) are greater than the resources available to satisfy those wants. The finiteness of resources is graphically portrayed by the PPF in Exhibit 4. The frontier tells us: "At this point in time, that's as far as you can go. You cannot go any farther. You are limited to choosing any combination of the two goods on the frontier or below it."

The PPF separates the production possibilities of an economy into two regions: (1) an *attainable region,* which consists of the points on the PPF itself and all points below it (this region includes points *A–F*) and (2) an *unattainable region,* which consists of the points above and beyond the PPF (such as point *G*). Recall that scarcity implies that some things are attainable and some things are unattainable. Point *A* on the PPF is attainable, as is point *F;* point *G* is not.

Choice and Opportunity Cost
Choice and opportunity cost are also shown in Exhibit 4. Note that within the attainable region, individuals must choose the combination of the two goods they want to produce. Obviously, hundreds of different combinations exist, but let's consider only two, represented

exhibit **4**

One PPF, Five Economic Concepts
The PPF illustrates five economic concepts: (1) Scarcity is illustrated by the frontier itself. Implicit in the concept of scarcity is the idea that we can have some things but not all things. The PPF separates an attainable region from an unattainable region. (2) Choice is represented by our having to decide among the many attainable combinations of the two goods. For example, will we choose the combination of goods represented by point *A* or by point *B*? (3) Opportunity cost is most easily seen as movement from one point to another, such as movement from point *A* to point *B*. More cars are available at point *B* than at point *A*, but fewer television sets are available. In short, the opportunity cost of more cars is fewer television sets. (4) Productive efficiency is represented by the points on the PPF (such as *A–E*), while productive inefficiency is represented by any point below the PPF (such as *F*). (5) Unemployment (in terms of resources being unemployed) exists at any productive inefficient point (such as *F*), whereas resources are fully employed at any productive efficient point (such as *A–E*).

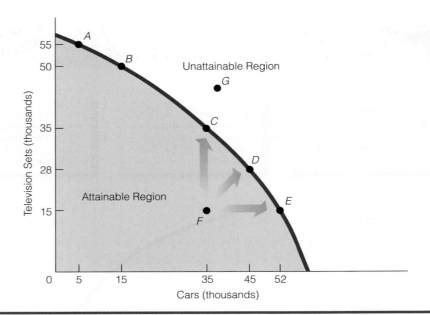

Productive Efficiency
The condition where the maximum output is produced with given resources and technology.

by points *A* and *B*. Which of the two will individuals choose? They can't be at both points; they must make a choice.

Opportunity cost is illustrated as we move from one point to another on the PPF in Exhibit 4. Suppose we are at point *A* and choose to move to point *B*. At *A*, we have 55,000 television sets and 5,000 cars, and at point *B*, we have 50,000 television sets and 15,000 cars. What is the opportunity cost of a car? Because 10,000 *more* cars come at a cost of 5,000 *fewer* television sets, the opportunity cost of 1 car is 1/2 television set.

Productive Efficiency
Economists often say that an economy is ~~productive efficient~~ if it is producing the maximum output with given resources and technology. In Exhibit 4, points *A, B, C, D,* and *E* are all productive efficient points. Notice that all these points lie *on* the production possibilities frontier. In other words, we are getting the most (in terms of output) from what we have (in terms of available resources and technology).

ANALYZING THE SCENE

Question from Setting the Scene: Why can't Bob get A's in both biology and calculus, and what does Jim's desire to produce "more time" tell us about life?
Bob says he has to choose between an A in biology and an A in calculus. To make that statement, Bob must be thinking in terms of his PPF for "producing grades." His "grades PPF" would look like the straight line in Exhibit 1. Bob's likely biology grade is on the vertical axis (starting with an F at the origin and moving up to an A), and his calculus grade is on the horizontal axis (again starting with an F at the origin and moving across to an A). When Bob says that he must choose where he wants to get an A, he is saying that there is no point on his "grades PPF" that represents an A in both courses (given his resources, such as time, and his state of technology, such as his ability to learn the material). In other words, the point that represents two A's is in his *unattainable region,* and the point that represents one A and, say, one B, is in his *attainable region.*

Jim's desire to produce "more time" tells us that he feels there is not enough of a particular resource (time) in which to accomplish all his goals. More resources means more goals can be met and fewer tradeoffs will be incurred.

Question from Setting the Scene: What do scarcity and choice have to do with the collapse of the Soviet Union and the reelection prospects of the President of the United States?

The first presidential advisor tells a story about Eduard Shevardnadze. The former Soviet foreign minister said the Soviet Union had collapsed because of a conflict between the Kremlin and the Soviet people. What was the conflict? The conflict concerned where the economy of the Soviet Union chose to be located on its PPF. The Kremlin wanted a point that represented "more guns" (more military goods) and "less butter" (fewer civilian or consumer goods), whereas the people wanted a point that represented "fewer guns" and "more butter."

Why tell the story? Because the first presidential advisor obviously believes that the President will pay a political cost if his policies are viewed as locating the U.S. economy at a point on the U.S. PPF that the vast majority of voting Americans do not prefer.

It follows that an economy is **productive inefficient** if it is producing *less* than the maximum output with given resources and technology. In Exhibit 4, point *F* is a productive inefficient point. It lies *below* the production possibilities frontier; it is below the outer limit of what is possible. In other words, we could produce more goods with the resources we have available to us. Or we can get more of one good without getting less of another good.

To illustrate, suppose we move from inefficient point *F* to efficient point *C.* We produce more television sets and no fewer cars. What if we move from *F* to *D?* We produce more television sets and more cars. Finally, if we move from *F* to *E,* we produce more cars and no fewer television sets. Thus, moving from *F* can give us more of at least one good and no less of another good. In short, *productive inefficiency implies that gains are possible in one area without losses in another.*

Unemployed Resources

When the economy exhibits productive inefficiency, it is not producing the maximum output with the available resources and technology. One reason may be that the economy is not using all its resources—that is, some of its resources are unemployed, as at point *F* in Exhibit 4.

When the economy exhibits productive efficiency, it is producing the maximum output with the available resources and technology. This means it is using all its resources to produce goods—its resources are fully employed, none are unemployed. At the productive efficient points *A–E* in Exhibit 4, there are no unemployed resources.

Economic Growth

Economic growth refers to the increased productive capabilities of an economy. It is illustrated by a shift outward in the production possibilities frontier. Two major factors that affect economic growth are an increase in the quantity of resources and an advance in technology.

With an increase in the quantity of resources (say, through a new discovery of resources), it is possible to produce a greater quantity of output. In Exhibit 5, an increase in the quantity of resources makes it possible to produce both more military goods and more civilian goods. Thus, the PPF shifts outward from PPF$_1$ to PPF$_2$.

Technology refers to the body of skills and knowledge concerning the use of resources in production. An advance in technology commonly refers to the ability to produce more output with a fixed quantity of resources or the ability to produce the same output with a smaller quantity of resources.

Productive Inefficiency
The condition where less than the maximum output is produced with given resources and technology. Productive inefficiency implies that more of one good can be produced without any less of another good being produced.

Technology
The body of skills and knowledge concerning the use of resources in production. An advance in technology commonly refers to the ability to produce more output with a fixed amount of resources or the ability to produce the same output with fewer resources.

---

exhibit 5

Economic Growth Within a PPF Framework
An increase in resources or an advance in technology can increase the production capabilities of an economy, leading to economic growth and a shift outward in the production possibilities frontier.

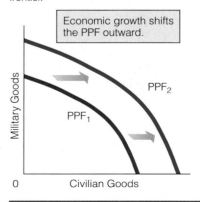

Economic growth shifts the PPF outward.

exhibit **6**

Economic Growth Ends Political Battles, for a While

The economy is at point A, but conservatives want to be at point C and liberals want to be at point B. As a result, there is a political tug-of-war. Both conservatives and liberals can get the quantity of the good they want through economic growth. This is represented by point D on PPF$_2$.

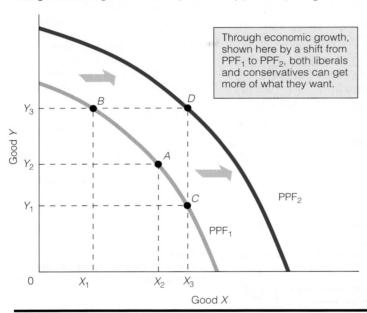

Through economic growth, shown here by a shift from PPF$_1$ to PPF$_2$, both liberals and conservatives can get more of what they want.

Liberals, Conservatives, and the PPF

Liberals and conservatives often pull in different economic directions. To illustrate, suppose our economy is currently at point A in Exhibit 6, producing X$_2$ of good X and Y$_2$ of good Y. Conservatives prefer point C to point A and try to convince the liberals and the rest of the nation to move to point C. The liberals, however, prefer point B to point A and try to persuade the conservatives and the rest of the nation to move to point B. Thus, we have a political tug-of-war.

Is there a way that both groups can get what they want? Yes, if there is economic growth so that the production possibilities frontier shifts outward from PPF$_1$ to PPF$_2$. On PPF$_2$, point D represents the quantity of X that conservatives want and the quantity of Y that liberals want. At point D, conservatives have X$_3$ units of good X, which is what they would have had at point C, and liberals have Y$_3$ units of good Y, which is what they would have had at point B. Through economic growth, both conservatives and liberals can get what they want. The political tug-of-war will cease—at least for a while.

We say "for a while" because even at point D, there is scarcity. The wants of liberals and conservatives are both greater than the resources available to satisfy those wants. Starting at point D, liberals might push for a movement up the production possibilities frontier and conservatives for a movement down it.

Question to ponder: Does an increase in a family's income have the same effect as economic growth in a society? Does it eliminate or reduce the family tug-of-war—at least for a while?

Suppose an advance in technology allows more military goods and more civilian goods to be produced with the same quantity of resources. As a result, the PPF in Exhibit 5 shifts outward from PPF$_1$ to PPF$_2$. The outcome is the same as when the quantity of resources is increased.

SELF-TEST *(Answers to Self-Test questions are in the Self-Test Appendix.)*

1. What does a straight-line production possibilities frontier (PPF) represent? What does a bowed-outward PPF represent?
2. What does the law of increasing costs have to do with a bowed-outward PPF?
3. A politician says, "If you elect me, we can get more of everything we want." Under what condition(s) is the politician telling the truth?
4. In an economy, only one combination of goods is productive efficient. True or false? Explain your answer.

TRADE OR EXCHANGE

Trade or exchange is the process of giving up one thing for something else. Usually, money is traded for goods and services. Trade is all around us; we are involved with it every day. Few of us, however, have considered the full extent of trade.

Trade (Exchange)
The process of giving up one thing for something else.

The Purpose of Trade

Why do people trade? Why do they exchange things? They do so in order to make themselves better off. When a person voluntarily trades $100 for a jacket, she is saying "I prefer to have the jacket instead of the $100." And, of course, when the seller of the jacket voluntarily sells the jacket for $100, he is saying, "I prefer to have the $100 instead of the jacket." In short, through trade or exchange, each person gives up something he or she values less for something he or she values more.

You can think of trade in terms of utility or satisfaction. Imagine a utility scale that goes from 1 to 10, with 10 being the highest utility you can achieve. Now suppose you currently have $40 in your wallet and you are at 7 on the utility scale. A few minutes later, you are in a store looking at some new CDs. The price of each is $10. You end up buying four CDs for $40.

Before you made the trade, you were at 7 on the utility scale. Are you still at 7 on the utility scale after you traded your $40 for the four CDs? The likely answer is no. If you expected to have the same utility after the trade as you did before, it is unlikely you would have traded your $40 for the four CDs. The only reason you entered into the trade is that you *expected* to be better off after the trade than you were before the trade. In other words, you thought trading your $40 for the four CDs would move you up the utility scale from 7 to, say, 8.

Periods Relevant to Trade

As the previous example makes clear, there are various time periods relevant to the trading process. We discuss the three relevant time periods next.

Before the Trade

Before a trade is made, a person is said to be in the ex ante position. For example, suppose Ramona has the opportunity to trade what she has, $2,000, for something she does not have, a big screen television set. In the ex ante position, she will think that she will be better off with either (1) the television set or (2) $2,000 worth of other goods. If she believes she will be better off with the television set than with $2,000 worth of other goods, she will make the trade. Individuals will make a trade only if they believe ex ante (before) the trade that the trade will make them better off.

Ex Ante
Phrase that means "before," as in before a trade.

At the Point of Trade

Suppose Ramona now gives $2,000 to the person in possession of the television set. Does Ramona still believe she will be better off with the television set than with the $2,000? Of course she does. Her action testifies to this fact.

After the Trade

After a trade is made, a person is said to be in the ex post position. Suppose two days have passed. Does Ramona still feel the same way about the trade as she did before the trade and at the point of trade? Maybe, maybe not. She may look back on the trade and regret it. She may say that if she had it to do over again, she would not trade the $2,000 for the big screen television set. In general, though, people expect a trade to make them better

Ex Post
Phrase that means "after," as in after a trade.

off, and usually the trade meets their expectations. But there are no guarantees that a trade will meet expectations because no one in the real world can see the future.

Trade and the Terms of Trade

Trade refers to the process whereby "things" (money, goods, services, and so on) are given up in order to obtain something else. The **terms of trade** refer to *how much* of one thing is given up for *how much* of something else. For example, if $30 is traded for a best-selling book, the terms of trade are 1 bestseller for $30. If the price of a loaf of bread is $2.50, the terms of trade are 1 loaf of bread for $2.50. Buyers and sellers can always think of more advantageous terms of exchange. Buyers prefer lower prices, sellers prefer higher prices.

! ANALYZING THE SCENE

Question from Setting the Scene: Why did Nancy buy the sweater if she felt she was being "ripped off"?
Nancy believes she was "ripped off," even though the sweater she bought was on sale. The connotation of "being ripped off" is negative—one has been made worse off. But Nancy would not have purchased the sweater if she thought she was going to be made worse off. No doubt she is better off having purchased the sweater than not purchasing it. When she says she believes she was "ripped off," she is probably expressing discontent over the *terms of trade* and not the trade itself. What buyer wouldn't prefer to pay a lower price than the price paid?

Costs of Trades

As always, economists consider both benefits and costs. They want to determine what costs are involved in a trade and whether the costs may prevent a trade from taking place.

Unexploited Trades

Suppose Smith wants to buy a red 1965 Ford Mustang in excellent condition. The maximum price she is willing and able to pay for the Mustang is $30,000. Also suppose that Jones owns a red 1965 Ford Mustang in excellent condition. The minimum price he is willing and able to sell the Mustang for is $23,000. Obviously, Smith's maximum buying price ($30,000) is greater than Jones's minimum selling price ($23,000), so a potential trade or exchange exists.

Will the potential trade between Smith and Jones become an actual exchange? The answer to this question may depend on the transaction costs. **Transaction costs** are the costs associated with the time and effort needed to search out, negotiate, and consummate a trade. To illustrate, neither Smith nor Jones may know that the other exists. Suppose Smith lives in Roanoke, Virginia, and Jones lives 40 miles away in Blacksburg, Virginia. Each needs to find the other, which may take time and money. Perhaps Smith can put an ad in the local Blacksburg newspaper stating that she is searching for a 1965 Ford Mustang in mint condition. Alternatively, Jones can put an ad in the local Roanoke newspaper stating that he has a 1965 Ford Mustang to sell. The ad may or may not be seen by the relevant party and then acted upon. Our point is a simple one: Transaction costs sometimes keep potential trades from turning into actual trades.

Consider another example. Suppose Kurt hates to shop for clothes because shopping takes too much time. He has to get in his car, drive to the mall, park the car, walk into the mall, look in different stores, try on different clothes, pay for the items, get back in his car, and drive home. Suppose Kurt spends an average of 2 hours when he shops and he estimates that an hour of his time is worth $30. It follows, then, that Kurt incurs

$60 worth of transaction costs when he buys clothes. Usually, he is not willing to incur the transaction costs necessary to buy a pair of trousers or a shirt.

Now, suppose we ask Kurt if he would be more willing to buy clothes if shopping were easier. Suppose, we say, the transaction costs associated with buying clothes could be lowered from $60 to less than $10. At lower transaction costs, Kurt says that he would be willing to shop more often.

How can transaction costs be lowered? Both people and computers can help lower the transaction costs of trades. For example, real estate brokers lower the transaction costs of selling and buying a house. Jim has a house to sell but doesn't know how to find a buyer. Karen wants to buy a house but doesn't know how to find a seller. Enter the real estate broker, who brings buyers and sellers together. In so doing, she lowers the transaction costs of buying and selling a house.

As another example, consider e-commerce on the Internet. Ursula can buy a book by getting in her car, driving to a bookstore, getting out of her car, walking into the bookstore, looking at the books on the shelves, taking a book to the cashier, paying for it, leaving the store, getting back in her car, and returning home. Or, Ursula can buy a book over the Internet. She can click on one of the online booksellers, search for the book by title, read a short description of the book, and then click on 1-Click Buying. Buying on the Internet has lower transaction costs than shopping at a store because online buying requires less time and effort. Before online book buying and selling, were there potential book purchases and sales that weren't being turned into actual book purchases and sales? There is some evidence that there were.

ANALYZING THE SCENE

Question from Setting the Scene: What did eBay do that really wasn't that hard?
On any given day, 16 million items in 27,000 different categories are listed for sale on eBay.com. What does eBay do? It brings buyers and sellers together.

Consider the situation years ago when the World Wide Web did not exist. Suppose a person in London found an old Beatles' record in his attic and decided he wanted to sell it. Unbeknownst to him, a person in Los Angeles wanted to buy exactly that old Beatles' record. But, alas, the record never changed hands because neither the seller nor the buyer knew how to find the other or even if the other existed. In short, the transaction costs of completing the trade were just too high.

Years later, the Web came along, and with it, eBay. What eBay actually did was use the Web to lower the transaction costs of trading. eBay basically told the world: If you're a seller and want a buyer or if you're a buyer and want a seller, come to us.

Today, the London seller of the old Beatles' record can inexpensively be matched with the Los Angeles buyer. eBay and the Web are the "matchmakers." The potential traders go online to eBay where they become actual traders. eBay charges a small fee for creating the place where buyer and seller can find each other.

Turning Potential Trades Into Actual Trades

Some people are always looking for ways to earn a profit. Can what you have learned about exchange and transaction costs help you earn money? It would seem that one way to earn a profit is to turn potential trades into actual trades by lowering transaction costs. Consider the following example. Buyer Smith is willing to pay a maximum price of $400 for good X; Seller Jones is willing to accept a minimum price of $200 for good X. Currently, the transaction costs of the exchange are $500, evenly split between Buyer Smith and Seller Jones.

Buyer Smith thinks, "Even if I pay the lowest possible price for good X, $200, I will still have to pay $250 in transaction costs, bringing my total to $450. The maximum price I am willing to pay for good X is $400, so I will not make this purchase."

Seller Jones thinks, "Even if I receive the highest possible price for good X, $400, I will still have to pay $250 in transaction costs, leaving me with only $150. The minimum price I am willing to accept for good X is $200, so I will not make this sale."

This potential trade will not become an actual trade, unless someone can lower the transaction costs. One role of an entrepreneur is to try *to turn potential trades into actual trades by lowering transaction costs.* Suppose Entrepreneur Brown can lower the transaction costs for Buyer Smith and Seller Jones to $10 each, asking $60 from each person for services rendered. Also, Entrepreneur Brown negotiates the price of good X at $300. Will the potential exchange become an actual exchange?

Buyer Smith thinks, "I am willing to pay a maximum of $400 for good X. If I purchase good X through Entrepreneur Brown, I will pay $300 to Seller Jones, $10 in transaction costs, and $60 to Brown. This is a total of $370, leaving me better off by $30. It is worthwhile for me to purchase good X."

Seller Jones thinks, "I am willing to sell good X for a minimum of $200. If I sell good X through Entrepreneur Brown, I will receive $300 from Buyer Smith and will have to pay $10 in transaction costs and $60 to Brown. That will leave me with $230, or $30 better off. It is worthwhile for me to sell good X."

Thus, an entrepreneur can earn a profit by finding a way to lower transaction costs. As a result, a potential exchange turns into an actual exchange.

SELF-TEST

1. What are transaction costs? Are the transaction costs of buying a house likely to be greater or less than those of buying a car? Explain your answer.
2. Smith is willing to pay a maximum of $300 for good X and Jones is willing to sell good X for a minimum of $220. Will Smith buy good X from Jones?

PRODUCTION, TRADE, AND SPECIALIZATION

The first section of this chapter discusses production; the second section discusses trade. From these two sections, you might conclude that production and trade are unrelated activities. However, they are not: Before you can trade, you need to produce something. This section ties production and trade together and also shows how the benefits one receives from trade can be affected by how one produces.

Producing and Trading

To show how a change in production can benefit traders, we eliminate anything and everything extraneous to the process. Thus, we eliminate money and consider a barter, or moneyless, economy.

In this economy, there are two individuals, Elizabeth and Brian. They live near each other and each engages in two activities: baking bread and growing apples. Let's suppose that within a certain period of time, Elizabeth can produce 20 loaves of bread and no apples, or 10 loaves of bread and 10 apples, or no bread and 20 apples. In other words, three points on Elizabeth's production possibilities frontier correspond to 20 loaves of bread and no apples, 10 loaves of bread and 10 apples, and no bread and 20 apples. As a consumer, Elizabeth likes to eat both bread and apples, so she decides to produce (and consume) 10 loaves of bread and 10 apples.

Within the same time period, Brian can produce 10 loaves of bread and no apples, or 5 loaves of bread and 15 apples, or no bread and 30 apples. In other words, these three

exhibit **7**

Elizabeth		Brian	
Bread	**Apples**	**Bread**	**Apples**
20	0	10	0
10	10	5	15
0	20	0	30

Production by Elizabeth and Brian
The exhibit shows the combinations of goods each can produce individually in a given time period.

combinations correspond to three points on Brian's production possibilities frontier. Brian, like Elizabeth, likes to eat both bread and apples, so he decides to produce and consume 5 loaves of bread and 15 apples. Exhibit 7 shows the combinations of bread and apples that Elizabeth and Brian can produce.

Elizabeth thinks that both she and Brian may be better off if each specializes in producing only one of the two goods and trading it for the other. In other words, Elizabeth should produce either bread or apples but not both. Brian thinks this may be a good idea but is not sure what good each person should specialize in producing.

An economist would advise each to produce the good that he or she can produce at a lower cost. In economics, a person who can produce a good at a lower cost than another person can is said to have a comparative advantage in the production of that good.

Comparative Advantage
The situation where someone can produce a good at lower opportunity cost than someone else can.

Exhibit 7 shows that for every 10 units of bread Elizabeth does not produce, she can produce 10 apples. In other words, the opportunity cost of producing one loaf of bread *(B)* is one apple *(A)*:

$$\text{Opportunity costs for Elizabeth: } 1B = 1A$$
$$1A = 1B$$

As for Brian, for every 5 loaves of bread he does not produce, he can produce 15 apples. So, for every 1 loaf of bread he does not produce, he can produce 3 apples. It follows, then, that for every one apple he chooses to produce, he forfeits 1/3 loaf of bread.

$$\text{Opportunity costs for Brian: } 1B = 3A$$
$$1A = \tfrac{1}{3}B$$

Comparing opportunity costs, we see that Elizabeth can produce bread at a lower opportunity cost than Brian can. (Elizabeth forfeits 1 apple when she produces 1 loaf of bread, whereas Brian forfeits 3 apples when he produces 1 loaf of bread.) On the other hand, Brian can produce apples at a lower opportunity cost than Elizabeth can. We conclude that Elizabeth has a comparative advantage in the production of bread and Brian has a comparative advantage in the production of apples.

Suppose each person specializes in the production of the good in which he or she has a comparative advantage. This means Elizabeth produces only bread and produces 20 loaves. Brian produces only apples and produces 30 apples.

Now suppose that Elizabeth and Brian decide to trade 8 loaves of bread for 12 apples. In other words, Elizabeth produces 20 loaves of bread and then trades 8 of the loaves for 12 apples. After the trade, Elizabeth consumes 12 loaves of bread and 12 apples. Compare this situation with what she consumed when she didn't specialize and didn't trade. In that situation, she consumed 10 loaves of bread and 10 apples. Clearly, Elizabeth is better off when she specializes and trades than when she does not. But what about Brian?

exhibit 8

Consumption for Elizabeth and Brian With and Without Specialization and Trade

A comparison of the consumption of bread and apples before and after specialization and trade shows that both Elizabeth and Brian benefit from producing the good in which each has a comparative advantage and trading for the other good.

		No Specialization and No Trade	Specialization and Trade	Gains From Specialization and Trade
Elizabeth	Consumption of Loaves of Bread	10	12	+ 2
	Consumption of Apples	10	12	+ 2
Brian	Consumption of Loaves of Bread	5	8	+ 3
	Consumption of Apples	15	18	+ 3

Brian produces 30 apples and trades 12 of them to Elizabeth for 8 loaves of bread. In other words, he consumes 8 loaves of bread and 18 apples. Compare this situation with what he consumed when he didn't specialize and didn't trade. In that situation, he consumed 5 loaves of bread and 15 apples. Thus, Brian is also better off when he specializes and trades than when he does not.

Exhibit 8 summarizes consumption for Elizabeth and Brian. It shows that both Elizabeth and Brian make themselves better off by specializing in the production of one good and trading for the other.

ANALYZING THE SCENE

Question from Setting the Scene: Why doesn't a smart guy with a Ph.D. know how to change the oil in his car?

Terrence wonders why Mark, a smart guy with a Ph.D., doesn't know how to change the oil in his car. The answer is simple: Mark is a specialist. Why should Mark take the time to learn how to change the oil in his car if his time is better spent doing something for which he will receive greater net benefits? Think again of Elizabeth and Brian. Perhaps after years of specializing in the production of bread, someone wonders why Elizabeth doesn't know how to produce apples. Well, it's not that Elizabeth can't produce both bread and apples, it's just that she is better off producing only bread and trading some of the bread for apples. Elizabeth doesn't produce apples, and Mark doesn't change the oil in his car. Same story.

Profit and a Lower Cost of Living

The last column of Exhibit 8 shows the gains from specialization and trade. One way to view these gains is in terms of Elizabeth and Brian being better off when they specialize and trade than when they do not specialize and do not trade. In short, specialization and trade make people better off.

Another way to view these gains is in terms of *profit* and a *lower cost of living*. To illustrate, let's look again at Elizabeth. Essentially, Elizabeth undertakes two actions by specializing and trading. The first action is to produce more of one good (loaves of bread) than she produces when she does not specialize. The second action is to trade, or "sell," some of the bread for a "price" higher than the cost of producing the bread. Specifically, she "sells" 8 of the loaves of bread (to Brian) for a "price" of 12 apples. In other words, she

Popular Culture Technology Everyday Life

POPULAR CULTURE

POPULAR CULTURE

POPULAR CULTURE

© Associated Press/AP

Elvis, Comparative Advantage, and Specialization

Elvis Presley was born on January 8, 1935, in Tupelo, Mississippi. As an adolescent, he moved with his parents to Memphis, Tennessee, and lived in a housing project. After graduating from high school, he drove a truck for the Crown Electric Company. One day, Elvis decided to cut a record—a record he wanted to give to his mother for her upcoming birthday. He went into Sun Studios, paid to cut a record, and the rest, as they say, is rock 'n' roll history.

In a way, the story of Elvis Presley is similar to the story of millions of people today, including you. Elvis pretty much did one thing, and only one thing, for most of his working life—he sang songs.[1] Most people today, in their everyday working lives, do one and only one thing. Some people only cut hair, others only write books, and still others only perform attorney services. The probability is high that for most of your working life you will do one and only one thing—whether it be working as a physician, school teacher, attorney, actor, or small business owner.

Just as Elvis specialized, so do most people.

But how do people decide on their specialization? Do they simply choose a profession or particular job at random? Did you choose your college major randomly? It's doubtful. Many people specialize in that activity for which they have a comparative advantage. That's because most people are motivated by profit. Think back to Elizabeth and Brian. Elizabeth's cost of producing 1 apple was 1 loaf of bread, but she could "sell" a loaf of bread to Brian for 1.5 apples. Because her price for bread (1.5 apples) was greater than her cost of producing bread (1 apple), she earned a profit. Because she earned a profit, Elizabeth specialized in producing bread. She specialized in producing what she had a comparative advantage in producing.

Although Elvis had a comparative advantage in singing songs, he never had a singing lesson in his life. He said he started singing for a "real audience" at a fairground in Tupelo, Mississippi, when he was 11 years old. He said he was "shaking like a leaf," but nothing could stop him from entering the talent contest at the fair.

---

1. He also acted in movies, but it is doubtful he would have acted in movies had he not sung in those movies.

"sells" each loaf of bread for a "price" of 1.5 apples. But, Elizabeth can produce a loaf of bread for a cost of 1 apple. So, she "sells" the bread for a "price" (1.5 apples) that's higher than the cost to her of producing the bread (1 apple). The difference is her profit.

Many people think that one person's profit is another person's loss. In other words, because Elizabeth earns a profit by specializing and trading, Brian must lose. But we know this is not the case. The cost to Brian of producing a loaf of bread is 3 apples. But he "buys" bread from Elizabeth for a "price" of only 1.5 apples. In other words, while Elizabeth is earning a profit, Brian's cost of living (what he has to forfeit to get a loaf of bread) is declining.

A Benevolent and All-Knowing Dictator Versus the Invisible Hand

Suppose a benevolent dictator governs the country where Brian and Elizabeth live. We assume that this benevolent dictator knows everything about almost every economic activity in his country. In other words, he knows Elizabeth's and Brian's opportunity costs of producing bread and apples.

Because the dictator is benevolent and because he wants the best for the people who live in his country, he orders Elizabeth to produce only loaves of bread and Brian

Economics In

Popular Culture   Technology   Everyday Life

POPULAR CULTURE

© CORBIS KIPA

Jerry Seinfeld, the Doorman, and Adam Smith

Oh, I get it. Why waste time making small talk with the door-man? I should just shut up and do my job, opening the door for you.
    —The doorman, speaking to Jerry, in an episode of *Seinfeld*

In a *Seinfeld* episode, Jerry comes across a doorman (played by actor Larry Miller) who seems to have a chip on his shoulder. While waiting for the elevator, Jerry sees the doorman reading a newspaper. Jerry looks over and says, "What about those Knicks?" (a reference to the New York Knicks professional basketball team). The doorman's response is, "What makes you think I wasn't reading the Wall Street page? Oh, I know, because I'm the uneducated doorman."

This exchange between the doorman and Jerry would be unlikely if Jerry had not lived in New York City or in some other large city. That's because doormen are usually found only in large cities. If you live in a city with a population less than 100,000, you may not find a single doorman in the entire city. There are few doormen even in cities with a population of 1 million.

This observation is not unique to us. It goes back to Adam Smith, who said that there is a direct relationship between the degree of specialization and the size of the market. Smith said:

> There are some sorts of industry, even of the lowest kind, which can be carried on nowhere but in a great town. A porter, for example, can find employment and subsistence in no other place. A village is by much too narrow a sphere for him; even an ordinary market town is scarce large enough to afford him constant occupation.[2]

Smith's observation that "some sorts of industry . . . can be carried on nowhere but in a great town" seems to be true. Some occupations and some goods can only be found in big cities. Try to find a doorman in North Adams, Michigan (population 514), or restaurant chefs who only prepare Persian, Yugoslavian, or Caribbean entreés in Ipswich, South Dakota (population 943).

2. *An Inquiry into the Nature and Causes of the Wealth of Nations,* Adam Smith. Ed. Edwin Cannan, New York: Modern Library, 1965.

---

to produce only apples. Next, he tells Elizabeth and Brian to trade 8 loaves of bread for 12 apples.

Afterward, he shows Exhibit 8 to Elizabeth and Brian. They are both surprised that they are better off having done what the benevolent dictator told them to do.

THINKING LIKE AN ECONOMIST *The layperson wonders how "anything good" can come from greed (which he often equates with self-interest.) The economist knows that self-interest can sometimes lead to socially desirable results. As Adam Smith said: "It is not from the benevolence of the butcher, the brewer, or the baker, that we expect our dinner, but from their regard to their own self-interest. We address ourselves, not to their humanity but to their self-love, and never talk to them of our own necessities, but of their advantages."*

Now in the original story about Elizabeth and Brian, there was no benevolent, all-knowing dictator. There were only two people who were guided by their self-interest to specialize and trade. In other words, self-interest did for Elizabeth and Brian what the benevolent dictator did for them.

Adam Smith, the eighteenth-century Scottish economist and founder of modern economics, spoke about the *invisible hand* that "guided" individuals' actions toward a positive outcome that he or she did not intend. That is what happened in the original story about Elizabeth and Brian. Neither intended to increase the overall output of society; each intended only to make himself or herself better off.

1. If George can produce either (a) 10X and 20Y or (b) 5X and 25Y, what is the opportunity cost to George of producing one more X?
2. Harriet can produce either (a) 30X and 70Y or (b) 40X and 55Y; Bill can produce either (c) 10X and 40Y or (d) 20X and 20Y. Who has a comparative advantage in the production of X? of Y? Explain your answers.

PRODUCING, TRADING, AND ECONOMIC SYSTEMS

Producing and trading are major economic activities in every country of the world, not just the United States. But the laws, regulations, traditions, and social institutions that affect producing and trading are not the same in all countries. This leads us to a discussion of economic systems.

Economic Systems

An **economic system** refers to the way in which a society decides to answer key economic questions—in particular those questions that relate to production and trade. Three questions that relate to production are:

- What goods will be produced?
- How will the goods be produced?
- For whom will the goods be produced?

Two questions that relate to trade are:

- What is the nature of trade?
- What function do prices serve?

There are hundreds of countries in the world but only two major economic systems: the *capitalist* (or market) economic system and the *socialist* economic system. One might think that every country's economy would fall neatly into one of these two categories, but things are not so simple. Most countries have chosen "ingredients" from both economic systems. These countries have economies that are neither purely capitalist nor purely socialist; instead, they are some mixture of both and are therefore called *mixed economies*. For example, the economic system that, to different degrees, exists in the United States, Canada, Australia, and Japan, among other countries, is generally known as **mixed capitalism.**

Think of capitalism and socialism as occupying opposite ends of an economic spectrum. Countries' economies lie along the spectrum. Some are closer to the capitalist end and some are closer to the socialist end.

But First, a Warning

In our discussion of the two major economic systems—capitalism and socialism—we *deliberately* present each system as the polar opposite of the other: If capitalism says no, then socialism says yes; if capitalism chooses black, then socialism chooses white; if capitalism is up, then socialism is down.

Unless you keep our premise in mind, you are likely to think, "But capitalist countries don't always do things the opposite way of socialist countries. Sometimes they do things similarly."

Remember we said that most countries of the world are neither purely capitalist nor purely socialist and that most countries fall somewhere between the two polar extremes.

Economic System
The way in which society decides to answer key economic questions—in particular those questions that relate to production and trade.

Mixed Capitalism
An economic system characterized by largely private ownership of factors of production, market allocation of resources, and decentralized decision making. Most economic activities take place in the private sector in this system, but government plays a substantial economic and regulatory role.

Thus, it naturally follows that there are elements of capitalism and socialism in most countries.

However, our purpose here is not to figure out the precise breakdown between capitalism and socialism for any given country. We are not interested in saying that the United States is X percent capitalist and Y percent socialist. Our purpose is to outline the two opposite ways of dealing with questions and issues that relate to production and trade. One of these ways is called capitalism; the other, socialism.

Three Economic Questions That Deal With Production

Every society must answer these three economic questions:

1. What goods will be produced?
2. How will the goods be produced?
3. For whom will the goods be produced?

Let's examine how these questions about production are answered in a capitalist economic system and in a socialist economic system.

What Goods Will Be Produced?

This question is really another way of asking, Where on its PPF will an economy operate? In a capitalist economic system, those goods will be produced that the market (buyers and sellers) want to be produced. If there are enough buyers who want to buy a particular good or service, then it is likely that the good or service will be produced and offered for sale. This is both a strength and weakness of capitalism, some people say.

People want to buy food, cars, houses, a night out at the opera, books, and so on, and under capitalism, these goods and services are produced. Furthermore, when preferences change and people want to buy more of one good and less of another, sellers usually respond accordingly.

In a socialist economic system, government plays a large role in determining what is produced. The degree to which ordinary citizens, working through their government, will have their buying preferences met largely depends on how responsive and open the government is.

How Will the Goods Be Produced?

Under capitalism, how the goods will be produced depends on the decisions of private producers. If private producers want to produce television sets with 10 units of capital and 100 units of labor, then so be it. If they want to produce television sets with robotics, then again it will be done. Private producers make the decisions as to how they will produce goods.

Under socialism, government plays a large role in determining how goods will be produced. For example, government might decide to have food produced on large collective farms instead of small private farms.

For Whom Will the Goods Be Produced?

Under capitalism, the goods will be produced for those persons who are able and willing to pay the prices for the goods. Government doesn't decide who will or will not have a television set, car, or house. If you want a television set and are able and willing to pay the price of the television set, then the television set is yours.

THINKING LIKE AN ECONOMIST *The layperson looks at countries and sees differences. For example, people speak French in France and English in the United States; the crime rate is higher in the United States than it is in Belgium; and so on. The economist knows that there are some things that are the same for all countries. The United States has to decide what goods to produce, and China has to decide what goods to produce. The United States has to decide how goods will be produced, and Brazil has to decide how goods will be produced. The United States has to deal with scarcity and its effects, and so do South Korea, Pakistan, India, and Canada.*

Under socialism, there is more government control over who gets what goods. For example, within a socialist economic system there may be a redistribution of funds from Smith to Jones. Or perhaps goods are given to Jones even though he is unable to pay the prices of these goods.

Trade

Consider an ordinary, everyday exchange of $100 for some clothes. Under capitalism, it is generally assumed that both the buyer and seller of the clothes benefit from the trade or else they would not have entered into it. Under socialism, the view often expressed is that one person in a trade is being made better off at the expense of the other person. In this example, perhaps the clothes seller took advantage of the buyer by charging too much money for the clothes.

Prices

When we buy something in a market—whether it is a car, a house, or a loaf of bread—we pay a price. Prices are a common market phenomenon. Under capitalism, price (1) rations goods and services, (2) conveys information, and (3) serves as an incentive to respond to information.

As discussed in Chapter 1, price is a rationing device. In a world of scarcity, where people's wants outstrip the resources available to satisfy those wants, some type of rationing device is necessary. It may be price, first-come-first-served, brute force, or something else. For capitalist thinkers, there needs to be some way of determining who gets what of the available resources, goods, and services. Price serves this purpose.

Now consider an example to see how price can convey information and serve as an incentive to respond to information. Suppose Tom buys a dozen oranges each week for 40 cents an orange. One day, a devastating freeze hits the Florida orange groves and destroys half the orange crop. As a result, there are fewer oranges in the world and price rises to 60 cents an orange. Tom notices the higher price of oranges and wonders what caused the price to rise. He does not know about the freeze, and even if he did, he might not connect the freeze with a reduced supply of oranges and higher orange prices. Nevertheless, Tom responds to the higher price of oranges by reducing his weekly purchase from 12 oranges to 8 oranges.

Let's consider the role price has played in this example. First, through an increase in price, the "information" of the freeze was conveyed to buyers. Specifically, price has transmitted information on the relative scarcity of a good. The higher price of oranges is saying: "There has been a cold spell in Florida resulting in fewer oranges."

Second, by rising, price has provided Tom with an incentive to reduce the quantity of oranges he consumes. Tom responds to the information of the increased relative scarcity of oranges, even without knowing about Florida weather conditions.

Under socialism, price is viewed as being set by greedy businesses with vast economic power. Perhaps because of this, socialists usually stand ready to "control" price. For example, under socialism it is not uncommon to pass a law making it illegal to charge more than a certain price for, say, gasoline or rental homes. It is also not uncommon to pass a law that makes it illegal to pay less than a certain dollar wage to a worker.

By passing laws that make it illegal to charge more than a certain price for certain goods and services, socialists seek to reduce some of the economic power that they believe sellers have over consumers. By passing laws that make it illegal to pay less than a certain wage to workers, socialists seek to reduce some of the economic power that they believe the owners of businesses have over workers.

PROPERTY RIGHTS

Economists often talk about *property rights*. To the layperson, this term usually relates to a person owning a piece of physical property—such as an acre of land. To an economist, property rights are much more inclusive. **Property rights** refer to the laws, regulations, rules, and social customs that define what an individual can and cannot do in society.

Economic Systems and Property Rights

While there is some overlap between the property rights of capitalism and socialism, more often than not the property rights assignments are different in the two economic systems. To simplify, suppose there are 26 property rights, *A* through *Z*. Some property rights are common to both capitalism and socialism (suppose they share *C, R,* and *W*), but many property rights are different in the two economic systems (suppose capitalism has *A, D,* and *F* and socialism has *G, X,* and *Z*). In short, economic systems are different to the extent that their property rights assignments are different. (What makes capitalism different from socialism? Answer: Capitalism has a different set of property rights than socialism has.)

To illustrate, a seller under capitalism has the property right to sell his or her good for the highest price it can fetch. This property right is modified under socialism. Price controls commonly exist under socialism, so a seller may have the property right to sell the good for no more than, say, $40. The capitalist-seller's property right in his good is more complete than is the socialist-seller's property right—that is, the capitalist seller is allowed to reach for some prices that the socialist seller is not.

Do Property Rights Matter?

Suppose only three countries exist in the world and each country has a completely different set of property rights. Would resources be allocated the same way in each country? Would the same kinds of incentives and disincentives exist in each country? More specifically, would your behavior be the same in each country?

The answer to all three questions is no. Property rights matter to how resources are allocated, what incentives and disincentives exist, and how individuals behave.

To illustrate, let's consider private property rights and communal property rights. Private property rights usually include the "right to exclude," but communal property rights do not. Instead, under communal property rights, the use of a resource is determined on a first-come-first-served basis.

The Canadian seal hunt of 1970 illustrates the difference in these two property rights assignments. The Canadian government specified that no more than 50,000 seals could be killed during the hunt. As a result, hunters killed seals as quickly as they could so each hunter could acquire as many seals as possible before the legal maximum of 50,000 seals was reached. In their attempts to kill seals quickly (before someone else got the seals), the hunters crushed baby seals' heads with heavy clubs. Pictures of hunters clubbing baby seals resulted in a public outcry against the seal hunt. The Canadian Minister of Fisheries told seal hunters that they had to kill the seals in a less crude and inhumane manner or the seal hunt would be ended.

The manner in which the hunters killed the seals was largely the result of the specified property rights in seals. The Canadian government had essentially said that the first to kill a seal, owned the seal. No wonder, then, that hunters would try to kill seals in the quickest manner possible and not necessarily in the most humane way.

If private property rights had existed in the seals, the private owner of the seals would have sold the seals for a price. Those persons who paid the price would own the seals (that is, the seals wouldn't be rationed on a first-come-first-served basis), and thus there would be no need to kill the seals quickly. A more time-consuming yet humane way of killing the seals could be used.

Property Rights and Scarce Resources

Private property rights are sometimes identified with antisocial behavior, while communal or state property rights are often identified with socially acceptable behavior. Let's look at two property rights assignments with respect to the resource oil and consider which is more likely to lead to a socially acceptable outcome.

Tex Baldwin is an oil producer who has private property rights in an oil field. He pumps crude oil from under his property and sells it to refineries. It costs him $30 to extract one barrel of oil and he sells each barrel for $35. At this price, he pumps and sells 1 million barrels of crude oil each year.

One day, Tex reads a report indicating that in five years, oil will be relatively more scarce than it is today; as a result, the price of oil will rise to $50 a barrel. Tex can continue to pump and sell oil today or he can leave the oil in the ground and pump and sell it in five years. Tex Baldwin is interested in maximizing his profits. Do you predict he will pump and sell now or pump and sell in five years?

Let's analyze Tex's situation. If he pumps and sells oil today, he earns a profit of $5 per barrel; if he pumps and sells oil five years from now, he will earn a profit of $20 per barrel.[3] Of course, if he leaves the oil in the ground, he cannot earn interest on the $5 profit per barrel. Suppose he can earn 5 percent interest on every $1 he saves. Thus, a profit of $5 a barrel today will return approximately $6.40 in five years. Comparing $6.40 a barrel with $20 a barrel, Tex realizes that he will maximize his profits by leaving the oil in the ground.

Instead of reducing the quantity of oil he supplies to the market from 1 million barrels to nothing, Tex decides to cut back to supplying 100,000 barrels. He needs some income to meet his annual financial obligations.

From a societal perspective, it is interesting that Tex, who only wants to maximize his profits, ends up conserving a resource (oil) that is expected to become relatively more scarce in the future. In fact, because of his desire for profit, oil in the future will likely be relatively less scarce than initially expected (after all, Tex is saving oil for the future). In this case, private property rights are not identified with antisocial behavior but rather further society's need to conserve resources.

What might the outcome have been had the oil been state owned? Would the state have conserved oil to the same degree that Tex Baldwin did? Probably not. Day-to-day operations of the state are largely under the control of elected politicians, who usually look at short-term results. Often, what politicians seek to maximize are votes at the next election. If the next election is only one year off, then the politician has to weigh the actual votes of voters one year from now against the "dollar votes" of consumers, say, five to ten years in the future. So what if oil will be relatively more scarce in five years, and, to some degree, consumers in the future would prefer to have some of today's oil reallocated to the future? Consumers of the future do not vote today; consumers today are the ones who vote. If voters today do not want oil conserved for the future but instead want a generous supply of oil today so that they can pay lower oil prices, then the politician seeking election or reelection will find it difficult to turn his back on what voters want today. In short, if voters today say "live for today and let the future take care of itself," then so will today's politicians.

---

3. We are assuming that the cost of extracting oil is not higher in five years than it is today.

1. What are the three economic questions that deal with production that every society must answer?
2. How is trade viewed in a capitalist economic system?
3. What does an economic system have to do with where on its PPF the economy operates?
4. What do price controls have to do with property rights?

A **READER ASKS**

How Will Economics Help Me If I'm a History Major?

I'm a history major taking my first course in economics. But quite frankly, I don't see how economics will be of much use in my study of history. Any thoughts on the subject?

Economics often plays a major role in historical events. For example, many social scientists argue that economics played a large role in the collapse of communism. If communism had been able to produce the quantity and variety of goods and services that capitalism produces, perhaps the Soviet Union would still exist.

Fact is, understanding economics may help you understand many historical events or periods. If, as a historian, you study the Great Depression, you will need to know something about the stock market, tariffs, and more. If you study the California Gold Rush, you will need to know about supply, demand, and prices. If you study the history of prisoner-of-war camps, you will need to know about how and why people trade and about money. If you study the Boston Tea Party, you will need to know about government grants of monopoly and about taxes.

Economics can also be useful in another way. Suppose you learn in your economics course what can and cannot cause inflation. We'll say you learn that X can cause inflation and that Y cannot. Then one day, you read an article in which a historian says that Y caused the high inflation in a certain country and that the high inflation led to a public outcry, which was then met with stiff government reprisals. Without an understanding of economics, you might be willing to accept what the historian has written. But with your understanding of economics, you know that events could not have happened as the historian reports because Y, which the historian claims caused the high inflation, could not have caused the high inflation.

In conclusion, a good understanding of economics will not only help you understand key historical events but also help you discern inaccuracies in recorded history.

Chapter Summary

An Economy's Production Possibilities Frontier

> An economy's production possibilities frontier (PPF) represents the possible combinations of two goods that the economy can produce in a certain period of time, under the conditions of a given state of technology and fully employed resources.

Increasing and Constant Opportunity Costs

> A straight-line PPF represents "constant opportunity costs:" increased production of one good comes at constant opportunity costs.
> A bowed-outward (concave-downward) PPF represents the law of "increasing opportunity costs:" increased production of one good comes at increased opportunity costs.

The Production Possibilities Frontier and Various Economic Concepts

> The PPF can be used to illustrate various economic concepts. Scarcity is illustrated by the frontier itself. Choice is illustrated by our knowing that we have to locate at some particular point either on the frontier or below it. In short, of the many attainable positions, one must be chosen. Opportunity cost is illustrated by a movement from one point on the PPF to another point on the PPF. Unemployed resources and productive inefficiency are illustrated by a point below the PPF. Productive efficiency and fully employed resources are illustrated by a point on the PPF. Economic growth is illustrated by a shift outward in the PPF.

Trade or Exchange

> People trade in order to make themselves better off. Exchange is a utility-increasing activity.
> The three time periods relevant to the trading process are (1) the ex ante period, which is the time before the trade is made; (2) the point of trade; and (3) the ex post period, which is the time after the trade has been made.
> There is a difference between trade and the terms of trade. Trade refers to the act of giving up one thing for something else. For example, a person may trade money for a car. The terms of trade refer to how much of one thing is traded for how much of something else. For example, how much money ($25,000? $30,000?) is traded for one car.

Transaction Costs

> Transaction costs are the costs associated with the time and effort needed to search out, negotiate, and consummate a trade. Some potential exchanges are not realized because of high transaction costs. Lowering transaction costs can turn a potential exchange into an actual exchange.
> One role of an entrepreneur is to try to lower transaction costs.

Comparative Advantage and Specialization

> Individuals can make themselves better off by specializing in the production of the good in which they have a comparative advantage and then trading some of that good for other goods. A person has a comparative advantage in the production of a good if he or she can produce the good at a lower opportunity cost than another person can.
> Individuals gain by specializing and trading. Specifically, they earn a profit by specializing in the production of the goods in which they have a comparative advantage.

Economic Systems

> An economic system refers to the way in which a society decides to answer key economic questions—in particular those questions that relate to production and trade.
> There are two major economic systems: the capitalist (or market) economic system and the socialist economic system.

> One of the key differences between capitalism and socialism is how decisions are made with respect to where on the PPF the economy will operate. Under capitalism, the market (buyers and sellers) largely determines at which point on the PPF the economy will operate. Under socialism, government plays a large role in determining at which point on the PPF the economy will operate.
> Three economic questions that relate to production that every society must answer are: (1) What goods will be produced? (2) How will the goods be produced? (3) For whom will the goods be produced?
> Under capitalism, price (1) rations goods and services, (2) conveys information, and (3) serves as an incentive to respond to information. Under socialism, price is viewed as being set by greedy businesses with vast economic power.

Property Rights

> Property rights refer to the laws, regulations, rules, and social customs that define what an individual can and cannot do in society.
> Property rights influence how resources are allocated, what incentives and disincentives exist, and how individuals behave.
> The set of property rights under capitalism is not the same as the set of property rights under socialism, although capitalism and socialism can hold some property rights in common.

Key Terms and Concepts

Production Possibilities Frontier (PPF)	Trade (Exchange)	Comparative Advantage
Law of Increasing Opportunity Costs	Ex Ante	Economic System
Productive Efficiency	Ex Post	Mixed Capitalism
Productive Inefficiency	Terms of Trade	Property Rights
Technology	Transaction Costs	

Questions and Problems

1. Describe how each of the following would affect the U.S. production possibilities frontier: (a) an increase in the number of illegal aliens entering the country; (b) a war; (c) the discovery of a new oil field; (d) a decrease in the unemployment rate; (e) a law that requires individuals to enter lines of work for which they are not suited.

2. Explain how the following can be represented in a PPF framework: (a) the finiteness of resources implicit in the scarcity condition; (b) choice; (c) opportunity cost; (d) productive efficiency; (e) unemployed resources.

3. What condition must hold for the production possibilities frontier to be bowed outward (concave downward)? to be a straight line?

4. Give an example to illustrate each of the following: (a) constant opportunity costs; (b) increasing opportunity costs.

5. Why are most production possibilities frontiers for goods bowed outward, or concave downward?

6. Within a PPF framework, explain each of the following: (a) a disagreement between a person who favors more domestic welfare spending and one who favors more national defense spending; (b) an increase in the population; (c) a technological change that makes resources less specialized.

7. Some people have said that during the Cold War, the Central Intelligence Agency (CIA) regularly estimated (a) the total quantity of output produced in the Soviet Union and (b) the total quantity of civilian goods produced in the Soviet Union. Of what interest would these data, or the information that might be deduced from them, be to the CIA? (Hint: Think in terms of the PPF.)

8. Suppose a nation's PPF shifts inward as its population grows. What happens, on average, to the material standard of living of the people? Explain your answer.

9. "A nation may be able to live beyond its means, but the world cannot." Do you agree or disagree? Explain your answer.

10. Use the PPF framework to explain something in your everyday life that was not mentioned in the chapter.

11. Describe the three time periods relevant to the trading process.

12. Are all exchanges or trades beneficial to both parties in the ex post position? Explain your answer.

13. If Donovan agrees to trade $50 for a painting, what can we say about the utility he gets from the $50 compared with the utility he expects to get from the painting?

14. A person who benefits from a trade can be disgruntled over the terms of trade. Do you agree or disagree? Explain your answer.

15. Give an example to illustrate that a change in property rights can change behavior.

16. A capitalist would be much less likely to support controls on prices and wages than would a socialist. Why?

17. Some people argue that capitalism and socialism are usually evaluated only on economic grounds, where capitalism has a clear advantage. But in order to evaluate the two economic systems evenhandedly, other factors should be considered as well—justice, fairness, the happiness of people living under both systems, the crime rate, the standard of living of those at the bottom of the economic ladder, and much more. Do you think this is the proper way to proceed? Why or why not?

18. The convergence hypothesis, first proposed by a Soviet economist, suggests that over time the capitalist economies will become increasingly socialistic and the socialist economies will become increasingly capitalistic. Do you believe the convergence hypothesis has merit? What real-world evidence can you cite to prove or disprove the hypothesis?

19. Consider two property right systems, A and B. Under A, an individual gets to keep 100 percent of the income he or she earns. Under B, an individual gets to keep 60 percent of the income he or she earns (and must pay 40 percent of the income in taxes). Under which property rights assignment does the individual have a stronger incentive to work and earn income? What does your answer tell you about the relationship between property rights and incentives?

Working With Numbers and Graphs

1. Tina can produce any of the following combinations of goods X and Y: (a) $100X$ and $0Y$, (b) $50X$ and $25Y$, and (c) $0X$ and $50Y$. David can produce any of the following combinations of goods X and Y: (a) $50X$ and $0Y$, (b) $25X$ and $40Y$, and (c) $0X$ and $80Y$. Who has a comparative advantage in the production of good X? of good Y? Explain your answer.

2. Using the data in Problem 1, prove that both Tina and David can be made better off through specialization and trade.

3. Exhibit 5 represents an advance in technology that made it possible to produce more of both military and civilian goods. Represent an advance in technology that makes it possible to produce more of only civilian goods. Does this indirectly make it possible to produce more military goods? Explain your answer.

4. In the following figure, which graph depicts a technological breakthrough in the production of good X only?

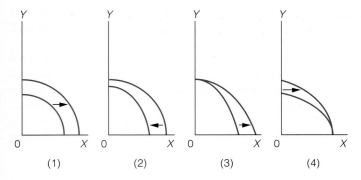

(1)   (2)   (3)   (4)

5. In the preceding figure, which graph depicts a change in the PPF that is a likely consequence of war?

6. If PPF_2 in the following graph is the relevant production possibilities frontier, then which points are unattainable? Explain your answer.

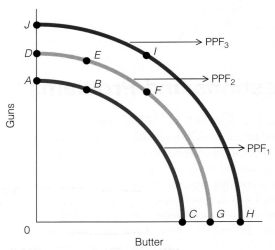

7. If PPF_1 in the figure above is the relevant production possibilities frontier, then which point(s) represent productive efficiency? Explain your answer.

© Digital Vision/Getty Images

chapter **3**

SUPPLY AND DEMAND

Setting the Scene

James Beider is a law student at Columbia Law School. He lives on the Upper West Side of Manhattan, about 30 blocks from the school. The following events occurred on a day not too long ago.

9:03 A.M.

James is sitting in front of a computer in the law library at Columbia University. He's not checking on books but on the current prices of three stocks he owns (Wal-Mart, Microsoft, and Dell). He also checks on the exchange rate between the dollar and the euro. He plans to take a trip to Europe in the summer and is hoping that the dollar will be stronger (against the euro) than it has been in the last few weeks. Last week, a person paid $1.10 for 1 euro; today, a person has to pay $1.28 for a euro. James mutters under his breath that if the dollar gets any weaker, he might have to cancel his trip.

1:30 P.M.

James is sitting in Tommy's Restaurant (three blocks from Columbia

University), eating lunch with a few friends. His last class of the day is at 2:00 P.M. He picks up his cell phone and calls his apartment supervisor. No answer. James frowns as he puts his phone away. "What's wrong?" one friend asks. "I've been trying to get this guy to fix my shower for two weeks now," James answers. "I'm just frustrated." "Ah, the joys of living in a rent-controlled apartment," his friend says.

4:55 P.M.

James and his girlfriend Kelly are in a taxi on their way to the Ed Sullivan Theater at 1697 Broadway to see the *Late Show with David Letterman*. James has wanted to see the show for two years and finally managed to get tickets. The tickets are free—but the wait time to obtain

two tickets is approximately nine months.

11:02 P.M.

James is watching the 11 o'clock news as he eats a slice of cold pizza.

The TV reporter says, "The mayor said today that he is concerned that the city's burglary rate has been rising."

Cut to mayor at today's news conference.

"This city and this mayor are not going to be soft on crime. We're going to do everything in our power to make sure that everyone knows that crime doesn't pay."

James says, "You tell 'em, mayor." Then he reaches for another slice of pizza.

How would an economist look at these events? Later in the chapter, discussions based on the following questions will help you analyze the scene the way an economist would.

- At the time James checks stock prices, Wal-Mart is selling for $52.42, Microsoft for $27.75, and Dell for $35.75. Why doesn't Dell sell for more than Wal-Mart? Why doesn't Microsoft sell for more than Dell?
- Why is the euro selling for $1.28 and not higher or lower?
- What does getting his shower fixed have to do with James living in a rent-controlled apartment?

- Why does it take so long (nine months) to get tickets to see the *Late Show with David Letterman?*
- Does the burglary rate have anything to do with how "hard" or "soft" a city is on crime?

A NOTE ABOUT THEORY

Chapter 1 discusses theory-building in economics, explaining that economists build theories in order to answer questions that do not have obvious answers. This chapter discusses one of the most famous and widely used theories in economics: the theory of supply and demand.

What questions does the supply-and-demand theory seek to answer? One important question is: What determines price? Specifically, why is the price of, say, a share of Wal-Mart stock $53 and not $43 or $67? How did the stock price come to be $53?

As you read through this chapter, think back to the discussion of theory in Chapter 1. Many of the topics discussed there will be applied here. For example, Chapter 1 states that when building theories, economists identify certain variables that they think will explain or predict what they seek to explain or predict. This chapter explains the variables that economists think are important to explaining and predicting prices.

DEMAND

Demand
The willingness and ability of buyers to purchase different quantities of a good at different prices during a specific time period.

The word **demand** has a precise meaning in economics. It refers to (1) the willingness and ability of buyers to purchase different quantities of a good (2) at different prices (3) during a specific time period (per day, week, and so on).[1] For example, we can express part of John's demand for magazines by saying that he is willing and able to buy 10 magazines a month at $4 per magazine and that he is willing and able to buy 15 magazines a month at $3 per magazine.

Remember this important point about demand: Unless *both* willingness and ability to buy are present, a person is not a buyer and there is no demand. For example, Josie may be willing to buy a computer but be unable to pay the price; Tanya may be able to buy a computer but be unwilling to do so. Neither Josie nor Tanya demands a computer.

The Law of Demand

Law of Demand
As the price of a good rises, the quantity demanded of the good falls, and as the price of a good falls, the quantity demanded of the good rises, *ceteris paribus*.

Will people buy more units of a good at lower prices than at higher prices? For example, will people buy more personal computers at $1,000 per computer than at $4,000 per computer? If your answer is yes, you instinctively understand the law of demand. The **law of demand** states that as the price of a good rises, the quantity demanded of the good falls, and as the price of a good falls, the quantity demanded of the good rises, *ceteris paribus*. Simply put, the law of demand states that the price of a good and the quantity demanded of the good are inversely related, *ceteris paribus*:

$$P\uparrow \ Q_d\downarrow$$
$$P\downarrow \ Q_d\uparrow \ ceteris \ paribus$$

THINKING LIKE AN ECONOMIST

When Bill says, "The more income a person has, the more expensive cars (Porsches, Corvettes) he will buy," he is not thinking like an economist. An economist knows that the ability to buy something does not necessarily imply the willingness to buy it. After all, Bill Gates, the billionaire cofounder of Microsoft, Inc., has the ability to buy many things that he chooses not to buy.

where P = price and Q_d = quantity demanded. Quantity demanded is the number of units of a good that individuals are willing and able to buy at a particular price during some time period. For example, suppose individuals are willing and able to buy 100 TV dinners per week at the price of $4 per dinner. Therefore, 100 units is the quantity demanded of TV dinners at $4.

---

1. Demand takes into account *services* as well as goods. Goods are tangible and include such things as shirts, books, and television sets. Services are intangible and include such things as dental care, medical care, and an economics lecture. To simplify the discussion, we refer only to *goods*.

Question from Setting the Scene: Does the burglary rate have anything to do with how "hard" or "soft" a city is on crime?

The law of demand holds for apples—raise the price of apples and fewer apples will be sold. But does the law of demand hold for burglary too? The mayor of New York City hinted that it does in a report on the 11 o'clock news. The mayor said, "This city and this mayor are not going to be soft on crime. We're going to do everything in our power to make sure that everyone knows that crime doesn't pay." He said these words in response to the rise in the city's burglary rate. Obviously, the mayor thinks that if the city raises the "price" a person has to pay for committing burglary (in terms of fines or jail time), there will be fewer burglaries. Do you agree? Why or why not?

Four Ways to Represent the Law of Demand

Economists use four ways to represent the law of demand.

- **In Words.** We can represent the law of demand in words; we have done so already. The law of demand states that as price rises, quantity demanded falls, and as price falls, quantity demanded rises, *ceteris paribus*.

- **In Symbols.** We can also represent the law of demand in symbols, which we have also done earlier. In symbols, the law of demand is:

$$P\uparrow \ Q_d\downarrow$$
$$P\downarrow \ Q_d\uparrow \ \textit{ceteris paribus}$$

- **In a Demand Schedule.** A demand schedule is the numerical representation of the law of demand. A demand schedule for good X is illustrated in Exhibit 1a.

- **As a Demand Curve.** In Exhibit 1b, the four price-quantity combinations in part (a) are plotted and the points connected, giving us a (downward-sloping) demand curve. A **(downward-sloping) demand curve** is the graphical representation of the inverse relationship between price and quantity demanded specified by the law of demand. In short, a demand curve is a picture of the law of demand.

Demand Schedule
The numerical tabulation of the quantity demanded of a good at different prices. A demand schedule is the numerical representation of the law of demand.

(Downward-sloping) Demand Curve
The graphical representation of the law of demand.

Demand Schedule for Good X

Price (dollars)	Quantity Demanded	Point in Part (b)
4	10	A
3	20	B
2	30	C
1	40	D

(a)

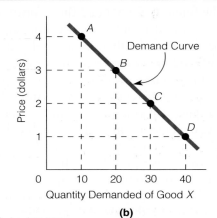

(b)

exhibit **1**

Demand Schedule and Demand Curve

Part (a) shows a demand schedule for good X. Part (b) shows a demand curve, obtained by plotting the different price-quantity combinations in part (a) and connecting the points. On a demand curve, the price (in dollars) represents price per unit of the good. The quantity demanded, on the horizontal axis, is always relevant for a specific time period (a week, a month, and so on).

Absolute and Relative Price

Absolute (Money) Price
The price of a good in money terms.

Relative Price
The price of a good in terms of another good.

In economics, there are absolute (or money) prices and relative prices. The **absolute price** of a good is the price of the good in money terms. For example, the absolute price of a car might be $30,000. The **relative price** of a good is the price of the good *in terms of another good*. For example, suppose the absolute price of a car is $30,000 and the absolute price of a computer is $2,000. The relative price of the car—that is, the price of the car in terms of computers—is 15 computers. A person gives up the opportunity to buy 15 computers when he or she buys a car.

$$\text{Relative price of a car (in terms of computers)} = \frac{\text{Absolute price of a car}}{\text{Absolute price of a computer}}$$

$$= \frac{\$30,000}{\$2,000}$$

$$= 15$$

Thus, the relative price of a car in this example is 15 computers.

Now let's compute the relative price of a computer, that is, the price of a computer in terms of a car:

$$\text{Relative price of a computer (in terms of cars)} = \frac{\text{Absolute price of a computer}}{\text{Absolute price of a car}}$$

$$= \frac{\$2,000}{\$30,000}$$

$$= \frac{1}{15}$$

Thus, the relative price of a computer in this example is 1/15 of a car. A person gives up the opportunity to buy 1/15 of a car when he or she buys a computer.

Now consider this question: What happens to the relative price of a good if its absolute price rises and nothing else changes? For example, if the absolute price of a car rises from $30,000 to $40,000 what happens to the relative price of a car? Obviously, it rises from 15 computers to 20 computers. In short, if the absolute price of a good rises and nothing else changes, then the relative price of the good rises too.

Knowing the difference between absolute price and relative price can help you understand some important economic concepts. In the next section, relative price is used in the explanation of why price and quantity demanded are inversely related.

Why Quantity Demanded Goes Down as Price Goes Up

The law of demand states that price and quantity demanded are inversely related, but it does not say why they are inversely related. We identify two reasons. The first reason is that *people substitute lower-priced goods for higher-priced goods*.

Often many goods serve the same purpose. Many different goods will satisfy hunger, and many different drinks will satisfy thirst. For example, both orange juice and grapefruit juice will satisfy thirst. Suppose that on Monday, the price of orange juice equals the price of grapefruit juice. Then on Tuesday, the price of orange juice rises. As a result, some people will choose to buy less of the relatively higher-priced orange juice and more of the relatively lower-priced grapefruit juice. In other words, a rise in the price of orange juice will lead to a decrease in the quantity demanded of orange juice.

The second reason for the inverse relationship between price and quantity demanded has to do with the **law of diminishing marginal utility**, which states that for a given time period, the marginal (additional) utility or satisfaction gained by consuming equal

Law of Diminishing Marginal Utility
For a given time period, the marginal (additional) utility or satisfaction gained by consuming equal successive units of a good will decline as the amount consumed increases.

Economics In

Popular Culture
Technology
Everyday Life
The World

© Susan Van Etten

U4E (((H))) ^5
Yours Forever, Big Hug, High Five

In December 2002, the average number of text messages sent by an American mobile subscriber was 5. In the same month and year in Singapore, the average number of text messages sent was 247; in the Philippines, it was 198; in Ireland, 70; in Norway, 62; in Spain, 45; and in Great Britain, 32.[2] These data point out what we have known for awhile: Americans do not send text messages as often as do residents of many other countries. But why? According to Alan Reiter, a telecommunications analyst in Chevy Chase, Maryland, "it's partly a cultural issue."[3]

When someone explains something by saying "it's a cultural issue," the economist believes the person simply doesn't know what the real explanation is. Saying "it's a cultural issue" is sort of like saying that the difference between Americans and others (when it comes to any particular activity) is explained by saying, "Americans are Americans and non-Americans are non-Americans." Sorry, but that's not much of an explanation.

Economists believe one of the things that explains the difference in the amount of text messaging is price. Consider a text message and a local phone call. In much of the world, people are charged for each local call they make. However, most Americans pay a set dollar amount for their local phone service. They pay the same amount each month whether they make 10 local phone calls or 100 local phone calls. (Most Americans will say, "Local calls are free," which prompts some to argue that "talk is cheap" in America.) For an American, it is cheaper to make a voice call than to text message because, unlike local phone calls, a price is charged for each text message.

Also, because local calls are "free" in the United States, people are much more likely to send instant messages (via their computers) than to text message. Although, instant messaging isn't a perfect substitute for text messaging because a computer is needed to send an instant message, it appears to be a "good enough" substitute that many Americans choose it over text messaging.

In addition, the actual dollar and cents price of sending a text message is higher in the United States than it is in many countries. For example, the price of a text message is roughly 5 to 10 cents in the United States, whereas it is generally 2 cents in much of Asia.

So, do Americans use text messaging less than most other people in the world because Americans are somehow culturally different? It's doubtful. The explanation is much more likely to be an economic one: where the price of text messaging is relatively low, people will buy more text messages than where the price is relatively high.

2. "No Text Please, We're American," *The Economist*, April 3, 2003.
3. "U.S. Cellphone Users Don't Seem To Get Message About Messaging," *The New York Times*, September 2, 2002.

successive units of a good will decline as the amount consumed increases. For example, you may receive more utility or satisfaction from eating your first hamburger at lunch than from eating your second and, if you continue on, more utility from your second hamburger than from your third.

What does this have to do with the law of demand? Economists state that the more utility you receive from a unit of a good, the higher price you are willing to pay for it; the less utility you receive from a unit of a good, the lower price you are willing to pay for it. According to the law of diminishing marginal utility, individuals obtain less utility from additional units of a good. It follows that they will only buy larger quantities of a good at lower prices. And this is the law of demand.

Individual Demand Curve and Market Demand Curve

An individual demand curve represents the price-quantity combinations of a particular good for a *single buyer*. For example, a demand curve could show Jones's demand for CDs.

exhibit **2**

Deriving a Market Demand Schedule and a Market Demand Curve
Part (a) shows four demand schedules combined into one table. The market demand schedule is derived by adding the quantities demanded at each price. In (b), the data points from the demand schedules are plotted to show how a market demand curve is derived. Only two points on the market demand curve are noted.

	Quantity Demanded			
Price	Jones	Smith	Other Buyers	All Buyers
$15	1	2	20	23
14	2	3	45	50
13	3	4	70	77
12	4 +	5 +	100 =	109
11	5 +	6 +	130 =	141
10	6	7	160	173

(a)

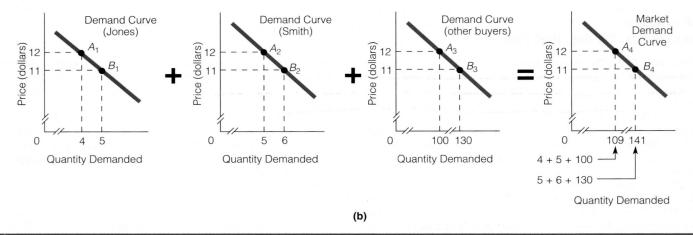

(b)

A market demand curve represents the price-quantity combinations of a particular good for *all buyers*. In this case, the demand curve would show all buyers' demand for CDs.

Exhibit 2 shows how a market demand curve can be derived by "adding" individual demand curves. The demand schedules for Jones, Smith, and other buyers are shown in part (a). The market demand schedule is obtained by adding the quantities demanded at each price. For example, at $12, the quantities demanded are 4 units for Jones, 5 units for Smith, and 100 units for other buyers. Thus, a total of 109 units are demanded at $12. In part (b), the data points for the demand schedules are plotted and "added" to produce a market demand curve. The market demand curve could also be drawn directly from the market demand schedule.

A Change in Quantity Demanded Versus a Change in Demand
Economists often talk about (1) a change in quantity demanded and (2) a change in demand. Although "quantity demanded" may sound like "demand," they are not the same. In short, a "change in quantity demanded" *is not* the same as a "change in demand." (Read the last sentence at least two more times.) We use Exhibit 1 to illustrate the difference between "a change in quantity demanded" and "a change in demand."

A Change in Quantity Demanded
Look at the horizontal axis in Exhibit 1, which is labeled "quantity demanded." Notice that quantity demanded is a number—such as 10, 20, 30, 40, and so on. More specifically, it is the number of units of a good that individuals are willing and able to buy at a particular price during some time period. In Exhibit 1, if the price is $4, then quantity

demanded is 10 units of good X; if the price is $3, then quantity demanded is 20 units of good X.

Quantity demanded = The *number* of units of a good that individuals are
willing and able to buy at a particular price

Now, again looking at Exhibit 1, what can change quantity demanded from 10 (which it is at point A) to 20 (which it is at point B)? Or, what has to change before quantity demanded will change? The answer is on the vertical axis of Exhibit 1. The only thing that can change the quantity demanded of a good is the price of the good, which is called **own price.**

Change in quantity demanded = A *movement* from one point to another point on the same
demand curve *caused* by a change in the price of the good

Own Price
The price of a good. For example, if the price of oranges is $1, this is (its) own price.

A Change in Demand
Let's look again at Exhibit 1, this time focusing on the demand curve. Demand is represented by the *entire* curve. When an economist talks about a "change in demand," he or she is actually talking about a change—or shift—in the entire demand curve.

Change in demand = Shift in demand curve

Demand can change in two ways: demand can increase and demand can decrease. Let's look first at an *increase* in demand. Suppose we have the following demand schedule.

Demand Schedule A

Price	Quantity Demanded
$20	500
$15	600
$10	700
$ 5	800

The demand curve for this demand schedule will look like the demand curve in Exhibit 1.
What does an increase in demand mean? It means that individuals are willing and able to buy more units of the good at each and every price. In other words, demand schedule A will change as follows:

Demand Schedule B (increase in demand)

Price	Quantity Demanded
$20	~~500~~ 600
$15	~~600~~ 700
$10	~~700~~ 800
$ 5	~~800~~ 900

Whereas individuals were willing and able to buy 500 units of the good at $20, now they are willing and able to buy 600 units of the good at $20; whereas individuals were willing and able to buy 600 units of the good at $15, now they are willing and able to buy 700 units of the good at $15; and so on.
As shown in Exhibit 3a, the demand curve that represents demand schedule B lies to the right of the demand curve that represents demand schedule A. We conclude that *an*

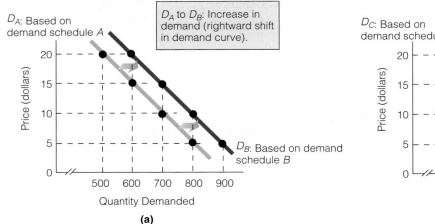

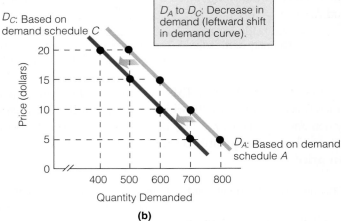

(a) **(b)**

Shifts in the Demand Curve
In part (a), the demand curve shifts rightward from DA to DB. This shift represents an increase in demand. At each price, the quantity demanded is greater than it was before. For example, the quantity demanded at $20 increases from 500 units to 600 units. In part (b), the demand curve shifts leftward from DA to DC. This shift represents a decrease in demand. At each price, the quantity demanded is less. For example, the quantity demand at $20 decreases from 500 units to 400 units.

increase in demand is represented by a rightward shift in the demand curve and means that individuals are willing and able to buy more of a good at each and every price.

Increase in demand = Rightward shift in the demand curve

Now let's look at a *decrease* in demand. What does a decrease in demand mean? It means that individuals are willing and able to buy less of a good at each and every price. In this case, demand schedule *A* will change as follows:

Demand Schedule C (decrease in demand)

Price	Quantity Demanded	
$20	~~500~~	400
$15	~~600~~	500
$10	~~700~~	600
$ 5	~~800~~	700

As shown in Exhibit 3b, the demand curve that represents demand schedule *C* obviously lies to the left of the demand curve that represents demand schedule *A*. We conclude that *a decrease in demand is represented by a leftward shift in the demand curve and means that individuals are willing and able to buy less of a good at each and every price.*

Decrease in demand = Leftward shift in the demand curve

What Factors Cause the Demand Curve to Shift?

We know what an increase and decrease in demand mean: An increase in demand means consumers are willing and able to buy more of a good at every price. A decrease in demand means consumers are willing and able to buy less of a good every price. We also know that an increase in demand is graphically portrayed as a rightward shift in a demand curve and a decrease in demand is graphically portrayed as a leftward shift in a demand curve.

But, what factors or variables can increase or decrease demand? What factors or variables can shift demand curves? We identify and discuss these factors or variables in this section.

Income

As a person's income changes (increases or decreases), his or her demand for a particular good may rise, fall, or remain constant.

For example, suppose Jack's income rises. As a consequence, his demand for CDs rises. For Jack, CDs are a normal good. For a **normal good,** as income rises, demand for the good rises, and as income falls, demand for the good falls.

Normal Good
A good the demand for which rises (falls) as income rises (falls).

$$X \text{ is a normal good:} \quad \text{If income} \uparrow \text{ then } D_X \uparrow$$
$$\text{If income} \downarrow \text{ then } D_X \downarrow$$

Now suppose Marie's income rises. As a consequence, her demand for canned baked beans falls. For Marie, canned baked beans are an inferior good. For an **inferior good,** as income rises, demand for the good falls, and as income falls, demand for the good rises.

Inferior Good
A good the demand for which falls (rises) as income rises (falls).

$$Y \text{ is an inferior good:} \quad \text{If income} \uparrow \text{ then } D_Y \downarrow$$
$$\text{If income} \downarrow \text{ then } D_Y \uparrow$$

Finally, suppose when George's income rises, his demand for toothpaste neither rises nor falls. For George, toothpaste is neither a normal good nor an inferior good. Instead, it is a neutral good. For a **neutral good,** as income rises or falls, the demand for the good does not change.

Neutral Good
A good the demand for which does not change as income rises or falls.

Preferences

People's preferences affect the amount of a good they are willing to buy at a particular price. A change in preferences in favor of a good shifts the demand curve rightward. A change in preferences away from the good shifts the demand curve leftward. For example, if people begin to favor Tom Clancy novels to a greater degree than previously, the demand for Clancy novels increases and the demand curve shifts rightward.

Prices of Related Goods

There are two types of related goods: substitutes and complements. Two goods are **substitutes** if they satisfy similar needs or desires. For many people, Coca-Cola and Pepsi-Cola are substitutes. If two goods are substitutes, as the price of one rises (falls), the demand for the other rises (falls). For instance, higher Coca-Cola prices will increase the demand for Pepsi-Cola as people substitute Pepsi for the higher-priced Coke (Exhibit 4a). Other examples of substitutes are coffee and tea, corn chips and potato chips, two brands of margarine, and foreign and domestic cars.

Substitutes
Two goods that satisfy similar needs or desires. If two goods are substitutes, the demand for one rises as the price of the other rises (or the demand for one falls as the price of the other falls).

$$X \text{ and } Y \text{ are substitutes:} \quad \text{If } P_X \uparrow \text{ then } D_Y \uparrow$$
$$\text{If } P_X \downarrow \text{ then } D_Y \downarrow$$

Two goods are **complements** if they are consumed jointly. For example, tennis rackets and tennis balls are used together to play tennis. If two goods are complements, as the price of one rises (falls), the demand for the other falls (rises). For example, higher tennis racket prices will decrease the demand for tennis balls, as Exhibit 4b shows. Other examples of complements are cars and tires, light bulbs and lamps, and golf clubs and golf balls.

Complements
Two goods that are used jointly in consumption. If two goods are complements, the demand for one rises as the price of the other falls (or the demand for one falls as the price of the other rises).

$$A \text{ and } B \text{ are complements:} \quad \text{If } P_A \uparrow \text{ then } D_B \downarrow$$
$$\text{If } P_A \downarrow \text{ then } D_B \uparrow$$

Number of Buyers

The demand for a good in a particular market area is related to the number of buyers in the area: More buyers, higher demand; fewer buyers, lower demand. The number of buyers may increase owing to a higher birthrate, increased immigration, the migration of people from

exhibit **4**

Substitutes and Complements
(a) Coca-Cola and Pepsi-Cola are substitutes: The price of one and the demand for the other are directly related. As the price of Coca-Cola rises, the demand for Pepsi-Cola increases. (b) Tennis rackets and tennis balls are complements: The price of one and the demand for the other are inversely related. As the price of tennis rackets rises, the demand for tennis balls decreases.

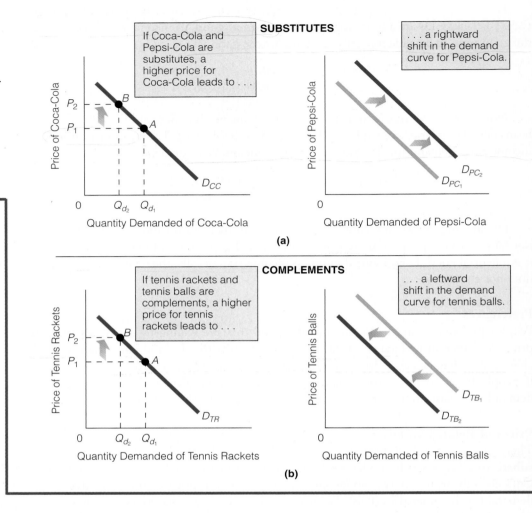

SUBSTITUTES

If Coca-Cola and Pepsi-Cola are substitutes, a higher price for Coca-Cola leads to . . .

. . . a rightward shift in the demand curve for Pepsi-Cola.

(a)

COMPLEMENTS

If tennis rackets and tennis balls are complements, a higher price for tennis rackets leads to . . .

. . . a leftward shift in the demand curve for tennis balls.

(b)

THINKING LIKE AN ECONOMIST

Economists analyze numerous curves as they look for answers to their questions. In their analyses, economists identify two types of factors related to curves: (1) factors that can move us along curves and (2) factors that can shift curves.

The factors that move us along curves are sometimes called movement factors. In many economic diagrams—such as the diagram of the demand curve in Exhibit 1—the movement factor is on the vertical axis.

The factors that actually shift the curves are sometimes called shift factors. The shift factors for the demand curve are income, preferences, the price of related goods, and so on. Often the shift factors do not appear in the economic diagrams. For example, in Exhibit 1, the movement factor—price—is on the vertical axis, but the shift factors do not appear anywhere in the diagram. We just know what they are and that they can shift the demand curve.

When you see a curve in this book, first ask what factor will move us along the curve. In other words, what is the movement factor? Second, ask what factors will shift the curve. In other words, what are the shift factors? Exhibit 5 summarizes the shift factors that can change demand and the movement factors that can change quantity demanded.

one region of the country to another, and so on. The number of buyers may decrease owing to a higher death rate, war, the migration of people from one region of the country to another, and so on.

Expectations of Future Price
Buyers who expect the price of a good to be higher next month may buy the good now—thus increasing the current demand for the good. Buyers who expect the price of a good to be lower next month may wait until next month to buy the good—thus decreasing the current demand for the good.

For example, suppose you are planning to buy a house. One day, you hear that house prices are expected to go down in a few months. Consequently, you decide to hold off your purchase of a house for a few months. Alternatively, if you hear that prices are expected to rise in a few months, you might go ahead and purchase a house now.

Popular Culture · Technology · Everyday Life · The World

Getting to Class on Time

Class starts at 10 o'clock in the morning. At 10:09, Pam Ferrario walks in late. She apologizes to the instructor, saying, "I've been on campus for 20 minutes, but I couldn't find a parking space." Her classmates nod, knowing full well what she is talking about. At Pam's university, especially between the hours of 8 A.M. and 2 P.M., parking spaces are hard to find.

This scene is replayed every day at many universities and colleges across the country. Students are late for class because on many days there isn't a parking space to be found. Why can't students find parking spaces? The immediate answer is because there is a shortage of parking spaces. But why is there a shortage of parking spaces? There is a shortage of parking spaces for the same reason there is any shortage: the equilibrium price is not being charged.

Who pays for the shortage of parking spaces? The students pay—not in money, but in time. Because students know parking spaces on campus are hard to find, they often leave home or work sooner than they would if there were no shortages. Or like Pam Ferrario, they pay by being late to class.

Are there alternatives to the *pay-in-time* and *pay-in-being-late-to-class* schemes for rationing campus parking spots? Some economists have suggested a *pay-in-price* scheme. For example, the university could install meters in the parking lot and raise the fee high enough so that between the hours of 8 A.M. and 2 P.M., the quantity demanded for parking spaces equals the quantity supplied.

Such suggestions are sometimes criticized on the basis that students must pay the parking fee, no matter how high, in order to attend classes. But that's not exactly true. Parking off campus and using public transportation are sometimes alternatives. But this is not really the main point. The issue isn't paying or not paying, but choosing *how* to pay—in dollar price, time, or being late for class.

Some economists have taken the pay-in-price scheme further and have argued that parking spots should be auctioned on a yearly basis. In other words, a student would rent a parking spot for a year. This way the student would always know that a parking spot would be open when he or she arrived at the campus. People who parked in someone else's spot would be ticketed by campus police.

Additionally, under this scheme, a student who rented a parking spot and chose not to use it between certain hours of the day could rent it to someone else during this period. So we would expect to see notices like this on campus billboards:

PARKING SPOT FOR RENT
Near Arts Building and Student Union. Ideal for liberal arts students. Available on a 2–12 hour basis between 12 noon and 12 midnight. Rate: $1 per hour. Call Jenny at 555–5309.

SELF-TEST   *(Answers to Self-Test questions are in the Self-Test Appendix.)*

1. As Sandi's income rises, her demand for popcorn rises. As Mark's income falls, his demand for prepaid telephone cards rises. What kinds of goods are popcorn and telephone cards for the people who demand each?
2. Why are demand curves downward-sloping?
3. Give an example that illustrates how to derive a market demand curve.
4. What factors can change demand? What factors can change quantity demanded?

SUPPLY

Just as the word *demand* has a specific meaning in economics, so does the word *supply.* **Supply** refers to (1) the willingness and ability of sellers to produce and offer to sell different quantities of a good (2) at different prices (3) during a specific time period (per day, week, and so on).

Supply
The willingness and ability of sellers to produce and offer to sell different quantities of a good at different prices during a specific time period.

exhibit **5**

A Change in Demand Versus a Change in Quantity Demanded
(a) A change in demand refers to a shift in the demand curve. A change in demand can be brought about by a number of factors (see the exhibit and text). (b) A change in quantity demanded refers to a movement along a given demand curve. A change in quantity demanded is brought about only by a change in (a good's) own price.

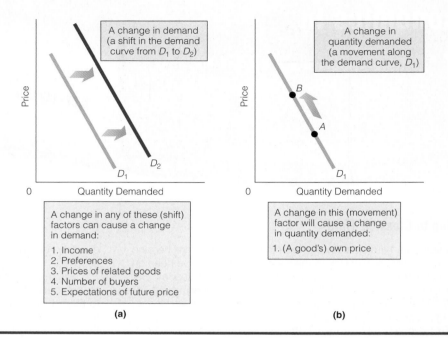

(a)

A change in demand
(a shift in the demand
curve from D_1 to D_2)

A change in
quantity demanded
(a movement along
the demand curve, D_1)

A change in any of these (shift) factors can cause a change in demand:

1. Income
2. Preferences
3. Prices of related goods
4. Number of buyers
5. Expectations of future price

A change in this (movement) factor will cause a change in quantity demanded:

1. (A good's) own price

(b)

Law of Supply
As the price of a good rises, the quantity supplied of the good rises, and as the price of a good falls, the quantity supplied of the good falls, *ceteris paribus*.

(Upward-sloping) Supply Curve
The graphical representation of the law of supply.

exhibit **6**

A Supply Curve
The upward-sloping supply curve is the graphical representation of the law of supply, which states that price and quantity supplied are directly related, *ceteris paribus*. On a supply curve, the price (in dollars) represents price per unit of the good. The quantity supplied, on the horizontal axis, is always relevant for a specific time period (a week, a month, and so on).

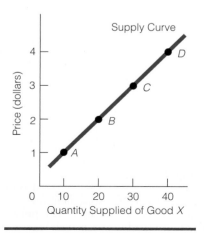

The Law of Supply

The **law of supply** states that as the price of a good rises, the quantity supplied of the good rises, and as the price of a good falls, the quantity supplied of the good falls, *ceteris paribus*. Simply put, the price of a good and the quantity supplied of the good are directly related, *ceteris paribus*. (Quantity supplied is the number of units of a good sellers are willing and able to produce and offer to sell at a particular price.) The **(upward-sloping) supply curve** is the graphical representation of the law of supply (see Exhibit 6).

The law of supply can be summarized as follows:

$$P \uparrow Q_S \uparrow$$
$$P \downarrow Q_S \downarrow \text{ ceteris paribus}$$

where P = price and Q_S = quantity supplied.

The law of supply holds for the production of most goods. It does not hold when there is no time to produce more units of a good. For example, suppose a theater in Atlanta is sold out for tonight's play. Even if ticket prices increased from $30 to $40, there would be no additional seats in the theater. There is no time to produce more seats. The supply curve for theater seats is illustrated in Exhibit 7a. It is fixed at the number of seats in the theater, 500.[4]

The law of supply also does not hold for goods that cannot be produced over any period of time. For example, the violinmaker Antonio Stradivari died in 1737. A rise in the price of Stradivarius violins does not affect the number of Stradivarius violins supplied, as Exhibit 7b illustrates.

Why Most Supply Curves Are Upward-Sloping

Think back to the discussion of the *law of increasing opportunity costs* in Chapter 2. That discussion shows that if the production possibilities frontier (PPF) is bowed outward, increasing costs exist. In other words, increased production of a good comes at increased

---

4. The vertical supply curve is said to be *perfectly inelastic*.

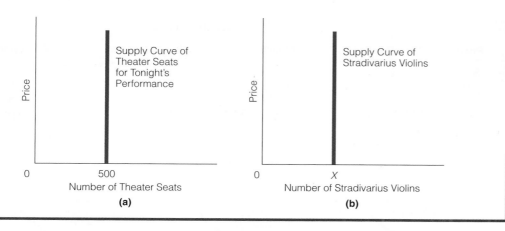

exhibit 7

Supply Curves When There Is No Time to Produce More or No More Can Be Produced
The supply curve is not upward-sloping when there is no time to produce additional units or when additional units cannot be produced. In those cases, the supply curve is vertical.

opportunity costs. An upward-sloping supply curve simply reflects the fact that costs rise when more units of a good are produced.

The Market Supply Curve

An individual supply curve represents the price-quantity combinations for a single seller. The market supply curve represents the price-quantity combinations for all sellers of a particular good. Exhibit 8 shows how a market supply curve can be derived by "adding" individual supply curves. In part (a), a **supply schedule,** the numerical tabulation of the quantity supplied of a good at different prices, is given for Brown, Alberts, and other suppliers. The market supply schedule is obtained by adding the quantities supplied at each price, *ceteris paribus.* For example, at $11, the quantities supplied are 2 units for Brown, 3 units for Alberts, and 98 units for other suppliers. Thus, a total of 103 units are supplied at $11. In part (b), the data points for the supply schedules are plotted and "added" to produce a market supply curve. The market supply curve could also be drawn directly from the market supply schedule.

Supply Schedule
The numerical tabulation of the quantity supplied of a good at different prices. A supply schedule is the numerical representation of the law of supply.

Changes in Supply Mean Shifts in Supply Curves

Just as demand can change, so can supply. The supply of a good can rise or fall. What does it mean if the supply of a good increases? It means that suppliers are willing and able to produce and offer to sell more of the good at all prices. For example, suppose that in January sellers are willing and able to produce and offer for sale 600 shirts at $25 each and that in February they are willing and able to produce and sell 900 shirts at $25 each. An increase in supply shifts the entire supply curve to the right, as shown in Exhibit 9a.

The supply of a good decreases if sellers are willing and able to produce and offer to sell less of the good at all prices. For example, suppose that in January sellers are willing and able to produce and offer for sale 600 shirts at $25 each and that in February they are willing and able to produce and sell only 300 shirts at $25 each. A decrease in supply shifts the entire supply curve to the left, as shown in Exhibit 9b.

What Factors Cause the Supply Curve to Shift?

We know the supply of any good can change. But what causes supply to change? What causes supply curves to shift? The factors that can change supply include (1) prices of relevant resources, (2) technology, (3) number of sellers, (4) expectations of future price, (5) taxes and subsidies, and (6) government restrictions.

Prices of Relevant Resources

Resources are needed to produce goods. For example, wood is needed to produce doors. If the price of wood falls, it becomes less costly to produce doors. How will door producers

exhibit **8**

Deriving a Market Supply Schedule and a Market Supply Curve

Part (a) shows four supply schedules combined into one table. The market supply schedule is derived by adding the quantities supplied at each price. In (b), the data points from the supply schedules are plotted to show how a market supply curve is derived. Only two points on the market supply curve are noted.

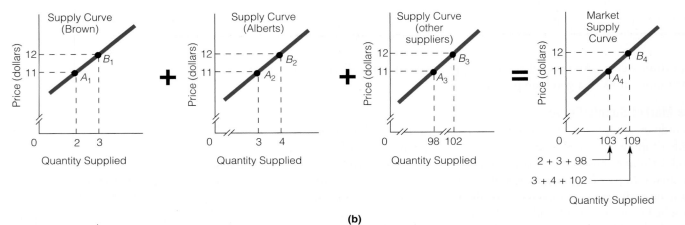

		Quantity Supplied		
Price	Brown	Alberts	Other Suppliers	All Suppliers
$10	1	2	96	99
11	2 +	3 +	98 =	103
12	3 +	4 +	102 =	109
13	4	5	106	115
14	5	6	108	119
15	6	7	110	123

(a)

(b)

---

exhibit **9**

Shifts in the Supply Curve

(a) The supply curve shifts rightward from S_1 to S_2. This represents an increase in the supply of shirts: At each price the quantity supplied of shirts is greater. For example, the quantity supplied at $25 increases from 600 shirts to 900 shirts. (b) The supply curve shifts leftward from S_1 to S_2. This represents a decrease in the supply of shirts: At each price the quantity supplied of shirts is less. For example, the quantity supplied at $25 decreases from 600 shirts to 300 shirts.

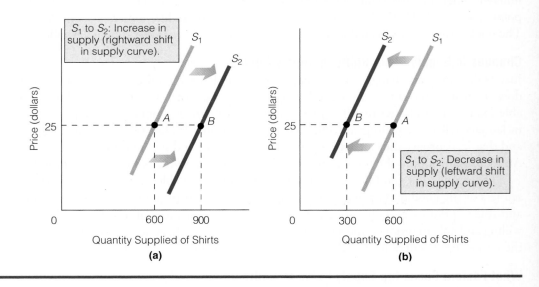

---

respond? Will they produce more doors, the same number of doors, or fewer doors? With lower costs and prices unchanged, the profit from producing and selling doors has increased; as a result, there is an increased incentive to produce doors. Door producers will produce and offer to sell more doors at each and every price. Thus, the supply of doors will increase and the supply curve of doors will shift rightward. If the price of wood rises, it becomes more costly to produce doors. Consequently, the supply of doors will decrease and the supply curve of doors will shift leftward.

Technology

In Chapter 2, technology is defined as the body of skills and knowledge concerning the use of resources in production. Also, an advance in technology refers to the ability to produce more output with a fixed amount of resources, thus reducing per-unit production costs. To illustrate, suppose it currently takes $100 to produce 40 units of a good. The per-unit cost is therefore $2.50. If an advance in technology makes it possible to produce 50 units at a cost of $100, then the per-unit cost falls to $2.00.

If per-unit production costs of a good decline, we expect the quantity supplied of the good at each price to increase. Why? The reason is that lower per-unit costs increase profitability and therefore provide producers with an incentive to produce more. For example, if corn growers develop a way to grow more corn using the same amount of water and other resources, it follows that per-unit production costs will fall, profitability will increase, and growers will want to grow and sell more corn at each price. The supply curve of corn will shift rightward.

Number of Sellers

If more sellers begin producing a particular good, perhaps because of high profits, the supply curve will shift rightward. If some sellers stop producing a particular good, perhaps because of losses, the supply curve will shift leftward.

Expectations of Future Price

If the price of a good is expected to be higher in the future, producers may hold back some of the product today (if possible; for example, perishables cannot be held back). Then, they will have more to sell at the higher future price. Therefore, the current supply curve will shift leftward. For example, if oil producers expect the price of oil to be higher next year, some may hold oil off the market this year to be able to sell it next year. Similarly, if they expect the price of oil to be lower next year, they might pump more oil this year than previously planned.

Taxes and Subsidies

Some taxes increase per-unit costs. Suppose a shoe manufacturer must pay a $2 tax per pair of shoes produced. This tax leads to a leftward shift in the supply curve, indicating that the manufacturer wants to produce and offer to sell fewer pairs of shoes at each price. If the tax is eliminated, the supply curve shifts rightward.

Subsidies have the opposite effect. Suppose the government subsidizes the production of corn by paying corn farmers $2 for every bushel of corn they produce. Because of the subsidy, the quantity supplied of corn is greater at each price and the supply curve of corn shifts rightward. Removal of the subsidy shifts the supply curve of corn leftward. A rough rule of thumb is that we get more of what we subsidize and less of what we tax.

(Production) Subsidy
A monetary payment by government to a producer of a good or service.

Government Restrictions

Sometimes government acts to reduce supply. Consider a U.S. import quota on Japanese television sets. An import quota, or quantitative restriction on foreign goods, reduces the supply of Japanese television sets in the United States. It shifts the supply curve leftward. The elimination of the import quota allows the supply of Japanese television sets in the United States to shift rightward.

Licensure has a similar effect. With licensure, individuals must meet certain requirements before they can legally carry out a task. For example, owner-operators of day-care centers must meet certain requirements before they are allowed to sell their services. No

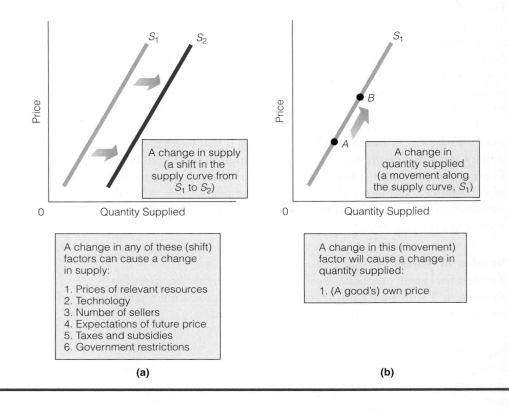

exhibit **10**

**A Change in Supply Versus
a Change in Quantity Supplied**
(a) A change in supply refers to a shift in
the supply curve. A change in supply can
be brought about by a number of factors
(see the exhibit and text). (b) A change in
quantity supplied refers to a movement
along a given supply curve. A change in
quantity supplied is brought about only
by a change in (a good's) own price.

A change in supply
(a shift in the
supply curve from
S_1 to S_2)

A change in
quantity supplied
(a movement along
the supply curve, S_1)

A change in any of these (shift)
factors can cause a change
in supply:

1. Prices of relevant resources
2. Technology
3. Number of sellers
4. Expectations of future price
5. Taxes and subsidies
6. Government restrictions

A change in this (movement)
factor will cause a change in
quantity supplied:

1. (A good's) own price

(a)

(b)

doubt this reduces the number of day-care centers and shifts the supply curve of day-care
centers leftward.

A Change in Supply Versus a Change in Quantity Supplied

Just as a change in demand is not the same as a change in quantity demanded, a change
in supply is not the same as a change in quantity supplied. A change in supply refers to a
shift in the supply curve, as illustrated in Exhibit 10a. For example, saying that the supply of oranges has increased is the same as saying that the supply curve for oranges has
shifted rightward. The factors that can change supply (shift the supply curve) include
prices of relevant resources, technology, number of sellers, expectations of future price,
taxes and subsidies, and government restrictions.

A change in quantity supplied refers to a movement along a supply curve, as in
Exhibit 10b. The only factor that can directly cause a change in the quantity supplied of
a good is a change in the price of the good, or own price.

SELF-TEST

1. What would the supply curve for houses (in a given city) look like for a time period of (a) the
next 10 hours and (b) the next 3 months?
2. What happens to the supply curve if each of the following occurs?
   a. There is a decrease in the number of sellers.
   b. A per-unit tax is placed on the production of a good.
   c. The price of a relevant resource falls.
3. "If the price of apples rises, the supply of apples will rise." True or false? Explain your
answer.

THE MARKET: PUTTING SUPPLY AND DEMAND TOGETHER

In this section, we put supply and demand together and discuss the market. The purpose of the discussion is to gain some understanding about how prices are determined.

Supply and Demand at Work at an Auction

Imagine you are at an auction where bushels of corn are bought and sold. At this auction, the auctioneer will adjust the corn price to sell all the corn offered for sale. The supply curve of corn is vertical, as in Exhibit 11. It intersects the horizontal axis at 40,000 bushels; that is, quantity supplied is 40,000 bushels. The demand curve for corn is downward-sloping. Furthermore, suppose each potential buyer of corn is sitting in front of a computer that immediately registers the number of bushels he or she wants to buy. For example, if Nancy Bernstein wants to buy 5,000 bushels of corn, she simply keys "5,000" into her computer. The auction begins. (Follow along in Exhibit 11 as we relay what is happening at the auction.) The auctioneer calls out the price:

- **$6.00.** The potential buyers think for a second, and then each registers the number of bushels he or she is willing and able to buy at that price. The total is 10,000 bushels, which is the quantity demanded of corn at $6.00. The auctioneer, realizing that 30,000 bushels of corn (40,000 − 10,000 = 30,000) will go unsold at this price, decides to lower the price per bushel to:
- **$5.00.** The quantity demanded increases to 20,000 bushels, but still the quantity supplied of corn at this price is greater than the quantity demanded. The auctioneer calls out:
- **$4.00.** The quantity demanded increases to 30,000 bushels, but the quantity supplied at $4.00 is still greater than the quantity demanded. The auctioneer drops the price down to:
- **$1.25.** At this price, the quantity demanded jumps to 60,000 bushels, but that is 20,000 bushels more than the quantity supplied. The auctioneer calls out a higher price:
- **$2.25.** The quantity demanded drops to 50,000 bushels, but buyers still want to buy more corn at this price than there is corn to be sold. The auctioneer calls out:

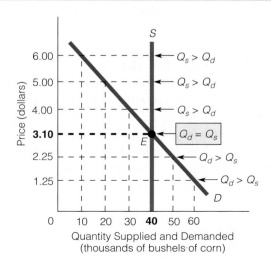

exhibit **11**

Supply and Demand at Work at an Auction
Q_d = quantity demanded; Q_s = quantity supplied. The auctioneer calls out different prices, and buyers record how much they are willing and able to buy. At prices of $6.00, $5.00, and $4.00, quantity supplied is greater than quantity demanded. At prices of $1.25 and $2.25, quantity demanded is greater than quantity supplied. At a price of $3.10, quantity demanded equals quantity supplied.

- **$3.10.** At this price, the quantity demanded of corn is 40,000 bushels and the quantity supplied of corn is 40,000 bushels. The auction stops. The 40,000 bushels of corn are bought and sold at $3.10 per bushel.

The Language of Supply and Demand: A Few Important Terms

If quantity supplied is greater than quantity demanded, a **surplus** or **excess supply** exists. If quantity demanded is greater than quantity supplied, a **shortage** or **excess demand** exists. In Exhibit 11, a surplus exists at $6.00, $5.00, and $4.00. A shortage exists at $1.25 and $2.25. The price at which quantity demanded equals quantity supplied is the **equilibrium price** or **market-clearing price.** In our example, $3.10 is the equilibrium price. The quantity that corresponds to the equilibrium price is the **equilibrium quantity.** In our example, it is 40,000 bushels of corn. Any price at which quantity demanded is not equal to quantity supplied is a **disequilibrium price.**

A market that exhibits either a surplus ($Q_s > Q_d$) or a shortage ($Q_d > Q_s$) is said to be in **disequilibrium.** A market in which quantity demanded equals quantity supplied ($Q_d = Q_s$) is said to be in **equilibrium** (identified by the letter E in Exhibit 11).

Moving to Equilibrium: What Happens to Price When There Is a Surplus or a Shortage?

What did the auctioneer do when the price was $6.00 and there was a surplus of corn? He lowered the price. What did the auctioneer do when the price was $2.25 and there was a shortage of corn? He raised the price. The behavior of the auctioneer can be summarized this way: If a surplus exists, lower price; if a shortage exists, raise price. This is how the auctioneer moved the corn market into equilibrium.

Not all markets have auctioneers. (When was the last time you saw an auctioneer in the grocery store?) But many markets act *as if* an auctioneer were calling out higher and lower prices until equilibrium price is reached. In many real-world auctioneerless markets, prices fall when there is a surplus and rise when there is a shortage. Why?

Why Does Price Fall When There Is a Surplus?

In Exhibit 12, there is a surplus at a price of $15: quantity supplied (150 units) is greater than quantity demanded (50 units). Suppliers will not be able to sell all they had hoped to sell at $15. As a result, their inventories will grow beyond the level they hold in preparation for demand changes. Sellers will want to reduce their inventories. Some will lower prices to do so, some will cut back on production, others will do a little of both. As shown in the exhibit, there is a tendency for price and output to fall until equilibrium is achieved.

Why Does Price Rise When There Is a Shortage?

In Exhibit 12, there is a shortage at a price of $5: quantity demanded (150 units) is greater than quantity supplied (50 units). Buyers will not be able to buy all they had hoped to buy at $5. Some buyers will bid up the price to get sellers to sell to them instead of to other buyers. Some sellers, seeing buyers clamor for the goods, will realize that they can raise the price of the goods they have for sale. Higher prices will also call forth added output. Thus, there is a tendency for price and output to rise until equilibrium is achieved.

Also, see Exhibit 13 which brings together much of what we have discussed about supply and demand.

Speed of Moving to Equilibrium

On January 9, 2004, at 1:28 P.M., the price of a share of IBM stock was $91.88. A few seconds later, the price had risen to $92.11. Obviously, the stock market is a market that

Surplus (Excess Supply)
A condition in which quantity supplied is greater than quantity demanded. Surpluses occur only at prices above equililbrium price.

Shortage (Excess Demand)
A condition in which quantity demanded is greater than quantity supplied. Shortages occur only at prices below equilibrium price.

Equilibrium Price (Market-Clearing Price)
The price at which quantity demanded of the good equals quantity supplied.

Equilibrium Quantity
The quantity that corresponds to equilibrium price. The quantity at which the amount of the good that buyers are willing and able to buy equals the amount that sellers are willing and able to sell, and both equal the amount actually bought and sold.

Disequilibrium Price
A price other than equilibrium price. A price at which quantity demanded does not equal quantity supplied.

Disequilibrium
A state of either surplus or shortage in a market.

Equilibrium
Equilibrium means "at rest." Equilibrium in a market is the price-quantity combination from which there is no tendency for buyers or sellers to move away. Graphically, equilibrium is the intersection point of the supply and demand curves.

Price	Q_s	Q_d	Condition
$15	150	50	Surplus
10	100	100	Equilibrium
5	50	150	Shortage

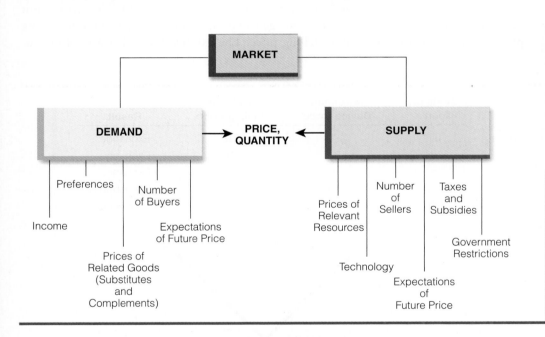

exhibit 12

Moving to Equilibrium
If there is a surplus, sellers' inventories rise above the level they hold in preparation for demand changes. Sellers will want to reduce their inventories. As a result, price and output fall until equilibrium is achieved. If there is a shortage, some buyers will bid up price to get sellers to sell to them instead of to others buyers. Some sellers will realize they can raise the price of the goods they have for sale. Higher prices will call forth added output. Price and output rise until equilibrium is achieved. (Note: Recall that price, on the vertical axis, is price per unit of the good, and quantity, on the horizontal axis, is for a specific time period. In this text, we do not specify this on the axes themselves, but consider it to be understood.)

exhibit 13

A Summary Exhibit of a Market (Supply and Demand)
This exhibit ties together the topics discussed so far in this chapter. A market is composed of both supply and demand, as shown. Also shown are the factors that affect supply and demand and therefore indirectly affect the equilibrium price and quantity of a good.

equilibrates quickly. If demand rises, then initially there is a shortage of the stock at the current equilibrium price. The price is bid up and there is no longer a shortage. All this happens in seconds.

Now consider a house offered for sale in any city in the country. It is not uncommon for the sale price of a house to remain the same even though the house does not sell for months. For example, a person offers to sell her house for $400,000. One month passes, no sale; two months pass, no sale; three months pass, no sale; and so on. Ten months later, the house has still not sold and the price is still $400,000.

Is $400,000 the equilibrium price of the house? Obviously not. At the equilibrium price, there would be a buyer for the house and a seller of the house (quantity demanded would equal quantity supplied). At a price of $400,000, there is a seller of the house but no buyer. The price of $400,000 is above equilibrium price. At $400,000, there is a surplus in the housing market; equilibrium has not been achieved.

Some people may be tempted to argue that supply and demand are at work in the stock market but not in the housing market. A better explanation, though, is that *not all markets equilibrate at the same speed.* While it may take only seconds for the stock market to go from surplus or shortage to equilibrium, it may take months for the housing market to do so.

Moving to Equilibrium: Maximum and Minimum Prices

The discussion of surpluses illustrates how a market moves to equilibrium, but there is another way to show this. Exhibit 14 shows the market for good *X*. Look at the first unit of good *X*. What is the *maximum price buyers would be willing to pay* for it? The answer is $70. This can be seen by following the dotted line up from the first unit of the good to the demand curve. What is the *minimum price sellers need to receive before they would be willing to sell* this unit of good *X*? It is $10. This can be seen by following the dotted line up from the first unit to the supply curve. Because the maximum buying price is greater than the minimum selling price, the first unit of good *X* will be exchanged.

What about the second unit? For the second unit, buyers are willing to pay a maximum price of $60 and sellers need to receive a minimum price of $20. The second unit of good *X* will be exchanged. In fact, exchange will occur as long as the maximum buying price is greater than the minimum selling price. The exhibit shows that a total of four

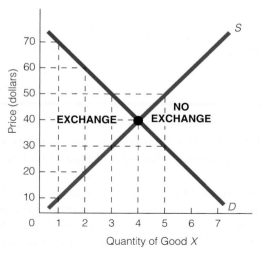

exhibit 14

Moving to Equilibrium in Terms of Maximum and Minimum Prices
As long as the maximum buying price is greater than the minimum selling price, an exchange will occur. This condition is met for units 1–4. The market converges on equilibrium through a process of mutually beneficial exchanges.

Units of Good X	Maximum Buying Price	Minimum Selling Price	Result
1st	$70	$10	Exchange
2d	60	20	Exchange
3d	50	30	Exchange
4th	40	40	Exchange
5th	30	50	No Exchange

units of good X will be exchanged. The fifth unit will not be exchanged because the maximum buying price ($30) is less than the minimum selling price ($50).

In the process just described, buyers and sellers trade money for goods as long as both benefit from the trade. The market converges on a quantity of 4 units of good X and a price of $40 per unit. This is equilibrium. In other words, mutually beneficial trade drives the market to equilibrium.

Equilibrium in Terms of Consumers' and Producers' Surplus

Equilibrium can be viewed in terms of two important economic concepts, consumers' surplus and producers' (or sellers') surplus. **Consumers' surplus** is the difference between the maximum buying price and the price paid by the buyer.

Consumers' surplus = Maximum buying price − Price paid

For example, if the highest price you would pay to see a movie is $10 and you pay $7 to see the movie, then you have received $3 consumers' surplus. Obviously, the more consumers' surplus consumers receive, the better off they are. Wouldn't you have preferred to pay, say, $4 to see the movie instead of $7? If you had paid only $4, your consumers' surplus would have been $6 instead of $3.

Producers' surplus is the difference between the price received by the producer or seller and the minimum selling price.

Producers' (sellers') surplus = Price received − Minimum selling price

Suppose the minimum price the owner of the movie theater would have accepted for admission is $5. But she doesn't sell admission for $5, but $7. Her producers' or sellers' surplus is $2. A seller prefers a large producers' surplus to a small one. The theater owner would have preferred to sell admission to the movie for $8 instead of $7 because then she would have received $3 producers' surplus.

Total surplus is the sum of the consumer's surplus and producer's surplus.

Total surplus = Consumers' surplus + Producers' surplus

In Exhibit 15a, consumers' surplus is represented by the shaded triangle. This triangle includes the area under the demand curve and above the equilibrium price. According to the definition, consumers' surplus is the highest price buyers are willing to pay (maximum buying price) minus the price they pay. For example, the window in (a) shows that buyers are willing to pay as high as $7 for the 50th unit, but only pay $5. Thus, the consumers' surplus on the 50th unit of the good is $2. If we add the consumers' surplus on each unit of the good between and including the first and the 100th (100 units being the equilibrium quantity), we obtain the shaded consumers' surplus triangle.

In Exhibit 15b, producers' surplus is represented by the shaded triangle. This triangle includes the area above the supply curve and under the equilibrium price. Keep in mind the definition of producers' surplus—the price received by the seller minus the lowest price the seller would accept for the good. For example, the window in (b) shows that sellers would have sold the 50th unit for as low as $3 but actually sold it for $5. Thus, the producers' surplus on the 50th unit of the good is $2. If we add the producers' surplus on each unit of the good between and including the first and the 100th, we obtain the shaded producers' surplus triangle.

Now consider consumers' surplus and producers' surplus at the equilibrium quantity. Exhibit 16 shows that consumers' surplus at equilibrium is equal to areas $A + B + C + D$,

Consumers' Surplus *(CS)*
The difference between the maximum price a buyer is willing and able to pay for a good or service and the price actually paid. CS = Maximum buying price − Price paid

Producers' (Sellers') Surplus *(PS)*
The difference between the price sellers receive for a good and the minimum or lowest price for which they would have sold the good. PS = Price received − Minimum selling price

Total Surplus *(TS)*
The sum of consumers' surplus and producers' surplus. $TS = CS + PS$

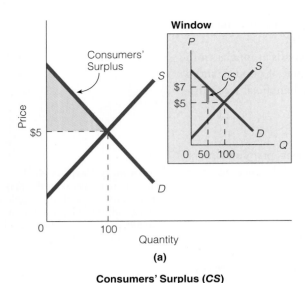

(a)

Consumers' Surplus (CS)

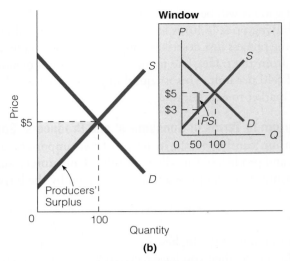

(b)

Producers' Surplus (PS)

and producers' surplus at equilibrium is equal to areas $E + F + G + H$. At any other exchangeable quantity, such as at 25, 50, or 75 units, both consumers' surplus and producers' surplus are less. For example, at 25 units, consumers' surplus is equal to area A and producers' surplus is equal to area E. At 50 units, consumers' surplus is equal to areas $A + B$ and producers' surplus is equal to areas $E + F$.

Is there a special property to equilibrium? At equilibrium, both consumers' surplus and producers' surplus are maximized. In short, total surplus is maximized.

What Can Change Equilibrium Price and Quantity?

Equilibrium price and quantity are determined by supply and demand. Whenever demand changes or supply changes or both change, equilibrium price and quantity change. Exhibit 17 illustrates eight different cases where this occurs. Cases (a)–(d) illustrate the four basic changes in supply and demand, where either supply or demand changes. Cases (e)–(h) illustrate changes in both supply and demand.

- (a) Demand rises (the demand curve shifts rightward), and supply is constant (the supply curve does not move). Equilibrium price rises, equilibrium quantity rises.
- (b) Demand falls, supply is constant. Equilibrium price falls, equilibrium quantity falls.
- (c) Supply rises, demand is constant. Equilibrium price falls, equilibrium quantity rises.
- (d) Supply falls, demand is constant. Equilibrium price rises, equilibrium quantity falls.
- (e) Demand rises and supply falls by an equal amount. Equilibrium price rises, equilibrium quantity is constant.
- (f) Demand falls and supply rises by an equal amount. Equilibrium price falls, equilibrium quantity is constant.
- (g) Demand rises by a greater amount than supply falls. Equilibrium price rises, equilibrium quantity rises.
- (h) Demand rises by a lesser amount than supply falls. Equilibrium price rises, equilibrium quantity falls.

Quantity (units)	Consumers' Surplus	Producers' Surplus
25	A	E
50	A + B	E + F
75	A + B + C	E + F + G
100 (Equilibrium)	A + B + C + D	E + F + G + H

(a)

(b)

exhibit 16

Equilibrium, Consumers' Surplus, and Producers' Surplus

Consumers' surplus is greater at equilibrium quantity (100 units) than at any other exchangeable quantity. Producers' surplus is greater at equilibrium quantity than at any other exchangeable quantity. For example, consumers' surplus is areas A + B + C at 75 units, but areas A + B + C + D at 100 units. Producers' surplus is areas E + F + G at 75 units, but areas E + F + G + H at 100 units.

ANALYZING THE SCENE

Questions from Setting the Scene: At the time James checks stock prices, Wal-Mart is selling for $52.42, Microsoft for $27.75, and Dell for $35.75. Why doesn't Dell sell for more than Wal-Mart? Why doesn't Microsoft sell for more than Dell? Why is the euro selling for $1.28 and not higher or lower?

The price of each stock is determined by supply and demand. The price of Wal-Mart stock is higher than the price of Dell stock because the demand for Wal-Mart stock is higher than the demand for Dell stock and/or the supply of Wal-Mart stock is lower than the supply of Dell stock. Similar reasoning explains why Microsoft stock sells for less than Dell stock does.

The exchange rate between the euro and the dollar is also determined by supply and demand. Just as there is a demand for and supply of apples, oranges, houses, and computers, there is a demand for and supply of various currencies (such as the dollar and the euro). The dollar price James has to pay for a euro has to do with the demand for and supply of euros. Thus, supply and demand may determine whether or not James takes a trip to Europe this summer.[5]

5. The supply and demand of currencies are analyzed in a later chapter.

SELF-TEST

1. When a person goes to the grocery store to buy food, there is no auctioneer calling out prices for bread, milk, and other items. Therefore, supply and demand cannot be operative. Do you agree or disagree? Explain your answer.
2. The price of a given-quality personal computer is lower today than it was five years ago. Is this necessarily the result of a lower demand for computers? Explain your answer.

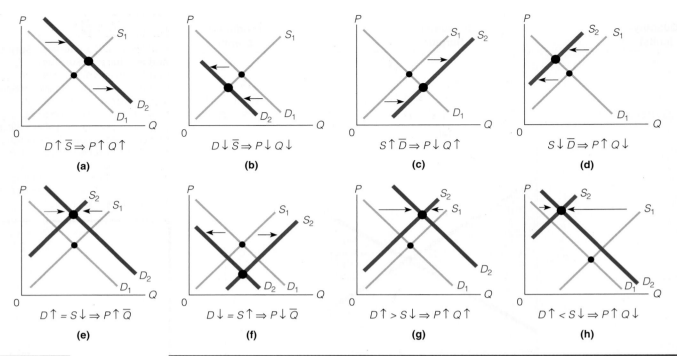

$$D\uparrow \bar{S} \Rightarrow P\uparrow Q\uparrow$$

(a)

$$D\downarrow \bar{S} \Rightarrow P\downarrow Q\downarrow$$

(b)

$$\bar{S}\uparrow \bar{D} \Rightarrow P\downarrow Q\uparrow$$

(c)

$$S\downarrow \bar{D} \Rightarrow P\uparrow Q\downarrow$$

(d)

$$D\uparrow = S\downarrow \Rightarrow P\uparrow \bar{Q}$$

(e)

$$D\downarrow = S\uparrow \Rightarrow P\downarrow \bar{Q}$$

(f)

$$D\uparrow > S\downarrow \Rightarrow P\uparrow Q\uparrow$$

(g)

$$D\uparrow < S\downarrow \Rightarrow P\uparrow Q\downarrow$$

(h)

exhibit 17

Equilibrium Price and Quantity Effects of Supply Curve Shifts and Demand Curve Shifts

The exhibit illustrates the effects on equilibrium price and quantity of a change in demand, a change in supply, or a change in both. Below each diagram the condition leading to the effects is noted, using the following symbols: (1) a bar over a letter means *constant* (thus, $\bar{S}$ means that supply is constant); (2) a downward-pointing arrow ($\downarrow$) indicates a fall; (3) an upward-pointing arrow ($\uparrow$) indicates a rise. A rise (fall) in demand is the same as a rightward (leftward) shift in the demand curve. A rise (fall) in supply is the same as a rightward (leftward) shift in the supply curve.

3. What is the effect on equilibrium price and quantity of the following?
   a. A decrease in demand that is greater than the increase in supply
   b. An increase in supply
   c. A decrease in supply that is greater than the increase in demand
   d. A decrease in demand
4. At equilibrium quantity, what is the relationship between the maximum buying price and the minimum selling price?
5. If the price paid is $40 and consumers' surplus is $6, then what is the maximum buying price? If the minimum selling price is $30 and producers' surplus is $4, then what is the price received by the seller?

PRICE CONTROLS

Because scarcity exists, there is a need for a rationing device—such as dollar price. But price is not always permitted to be a rationing device. Sometimes price is controlled. There are two types of price controls: price ceilings and price floors. In the discussion of price controls, the word *price* is used in the generic sense. It refers to the price of an apple, for example, the price of labor (wage), the price of credit (interest rate), and so on.

Price Ceiling: Definition and Effects

A **price ceiling** is a government-mandated maximum price above which legal trades cannot be made. For example, suppose the government mandates that the maximum price at which good X can be bought and sold is $8. It follows that $8 is a price ceiling. If $8 is below the equilibrium price of good X, as in Exhibit 18, any or all of the following effects may arise.[6]

Price Ceiling
A government-mandated maximum price above which legal trades cannot be made.

---

6. If the price ceiling is above the equilibrium price (say, $8 is the price ceiling and $4 is the equilibrium price), it has no effects. Usually, however, a price ceiling is below the equilibrium price. The price ceilings discussed here hold for a particular market structure and not necessarily for all market structures. The relevant market structure is usually referred to as a perfectly competitive market, a price-taker market, or a perfect market. In this market, there are enough buyers and sellers so that no single buyer can influence price.

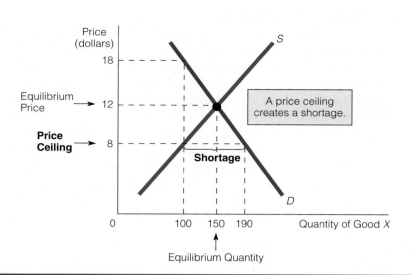

exhibit 18

A Price Ceiling
The price ceiling is $8 and the equilibrium price $12. At $12, quantity demanded = quantity supplied. At $8, quantity demanded > quantity supplied. (Recall that price, on the vertical axis, always represents price per unit. Quantity, on the horizontal axis, always holds for a specific time period.)

Shortages

At the $12 equilibrium price in Exhibit 18, the quantity demanded of good X (150) is equal to the quantity supplied (150). At the $8 price ceiling, a shortage exists. The quantity demanded (190) is greater than the quantity supplied (100). When a shortage exists, there is a tendency for price and output to rise to equilibrium. But when a price ceiling exists, this tendency cannot be realized because it is unlawful to trade at the equilibrium price.

Fewer Exchanges

At the equilibrium price of $12 in Exhibit 18, 150 units of good X are bought and sold. At the price ceiling of $8, 100 units of good X are bought and sold. (Buyers would prefer to buy 190 units, but only 100 are supplied.) We conclude that price ceilings cause fewer exchanges to be made.

Notice in Exhibit 18 that the demand curve is above the supply curve for all quantities less than 150 units. (At 150 units, the demand curve and the supply curve intersect and thus share the same point in the two dimensional space.) This means the maximum buying price is greater than the minimum selling price for all units less than 150 units. In particular, the maximum buying price is greater than the minimum selling price for units 101 to 149. For example, buyers might be willing to pay $17 for the 110th unit, and sellers might be willing to sell the 110th unit for $10. But no unit after the 100th unit (not the 110th unit, not the 114th unit, not the 130th unit) will be produced and sold because of the price ceiling. In short, the price ceiling prevents mutually advantageous trades from being realized.

Nonprice Rationing Devices

If the equilibrium price of $12 fully rationed good X before the price ceiling was imposed, it follows that a (lower) price of $8 can only partly ration this good. In short, price ceilings prevent price from rising to the level sufficient to ration goods fully. But if price is responsible for only part of the rationing, what accounts for the rest? The answer is some other (nonprice) rationing device, such as first-come-first-served (FCFS).

In Exhibit 18, 100 units of good X will be sold at $8 although buyers are willing to buy 190 units at this price. What happens? Possibly, good X will be sold on an FCFS basis for $8 per unit. In other words, to buy good X, a person must not only pay $8 per unit but also be one of the first people in line.

Buying and Selling at a Prohibited Price

Buyers and sellers may regularly circumvent a price ceiling by making their exchanges "under the table." For example, some buyers may offer some sellers more than $8 per unit for good X. No doubt some sellers will accept the offers. But why would some buyers offer more than $8 per unit when they can buy good X for $8? The answer is because not all buyers can buy the amount of good X they want at $8. As Exhibit 18 shows, there is a shortage. Buyers are willing to buy 190 units at $8, but sellers are willing to sell only 100 units. In short, 90 fewer units will be sold than buyers would like to buy. Some buyers will go unsatisfied. How, then, does any one buyer make it more likely that sellers will sell to him or her instead of to someone else? The answer is by offering to pay a higher price. Because it is illegal to pay a higher price, the transaction must be made "under the table."

Tie-in Sales

In Exhibit 18, the maximum price buyers would be willing and able to pay per unit for 100 units of good X is $18. (This is the price on the demand curve at a quantity of 100 units.) The maximum legal price, however, is $8. This difference between two prices often prompts a **tie-in sale,** a sale whereby one good can be purchased only if another good is also purchased. For example, if Ralph's Gas Station sells gasoline to customers only if they buy a car wash, the two goods are linked together in a tie-in sale.

Suppose that the sellers of good X in Exhibit 18 also sell good Y. They might offer to sell buyers good X at $8 only if the buyers agree to buy good Y at, say, $10. We choose $10 as the price for good Y because $10 is the difference between the maximum per-unit price buyers are willing and able to pay for 100 units of good X ($18) and the maximum legal price ($8).

In New York City and other communities with rent-control laws, tie-in sales sometimes result from rent ceilings on apartments. Occasionally, in order to rent an apartment, an individual must agree to buy the furniture in the apartment.

Tie-in Sale
A sale whereby one good can be purchased only if another good is also purchased.

! ANALYZING THE SCENE

Questions from Setting the Scene: What does getting his shower fixed have to do with James living in a rent-controlled apartment? Why does it take so long (nine months) to get tickets to see the *Late Show with David Letterman*?

Both these questions relate to disequilibrium prices. James has been trying for two weeks to get his apartment supervisor to fix his shower. James's friend thinks it has taken so long because James lives in a rent-controlled apartment. (A rent-controlled apartment has a rent ceiling; James's rent is lower than the equilibrium, or market-clearing rent.) Is James's friend right? With a rent ceiling, the quantity demanded of apartments is greater than the quantity supplied, that is, a shortage of apartments exists. The apartment supervisor knows there is a shortage of apartments, and realizes he could rent the apartment easily if James moved. The supervisor is likely to be less responsive to James's request to fix the shower than he would be if the rental market were in equilibrium or surplus.

For the second question, let's recall the facts and do some economic analyzing. We know that the price of a ticket is zero (which is not the equilibrium or market-clearing price). At a price of zero, the quantity demanded of tickets is much greater than quantity supplied. How are the tickets rationed? They're rationed on a first-come-first-served basis. James had to "stand in line" or "wait" for nine months to get tickets to see the show. That's one long line.

Supply and Demand on a Freeway

What does a traffic jam on a busy freeway in any large city have to do with supply and demand? Actually, it has quite a bit to do with supply and demand. Look at it this way: There is a demand for driving on the freeway and a supply of freeway space. The supply of freeway space is fixed (freeways do not expand and contract over a day, week, or month). The demand, however, fluctuates. It is higher at some times than at other times. For example, we would expect the demand for driving on the freeway to be higher at 8 A.M. (rush hour) than at 11 P.M. But even though the demand may vary, the money price for driving on the freeway is always the same—zero. A zero money price means that motorists do not pay tolls to drive on the freeway.

Exhibit 19 shows two demand curves for driving on the freeway: $D_{8A.M.}$ and $D_{11P.M.}$ We have assumed the demand at 8 A.M. is greater than at 11 P.M. We have also assumed that at $D_{11P.M.}$ and zero money price the freeway market clears: Quantity demanded of freeway space equals quantity supplied of freeway space. At the higher demand, $D_{8A.M.}$, however, this is not the case. At zero money price, a shortage of freeway space exists: Quantity demanded of freeway space is greater than quantity supplied of freeway space. The shortage appears in the form of freeway congestion, bumper-to-bumper traffic. One way to eliminate the shortage is through an increase in the money price of driving on the freeway at 8 A.M. For example, as Exhibit 19 shows, a toll of 70 cents would clear the freeway market at 8 A.M.

If charging different prices (tolls) at different times of the day on freeways sounds like an unusual idea, consider how Miami Beach hotels price their rooms. They charge different prices for their rooms at different times of the year. During the winter months when the demand for vacationing in Miami Beach is high, the hotels charge higher prices than when the demand is (relatively) low. If different prices were charged for freeway space at different times of the day, freeway space would be rationed the same way Miami Beach hotel rooms are rationed.

Before we leave this topic, let's consider the three alternatives usually proposed for freeway congestion. Some people propose tolls, some propose building more freeways, and others propose

encouraging carpooling. Tolls deal with the congestion problem by adjusting price to its equilibrium level, as shown in Exhibit 19. Building more freeways deals with the problem by increasing supply. In Exhibit 19, it would be necessary to shift the supply curve of freeway space to the right so there is no longer any shortage of space at 8 A.M. More carpooling deals with the problem by decreasing demand. Two people in one car takes up less space on a freeway than two people in two cars. In Exhibit 19, if through carpooling the demand at 8 A.M. begins to look like the demand at 11 P.M., then there is no longer a shortage of freeway space at 8 A.M.

exhibit 19

Freeway Congestion and Supply and Demand
The demand for driving on the freeway is higher at 8 A.M. than at 11 P.M. At zero money price and $D_{11\,P.M.}$, the freeway market clears. At zero money price and $D_{8\,A.M.}$, there is a shortage of freeway space, which shows up as freeway congestion. At a price (toll) of 70 cents, the shortage is eliminated and freeway congestion disappears.

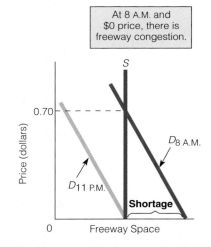

At 8 A.M. and $0 price, there is freeway congestion.

Do Buyers Prefer Lower Prices to Higher Prices?

"Of course," someone might say, "buyers prefer lower prices to higher prices. What buyer would want to pay a higher price for anything?" But wait a minute. Price ceilings are often lower than equilibrium prices. Does it follow that buyers prefer price ceilings to equilibrium prices? Not necessarily. Price ceilings have effects that equilibrium prices do not:

exhibit **20**

A Price Floor
The price floor is $20 and the equilibrium price is $15. At $15, quantity demanded = quantity supplied. At $20, quantity supplied > quantity demanded.

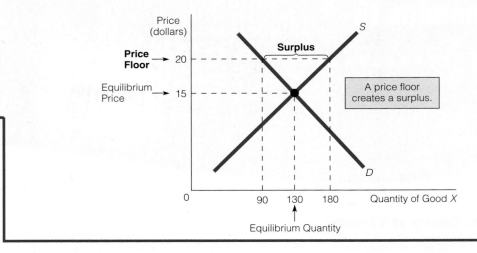

Price Floor
A government-mandated minimum price below which legal trades cannot be made.

shortages, use of first-come-first-served as a rationing device, tie-in sales, and so on. A buyer could prefer to pay a higher price (an equilibrium price) than to pay a lower price and have to deal with the effects of a price ceiling. All we can say for certain is that buyers prefer lower prices to higher prices, *ceteris paribus*. As in many cases, the *ceteris paribus* condition makes all the difference.

Price Floor: Definition and Effects

A **price floor** is a government-mandated minimum price below which legal trades cannot be made. For example, suppose the government mandates that the minimum price at which good X can be sold is $20. It follows that $20 is a price floor (see Exhibit 20). If the price floor is above the equilibrium price, the following two effects arise.[7]

Surpluses

At the $15 equilibrium price in Exhibit 20, the quantity demanded of good X (130) is equal to the quantity supplied (130). At the $20 price floor, a surplus exists. The quantity supplied (180) is greater than the quantity demanded (90). A surplus is usually a temporary state of affairs. When a surplus exists, there is a tendency for price and output to fall to equilibrium. But when a price floor exists, this tendency cannot be realized because it is unlawful to trade at the equilibrium price.

Fewer Exchanges

At the equilibrium price in Exhibit 20, 130 units of good X are bought and sold. At the price floor, 90 units are bought and sold. (Sellers want to sell 180 units, but buyers buy only 90.) We conclude that price floors cause fewer exchanges to be made.

SELF-TEST

1. Do buyers prefer lower prices to higher prices?
2. "When there are long-lasting shortages, there are long lines of people waiting to buy goods. It follows that the shortages cause the long lines." Do you agree or disagree? Explain your answer.
3. Who might argue for a price ceiling? a price floor?

---

7. If the price floor is below the equilibrium price (say, $20 is the price floor and $25 is the equilibrium price), it has no effects. Usually, however, a price floor is above the equilibrium price. As with price ceilings, the price floor effects discussed here hold for a perfectly competitive market. See footnote 6.

Some things are interesting but not useful. Other things are useful but not interesting. For example, supply and demand are interesting, but not useful. Learning how to fix a car is useful, but not particularly interesting. Am I wrong? Have I missed something? Is knowledge of supply and demand useful? If it is, what can you do with it?

A knowledge of supply and demand can be used both to explain and to predict. Let's look at prediction first. Suppose you learn that the federal government is going to impose a quota on imported television sets. What will happen when the quota is imposed? With your knowledge of supply and demand, you can predict that the price of television sets will rise. In other words, you can use your knowledge of supply and demand to predict what will happen. Stated differently, you can use your knowledge of supply and demand to see into the future. Isn't the ability to see into the future useful?

Supply and demand also allows you to develop richer and fuller explanations of events. To illustrate, suppose there is a shortage of apples in country *X*. The cause of the shortage, someone says, is that apple growers in the country are simply growing too few apples. Well, of course, it's true that apple growers are growing "too

few" apples as compared to the number of apples consumers want to buy. But does this explanation completely account for the shortage of apples? Your knowledge of supply and demand will prompt you to ask why apple growers are growing too few apples. When you understand that quantity supplied is related to price, you understand that apple growers will grow more apples if the price of apples is higher. What is keeping the price of apples down? Could it be a price ceiling? Without a price ceiling, the price of apples would rise, and apple growers would grow (and offer to sell) more apples. The shortage of apples will vanish.

In other words, without a knowledge of supply and demand you may have been content to explain the shortage of apples by saying that apple growers are growing too few apples. With your knowledge of supply and demand, you delve deeper into *why* apple growers are growing too few apples.

Chapter Summary

Demand

> The law of demand states that as the price of a good rises, the quantity demanded of the good falls, and as the price of a good falls, the quantity demanded of the good rises, *ceteris paribus*. The law of demand holds that price and quantity demanded are inversely related.

> Quantity demanded is the total number of units of a good that buyers are willing and able to buy at a particular price.

> A (downward-sloping) demand curve is the graphical representation of the law of demand.

> Factors that can change demand and cause the demand curve to shift include income, preferences, prices of related goods (substitutes and complements), number of buyers, and expectations of future price.

> The only factor that can directly cause a change in the quantity demanded of a good is a change in the good's own price.

Absolute Price and Relative Price

> The absolute price of a good is the price of the good in money terms.

> The relative price of a good is the price of the good in terms of another good.

Supply

> The law of supply states that as the price of a good rises, the quantity supplied of the good rises, and as the price of a good

falls, the quantity supplied of the good falls, *ceteris paribus*. The law of supply asserts that price and quantity supplied are directly related.

> The law of supply does not hold when there is no time to produce more units of a good or when goods cannot be produced at all (over any period of time).

> The upward-sloping supply curve is the graphical representation of the law of supply. More generally, a supply curve (no matter how it slopes) represents the relationship between price and quantity supplied.

> Factors that can change supply and cause the supply curve to shift include prices of relevant resources, technology, number of sellers, expectations of future price, taxes and subsidies, and government restrictions.

> The only factor that can directly cause a change in the quantity supplied of a good is a change in the good's own price.

The Market

> Demand and supply together establish equilibrium price and equilibrium quantity.

> A surplus exists in a market if, at some price, quantity supplied is greater than quantity demanded. A shortage exists if, at some price, quantity demanded is greater than quantity supplied.

> Mutually beneficial trade between buyers and sellers drives the market to equilibrium.

Consumers' Surplus, Producers' Surplus, and Total Surplus

> Consumers' surplus is the difference between the maximum buying price and price paid by the buyer.

Consumers' surplus = Maximum buying price − Price paid

> Producers' (or sellers') surplus is the difference between the price the seller receives and minimum selling price.

Producers' surplus = Price received − Minimum selling price

> The more consumers' surplus that buyers receive, the better off they are. The more producers' surplus that sellers receive, the better off they are.
> Total surplus is the sum of consumers' surplus and producers' surplus.
> Total surplus (the sum of consumers' surplus and producers' surplus) is maximized at equilibrium.

Price Ceilings

> A price ceiling is a government-mandated maximum price. If a price ceiling is below the equilibrium price, some or all of the following effects arise: shortages, fewer exchanges, nonprice rationing devices, buying and selling at prohibited prices, and tie-in sales.
> Consumers do not necessarily prefer (lower) price ceilings to (higher) equilibrium prices. They may prefer higher prices and none of the effects of price ceilings to lower prices and some of the effects of price ceilings. All we can say for sure is that consumers prefer lower prices to higher prices, *ceteris paribus*.

Price Floors

> A price floor is a government-mandated minimum price. If a price floor is above the equilibrium price, the following effects arise: surpluses and fewer exchanges.

Key Terms and Concepts

Demand	Substitutes	Equilibrium Quantity
Law of Demand	Complements	Disequilibrium Price
Demand Schedule	Supply	Disequilibrium
Demand Curve	Law of Supply	Equilibrium
Absolute (Money) Price	Supply Curve	Consumers' Surplus
Relative Price	Supply Schedule	Producers' (Sellers') Surplus
Law of Diminishing Marginal Utility	Subsidy	Total Surplus
Own Price	Surplus (Excess Supply)	Price Ceiling
Normal Good	Shortage (Excess Demand)	Tie-in Sale
Inferior Good	Equilibrium Price (Market-Clearing	Price Floor
Neutral Good	Price) `	

Questions and Problems

1. True or false? As the price of oranges rises, the demand for oranges falls, *ceteris paribus*. Explain your answer.
2. "The price of a bushel of wheat, which was $3.00 last month, is $3.70 today. The demand curve for wheat must have shifted rightward between last month and today." Discuss.
3. "Some goods are bought largely because they have 'snob appeal.' For example, the residents of Beverly Hills gain prestige by buying expensive items. In fact, they won't buy some items unless they are expensive. The law of demand, which holds that people buy more at lower prices than higher prices, obviously doesn't hold for the residents of Beverly Hills. The following rules apply in Beverly Hills: high prices, buy; low prices, don't buy." Discuss.
4. "The price of T-shirts keeps rising and rising, and people keep buying more and more. T-shirts must have an upward-sloping demand curve." Identify the error.
5. Predict what would happen to the equilibrium price of marijuana if it were legalized.
6. Compare the ratings for television shows with prices for goods. How are ratings like prices? How are ratings different from prices? (Hint: How does rising demand for a particular television show manifest itself?)

7. Must consumers' surplus equal producers' surplus at equilibrium price? Explain your answer.
8. Many movie theaters charge a lower admission price for the first show on weekday afternoons than they do for a weeknight or weekend show. Explain why.
9. A Dell computer is a substitute for a Compaq computer. What happens to the demand for Compaqs and the quantity demanded of Dells as the price of a Dell falls?
10. Describe how each of the following will affect the demand for personal computers: (a) a rise in incomes (assuming computers are a normal good); (b) a lower expected price for computers; (c) cheaper software; (d) computers become simpler to operate.
11. Describe how each of the following will affect the supply of personal computers: (a) a rise in wage rates; (b) an increase in the number of sellers of computers; (c) a tax placed on the production of computers; (d) a subsidy placed on the production of computers.
12. The law of demand specifies an inverse relationship between price and quantity demanded, *ceteris paribus*. Is the "price" in the law of demand absolute price or relative price? Explain your answer.
13. Use the law of diminishing marginal utility to explain why demand curves slope downward.

14. Explain how the market moves to equilibrium in terms of shortages and surpluses and in terms of maximum buying prices and minimum selling prices.
15. Identify what happens to equilibrium price and quantity in each of the following cases:
    a. Demand rises and supply is constant
    b. Demand falls and supply is constant
    c. Supply rises and demand is constant
    d. Supply falls and demand is constant
    e. Demand rises by the same amount that supply falls
    f. Demand falls by the same amount that supply rises
    g. Demand falls by less than supply rises
    h. Demand rises by more than supply rises
    i. Demand rises by less than supply rises
    j. Demand falls by more than supply falls
    k. Demand falls by less than supply falls
16. Many of the proponents of price ceilings argue that government-mandated maximum prices simply reduce producers' profits and do not affect the quantity supplied of a good on the market. What must the supply curve look like before a price ceiling does not affect quantity supplied?

Working With Numbers and Graphs

1. If the absolute price of good X is $10 and the absolute price of good Y is $14, then what is (a) the relative price of good X in terms of good Y and (b) the relative price of good Y in terms of good X?
2. Price is $10, quantity supplied is 50 units, and quantity demanded is 100 units. For every $1 rise in price, quantity supplied rises by 5 units and quantity demanded falls by 5 units. What is the equilibrium price and quantity?
3. Draw a diagram that shows a larger increase in demand than the decrease in supply.
4. Draw a diagram that shows a smaller increase in supply than the increase in demand.
5. At equilibrium in the following figure, what area(s) does consumers' surplus equal? producers' surplus?

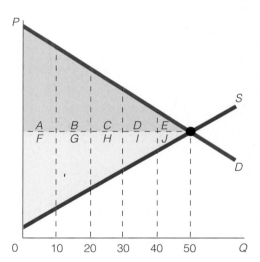

6. At what quantity in the preceding figure is the maximum buying price equal to the minimum selling price?
7. Diagrammatically explain why there are no exchanges in the area where the supply curve is above the demand curve.
8. In the following figure, can the movement from point 1 to point 2 be explained by a combination of an increase in the price of a substitute and a decrease in the price of nonlabor resources? Explain your answer.

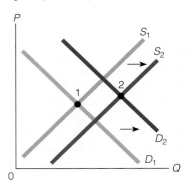

9. The demand curve is downward-sloping, the supply curve is upward-sloping, and the equilibrium quantity is 50 units. Show on a graph that the difference between the maximum buying price and minimum selling price is greater at 25 units than at 33 units.
10. Diagrammatically show and explain why a price ceiling that is above the equilibrium price will not prompt a tie-in sale.
11. Xavier is willing and able to pay up to $40 for a good that he buys for $22. Keri is willing and able to sell the good to Xavier for no less than $21. What does consumers' surplus equal? What does producers' (sellers') surplus equal?

Setting the Scene

The following events occurred on a day in January 2004.

7:42 A.M.

It's Thursday, and Franklin Smithies has just gotten off the subway at Park Place, in the heart of the Financial District in Lower Manhattan. He sips his morning cup of coffee as he walks toward his office. As he walks, he thinks about what awaits him. Franklin manages the stock portfolio of one of the largest pension funds in the country, and in a little less than an hour, the U.S. Department of Labor, Bureau of Labor Statistics (BLS) will issue a summary report on prices. What that report says will have much to do with how he spends the rest of his day.

8:30 A.M.

The BLS releases this statement: The Consumer Price Index for All Urban Consumers (CPI-U) decreased 0.1 percent in December, before seasonal adjustment. The December level of 184.3 (1982–84 = 100) was 2.8 percent higher than in December 2004.

3:18 P.M.

Catherine Lincoln picks up the phone to call her parents, both of whom are retired. When her father answers the phone, Catherine blurts out, "I got the job. And I got the salary I asked for—$50,000 a year." Her father replies, "That's a great salary—you're rich. You can easily live on that salary. After all, your mother and I lived comfortably on my first salary of $8,000 a year."

4:24 P.M., Inside a house in Carbondale, Illinois

Owner of the house:
  How much do I owe you?

Plumber:
  The bill comes to $185. I was wondering if you could pay me in cash. Would that be okay?

5:07 P.M., Drug Enforcement Agency (DEA) Headquarters

First DEA official:
  We just got a report that the banks in Miami are experiencing an unusually high demand for cash.

Second DEA official:
  I'll call the Miami office.

? **How would an economist look at these events? Later in the chapter, discussions based on the following questions will help you analyze the scene the way an economist would.**

- What does a report on prices have to do with what Franklin Smithies will do at work?
- How does the BLS compute the consumer price index, and what does it matter whether prices are rising or falling?

- Will Catherine be rich? How does her salary of $50,000 compare to her father's first salary of $8,000?
- Why does the plumber want to be paid in cash?
- Why does the DEA care that people are demanding cash from banks in Miami?

MACROECONOMIC MEASUREMENTS

A doctor often takes your temperature and blood pressure and, in some cases, may order a few tests. The doctor uses these measurements to learn about the condition of your body.

In a way, economists are the physicians of the economy. They often want to take the "temperature" or "blood pressure" of the economy. Their objective in taking such measurements is to find out how the economy is doing. Is it well and healthy? Is it getting sick? If it is getting sick, is there any "medicine" that can be prescribed?

Some of the things that economists measure are prices (Are prices rising or falling?), the unemployment rate (Is the unemployment rate rising or falling?), and the total market value of all final goods and services produced in the economy (Is the economy producing more goods or fewer goods?).

This chapter explains how economists measure prices, the unemployment rate, and the market value of the goods and services the economy produces.

MEASURING PRICES

Price in macroeconomics does not usually refer to a single price, such as the price of cars or the price of computers. Price in macroeconomics usually refers to an *aggregate price,* a *price level,* a *price index,* or an *average price.*

For example, suppose books and pens are the only two goods in an economy. Books are priced at $10 each and pens at $1 each. Without considering the quantity of each good, the *average price* in this tiny economy is $5.50. When economists talk about *price stability,* they are referring to the average price, price level, or price index remaining constant.

Measuring Prices Using the CPI

Price Level
A weighted average of the prices of all good and services

Price Index
A measure of the price level.

The **price level** is a weighted average of the prices of all goods and services. Economists measure the price level by constructing a **price index.** One major price index is the **consumer price index (CPI).**

Computing the CPI

Consumer Price Index (CPI)
A widely cited index number for the price level; the weighted average of prices of a specific set of goods and services purchased by a typical household.

The CPI is calculated by the Bureau of Labor Statistics (BLS) through its sampling of thousands of households and businesses. When a news report says that the "cost of living" increased by, say, 7 percent, it is usually referring to the CPI.[1] The CPI is based on a representative group of goods and services purchased by a typical household. This representative group of goods is called the *market basket.*

To simplify our discussion, we assume the market basket includes only three goods instead of the many goods it actually contains. Our market basket consists of 10 pens, 5 shirts, and 3 pairs of shoes.

Base Year
The year chosen as a point of reference or basis of comparison for prices in other years; a benchmark year.

To calculate the CPI, we must first calculate the total dollar expenditure on the market basket in two years: the current year and the base year. The **base year** is a benchmark year that serves as a basis of comparison for prices in other years.

In Exhibit 1, we multiply the quantity of each good in the market basket (column 1) times its current-year price (column 2) to compute the current-year expenditure on each good (column 3). By adding the dollar amounts in column 3, we obtain the total dollar expenditure on the market basket in the current year. This amount is $167.

---

1. Although changes in the CPI are often used to compute the change in the "cost of living," one's cost of living usually involves more than is measured by the CPI. For example, the CPI does not include income taxes, yet income taxes are a part of the cost of living for most people.

(1) Market Basket		(2) Current-Year Prices (per item)		(3) Current-Year Expenditures	(1A) Market Basket		(2A) Base-Year Prices (per item)		(3A) Base-Year Expenditures
10 pens	×	$ .70	=	$ 7.00	10 pens	×	$ .20	=	$ 2.00
5 shirts	×	14.00	=	70.00	5 shirts	×	7.00	=	35.00
3 pairs of shoes	×	30.00	=	90.00	3 pairs of shoes	×	10.00	=	30.00
				$167.00					**$67.00**
				Total dollar expenditure on market basket in current year					Total dollar expenditure on market basket in base year

$$CPI = \left(\frac{\text{Total dollar expenditure on market basket in current year}}{\text{Total dollar expenditure on market basket in base year}} \right) \times 100$$

$$= \left(\frac{\$167}{\$67} \right) \times 100$$

$$= 249$$

exhibit 1

Computing the Consumer Price Index
The exhibit uses hypothetical data to show how the CPI is computed. To find the "total dollar expenditure on market basket in current year," we multiply the quantities of goods in the market basket times their current-year prices and add these products. This gives us $167. To find the "total dollar expenditure on market basket in base year," we multiply the quantities of goods in the market basket times their base-year prices and add these products. This gives us $67. We then divide $167 by $67 and multiply the quotient times 100.

To find the total expenditure on the market basket in the base year, we multiply the quantity of each good in the market basket (column 1A) times its base-year price (column 2A) and then add these products (column 3A). This gives us $67.

To find the CPI, we use the formula:

$$CPI = \frac{\text{Total dollar expenditure on market basket in current year}}{\text{Total dollar expenditure on market basket in base year}} \times 100$$

As shown in Exhibit 1, the CPI for our tiny economy is 249.

The consumer price index for the United States for the years 1960 to 2005 is shown in Exhibit 2.

More About the Base Year

Recall that the base year is a benchmark year that serves as a basis of comparison for prices in other years. The CPI in the base year is 100. How do we know this? Well, look again at the formula for calculating the CPI. The numerator is the "total dollar expenditure on market basket in current year" and the denominator is the "total dollar expenditure on market basket in base year." In the base year, the current year *is* the base year so the numerator and denominator are the same. The ratio is 1, and $1 \times 100 = 100$.

But if you look at Exhibit 2, you will notice that there is no year where the CPI is 100. Does this mean that there is no base year? Not at all. The base year has been defined by the government to be the period 1982–84. Look at the CPI in each of the years 1982, 1983, and 1984. If we add the CPIs for the three years and divide by 3, we get 100: $(96.5 + 99.6 + 103.9) \div 3 = 100$.

When We Know the CPI for Various Years, We Can Compute the Percentage Change in Prices

To find the percentage change in prices between any two years, we use the following formula:

$$\text{Percentage change in prices} = \left(\frac{CPI_{\text{later year}} - CPI_{\text{earlier year}}}{CPI_{\text{earlier year}}} \right) \times 100$$

exhibit **2**

CPI, 1959–2004
Source: The data were reported at the Web
site for the U.S. Department of Labor, Bureau
of Labor Statistics. Site address:
http://www.bls.gov/home.htm

Year	CPI	Year	CPI
1960	29.6	1983	99.6
1961	29.9	1984	103.9
1962	30.2	1985	107.6
1963	30.6	1986	109.6
1964	31.0	1987	113.6
1965	31.5	1988	118.3
1966	32.4	1989	124.0
1967	33.4	1990	130.7
1968	34.8	1991	136.2
1969	36.7	1992	140.3
1970	38.8	1993	144.5
1971	40.5	1994	148.2
1972	41.8	1995	152.4
1973	44.4	1996	156.9
1974	49.3	1997	160.5
1975	53.8	1998	163.0
1976	56.9	1999	166.6
1977	60.6	2000	172.2
1978	65.2	2001	177.1
1979	72.6	2002	179.9
1980	82.4	2003	184.0
1981	90.9	2004	190.3
1982	96.5	2005	198.9

For example, Exhibit 2 shows that the CPI in 1990 was 130.7 and the CPI in 2003 was 184.0. What was the percentage change in prices over this period of time? It was 40.78 percent: [(184.0 − 130.7) ÷ 130.7] × 100 = 40.78. This means that from 1990 to 2003, prices increased 40.78 percent. You can think of the percentage change in prices this way: What cost $1 in 1990 cost approximately $1.41 in 2003.

Consider another time period. Between 1980 and 2000, prices in the United States increased more than 108 percent: [(172.2 − 82.4) ÷ 82.4] × 100 = 108.98. Does this mean that the price of every good increased by this percentage? No. Some increased by more and some increased by less. For example, food and beverage prices increased 94 percent, housing prices increased 109 percent, telephone service prices increased 26 percent, and motor fuel prices increased 32 percent. Two of the bigger price increases during this period were in medical care and college tuition. Medical care costs increased 248 percent, and college tuition increased 368 percent.

Inflation and the CPI

Inflation is an increase in the price level and is usually measured on an annual basis. The *inflation rate* is the positive percentage change in the price level on an annual basis. For example, the inflation rate for 2000 is the percentage change in prices from the end of December 1999 through the end of December 2000. Although we do not show these data in a table, the CPI in December 1999 was 168.9 and the CPI in December 2000 was 174.6. This means the inflation rate in 2000 was approximately 3.4 percent.

When you know the inflation rate, you can find out whether your income is (1) keeping up with, (2) not keeping up with, or (3) more than keeping up with inflation. How you are doing depends on whether your income is rising by (1) the same percentage as, (2) a lesser percentage than, or (3) a greater percentage than the inflation rate, respectively. Another way to look at this is to compute and compare your real income for different years. **Real income** is a person's **nominal income** (or money income) adjusted for any change in prices. Real income is computed as follows:

$$\text{Real income} = \left(\frac{\text{Nominal income}}{\text{CPI}} \right) \times 100$$

ANALYZING THE SCENE

Questions from Setting the Scene: How does the BLS compute the consumer price index, and what does it matter whether prices are rising or falling? What does a report on prices have to do with what Franklin Smithies will do at work?

This section shows how to compute the CPI: define the market basket of goods, collect prices in the base year and current year, and carry out some simple arithmetic operations. Does it matter whether prices rise or fall? As you will find out in later chapters, it does. For now, though, let's consider what a report on prices (and whether prices are rising or falling) has to do with what Franklin Smithies will do at work.

Franklin manages the stock portfolio of one of the largest pension funds in the country. Often stock portfolio managers use price reports to get a hint of what the Federal Reserve will do in the near future. (The Federal Reserve is the monetary authority of the United States, capable of increasing and decreasing the money supply, influencing interest rates, and so on.) For example, Franklin might reason: If prices have recently risen sharply, the Federal Reserve may try to slow down price rises by raising interest rates. Higher interest rates may adversely affect the stocks I recently purchased, so the best thing for me to do is to sell some stocks.

Case 1. Keeping Up With Inflation: Real Income Stays Constant

Jim earns $50,000 in year 1 and $55,000 in year 2. The CPI is 100 in year 1 and 110 in year 2. Jim's income has risen by 10 percent [(($55,000 – $50,000)/$50,000) × 100 = 10], and the inflation rate is 10 percent [((110 – 100)/100) × 100 = 10]. Jim's income has risen by the same percentage as the inflation rate, so he has kept up with inflation. This is evident when we see that Jim's real income is the same in the two years. In year 1, it is $50,000, and in year 2, it is $50,000 too.

Real income year 1 = ($50,000/100) × 100 = $50,000
Real income year 2 = ($55,000/110) × 100 = $50,000

Case 2. Not Keeping Up With Inflation: Real Income Falls

Karen earns $50,000 in year 1 and $52,000 in year 2. The CPI is 100 in year 1 and 110 in year 2. Karen's income has risen by 4 percent, and the inflation rate is 10 percent. Her income has risen by a lesser percentage than the inflation rate, so she has not kept up with inflation. Karen's real income has fallen from $50,000 in year 1 to $47,273 in year 2.

Real income year 1 = ($50,000/100) × 100 = $50,000
Real income year 2 = ($52,000/110) × 100 = $47,273

Case 3. More Than Keeping Up With Inflation: Real Income Rises

Carl earns $50,000 in year 1 and $60,000 in year 2. The CPI is 100 in year 1 and 110 in year 2. Carl's income has risen by 20 percent, and the inflation rate is 10 percent. His income has risen by a greater percentage than the inflation rate, so he has more than kept up with inflation. Carl's real income has risen from $50,000 in year 1 to $54,545 in year 2.

Real income year 1 = ($50,000/100) × 100 = $50,000
Real income year 2 = ($60,000/110) × 100 = $54,545

Inflation
An increase in the price level.

Real Income
Nominal income adjusted for price changes.

Nominal Income
The current-dollar amount of a person's income.

GDP Implicit Price Deflator

Besides the CPI, there is another price index that is often cited—the *GDP deflator* or the *GDP implicit price deflator*. As you know, the CPI is based on a representative group of goods and services (the market basket) purchased by a typical household. Obviously, there are more goods and services produced in an economy than find their way into the market basket. The GDP implicit price deflator, unlike the CPI, is based on all goods and services produced in an economy.

THINKING LIKE AN ECONOMIST *Comparing one thing with something else can be extremely useful. For example, in each of these three cases, we compared the percentage change in a person's nominal income with the inflation rate. Through this comparison, we learned something that we could not have learned by looking at either factor alone: how a person fared under inflation. Making comparisons is part of the economic way of thinking.*

Converting Dollars From One Year to Another

Suppose someone says to you, "Back in 1960, I had an annual salary of $10,000 a year. That sure isn't much these days." Of course, the person is right in one sense: an annual salary of $10,000 doesn't buy much these days. But was $10,000 a good salary back in 1960? It certainly could have been because prices in 1960 weren't as high as they are today. For example, the CPI was 29.6 in 1960 and it was 184.0 in 2003. In other words, one of the things that make a salary "good" or "not so good" is what the salary can buy.

Now suppose someone tells you that a $10,000 salary in 1960 is the same as a $67,195 salary today. Would you then better understand the 1960 $10,000 salary? Of course you would because you understand what it means to earn $67,195 today. Economists convert a past salary into a salary today by using this formula:

$$\text{Salary in today's (current) dollars} = \text{Salary}_{\text{earlier year}} \times \left(\frac{\text{CPI}_{\text{current year}}}{\text{CPI}_{\text{earlier year}}}\right)$$

Assume the CPI today is the same as the most recent CPI in Exhibit 2 (which is the CPI for 2005). Using the formula, we get:

$$\text{Salary in 2005 dollars} = \$10,000 \times \left(\frac{198.9}{29.6}\right)$$
$$= \$67,195$$

ANALYZING THE SCENE

Questions from Setting the Scene: Will Catherine be rich? How does her salary of $50,000 compare to her father's first salary of $8,000?

The questions about Catherine's salary and her father's salary are related to comparing dollars in one year to dollars in a different year. Catherine's father is quite happy about Catherine's salary of $50,000. He thinks Catherine is rich because her salary is a lot larger than his first starting salary of $8,000. But when Catherine's father earned $8,000, prices were lower than prices were in 2005. Suppose Catherine's father earned the $8,000 in, say, 1960. By converting 1960 dollars into 2005 dollars, we find that earning $8,000 in 1960 is equivalent to earning $53,756 today. So, Catherine's salary is $3,756 less than her father earned in 1960.

SELF-TEST *(Answers to Self-Test questions are in the Self-Test Appendix.)*

1. Explain how the CPI is calculated.
2. If the CPI at the end of December in year 1 is 132.5 and the CPI at the end of December in year 2 is 143.2, what is the inflation rate?
3. In year 1, your annual income is $45,000 and the CPI is 143.6; in year 2, your annual income is $51,232 and the CPI is 150.7. Has your real income risen, fallen, or remained constant? Explain your answer.

MEASURING UNEMPLOYMENT

Every month, the government surveys thousands of households to gather information about labor market activities. It uses the information from the survey to derive the number of Americans unemployed.

Who Are the Unemployed?

The total population of the United States can be divided into two broad groups (Exhibit 3). One group consists of persons who are (1) under 16 years of age, (2) in the armed forces, or (3) institutionalized—that is, they are in a prison, mental institution, or home for the aged. The second group, which consists of all others in the total population, is called the *civilian noninstitutional population.*

The civilian noninstitutional population, in turn, can be divided into two groups: persons *not in the labor force* and persons in the *civilian labor force.* (Economists often refer to the "labor force" instead of the "civilian labor force.")

Civilian noninstitutional population = Persons not in the labor force + Persons in the labor force

Economics In

Popular Culture   Technology   Everyday Life

© Bettmann/CORBIS

Who Earned More as President: John F. Kennedy or George W. Bush?

You know how to compute the CPI and how to use it to find the percentage change in prices between years. We can do something else with the CPI. We can use it to find out who earned more as president—John F. Kennedy or George W. Bush.

John F. Kennedy was president in 1961; his annual salary that year was $100,000. George W. Bush was president in 2005; his annual salary that year was $400,000. It seems clear that Bush earned more as president than Kennedy did.

But wait; have we considered everything? No. The dollars Kennedy was paid as president had greater purchasing power than the dollars Bush was paid as president. One dollar in 1961 bought more goods and services than one dollar in 2005 did. To accurately compare their salaries, we need to convert Kennedy's 1961 salary of $100,000 into 2005 dollars.

$$\text{Kennedy's salary in 2005 dollars} = \$100,000 \times \left(\frac{198.9}{29.9}\right)$$
$$= \$665,217$$

So, in 2005 dollars, Kennedy earned $638,175; Bush, of course, earned $400,000 in 2005.

Those persons not in the labor force are neither working nor looking for work. For example, people who are retired, who are engaged in own-home housework, or who choose not to work fall into this category.

Persons in the civilian labor force fall into one of two categories: *employed* or *unemployed.*

Civilian labor force = Employed persons + Unemployed persons

According to the BLS, employed persons consist of:

- All persons who did any work for pay or profit during the survey reference week.
- All persons who did at least 15 hours of unpaid work in a family-operated enterprise.

exhibit 3

Breakdown of the U.S. Population and the Labor Force

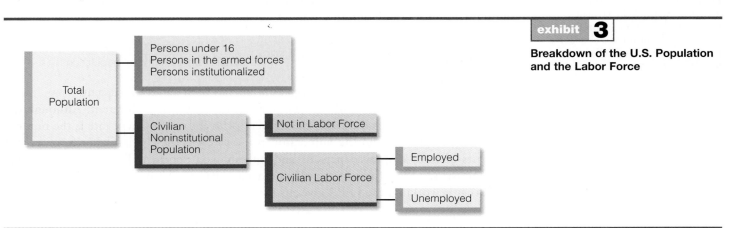

- All persons who were temporarily absent from their regular jobs because of illness, vacation, bad weather, industrial dispute, or various personal reasons.

According to the BLS, unemployed persons consist of:

- All persons who did not have jobs, made specific active efforts to find a job during the prior four weeks, and were available for work.
- All persons who were not working and were waiting to be called back to a job from which they had been temporarily laid off.

The Unemployment and Employment Rates

Unemployment Rate
The percentage of the civilian force that is unemployed: Unemployment rate = Number of unemployed persons /Civilian labor force.

The **unemployment rate** is the percentage of the civilian labor force that is unemployed. It is equal to the number of unemployed persons divided by the civilian labor force.

$$\text{Unemployment rate } (U) = \frac{\text{Number of unemployed persons}}{\text{Civilian labor force}}$$

In June 2005, the civilian labor force consisted of 149.1 million people. The number of unemployed persons totaled 7.7 million, so the unemployment rate was 5.16 percent.

Employment Rate
The percentage of the civilian noninstitutional population that is employed: Employment rate = Number of employed persons/Civilian noninstitutional population.

The **employment rate** (sometimes referred to as the *employment/population ratio*) is the percentage of the civilian noninstitutional population that is employed. It is equal to the number of employed persons divided by the civilian noninstitutional population:

$$\text{Employment rate } (E) = \frac{\text{Number of employed persons}}{\text{Civilian noninstitutional population}}$$

In recent years, the employment rate has ranged between 61 and 64 percent. In other words, between 61 and 64 percent of the civilian noninstitutional population is employed.

Notice that the sum of the unemployment rate and the employment rate is *not* 100 percent. In other words if the unemployment rate is 6 percent, it does *not* follow that the employment rate is 94 percent. The denominator of the unemployment rate and the denominator of the employment rate are not the same, so the two rates are percentages of different totals. The unemployment rate is a percentage of the civilian labor force. The employment rate is a percentage of the civilian noninstitutional population, which is a larger number than the civilian labor force.

Labor Force Participation Rate
The percentage of the civilian noninstitutional population that is in the civilian labor force. Labor force participation rate = Civilian labor force/Civilian noninstitutional population.

Finally, the **labor force participation rate** (LFPR) is the percentage of the civilian noninstitutional population that is in the civilian labor force.

$$\text{Labor force participation rate (LFPR)} = \frac{\text{Civilian labor force}}{\text{Civilian noninstitutional population}}$$

In recent years the labor force participation rate has been about 67 percent.

The LFPR may sound like the employment rate, but it is different. Although the denominator in both is the same, the numerator in the employment rate is the number of employed persons and the numerator in the LFPR is the civilian labor force (which consists of both employed persons and unemployed persons). For this reason, some economists say that while the employment rate gives us the percentage of the population that is working, the LFPR gives us the percentage of the population that is *willing to work*.

Economics In

What Explains the Increasing Percentage of Women in the Labor Force?

The BLS reports that in 1948 in the United States, 31 percent of all women 20 years old and older were working in the labor force. In 2003, that percentage had risen to 57.2 percent. In fact, in the years from 1948 to 2003, the percentage of women in the labor force has increased almost every year.

The same trend is visible in many other countries. In 1984, 52.8 percent of the adult female population in Australia worked in the labor force, and in 1994, the percentage had increased to 63.4 percent. During the same time period, the percentage rose from 62.7 percent to 80.0 percent in Iceland, from 33.2 percent to 44.1 percent in Spain, and from 57.2 to 62.1 percent in Japan.

What explains the percentage increase of women in the work force over the last half of the twentieth century? One explanation is that the "work culture" has changed during this time period. Whereas once it was widely accepted that a woman's place was primarily in the home, this view has changed over time. Often, in the United States in particular, the women's movement and feminism are given credit for this change in attitude.

There is, however, another explanation—one that has nothing to do with a changing culture but is purely economic in nature. Women have joined the work force in record numbers at the same time that it has become monetarily more advantageous to join the work force.

To illustrate, let's consider life at the end of the nineteenth century. In 1895, the average worker had to work 260 hours to earn enough money to buy a one-speed bicycle, 24 hours to earn enough to buy a cushioned chair, and 44 hours to earn enough to buy a 100-piece dinner set. More than 100 years later, in 2000, the average worker had to work only 7.2 hours to earn enough money to buy a one-speed bicycle, only 2.0 hours to earn enough to buy a cushioned chair, and only 3.6 hours to earn enough to buy a 100-piece dinner set. In other words, the average worker did not have to work as many hours in 2000 as in 1895 to buy the same goods. This conclusion also holds for goods other than bicycles, cushioned chairs, and dinner sets. In fact, it holds for many if not most goods. Here are a few:[2]

Time Needed for the Average Worker to Earn the Purchase Price of Various Goods

	Time to Earn in 1895 (hours)	Time to Earn in 2000 (hours)
One-speed bicycle	260	7.2
Cushioned office chair	24	2.0
100-piece dinner set	44	3.6
Hairbrush	16	2.0
Cane rocking chair	8	1.6
Solid gold locket	28	6.0
Encyclopedia Britannica	140	33.8
Steinway piano	2,400	1,107.6

When the average worker has to work only 7.2 hours to earn enough money to buy a bicycle, as compared to 260 hours, it follows that it is much more advantageous to work. Stated differently, using bicycles as our good, one hour of work in 1895 got the average worker 1/260 of a bicycle; but in 2000, it got the average worker about 1/7 of a bicycle. In other words, the hourly pay (in terms of bicycles) was much higher in 2000 than in 1895.

Economists would predict that more people would want to work the higher the wage rate for working (in terms of goods). In other words, the greater the benefits from working, the more people would choose to work. And this is exactly what we see. As the wage rate for working (in terms of bicycles, office chairs, dinner sets) has increased, women have joined the labor force in record numbers.

---

2. The data here are from Brad DeLong, an economist at the University of California, Berkeley, in his work-in-progress *The Economic History of the Twentieth Century: Slouching Towards Utopia.* The work can be found at http://www.j-bradford-delong.net/TCEH/2000/TCEH_title.html.

Types of Unemployment

This section describes a few types of unemployment.

Frictional Unemployment

Every day, demand conditions change in some markets, causing qualified individuals with transferable skills to leave some jobs and move to others. To illustrate, suppose there are two computer firms, *A* and *B*. For some reason, the demand falls for firm *A*'s computers and the demand rises for firm *B*'s computers. Consequently, firm *A* produces fewer computers. With fewer computers being produced, firm *A* doesn't need as many employees, so it fires some employees. On the other hand, firm *B* produces more computers. With more computers being produced, firm *B* hires additional employees. The employees fired from firm *A* have skills that they can transfer to firm *B*—after all, both firms produce computers. However, it takes time for people to transfer from one firm to another. During this time, they are said to be frictionally unemployed.

The unemployment owing to the natural "frictions" of the economy, which is caused by changing market conditions and is represented by qualified individuals with transferable skills who change jobs, is called **frictional unemployment.** We use the symbol U_F to designate the frictional unemployment rate, which is the percentage of the labor force that is frictionally unemployed.

In a dynamic, changing economy like ours, there will always be frictional unemployment. Many economists believe that the basic cause of frictional unemployment is imperfect or incomplete information, which prevents individuals from leaving one job and finding another instantly.

Structural Unemployment

Structural unemployment is unemployment due to structural changes in the economy that eliminate some jobs and create others for which the unemployed are unqualified. Most economists argue that structural unemployment is largely the consequence of automation (laborsaving devices) and long-lasting shifts in demand. The major difference between the frictionally unemployed and the structurally unemployed is that the latter do not have transferable skills. Their choice is between prolonged unemployment and retraining. For example, suppose there is a pool of unemployed automobile workers and a rising demand for computer analysts. If the automobile workers do not currently have the skills necessary to become computer analysts, they are structurally unemployed. We use the symbol U_S to designate the structural unemployment rate, which is the percentage of the labor force that is structurally unemployed.

Natural Unemployment

Adding the frictional unemployment rate and the structural unemployment rate gives the **natural unemployment** rate (or natural rate of unemployment). We use the symbol U_N to designate the natural unemployment rate. Currently, most economists estimate the natural unemployment rate at between 4 and 6.5 percent.

$$\text{Natural unemployment rate } (U_N) =$$
$$\text{Frictional unemployment rate } (U_F) + \text{Structural unemployment rate } (U_S)$$

What Is Full Employment?

What do you think of when you hear the term *full employment*? Most people think full employment means that the actual or reported unemployment rate is zero. But a dynamic, changing economy can never have full employment of this type due to the frictional and structural changes that continually occur. In fact, it is natural for some unemployment to

---

Frictional Unemployment
Unemployment due to the natural "frictions" of the economy, which is caused by changing market conditions and is represented by qualified individuals with transferable skills who change jobs.

Structural Unemployment
Unemployment due to structural changes in the economy that eliminate some jobs and create others for which the unemployed are unqualified.

Natural Unemployment
Unemployment caused by frictional and structural factors in the economy. Natural unemployment rate = Frictional unemployment rate + Structural unemployment rate

exist—some natural unemployment, that is. For this reason, economists *do not* equate full employment with a zero unemployment rate. Instead, for economists, **full employment** *exists when the economy is operating at its natural unemployment rate.* For example, if the natural unemployment rate is 5 percent, then full employment exists when the unemployment rate (in the economy) is 5 percent. In other words, the economy can be operating at full employment and some people will be unemployed.

Full Employment
The condition that exists when the unemployment rate is equal to the natural unemployment rate.

Cyclical Unemployment

The unemployment rate that exists in the economy is not always the natural rate. The difference between the existing unemployment rate and the natural unemployment rate is the **cyclical unemployment rate** (U_C).

Cyclical Unemployment Rate
The difference between the unemployment rate and the natural unemployment rate.

Cyclical unemployment rate (U_C) = Unemployment rate (U) – Natural unemployment rate (U_N)

When the unemployment rate (U) that exists in the economy is greater than the natural unemployment rate (U_N), the cyclical unemployment rate (U_C) is positive. For example, if $U = 8$ percent and $U_N = 5$ percent, then $U_C = 3$ percent. When the unemployment rate that exists in the economy is less than the natural unemployment rate, the cyclical unemployment rate is negative. For example, if $U = 4$ percent and $U_N = 5$ percent, then $U_C = -1$ percent.

SELF-TEST

1. What is the major difference between a person who is frictionally unemployed and one who is structurally unemployed?
2. If the cyclical unemployment rate is positive, what does this imply?

GROSS DOMESTIC PRODUCT

In any given year, people in the United States produce goods and services. They produce television sets, books, pencil sharpeners, tape recorders, attorney services, haircuts, and much more. Have you ever wondered what the total dollar value of all those goods and services is? In 2004, it was $11.9 trillion. In other words, in 2004, people living and working in the United States produced $11.9 trillion worth of goods and services. That dollar amount—$11.9 trillion—is what economists call the gross domestic product. Simply put, **gross domestic product (GDP)** is the *total market value of all final goods and services produced annually within a country's borders.*

Gross Domestic Product (GDP)
The total market value of all final goods and services produced annually within a country's borders.

Three Ways to Compute GDP

Consider a simple economy in which one good is produced and sold. Bob finds a seed and plants it. Sometime later an orange tree appears. Bob pays Harry $5 in wages to pick and box the oranges. Next, Bob sells the oranges to Jim for $8. Jim turns the oranges into orange juice and sells the orange juice to Caroline for $10. Caroline drinks the juice. What is the GDP in this simple economy? Is it $5, $13, $10, $18, or some other dollar amount?

Economists use three approaches to compute GDP—the expenditure approach, the income approach, and the value-added approach. The following paragraphs describe each approach in terms of our simple economy.

Expenditure Approach

To compute GDP using the expenditure approach, add the amount of money spent by buyers on *final goods and services.* The words "final goods and services" are important in computing GDP because not all goods are final goods. Some goods are *intermediate goods.*

Final Good
A good in the hands of its final user.

A **final good** (or service) is a good in the hands of the final user or ultimate consumer. Think of buyers standing in line, one after another. The first buyer in our simple economy was Jim. He bought oranges from Bob. The second buyer was Caroline, who bought orange juice from Jim.

Caroline is the final buyer in this economy; she is the final user, the ultimate consumer. No buyer comes after her. The good that she buys is the final good. In other words, the orange juice is the final good.

So, then, what are the oranges? Aren't they a final good too? No, the oranges are an *intermediate good*. An **intermediate good** is an input in the production of a final good. In other words, the oranges were used to produce orange juice (the final good).

Intermediate Good
A good that is an input in the production of a final good.

So, what does GDP equal if we use the expenditure approach to compute it? Again, it is the dollar amount spent by buyers for *final* goods and services. In our simple economy, there is only one buyer (Caroline) who spends $10 on one final good (orange juice). Thus, GDP in our tiny economy is $10.

You may be wondering why expenditures on only final goods are counted when computing GDP. The reason is because we would be *double counting* if we counted expenditures on both final goods *and* intermediate goods. **Double counting** refers to counting a good more than once when computing GDP. To illustrate, if we count both Caroline's purchase of the orange juice ($10) and Jim's purchase of the oranges ($8), we count the purchase of the oranges *twice*—once when the oranges are purchased by Jim and once when the oranges are in the orange juice.

Double Counting
Counting a good more than once when computing GDP.

Consider another example. Some of the intermediate goods used to make a book are glue, ink, and paper. In one sense, *a book is simply another name for glue, ink, and paper together*. In equation form, book = glue + ink + paper. Now, when computing GDP, if we count the purchase of the book *and* the purchases of glue, ink, and paper, we are counting what is on the left side of the equal sign in the equation (that is, the book) and then adding it to what is on the right side of the equal sign in the equation (that is, glue + ink + paper). That would be like saying 2 = 1 + 1 and counting both the 2 and the 1 + 1 to give us a total of 4. Counting the "2" is enough; adding the "2" and the "1 + 1" is double counting.

Income Approach

In our simple economy, income consists of wages and profits.[3] To compute GDP using the income approach, simply find the sum of all the wages and profits.

First, Harry earns $5 in wages.

Second, Bob's profit is $3: (1) Bob pays $5 to Harry, so the $5 is a cost to Bob; (2) Bob receives $8 for the oranges he sells to Jim; (3) $8 in revenue minus $5 in costs leaves Bob with $3 profit.

Third, Jim's profit is $2: (1) Jim pays $8 to Bob for the oranges, so the $8 is a cost to Jim; (2) Jim receives $10 for the orange juice he sells to Caroline; (3) $10 in revenue minus $8 in costs leaves Jim with $2 profit.

In our simple economy, the sum of Harry's wages, Bob's profit, and Jim's profit is $10. So GDP is equal to $10.

Value-Added Approach

In our tiny economy, orange juice is sold for, or has a market value of, $10. How much of the $10 market value is attributable to Jim? Stated differently, how much of the $10

---

3. Later in the chapter, you will learn that in a large economy, such as the U.S. economy, income consists of more than wages and profits. To simplify the explanation, we have defined a tiny economy where only wages and profits exist.

market value is *value added* by Jim? If your intuition tells you $2, then your intuition is correct. **Value added** is the dollar value contributed to a final good at each stage of production. That is, it is the difference between the dollar value of the output the producer sells and the dollar value of the intermediate goods the producer buys.

To compute GDP using the value-added approach, find the sum of the values added at all the stages of production. Bob buys no intermediate goods (he simply found a seed, planted it, and then hired Harry to pick and box oranges), but he sells the oranges to Jim for $8. In other words, valued added at this stage of production is $8.

Jim takes the oranges (an intermediate good he buys from Bob for $8) and turns them into orange juice that he sells to Caroline for $10. Value added at this stage of production is $2.

The sum of the values added at all (two) stages of production is $10, so GDP is equal to $10.

Value Added
The dollar value contributed to a final good at each stage of production.

What GDP Omits

Some exchanges that take place in an economy are not included in GDP. As the following paragraphs indicate, these trades range from sales of used cars to illegal drug deals.

Certain Nonmarket Goods and Services

If a family hires a person through the classified section of the newspaper to cook and clean, the service is counted in GDP. If family members perform the same tasks, however, their services are not counted in GDP. The difference is that, in the first case, a service is actually bought and sold for a price in a market setting, and in the other, it is not.

Some nonmarket goods are included in GDP. For example, the market value of food produced on a farm and consumed by the farm family is estimated, and this imputed value is part of GDP.

Underground Activities, Both Legal and Illegal

The underground economy consists of unreported exchanges that take place outside the normal recorded market channels. Some underground activities involve illegal goods (such as cocaine), and others involve legal goods and tax evasion.

Illegal goods and services are not counted in GDP because no record exists of such transactions. There are no written records of illegal drug sales, illegal gambling, and illegal prostitution. Neither are there written records of some legal activities that individuals want to keep from government notice. For example, a gardener might agree to do some gardening work only on the condition that he is paid in cash. Obviously, it is not illegal for a person to buy or sell gardening services, but still the transaction might not be recorded if one or both parties do not want it to be. Why might the gardener want to be paid in cash? Perhaps he doesn't want to pay taxes on the income received—an objective more easily accomplished if there is no written record of the income being generated.

Sales of Used Goods

GDP measures *current production* (that is, occurring during the current year). A used car sale, for example, does not enter into the current-year statistics because the car was counted when it was originally produced.

Financial Transactions

The trading of stocks and bonds is not counted in GDP because it does not represent the production of new assets, but simply the trading of existing assets (the exchange of stocks or bonds for money).

Government Transfer Payments

Transfer Payment
A payment to a person that is not made in return for goods and services currently supplied.

A **transfer payment** is a payment to a person that is not made in return for goods and services currently supplied. Government transfer payments—such as Social Security benefits and veterans' benefits—are not counted in GDP because they do not represent payments to individuals for *current production.*

Leisure

Leisure is a good, in much the same way that cars, houses, and shoes are goods. New cars, houses, and shoes are counted in GDP, but leisure is not because it is too difficult to quantify. The length of the workweek has fallen in the United States over the past years, indicating that the leisure time individuals have to consume has increased. But GDP computations do not take this into account.

ANALYZING THE SCENE

Questions from Setting the Scene: Why does the plumber want to be paid in cash? Why does the DEA care that people are demanding cash from banks in Miami?

Both of these questions relate to the underground economy where exchanges take place outside recorded market channels. Economists argue that the greater the demand for cash transactions relative to check and credit transactions, the more likely individuals want to transact business in the underground economy (outside the view of government). One reason to operate in the underground economy is because you do not want to pay taxes on income earned. This is likely the reason why the plumber wants to be paid in cash.

Another reason to operate in the underground economy is because what you are buying or selling is illegal. The mission of the Drug Enforcement Administration (DEA) is to "bring to the criminal and civil justice system of the United States . . . those organizations and principal members of organizations, involved in the growing, manufacture, or distribution of controlled substances appearing in or destined for illicit traffic in the United States."[4] Illegal drugs are bought and sold for cash. (No checks or credit cards, please.) The fact that increasingly more cash was being withdrawn from Miami banks could be indicative of increased illegal drug purchases and sales in Miami. This is something that would obviously interest the DEA.

Is Either GDP or Per Capita GDP a Measure of Happiness or Well-Being?

Are the people in a country with a higher GDP or higher per capita GDP (GDP divided by population) better off or happier than the people in a country with a lower GDP or lower per capita GDP? We cannot answer that question because well-being and happiness are subjective. A person with more goods may be happier than a person with fewer goods, but possibly not. The person with fewer goods but a lot of leisure, little air pollution, and a relaxed way of life may be much happier than the person with many goods, little leisure, and a polluted, stressful environment.

We make this point to warn against reading too much into GDP figures. GDP figures are useful for obtaining an estimate of the productive capabilities of an economy, but they do not necessarily measure happiness or well-being.

---

4. From the DEA Mission Statement.

SELF-TEST

1. Why aren't transfer payments included in GDP?
2. Suppose the GDP for a country is $0. Does this mean that there was no productive activity in the country? Explain your answer.

THE EXPENDITURE APPROACH TO COMPUTING GDP FOR A REAL-WORLD ECONOMY

The last section explains the expenditure, income, and value-added approaches to computing GDP for a simple economy. This simple economy consisted of one person producing oranges, one person producing orange juice, and one person buying orange juice. Obviously, the U.S. economy is much more complex than this tiny economy is.

This section explains how the expenditure approach is used to compute GDP in a real-world economy like the U.S. economy.

Expenditures in a Real-World Economy

Economists often talk about four sectors of the economy: (1) household sector, (2) business sector, (3) government sector, and (4) foreign sector. Economic actors in these sectors buy goods and services; in other words, they spend. The expenditures of the sectors are called, respectively, (1) *consumption;* (2) gross private domestic investment, or simply *investment;* (3) government consumption expenditures and gross investment, or simply *government purchases;* and (4) *net exports.*

Consumption

Consumption *(C)* includes (1) spending on durable goods, (2) spending on nondurable goods, and (3) spending on services. Durable goods are goods that are expected to last for more than three years, such as refrigerators, ovens, or cars. Nondurable goods are goods that are not expected to last for more than three years, such as food. Services are intangible items such as lawn care, car repair, and entertainment. In 2004, consumption expenditures in the United States accounted for approximately 70.6 percent of GDP. In short, consumption is the largest spending component of GDP.

Consumption
The sum of spending on durable goods, nondurable goods, and services.

Investment

Investment *(I)* is the sum of (1) the purchases of newly produced capital goods, (2) changes in business inventories, sometimes referred to as **inventory investment,** and (3) the purchases of new residential housing.[5] The sum of the purchases of newly produced capital goods and the purchases of new residential housing is often referred to as **fixed investment.** In other words, investment = fixed investment + inventory investment. Fixed investment is the larger of the two components of investment.

Investment
The sum of all purchases of newly produced capital goods, changes in business inventories, and purchases of new residential housing.

Inventory Investment
Changes in the stock of unsold goods.

Fixed Investment
Business purchases of capital goods, such as machinery and factories, and purchases of new residential housing.

Government Purchases

Government purchases *(G)* include federal, state, and local government purchases of goods and services and gross investment in highways, bridges, and so on. **Government transfer payments,** which are payments to persons that are not made in return for goods and services currently supplied, are not included in government purchases. Social Security

Government Purchases
Federal, state, and local government purchases of goods and services and gross investment in highways, bridges, and so on.

Government Transfer Payments
Payments to persons that are not made in return for goods and services currently supplied.

---

5. For purposes of computing GDP, the purchases of new residential housing (although undertaken by members of the household sector) are considered investment.

benefits and welfare payments are two examples of transfer payments; neither is a payment for current productive efforts.

Net Exports

Imports
Total domestic (U.S.) spending on foreign goods.

Exports
Total foreign spending on domestic (U.S.) goods.

Net Exports
Exports minus imports.

People, firms, and governments in the United States sometimes purchase foreign-produced goods. These purchases are referred to as **imports** *(IM)*. Foreign residents, firms, and governments sometimes purchase U.S.-produced goods. These purchases are referred to as **exports** *(EX)*. If imports are subtracted from exports, we are left with **net exports** *(NX)*.

$$NX = EX - IM$$

Obviously, net exports *(NX)* can be positive or negative. If exports are greater than imports, then *NX* is positive; if imports are greater than exports, then *NX* is negative.

Computing GDP Using the Expenditure Approach

The expenditure approach to computing GDP sums the purchases of final goods and services made by the four sectors of the economy. This may give you reason to pause because our earlier definition of GDP did not mention *purchases* of final goods and services. Rather, we defined GDP as the total market value of all final goods and services *produced* annually within a nation's borders.

The discrepancy is cleared up quickly when we note that national income accountants (those persons who compute GDP for the government) assume that anything that is produced but not sold to consumers is "bought" by the firm that produced it. In other words, if a car is produced but not sold, it goes into business inventory and is consider to be "purchased" by the firm that produced it. Thus, we can compute GDP by summing the purchases made by the four sectors of the economy. GDP equals consumption *(C)* plus investment *(I)* plus government purchases *(G)* plus net exports *(EX − IM)*.

$$GDP = C + I + G + (EX - IM)$$

Exhibit 4 shows the dollar amounts of the four components of GDP for the United States in 2004.

---

exhibit | **4**

**Components of GDP
(Expenditure Approach)**
The expenditure approach to computing GDP sums the purchases made by final users of goods and services. The expenditure components include consumption, investment, government purchases, and net exports. The data are for 2004.

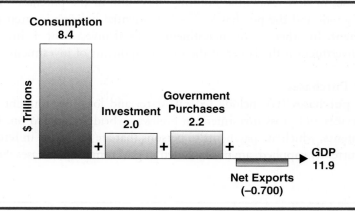

SELF-TEST

1. Describe the expenditure approach to computing GDP in a real-world economy.
2. Will GDP be smaller than the sum of consumption, investment, and government purchases if net exports are negative? Explain your answer.
3. If GDP is $400 billion, and the country's population is 100 million, does it follow that each individual in the country has $40,000 worth of goods and services?

REAL GDP

This section defines Real GDP, shows how to compute it, and then explains how it is used to measure economic growth.

Why We Need Real GDP

In 2003, U.S. GDP was $11.2 trillion. One year later, in 2004, GDP was $11.9 trillion. Although you know GDP was higher in 2004 than in 2003, do you know *the reason why* GDP was higher in 2004 than in 2003?

As you think about your answer, let's look at GDP in a one-good economy. Suppose 10 units of this good are produced and each unit is sold for $10, so GDP in the economy is $100.

$$GDP = \$10 \times 10 \text{ units} = \$100$$

Now suppose GDP rises from $100 to $250. What caused it to rise? It could be because price increased from $10 to $25:

$$GDP = \boxed{\$25} \times 10 \text{ units} = \$250$$

Or, it could be because quantity of output produced increased from 10 units to 25 units:

$$GDP = \$10 \times \boxed{25} \text{ units} = \$250$$

Or, it could be because price increased to $12.50 and quantity increased to 20 units:

$$GDP = \boxed{\$12.50} \times \boxed{20 \text{ units}} = \$250$$

To gauge the health of the economy, economists want to know the *reason* for an increase in GDP. If GDP increased simply because price increased, then the economy is not growing. For an economy to grow, more output must be produced.

Because an increase in GDP can be due in part to simply an increase in price, a more meaningful measure is Real GDP. **Real GDP** is GDP adjusted for price changes.

Real GDP
The value of the entire output produced annually within a country's borders, adjusted for price changes.

Computing Real GDP

One way to compute Real GDP is to find the value of the output for the different years in terms of the same prices, the prices that existed in the base year. Let's look again at our one-good economy. Consider the following data.

Year	Price of Good X	Quantity Produced of Good X (units)	GDP
1	$10	100	$10 × 100 = **$1,000**
2	$12	120	$12 × 120 = **$1,440**
3	$14	140	$14 × 140 = **$1,960**

Popular Culture   Technology   **Everyday Life**   The World

Does the State of the Economy Influence How People Vote?

A presidential election is held in the United States every four years. There are usually two major presidential candidates (one from the Democratic party and one from the Republican party) and a number of third-party candidates. In the months before the presidential election, journalists follow the two major candidates across the country and record their every action and word. Not only is what they say about the issues reported, but every misstep, scandal, and piece of gossip is reported as well. Then, on election day, the voters go to the polls and elect or reelect a president.

After the results are in, news commentators analyze why the voters voted the way they did. Some commentators may say that the people voted for *X* over *Y* because *X* has a better foreign policy and people are worried about foreign affairs these days. Some commentators may say that the people voted for *X* over *Y* because *X* is more self-confident, more personable, or more charismatic. Commentators often present many different reasons to explain why the voters voted the way they did.

But suppose none of these reasons really matter. Suppose the only thing that determines how people vote is the state of the economy prior to the election. If the economy is good, then they vote for the incumbent or the incumbent's party. If the economy is bad, then they vote for the challenger.

Some economists have developed models suggesting that only economic variables influence how people vote. One model, the Fair Model, was developed by Ray Fair, an economist at Yale University. The equation he has developed to predict the outcome of presidential elections is:

$$V = 55.57 + 0.691g_3 - 0.775p_{15} + 0.837n$$

In the equation, V equals the Democratic share of the two-party presidential vote; g_3 equals the growth rate of per capita Real GDP in the three quarters prior to the election; p_{15} equals the growth rate of the GDP implicit price deflator in the 15 quarters prior to the election; n equals the number of quarters in the 15 quarters mentioned in which the growth rate of per capita Real GDP is greater than a 3.2 percent annual rate.

Fair's model has not always predicted accurately in the past, but it does have a fairly significant success rate. Thus, the state of the economy—as measured by per capita Real GDP, and so on—seems to matter to how people vote.

The data show *why* GDP is higher in subsequent years: GDP is higher because both price and quantity have increased. In other words, GDP rises because both price *and* quantity rise. Suppose we want to separate the part of GDP that is higher because quantity is higher from the part of GDP that is higher because price is higher. What we want then is Real GDP because Real GDP is the part of GDP that is higher because quantity (of output) is higher.

To compute Real GDP for any year, we simply multiply the quantity of the good produced in a given year by the price in the base year. Suppose we choose year 1 as the base year. So, to compute Real GDP in year 2, we simply multiply the quantity of the good produced in year 2 by the price of the good in year 1. To find Real GDP in year 3, we simply multiply the quantity of the good produced in year 3 by the price of the good in year 1.

Year	Price of Good X	Quantity Produced of Good X (units)	GDP	Real GDP
1 (Base Year)	$10	100	$10 × 100 = **$1,000**	$10 × 100 = **$1,000**
2	$12	120	$12 × 120 = **$1,440**	$10 × 120 = **$1,200**
3	$14	140	$14 × 140 = **$1,960**	$10 × 140 = **$1,400**

The General Equation for Real GDP

In the real world, there is more than one good and more than one price. The general equation used to compute Real GDP is:

$$\text{Real GDP} = \Sigma \text{ (Base-year prices} \times \text{Current-year quantities)}$$

Σ is the Greek capital letter *sigma*. Here it stands for *summation*. Thus, Real GDP is "the sum of all the current-year quantities times their base-year prices." In 2004, Real GDP in the United States was $10.9 trillion.

What Does It Mean if Real GDP Is Higher in One Year Than in Another Year?

If GDP is, say, $9 trillion in year 1 and $9.5 trillion in year 2, we cannot be sure why it has increased. Obviously, GDP can rise from one year to the next if: (1) prices rise and output remains constant; (2) output rises and prices remain constant; or (3) prices and output rise.

However, if Real GDP is, say, $8 trillion in year 1 and $8.3 trillion in year 2, we *know* why it has increased. Real GDP rises only if output rises. In other words, Real GDP rises only if more goods and services are produced.

Real GDP, Economic Growth, and Business Cycles

Suppose there are two countries, *A* and *B*. In country *A*, Real GDP grows by 3 percent each year. In country *B*, Real GDP is the same each year: if Real GDP was $500 billion last year, it is $500 billion in the current year, and it will be $500 billion next year. In which of the two countries would you prefer to live, *ceteris paribus?*

Now consider another situation. Again suppose there are two countries, *C* and *D*. In country *C*, Real GDP takes a roller coaster ride: it alternates between rising and falling. It rises for some months, then falls, then rises again, then falls, and so on. In country *D*, Real GDP simply rises year after year. In which of the two countries would you prefer to live, *ceteris paribus?*

If you chose one country over the other in each of these two cases, then you are implicitly saying that Real GDP matters to you. One of the reasons economists study Real GDP is simply because Real GDP matters to you and others. In other words, because Real GDP is important to you, it is important to economists too.

Economists study two major macroeconomic topics that have to do with Real GDP. One topic is *economic growth;* the other is *business cycles.*

Economic Growth

Annual **economic growth** has occurred if Real GDP in one year is higher than Real GDP in the previous year. For example, if Real GDP is $8.1 trillion in one year and $8.3 trillion in the next, the economy has witnessed economic growth. The growth rate is equal to the (positive) percentage change in Real GDP. The growth rate is computed using the following formula:

Economic Growth
Increases in Real GDP.

$$\text{Percentage change in Real GDP} = \left(\frac{\text{Real GDP}_{\text{later year}} - \text{Real GDP}_{\text{earlier year}}}{\text{Real GDP}_{\text{earlier year}}} \right) \times 100$$

The Phases of the Business Cycle
The phases of a business cycle include the peak, contraction, trough, recovery, and expansion. A business cycle is measured from peak to peak.

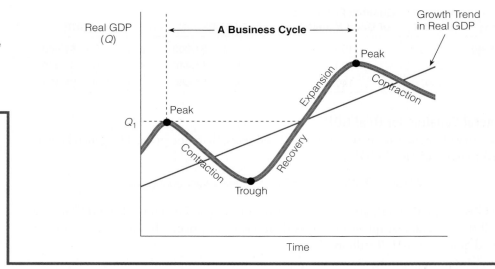

Business Cycle
Recurrent swings (up and down) in Real GDP.

The "Ups and Downs" in the Economy, or the Business Cycle

If Real GDP is on a roller coaster—rising and falling and rising and falling—the economy is said to be incurring a **business cycle.** Economists usually talk about four or five phases of the business cycle. We identify five phases below and in Exhibit 5.

1. **Peak.** At the *peak* of the business cycle, Real GDP is at a temporary high. In Exhibit 5, Real GDP is at a temporary high at Q_1.

2. **Contraction.** The *contraction* phase represents a decline in Real GDP. According to the standard definition of *recession,* two consecutive quarter declines in Real GDP constitute a recession.

3. **Trough.** The low point in Real GDP, just before it begins to turn up, is called the *trough* of the business cycle.

4. **Recovery.** The *recovery* is the period when Real GDP is rising. It begins at the trough and ends at the initial peak. The recovery in Exhibit 5 extends from the trough until Real GDP is again at Q_1.

5. **Expansion.** The *expansion* phase refers to increases in Real GDP beyond the recovery. In Exhibit 5, it refers to increases in Real GDP above Q_1.

An entire business cycle is measured from peak to peak. The typical business cycle is approximately four to five years, although a few have been shorter and some have been longer.

NBER and Recessions

In the contraction stage of the business cycle, we state that the "standard" definition of a recession is two consecutive quarter declines in Real GDP. This is not, however, the only definition of a recession.

On November 26, 2001, the National Bureau of Economic Research, which dates the business cycle, issued a press release. The first paragraph read:

The NBER's Business Cycle Dating Committee has determined that a peak in business activity occurred in the U.S. economy in March 2001. A peak marks the end of an expansion and the beginning of a recession. The determination of a peak date in March is thus a determination that the expansion that began in March 1991 ended in March 2001 and a recession began. The expansion lasted exactly 10 years, the longest in the NBER's chronology.

According to this statement, the U.S. economy entered a recession in March 2001. That's because according to the NBER "a peak marks the end of an expansion and the beginning of a recession" and March 2001 was dated by the NBER as the peak of the business cycle. In other words, the U.S. economy was in a recession even though Real GDP had not declined for two consecutive quarters.

The NBER definition of a recession is different from the standard definition of a recession. According to the NBER, " a recession is a significant decline in activity spread across the economy, lasting more than a few months, visible in industrial production, employment, real income, and wholesale-retail trade."

SELF-TEST

1. Suppose GDP is $6 trillion in year 1 and $6.2 trillion in year 2. What has caused the rise in GDP?
2. Suppose Real GDP is $5.2 trillion in year 1 and $5.3 trillion in year 2. What has caused the rise in Real GDP?
3. Can an economy be faced with endless business cycles and still have its Real GDP grow over time? Explain your answer.

A READER ASKS   ***Where Do I Go to Learn the Specifics of Jobs and Wages?***

I'm a math major and I'll graduate from college in about a year. Is there a way for me to find out how much mathematicians earn and what types of jobs they perform?

No matter what your major is, you can learn about jobs and wages from the *Occupational Outlook Handbook.* The *Handbook* is on the Bureau of Labor Statistics Web site at *http://stats.bls.gov/emp/*.

According to the *Handbook,* mathematicians usually work as part of a team that includes economists, engineers, computer scientists, physicists, and others. In 2000, mathematicians held about 3,600 jobs. In addition, about 20,000 persons held faculty positions in mathematics at colleges and universities.

Many nonfaculty mathematicians work for the federal and state governments. The biggest employer of mathematicians in the federal government is the Department of Defense. In the private sector, major employers include research and testing services, educational services, security and commodity exchanges, and management and public relations services. In manufacturing, the pharmaceutical industry is the primary employer. Some mathematicians also work for banks, insurance companies, and public utilities.

Median annual earnings of mathematicians were $68,640 in 1998. The middle 50 percent earned between $50,740 and $85,520. The lowest 10 percent had earnings of less than $35,390, while the top 10 percent earned more than $101,900.

According to the *Handbook,* "employment of mathematicians is expected to decline through 2010, because very few jobs with the title mathematician are available. However, master's and Ph.D. degree holders with a strong background in mathematics and a related discipline, such as engineering or computer science, should have good job opportunities. However, many of these workers have job titles that reflect their occupation, rather than the title mathematician."

Finally, according to a 2001 survey by the National Association of Colleges and Employers, starting salary offers averaged about $46,466 a year for mathematics graduates with a bachelor's degree and $53,440 for those with a master's degree. Doctoral degree candidates averaged $55,938. The average annual salary in 1999 for mathematicians employed by the federal government in supervisory, nonsupervisory, and managerial positions was $76,460, for mathematics statisticians it was $76,530, and for cryptoanalysts it was $70,840.

Chapter Summary

Measuring Prices

> One major price index is the consumer price index (CPI).

> $$\text{CPI} = \left(\frac{\begin{array}{c} \text{Total dollar expenditure on} \\ \text{market basket in current year} \end{array}}{\begin{array}{c} \text{Total dollar expenditure on} \\ \text{market basket in base year} \end{array}} \right) \times 100$$

> Percentage change in prices $=$
$$\left(\frac{\text{CPI}_{\text{later year}} - \text{CPI}_{\text{earlier year}}}{\text{CPI}_{\text{earlier year}}} \right) \times 100$$

> Inflation is an increase in the price level or price index.

> $$\text{Real income} = \left(\frac{\text{Nominal income}}{\text{CPI}} \right) \times 100$$

> A given dollar amount in an earlier year does not have the same purchasing power in a later year (or current year) if prices are different in the two years. To convert a dollar amount in an earlier year into today's (or current) dollars, we use the formula:

Dollar amount in today's (current) dollars $=$

Dollar amount$_{\text{earlier year}}$ $\times \left(\dfrac{\text{CPI}_{\text{current year}}}{\text{CPI}_{\text{earlier year}}} \right)$

Unemployment and Employment

> Unemployment rate $(U) = \dfrac{\begin{array}{c}\text{Number of} \\ \text{unemployed persons}\end{array}}{\begin{array}{c}\text{Civilian labor} \\ \text{force}\end{array}}$

> Employment rate $(E) = \dfrac{\begin{array}{c}\text{Number of} \\ \text{employed persons}\end{array}}{\begin{array}{c}\text{Civilian noninstitutional} \\ \text{population}\end{array}}$

> Frictional unemployment, due to the natural "frictions" of the economy, is caused by changing market conditions and is represented by qualified individuals with transferable skills who change jobs.

> Structural unemployment is due to structural changes in the economy that eliminate some jobs and create others for which the unemployed are unqualified.

> Natural unemployment is caused by frictional and structural factors in the economy. The natural unemployment rate equals the sum of the frictional unemployment rate and the structural unemployment rate.

> Full employment is the condition that exists when the unemployment rate is equal to the natural unemployment rate.

> The cyclical unemployment rate is the difference between the existing unemployment rate and the natural unemployment rate.

Gross Domestic Product

> Gross domestic product (GDP) is the total market value of all final goods and services produced annually within a country's borders.

> Any one of the following can be used to compute GDP: (1) expenditure approach, (2) income approach, or (3) value-added approach.

> To avoid the problem of double counting, only final goods and services are counted in GDP.

> GDP omits certain nonmarket goods and services, both legal and illegal underground activities, the sale of used goods, financial transactions, transfer payments, and leisure (even though leisure is a good).

Expenditures

> The expenditures on U.S. goods and services include consumption; gross private domestic investment, or investment; government consumption expenditures and gross investment, or government purchases; and net exports (exports – imports).

> Consumption includes spending on durable goods, nondurable goods, and services.

> Investment includes purchases of newly produced capital goods (fixed investment), changes in business inventories (inventory investment), and the purchases of new residential housing (also fixed investment).

> Government purchases include federal, state, and local government purchases of goods and services and gross investment in highways, bridges, and so on. Government purchases do not include transfer payments.

> Net exports equal the total foreign spending on domestic goods (exports) minus the total domestic spending on foreign goods (imports).

Computing GDP

> Using the expenditure approach, GDP $= C + I + G + (EX - IM)$. In other words, GDP equals consumption plus investment plus government purchases plus net exports.

Real GDP

> Real GDP is GDP adjusted for price changes. It is GDP in base-year dollars.

Economic Growth and Business Cycles

> Annual economic growth has occurred if Real GDP in one year is higher than Real GDP in the previous year.

> There are five phases to the business cycle: peak, contraction, trough, recovery, and expansion. A complete business cycle is measured from peak to peak.

Key Terms and Concepts

Price Level
Price Index
Consumer Price Index (CPI)
Base Year
Inflation
Real Income
Nominal Income
Unemployment Rate
Employment Rate
Labor Force Participation Rate
Frictional Unemployment

Structural Unemployment
Natural Unemployment
Full Employment
Cyclical Unemployment Rate
Gross Domestic Product (GDP)
Final Good
Intermediate Good
Double Counting
Value Added
Transfer Payment
Consumption

Investment
Inventory Investment
Fixed Investment
Government Purchases
Government Transfer Payments
Imports
Exports
Net Exports
Real GDP
Economic Growth
Business Cycle

Questions and Problems

1. What does the CPI in the base year equal? Explain your answer.
2. Show that if the percentage rise in prices is equal to the percentage rise in nominal income, then one's real income does not change.
3. How does structural unemployment differ from frictional unemployment?
4. What does it mean to say that the country is operating at full employment?
5. What is "natural" about natural unemployment?
6. What is the difference between the employment rate and the labor force participation rate?
7. If the unemployment rate is 4 percent, it does not follow that the employment rate is 96 percent. Explain why.
8. "I just heard on the news that GDP is higher this year than it was last year. This means that we're better off this year than last year." Comment.
9. Which of the following are included in the calculation of this year's GDP? (a) Twelve-year-old Johnny mowing his family's lawn; (b) Dave Malone buying a used car; (c) Barbara Wilson buying a bond issued by General Motors; (d) Ed Ferguson's receipt of a Social Security payment; (e) the illegal drug transaction at the corner of Elm and Fifth.
10. Discuss the problems you see in comparing the GDPs of two countries, say, the United States and the People's Republic of China.

11. The manuscript for this book was keyed by the author. Had he hired someone to do the keying, GDP would have been higher than it was. What other activities would increase GDP if they were done differently? What activities would decrease GDP if they were done differently?
12. Why does GDP omit the sales of used goods? of financial transactions? of government transfer payments?
13. A business firm produces a good this year that it doesn't sell. As a result, the good is added to the firm's inventory. How does this inventory good find its way into GDP?
14. Economists prefer to compare Real GDP figures for different years instead of comparing GDP figures. Why?
15. Define each of the following terms:
    a. Contraction
    b. Business cycle
    c. Trough
16. Explain why GDP can be computed either by measuring spending or by measuring income.
17. In the first quarter of the year, Real GDP was $400 billion; in the second quarter, it was $398 billion; in the third quarter, it was $399 billion; and in the fourth quarter, it was $395 billion. Has there been a recession? Explain your answer.

Working With Numbers and Graphs

1. Suppose there are 60 million people employed, 10 million unemployed, and 30 million not in the labor force. What does the civilian noninstitutional population equal?
2. Suppose there are 100 million people in the civilian labor force and 90 million people employed. How many people are unemployed? What is the unemployment rate?

3. Change the current-year prices in Exhibit 1 to $1 for pens, $28 for shirts, and $32 for a pair of shoes. What is the CPI for the current year based on these prices?
4. Jim earned an annual salary of $15,000 in 1965. What is this equivalent to in 2002 dollars? (Use Exhibit 2 to find the CPI in the years mentioned.)

5. Using the following data, compute (a) the unemployment rate, (b) the employment rate, and (c) the labor force participation rate.

   Civilian noninstitutional population = 200 million
   Number of employed persons = 126 million
   Number of unemployed persons = 8 million

6. Based on the following data, compute (a) the unemployment rate, (b) the structural unemployment rate, and (c) the cyclical unemployment rate.

   Frictional unemployment rate = 2 percent
   Natural unemployment rate = 5 percent
   Civilian labor force = 100 million
   Number of employed persons = 82 million

7. Using Exhibit 2, compute the percentage change in prices between (a) 1966 and 1969, (b) 1976 and 1986, and (c) 1990 and 1999.

8. If the CPI is 150 and nominal income is $100,000, what does real income equal?

9. Net exports are –$114 billion and exports are $857 billion. What are imports?

10. Consumption spending is $3.708 trillion, spending on non-durable goods is $1.215 trillion, and spending on services is $2.041 trillion. What does spending on durable goods equal?

11. Inventory investment is $62 billion and (total) investment is $1.122 trillion. What does fixed investment equal?

12. In year 1, the prices of goods X, Y, and Z are $2, $4, and $6 per unit, respectively. In year 2, the prices of goods X, Y, and Z are $3, $4, and $7, respectively. In year 2, twice as many units of each good are produced as in year 1. In year 1, 20 units of X, 40 units of Y, and 60 units of Z are produced. If year 1 is the base year, what does Real GDP equal in year 2?

13. Nondurable goods spending = $400 million, durable goods spending = $300 million, new residential housing spending = $200 million, and spending on services = $500 million. What does consumption equal?

14. If Real GDP in year 1 is $487 billion and it is $498 billion in year 2, what is the economic growth rate equal to?

chapter 5

AGGREGATE DEMAND AND AGGREGATE SUPPLY

© Frank Siteman/Photo Edit

Setting the Scene

The following events occurred on a day in February.

10:13 A.M.

Toby Perkins, 22 years old, is looking at a car on a dealer's lot. He examines the right side of the car and then walks around to the left side. He opens the door and sits in the driver's seat. Just then, a car salesman walks up to the car. "That's a really nice car," are the salesman's first words. "I know," says Toby. "I wish interest rates were a little lower so I could buy it today." The car salesman says, "Oh, I'm sure we can work something out."

11:53 A.M.

Marcy, 23 years old, is sitting at the kitchen table looking at travel brochures—the ones for Ireland, England, France, Belgium, and Germany. Her mother enters the kitchen and asks, "Excited about your big trip?" "I guess," says Marcy. "Of course, the trip is getting more expensive by the minute." "What do you mean?" her mother asks. "The exchange rate," Marcy answers. "It's killing me. A couple of months ago, I could get euros for $1.10 each, today I'd have to pay $1.25 each. Two months ago, I could buy a British pound for $1.65, today I'd have to pay $1.85. If this trend continues, the trip will be too expensive and I don't think I can go."

12:01 P.M.

Catherine Zavier walks by her economic professor's office. A notice is posted on the bulletin board next to the office door. She stops to read it: *Economics won't keep you out of the unemployment line, but at least if you're there, you'll know why.*

3:34 P.M.

An economist is sitting in the Oval Office of the White House, across the desk from the president of the United States. The president asks, "How does unemployment look for the next quarter?" The economist answers, "It's not good. I don't think Real GDP is going to be as high as we initially thought. The problem seems to be foreign income—it's just not growing at the rate we thought it was going to grow."

How would an economist look at these events? Later in the chapter, discussions based on the following questions will help you analyze the scene the way an economist would.

- Why does Toby wish interest rates were lower? How can a change in interest rates affect a person's life?
- Why is Marcy's trip to Europe getting more expensive? How can a change in exchange rates affect a person's life?
- If you study economics and still end up in the unemployment line, will you really know why you're there?
- How can foreign income affect U.S. unemployment?

Aggregate Demand
The quantity demanded of all goods and services (Real GDP) at different price levels, *ceteris paribus.*

Aggregate Demand (*AD*) Curve
A curve that shows the quantity demanded of all goods and services (Real GDP) at different price levels, *ceteris paribus.*

Real Balance Effect
The change in the purchasing power of dollar-denominated assets that results from a change in the price level.

Monetary Wealth
The value of a person's monetary assets. Wealth, as distinguished from monetary wealth, refers to the value of all assets owned, both monetary and nonmonetary. In short, a person's wealth equals his or her monetary wealth (such as $1,000 cash) plus nonmonetary wealth (a car or a house).

Purchasing Power
The quantity of goods and services that can be purchased with a unit of money. Purchasing power and the price level are inversely related: As the price level goes up (down), purchasing power goes down (up).

The Aggregate Demand Curve
The aggregate demand curve is downward-sloping, specifying an inverse relationship between the price level and the quantity demanded of Real GDP.

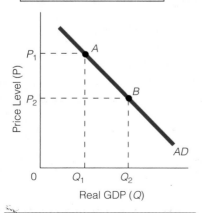

THE TWO SIDES TO AN ECONOMY

Just as there are two sides to a market, a buying side (demand) and a selling side (supply), there are two sides to an economy. There is a demand side and a supply side. The demand in an economy is referred to as *aggregate demand (AD);* the supply in an economy is referred to as *aggregate supply (AS).*

Macroeconomists often use the *AD-AS* framework of analysis to discuss the price level, GDP, Real GDP, unemployment, economic growth, and other major macroeconomic topics. In other words, all these topics can be and are discussed within the same framework. Discussing so many important economic topics within one framework, or with the same tools of analysis, often makes things easier for the student who is just beginning to study macroeconomics. The *AD-AS* framework has three parts: (1) aggregate demand (*AD*), (2) short-run aggregate supply (*SRAS*), and (3) long-run aggregate supply (*LRAS*).

AGGREGATE DEMAND

Recall from the last chapter that people, firms, and governments buy U.S. goods and services. **Aggregate demand** refers to the quantity demanded of these (U.S.) goods and services, or the quantity demanded of (U.S.) Real GDP, at various price levels, *ceteris paribus.* For example, the following whole set of data represents aggregate demand:

Aggregate Demand

Price Index	Quantity Demanded of Goods and Services (Quantity Demanded of Real GDP)
100	$1,200 billion worth of goods and services
110	$1,000 billion worth of goods and services
120	$800 billion worth of goods and services

An **aggregate demand (*AD*) curve** is the graphical representation of aggregate demand. An *AD* curve is shown in Exhibit 1. Notice that it is downward-sloping, indicating an inverse relationship between the price level (*P*) and the quantity demanded of Real GDP (*Q*): as the price level rises, the quantity demanded of Real GDP falls, and as the price level falls, the quantity demanded of Real GDP rises, *ceteris paribus.*

Why Does the Aggregate Demand Curve Slope Downward?

Asking why the *AD* curve slopes downward is the same as asking why there is an inverse relationship between the price level and the quantity demanded of Real GDP. This inverse relationship, and the resulting downward slope of the *AD* curve, is explained by the real balance effect.

The **real balance effect** states that the inverse relationship between the price level and the quantity demanded of Real GDP is established through changes in the value of **monetary wealth,** or money holdings.

To illustrate, consider a person who has $50,000 in cash. Suppose the price level falls. As this happens, the **purchasing power** of the person's $50,000 rises. That is, the $50,000, which once could buy 100 television sets at $500 each, can now buy 125 sets at $400 each. An increase in the purchasing power of the person's $50,000 is identical to saying that his monetary wealth has increased. (After all, isn't the $50,000 more valuable when it can buy more than when it can buy less?) And as he becomes wealthier, he buys more goods.

In summary, a fall in the price level causes purchasing power to rise, which increases a person's monetary wealth. As people become wealthier, the quantity demanded of Real GDP rises.

Suppose the price level rises. As this happens, the purchasing power of the $50,000 falls. That is, the $50,000, which once could buy 100 television sets at $500 each, can now buy 80 sets at $625 each. A decrease in the purchasing power of the person's $50,000 is identical to saying that his monetary wealth has decreased. And as he becomes less wealthy, he buys fewer goods.

In summary, a rise in the price level causes purchasing power to fall, which decreases a person's monetary wealth. As people become less wealthy, the quantity demanded of Real GDP falls.

A Change in the Quantity Demanded of Real GDP Versus a Change in Aggregate Demand

Chapter 3 explains the difference between a change in quantity demanded and a change in demand. Similarly, there is a difference between a change in the quantity demanded of Real GDP and a change in aggregate demand.

A change in the quantity demanded of Real GDP is brought about by a change in the price level. As the price level falls, the quantity demanded of Real GDP rises, *ceteris paribus*. In Exhibit 2a, a change in the quantity demanded of Real GDP is represented as a *movement* from one point (*A*) on AD_1 to another point (*B*) on AD_1.

A change in aggregate demand is represented in Exhibit 2b as a *shift* in the aggregate demand curve from AD_1 to AD_2. Notice that when the aggregate demand curve shifts, the quantity demanded of Real GDP changes even though the price level remains constant. For example, at a price level (index number) of 180, the quantity demanded of Real GDP

THINKING LIKE AN ECONOMIST

Economists deal with curves—demand curves, supply curves, aggregate demand curves, and so on. An economist looks at a curve and asks: (1) What can move us from one point on the curve to another point on the same curve and (2) what can shift the curve? In economics, only one factor can move us from one point on a curve to another point on the same curve: A change in the factor that is identified on the vertical axis. For example, only a change in the price level can move the economy from one point on a given AD curve to another point on the same AD curve. In contrast, a shift in a curve can often be brought about by many factors.

exhibit **2**

A Change in the Quantity Demanded of Real GDP Versus a Change in Aggregate Demand
(a) A change in the quantity demanded of Real GDP is graphically represented as a *movement* from one point, *A*, on AD_1 to another point, *B*, on AD_1. A change in the quantity demanded of Real GDP is the result of a change in the price level. (b) A change in aggregate demand is graphically represented as a *shift* in the aggregate demand curve from AD_1 to AD_2.

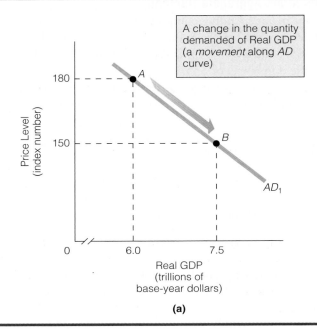

A change in the quantity demanded of Real GDP (a *movement* along *AD* curve)

(a)

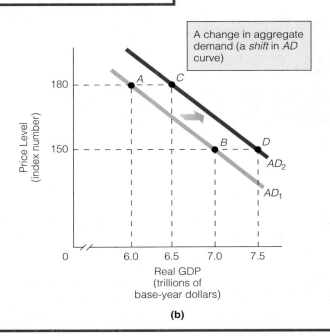

A change in aggregate demand (a *shift* in *AD* curve)

(b)

on AD_1 in Exhibit 2b is $6.0 trillion. But at the same price level (180), the quantity demanded of Real GDP on AD_2 is $6.5 trillion.

Changes in Aggregate Demand—Shifts in the *AD* Curve

What can change aggregate demand? In other words, what can cause aggregate demand to rise and what can cause it to fall?

The simple answer is that aggregate demand changes when the spending on U.S. goods and services changes. If spending increases at a given price level, aggregate demand rises; if spending decreases at a given price level, aggregate demand falls. For example, suppose the price level in the economy is represented by the consumer price index and the index is currently 150 (CPI = 150). At this price level, U.S. residents, firms, and governments, along with foreigners, foreign firms, and foreign governments, want to buy, say, $7.0 trillion worth of U.S. goods and services. Then something changes and, all of a sudden, they want to buy $7.5 trillion worth of U.S. goods and services. Now before you conclude that they want to buy more goods and services because the prices of goods and services have fallen, keep in mind that we haven't lowered the price level. The price level is still represented by the CPI and it is still 150. In other words, all these people, firms, and governments want to buy more U.S. goods even though the prices of the goods and services have not changed.

When individuals, firms, and governments want to buy more U.S. goods and services, even though the prices of these goods have not changed, then we say that aggregate demand has increased. As a result, the *AD* curve shifts to the right. Of course, when individuals, firms, and governments want to buy fewer U.S. goods and services at a given price level, then we say that aggregate demand has decreased. As a result, the *AD* curve shifts to the left.

Let's look again at Exhibit 2b, which shows a change in aggregate demand (a shift in the *AD* curve). At point *B*, the price level is 150 and total expenditures on U.S. goods and services is $7.0 trillion. At point *D*, the price level is still 150 but total expenditures on U.S. goods and services has increased to $7.5 trillion. Why has aggregate demand moved from point *B* to point *D*; that is, what has caused the increase in total expenditures? To find out, we have to look at the components of total expenditures.

How Spending Components Affect Aggregate Demand

The last chapter identifies four major spending components—consumption, investment, government purchases, and net exports. Let's keep the numbers simple and let $C = \$100$, $I = \$100$, $G = \$100$, $EX = \$50$, and $IM = \$15$. If $EX = \$50$ and $IM = \$15$, it follows that net exports (*NX*) equal the difference, or $35.

Using these dollar figures, we calculate that $335 is spent on U.S. goods and services. We get this dollar amount by finding the sum of consumption, investment, government purchases, and net exports.

Total expenditures on U.S. goods and services = *C* + *I* + *G* + *NX*

Obviously, this dollar amount will go up if (1) *C* rises, (2) *I* rises, (3) *G* rises, or (4) *NX* rises. In other words, a rise in consumption, investment, government purchases, or net exports will raise spending on U.S. goods and services:

C↑, *I*↑, *G*↑, *NX*↑ → Total expenditures on U.S. goods and services↑

Now what will cause spending on U.S. goods to go down? Obviously, it will decline if (1) *C* falls, (2) *I* falls, (3) *G* falls, or (4) *NX* falls.

C↓, *I*↓, *G*↓, *NX*↓ → Total expenditures on U.S. goods or services↓

Because we now know what causes total expenditures on U.S. goods and services to change, we can relate the components of spending to (U.S.) aggregate demand. If, *at a given price level,* consumption, investment, government purchases, or net exports rise, aggregate demand will rise and the *AD* curve will shift to the right. If, *at a given price level,* consumption, investment, government purchases, or net exports fall, aggregate demand will fall and the *AD* curve will shift to the left. We can write these relationships as:

If, at a given price level, $C\uparrow$, $I\uparrow$, $G\uparrow$, $NX\uparrow$ then $AD\uparrow$
If, at a given price level, $C\downarrow$, $I\downarrow$, $G\downarrow$, $NX\downarrow$ then $AD\downarrow$

The flow charts in Exhibit 3 show how changes in spending components affect aggregate demand.

Factors That Can Change *C, I, G,* AND *NX* (*EX − IM*), and Therefore Can Change *AD*

What can change aggregate demand (*AD*) in the economy? You know that the answer is a change in consumption, investment, government purchases, or net exports (exports minus imports). So, for example, if someone asks you why *AD* increased, you may say because consumption (*C*) increased.

But suppose the person then asks, "But what caused consumption to increase?" In other words, your answer to one question simply leads to another question. If a change in consumption changes aggregate demand, what changes consumption? The same question can be asked about changes in investment, government purchases, and net exports (which means exports and imports). For example, if aggregate demand increased because investment increased, then what caused investment to increase?

This section looks at some of the (many) factors that can change consumption, investment, and net exports. A later chapter considers the factors that can change government purchases.

Consumption

Four factors that can affect consumption are wealth, expectations about future prices and income, the interest rate, and income taxes.

exhibit 3

Changes in Aggregate Demand
The flow charts show how aggregate demand changes given changes in various spending components.
C = Consumption, *I* = Investment, *G* = Government purchases, *NX* = Net exports, *EX* = Exports, *IM* = Imports. Keep in mind that *NX* = *EX* − *IM*.

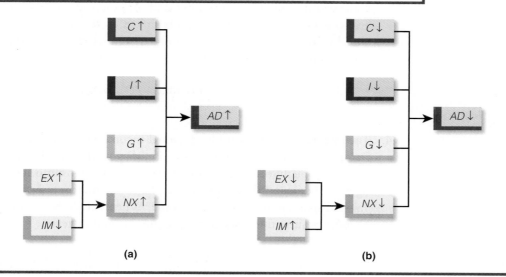

(a)   (b)

Wealth
The value of all assets owned, both monetary and nonmonetary.

1. **Wealth.** Individuals consume not only on the basis of their present income but also on the basis of their **wealth.** Consider two individuals, each receiving an income of $50,000 a year. One has $75,000 in the bank, and the other has no assets at all. Which would you expect to spend more of her income on consumption goods this year? We would expect the person with the $75,000 in the bank to consume more. Greater wealth makes individuals feel financially more secure and thus more willing to spend. Increases in wealth lead to increases in consumption. If consumption increases, then aggregate demand rises and the *AD* curve shifts to the right. What will happen if wealth decreases? Decreases in wealth lead to a fall in consumption, which leads to a fall in aggregate demand. Consequently, the *AD* curve shifts to the left.

$$\text{Wealth}\uparrow \rightarrow C\uparrow \rightarrow AD\uparrow$$
$$\text{Wealth}\downarrow \rightarrow C\downarrow \rightarrow AD\downarrow$$

2. **Expectations about future prices and income.** If individuals expect higher prices in the future, they increase current consumption expenditures in order to buy goods at the lower current prices. This increase in consumption leads to an increase in aggregate demand. If individuals expect lower prices in the future, they decrease current consumption expenditures. This reduction in consumption leads to a decrease in aggregate demand.

   Similarly, expectation of a higher future income increases consumption, which leads to an increase in aggregate demand. Expectation of a lower future income decreases consumption, which leads to a decrease in aggregate demand.

$$\text{Expect higher future prices} \rightarrow C\uparrow \rightarrow AD\uparrow$$
$$\text{Expect lower future prices} \rightarrow C\downarrow \rightarrow AD\downarrow$$
$$\text{Expect higher future income} \rightarrow C\uparrow \rightarrow AD\uparrow$$
$$\text{Expect lower future income} \rightarrow C\downarrow \rightarrow AD\downarrow$$

3. **Interest rate.** Current empirical work shows that spending on consumer durables is sensitive to the interest rate. Many of these items are financed by borrowing, so an increase in the interest rate increases the monthly payment amounts linked to their purchase and thereby reduces their consumption. This reduction in consumption leads to a decline in aggregate demand. Alternatively, a decrease in the interest rate reduces monthly payment amounts linked to the purchase of durable goods and thereby increases their consumption. This increase in consumption leads to an increase in aggregate demand.

$$\text{Interest rate}\uparrow \rightarrow C\downarrow \rightarrow AD\downarrow$$
$$\text{Interest rate}\downarrow \rightarrow C\uparrow \rightarrow AD\uparrow$$

4. **Income Taxes.** Let's consider personal income taxes, the tax a person pays on the income he earns. As income taxes rise, disposable (or after-tax) income decreases. When people have less take-home pay to spend, consumption falls. Consequently, aggregate demand decreases. A decrease in income taxes has the opposite effect; it raises disposable (or after-tax) income. When people have more take-home pay to spend, consumption rises and aggregate demand increases.

$$\text{Income taxes}\uparrow \rightarrow C\downarrow \rightarrow AD\downarrow$$
$$\text{Income taxes}\downarrow \rightarrow C\uparrow \rightarrow AD\uparrow$$

Popular Culture   Technology   Everyday Life

EVERYDAY LIFE   EVERYDAY LIFE   EVERYDAY LIFE

© Photodisc/Getty Images

Looking at Consumption

Consumption spending is a large part of total spending. For example, in 2003, consumption spending was approximately 70 percent of all spending. Stated differently, consumption is a large slice of the aggregate demand pie. Just how much do households spend? The total dollar amount of consumption spending in each of four years is as follows:

2000	2001	2002	2003
$6.74 trillion	$7.04 trillion	$7.38 trillion	$7.75 trillion

Most of the consumption dollars are spent to purchase services (as opposed to durable and nondurable goods). For example, in 2003, households spent $4.6 trillion on services (recreational services, medical services, and so on), $2.2 trillion on nondurable goods (food, clothing, gasoline, and so on), and $950 billion on durable goods (cars, household equipment, and so on). So in 2003, services spending accounted for almost 60 percent of consumption spending; nondurable goods spending, about 28 percent; and durable spending, about 12 percent.

Let's break down consumption into particular expenditures on particular goods. The following table shows the dollar amounts that households spent on various goods in each of four years. The percentage each dollar amount is of total consumption spending is shown in parentheses.

Good	2000	2001	2002	2003
Food (exclusive of alcohol)	$816 billion (12.1%)	$852 billion (12.1%)	$889 billion (12.0%)	$940 billion (12.1%)
Alcoholic Beverages	$108 billion (1.6%)	$111 billion (1.6%)	$116 billion (1.6%)	$123 billion (1.6%)
Tobacco Products	$78 billion (1.2%)	$83 billion (1.2%)	$89 billion (1.2%)	$89 billion (1.1%)
Medical Care	$1.22 trillion (18.1%)	$1.32 trillion (18.8%)	$1.44 trillion (19.5%)	$1.56 trillion (20.1%)
Clothing and Jewelry	$396 billion (5.9%)	$396 billion (5.6%)	$405 billion (5.5%)	$415 billion (5.3%)
Religious and Welfare Activities	$172 billion (2.6%)	$186 billion (2.6%)	$202 billion (2.7%)	$207 billion (2.7%)

Notice that more was spent in each category in later years than in earlier years. For example, $396 billion was spent on clothing and jewelry in 2000 and $415 billion was spent on clothing and jewelry in 2003. But clothing and jewelry spending fell from 5.9 percent in 2000 to 5.3 percent in 2003. In other words, more was being spent on clothing and jewelry at the same time that spending on clothing and jewelry was becoming a smaller slice (percentage) of the consumption spending pie.

Also notice that while the percentage of total spending for some categories increased over the period 2000–2003, spending in other categories fell, and spending in still other categories remained nearly constant. For example, while spending on clothing and jewelry fell as a percentage of total consumption spending during the period, spending on medical care increased as a percentage of total consumption spending.

A change in relative spending can be brought about by a change in price, holding total spending constant. To illustrate, suppose the price of good X rises and people end up spending a greater total dollar amount on good X, say, $10 million instead of $9 million. Then they will have $1 million less to spend on good Y.

Alternatively, a change in relative spending may accompany a change in total spending. Suppose that when total spending is $100, $30 is spent on good X and $70 is spent on good Y. This means 30 percent of total spending goes for good X and 70 percent goes for good Y. Now total spending rises to $110 because of an increase in income. Suppose spending on good X rises to $37 and spending on good Y rises to $73. Then, spending on good X has risen from 30 percent to 33.6 percent of total spending, and spending on good Y has fallen from 70 percent to 66.4 percent.

Investment

Three factors that can change investment are the interest rate, expectations about future sales, and business taxes.

1. **Interest rate.** Changes in interest rates affect business decisions. As the interest rate rises, the cost of a given investment project rises and businesses invest less. As investment decreases, aggregate demand decreases. On the other hand, as the interest rate falls, the cost of a given investment project falls and businesses invest more. Consequently, aggregate demand increases.

    $$\text{Interest rate}\uparrow \rightarrow I\downarrow \rightarrow AD\downarrow$$
    $$\text{Interest rate}\downarrow \rightarrow I\uparrow \rightarrow AD\uparrow$$

2. **Expectations about future sales.** Businesses invest because they expect to sell the goods they produce. If businesses become optimistic about future sales, investment spending grows and aggregate demand increases. If businesses become pessimistic about future sales, investment spending contracts and aggregate demand decreases.

    $$\text{Businesses become optimistic about future sales} \rightarrow I\uparrow \rightarrow AD\uparrow$$
    $$\text{Businesses become pessimistic about future sales} \rightarrow I\downarrow \rightarrow AD\downarrow$$

3. **Business taxes.** Businesses naturally consider expected after-tax profits when making their investment decisions. An increase in business taxes lowers expected profitability. With less profit expected, businesses invest less. As investment spending declines, aggregate demand declines. A decrease in business taxes, on the other hand, raises expected profitability and investment spending. This increases aggregate demand.

    $$\text{Business Taxes}\uparrow \rightarrow I\downarrow \rightarrow AD\downarrow$$
    $$\text{Business Taxes}\downarrow \rightarrow I\uparrow \rightarrow AD\uparrow$$

Net Exports

Two factors that can change net exports are foreign real national income and the exchange rate.

1. **Foreign real national income.** Just as Americans earn a national income, so do people in other countries. There is a foreign national income. By adjusting this foreign national income for price changes, we obtain foreign real national income. As foreign real national income rises, foreigners buy more U.S. goods and services. Thus, U.S. exports (*EX*) rise. As exports rise, net exports rise, *ceteris paribus*. As net exports rise, aggregate demand increases.

    This process works in reverse too. As foreign real national income falls, foreigners buy fewer U.S. goods and exports fall. This lowers net exports, which reduces aggregate demand.

    $$\text{Foreign real national income}\uparrow \rightarrow \text{U.S. exports}\uparrow \rightarrow \text{U.S. net exports}\uparrow \rightarrow AD\uparrow$$
    $$\text{Foreign real national income}\downarrow \rightarrow \text{U.S. exports}\downarrow \rightarrow \text{U.S. net exports}\downarrow \rightarrow AD\downarrow$$

Exchange Rate
The price of one currency in terms of another currency.

Appreciation
An increase in the value of one currency relative to other currencies.

Depreciation
A decrease in the value of one currency relative to other currencies.

2. **Exchange rate.** The **exchange rate** is the price of one currency in terms of another currency; for example, $1.25 = 1 euro. A currency has **appreciated** in value if more of a foreign currency is needed to buy it. A currency has **depreciated** in value if more of it is needed to buy a foreign currency. For example, a change in the exchange rate from $1.25 = 1 euro to $1.50 = 1 euro means that that more dollars

are needed to buy one euro and the euro has appreciated. And because more dollars are needed to buy one euro, the dollar has depreciated.

A depreciation in a nation's currency makes foreign goods more expensive. Consider an Irish coat that is priced at 200 euros when the exchange rate is $1.25 = 1 euro. To buy the Irish coat for 200 euros, an American has to pay $250 ($1.25 for each of 200 euros for a total of $250). Now suppose the dollar depreciates to $1.50 = 1 euro. The American has to pay $300 for the coat.

This process is symmetrical, so an appreciation in a nation's currency makes foreign goods cheaper. For example, if the exchange rate goes from $1.25 = 1 euro to $1 = 1 euro, the Irish coat will cost the American $200.

The depreciation and appreciation of the U.S. dollar affect net exports. As the dollar depreciates, foreign goods become more expensive, Americans cut back on imported goods, and foreigners (whose currency has appreciated) increase their purchases of U.S. exported goods. If exports rise and imports fall, net exports increase and aggregate demand increases.

As the dollar appreciates, foreign goods become cheaper, Americans increase their purchases of imported goods, and foreigners (whose currency has depreciated) cut back on their purchases of U.S. exported goods. If exports fall and imports rise, net exports decrease, thus lowering aggregate demand.

Dollar depreciates → U.S. exports↑ and U.S. imports↓ → U.S. net exports↑ → AD↑
Dollar appreciates → U.S. exports↓ and U.S. imports↑ → U.S. net exports↓ → AD↓

See Exhibit 4 for a summary of the factors that change aggregate demand.

The Interest Rate and the Loanable Funds Market

Changes in consumption, investment, government purchases, and net exports can change total expenditures. Also, a change in the interest rate can change both consumption and investment and therefore change total expenditures. But, what can cause a change in interest rates?

Interest rates are a market phenomenon—that is, interest rates are determined in the *loanable funds market.* There is a demand for loanable funds and a supply of loanable funds. The demanders of loanable funds are borrowers; the suppliers of loanable funds are lenders. Supply and demand in the loanable funds market is a form of the supply and demand described in Chapter 3.

As shown in Exhibit 5, the demand curve for loanable funds is downward-sloping; borrowers will borrow more loanable funds the lower the interest rate. For example, Jim might borrow $10,000 if the interest rate is 5 percent but be willing to borrow $15,000 if the interest rate is 4 percent. To a borrower, the interest rate is the cost of borrowing and the lower the cost, the more will be borrowed, *ceteris paribus.*

The supply curve of loanable funds, as shown in Exhibit 5, is upward-sloping; lenders will lend more loanable funds the higher the interest rate. For example, Stephanie might lend $20,000 if the interest rate is 6 percent but be willing to lend $25,000 if the interest rate is 7 percent. To a lender, the interest rate is the reward for lending and the higher the reward, the more will be lent, *ceteris paribus.*

So, the interest rate will change if there is a change in either the demand for loanable funds or the supply of loanable funds. But what causes the demand for loanable funds to change and what causes the supply of loanable funds to change? In other words, what factors shift the demand curve for loanable funds and what factors shift the supply curve of loanable funds? We discuss these factors next.

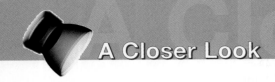

exhibit **4**

Factors That Change Aggregate Demand

Aggregate demand (AD) changes whenever consumption (C), investment (I), government purchases (G), or net exports (EX − IM) change. The factors that can affect C, I, and EX − IM, thereby indirectly affecting aggregate demand, are listed.

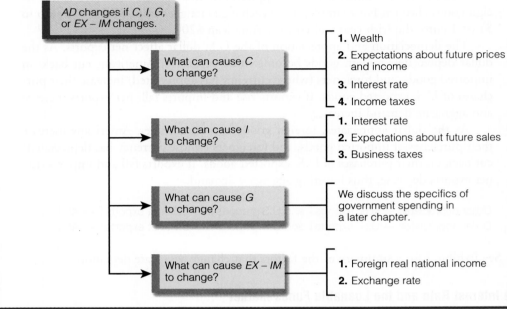

AD changes if C, I, G, or EX − IM changes.

What can cause C to change?
1. Wealth
2. Expectations about future prices and income
3. Interest rate
4. Income taxes

What can cause I to change?
1. Interest rate
2. Expectations about future sales
3. Business taxes

What can cause G to change?
We discuss the specifics of government spending in a later chapter.

What can cause EX − IM to change?
1. Foreign real national income
2. Exchange rate

exhibit **5**

The Loanable Funds Market

The demand curve for loanable funds is downward-sloping, and the supply curve of loanable funds is upward-sloping. As the interest rate rises, the quantity demanded of loanable funds falls and the quantity supplied of loanable funds rises. As the interest rate falls, the quantity demanded of loanable funds rises and the quantity supplied of loanable funds falls. See the text for the factors that can shift the two curves.

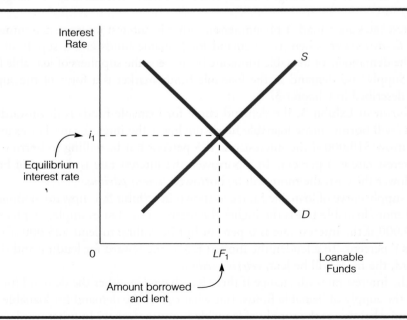

The Demand for Loanable Funds

Generally, anything that prompts one or more of the four sectors of the economy to borrow more funds shifts the demand curve for loanable funds rightward; anything that causes one or more of the four sectors to borrow fewer funds shifts the demand curve leftward.

For example, suppose that businesses expect consumers to buy more goods next year than they are buying this year. This would prompt businesses to want to borrow more in order to invest in more capital goods (more factories, more machinery, and so on). What would happen to the interest rate as a result? An increase in the demand for loanable funds would shift the demand curve to the right, and with no change in the supply of loanable funds, the interest rate would rise.

As another example, suppose the government budget is initially balanced, but then government purchases rise with no change in tax revenues. The budget would go from being balanced to being in a state of deficit. How would government finance the deficit? Obviously, it would have to borrow funds to pay for the amount of purchases not paid for by tax revenues. (In other words, it would have to borrow funds to pay for the deficit.) What would this do to the demand for loanable funds? It would increase the demand for loanable funds and shift the demand curve rightward. In turn, the interest rate would rise, *ceteris paribus.*

Be careful. There is a tendency to say that a decrease in the interest rate (say, from 5 percent to 4 percent) will increase the demand for loanable funds. This is incorrect. A change in the interest rate does not change the demand for loanable funds and therefore does not shift the demand curve for loanable funds. Instead, it changes the *quantity demanded* of loanable funds. In other words, a change in the interest rate causes a *movement* from one point on a given demand curve for loanable funds to another point on the *same* curve.

The Supply of Loanable Funds

Generally, anything that prompts one or more of the four sectors of the economy to lend more funds shifts the supply curve of loanable funds to the right; anything that causes one or more of the four sectors to lend fewer funds shifts the supply curve of loanable funds to the left.

For example, suppose a change in the law makes interest income exempt from taxation. This would increase the reward for saving, and we would expect people would want to save more at every given interest rate. In short, the supply curve of loanable funds would shift rightward. And a rightward shift in the supply curve of loanable funds would lower the interest rate, *ceteris paribus.*

Or suppose that government were to increase Social Security benefits. This might prompt workers to save less on their own. After all, if Social Security benefits were increased, there would be less need to save (privately) for retirement. As a result, the supply curve of loanable funds would shift leftward, and the interest rate would rise, *ceteris paribus.*

Again, be careful. There is a tendency to say that an increase in the interest rate (say, from 5 percent to 6 percent) will increase the supply of loanable funds. This is incorrect. A change in the interest rate does not change the supply of loanable funds and therefore does not shift the supply curve of loanable funds. Instead, it changes the *quantity supplied* of loanable funds. In other words, a change in the interest rate causes a *movement* from one point on a given supply curve of loanable funds to another point on the *same* curve.

Questions from Setting the Scene: Why does Toby wish interest rates were lower? How can a change in interest rates affect a person's life?

Why is Marcy's trip to Europe getting more expensive? How can a change in exchange rates affect a person's life?

The loanable funds market is a large market. Many millions of borrowers and lenders make up this market in which an equilibrium interest rate is determined. How might what happens in the loanable funds market affect you? How does it affect Toby who is interested in buying a car? Obviously, Toby plans to take out a loan to buy a car. If interest rates were lower, he would be more likely to buy the car. Whether or not Toby drives home in a new car that particular day is influenced by the millions of borrowers and lenders in the loanable funds market.

Exchange rates are determined much the same way that interest rates are determined—by the forces of supply and demand. The price Marcy will pay for the goods and services she buys in Europe is affected by the dollar price she has to pay for the euro and the British pound. For example, suppose Marcy has reservations at a hotel in London that charges £70 a night. At an exchange rate £1 = $1.65, Marcy would pay $115.50 a night. But at an exchange rate of £1 = $1.85, she would have to pay $129.50 a night.

Can a change in supply and demand (whether the change is in the demand for and supply of loanable funds or in the demand for and supply of a particular currency) affect us? It sure can.

Can a Change in the Money Supply Change Aggregate Demand?

Changes in such factors as interest rates, business taxes, exchange rates, and so on can change aggregate demand (indirectly) by directly changing consumption, investment, and net exports. What about the money supply? Can a change in the money supply lead to a change in aggregate demand?

Suppose the money supply rises from, say, $1,350 billion to $1,400 billion. Will this result in an increase in aggregate demand? Most economists would say that it does, but they differ as to how the change in the money supply affects aggregate demand. One way to explain the effect (within the context of our discussion) is as follows: (1) A change in the money supply affects interest rates. (2) A change in interest rates changes consumption and investment. (3) A change in consumption and investment affects aggregate demand. Therefore, a change in the money supply is a catalyst in a process that ends with a change in aggregate demand. (We will have much more to say about the money supply and interest rates in later chapters.)

SELF-TEST *(Answers to Self-Test questions are in the Self-Test Appendix.)*

1. Explain the real balance effect.
2. Explain what happens to the *AD* curve if the dollar appreciates relative to other currencies.
3. Explain what happens to the *AD* curve if personal income taxes decline.
4. What happens to the demand for loanable funds and the interest rate if the budget deficit becomes smaller (but not zero)? Explain your answer.

SHORT-RUN AGGREGATE SUPPLY

Aggregate Supply
The quantity supplied of all goods and services (Real GDP) at different price levels, *ceteris paribus.*

Aggregate demand is one side of the economy; aggregate supply is the other side. **Aggregate supply** refers to the quantity supplied of all goods and services (Real GDP) at various price levels, *ceteris paribus.* Aggregate supply includes both short-run aggregate supply (*SRAS*) and long-run aggregate supply (*LRAS*). Short-run aggregate supply is discussed in this section.

Short-Run Aggregate Supply Curve: What It Is and Why It Is Upward-Sloping

A **short-run aggregate supply *(SRAS)* curve** is illustrated in Exhibit 6. It shows the quantity supplied of all goods and services (Real GDP or output) at different price levels, *ceteris paribus*. Notice that the *SRAS* curve is upward-sloping: as the price level rises, firms increase the quantity supplied of goods and services; as the price level drops, firms decrease the quantity supplied of goods and services. Why is the *SRAS* curve upward-sloping? Two explanations are the sticky-wage explanation and the worker-misperceptions explanation. We outline the details of the sticky-wage explanation in terms of a fall in the price level and the details of the worker-misperceptions explanation in terms of a rise in the price level.

Sticky Wages

Some economists believe that wages are sticky or inflexible. This may be because wages are "locked in" for a few years due to labor contracts entered into by workers and management. For example, management and labor may agree to lock in wages for the next one to three years. Both labor and management may see this as in their best interest. Management has some idea what its labor costs will be during the time of the contract, and workers may have a sense of security knowing that their wages can't be lowered. Alternatively, wages may be sticky because of certain social conventions or perceived notions of fairness. Whatever the specific reason for sticky wages, let's see how it provides an explanation of an upward-sloping *SRAS* curve.

Firms pay *nominal wages* (for example, $30 an hour), but they often decide how many workers to hire based on real wages. *Real wages* are nominal wages divided by the price level.

$$\text{Real wage} = \frac{\text{Nominal wage}}{\text{Price level}}$$

For example, suppose the nominal wage is $30 an hour and the price level as measured by a price index is 1.50.[1] The real wage is therefore $20.

The quantity supplied of labor is *directly related* to the real wage: as the real wage rises, the quantity supplied of labor rises; as the real wage falls, the quantity supplied of labor falls. In short, more individuals are willing to work, and current workers are willing to work more, at higher than at lower real wages.

Real wage↑ → *Quantity supplied* of labor↑
Real wage↓ → *Quantity supplied* of labor↓

The quantity demanded of labor is *inversely related* to the real wage: as the real wage rises, the quantity demanded of labor falls; as the real wage falls, the quantity demanded of labor rises. Firms will employ more workers the cheaper it is to hire them.

Real wage↑ → *Quantity demanded* of labor↓
Real wage↓ → *Quantity demanded* of labor↑

With this as background, suppose that a firm has agreed to pay its workers $30 an hour for the next three years and that it has hired 1,000 workers. When it agreed to this

1. Alternatively, you can view the price index as 1.50 times 100, or 150. In this case, the formula for the real wage would change to Real wage = (Nominal wage/Price level) × 100.

exhibit 6

The Short-Run Aggregate Supply Curve

The short-run aggregate supply curve is upward-sloping, specifying a direct relationship between the price level and the quantity supplied of Real GDP.

> **Short-Run Aggregate Supply Curve**
> The price level and quantity supplied of Real GDP are directly related.

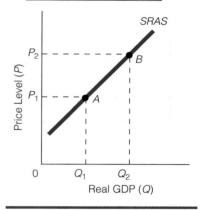

Short-Run Aggregate Supply (SRAS) Curve

A curve that shows the quantity supplied of all goods and services (Real GDP) at different price levels, *ceteris paribus*.

nominal wage, it thought the price index would remain at 1.50 and that the real wage would stay at $20.

Now suppose the price index *falls* to 1.25. When the price level falls to an index of 1.25, the real wage rises to $24 ($30/1.25). This is a higher real wage than the firm expected when it agreed to lock in nominal wages at $30 an hour. If the firm had known that the real wage would turn out to be $24 (and not remain at $20), it would never have hired 1,000 workers. It would have hired, say, 800 workers instead.

So what does the firm do? As we stated above, there is an inverse relationship between the real wage and the quantity demanded of labor (the number of workers that firms want to hire). Now that the real wage has risen (from $20 to $24), the firm cuts back on its labor (say, from 1,000 workers to 800 workers). With fewer workers working, less output is produced.

In conclusion, if wages are sticky, a decrease in the price level (which pushes real wages up) will result in a decrease in output. This is what an upward-sloping *SRAS* curve represents: as the price level falls, the quantity supplied of goods and services declines.

Worker Misperceptions

Workers may misperceive real wage changes. To illustrate, suppose the nominal wage is $30 an hour and the price level as measured by a price index is 1.50. It follows that the real wage is $20. Now suppose the nominal wage rises to $40 and the price level rises to 2.00. The real wage is still $20, but workers may not know this. They will know their nominal wage has risen (they see a bigger paycheck), but they may be unaware (at least for some time) that the price level has risen from 1.50 to 2.00. For some time then, they may calculate their new real wage at $26.67 ($40/1.50) instead of $20 ($40/2.00). In response to (the misperceived) rising real wage, workers may increase the quantity of labor they are willing to supply. With more workers (resources), firms will end up producing more.

In conclusion, if workers misperceive real wage changes, then a rise in the price level will bring about a rise in output, which is illustrative of an upward-sloping *SRAS* curve.

What Puts the "Short Run" in *SRAS?*

According to most macroeconomists, the *SRAS* curve slopes upward because of sticky wages or worker misperceptions. No matter which explanation of the upward-sloping *SRAS* curve we accept, though, things are likely to change over time. Wages will not be sticky forever (labor contracts will expire) and workers will figure out that they misperceived real wage changes. It is only for a period of time—identified as the short run—that these issues are likely to be relevant.

Changes in Short-Run Aggregate Supply—Shifts in the *SRAS* Curve

A change in the quantity supplied of Real GDP is brought about by a change in the price level. A change in quantity supplied is shown as a *movement* along the *SRAS* curve. But what can change short-run aggregate supply? What can *shift* the *SRAS* curve? The factors that can shift the *SRAS* curve include wage rates, prices of nonlabor inputs, productivity, and supply shocks.

Wage Rates

Changes in wage rates have a major impact on the position of the *SRAS* curve because wage costs are usually a firm's major cost item. The impact of a rise or fall in equilibrium wage rates can be understood in terms of the following equation:

$$\text{Profit per unit} = \text{Price per unit} - \text{Cost per unit}$$

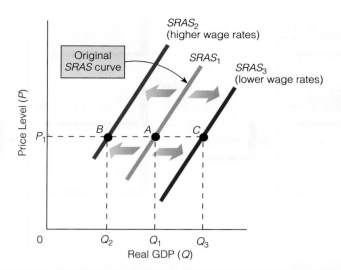

exhibit 7

Wage Rates and a Shift in the Short-Run Aggregate Supply Curve
A rise in wage rates shifts the short-run aggregate supply curve leftward. A fall in wage rates shifts the short-run aggregate supply curve rightward.

Higher wage rates mean higher costs and, at constant prices, translate into lower profits and a reduction in the number of goods managers of firms will want to produce. Lower wage rates mean lower costs and, at constant prices, translate into higher profits and an increase in the number of goods managers will decide to produce.

The impact of higher and lower equilibrium wages is shown in Exhibit 7. At the given price level, P_1 on $SRAS_1$, the quantity supplied of Real GDP is Q_1. When higher wage rates are introduced, a firm's profits at a given price level decrease. Consequently, the firm reduces production. In the diagram, this corresponds to moving from Q_1 to Q_2, which at the given price level is point B. Point B represents a point on a new aggregate supply curve ($SRAS_2$). Thus, a rise in equilibrium wage rates leads to a leftward shift in the aggregate supply curve. The steps are simply reversed for a fall in equilibrium wage rates.

Prices of Nonlabor Inputs

There are other inputs to the production process besides labor. Changes in their prices affect the *SRAS* curve in the same way as changes in wage rates do. An increase in the price of a nonlabor input (say, oil) shifts the *SRAS* curve leftward; a decrease in the price of a nonlabor input shifts the *SRAS* curve rightward.

Productivity

Productivity describes the output produced per unit of input employed over some period of time. While various inputs can become more productive, let's consider the input labor. An increase in labor productivity means businesses will produce more output with the same amount of labor. This causes the *SRAS* curve to shift rightward. A decrease in labor productivity means businesses will produce less output with the same amount of labor. This causes the *SRAS* curve to shift leftward. A host of factors lead to increased labor productivity, including a more educated labor force, a larger stock of capital goods, and technological advancements.

Supply Shocks

Major natural or institutional changes on the supply side of the economy that affect aggregate supply are referred to as *supply shocks*. Bad weather that wipes out a large part of the midwestern wheat crop would be considered a supply shock. So would a major cutback in the supply of oil coming to the United States from the Middle East.

exhibit **8**

Changes in Short-Run Aggregate Supply
The flow charts show how short-run aggregate supply changes given changes in several factors.

Wage Rates ↓				Wage Rates ↑		
Prices of Nonlabor Inputs ↓	→	SRAS ↑		Prices of Nonlabor Inputs ↑	→	SRAS ↓
Productivity ↑				Productivity ↓		
Beneficial Supply Shock				Adverse Supply Shock		

(a)   (b)

Supply shocks are of two varieties. *Adverse supply shocks* (such as the examples just given) shift the *SRAS* curve leftward, and *beneficial supply shocks* shift it rightward. Examples of the latter include a major oil discovery and unusually good weather leading to increased production of a food staple. These supply shocks are reflected in resource or input prices.

Exhibit 8 summarizes the factors that affect short-run aggregate supply.

SELF-TEST

1. If wage rates decline, explain what happens to the short-run aggregate supply (*SRAS*) curve.
2. Give an example of an increase in labor productivity.

PUTTING *AD* AND *SRAS* TOGETHER: SHORT-RUN EQUILIBRIUM

In this section, we put aggregate demand and short-run aggregate supply together to achieve short-run equilibrium in the economy. Aggregate demand and short-run aggregate supply determine the price level, Real GDP, and the unemployment rate in the short run.

How Short-Run Equilibrium in the Economy Is Achieved
Exhibit 9 shows an aggregate demand (*AD*) curve and a short-run aggregate supply (*SRAS*) curve. We consider the quantity demanded of Real GDP and the quantity supplied of Real GDP at three different price levels: P_1, P_2, and P_E.

At P_1, the quantity supplied of Real GDP (Q_2) is greater than the quantity demanded (Q_1). There is a surplus of goods. As a result, the price level drops, firms decrease output, and consumers increase consumption. Why do consumers increase consumption as the price level drops? (Hint: Think of the real balance effect.)

At P_2, the quantity supplied of Real GDP (Q_1) is less than the quantity demanded (Q_2). There is a shortage of goods. As a result, the price level rises, firms increase output, and consumers decrease consumption.

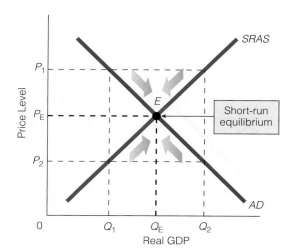

exhibit 9

Short-Run Equilibrium
At P_1, the quantity supplied of Real GDP is greater than the quantity demanded. As a result, the price level falls and firms decrease output. At P_2, the quantity demanded of Real GDP is greater than the quantity supplied. As a result, the price level rises and firms increase output. Short-run equilibrium occurs at point E, where the quantity demanded of Real GDP equals the (short-run) quantity supplied. This is at the intersection of the aggregate demand (*AD*) curve and the short-run aggregate supply (*SRAS*) curve. (Note: Although real-world *AD* and *SRAS* curves can, and likely do, have some curvature to them, we have drawn both as straight lines. This does not affect the analysis. Whenever the analysis is not disturbed, we follow suit throughout this text.)

In instances of both surplus and shortage, economic forces are moving the economy toward E, where the quantity demanded of Real GDP equals the (short-run) quantity supplied of Real GDP. This is the point of **short-run equilibrium.** P_E is the short-run equilibrium price level; Q_E is the short-run equilibrium Real GDP.

A change in aggregate demand or short-run aggregate supply or both will obviously affect the price level and/or Real GDP. For example, an increase in aggregate demand raises the equilibrium price level and, in the short run, Real GDP (Exhibit 10a). An increase in short-run aggregate supply lowers the equilibrium price level and raises Real GDP (Exhibit 10b). A decrease in short-run aggregate supply raises the equilibrium price level and lowers Real GDP (Exhibit 10c).

Short-Run Equilibrium
The condition that exists in the economy when the quantity demanded of Real GDP equals the (short-run) quantity supplied of Real GDP. This condition is met where the aggregate demand curve intersects the short-run aggregate supply curve.

The Unemployment Rate in the Short Run

When a change occurs in aggregate demand, short-run aggregate supply, or both, the price level and Real GDP are not the only economic variables affected. Because Real GDP changes, the unemployment rate can also change.

Changes in Real GDP and Changes in the Unemployment Rate

There is always some unemployment in the economy. And no matter what the unemployment rate (U) is—5 percent, 6 percent, or whatever—some Real GDP (Q) is being produced at that particular unemployment rate.

All other things held constant, we expect a higher Real GDP level to be associated with a lower unemployment rate and a lower Real GDP level to be associated with a higher unemployment rate. In other words, Real GDP and the unemployment rate are inversely related: as one goes up, the other goes down.

But why? The reason is that more workers are needed to produce more output and fewer workers are needed to produce less output, *ceteris paribus*. Because more workers are needed to produce more output (more Real GDP), fewer people remain unemployed

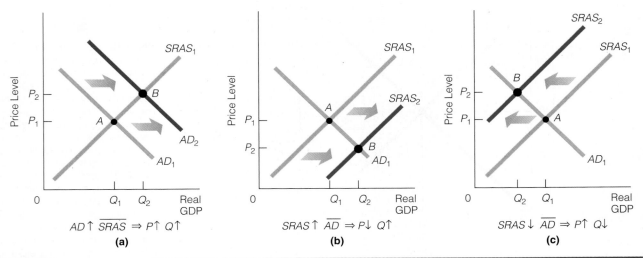

$$AD \uparrow \overline{SRAS} \Rightarrow P \uparrow Q \uparrow$$

(a)

$$SRAS \uparrow \overline{AD} \Rightarrow P \downarrow Q \uparrow$$

(b)

$$SRAS \downarrow \overline{AD} \Rightarrow P \uparrow Q \downarrow$$

(c)

**Changes in Short-Run Equilibrium
in the Economy**
(a) An increase in aggregate demand
increases the price level and Real GDP.
(b) An increase in short-run aggregate
supply decreases the price level and
increases Real GDP. (c) A decrease in
short-run aggregate supply increases the
price level and decreases Real GDP.

and the unemployment rate drops, *ceteris paribus*. Because fewer workers are needed to produce less output, more people are unemployed and the unemployment rate rises, *ceteris paribus*.

Ceteris Paribus Makes All the Difference in the Relationship Between Real GDP and the Unemployment Rate

Do the data substantiate the inverse relationship between Real GDP and the unemployment rate? In 1997, Real GDP was $8.2 trillion and the unemployment rate was 4.9 percent. In 1998, Real GDP had risen to $8.5 trillion and the unemployment rate had fallen to 4.5 percent. Obviously, these data support the inverse relationship between Real GDP and the unemployment rate.

But here are some data that do not: In 1991, Real GDP was $6.7 trillion and the unemployment rate was 6.8 percent. In 1992, Real GDP had risen to $6.9 trillion and the unemployment rate had risen to 7.5 percent.

Conclusion: The 1997–1998 data support the inverse relationship between Real GDP and the unemployment rate, but the 1991–1992 data do not. What explains these inconsistent findings?

Recall that the inverse relationship between Real GDP and the unemployment rate is conditioned upon *ceteris paribus,* or nothing else changing. If some other things do change, it may appear as if the inverse relationship between Real GDP and the unemployment rate does not hold.

To illustrate, let's look at the unemployment rate, which is computed by dividing the number of unemployed persons by the civilian labor force. For example, if 100,000 people are unemployed and the civilian labor force is 1 million, the unemployment rate is 10 percent. Let's say that at this 10 percent unemployment rate, Real GDP is $9.0 trillion.

Now suppose Real GDP rises to $9.5 trillion. If nothing else changes, we would expect the unemployment rate to drop. But suppose something else does change. Suppose that as the number of unemployed falls to 98,000, the civilian labor force does not stay constant at 1 million, but falls to 900,000 persons. When we divide the number of unemployed persons (98,000) by the civilian labor force (900,000), we get an unemployment rate of 10.9 percent. In other words, we witness a rising Real GDP (from

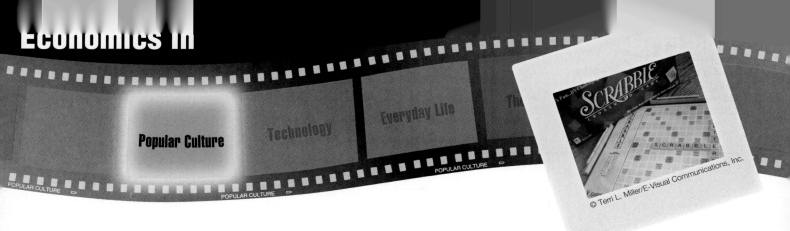

Aggregate Demand, the Great Depression, and Scrabble

Economist Christina Romer writes, "At the broadest conceptual level, the Great Depression in the United States can be analyzed quite well with the simple aggregate supply-aggregate demand model familiar to introductory economics students. Between 1929 and 1933, a series of shocks caused aggregate demand to decline repeatedly in the United States. [In other words, the *AD* curve repeatedly shifted to the left.] These declines in aggregate demand moved the economy down along an upward-sloping aggregate supply curve. The net result was both progressively worsening unemployment and deflation."[2]

Certainly a fall in aggregate demand can cause a rise in unemployment and a fall in prices. But can a repeated fall in aggregate demand lead to anything else? In an indirect way, it can. In fact, if it weren't for falling aggregate demand and the ensuing Great Depression, we might not have one of the more popular games people play—Scrabble.

Scrabble was invented by Alfred M. Butts of Poughkeepsie, New York. Before Butts invented Scrabble he was an architect.

Because of the Great Depression, Butts lost his job and couldn't find another. Wondering what to do with his time, he started analyzing different board games. He found that every game fell into one of three categories: number games, such as dice and bingo; move games, such as chess and checkers; and word games, such as anagrams.

Alfred Butts set out to create a board game that would combine chance and skill. He combined features of anagrams and crossword puzzles and called his game "Criss Cross Word." The first boards of his Criss Cross Word game were hand drawn with his architectural drafting equipment. In time, Butts's game was purchased and renamed "Scrabble."

---

2. Christina Romer, "The Nation in Depression," *Journal of Economic Perspectives* (Spring 1993):25

$9.0 trillion to $9.5 trillion) associated with a rising unemployment rate (from 10 percent to 10.9 percent).

To repeat: the *ceteris paribus* condition makes all the difference. A higher Real GDP is associated with a lower unemployment rate, and a lower Real GDP is associated with a higher unemployment rate, *ceteris paribus.*

ANALYZING THE SCENE

Questions from Setting the Scene: If you study economics and still end up in the unemployment line, will you really know why you're there? How can foreign income affect U.S. unemployment?

You should have a better idea of why you might be in the unemployment line after reading this chapter than you did before you read it. According to the *AD-SRAS* framework in this chapter, changes in either *AD* or *SRAS* will change Real GDP in the short run. And changes in Real GDP will affect the unemployment rate. You might be standing in the unemployment line because the economy's *AD* curve shifted to the left.

Similarly, foreign income is linked to the unemployment rate in the United States through changes in Real GDP. If foreign income falls, foreigners may buy fewer exports from the United States. And if U.S. export spending declines, so does aggregate demand for U.S. produced goods and services. A decline in aggregate demand, in turn, leads to lower Real GDP in the short run. And a lower Real GDP is likely to come with a higher unemployment rate.

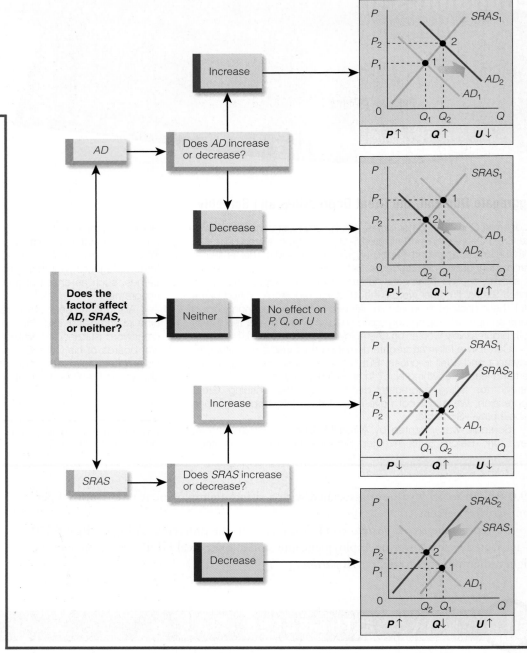

exhibit 11

How a Factor Affects the Price Level, Real GDP, and the Unemployment Rate in the Short Run
In the exhibit, P = price level, Q = Real GDP, and U = unemployment rate.

Thinking in Terms of Short-Run Equilibrium Changes in the Economy

Earlier you learned that certain factors can lead to a change in aggregate demand. You also learned that certain factors can lead to a change in short-run aggregate supply. Then you learned that if either aggregate demand or short-run aggregate supply changes, the price level, Real GDP, and the unemployment rate will all change in the short run. Exhibit 11 puts all this information together in a flow chart.

Let's see how it works. With one eye on the exhibit, consider an adverse supply shock that hits the economy. Question: Does an adverse supply shock affect AD, $SRAS$, or neither? Answer: It affects $SRAS$.

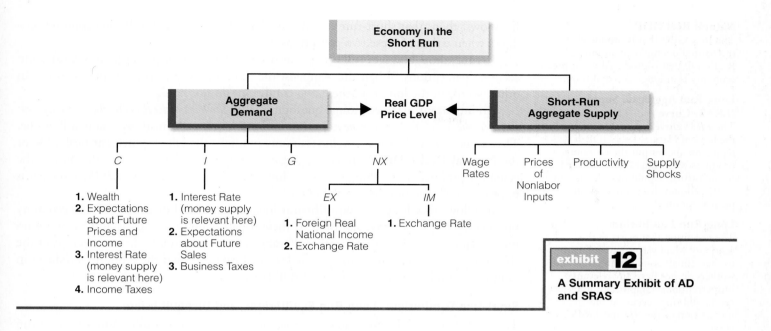

exhibit **12**

A Summary Exhibit of AD and SRAS

Next question: Does it cause *SRAS* to increase or decrease? Answer: Decrease. We then see that as a result of the adverse supply shock, the price level (*P*) rises and Real GDP (*Q*) falls in the short run. And earlier you learned that when Real GDP falls, the unemployment rate (*U*) rises, *ceteris paribus*.

Exhibit 12 summarizes much of the discussion in this chapter up to this point.

SELF-TEST

1. Identify what will happen to the price level and Real GDP (in the short run) as a result of each of the following:
   a. *SRAS* rises
   b. *SRAS* falls
   c. *AD* rises
   d. *AD* falls
   e. *AD* rises by more than *SRAS* rises
   f. *AD* falls by less than *SRAS* falls
2. Explain Exhibit 11 in your own words.

THINKING LIKE AN ECONOMIST

In the flow chart in Exhibit 11, it is easy to see how one thing is related to another. For example, you can see how the change in Real GDP shown in the large box at the lower right of the exhibit is related to a change in a factor (represented in the middle far-left box). Lines in a flow chart connect factors that are linked in real life—thus visually establishing connections or causes and effects.

To a large degree, economists naturally think in terms of flow charts. Economics is about establishing a connection or link between an effect (such as a fall in Real GDP) and a correct cause (such as an adverse supply shock that shifts the SRAS curve to the left). A flow chart is simply the graphical representation of the economic way of thinking.

LONG-RUN AGGREGATE SUPPLY

In this section, we discuss long-run aggregate supply and draw a long-run aggregate supply (*LRAS*) curve. We also discuss long-run equilibrium and explain how it differs from short-run equilibrium.

Going From the Short Run to the Long Run

Graphically, short-run equilibrium is at the intersection of the *AD* curve and the (upward-sloping) *SRAS* curve. As an earlier section explains, economists give different reasons for an upward-sloping *SRAS* curve. Recall that those reasons have to do with:

1. Sticky wages
2. Worker misperceptions

Natural Real GDP
The Real GDP that is produced at the natural unemployment rate. The Real GDP that is produced when the economy is in long-run equilibrium.

Long-Run Aggregate Supply (LRAS) Curve
The *LRAS* curve is a vertical line at the level of Natural Real GDP. It represents the output the economy produces when wages have adjusted to their (final) equilibrium levels and workers do not have any relevant misperceptions.

Long-Run Equilibrium
The condition that exists in the economy when wages have adjusted to their (final) equilibrium levels and workers do not have any relevant misperceptions. Graphically, long-run equilibrium occurs at the intersection of the *AD* and *LRAS* curves.

exhibit 13

Long-Run Aggregate Supply (LRAS) Curve
The *LRAS* curve is a vertical line at the level of Natural Real GDP. It represents the output the economy produces when all economy-wide adjustments have taken place and no economic agents have any (relevant) misperceptions.

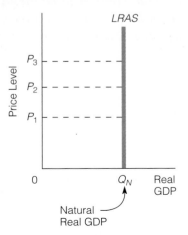

It follows, then, that short-run equilibrium identifies the Real GDP the economy produces when either of these two conditions holds.

In time, though, wages will become unstuck and worker misperceptions will turn into accurate perceptions. When this happens, the economy is said to be in the *long run*. In other words, in the long run, these two conditions do not hold.

An important macroeconomic question is: *Will the level of Real GDP the economy produces in the long run be the same as in the short run?* Most economists say that it will not be. They argue that in the long run, the economy produces the full-employment Real GDP or the **Natural Real GDP** (Q_N). The aggregate supply curve that identifies the output the economy produces in the long run is the **long-run aggregate supply (LRAS) curve.** It is portrayed as the vertical line in Exhibit 13.

It follows that **long-run equilibrium** identifies the level of Real GDP the economy produces when wages have adjusted to their (final) equilibrium levels and there are no misperceptions on the part of workers. Graphically, this occurs at the intersection of the *AD* and *LRAS* curves. Furthermore, the level of Real GDP that the economy produces in long-run equilibrium is Natural Real GDP (Q_N).

Short-Run Equilibrium, Long-Run Equilibrium, and Disequilibrium

There are two equilibrium states in an economy—short-run equilibrium and long-run equilibrium. These two equilibrium states are graphically shown in Exhibit 14.

In Exhibit 14a, the economy is at point 1, producing Q_1 amount of Real GDP. Notice that at point 1, the quantity supplied of Real GDP (in the short run) is equal to the quantity demanded of Real GDP and both are Q_1. The economy is in short-run equilibrium.

In Exhibit 14b, the economy is at point 1, producing Q_N. In other words, it is producing Natural Real GDP. The economy is in long-run equilibrium when it produces Q_N.

When the economy is in neither short-run equilibrium nor long-run equilibrium, it is said to be in *disequilibrium*. Essentially, disequilibrium is the state of the economy as it moves from one short-run equilibrium to another or from short-run equilibrium to long-run equilibrium. The next chapter discusses how the economy moves from short-run equilibrium to long-run equilibrium.

SELF-TEST

1. What is the difference between short-run equilibrium and long-run equilibrium?
2. Diagrammatically represent an economy that is in neither short-run equilibrium nor long-run equilibrium.

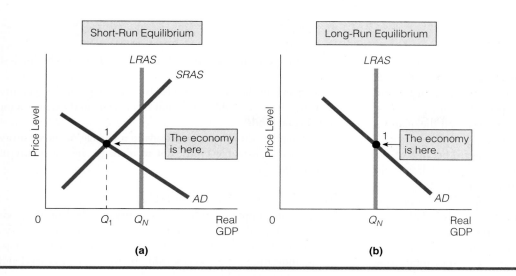

exhibit **14**

Equilibrium States of the Economy
There are two equilibrium states in the
economy: short-run equilibrium, shown in
part (a), and long-run equilibrium, shown
in part (b). During the time an economy
moves from one equilibrium to another, it
is said to be in disequilibrium.

A **READER ASKS** *Do My Job Prospects Depend on AD and SRAS?*

Aggregate demand (*AD*) and short-run aggregate supply (*SRAS*) appear to determine Real GDP
in the short run. Will *AD* and *SRAS* also influence my job prospects after I graduate from college?

Your job prospects will depend in part on your major, your grades,
and your performance in job interviews. But your prospects will
also depend on where the *AD* curve and the *SRAS* curve "intersect."
That is, your job prospects will depend on whether *AD* and *SRAS*
have been increasing, decreasing, or remaining constant.

To illustrate, suppose that some months before you graduate,
interest rates rise and the dollar appreciates. An increase in interest
rates tends to reduce durable goods spending and investment
spending—so both consumption and investment decline. If the
dollar appreciates, U.S. goods become more expensive for foreigners, so they buy less. Also, foreign goods become cheaper for
Americans, so they buy more. The result is that exports fall and
imports rise, or net exports decline.

If consumption, investment, and net exports fall, aggregate
demand in the U.S. economy declines. In other words, the *AD*
curve shifts to the left.

As a result of declining aggregate demand in the economy,
there is a new short-run equilibrium. The new short-run equilibrium is at a lower Real GDP level. In other words, firms have cut
back on the quantity of the goods and services they produce. Many
of the firms that cut back may be the ones at which you hope to
find a job after college. Your job prospects look slightly less rosy
than they did before the changes in the economy.

A statement in the magazine *The Economist* provides further
evidence of the connection between the state of the economy
and your job prospects. In its November 1, 2001, edition, the
magazine stated, "the downturn [in the economy] is plainly
bad news for the [MBA] students, especially since banking
and consulting—two of the industries which, in less interesting
times, reliably hire hundreds of MBAs—have curtailed their
recruiting."

Chapter Summary

Aggregate Demand

> Aggregate demand refers to the quantity demanded of all goods and services (Real GDP) at different price levels, *ceteris paribus*.

> The aggregate demand (*AD*) curve slopes downward, indicating an inverse relationship between the price level and the quantity demanded of Real GDP.

> The aggregate demand curve slopes downward because of the real balance effect, which states that the inverse relationship between the price level and the quantity demanded of Real GDP is established through changes in the value of a person's monetary wealth or money holdings. Specifically, a fall in the price level causes purchasing power to rise, which increases a person's monetary wealth. As people become wealthier, they buy more goods. A rise in the price level causes purchasing power to fall, which reduces a person's monetary wealth. As people become less wealthy, they buy fewer goods.

> At a given price level, a rise in consumption, investment, government purchases, or net exports will increase aggregate demand and shift the *AD* curve to the right. At a given price level, a fall in consumption, investment, government purchases, or net exports will decrease aggregate demand and shift the *AD* curve to the left.

Factors That Can Change C, I, and NX (EX − IM) and Therefore Can Change AD

> The following factors can change consumption: wealth, expectations about future prices and income, the interest rate, and income taxes. The following factors can change investment: the interest rate, expectations about future sales, and business taxes. The following factors can change net exports (exports − imports): foreign real national income and the exchange rate. A change in the money supply can affect one or more spending components (e.g., consumption) and therefore affect aggregate demand.

Interest Rates and the Loanable Funds Market

> A change in interest rates can change both consumption and investment and therefore change aggregate demand.

> The interest rate is determined in the loanable funds market. In this market, there is a downward-sloping demand curve for loanable funds and an upward-sloping supply curve of loanable funds.

> An increase in the demand for loanable funds raises the interest rate.

> A decrease in the demand for loanable funds lowers the interest rate.

> An increase in the supply of loanable funds lowers the interest rate.

> A decrease in the supply of loanable funds raises the interest rate.

> A change in the interest rate leads to a change in the quantity demanded of loanable funds, not to a change in the demand for loanable funds.

> A change in the interest rate leads to a change in the quantity supplied of loanable funds, not to a change in the supply of loanable funds.

Short-Run Aggregate Supply

> Aggregate supply refers to the quantity supplied of all goods and services (Real GDP) at different price levels, *ceteris paribus*.

> The short-run aggregate supply (*SRAS*) curve is upward-sloping, indicating a direct relationship between the price level and the quantity supplied of Real GDP.

> A decrease in wage rates, a decrease in the price of nonlabor inputs, an increase in productivity, and beneficial supply shocks all shift the SRAS curve to the right. An increase in wage rates, an increase in the price of nonlabor inputs, a decrease in productivity, and adverse supply shocks all shift the SRAS curve to the left.

Short-Run Equilibrium

> Graphically, short-run equilibrium exists at the intersection of the *AD* and *SRAS* curves. A shift in either or both of these curves can change the price level and Real GDP. For example, an increase in aggregate demand increases the price level and Real GDP, *ceteris paribus*.

The Unemployment Rate in the Short Run

> A higher Real GDP level is associated with a lower unemployment rate, and a lower Real GDP level is associated with a higher unemployment rate, *ceteris paribus*.

Long-Run Aggregate Supply and Long-Run Equilibrium

> The long-run aggregate supply (*LRAS*) curve is vertical at the Natural Real GDP level.

> Graphically, long-run equilibrium exists at the intersection of the *AD* and *LRAS* curves. It is the condition that exists in the economy when all economy-wide adjustments have taken place and no economic agents hold any (relevant) misperceptions. In long-run equilibrium, quantity demanded of Real GDP = quantity supplied of Real GDP = Natural Real GDP.

Three States of an Economy

> An economy can be in short-run equilibrium, long-run equilibrium, or disequilibrium.

Key Terms and Concepts

Aggregate Demand
Aggregate Demand (*AD*) Curve
Real Balance Effect
Monetary Wealth
Purchasing Power
Wealth

Exchange Rate
Appreciation
Depreciation
Aggregate Supply
Short-Run Aggregate Supply (*SRAS*)
  Curve

Short-Run Equilibrium
Natural Real GDP
Long-Run Aggregate Supply (*LRAS*)
  Curve
Long-Run Equilibrium

Questions and Problems

1. Is aggregate demand a specific dollar amount? For example, would it be correct to say that aggregate demand is $9 trillion this year?
2. Explain why the AD curve slopes downward.
3. Graphically portray each of the following: (a) a change in the quantity demanded of Real GDP and (b) a change in aggregate demand.
4. The amount of Real GDP (real output) that households are willing and able to buy may change if there is a change in either (a) the price level, or (b) some nonprice factor, such as wealth, interest rates, and so on. Do you agree or disagree? Explain your answer.
5. Explain what happens to aggregate demand in each of the following cases:
   a. The interest rate rises.
   b. Wealth falls.
   c. The dollar depreciates relative to foreign currencies.
   d. Households expect lower prices in the future.
   e. Business taxes rise.
6. Suppose the budget deficit grows and the government borrows more loanable funds. How will this affect the interest rate? How will this affect consumption spending? How will this affect investment spending?
7. Which of the following two statements is correct and why?
   Statement 1: A change in the demand for loanable funds leads to a change in the interest rate which, in turn, leads to a change in the quantity demanded of loanable funds.
   Statement 2: A change in the interest rate leads to a change in the demand for loanable funds which, in turn, leads to a change in the quantity demanded of loanable funds.

8. Explain how each of the following will affect short-run aggregate supply:
   a. An increase in wage rates
   b. A beneficial supply shock
   c. An increase in the productivity of labor
   d. A decrease in the price of a nonlabor resource (such as oil)
9. What is the difference between a change in the quantity supplied of Real GDP and a change in short-run aggregate supply?
10. A change in the price level affects which of the following?
    a. The quantity demanded of Real GDP
    b. Aggregate demand
    c. Short-run aggregate supply
    d. The quantity supplied of Real GDP
11. In the short run, what is the impact on the price level, Real GDP, and the unemployment rate of each of the following:
    a. An increase in consumption brought about by a decrease in interest rates
    b. A decrease in exports brought about by an appreciation of the dollar
    c. A rise in wage rates
    d. A beneficial supply shock
    e. An adverse supply shock
    f. A decline in productivity
12. Explain why there is an inverse relationship between Real GDP and the unemployment rate, *ceteris paribus*.
13. Identify the details of each of the following explanations for an upward-sloping *SRAS* curve:
    a. Sticky-wage explanation
    b. Worker-misperception explanation
14. What is the difference between short-run equilibrium and long-run equilibrium?

Working With Numbers and Graphs

1. Suppose that at a price index of 154, the quantity demanded of (U.S.) Real GDP is $10.0 trillion worth of goods. Do these data represent aggregate demand or a point on an aggregate demand curve? Explain your answer.

2. Diagrammatically represent the effect on the price level and Real GDP in the short run of each of the following:

    a. An increase in wealth

    b. An increase in wage rates

    c. An increase in labor productivity

3. Diagrammatically represent the following and identify the effect on Real GDP and the price level in the short run:

    a. An increase in $SRAS$ that is greater than the increase in AD

    b. A decrease in AD that is greater than the increase in $SRAS$

    c. An increase in $SRAS$ that is less than the increase in AD

4. In the following figure, which part is representative of each of the following:

    a. A decrease in wage rates

    b. An increase in the price level

    c. A beneficial supply shock

    d. An increase in the price of nonlabor inputs

5. In the following figure, which of the points is representative of each of the following:

    a. The lowest unemployment rate

    b. The highest unemployment rate

    c. A decrease in $SRAS$ that is greater than an increase in AD

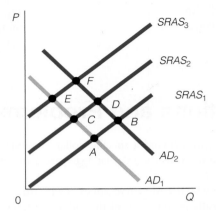

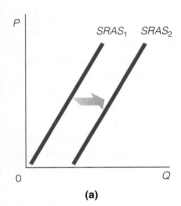

(a)

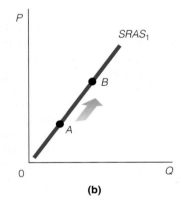

(b)

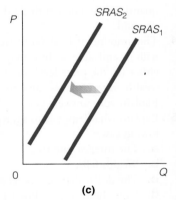

(c)

© Bill Aron/PhotoEdit

Setting the Scene

Each weekday morning, approximately 100,000 New Yorkers ride the train from their homes on Long Island to their workplaces in Manhattan. Each weekday afternoon, those same 100,000 people take the return trip. Listen to a few conversations that occurred on a return trip one day in June. The time is 5:16 P.M.

First Conversation

Yvonne:

I don't know. Wages are rising, but then so is the unemployment rate. I may be the next to go. If I am, then I may have to move back in with my parents for awhile.

Wendy:

That would be a shame after all you've been through these last few months.

Yvonne:

I know.

Second Conversation

Robert:

I read today that people are starting to save more than they have in the past. I'm not sure that's good for the economy.

Charles:

Why wouldn't it be?

Robert:

Well, if everyone is saving more, who's going to be spending? Cut down on spending and we might just head straight into a recession.

Third Conversation

Priscilla:

I read in the *Journal* that the president wants to lower taxes for businesses. That might stimulate production in the economy, but I'm not sure it will do anything for consumption. Don't people have to be able to buy the goods that businesses produce?

Jeff:

You remember Say's law from college, don't you? Supply creates its own demand.

Priscilla:

I'm not sure I ever believed that.

Fourth Conversation

José:

I think it's a little like when you have a cold or the flu. You don't need to see a doctor. In time, your body heals itself. That's sort of the way the economy works too. We don't really need government "coming to our rescue" every time the economy gets a cold.

Mark:

But what happens if the economy gets really sick? Can it heal itself then?

How would an economist look at these conversations? Later in the chapter, discussions based on the following questions will help you analyze the scene the way an economist would.

- What does the economy have to do with Yvonne possibly having to move back in with her parents?
- Can people saving more be bad for the economy?
- What is Say's law and what does it say about production and consumption?
- According to José, how does the economy work?

THE CLASSICAL VIEW

The term *classical economics* is often used to refer to an era in the history of economic thought that stretched from about 1750 to the late 1800s or early 1900s. Although classical economists lived and wrote many years ago, their ideas are often employed by some modern-day economists.

Classical Economists and Say's Law

You know from your study of supply and demand that there can be temporary shortages and surpluses in markets. For example, there may be a surplus in the apple market. But can there be a general surplus (a general glut of goods and services) in the economy? The classical economists thought not, largely because they believed in Say's law. In its simplest version, **Say's law** says that supply creates its own demand.

Say's law is most easily understood in terms of a barter economy. Consider a person baking bread in a barter economy; he is a supplier of bread. According to Say, the baker works at his trade because he plans to demand other goods. As he is baking his bread, the baker is thinking of the goods and services he will obtain in exchange for it. Thus, his act of supplying bread is linked to his demand for other goods. Supply creates its own demand.

If the supplying of some goods is simultaneously the demanding of other goods, then Say's law implies that there cannot be either (1) a general overproduction of goods (where supply in the economy is greater than demand in the economy) or (2) a general underproduction of goods (where demand in the economy is greater than supply in the economy).

Now suppose the baker is baking bread in a money economy. Does Say's law hold? Over a period of time, the baker earns an income as a result of his supplying bread. But what does he do with his income? One thing he does is buy goods and services. However, his demand for goods and services does not necessarily match the income that he generates through his actions as a supplier of bread. The baker may spend less than his full income because he engages in saving. Noting this, we might think that Say's law does not hold in a money economy because the act of supplying goods and services, and thus earning income, need not create an equal amount of demand.

But the classical economists disagreed. They argued that even in a money economy, where individuals sometimes spend less than their full incomes, Say's law still holds. Their argument was partly based on the assumption of interest rate flexibility.

Say's Law
Supply creates its own demand. Production creates demand sufficient to purchase all goods and services produced.

⚠ ANALYZING THE SCENE

Question from Setting the Scene: What is Say's law and what does it say about production and consumption?
According to Say's law, supply creates its own demand. Specifically, Say's law holds that the act of supplying goods (production) is linked to the act of demanding goods (consumption). People don't produce without thinking about how they'll consume. Believers in Say's law often argue that a key way to stimulate consumption in the economy is to make it easier for businesses to produce more. They argue that more production leads to more consumption.

Classical Economists and Interest Rate Flexibility

For Say's law to hold in a money economy, funds saved must give rise to an equal amount of funds invested; that is, what leaves the spending stream through one door must enter through another door. If not, then some of the income earned from supplying goods may not be used to demand goods (goodbye Say's law). As a result, there will be an overproduction of goods.

The classical economists argued that saving is matched by an equal amount of investment because of interest rate flexibility in the credit market. We explain their argument using Exhibit 1, where I represents investment and S represents saving.

Notice that I_1 is downward-sloping, indicating an inverse relationship between the amount of funds firms invest and the interest rate (i). The reason for this is straightforward. The interest rate is the cost of borrowing funds. The higher the interest rate, the fewer funds firms borrow and invest; the lower the interest rate, the more funds firms borrow and invest.

Notice that S_1 is upward-sloping, indicating a direct relationship between the amount of funds households save and the interest rate. The reason is that the higher the interest rate, the higher the reward for saving (or the higher the opportunity cost of consuming) and, therefore, the fewer funds consumed and the more funds saved. Market-equilibrating forces move the credit market to interest rate i_1 and equilibrium point E_1. At E_1, the number of dollars households save ($100,000) equals the number of dollars firms invest ($100,000).

Suppose now that saving increases at each interest rate. In Exhibit 1, we represent this by a rightward shift in the saving curve from S_1 to S_2. The classical economists believed that an increase in saving will put downward pressure on the interest rate, moving it to i_2,

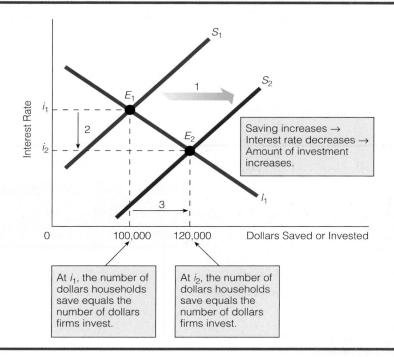

exhibit 1

The Classical View of the Credit Market
In classical theory, the interest rate is flexible and adjusts so that saving equals investment. Thus, if saving increases and the saving curve shifts rightward from S_1 to S_2 (arrow 1), the increase in saving eventually puts pressure on the interest rate and moves it downward from i_1 to i_2 (arrow 2). A new equilibrium is established at E_2 (arrow 3), where once again the amount households save equals the amount firms invest.

Saving increases →
Interest rate decreases →
Amount of investment increases.

At i_1, the number of dollars households save equals the number of dollars firms invest.

At i_2, the number of dollars households save equals the number of dollars firms invest.

thereby increasing the number of dollars firms invest. Ultimately, the number of dollars households save ($120,000) will once again equal the number of dollars firms invest ($120,000). Interest rate flexibility ensures that saving equals investment. (What goes out one door comes in the other door.) In short, changes in the interest rate uphold Say's law in a money economy where there is saving.

Let's use a few numbers to show exactly what classical economists were saying. Suppose that at a given price level, total expenditures (TE) in a very tiny economy are $5,000. We know that total expenditures (total spending on domestic goods and services) equal the sum of consumption (C), investment (I), government purchases (G), and net exports ($EX - IM$). If C = $3,000, I = $600, G = $1,200, and $EX - IM$ = $200, then

$$TE = C + I + G + (EX - IM)$$
$$\$5,000 = \$3,000 + \$600 + \$1,200 + \$200$$

Furthermore, let's assume the $5,000 worth of goods and services that the four sectors of the economy want to purchase also happens to be the exact dollar amount of goods and services that suppliers want to sell.

Next, let's increase saving in the economy. Saving (S) is equal to the amount of a person's disposable (after-tax) income (Y_d) minus consumption (C). For example, if Harriet earns a disposable income of $40,000 a year and spends $38,000, she saves $2,000.

$$\text{Saving } (S) = \text{Disposable income } (Y_d) - \text{Consumption } (C)$$

For saving to increase, consumption must decrease. Let's say saving increases by $100; then, consumption must fall from $3,000 to $2,900. At first glance, this seems to imply that total expenditures will fall to $4,900. But classical economists disagreed. They said that investment will increase by $100, going from $600 to $700. Total expenditures will remain constant at $5,000 and will be equal to the dollar amount of goods and services suppliers want to sell.

$$TE = C + I + G + (EX - IM)$$
$$\$5,000 = \$2,900 + \$700 + \$1,200 + \$200$$

Exhibit 2 summarizes this discussion.

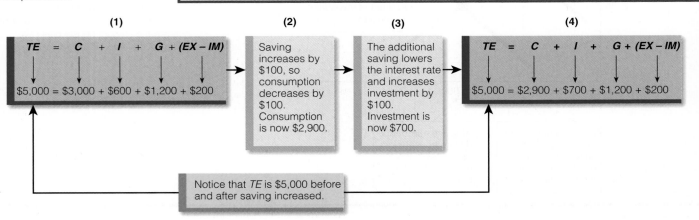

According to the classical view of the economy, then, Say's law holds both in a barter economy and in a money economy. In a money economy, according to classical economists, interest rates will adjust to equate saving and investment. Therefore, any fall in consumption (and consequent rise in saving) will be matched by an equal rise in investment. In essence, at a given price level, total expenditures will not decrease as a result of an increase in saving.

What does an increase in saving imply for aggregate demand (*AD*)? An earlier chapter explains that aggregate demand changes only if total spending in the economy changes at a given price level. Therefore, because there is no change in total spending as a result of an increase in saving, there is no change in aggregate demand.

ANALYZING THE SCENE

Question from Setting the Scene: Can people saving more be bad for the economy?
According to classical economists, if, say, households save more (and spend less), the interest rate will fall, prompting businesses to spend more. More importantly, the decline in household spending will be matched by an equal rise in business spending. In short, for classical economists, saving more does not lead to less spending in the economy. Saving more simply leads to a different configuration of spending (less consumption, more investment).

Classical Economists on Prices and Wages

Classical economists believed that most, if not all, markets are competitive. That is, supply and demand are operational in all markets. If, for example, there is a surplus of labor in the labor market, it will be temporary. Soon, the wage rate will decline and the quantity supplied of labor will equal the quantity demanded of labor. Similarly, if there is a shortage of labor in the labor market, the wage rate will rise and the quantity supplied will equal the quantity demanded.

What holds for wages in the labor market, holds for prices in the goods and services market. Prices will adjust quickly to any surpluses or shortages and equilibrium will be quickly reestablished.

SELF-TEST *(Answers to Self-Test Questions are in the Self-Test Appendix.)*

1. Explain Say's law in terms of a barter economy.
2. According to classical economists, if saving rises and consumption spending falls, will total spending in the economy decrease? Explain your answer.
3. What is the classical position on prices and wages?

THREE STATES OF THE ECONOMY

You will need the basic background information provided in this section before we discuss the views of economists who believe the economy is self-regulating. Specifically, we discuss three states of the economy, the correspondence between the labor market and the three states of the economy, and more in this section.

Real GDP and Natural Real GDP: Three Possibilities

In the last chapter, Natural Real GDP is defined as the Real GDP that is produced at the natural unemployment rate. It is the Real GDP that is produced when the economy is in long-run equilibrium.

Economists often refer to the three states of an economy that are possible when we consider the relationship between Real GDP and Natural Real GDP. The possibilities are an economy operating at a level of Real GDP (1) less than Natural Real GDP, (2) greater than Natural Real GDP, or (3) equal to Natural Real GDP.

Three possible states of an economy are:

- Real GDP is less than Natural Real GDP.
- Real GDP is greater than Natural Real GDP.
- Real GDP is equal to Natural Real GDP.

Let's now give a name to each of these three possible states of the economy and graphically portray each.

Real GDP Is Less Than Natural Real GDP (Recessionary Gap)

Exhibit 3a shows an *AD* curve, an *SRAS* curve, and the *LRAS* curve. It also shows that Natural Real GDP (Q_N) is produced in the long run.

Short-run equilibrium is at the intersection of the *AD* and *SRAS* curves, so in part (a), short-run equilibrium is at point 1. The Real GDP level that the economy is producing at point 1 is designated by Q_1.

Now compare Q_1 with Q_N. Obviously, Q_1 is less than Q_N. In other words, the economy is currently producing a level of Real GDP in the short run that is less than its Natural Real GDP level.

When the Real GDP the economy is producing is less than its Natural Real GDP, the economy is said to be in a **recessionary gap.**

Real GDP Is Greater Than Natural Real GDP (Inflationary Gap)

In Exhibit 3b, the *AD* and *SRAS* curves intersect at point 1, so short-run equilibrium is at point 1. The Real GDP level the economy is producing at point 1 is designated by Q_1.

Compare Q_1 with Q_N. Obviously, Q_1 is greater than Q_N. In other words, the economy is currently producing a level of Real GDP in the short run that is greater than its Natural Real GDP level or potential output.

Recessionary Gap
The condition where the Real GDP the economy is producing is less than the Natural Real GDP and the unemployment rate is greater than the natural unemployment rate.

Real GDP and Natural Real GDP: Three Possibilities

In (a), the economy is currently in short-run equilibrium at a Real GDP level of Q_1. Q_N is Natural Real GDP or the potential output of the economy. Notice that $Q_1 < Q_N$. When this condition ($Q_1 < Q_N$) exists, the economy is said to be in a recessionary gap.

In (b), the economy is currently in short-run equilibrium at a Real GDP level of Q_1. Q_N is Natural Real GDP or the potential output of the economy. Notice that $Q_1 > Q_N$. When this condition ($Q_1 > Q_N$) exists, the economy is said to be in an inflationary gap.

In (c), the economy is currently operating at a Real GDP level of Q_1, which is equal to Q_N. In other words, the economy is producing its Natural Real GDP or potential output. When this condition ($Q_1 = Q_N$) exists, the economy is said to be in long-run equilibrium.

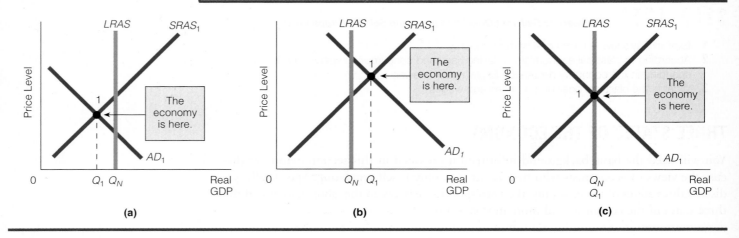

(a)   (b)   (c)

When the Real GDP the economy is producing is greater than its Natural Real GDP, the economy is said to be in an **inflationary gap.**

Real GDP Is Equal to Natural Real GDP (Long-Run Equilibrium)

In Exhibit 3c, the *AD* and *SRAS* curves indicate that short-run equilibrium is at point 1. The Real GDP level the economy is producing at point 1 is designated by Q_1.

Again compare Q_1 and Q_N. This time Q_1 is equal to Q_N. In other words, the economy is currently producing a level of Real GDP that is equal to its Natural Real GDP or potential output.

When the Real GDP the economy is producing is equal to its Natural Real GDP, the economy is in *long-run equilibrium.*

The Labor Market and the Three States of the Economy

If the economy can be in three possible states, so can the labor market. We identify the three possible states of the labor market, and then tie each state to a possible state of the economy.

We know that the labor market consists of the demand for labor and the supply of labor. Like a goods market, the labor market can manifest (1) equilibrium, (2) a shortage, or (3) a surplus.

Three possible states of the labor market are:

- Equilibrium
- Shortage
- Surplus

When equilibrium exists in the labor market, there are the same number of jobs available as the number of people who want to work. That is, the quantity demanded of labor is equal to the quantity supplied of labor.

When there is a shortage in the labor market, there are more jobs available than there are people who want to work. That is, the quantity demanded of labor is greater than the quantity supplied of labor.

When there is a surplus in the labor market, there are more people who want to work than there are jobs available; the quantity supplied of labor is greater than the quantity demanded of labor.

Recessionary Gap and the Labor Market

If the economy is in a recessionary gap, is the labor market in equilibrium, shortage, or surplus? To simplify, suppose the economy is in a recessionary gap producing a Real GDP level of $9 trillion (worth of goods and services) when Natural Real GDP, or potential output, is $10 trillion.

The unemployment rate that exists when the economy produces Natural Real GDP is, of course, the natural unemployment rate. Is the unemployment rate that exists when the economy is in a recessionary gap producing $9 trillion worth of goods and services greater or less than the natural unemployment rate that exists when the economy is producing $10 trillion worth of goods and services? The answer is that the unemployment rate is greater than the natural unemployment rate because fewer workers are needed to produce a Real GDP of $9 trillion than are needed to produce a Real GDP of $10 trillion. *Ceteris paribus,* the unemployment rate will be higher at a Real GDP level of $9 trillion than it is at a level of $10 trillion.

Inflationary Gap
The condition where the Real GDP the economy is producing is greater than the Natural Real GDP and the unemployment rate is less than the natural unemployment rate.

© AP/Wide World Photos

We conclude that when the economy is in a recessionary gap, the unemployment rate is *higher* than the natural unemployment rate. This implies there is a surplus in the labor market: quantity supplied of labor is greater than quantity demanded, or there are more people who want to work than there are jobs available.

> If the economy is in a recessionary gap, the unemployment rate is higher than the natural unemployment rate and a surplus exists in the labor market.

Inflationary Gap and the Labor Market

Now suppose the economy is in an inflationary gap producing a Real GDP level of $11 trillion (worth of goods and services) when Natural Real GDP, or potential output, is $10 trillion.

Again, the unemployment rate that exists when the economy produces Natural Real GDP is the natural unemployment rate. Is the unemployment rate that exists when the economy is producing $11 trillion worth of goods and services greater or less than the natural unemployment rate that exists when the economy is producing $10 trillion worth of goods and services? The answer is that the unemployment rate is less than the natural unemployment rate because more workers are needed to produce a Real GDP of $11 trillion than are needed to produce a Real GDP of $10 trillion. *Ceteris paribus,* the unemployment rate will be lower at a Real GDP level of $11 trillion than it is at a level of $10 trillion.

We conclude that when the economy is in an inflationary gap, the unemployment rate is *lower* than the natural unemployment rate. This implies that there is a shortage in the labor market: quantity demanded of labor is greater than quantity supplied, or there are more jobs available than there are people who want to work.

> If the economy is in an inflationary gap, the unemployment rate is less than the natural unemployment rate and a shortage exists in the labor market.

Long-Run Equilibrium and the Labor Market

Finally, suppose the economy is in long-run equilibrium. In other words, it is producing a Real GDP level equal to Natural Real GDP. It follows that in this state, the unemployment rate (that exists in the economy) is the same as the natural unemployment rate. This implies that there is neither a shortage nor a surplus in the labor market; instead, equilibrium exists in the labor market.

> If the economy is in long-run equilibrium, the unemployment rate equals the natural unemployment rate and equilibrium exists in the labor market.

The following table summarizes three possible states of the economy and the related states of the labor market.

State of the Economy	What Do We Call It?	Relationship Between Unemployment Rate and Natural Unemployment Rate	State of the Labor Market
Real GDP < Natural Real GDP	Recessionary gap	Unemployment rate > Natural unemployment rate	Surplus exists
Real GDP > Natural Real GDP	Inflationary gap	Unemployment rate < Natural unemployment rate	Shortage exists
Real GDP = Natural Real GDP	Long-run equilibrium	Unemployment rate = Natural unemployment rate	Equilibrium exists

One Nagging Question: How Can the Unemployment Rate Be Less Than the Natural Unemployment Rate?

Recall that when the economy is in an inflationary gap, the unemployment rate is less than the natural unemployment rate. For example, if the natural unemployment rate is 5 percent, the unemployment rate may be 4 percent.

You may have wondered how the economy can do better than the natural unemployment rate, which, after all, is equated with full employment or potential output. To explain, we need to use two production possibilities frontiers.

In Exhibit 4, the two production possibilities frontiers are the physical PPF (purple curve) and the institutional PPF (blue curve). The physical PPF illustrates different combinations of goods the economy can produce given the physical constraints of (1) finite resources and (2) the current state of technology.

The institutional PPF illustrates different combinations of goods the economy can produce given the physical constraints of (1) finite resources, (2) the current state of technology, and (3) any institutional constraints. Broadly defined, an institutional constraint is anything that prevents economic agents from producing the maximum Real GDP physically possible.

For example, the minimum wage law, which is an institutional constraint, specifies that workers must be paid a wage rate at least equal to the legislated minimum wage. One effect of this law is that unskilled persons whose value to employers falls below the legislated minimum wage will not be hired. Fewer workers means less output produced, *ceteris paribus*. (This is why the institutional PPF lies closer to the origin than the physical PPF.)

Within the confines of society's physical and institutional constraints, there is a natural unemployment rate. This state of affairs is represented by any point on the institutional PPF. In the exhibit, points *A, B,* and *C* are all such points.

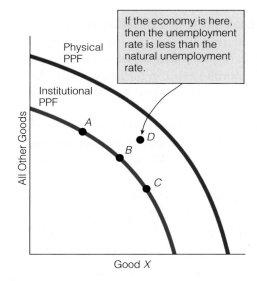

exhibit **4**

The Physical and Institutional PPFs
A society has both a physical PPF and an institutional PPF. The physical PPF illustrates different combinations of goods the economy can produce given the physical constraints of (1) finite resources and (2) the current state of technology. The institutional PPF illustrates different combinations of goods the economy can produce given the physical constraints of (1) finite resources, (2) the current state of technology, and (3) any institutional constraints. The economy is at the natural unemployment rate if it is located on its institutional PPF, such as at points *A, B,* or *C*. An economy can never operate beyond its physical PPF, but it is possible for it to operate beyond its institutional PPF because institutional constraints are not always equally effective. If the economy does operate beyond its institutional PPF, such as at point *D,* then the unemployment rate in the economy is lower than the natural unemployment rate.

An economy can never operate beyond its physical PPF, but it is possible for it to operate beyond its institutional PPF. For example, suppose inflation reduces the purchasing power of the minimum wage, thus reducing or eliminating the constraining properties of the minimum wage law on the unskilled labor market.[1] This would make one of society's institutional constraints ineffective, allowing the economy to temporarily move beyond the institutional constraint.

Logic dictates that if the economy is operating at the natural unemployment rate when it is located on its institutional PPF, then it must be operating at an unemployment rate lower than the natural rate when it is located beyond its institutional PPF (but below its physical PPF). Because society's institutional constraints are not always equally effective, it is possible for an economy to be operating at an unemployment rate below the natural rate.

SELF-TEST

1. What is a recessionary gap? an inflationary gap?
2. What is the state of the labor market when the economy is in a recessionary gap? in an inflationary gap?
3. If the economy is in an inflationary gap, locate its position in terms of the two PPFs discussed in this section.

THE SELF-REGULATING ECONOMY

Some economists believe that the economy is self-regulating. This means that if the economy is not at the natural unemployment rate (or full employment)—that is, it is not producing Natural Real GDP—then it can move itself to this position. The notion of a self-regulating economy is a very classical notion, but is also a view held by some modern-day economists. This section describes how a self-regulating economy works.

What Happens if the Economy Is in a Recessionary Gap?

If the economy is in a recessionary gap, (1) it is producing a Real GDP level that is less than Natural Real GDP, (2) the unemployment rate is greater than the natural unemployment rate, and (3) a surplus exists in the labor market. Exhibit 5a illustrates this case for a Real GDP of $9 trillion and a Natural Real GDP of $10 trillion. What, if anything, happens in the economy?

According to economists who believe the economy is self-regulating, the surplus in the labor market begins to exert downward pressure on wages.[2] In other words, as old wage contracts expire, business firms will negotiate contracts that pay workers lower wage rates.

Recall from the last chapter that as wage rates fall, the *SRAS* curve begins to shift to the right, ultimately moving from *SRAS*$_1$ to *SRAS*$_2$ in Exhibit 5b. As a result of the increase in short-run aggregate supply, the price level falls. But as the price level falls, the

---

1. Inflation reduces the real (inflation-adjusted) minimum wage. If the minimum wage is $6 and the price level is 1.00, the real minimum wage is $6 ($6 divided by the price level, 1.00). If the price level rises to 2.00, then the real minimum wage falls to $3. The lower the real minimum wage, the greater the number of unskilled workers that employers will hire because the demand curve for unskilled workers is downward-sloping.
2. In this discussion of how the self-regulating economy eliminates a recessionary gap, we have emphasized wages (in the labor market) adjusting downward. Other resource prices besides wages may fall as well.

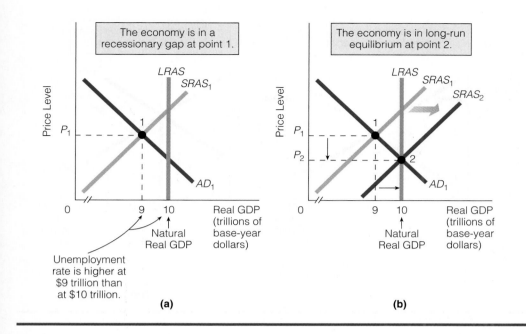

The economy is in a recessionary gap at point 1.

The economy is in long-run equilibrium at point 2.

Unemployment rate is higher at $9 trillion than at $10 trillion.

(a)

(b)

The Self-Regulating Economy: Removing a Recessionary Gap

(a) The economy is at P_1 and Real GDP of $9 trillion. Because Real GDP is less than Natural Real GDP ($10 trillion), the economy is in a recessionary gap and the unemployment rate is higher than the natural unemployment rate. (b) Wage rates fall, and the short-run aggregate supply curve shifts from $SRAS_1$ to $SRAS_2$. As the price level falls, the real balance effect increases the quantity demanded of Real GDP. Ultimately, the economy moves into long-run equilibrium at point 2.

quantity demanded of Real GDP rises due to the real balance effect (discussed in the last chapter). As the price level falls, the economy moves from one point on the *AD* curve to a point farther down the same curve. In Exhibit 5b, this is a move from point 1 to point 2.

As long as the economy's Real GDP is less than its Natural Real GDP, the price level will continue to fall. Ultimately, the economy moves to long-run equilibrium at point 2, corresponding to P_2 and a Natural Real GDP of $10 trillion.

> Recessionary gap →
> Unemployment rate > Natural unemployment rate →
> Surplus in labor market → Wages fall → *SRAS* curve shifts to the right →
> Economy moves into long-run equilibrium

What Happens if the Economy Is in an Inflationary Gap?

If the economy is in an inflationary gap, (1) it is producing a Real GDP level that is greater than Natural Real GDP, (2) the unemployment rate is less than the natural unemployment rate, and (3) a shortage exists in the labor market. Exhibit 6a illustrates this case for a Real GDP of $11 trillion and a Natural Real GDP of $10 trillion. What happens in the economy in this situation?

Again, according to economists who believe the economy is self-regulating, the shortage in the labor market begins to exert upward pressure on wages. In other words, as old wage contracts expire, business firms will negotiate contracts that pay workers higher wage rates.

As wage rates rise, the *SRAS* curve begins to shift to the left, ultimately moving from $SRAS_1$ to $SRAS_2$ in Exhibit 6b. As a result of the decrease in short-run aggregate supply, the price level rises. But as the price level rises, the quantity demanded of Real GDP falls due to the real balance effect. As the price level rises, the economy moves from one point

The Self-Regulating Economy   Chapter 6   **155**

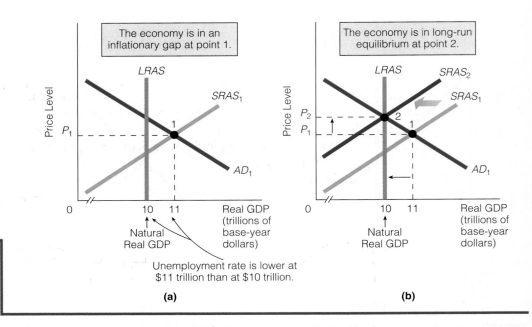

 exhibit 6

The Self-Regulating Economy: Removing an Inflationary Gap

(a) The economy is at P_1 and Real GDP of $11 trillion. Because Real GDP is greater than Natural Real GDP ($10 trillion), the economy is in an inflationary gap and the unemployment rate is lower than the natural unemployment rate.

(b) Wage rates rise, and the short-run aggregate supply curve shifts from $SRAS_1$ to $SRAS_2$. As the price level rises, the real balance effect decreases the quantity demanded of Real GDP. Ultimately, the economy moves into long-run equilibrium at point 2.

on the *AD* curve to a point farther up the same curve. In Exhibit 6b, this is a move from point 1 to point 2.

As long as the economy's Real GDP is greater than its Natural Real GDP, the price level will continue to rise. Ultimately, the economy moves to long-run equilibrium at point 2, corresponding to P_2 and a Natural Real GDP of $10 trillion.

Inflationary gap →
Unemployment rate < Natural unemployment rate →
Shortage in labor market → Wages rise → *SRAS* curve shifts to the left →
Economy moves into long-run equilibrium

! ANALYZING THE SCENE

Question from Setting the Scene: What does the economy have to do with Yvonne possibly having to move back in with her parents?

Yvonne says that wages are rising but so is the unemployment rate. This is what happens if the economy is self-regulating and is removing itself from an inflationary gap. In an inflationary gap, the unemployment rate is below the natural unemployment rate. In time, wages rise and the *SRAS* curve shifts leftward. As the *SRAS* curve shifts leftward, Real GDP declines and the unemployment rate rises. Bottom line: Some people will become unemployed as the economy stabilizes itself at the natural unemployment rate. If Yvonne is one of these people, then she may have to move back in with her parents for a while.

The Self-Regulating Economy: A Recap

We have shown that if the economy is in a recessionary gap, wage rates fall (along with other resource prices) and the *SRAS* curve shifts to the right. As this happens, the price level falls and the economy moves down the *AD* curve. The economy moves in the direction of long-run equilibrium, ultimately achieving the Natural Real GDP level.

156 *Part 3 Macroeconomic Stability and Instability*

If the economy is in an inflationary gap, wage rates rise (along with other resource prices) and the *SRAS* curve shifts to the left. As this happens, the price level rises and the economy moves up the *AD* curve. The economy moves in the direction of long-run equilibrium, ultimately achieving the Natural Real GDP level.

Flexible wage rates (and other resource prices) play a critical role in the self-regulating economy. For example, suppose wage rates are not flexible and do not fall in a recessionary gap. Then, the *SRAS* curve will not shift to the right. But if the *SRAS* curve does not shift to the right, the price level will not fall. And if the price level does not fall, the economy won't move down the *AD* curve toward long-run equilibrium. Similarly, if wage rates are not flexible and do not rise in an inflationary gap, then the economy won't move up the *AD* curve toward long-run equilibrium.

The economists who believe in a self-regulating economy—classical economists, monetarists, and new classical economists—believe that wage rates and other resource prices are *flexible* and move up and down in response to market conditions. Thus, these economists believe that *wage rates will fall* when there is a *surplus of labor.* They believe that *wage rates will rise* when there is a *shortage of labor.* You will see in the next chapter that the flexible wages and prices position taken by these economists has not gone unchallenged.

ANALYZING THE SCENE

Question from Setting the Scene: According to José, how does the economy work?
José says, "I think it's a little like when you have a cold or the flu. You don't need to see a doctor. In time, your body heals itself. That's sort of the way the economy works too." Obviously, José believes the economy is self-regulating and will heal itself. The economy will move itself out of either an inflationary gap or a recessionary gap and will settle down (eventually) in long-run equilibrium at the natural unemployment rate and Natural Real GDP.

The following table summarizes how a self-regulating economy works for three possible states of the economy.

State of the Economy	What Happens If the Economy Is Self-Regulating?
Recessionary gap (Real GDP < Natural Real GDP)	Wages fall and *SRAS* curve shifts to the right until Real GDP = Natural Real GDP.
Inflationary gap (Real GDP > Natural Real GDP)	Wages rise and *SRAS* curve shifts to the left until Real GDP = Natural Real GDP.
Long-run equilibrium (Real GDP = Natural Real GDP)	No change in wages and no change in *SRAS*.

Policy Implication of Believing the Economy Is Self-Regulating

Classical, new classical, and monetarist economists believe that the economy is self-regulating. For these economists, full employment is the norm: the economy always moves back to Natural Real GDP. Stated differently, if the economy becomes "ill"—in the form of a recessionary or an inflationary gap—it certainly is capable of healing itself through changes in wages and prices. This belief in how the economy works has led these economists to advocate a macroeconomic policy of **laissez-faire,** or noninterference. In

Laissez-faire
A public policy of not interfering with market activities in the economy.

© Photodisc/Getty Images

The Natural Unemployment Rate, Technology, and Policy Errors

Recall that the natural unemployment rate is equal to the frictional unemployment rate plus the structural unemployment rate. Thus, anything that lowers either the frictional or the structural unemployment rate will also lower the natural unemployment rate. Let's consider how the frictional unemployment rate might be lowered.

Frictional unemployment occurs when changing market conditions cause qualified individuals with transferable skills to change jobs. A person's frictional unemployment lasts only as long as it takes her to find another job. The length of time it takes to find another job is a function of many things—one of which is the amount of information the individual has about jobs that she can perform.

Have advances in technology influenced the amount of information available to job seekers? For example, suppose telephones and newspapers did not exist. In this situation, the frictionally unemployed person would be likely to stay unemployed longer than if she could use telephones and newspapers to obtain information.

In recent years, technology has provided another way for a frictionally unemployed person to obtain information and find a job. She can post her résumé on the Internet and can use the Internet to easily look for jobs all across the country. By using the Internet, a frictionally unemployed person is likely to stay unemployed for a shorter time. As a result, the frictional unemployment rate will fall, as will the natural unemployment rate.

Suppose technology lowers the natural unemployment rate in the way we have described, but this is as yet unknown to policymakers. Will errors in policy be made?

To illustrate, there is some evidence that the monetary authority in the United States—the Federal Reserve, or simply the Fed—sometimes uses the natural unemployment rate when making monetary policy. Specifically, it sometimes compares the actual unemployment rate to the natural unemployment rate in order to get an idea of the direction it should take in monetary policy.

Suppose the natural unemployment rate has fallen to 4.5 percent because of improvements in technology, but this is not yet known by the Fed. The Fed thinks the natural unemployment rate is 5 percent. Now assume the actual unemployment rate falls from 5.0 to 4.8 percent. The Fed believes the economy has gone below its natural unemployment rate (it is in an inflationary gap) and if the Fed does nothing, the price level will soon rise. In order to offset the potential rise in prices down the road, the Fed decides to try to reduce aggregate demand by lowering the growth rate of the money supply.

Let's summarize the situation: The economy is still operating at an unemployment rate (4.8 percent) above the true natural unemployment rate (4.5 percent), but the Fed thinks the economy is operating at an unemployment rate (4.8 percent) below the natural unemployment rate (5.0 percent). Stated differently, while the economy is still in a recessionary gap, the Fed thinks it is in an inflationary gap.

By cutting back the rate of growth in the money supply, the Fed will lower aggregate demand and keep the unemployment rate above the natural unemployment rate. Thus, the economy will stay in a recessionary gap for longer than would have been the case if the Fed had not made the mistake that it did.

---

the view of these economists, government does not have an economic management role to play.

Changes in a Self-Regulating Economy: Short Run and Long Run

Let's consider how a change in aggregate demand affects the economy in the short run and the long run if the economy is self-regulating. In Exhibit 7a, the economy is initially in long-run equilibrium at point 1. Suppose there is an increase in aggregate demand brought about by, say, an increase in government purchases (this possibility is discussed in the last chapter). The AD curve shifts right from AD_1 to AD_2 and in the short run, the economy moves to point 2 with both Real GDP and the price level higher than each was at point 1.

Now at point 2, the economy is in an inflationary gap. If the economy is self-regulating, wages will soon rise and the *SRAS* curve will shift to the left—ultimately from $SRAS_1$ to $SRAS_2$. The economy will end up at point 3 in long-run equilibrium.

Now let's examine the changes in the short run and in the long run. As a result of an increase in aggregate demand, Real GDP rises and the price level rises in the short run. In addition, because Real GDP rises, the unemployment rate falls. In the long run, when the economy is at point 3, it is producing exactly the same level of Real GDP that it was producing originally (Q_N) but at a higher price level.

Conclusion: If the economy is self-regulating, an increase in aggregate demand can raise the price level and Real GDP in the short run but in the long run, the only effect of an increase in aggregate demand is a rise in the price level. In other words, in the long run all that we have to show for an increase in aggregate demand is higher prices.

Now let's consider what happens if aggregate demand falls. In Exhibit 7b, the economy is initially in long-run equilibrium at point 1. Suppose there is a decrease in aggregate demand. The *AD* curve shifts left from AD_1 to AD_2 and in the short run, the economy moves to point 2 with both Real GDP and the price level lower than each was at point 1.

Now at point 2, the economy is in a recessionary gap. If the economy is self-regulating, wages will soon fall and the *SRAS* curve will shift to the right—ultimately from $SRAS_1$ to $SRAS_2$. The economy will end up at point 3 in long-run equilibrium.

Again, let's examine the changes in the short run and in the long run. As a result of a decrease in aggregate demand, Real GDP falls and the price level falls in the short run. In addition, because Real GDP falls, the unemployment rate rises. In the long run, when the economy is at point 3, it is producing exactly the same level of Real GDP that it was producing originally (Q_N) but at a lower price level.

Conclusion: If the economy is self-regulating, a decrease in aggregate demand can lower the price level and Real GDP in the short run but in the long run, the only effect of a decrease in aggregate demand is a lower price level.

Change in *AD*	In the Short Run,	In the Long Run,
$AD\uparrow$	$P\uparrow$, $Q\uparrow$	$P\uparrow$, Q does not change
$AD\downarrow$	$P\downarrow$, $Q\downarrow$	$P\downarrow$, Q does not change

Let's return to Exhibit 7a to clarify a point about long-run equilibrium. In the exhibit, the economy starts at point 1 in long-run equilibrium and then moves to point 2. At point

exhibit **7**

Changes in a Self-Regulating Economy: Short Run and Long Run

In (a) the economy is initially at point 1 in long-run equilibrium. Aggregate demand rises and the *AD* curve shifts right from AD_1 to AD_2. The economy is at point 2 in the short run, with a higher Real GDP and a higher price level than at point 1. The economy is also in an inflationary gap at point 2. If the economy is self-regulating, wages will soon rise, the *SRAS* curve will shift left from $SRAS_1$ to $SRAS_2$, and the economy will be in long-run equilibrium at point 3. At point 3, the economy is producing the same Real GDP as it did at point 1. In other words, in the long run, an increase in aggregate demand only raises the price level. In (b) the economy is initially at point 1 in long-run equilibrium. Aggregate demand falls and the *AD* curve shifts left from AD_1 to AD_2. The economy is at point 2 in the short run, with a lower Real GDP and a lower price level than at point 1. The economy is also in a recessionary gap. If the economy is self-regulating, wages will soon fall, the *SRAS* curve will shift right from $SRAS_1$ to $SRAS_2$, and the economy will be in long-run equilibrium at point 3. At point 3, the economy is producing the same Real GDP as it did at point 1. In other words, in the long run, a decrease in aggregate demand only lowers the price level.

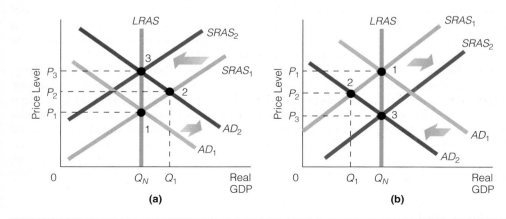

(a)　　　　　　　　(b)

THINKING LIKE AN ECONOMIST

Like other scientists, economists are often interested in knowing whether the phenomena they are studying have a natural resting place. For example, the natural resting place for a ball thrown high into the air is the ground. Gravity pulls the ball downward. Where is the natural resting place for a competitive market? It is where the quantity demanded of a good equals the quantity supplied of the good. Markets are "at rest" when they are in equilibrium.

Macroeconomists want to know if the economy has a natural resting place. Some economists think it does. They think the natural resting place for the economy is where Natural Real GDP is being produced and the natural unemployment rate exists. Economists who believe that the economy can eliminate both recessionary and inflationary gaps smoothly and quickly by itself, and thus return to its natural state, use the analogy of a person's normal body temperature.

When a person's body temperature rises above normal, he has a fever. In most cases, the body itself eliminates the fever in time; that is, the temperature returns to normal. When the person's body temperature is below normal, in most cases this is an aberration and his temperature will edge back up to normal in time. In short, a below-normal temperature and an above-normal temperature are temporary states. Just as the body has a natural resting place—at 98.6 degrees—so does the economy, some economists say. Thinking in terms of a "natural resting place," an "equilibrium," or a "benchmark" is part of some economists' way of thinking. However, not all economists agree on where the natural resting place of the economy is.

2, both the price level and Real GDP are higher than they were at point 1. In other words, if *AD* rises, both the price level and Real GDP rise in the short run. If the economy is self-regulating, it will not remain at point 2. Instead it will move to point 3, where it is again in long-run equilibrium. At point 3, the price level is higher than it was at point 2 but Real GDP is lower. Why, then, don't we say that Real GDP is lower in the long run than it is in the short run instead of saying that Real GDP does not change in the long run? The answer is that the long run is measured from one long-run equilibrium point to another long-run equilibrium point. In terms of Exhibit 7a, we look at the long run by comparing point 1 and point 3. When we make this comparison, we notice two things: The price level is higher at point 3 than at point 1, and Real GDP is the same at both points.

SELF-TEST

1. If the economy is self-regulating, what happens if it is in a recessionary gap?
2. If the economy is self-regulating, what happens if it is in an inflationary gap?
3. If the economy is self-regulating, how do changes in aggregate demand affect the economy in the long run?

A READER ASKS — *Why Don't All Economists Agree?*

According to the text, not all economists believe the economy is self-regulating. Why don't all economists agree on how the economy works?

One reason (but not the only reason) is because economists can't undertake controlled experiments. In a controlled experiment, it is possible to change one variable, leave all other variables unchanged, and then see what happens. Whatever happens must be the result of the one variable you changed.

To illustrate, suppose you want to know whether or not increasing your intake of vitamin C will reduce the number of colds you get in a year. In a controlled experiment, you would increase your intake of vitamin C and everything else in your life would stay the same—the amount of sleep you get each night, the amount of exercise you get, the people you are around, and so on. Then you would observe whether or not you got fewer colds. If you did get fewer colds, then you could be reasonably sure that it was because of your higher intake of vitamin C.

Now let's see what happens in economics because economists cannot run controlled experiments. Suppose Real GDP falls in

February 2003. Economist *A* argues that the decline in Real GDP was due to higher interest rates in July 2002 and not to higher taxes in August 2002. Economist *B* argues just the opposite: the decline in Real GDP was due to higher taxes in August 2002 and not to higher interest rates in July 2002.

Obviously, economist *A* has a theory that states that a change in interest rates affects Real GDP but a change in taxes does not. Economist *B* has a theory that states that a change in taxes affects Real GDP but a change in interest rates does not. It would be nice to test each theory in a controlled environment: change taxes and nothing else, and see what happens; change interest rates and nothing else, and see what happens. You can see that if we could do this, some of the disagreements between economists *A* and *B* are likely to disappear.

Chapter Summary

Say's Law

> Say's law states that supply creates its own demand. All economists believe that Say's law holds in a barter economy. Here, there can be no general overproduction or underproduction of goods. Classical economists believed that Say's law also holds in a money economy. In their view, even if consumption drops and saving rises, economic forces are at work producing an equal and offsetting increase in investment. According to classical economists, interest rates are flexible and equate the amount of saving and investment in an economy.

Classical Economists on Markets, Wages, and Prices

> Classical economists believed that most, if not all, markets are competitive and that wages and prices are flexible.

Three States of the Economy

> Natural Real GDP is the level of Real GDP that is produced when the economy is operating at the natural unemployment rate.
> The economy can be producing a Real GDP level that (1) is equal to Natural Real GDP, (2) is greater than Natural Real GDP, or (3) is less than Natural Real GDP. In other words, the economy can be in (1) long-run equilibrium, (2) an inflationary gap, or (3) a recessionary gap, respectively.
> In long-run equilibrium, the Real GDP that the economy is producing is equal to the Natural Real GDP. The unemployment rate that exists in the economy is equal to the natural unemployment rate, and the labor market is in equilibrium.
> In a recessionary gap, the Real GDP that the economy is producing is less than the Natural Real GDP. The unemployment rate that exists in the economy is greater than the natural unemployment rate, and a surplus exists in the labor market.
> In an inflationary gap, the Real GDP that the economy is producing is greater than the Natural Real GDP. The unemployment rate that exists in the economy is less than the natural unemployment rate, and a shortage exists in the labor market.

The Institutional and Physical Production Possibilities Frontiers

> The physical PPF illustrates different combinations of goods the economy can produce given the physical constraints of (1) finite resources and (2) the current state of technology. The institutional PPF illustrates different combinations of goods the economy can produce given the physical constraints of (1) finite resources, (2) the current state of technology, and (3) any institutional constraints.
> If an economy is operating on its institutional PPF, it is operating at the natural unemployment rate. If it is operating at a point beyond the institutional PPF but below the physical PPF, it is operating at an unemployment rate less than the natural unemployment rate.

The Self-Regulating Economy

> Some economists (classical, new classical, monetarists) contend that the economy can eliminate both recessionary and inflationary gaps smoothly and quickly by itself.
> If the economy is self-regulating and in a recessionary gap, then: The unemployment rate in the economy is greater than the natural unemployment rate, and a surplus exists in the labor market. As old wage contracts expire, wage rates fall. As a result, the SRAS curve shifts to the right and the price level falls. As the price level falls, the quantity demanded of Real GDP rises. Ultimately, the economy will move into long-run equilibrium where it is producing Natural Real GDP.
> If the economy is self-regulating and in an inflationary gap, then: The unemployment rate in the economy is less than the natural unemployment rate, and a shortage exists in the labor market. As old wage contracts expire, wage rates rise. As a result, the SRAS curve shifts to the left and the price level rises. As the price level rises, the quantity demanded of Real GDP falls. Ultimately, the economy will move into long-run equilibrium where it is producing Natural Real GDP.

Key Terms and Concepts

Say's Law
Recessionary Gap
Inflationary Gap
Laissez-faire

Questions and Problems

1. What is the classical economics position with respect to (a) wages, (b) prices, and (c) interest rates?
2. According to classical economists, does Say's law hold in a money economy? Explain your answer.
3. According to classical economists, does an increase in saving shift the AD curve to the left? Explain your answer.
4. What does it mean to say the economy is in a recessionary gap? in an inflationary gap? in long-run equilibrium?

5. Describe the relationship of the (actual) unemployment rate to the natural unemployment rate in each of the following economic states: (a) a recessionary gap, (b) an inflationary gap, and (c) long-run equilibrium.
6. Diagrammatically represent an economy in (a) an inflationary gap, (b) a recessionary gap, and (c) long-run equilibrium.
7. Explain how an economy can operate beyond its institutional PPF but not beyond its physical PPF.
8. According to economists who believe in a self-regulating economy, what happens—step by step—when the economy is in a recessionary gap? What happens when the economy is in an inflationary gap?
9. If wage rates are not flexible, can the economy be self-regulating? Explain your answer.
10. Explain the importance of the real balance effect to long-run (equilibrium) adjustment in the economy.

11. Suppose the economy is self-regulating, the price level is 132, the quantity demanded of Real GDP is $4 trillion, the quantity supplied of Real GDP in the short run is $3.9 trillion, and the quantity supplied of Real GDP in the long run is $4.3 trillion. Is the economy in short-run equilibrium? Will the price level in long-run equilibrium be greater than, less than, or equal to 132? Explain your answers.
12. Suppose the economy is self-regulating, the price level is 110, the quantity demanded of Real GDP is $4 trillion, the quantity supplied of Real GDP in the short run is $4.9 trillion, and the quantity supplied of Real GDP in the long run is $4.1 trillion. Is the economy in short-run equilibrium? Will the price level in long-run equilibrium be greater than, less than, or equal to 110? Explain your answers.

Working With Numbers and Graphs

1. In the following figure, which point is representative of:
   a. The economy on its *LRAS* curve
   b. The economy in a recessionary gap
   c. The economy in an inflationary gap

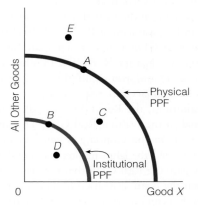

2. In the following figure, which of parts (a)–(c) is consistent with or representative of:

a. The economy operating at the natural unemployment rate
b. A surplus in the labor market
c. A recessionary gap
d. A cyclical unemployment rate of zero

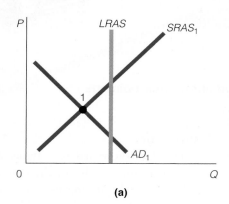

(a)

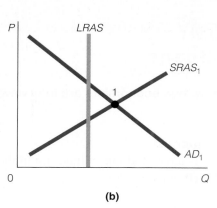

(b)

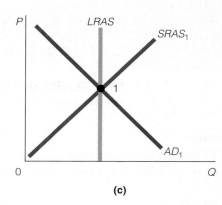

(c)

3. Diagrammatically represent the following:

a. An economy in which AD increases as it is self-regulating out of a recessionary gap
b. An economy in which AD decreases as it is self-regulating out of an inflationary gap

4. Economist Jones believes that there is always sufficient (aggregate) demand in the economy to buy all the goods and services supplied at full employment. Diagrammatically represent what the economy looks like for Jones.

5. Diagrammatically show what happens when the institutional constraints in the economy become less effective.

chapter 7

ECONOMIC INSTABILITY
A CRITIQUE OF THE
SELF-REGULATING ECONOMY

Setting the Scene

© SIE Productions/CORBIS

On a Sunday talk show, two economists are interviewed about their opinions on the economy.

Moderator:
The nation's unemployment rate has just risen. Will it continue to rise?

Economist 1:
I think it will remain where it is for some time. We'll need to stimulate the economy in order to bring down the unemployment rate.

Economist 2:
I disagree. The economy is self-regulating and the unemployment rate will soon begin to fall. There are already a few signs that wages are beginning to decline.

Moderator:
This week in the Congress, various spending proposals were discussed. Some say that enacting these spending proposals will go a long way to raising spending in this country. Do you agree?

Economist 1:
I agree. I think a huge multiplier effect will kick in.

Economist 2:
Again, I would have to disagree. I think the multiplier effect will be rather small.

Moderator:
Well, then, what about the effect of the spending on output and prices? Will the additional spending lead to higher output and higher prices?

Economist 1:
I think it will lead to largely higher output with only a very tiny increase in the price level.

Economist 2:
I think it will lead to almost no change in output and to a significant uptick in the price level.

Moderator:
The data show that the savings rate is beginning to rise in the country. People are beginning to save a large slice of their paychecks. Will this help the economy?

Economist 1:
I'm not so sure it will. When people save more, they spend less, and a decline in overall spending could be hurtful at this time.

Economist 2:
I don't agree. An increase in saving will put downward pressure on interest rates and businesses will invest more at lower interest rates. I don't see saving in as negative a way as my colleague.

How would a third economist look at this interview? Later in the chapter, discussions based on the following questions will help you analyze the scene the way an economist would.

- Why do the two economists disagree over the predicted change in the unemployment rate?
- Why do the two economists disagree over the predicted change in spending?
- Why do the two economists disagree over the predicted change in output (Real GDP) and the price level?
- Why do the two economists disagree over the effect on spending of a rise in savings?

QUESTIONING THE CLASSICAL POSITION

John Maynard Keynes, the English economist, changed the way many economists viewed the economy. Keynes's major work, *The General Theory of Employment, Income and Money,* was published in 1936. Just prior to its publication, the Great Depression had plagued many countries of the world. Looking around at the world during that time, one had to wonder if the classical view of the economy wasn't wrong. After all, unemployment was sky high in many countries and numerous economies had been contracting. Where was Say's law with its promise that there would not be general gluts? Where was the self-regulating economy healing itself of its depression illness? Where was full employment? And given the depressed state of the economy, could anyone any longer believe that laissez-faire was the right policy stance?

© Hulton-Deutsch Collection/CORBIS

With the Great Depression as recent history, Keynes and the Keynesians thought that while their theory may not be right with respect to every detail, there certainly was enough evidence to say that the classical view of the economy was wrong.

Keynes challenged all four of the following beliefs on which the classical position of the economy was based: (1) Say's law holds, so insufficient demand in the economy is unlikely. (2) Wages, prices, and interest rates are flexible. (3) The economy is self-regulating. (4) Laissez-faire is the right and sensible economic policy to implement.

Keynes's Criticism of Say's Law in a Money Economy

Let's review the position expressed by classical economists on Say's law in a money economy. According to classical economists, if consumption spending fell because saving increased, then total spending would not fall because the added saving would simply bring about more investment spending. This would happen through changes in the interest rate. The added saving would put downward pressure on the interest rate, and at a lower interest rate, businesses would borrow and invest more. Through changes in the interest rate, the amount of saving would always equal the amount invested.

Keynes disagreed. He didn't think that added saving would necessarily stimulate an equal amount of added investment spending. Exhibit 1 illustrates Keynes's point of view.

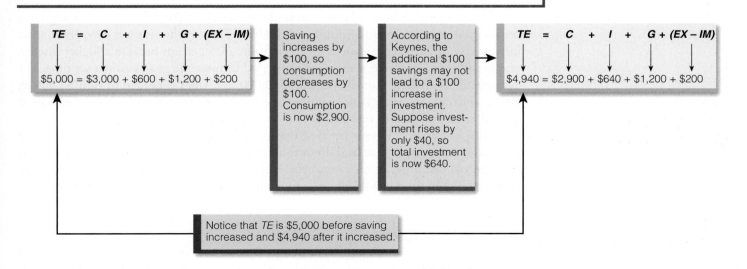

$$TE = C + I + G + (EX - IM)$$

$$\$5{,}000 = \$3{,}000 + \$600 + \$1{,}200 + \$200$$

Saving increases by $100, so consumption decreases by $100. Consumption is now $2,900.

According to Keynes, the additional $100 savings may not lead to a $100 increase in investment. Suppose investment rises by only $40, so total investment is now $640.

$$TE = C + I + G + (EX - IM)$$

$$\$4{,}940 = \$2{,}900 + \$640 + \$1{,}200 + \$200$$

Notice that *TE* is $5,000 before saving increased and $4,940 after it increased.

As in the last chapter, we let consumption = $3,000, investment = $600, government purchases = $1,200, and net exports = $200. Then saving increases by $100, which lowers consumption to $2,900. According to the classical economists, investment rose by $100 at the same time, going from $600 to $700. Keynes asked: What guarantee is there that an increase in saving will be equally matched by an increase in investment? What if saving rises by $100 (which means consumption goes down by $100), but investment rises by, say, only $40 (instead of $100)? In this situation, the equation $TE = C + I + G + (EX - IM)$ changes from

$$TE = \$3,000 + \$600 + \$1,200 + \$200$$
$$= \$5,000$$

to:

$$TE = \$2,900 + \$640 + \$1,200 + \$200$$
$$= \$4,940$$

Thus, total expenditures decrease from $5,000 to $4,940. And if, at a given price level, total spending falls, so will aggregate demand. In other words, according to Keynes, it was possible for saving to increase and aggregate demand to fall.

Of course, a classical economist would retort that, as a result of a $100 increase in saving, interest rates would fall enough to guarantee that investment would increase by $100. But Keynes countered by saying that individuals save and invest for a host of reasons and that no single factor, such as the interest rate, links these activities.

Furthermore, Keynes believed that saving is more responsive to changes in income than to changes in the interest rate and that investment is more responsive to technological changes, business expectations, and innovations than to changes in the interest rate. In summary, whereas the classical economists believed that saving and investment depend on the interest rate, Keynes believed that both saving and investment depend on a number of factors that may be far more influential than the interest rate.

Consider the difference between Keynes and the classical economists on saving. As noted earlier, the classical economists held that saving is directly related to the interest rate: As the interest rate goes up, saving rises; as the interest rate goes down, saving falls, *ceteris paribus.*

Keynes thought this might not always be true. Suppose individuals are saving for a certain goal—say, a retirement fund of $100,000. They might save less per period at an interest rate of 12 percent than at an interest rate of 5 percent because a higher interest rate means that less saving is required per period to meet the goal within a set time. For example, if the interest rate is 5 percent, $50,000 in savings is needed to earn $2,500 in interest income per year. If the interest rate is 10 percent, only $25,000 in savings is needed to earn $2,500 in interest.

As to investment, Keynes believed that the interest rate is important in determining the level of investment, but he did not think it is as important as other variables, such as the expected rate of profit on investment. Keynes argued that if business expectations are pessimistic, then there is unlikely to be much investment, regardless of how low the interest rate is.

Keynes on Wage Rates

In the last chapter, we state that if the unemployment rate in the economy is greater than the natural unemployment rate, a surplus exists in the labor market: the number of job

Question from Setting the Scene: Why do the two economists disagree over the effect on spending of a rise in savings?

Economist 1 believes an increase in saving may lead to a decline in total spending, and Economist 2 believes an increase in saving will not lead to a decline in total spending. What is at the heart of their difference? Economist 1 may believe that although an increase in saving will lead to a decline in the interest rate, investment spending is not responsive to the lower interest rate at this time. Economist 2 may believe the opposite: As saving rises, downward pressure on the interest rate will cause businesses to invest more at the lower interest rate, thus offsetting the decline in household spending.

seekers is high relative to the number of jobs available. Consequently, according to classical economists, wage rates will fall.

Keynes didn't believe the adjustment was so simple. Instead, he said, employees will naturally resist an employer's efforts to cut wages. Similarly, labor unions may resist wage cuts. In short, wage rates may be inflexible in a downward direction.

Suppose Keynes is correct and wage rates won't fall. Does this mean that if the economy is in a recessionary gap, it can't get itself out? The unequivocal answer is yes. If employee and labor union resistance prevent wage rates from falling, then the *SRAS* curve will not shift to the right. If the *SRAS* curve doesn't shift to the right, the price level won't come down. If the price level doesn't come down, buyers will not purchase more goods and services and remove the economy from a recessionary gap. In terms of Exhibit 2, the economy is stuck at point 1. It cannot get to point 2.

In summary, Keynes believed that the economy was inherently unstable—it may not automatically cure itself of a recessionary gap. It may not be self-regulating.

New Keynesians and Wage Rates

Many economists criticized early versions of the Keynesian theory on the ground that it didn't offer a rigorous and complete explanation for inflexible wages. Some of the later versions—put forth by New Keynesian economists—made up for this deficiency by

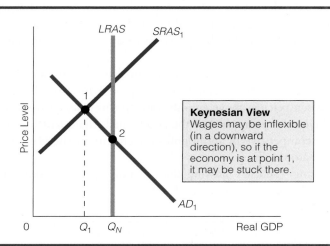

exhibit 2

The Economy Gets "Stuck" in a Recessionary Gap

If the economy is in a recessionary gap at point 1, Keynes held that wage rates may not fall. The economy may be stuck in the recessionary gap.

Keynesian View
Wages may be inflexible (in a downward direction), so if the economy is at point 1, it may be stuck there.

focusing on, among other things, long-term contracts and efficiency reasons for firms paying higher-than-market wages.

For example, New Keynesians argue that long-term labor contracts are often advantageous for both employers and workers. Firms may perceive such benefits as (1) fewer labor negotiations (labor negotiations can be costly) and (2) a decreased likelihood of worker strikes (the firms avoid strikes during the time of the contract). Workers may perceive such benefits as (1) fewer strikes (which can be costly for them too) and (2) the sense of security long-term contracts provide.

Long-term contracts have costs as well as benefits for both firms and workers, but some economists believe that in many instances the benefits outweigh the costs and that firms and workers enter into the long-term contracts for mutually advantageous reasons. When they do, wage rates are "locked in" for the period of the contract and therefore cannot adjust downward. As a result, the economy may get stuck at point 1 in Exhibit 2 for a long time and experience high levels of unemployment for many years.

Efficiency Wage Models
These models hold that it is sometimes in the best interest of business firms to pay their employees higher-than-equilibrium wage rates.

As another example, New Keynesian economists who work with **efficiency wage models** believe there are solid microeconomic reasons for inflexible wages. They argue that firms sometimes find it in their best interest to pay wage rates above market-clearing levels. According to efficiency wage models, labor productivity depends on the wage rate the firm pays its employees. Specifically, a cut in wages can cause labor productivity to decline, which, in turn, raises the firm's costs. (Basically, these models say that you are more productive when you are paid a higher wage than when you are paid a lower wage.) By paying a higher-than-market wage, firms provide an incentive to workers to be productive and do less shirking, among other things. If shirking declines, so do the monitoring (management) costs of the firm.

The economist Robert Solow has argued that "the most interesting and important line of work in current macroeconomic theory is the attempt to reconstruct plausible microeconomic underpinnings for a recognizably Keynesian macroeconomics."[1] Many Keynesian economists believe efficiency wage models can perform this task. They believe these models provide a solid microeconomic explanation for inflexible wages and thus are capable of explaining why continuing unemployment problems exist in some economies.

Keynes on Prices

Again, think back to the process classical economists (among others) believe occurs when a recessionary gap exists. Wage rates fall, the *SRAS* curve shifts to the right, and the price level begins to decrease . . . Now stop right there! Notice that we said ". . . and the price level begins to decrease." This phrase tells us that classical economists believe that prices in the economy are flexible: they move up and down in response to market forces.

Keynes said that the internal structure of an economy is not always competitive enough to allow prices to fall. Recall from Chapter 3 how the forces of supply and demand operate when price is above equilibrium. In this case, a surplus is generated and price falls until the quantity supplied of the good equals the quantity demanded. Keynes suggested that anticompetitive or monopolistic elements in the economy would sometimes prevent price from falling.

Before continuing, use the following chart to quickly review some of the differences in the views of the classical economists and Keynes.

---

1. Robert Solow, "Another Possible Source of Wage Stickiness," in *Efficiency Wage Models of the Labor Market*, ed. George Akerlof and Janet Yellen (Cambridge: Cambridge University Press, 1986), 41.

	Classical Economists	Keynes
Say's Law	Holds in a money economy. In other words, all output produced will be demanded.	May not hold in a money economy. In other words, more output may be produced than will be demanded.
Savings	Amount saved and interest rate are directly related. Savers save more at higher interest rates and save less at lower interest rates.	Savers may not save more at higher interest rates or save less at lower interest rates. If savers have a savings goal in mind, then a higher interest rate means savers can save less and still reach their goal.
Investment	Amount invested is inversely related to interest rate. Businesses invest more at lower interest rates and invest less at higher interest rates.	If expectations are pessimistic, a lower interest rate may not stimulate additional investment.
Wages	Flexible	May be inflexible downward
Prices	Flexible	May be inflexible downward

Is It a Question of the Time It Takes for Wages and Prices to Adjust?

Classical economists believed that both wages and prices are flexible and adjust downward in a recessionary gap. Keynes, however, suggested that wages and prices are not flexible (in a downward direction) and may not adjust downward in a recessionary gap.

Many economists today take a position somewhere between Keynes and the classical economists. For them, the question is not whether wages and prices are flexible downward, but *how long it takes for wages and prices to adjust downward.*

Consider Exhibit 3. Suppose the economy is currently in a recessionary gap at point 1. The relevant short-run aggregate supply curve is $SRAS_1$, where the wage rate is $10 per hour and the price level is P_1. Now classical economists said the wage rate and price level would fall, while Keynes said this may not happen.

Did Keynes mean that if the economy is in a recessionary gap, *the wage rate will never fall and the price level will never adjust downward?* Most economists think not. The question is *how long* the wage rate and price level will take to fall. Will they fall in just a few weeks? Will they fall in a few months? Or will they take five years to fall? The question is relevant because the answer determines how long an economy will be in a recessionary gap, and thus how long the economy takes to self-regulate.

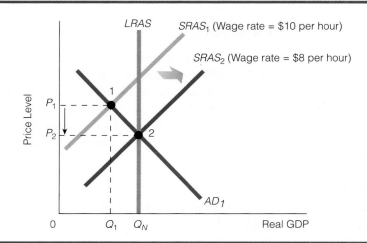

exhibit **3**

A Question of How Long It Takes for Wage Rates and Prices to Fall
Suppose the economy is in a recessionary gap at point 1. Wage rates are $10 per hour, and the price level is P_1. The issue may not be whether wage rates and the price level fall, but how long they take to reach long-run levels. If they take a short time, then classical economists are right: the economy is self-regulating. If they take a long time—perhaps years—then Keynes is right: the economy is not self-regulating over any reasonable period of time.

Let's look at things this way: If it takes only a few weeks or months for wage rates to fall (say, to $8 an hour) and shift the short-run aggregate supply curve from $SRAS_1$ to $SRAS_2$ and for the price level to fall from P_1 to P_2, then for all practical matters the economy is almost instantaneously self-regulating. But if it takes years for this to happen, the economy can hardly be considered self-regulating over any reasonable amount of time.

The classical position is that the time required before wages and prices adjust downward is short enough to call the economy self-regulating. The Keynesian position is that the time is long enough to say that the economy is not self-regulating. Instead, the Keynesians believe that the economy is inherently unstable: it can exist in a recessionary gap for a long time.

ANALYZING THE SCENE

Question from Setting the Scene: Why do the two economists disagree over the predicted change in the unemployment rate?
Economist 1 believes the unemployment rate will remain at its current level unless something is done. Economist 2 believes the unemployment rate will soon decline. He says that wages are already beginning to fall. Economist 1 probably believes that the economy is not self-regulating and that the economy is stuck in a recessionary gap. Either that, or he believes that wages and prices are not likely to come down any time soon so the "self-regulating" property of the economy isn't likely to be operable any time soon. Economist 2 seems to believe that lower wages will shift the $SRAS$ curve rightward, lowering the price level, and thus move the economy out of a recessionary gap. As the economy comes out of a recessionary gap, the unemployment rate will decline. In short, Economist 2 believes the economy is self-regulating (at Natural Real GDP) and Economist 1 does not.

SELF-TEST *(Answers to Self-Test questions are in the Self-Test Appendix.)*

1. What do Keynesians mean when they say the economy is inherently unstable?
2. "What matters is not whether the economy is self-regulating or not, but whether prices and wages are flexible and adjust quickly." Comment.
3. According to Keynes, why might aggregate demand be too low?

THE SIMPLE KEYNESIAN MODEL

Economists build models and theories for the purpose of better understanding the economic world. An economics student will find many models and theories in economics. We have already discussed a few in this book—the theory of supply and demand, the theory of comparative advantage, and the classical theory on interest rates.

We turn now to a prominent macroeconomics model—the simple Keynesian model. In this section, we identify and discuss a few of the key components and themes of the model.

Assumptions

In the simple Keynesian model, certain simplifying assumptions hold. First, the price level is assumed to be constant until the economy reaches its full-employment or Natural Real GDP level.

Second, there is no foreign sector. In other words, the model is representative of a *closed economy*, not an *open economy*. It follows that total spending in the economy is the sum of consumption, investment, and government purchases.

Third, the monetary side of the economy is excluded.

The Consumption Function

Although Keynes was interested in the level of total spending in general, he was particularly concerned about consumption. Consumption (C) was of major concern because it is by far the largest slice of the total spending pie.

Keynes made three basic points about consumption:

1. Consumption depends on disposable income. (Disposable income is income minus taxes.)
2. Consumption and disposable income move in the same direction.
3. When disposable income changes, consumption changes by less.

These three points make a specific statement about the relationship between consumption and disposable income. The statement specifying this relationship is called the **consumption function.** We can write the consumption function as:

$$C = C_0 + (MPC)(Y_d)$$

To understand the consumption function, you need to know what the variables represent. You know that C is consumption, and we use Y_d to specify disposable income. Let's look at MPC and C_0.

MPC stands for **marginal propensity to consume,** which is the ratio of the change in consumption to the change in disposable income:

Marginal propensity to consume = Change in consumption/Change in disposable income
$$MPC = \Delta C/\Delta Y_d$$

The symbol Δ stands for "change in." Thus, the MPC is equal to the change in consumption divided by the change in disposable income. To illustrate, suppose consumption rises from $800 to $900 as disposable income rises from $1,000 to $1,200. If we divide the change in consumption, which is $100, by the change in disposable income, which is $200, we see that the MPC equals 0.50. (Notice that the MPC is always a positive number between zero and one because of Keynes's points 2 and 3 above.)

C_0 is **autonomous consumption.** Autonomous consumption does not change as disposable income changes; it changes due to factors other than disposable income. Think of consumption (as specified by the consumption function) as being made up of two parts. One part—the C_0 part—which is independent of disposable income, is called *autonomous consumption.* The second part—the $MPC(Y_d)$ part—which depends on disposable income, is called *induced consumption.*

The difference between autonomous consumption and induced consumption can be illustrated by example. Suppose your taxes are lowered; consequently, your disposable income rises. With more disposable income, you buy more goods and services (entertainment, books, DVDs). The increase in disposable income has *induced* you to consume more, hence the name *induced consumption.* Next, suppose your disposable income has not changed but, for some reason, you are consuming more. You might be consuming more medicine because you have recently become ill, or you might be consuming more car maintenance services because your car recently broke down. In short, you are consuming more of various goods and services even though your disposable income has not changed at all.

Consumption Function
The relationship between consumption and disposable income. In the consumption function used here, consumption is directly related to disposable income and is positive even at zero disposable income: $C = C_0 + (MPC)(Y_d)$.

Marginal Propensity to Consume (MPC)
The ratio of the change in consumption to the change in disposable income: $MPC = \Delta C/\Delta Y_d$.

Autonomous Consumption
The part of consumption that is independent of disposable income.

This type of consumption is autonomous (independent) of disposable income, hence the name *autonomous consumption.*

Now, let's look again at the consumption function:

Consumption = Autonomous consumption
+ (Marginal propensity to consume)(Disposable income)

$$C = C_0 + (MPC)(Y_d)$$

Suppose $C_0 = \$800$, $MPC = 0.80$, and $Y_d = \$1,500$. By substituting these numbers into the consumption function, we find that $C = \$800 + (0.80)(\$1,500) = \$800 + \$1,200 = \$2,000$.

What will cause an increase in consumption? Consumption, C, will increase if any of the variables, C_0, MPC, or Y_d, increases. Thus, C can be increased in three ways:

1. **Raise autonomous consumption.** Suppose in our example that autonomous consumption, C_0, goes from $800 to $1,000. This would raise consumption to $2,200: $C = \$1,000 + (0.80)(\$1,500) = \$2,200$.
2. **Raise disposable income.** Suppose disposable income, Y_d, goes from $1,500 to $1,800. This would raise consumption to $2,240: $C = \$800 + (0.80)(\$1,800) = \$2,240$. This increase in consumption from $2,000 to $2,240 is due to an increase of $240 in induced consumption. Specifically, the increased consumption was induced by an increase in disposable income.
3. **Raise the *MPC.*** Suppose the *MPC* rises to 0.90. This would raise consumption to $2,150: $C = \$800 + (0.90)(\$1,500) = \$2,150$.

In Exhibit 4, we set C_0 equal to $200 billion and the *MPC* equal to 0.80; thus, $C = \$200$ billion $+ (0.8)(Y_d)$. We then calculated different levels of consumption (column 3) for different levels of disposable income (column 1).

Consumption and Saving

In Exhibit 4, we also calculated the saving levels (column 5) at the different disposable income levels. How did we calculate this? We know that $C = C_0 + (MPC)(Y_d)$, and we also know that households can only consume or save. So it follows that saving, S, is the difference between disposable income and consumption:

Saving = Disposable Income − Consumption
= Disposable Income − [Autonomous consumption
+ (Marginal propensity to consume)(Disposable income)]

$$S = Y_d - [C_0 + (MPC)(Y_d)].$$

<table>
<tr><td>exhibit 4</td></tr>
</table>

Consumption and Saving at Different Levels of Disposable Income (in billions)
Our consumption function is $C = C_0 + (MPC)(Y_d)$, where C_0 has been set at $200 billion and $MPC = 0.80$. Saving is the difference between Y_d and C: $S = Y_d - [C_0 + (MPC)(Y_d)]$. All dollar amounts are in billions.

(1) Disposable Income Y_d	(2) Change in Disposable Income ΔY_d	(3) Consumption $C = C_0 + (MPC)(Y_d)$	(4) Change in Consumption	(5) Saving $S = Y_d - [C_0 + (MPC)(Y_d)]$	(6) Change in Saving
$ 800	$___	$ 840	$___	−$40	$___
1,000	200	1,000	160	0	40
1,200	200	1,160	160	40	40
1,400	200	1,320	160	80	40
1,600	200	1,480	160	120	40
1,800	200	1,640	160	160	40

The **marginal propensity to save (MPS)** is the ratio of the change in saving to the change in disposable income:

Marginal Propensity to Save
(MPS)
The ratio of the change in saving to the change in disposable income: $MPS = \Delta S/\Delta Y_d$.

$$\text{Marginal propensity to save} = \text{Change in saving/Change in disposable income}$$
$$MPS = \Delta S/\Delta Y_d$$

Disposable income can be used only for consumption or saving, that is, $C + S = Y_d$. So, any change to disposable income can only change consumption or saving. It follows that the marginal propensity to consume (*MPC*) plus the marginal propensity to save (*MPS*) must equal 1.

$$\text{Marginal propensity to consume} + \text{Marginal propensity to save} = 1$$
$$MPC + MPS = 1$$

In Exhibit 4, the *MPC* is 0.80, so the *MPS* is 0.20.

The Multiplier

We know from the consumption function that a rise in autonomous consumption (C_0) will raise consumption (C) and, in turn, raise total spending. But, *how much* will total spending rise? If C_0 rises by $40 billion, will total spending rise by $40 billion? According to Keynes, total spending would not rise by $40 billion in this case. The rise in C_0 will act as a catalyst to additional spending, and total spending will rise by *more than* $40 billion.

Let's illustrate with a simple example. Suppose there are 10 people in the economy, represented by the letters A–J. Person *A* increases his autonomous consumption—specifically, he buys $40 more additional goods from person *B*. Now person *B* has witnessed an increase in his income; his income has risen by $40. According to Keynes, person *B* will spend some fraction of this additional income. How much he spends depends on his marginal propensity to consume (*MPC*). If his *MPC* is 0.80, then he will spend 80 percent of $40 or $32. Let's say he spends this additional $32 on goods he purchases from person *C*. Thus, person *C*'s income rises by $32, and now she will spend some percentage of this additional income. Again, how much she will spend of the additional income depends on her *MPC*. If we again assume that the *MPC* is 0.80, then person *C* spends $25.60.

> Person A increases his *autonomous consumption* by $40 →
> This generates $40 *additional income* for person B →
> Person B increases his *consumption* by $32 →
> This generates $32 *additional income* for person C →
> Person C increases her *consumption* by $25.60 →
> And so on and so on.

The process whereby an initial rise in autonomous consumption leads to a rise in consumption for one person, generating additional income for another person, and leading to additional consumption spending by that person, and so on and so on is called the *multiplier process*.

Suppose we sum the initial rise in autonomous spending ($40) and all the additional spending it generated through the multiplier process. When the multiplier process ends, how much additional spending will have been generated? In other words, by how much will total expenditures rise?

Multiplier
The number that is multiplied by the change in autonomous spending to obtain the overall change in total spending. The multiplier (m) is equal to $1/(1 - MPC)$. If the economy is operating below Natural Real GDP, then the multiplier turns out to be the number that is multiplied by the change in autonomous spending to obtain the change in Real GDP.

The answer depends on the value of the multiplier. The **multiplier** (m) is equal to 1 divided by $1 - MPC$.

$$\text{Multiplier } (m) = \frac{1}{1 - MPC}$$

For example, if the $MPC = 0.80$ (in each round of spending), then the multiplier equals 5:

$$\text{Multiplier } (m) = \frac{1}{1 - MPC}$$
$$= \frac{1}{1 - 0.80}$$
$$= \frac{1}{0.20}$$
$$= 5$$

Our original increase in autonomous consumption ($40) multiplied by the multiplier (5) equals $200. So in our example, a $40 increase in autonomous consumption would increase total spending $200.

Just as consumption has an autonomous spending component, so do investment and government purchases. The multiplier process holds for these sectors too. The process also holds for a decrease in autonomous spending by one of the sectors of total spending. So, in general,

Change in total spending = Multiplier × Change in autonomous spending

To illustrate, suppose many business owners become optimistic about the future of the economy. They believe that members of the household and government sectors will soon start buying more goods and services. In expectation of "better times," businesses buy more factories and capital goods and so investment spending rises. Investment spending has risen even though there has been no change in income or Real GDP; hence, the rise is in autonomous investment spending. According to the multiplier analysis, this additional autonomous investment spending will change total spending by some multiple. For example, if the multiplier is 5, then a $1 increase in autonomous investment will raise total spending by $5.

ANALYZING THE SCENE

Question from Setting the Scene: Why do the two economists disagree over the predicted change in spending?
Economist 1 believes that an initial rise in (autonomous) spending will lead to a large change in total spending, and Economist 2 believes it will not. What is at the heart of their disagreement? It could be that the two economists disagree on the current value of the marginal propensity to consume (*MPC*). The higher the *MPC*, the larger the multiplier and the larger the increase in total spending given an initial rise in autonomous spending. To illustrate, suppose Economist 1 believes the *MPC* is 0.80 and Economist 2 believes the *MPC* is 0.40. For Economist 1, the multiplier is 5, but for Economist 2, it is 1.67. This means Economist 1 believes that an increase in autonomous spending of $1 will end up increasing total spending by $5 and Economist 2 believes that an increase in autonomous spending of $1 will end up increasing total spending by $1.67.

© Myrleen Ferguson Cate/Photo Edit

The Multiplier Goes on Spring Break

During the week-long spring break, many college students put away their books, pack their shorts, swimsuits, and tanning oil, jump into their cars, and head for the beaches. As they are driving to Fort Lauderdale, Galveston, Myrtle Beach, Daytona Beach, San Diego, and other coastal cities, the multiplier is getting ready to go to work.

Look at it this way. When college students from around the country head for, say, Daytona Beach, they have dollars in their pockets. They will spend many of these dollars in Daytona Beach—on food and drink, motel rooms, dance clubs, and so on. As far as Daytona Beach is concerned, those dollars represent autonomous spending. More importantly, those dollars can raise the total income of Daytona Beach by some multiple of itself. College students buy pizzas, beer, and sodas. The people who sell these items find their

incomes rising. They, in turn, spend some fraction of their increase in income, which generates additional income for still others, who spend some fraction of their increase in income, and so on and so on.

Let's take a hypothetical example. Suppose college students spend $7 million in Daytona Beach during spring break. If the *MPC* is, say, 0.60 in Daytona Beach and all the added income generated is spent in Daytona Beach, then college students will increase (nominal) income in Daytona Beach by $17.5 million.

Do the people who live in Daytona Beach want college students to visit their city during spring break? Many of them do because it means extra dollars in their pockets. College students from out of town, together with the multiplier, often make for robust economic times!

The Multiplier and Reality

We have discussed the multiplier in simple terms: A change in autonomous spending leads to a *greater change* in total spending. Also, in the simple Keynesian model, the change in total spending is *equal to* the change in Real GDP (assuming the economy is operating below Natural Real GDP). That's because prices in the model are assumed to be constant until Natural GDP is reached; so any change in (nominal) total spending is equal to the change in *real* total spending.

We must note two points, however. First, the multiplier takes time to have an effect. In a textbook, it takes only seconds to go from an initial increase in autonomous spending to a multiple increase in either total spending or Real GDP. In the real world, this process takes many months.

Second, for the multiplier to increase Real GDP, *idle resources must exist at each spending round.* After all, if Real GDP is increasing (output is increasing) at each spending round, *idle resources must be available to be brought into production.* If this were not the case, then increased spending would simply result in higher prices without an increase in Real GDP. Simply put, there would be an increase in GDP but not in Real GDP.

SELF-TEST

1. How is autonomous consumption different from consumption?
2. If the *MPC* is 0.70, what does the multiplier equal?

THE SIMPLE KEYNESIAN MODEL IN THE *AD-AS* FRAMEWORK

The first section of this chapter presents a few of Keynes's criticisms of the self-regulating economy or classical position. The second section identifies and discusses some of the key components of the simple Keynesian model—in particular the consumption function and the multiplier. In this section, we analyze the simple Keynesian model in terms of the aggregate demand and aggregate supply (*AD-AS*) framework. In the next section, we discuss the simple Keynesian model in terms of the total expenditures and total production (*TE-TP*) framework.[2]

SHIFTS IN THE AGGREGATE DEMAND CURVE

Because there is no foreign sector in the simple Keynesian model, total spending consists of consumption (C), investment (I), and government purchases (G). Because there is no monetary side of the economy, it follows that changes in any of these variables (C, I, G) can shift the *AD* curve. For example, a rise in consumption will shift the *AD* curve to the right; a decrease in investment will shift the *AD* curve to the left.

Now let's consider aggregate demand in terms of what we know about the consumption function and the multiplier. We know that a rise in autonomous consumption (C_0) will raise consumption (C) and therefore shift the *AD* curve to the right.

$$C_0\uparrow \rightarrow C\uparrow \rightarrow AD\uparrow$$

How much the *AD* curve will shift due to the rise in autonomous consumption depends on the multiplier. Recall our earlier example in which autonomous consumption C_0 increases $40 and the multiplier ($m$) is 5.

$$\text{Change in total spending} = \text{Multiplier} \times \text{Change in autonomous spending}$$
$$= m \times \Delta C_0$$
$$= 5 \times \$40$$
$$= \$200$$

Exhibit 5 illustrates how the *AD* curve shifts in this situation. We start with the original aggregate demand curve AD_1. Now, autonomous consumption (C_0) rises by $40. This shifts the aggregate demand curve to AD_1'. Does the *AD* curve stay here? No. Because of the multiplier, the initial autonomous consumption spending generates more spending, eventually pushing the *AD* curve to AD_2. In other words, at the end of the process, the *AD* curve has shifted from AD_1 to AD_2. Part of this shift ($40) is due to the initial rise in autonomous consumption and part of this shift ($160) is due to the multiplier.

The Keynesian Aggregate Supply Curve

Earlier we note that in the simple Keynesian model "the price level is assumed to be constant until it reaches its full-employment or Natural Real GDP level." What does this tell us about the Keynesian aggregate supply curve?

Think back to the discussions of aggregate demand and aggregate supply in the last two chapters and in the first section of this chapter. In these discussions, the *AD* curve is downward-sloping and the *SRAS* curve is upward-sloping. Given that the *SRAS* curve is upward-sloping, any shift in the *AD* curve (rightward or leftward) will automatically

---

2. Some instructors may choose to assign only one of these two sections. It is clear at the end of the chapter which questions and problems go with which sections of this chapter.

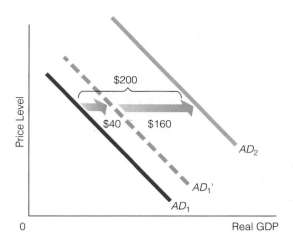

exhibit 5

The Multiplier and Aggregate Demand
An initial increase in autonomous consumption raises total spending and shifts the aggregate demand curve from AD_1 to AD_1'. The AD curve does not remain here, however. Because of the multiplier, the increase in autonomous spending generates additional income and additional spending, shifting the aggregate demand curve to AD_2.

change (raise or lower) the price level. If the price level is assumed to be constant, then the Keynesian aggregate supply curve must have a horizontal section to it.

As shown in Exhibit 6, the Keynesian aggregate supply curve (outlined in this chapter and implicit in the simple Keynesian model) has both a horizontal section and a vertical section. The aggregate supply curve is horizontal until Q_N or Natural Real GDP because the simple Keynesian model assumes the price level is constant until Q_N is reached. With this AS curve, what happens in the economy when the AD curve shifts?

An increase in aggregate demand from AD_1 to AD_2 raises Real GDP from Q_1 to Q_2, but does not change the price level. (The price level remains at P_1). On the other hand, once the economy has reached Q_N, any increases in aggregate demand do change the price level. For example, an increase in aggregate demand from AD_3 to AD_4 raises the price level from P_2 to P_3.

According to Keynes, a change in autonomous spending (such as a change in autonomous consumption) will stimulate additional spending in the economy. In our example, a rise in autonomous consumption of $40 generated an additional $160 worth of spending so that total spending increased by $200. (The multiplier was 5 because we assumed the MPC was 0.80.)

Consider this question: Under what condition will a $200 *increase in total spending* lead to a $200 *increase in Real GDP?* The answer is when the aggregate supply curve is

ANALYZING THE SCENE

Question from Setting the Scene: Why do the two economists disagree over the predicted change in output (Real GDP) and the price level?
Economist 1 believes the additional spending in the economy will lead to a large change in output and almost no change in the price level. Economist 2 believes the additional spending in the economy will lead to almost no change in output and to a substantial change in the price level. What is at the heart of their difference? Economist 1 views the increased spending as occurring within the horizontal section of the Keynesian aggregate supply (AS) curve. After all, if aggregate demand rises within the horizontal section of the AS curve, Real GDP will rise but the price level will not. Economist 2 views the increased spending as occurring within the vertical section of the Keynesian AS curve. In this case, a rise in aggregate demand leaves Real GDP unchanged but raises the price level.

The *AS* Curve in the Simple Keynesian Model

The *AS* curve in the simple Keynesian model is horizontal until Q_N (Natural Real GDP) and vertical at Q_N. It follows that any changes in aggregate demand in the horizontal section do not change the price level but any changes in aggregate demand in the vertical section do change the price level.

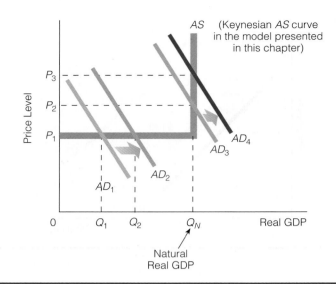

horizontal, which means (in the simple Keynesian model) when the economy is currently producing less than Natural Real GDP. In other words, the *AD* curve in the economy must be shifting rightward (due to the increased spending) but must be within the *horizontal section* of the Keynesian *AS* curve.

The Economy in a Recessionary Gap

According to classical and other economists, the economy is self-regulating. A recessionary gap or an inflationary gap is only a temporary state of affairs. In time, the economy moves into long-run equilibrium and produces Natural Real GDP (Q_N).

Keynes did not believe that the economy always works this way. He believed the economy could get stuck in a recessionary gap. As shown in Exhibit 7, this means the economy could be stuck at Q_1 (its equilibrium position) and be unable to get to Q_N on its own. In other words, the economy is at point *A* and it is not able to get to point *B*. Keynes believed that the private sector—consisting of the household sector and business sector—may not be able to move the economy from point *A* to point *B*. Stated differently, neither consumption nor investment would rise enough to shift the aggregate demand from its current position (AD_1).

But suppose the interest rate in the economy falls. Won't this be enough to get businesses to invest more and thus won't the *AD* curve begin to shift rightward, headed for point *B?* Not necessarily said Keynes. Remember, Keynes didn't always believe that investment spending was responsive to changes in interest rates. For example, suppose businesses are pessimistic about future sales and the interest rate drops. Are businesses going to invest more just because interest rates have dropped, or might their pessimistic expectations of future sales be so strong that they don't invest more at the lower interest rate? Keynes believed that the latter scenario could be the case.

Government's Role in the Economy

In the self-regulating economy of the classical economists, government did not have a management role to play in the economy. The private sector (households and businesses) was capable of self-regulating the economy at its Natural Real GDP level.

Keynes believed the economy was not self-regulating, that economic instability was a possibility. In other words, it was possible for the economy to get stuck in a recessionary gap.

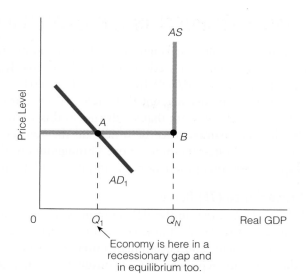

AS

Price Level

A

B

AD_1

0   Q_1 Q_N Real GDP

Economy is here in a
recessionary gap and
in equilibrium too.

exhibit 7

Can the Private Sector Remove the Economy From a Recessionary Gap?
The economy is at point A producing Q_1. Q_1 is less than Q_N, so the economy is in a recessionary gap. The question is whether the private sector (consisting of consumption and investment spending) can remove the economy from the recessionary gap by increasing spending enough to shift the aggregate demand curve rightward to go through point B. Keynes believed that sometimes it could not. No matter how low interest rates fell, investment spending would not rise because of pessimistic business expectations with respect to future sales.

Economic instability opens the door to government playing a role in the economy. According to Keynes, and to many Keynesians, if the private sector cannot self-regulate the economy at its Natural Real GDP level, then maybe it is incumbent for the government to help. In terms of Exhibit 7, maybe the government has a role to play in shifting the AD curve rightward so that it goes through point B. We discuss the role government might play in the economy in a later chapter.

THINKING LIKE AN ECONOMIST

An economist's view of the economy and his policy suggestions are often linked. For example, classical economists and their modern-day counterparts, who view the economy as inherently stable, believe in a policy of laissez-faire: Government should keep its hands off the economy. Keynesians, however, who view the economy as inherently unstable, suggest that government has an economic role to play. In short, policy suggestions are sometimes a consequence of how one views the internal or inherent workings of an economy.

The Theme of the Simple Keynesian Model

As portrayed in terms of AD and AS, the essence of the simple Keynesian model is:

1. The price level is constant until Natural Real GDP is reached.
2. The AD curve shifts if there are changes in C, I, or G.
3. According to Keynes, it is possible for the economy to be in equilibrium and in a recessionary gap too. In other words, the economy can be at point A in Exhibit 7.
4. The private sector may not be able to get the economy out of a recessionary gap. In other words, the private sector (households and businesses) may not be able to increase C or I enough to get the AD curve in Exhibit 7 to intersect the AS curve at point B.
5. The government may have a management role to play in the economy. According to Keynes, government may have to raise aggregate demand enough to stimulate the economy out of the recessionary gap and move it to its Natural Real GDP level.

SELF-TEST

1. What was Keynes's position with respect to the self-regulating properties of an economy?
2. What will happen to Real GDP if autonomous spending rises and the economy is operating in the horizontal section of the Keynesian AS curve? Explain your answer.
3. An economist who believes the economy is self-regulating is more likely to advocate laissez-faire than an economist who believes the economy is inherently unstable. Do you agree or disagree? Explain your answer.

THE SIMPLE KEYNESIAN MODEL IN THE *TE-TP* FRAMEWORK

A story can be translated into different languages and an economic model can be presented in various frameworks. The last section presents the simple Keynesian model in terms of the familiar (diagrammatic) *AD-AS* framework of analysis.

But the simple Keynesian model was not first presented in terms of *AD-AS*. It was first presented in terms of the framework that we discuss in this section. This framework has been known by different names, three of which are the Keynesian cross, income-expenditure, and total expenditure-total production. Throughout our discussion, we shall refer to it as total expenditure-total production, or simply *TE-TP* framework.

Deriving a Total Expenditures (*TE*) Curve

Just as we derived *AD* and *AS* curves in the *AD-AS* framework, we want to derive a total expenditures (*TE*) curve in the *TE-TP* framework. Total expenditures is the sum of its parts—consumption, investment, and government purchases. To derive a *TE* curve, we must first derive a diagrammatic representation of consumption, investment, and government purchases, as shown in Exhibit 8 and explained below.

1. **Consumption.** As disposable income rises, so does consumption. This is shown arithmetically in columns (1) and (3) of Exhibit 4. Exhibit 4 also shows that because the *MPC* is less than 1, consumption rises by less than disposable income rises. Consumption also rises as Real GDP rises, but, again, by a smaller percentage. For example, if Real GDP rises by $100, consumption may rise by $80. In Exhibit 8a, we have drawn consumption as an upward-sloping curve. Notice that as Real GDP rises from Q_1 to Q_2, consumption rises from $7 trillion to $7.5 trillion.
2. **Investment.** We are going to simplify things in deriving *TE*. Look at the investment curve in Exhibit 8b. We assume investment is constant at $1 trillion, no matter whether Real GDP is Q_1 or Q_2.
3. **Government purchases.** We simplify the government spending curve too. In Exhibit 8c, government purchases are constant at $1.5 trillion, regardless of the amount of Real GDP.

In Exhibit 8d, we have derived a *TE* curve. We simply added the components of total expenditures at the two Real GDP levels, Q_1 and Q_2, plotted the relevant points, and then drew a line through the points. We see that at Q_1, total expenditures are $9.5 trillion; and at Q_2, they are $10.0 trillion. The *TE* curve is upward-sloping.

What Will Shift the *TE* Curve?

The *TE* curve in the *TE-TP* framework plays the same role as the *AD* curve in the *AD-AS* framework. Just as the *AD* curve shifts if there is a change in *C, I,* or *G,* the *TE* curve shifts if there is a change in *C, I,* or *G.* For example, a rise in *C* will shift the *TE* curve upward; a decline in *I* will shift the *TE* curve downward.

Comparing Total Expenditures (*TE*) and Total Production (*TP*)

Businesses produce the goods and services that are bought by the three sectors of the economy (household, business, and government). Sometimes, though, businesses produce too much or too little in comparison to what the three sectors buy. For example, suppose businesses produce $10 trillion worth of goods and services, but the three sectors of the economy buy only $9.5 trillion worth of goods and services. In this case, businesses have produced too much relative to what the three sectors of the economy buy.

Or, possibly, businesses produce $10 trillion worth of goods and services, but the three sectors of the economy buy $10.5 trillion worth of goods and services. In this case,

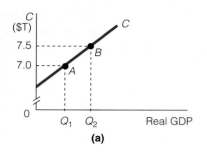

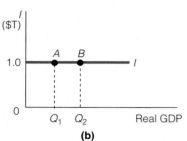

exhibit 8

The Derivation of the Total Expenditures (*TE*) Curve
At different levels of Real GDP, we sum consumption (a), investment (b), and government purchases (c) to derive the *TE* curve (d).

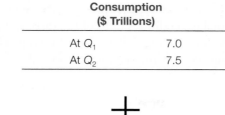

**Consumption
($ Trillions)**

At Q_1	7.0
At Q_2	7.5

**Investment
($ Trillions)**

At Q_1	1.0
At Q_2	1.0

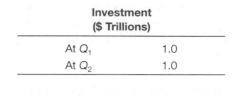

**Government Purchases
($ Trillions)**

At Q_1	1.5
At Q_2	1.5

**Total Expenditures
($ Trillions)**

At Q_1	9.5
At Q_2	10.0

businesses have produced too little relative to what the three sectors of the economy buy. (If you are wondering how the three sectors of the economy can possibly buy more than business produce, the answer has to do with goods that businesses hold in inventory. We will soon explain the process.)

Finally, it is possible for businesses to produce $10 trillion worth of goods and services, and for the three sectors of the economy to buy exactly $10 trillion worth of goods and services. In this case, businesses have produced exactly the right amount of goods and services.

Thus, there are three possible states of the economy in the *TE-TP* framework. The total expenditures (*TE*) of the three sectors of the economy can be less than, greater than, or equal to the dollar value of total production (*TP*). In other words, each of the following states of the economy is possible:

$$TE < TP$$
$$TE > TP$$
$$TE = TP$$

According to many economists, if the economy is currently operating where $TE < TP$ or $TE > TP$ (both states are described as disequilibrium), it will eventually move to where $TE = TP$ (where the economy is in equilibrium). The next section explains how this happens.

Moving From Disequilibrium to Equilibrium

Business firms hold an inventory of their goods to guard against unexpected changes in the demand for their product. For example, General Motors may hold an inventory of a certain type of car in case the demand for that car suddenly increases unexpectedly.

Although we know why business firms hold an inventory of their goods, we don't know *how much* inventory they will hold. For example, we don't know if General Motors will hold an inventory of 1,000 cars, 2,000 cars, or 10,000 cars. (Inventories are usually held in terms of, say, a 45- or 60-day supply, but we have simplified things here.) However, we do know that for General Motors, and all other business firms, there is some *optimum inventory.* This is "just the right amount" of inventory—not too much and not too little. With this in mind, consider two cases that illustrate how business inventory levels play an important role in the economy's adjustment from disequilibrium to equilibrium in the *TE-TP* framework.

Case 1: $TE < TP$

Assume business firms hold an optimum inventory level of $300 billion worth of goods. Then firms produce $11 trillion worth of goods and services, and the three sectors of the economy buy $10.8 trillion worth of goods and services. Thus, producers produce more than individuals buy ($TE < TP$). The difference adds to inventories, and inventory levels rise unexpectedly to $500 billion, which is $200 billion more than the $300 billion firms see as optimal.

This unexpected rise in inventories signals to firms that they have *overproduced.* Consequently, they cut back on the quantity of goods they produce. The cutback in production causes Real GDP to fall, bringing Real GDP closer to the (lower) output level that the three sectors of the economy are willing and able to buy. Ultimately, *TP* will equal *TE*.

Case 2: $TE > TP$

Assume business firms hold their optimum inventory level, $300 billion worth of goods. Then firms produce $10.4 trillion worth of goods, and members of the three sectors buy $10.6 trillion worth of goods. But how can individuals buy more than firms produce? The answer is that firms make up the difference out of inventory. In our example, inventory levels fall from $300 billion to $100 billion because individuals purchase $200 billion more of goods than firms produced (to be sold). This example illustrates why firms maintain inventories in the first place: to be able to meet an unexpected increase in sales.

The unexpected fall in inventories signals to firms that they have *underproduced.* Consequently, they increase the quantity of goods they produce. The rise in production causes Real GDP to rise, in the process bringing Real GDP closer to the (higher) real output that the three sectors are willing and able to buy. Ultimately, *TP* will equal *TE.*

The Graphical Representation of the Three States of the Economy in the *TE-TP* Framework

The three states of the economy are represented in Exhibit 9. Notice that there is a *TE* curve, which we derived earlier, and a *TP* curve, which is simply a 45-degree line. (It is called a 45-degree line because it bisects the 90-degree angle at the origin.) It is important to notice that at any point on the *TP* curve, total production is equal to Real GDP (*TP* = Real GDP).[3] This is because *TP* and Real GDP are different names for the same thing. Real GDP, remember, is simply the total market value of all final goods and services produced annually within a country's borders, adjusted for price changes.

Now let's look at three different Real GDP levels in the exhibit. We start with Q_1, where Real GDP = $11 trillion. At this Real GDP level, what does *TE* equal? What does *TP* equal? We see that *TE* is $10.8 trillion and *TP* is $11 trillion. This illustrates Case 1, in which producers produce more than individuals buy (*TE* < *TP*). The difference adds to inventories. This unexpected rise in inventories signals to firms that they have over-produced. Consequently, they cut back on the quantity of goods they produce. The cut-back in production causes Real GDP to fall, ultimately bringing Real GDP down to Q_E ($10.7 trillion in the exhibit).

Now we look at Q_2, where Real GDP = $10.4 trillion. At this Real GDP level, *TE* equals $10.6 trillion and *TP* equals $10.4 trillion. This illustrates Case 2, in which the three sectors of the economy buy more goods and services than business firms have produced (*TE* > *TP*). Business firms make up the difference between what they have produced and what the three sectors of the economy buy through inventories. Inventories fall below optimum levels. Consequently, businesses increase the quantity of goods they produce. The rise in production causes Real GDP to rise, ultimately moving Real GDP up to Q_E ($10.7 trillion in the exhibit).

When the economy is producing Q_E, or $10.7 trillion worth of goods and services, it is in equilibrium. At this Real GDP level, *TP* and *TE* are the same, $10.7 trillion. The following table summarizes some key points about the state of the economy in the *TE-TP* framework.

State of the Economy	What Happens to Inventories?	What Do Firms Do?
TE < *TP* Individuals are buying less output than firms produce.	Inventories rise above optimum levels.	Firms cut back production to reduce inventories to their optimum levels.
TE > *TP* Individuals are buying more output than firms produce.	Inventories fall below optimum levels.	Firms increase production to raise inventories to their optimum levels.
TE = *TP*	Inventories are at their optimum levels.	Firms neither increase nor decrease production.

3. Earlier we said that the *TE* curve plays the role in the *TE-TP* framework that the *AD* curve plays in the *AD-AS* framework. In other words, roughly speaking, the *AD* curve is the *TE* curve. Similarly, the *TP* curve plays the role in the *TE-TP* framework that the *AS* curve plays in the *AD-AS* framework. In other words, roughly speaking, the *TP* curve is the *AS* curve. In the *AD-AS* framework, equilibrium is at the intersection of the *AD* and *AS* curves. As you will soon learn, in the *TE-TP* framework, equilibrium is at the intersection of the *TE* and *TP* curves.

exhibit 9

The Three States of the Economy in the *TE-TP* Framework

At Q_E, $TE = TP$ and the economy is in equilibrium. At Q_1, $TE < TP$. This results in an unexpected increase in inventories, which signals firms that they have overproduced, which leads firms to cut back production. The cutback in production reduces Real GDP. The economy tends to move from Q_1 to Q_E. At Q_2, $TE > TP$. This results in an unexpected decrease in inventories, which signals firms that they have underproduced, which leads firms to raise production. The increased production raises Real GDP. The economy tends to move from Q_2 to Q_E.

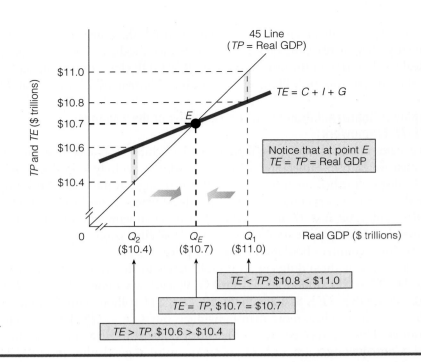

Notice that at point E
$TE = TP = $ Real GDP

$TE < TP$, $10.8 < 11.0$

$TE = TP$, $10.7 = 10.7$

$TE > TP$, $10.6 > 10.4$

THINKING LIKE AN ECONOMIST

Economists often think in threes. For example, this section describes three possible states of the economy: (1) TE less than TP, (2) TE greater than TP, or (3) TE equal to TP. The last chapter also identifies three possible states of the economy: (1) Real GDP less than Natural Real GDP, (2) Real GDP greater than Natural Real GDP, or (3) Real GDP equal to Natural Real GDP. Chapter 3, which discusses supply and demand, describes three possible market conditions: (1) quantity demanded greater than quantity supplied, (2) quantity demanded less than quantity supplied, or (3) quantity demanded equal to quantity supplied. Economists often think in threes because economists often think in terms of equilibrium and disequilibrium—and usually there is one equilibrium position and two (categorically different) disequilibria positions.

The Economy in a Recessionary Gap and the Role of Government

According to Keynes, the economy can be in equilibrium and in a recessionary gap too. We saw this in the last section for the simple Keynesian model in the *AD-AS* framework. (To review, look back at Exhibit 7.) Can the same situation exist in the *TE-TP* framework? Yes it can. For example, in Exhibit 9, the economy equilibrates at point *E*, and thus produces a Real GDP level of $10.7 trillion worth of goods and services. Is there any guarantee that the Real GDP level of $10.7 trillion is the Natural Real GDP level? Not at all. The economy could be in a situation like that shown in Exhibit 10. The economy is in equilibrium, at point *A*, producing Q_E, but the Natural Real GDP level is Q_N. Because the economy is producing at a Real GDP level that is less than Natural Real GDP, it is in a recessionary gap.

How does the economy get out of the recessionary gap? Will the private sector (households and businesses) be capable of pushing the *TE* curve in Exhibit 10 upward so that it goes through point *B* and thus Q_N is produced? According to Keynes, not necessarily. Keynes believed government may be necessary to get the economy out of a recessionary gap. For example, government may have to raise its purchases (raise *G*) so that the *TE* curve shifts upward and goes through point *B*.

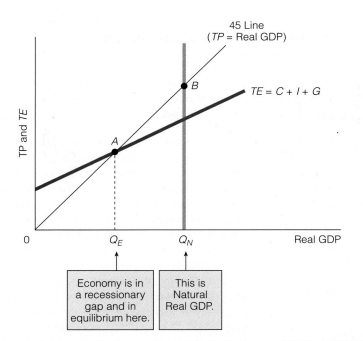

exhibit 10

The Economy: In Equilibrium and in a Recessionary Gap Too
Using the *TE-TP* framework, the economy is currently in equilibrium at point *A*, producing Q_E. Natural Real GDP, however, is greater than Q_E, so the economy is in a recessionary gap as well as being in equilibrium.

The Theme of the Simple Keynesian Model

As portrayed in terms of *TE* and *TP,* the essence of the simple Keynesian model is:

1. The price level is constant until Natural Real GDP is reached.
2. The *TE* curve shifts if there are changes in *C, I,* or *G.*
3. According to Keynes, it is possible for the economy to be in equilibrium and in a recessionary gap too. In other words, the economy can be at point *A* in Exhibit 10.
4. The private sector may not be able to get the economy out of a recessionary gap. In other words, the private sector (households and businesses) may not be able to increase *C* or *I* enough to get the *TE* curve in Exhibit 10 to rise and pass through point *B.*
5. The government may have a management role to play in the economy. According to Keynes, government may have to raise *TE* enough to stimulate the economy out of the recessionary gap and move it to its Natural Real GDP level.

SELF-TEST

1. What happens in the economy if total production (*TP*) is greater than total expenditures (*TE*)?
2. What happens in the economy if total expenditures (*TE*) are greater than total production (*TP*)?

Even before I enrolled in an economics course, I heard of the economist John Maynard Keynes. Could you tell me a little about his life? Also, I'd like to know if economists consider him a revolutionary in economics? If so, what did he revolutionize?

John Maynard Keynes was born in Cambridge, England, on June 5, 1883, and died at Tilton (in Sussex) on April 21, 1946. His father was John Neville Keynes, an eminent economist and author of *The Scope and Method of Political Economy.* Keynes's mother was one of the first female students to attend Cambridge University and for a time presided as mayor of the city of Cambridge.

Keynes was educated at Eton and at King's College, Cambridge, where he received a degree in mathematics in 1905. At Cambridge, he studied under the well-known and widely respected economist, Alfred Marshall. In 1925, Keynes married the Russian ballerina Lydia Lopokova. He was prominent in British social and intellectual circles and enjoyed art, theater, opera, debate, and collecting rare books.

Many economists rank Keynes's *The General Theory of Employment, Interest and Money* alongside Adam Smith's *Wealth of Nations* and Karl Marx's *Das Kapital* as one of the most influential economic treatises ever written. The book was published on February 4, 1936.

Before the publication of the *General Theory,* Keynes presented the ideas contained in the work in a series of university lectures that he gave between October 10, 1932, and December 2, 1935. Ten days after his last lecture, he sent off the manuscript of what was to become the *General Theory.*

Keynes's lectures were said to be both shocking (he was pointing out the errors of the Classical School) and exciting (he was proposing something new). One of the students at these lectures was Lorie Tarshis, who later wrote the first Keynesian introductory textbook, *The Elements of Economics.* In another venue, Tarshis wrote about the Keynes lectures and specifically about why Keynes's ideas were revolutionary.

I attended that first lecture, naturally awed but bothered. As the weeks passed, only a stone would not have responded to the growing excitement these lectures generated. So I missed only two over the four years—two out of the thirty lectures. And like others, I would feel the urgency of the task. No wonder! These were the years when everything came loose; when sober dons and excitable students seriously discussed such issues as: Was capitalism not doomed? Should Britain not take the path of Russia or Germany to create jobs? Keynes obviously believed his analysis led to a third means to prosperity far less threatening to the values he prized, but until he had developed the theory and offered it in print, he knew that he could not sway government. So he saw his task as supremely urgent. I was also a bit surprised by his concern over too low a level of output. I had been assured by all I had read that the economy would bob to the surface, like a cork held under water—and output would rise, of its own accord, to an acceptable level. But Keynes proposed something far more shocking: that the economy could reach an equilibrium position with output far below capacity. That was an exciting challenge, sharply at variance with the views of Pigou and Marshall who represented "The Classical (Orthodox) School" in Cambridge, and elsewhere.[4]

---

4. L. Tarshis, "Keynesian Revolution" in *The New Palgrave: A Dictionary of Economics,* vol. 3 (London: The Macmillan Press, 1987), 48.

Chapter Summary

Keynes on Wage Rates and Prices

> Keynes believed that wage rates and prices may be inflexible downwards. He said that employees and labor unions would resist employer's wage cuts and that because of anticompetitive or monopolistic elements in the economy, prices would not fall.

Keynes on Say's Law

> Keynes did not agree that Say's law would necessarily hold in a money economy. He thought it was possible for consumption to fall (saving to increase) by more than investment increased. Consequently, a decrease in consumption (or increase in saving) could lower total expenditures and aggregate demand in the economy.

Consumption Function

> Keynes made three points about consumption and disposable income: (1) Consumption depends on disposable income. (2) Consumption and disposable income move in the same direction. (3) As disposable income changes, consumption changes by less. These three ideas are incorporated into the consumption function, $C = C_0 + (MPC)(Y_d)$, where C_0 is autonomous consumption, MPC is the marginal propensity to consume, and Y_d is disposable income.

The Multiplier

> A change in autonomous spending will bring about a multiple change in total spending. The overall change in spending is

equal to $1/(1 - MPC)$ (the multiplier) times the change in autonomous spending.

The Simple Keynesian Model in the *AD-AS* Framework

> Changes in consumption, investment, and government purchases will change aggregate demand.
> A rise in *C, I,* or *G* will shift the *AD* curve to the right.
> A decrease in *C, I,* or *G* will shift the *AD* curve to the left.
> The aggregate supply curve in the simple Keynesian model has both a horizontal section and a vertical section. The "kink" between the two sections is at the Natural Real GDP level. If aggregate demand changes in the horizontal section of the curve (when the economy is operating below Natural Real GDP), there is a change in Real GDP but no change in the price level. If aggregate demand changes in the vertical section of the curve (when the economy is operating at Natural Real GDP), there is a change in the price level but no change in Real GDP.

The Simple Keynesian Model in the *TE-TP* Framework

> Changes in consumption, investment, and government purchases will change total expenditures.

> A rise in *C, I,* or *G* will shift the *TE* curve upward.
> A decrease in *C, I,* or *G* will shift the *TE* curve downward.
> If total expenditures (*TE*) equal total production (*TP*), the economy is in equilibrium. If *TE* < *TP*, the economy is in disequilibrium and inventories unexpectedly rise, signaling firms to cut back production. If *TE* > *TP*, the economy is in disequilibrium and inventories unexpectedly fall, signaling firms to increase production.
> Equilibrium occurs where *TE* = *TP*. The equilibrium level of Real GDP may be less than the Natural Real GDP level and the economy may be stuck at this lower level of Real GDP.

A Keynesian Theme

> Keynes proposed that the economy could reach its equilibrium position with Real GDP below Natural Real GDP; that is, the economy can be in equilibrium and in a recessionary gap too. Furthermore, he argued that the economy may not be able to get out of a recessionary gap by itself. Government may need to play a management role in the economy.

Key Terms and Concepts

Efficiency Wage Models
Consumption Function

Marginal Propensity to Consume (*MPC*)
Autonomous Consumption

Marginal Propensity to Save (*MPS*)
Multiplier

Questions and Problems

Questions 1–4 are based on the first section of the chapter; questions 5–7, on the second section; questions 8–14, on the third section; and questions 15–19, on the fourth section.

1. How is Keynes's position different from the classical position with respect to wages, prices, and Say's law?
2. Classical economists assumed that wage rates, prices, and interest rates were flexible and would adjust quickly. Consider an extreme case: Suppose classical economists believed wage rates, prices, and interest rates would adjust instantaneously. What would this imply the classical aggregate supply (*AS*) curve would look like? Explain your answer.
3. Give two reasons why wage rates may not fall.
4. According to New Keynesian economists, why might business firms pay wage rates above market-clearing levels?
5. Given the Keynesian consumption function, how would a cut in income tax rates affect consumption? Explain your answer.

6. Explain how a rise in autonomous spending can increase total spending by some multiple.
7. A change in what factors will lead to a change in consumption?
8. According to Keynes, can an increase in saving shift the *AD* curve to the left? Explain your answer.
9. What factors will shift the *AD* curve in the simple Keynesian model?
10. According to Keynes, an increase in saving and decrease in consumption may lower total spending in the economy. But how could this happen if the increased saving lowers interest rates (as shown in the last chapter)? Wouldn't a decrease in interest rates increase investment spending, thus counteracting the decrease in consumption spending?
11. Can a person believe that wages are inflexible downward for, say, one year and also believe in a self-regulating economy? Explain your answer.
12. According to Keynes, can the private sector always remove the economy from a recessionary gap? Explain your answer.

13. What does the aggregate supply curve look like in the simple Keynesian model?

14. Suppose consumption rises and investment and government purchases remain constant. How will the *AD* curve shift in the simple Keynesian model? Under what condition will the rise in Real GDP be equal to the rise in total spending?

15. Explain how to derive a total expenditures (*TE*) curve.

16. What role do inventories play in the equilibrating process in the simple Keynesian model (as described in the *TE-TP* framework)?

17. Identify the three states of the economy in terms of *TE* and *TP*.

18. If Real GDP is $10.4 trillion in Exhibit 9, what is the state of business inventories?

19. How will a rise in government purchases change the *TE* curve in Exhibit 9?

Working With Numbers and Graphs

Questions 1–2 are based on the second section of the chapter, questions 3–4 are based on the third section, and questions 5–8 are based on the fourth section.

1. Compute the multiplier in each of the following cases:
  a. *MPC* = 0.60
  b. *MPC* = 0.80
  c. *MPC* = 0.50

2. Write an investment function (equation) that specifies two components: (a) autonomous investment spending and (b) induced investment spending.

3. Economist Smith believes that changes in aggregate demand affect only the price level, and economist Jones believes that changes in aggregate demand affect only Real GDP. What do the *AD* and *AS* curves look like for each economist?

4. Explain the following using the figure below.
  a. According to Keynes, aggregate demand may be insufficient to bring about the full-employment output level (or Natural Real GDP).
  b. A decrease in consumption (due to increased saving) is not matched by an increase in investment spending.

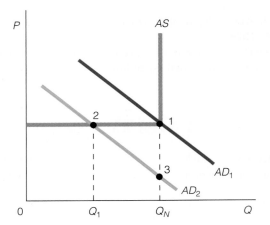

5. The *TE* curve in Exhibit 8d is upward-sloping because the consumption function is upward-sloping. Explain.
6. Look at Exhibit 8d. What does the vertical distance between the origin and the point at which the *TE* curve cuts the vertical axis represent?
7. In the following figure, explain what happens if:
   a. The economy is at Q_1
   b. The economy is at Q_2

8. In the previous figure, if Natural Real GDP is Q_2, what state is the economy in at point *A*?

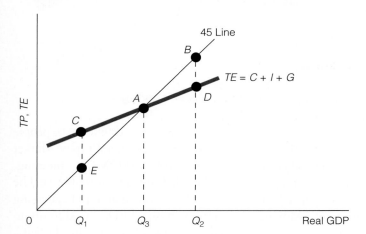

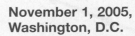
© Archivo Iconografico S.A./CORBIS

Setting the Scene

The following events occurred at various times.

April 7, 1787, Vienna, Austria

Ludwig van Beethoven, 16, arrives to take music lessons from Wolfgang Amadeus Mozart, 31. Mozart composes his "Quintet in C for Strings" this month.

Sometime in 1885, Edinburgh, Scotland

Robert Louis Stevenson is having a nightmare. His wife wakes him up. He asks her why she woke him up. For Stevenson, this nightmare is the beginning of what will turn out to be *The Strange Case of Dr. Jekyll and Mr. Hyde.* Here is a passage from the book: "It was on the moral side, and in my own person, that I learned to recognise the thorough and primitive duality of man; I saw that, of the two natures that contended in the field of my consciousness, even if I could rightly be said to be either, it was only because I was radically both; and from an early date . . . I had learned to dwell with pleasure, as a

beloved daydream, on the thought of the separation of these elements."

June 27, 1905, Bern, Switzerland

Albert Einstein is sitting in a chair in his home. In three days, on June 30, 1905, he will submit his paper "On the Electrodynamics of Moving Bodies" to the leading German physics journal. The first few lines of that paper read: "It is known that Maxwell's electrodynamics—as usually understood at the present time—when applied to moving bodies, leads to asymmetries which do not appear to be inherent in the phenomena. Take, for example, the reciprocal electrodynamic action of a magnet and a conductor. The observable phenomenon here depends only on the relative motion of the conductor and the magnet, whereas the customary view draws a sharp distinction between the two cases in which either the one or the other of these bodies is in motion."

November 1, 2005, Washington, D.C.

Between 8:45 and 9:00 A.M., people arrive for the Federal Open Market Committee (FOMC) meeting, scheduled to begin at 9:00 A.M. The FOMC is the major policymaking group in the FED. In addition to the 12 members of the FOMC, about 37 other people are present for the meeting. The meeting commences with a discussion of the financial and foreign exchange markets, including details about open market operations. After the latest U.S. economic data are reviewed and discussed, the 12 FOMC members present their views of local and national economic conditions. The Chairman of the Board of Governors gives his opinion of the economy and of possible actions that might be taken by the FOMC. After a discussion, the members vote on the various options for FOMC action.

How would an economist look at these events? Later in the chapter, discussions based on the following questions will help you analyze the scene the way an economist would.

- What do Ludwig van Beethoven, Wolfgang Amadeus Mozart, Robert Louis Stevenson, and Albert Einstein have to do with money evolving out of a barter economy?

- How does the Fed expand or contract the money supply?

MONEY: WHAT IS IT AND HOW DID IT COME TO BE?

The story of money starts with a definition and a history lesson. This section discusses what money is and isn't (the definition) and how money came to be (the history lesson).

Money: A Definition

To the layperson, the words *income, credit,* and *wealth* are synonyms for *money.* In each of the next three sentences, the word *money* is used incorrectly; the word in parentheses is the word an economist would use.

1. "How much money (income) did you earn last year?"
2. "Most of her money (wealth) is tied up in real estate."
3. "It sure is difficult to get much money (credit) in today's tight mortgage market."

In economics, the words *money, income, credit,* and *wealth* are not synonyms. The most general definition of **money** is any good that is widely accepted for purposes of exchange (payment for goods and services) and in the repayment of debts.

Money
Any good that is widely accepted for purposes of exchange and in the repayment of debt.

Three Functions of Money

Money has three major functions. It functions as a medium of exchange, a unit of account, and a store of value.

Money as a Medium of Exchange

If money did not exist, goods would have to be exchanged by **barter.** Suppose you wanted a shirt. You would have to trade some good in your possession, say, a jackknife, for the shirt. But first, you would have to locate a person who has a shirt and wants to trade it for a knife. In a money economy, this step is not necessary. You can simply (1) exchange money for a shirt or (2) exchange the knife for money and then the money for the shirt. The buyer of the knife and the seller of the shirt do not have to be the same person. Money is the medium through which exchange occurs; hence, it is a **medium of exchange.** As such, money reduces the *transaction costs* of making exchanges. Exchange is easier and less time-consuming in a money economy than in a barter economy.

Barter
Exchanging goods and services for other goods and services without the use of money.

Medium of Exchange
Anything that is generally acceptable in exchange for goods and services. A function of money.

Money as a Unit of Account

A **unit of account** is a common measure in which values are expressed. Consider a barter economy. The value of every good is expressed in terms of all other goods, and there is no common unit of measure. For example, one horse might equal 100 bushels of wheat, or 200 bushels of apples, or 20 pairs of shoes, or 10 suits, or 55 loaves of bread, and so on. In a money economy, a person doesn't have to know the price of an apple in terms of oranges, pizzas, chickens, or potato chips, as would be the case in a barter economy. He or she only needs to know the price in terms of money. And because all goods are denominated in money, determining relative prices is easy and quick. For example, if 1 apple is $1 and 1 orange is 50 cents, then 1 apple = 2 oranges.

Unit of Account
A common measure in which relative values are expressed. A function of money.

Money as a Store of Value

The **store of value** function refers to a good's ability to maintain its value over time. This is the least exclusive function of money because other goods—for example,

Store of Value
The ability of an item to hold value over time. A function of money.

paintings, houses, and stamps—can do this too. At times, money has not maintained its value well, such as during high inflationary periods. For the most part, though, money has served as a satisfactory store of value. This allows us to accept payment in money for our productive efforts and to keep that money until we decide how we want to spend it.

From a Barter to a Money Economy: The Origins of Money

The thing that differentiates man and animals is money.

—Gertrude Stein

At one time, there was trade but no money. Instead, people bartered. They would trade an apple for two eggs, a banana for a peach.

Today we live in a money economy. How did we move from a barter to a money economy? Did some king or queen issue the edict "Let there be money"? Not likely. Money evolved in a much more natural, market-oriented manner.

Making exchanges takes longer (on average) in a barter economy than in a money economy. That's because the *transaction costs* of making exchanges are higher in a barter economy than they are in a money economy. Stated differently, the time and effort one has to incur to consummate an exchange is greater in a barter economy than in a money economy. To illustrate, suppose Smith, living in a barter economy, wants to trade apples for oranges. He locates Jones, who has oranges. Smith offers to trade apples for oranges, but Jones tells Smith that she does not like apples and would rather have peaches.

In this situation, Smith must either (1) find someone who has oranges and wants to trade oranges for apples or (2) find someone who has peaches and wants to trade peaches for apples, after which he must return to Jones and trade peaches for oranges.

Suppose Smith continues to search and finds Brown, who has oranges and wants to trade oranges for (Smith's) apples. In economics terminology, Smith and Brown are said to have a **double coincidence of wants.** Two people have a double coincidence of wants if what the first person wants is what the second person has and what the second person wants is what the first person has. A double coincidence of wants is a necessary condition for trade to take place.

In a barter economy, some goods are more readily accepted in exchange than other goods are. This may originally be the result of chance, but when traders notice the difference in marketability, their behavior tends to reinforce the effect. Suppose there are 10 goods, *A–J,* and that good *G* is the most marketable of the 10. On average, good *G* is accepted 5 out of every 10 times it is offered in an exchange, while the remaining goods are accepted, on average, only 2 out of every 10 times. Given this difference, some individuals accept good *G* simply because of its relatively greater acceptability, even though they have no plans to consume it. They accept good *G* because they know that it can easily be traded for most other goods at a later time (unlike the item originally in their possession).

The effect snowballs. The more people accept good *G* for its relatively greater acceptability, the greater its relative acceptability becomes, which in turn causes more people to agree to accept it. This is how money evolved. When good *G*'s acceptance evolves to the point where good *G* is widely accepted for purposes of exchange, good *G* is money. Historically, goods that have evolved into money include gold, silver, copper, cattle, salt, cocoa beans, and shells.

Double Coincidence of Wants
In a barter economy, a requirement that must be met before a trade can be made. It specifies that a trader must find another trader who is willing to trade what the first trader wants and at the same time wants what the first trader has.

English and Money

In a world of barter, some goods are more widely accepted than other goods.

In a world of languages, some languages may be more widely used than other languages. Today, the most widely used language appears to be English.

English is spoken not only by native English speakers but by many other people around the world. English is the language of computers and the Internet. You can see English on posters everywhere in the world. You can hear English in pop songs sung in Tokyo. English is the working language of the Asian trade group ASEAN (Association of South East Asian Nations). It is the language of 98 percent of German research physicists and 83 percent of German research chemists. It is the official language of the European Central Bank, even though the bank is in Frankfurt, Germany. It is found in official documents in Phnom Penh, Cambodia. Singers all over the world sing in English. Alcatel, a French telecommunications company, uses English as its internal language. By 2050, half the world's population is expected to be proficient in English.

In a barter economy, if more people accept a particular good in exchange, then more people will want to accept that good. Might the same be true of a language? In other words, if more people speak English, then more non-English-speaking people will want to learn English. Just as money lowers the transaction costs of making exchanges, English might lower the transaction costs of communicating.

Is the world evolving toward one universal language and is that language English?

ANALYZING THE SCENE

Question from Setting the Scene: What do Ludwig van Beethoven, Wolfgang Amadeus Mozart, Robert Louis Stevenson, and Albert Einstein have to do with money evolving out of a barter economy?

All of the individuals mentioned worked at one thing and one thing only. Beethoven and Mozart composed music, Robert Louis Stevenson wrote novels, and Einstein thought and wrote about the physical world. Would anyone have done what he did had he lived in a barter economy instead of in a money economy? It is doubtful. In a money economy, individuals usually specialize in the production of one good or service because they can do so. In a barter economy, specializing is extremely costly. For Beethoven, it would mean writing music all day and then going out and trying to trade what he had written that day for apples, oranges, chickens, and bread. Would the baker trade two loaves of bread for two pages of music? Einstein, living in a barter economy, would soon learn that he did not have a double coincidence of wants with many people, and therefore if he was going to eat and be housed, he would need to spend time baking bread, raising chickens, and building shelter instead of thinking about space and time. In a barter economy, trade is difficult, so people produce for themselves. In a money economy, trade is easy, and so individuals produce one thing, sell it for money, and then buy what they want with the money. The Beethoven who lived in a barter economy would spend his days very differently than the Beethoven who lived in Vienna in 1787.

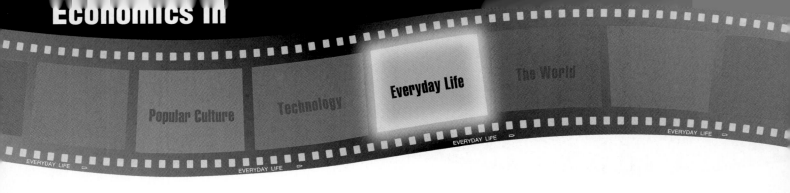

Is Money the Best Gift?

Consider what happens when one person gives another person a gift. First, the gift giver has to decide how much money to spend on the gift. Is it an amount between $10 and $20 or between $50 and $80? After the dollar range has been decided, the gift giver has to decide what to buy. Will it be a book, a shirt, a gift certificate to a restaurant, or what? Deciding what to buy requires the gift giver to guess the preferences of the gift recipient. This is no easy task, even if the gift giver knows the gift recipient fairly well. Often, guessing preferences is done poorly, which means that each year hundreds of thousands of people end up with gifts they would prefer not to have received. Every year, shirts go unworn, books go unread, and closets fill up with unwanted items.

At the end of a holiday season in 1993, Joel Waldfogel, then an economist at Yale University, asked a group of students two

questions. First, he asked them what dollar value they would estimate was paid by the gift givers for all the holiday gifts they (the students) received. Second, he asked the students how much *they* would have paid to get the gifts they received. What Waldfogel learned was that, on average, gift recipients were willing to pay less for the gifts they received than gift givers paid for the gifts. For example, a gift recipient might be willing to pay $25 for a book that a gift giver bought for $30. The most conservative estimate put the average gift recipient's valuation at 90 percent of the buying price. This means that if the gift giver had given the cash value of the purchase instead of the gift itself, the recipient could then buy what was really wanted and been better off at no additional cost. In other words, some economists have concluded that when you don't know the preferences of the gift recipient very well, it just may be better to give money.

DEFINING THE MONEY SUPPLY

Money is any good that is widely accepted for purposes of exchange. Is a ten-dollar bill money? Is a dime money? Is a checking account or a savings account money? What does money include? In other words, what is included in the money supply? Two of the more frequently used definitions of the money supply are M1 and M2.

M1

M1
Includes currency held outside banks + checkable deposits + traveler's checks.

M1 is sometimes referred to as the *narrow definition of the money supply* or as *transactions money.* It is money that can be directly used for everyday transactions—to buy gas for the car, groceries to eat, and clothes to wear. **M1** consists of currency held outside banks (by members of the public for use in everyday transactions), checkable deposits, and traveler's checks.

$$M1 = \text{Currency held outside banks} \\ + \text{ Checkable deposits} \\ + \text{ Traveler's checks}$$

Currency
Coins and paper money.

Federal Reserve Notes
Paper money issued by the Fed.

Checkable Deposits
Deposits on which checks can be written.

How are the components of M1 defined? **Currency** includes coins minted by the U.S. Treasury and paper money. About 99 percent of the paper money in circulation is **Federal Reserve notes** issued by the Federal Reserve District Banks. **Checkable deposits** are deposits on which checks can be written. There are different types of checkable deposits, including demand deposits, which are checking accounts that pay no interest, and NOW (negotiated order of withdrawal) and ATS (automatic transfer from savings) accounts, which do pay interest on their balances.

In June 2005, checkable deposits equaled $660 billion, currency held outside banks equaled $710 billion, and traveler's checks were $7 billion. M1, the sum of these figures, was $1,377 billion.

M2

M2 is sometimes referred to as the (most common) *broad definition of the money supply.* **M2** is made up of M1 plus savings deposits (including money market deposit accounts), small-denomination time deposits, and money market mutual funds (noninstitutional). In June 2005, M2 was $6,510 billion.

$$M2 = M1$$
+ Savings deposits (including money market deposit accounts)
+ Small-denomination time deposits
+ Money market mutual funds (noninstitutional)

Let's look at some of the components of M2. A **savings deposit,** sometimes called a *regular savings deposit,* is an interest-earning account at a commercial bank or thrift institution. (Thrift institutions include savings and loan associations, mutual savings banks, and credit unions.) Normally, checks cannot be written on savings deposits, and the funds in savings deposits can be withdrawn (at any time) without a penalty payment.

A **money market deposit account** (MMDA) is an interest-earning account at a bank or thrift institution. Usually, a minimum balance is required for an MMDA. Most MMDAs offer limited check-writing privileges. For example, the owner of an MMDA might be able to write only a certain number of checks each month, and/or each check may have to be above a certain dollar amount (say, $500).

A **time deposit** is an interest-earning deposit with a *specified maturity date.* Time deposits are subject to penalties for early withdrawal. Small-denomination time deposits are deposits of less than $100,000.

A **money market mutual fund** (MMMF) is an interest-earning account at a *mutual fund company.* MMMFs held by large institutions are referred to as institutional MMMFs. MMMFs held by all others (for example, the MMMF held by an individual) are referred to as noninstitutional MMMFs. *Only noninstitutional MMMFs are part of M2.* Usually, a minimum balance is required for an MMMF account. Most MMMF accounts offer limited check-writing privileges.

Where Do Credit Cards Fit In?

Credit cards are commonly referred to as money—plastic money. But they are not money. A credit card is an instrument or document that makes it easier for the holder to obtain a loan. When Tina Ridges hands the department store clerk her MasterCard or Visa, she is, in effect, spending someone else's money (that already existed). The department store submits the claim to the bank, the bank pays the department store, and then the bank bills the holder of its credit card. By using her credit card, Tina has spent someone else's money, and she ultimately must repay her credit card debt with money. These transactions shift around the existing quantity of money between various individuals and firms but do not change the total.

THINKING LIKE AN ECONOMIST *When a layperson hears the word money, she usually thinks of currency—paper money (dollar bills) and coins. For example, if you're walking along a dark street at night and a thief stops you and says, "Your money or your life," you can be sure he wants your currency. To an economist, though, money is more than simply currency. One definition of money (the M1 definition) is that it is currency, checkable deposits, and traveler's checks. (Still, if stopped by a thief, an economist would be unlikely to hand over his currency and then write a check too.)*

M2
Includes M1 + savings deposits (including money market deposit accounts) + small-denomination time deposits + money market mutual funds (noninstitutional).

Savings Deposit
An interest-earning account at a commercial bank or thrift institution. Normally, checks cannot be written on savings deposits and the funds in a savings deposit can be withdrawn (at any time) without a penalty payment.

Money Market Deposit Account
An interest-earning account at a bank or thrift institution. Usually a minimum balance is required for an MMDA. Most MMDAs offer limited check-writing privileges.

Time Deposit
An interest-earning deposit with a specified maturity date. Time deposits are subject to penalties for early withdrawal. Small-denomination time deposits are deposits of less than $100,000.

Money Market Mutual Fund
An interest-earning account at a mutual fund company. Usually a minimum balance is required for an MMMF account. Most MMMF accounts offer limited check-writing privileges. Only noninstitutional MMMFs are part of M2.

Popular Culture   Technology   Everyday Life

© API/Wide World Photos

POPULAR CULTURE

Economics on the Yellow Brick Road

I'll get you, my pretty.
— Wicked Witch of the West in *The Wizard of Oz*

In 1893, the United States fell into economic depression: the stock market crashed, banks failed, workers were laid off, and many farmers lost their farms. Some people blamed the depression on the gold standard. They proposed that instead of only gold backing U.S. currency, there should be a bimetallic monetary standard where both gold and silver backed the currency. This would lead to an increase in the money supply. Many people thought that with more money in circulation, the economic hard times would soon be a thing of the past.

One of the champions of silver was William Jennings Bryan, who was the Democratic candidate for the U.S. Presidency in 1896. Bryan had established himself as a friend to the many Americans who had been hurt by the economic depression— especially farmers and industrial workers. Bryan's views were shared by L. Frank Baum, the author of *The Wonderful Wizard of Oz,* the book that was the basis for the 1939 movie *The Wizard of Oz.*

Baum blamed the gold standard for the hardships faced by farmers and workers during the depression. Baum saw farmers and industrial workers as the "common man," and he saw William Jennings Bryan as the best possible hope for the common man in this country.

Numerous persons believe that Baum's most famous work, *The Wonderful Wizard of Oz,* is an allegory for the presidential election of 1896.[1] Some say that Dorothy, in the book and the movie, represents Bryan. Both Dorothy and Bryan were young (Bryan was a 36-year-old presidential candidate). Like the cyclone in the movie that transported Dorothy to the Land of Oz, the delegates at the 1896 Democratic convention lifted Bryan into a new political world, the world of presidential politics.

As Dorothy begins her travels to the Emerald City (Washington, D.C.) with Toto (who represents the Democratic Party) to meet the Wizard of Oz, she travels down a yellow brick road (the gold standard). On her way, she meets the scarecrow (who represents the farmer), the tin man (who represents the industrial worker), and the cowardly lion, who some believe represents the Populist Party of the time. (The Populist Party was sometimes represented as a lion in cartoons of the time. It was a "cowardly" lion because, some say, it did not have the courage to fight an independent campaign for the presidency in 1896.) The message is clear: Bryan, with the help of the Democratic and Populist parties and the votes of the farmers and the industrial workers, will travel to Washington.

But then, when Dorothy and the others reach the Emerald City, they are denied their wishes, just as Bryan is denied the presidency. He loses the election to William McKinley.

But all is not over. There is still the battle with the Wicked Witch of the West, who wears a golden cap (gold standard). When the Wicked Witch sees Dorothy's silver shoes—they were changed to ruby shoes in the movie—she desperately wants them for their magical quality. But that is not to be. Dorothy kills the Wicked Witch of the West; she then clicks her silver shoes together and they take her back home, where all is right with the world.

1. The interpretation here is based on "William Jennings Bryan on the Yellow Brick Road" by John Geer and Thomas Rochon (*Journal of American Culture,* Winter 1993) and "The Wizard of Oz: Parable on Populism" by Henry Littlefield (*American Quarterly,* 1964).

SELF-TEST *(Answers to Self-Test questions are in the Self-Test Appendix.)*

1. Why (not how) did money evolve out of a barter economy?
2. If individuals remove funds from their checkable deposits and transfer them to their money market accounts, will M1 fall and M2 rise? Explain your answer.
3. How does money reduce the transaction costs of making trades?

THE MONEY CREATION PROCESS

This section describes the important money supply process, specifically, how the banking system, working under a **fractional reserve banking** arrangement, creates money.

The Federal Reserve System

The next section discusses the structure of **the Fed** (the popular name for the **Federal Reserve System**) and the tools it uses to change the money supply. For now, we need only note that the Federal Reserve System is the central bank; essentially, it is a bank's bank. Its chief function is to control the nation's money supply.

The Bank's Reserves and More

Many banks have an account with the Fed, in much the same way that an individual has a checking account with a commercial bank. Economists refer to this account with the Fed as either a reserve account or bank deposits at the Fed. Banks also have currency or cash in their vaults—simply called vault cash—on the bank premises. The sum of (1) bank deposits at the Fed and (2) the bank's vault cash is (total bank) **reserves.**

$$\text{Reserves} = \text{Bank deposits at the Fed} + \text{Vault cash}$$

For example, if a bank currently has $4 million in deposits at the Fed and $1 million in vault cash, it has $5 million in reserves.

The Required Reserve Ratio and Required Reserves

The Fed mandates that member commercial banks must hold a certain fraction of their checkable deposits in reserve form. What does "reserve form" mean here? It means in the form of "bank deposits at the Fed" and/or "vault cash" because the sum of these two equals reserves.

The fraction of checkable deposits that banks must hold in reserve form is called the **required reserve ratio (r).** The actual dollar amount of deposits held in reserve form is called **required reserves.** In other words, to find the required reserves for a given bank, multiply the required reserve ratio by checkable deposits (in the bank):

$$\text{Required reserves} = r \times \text{Checkable deposits}$$

For example, assume that customers have deposited $40 million in a neighborhood bank and that the Fed has set the required reserve ratio at 10 percent. It follows that required reserves for the bank equal $4 million ($0.10 \times \$40$ million = $4 million).

Excess Reserves

The difference between a bank's (total) reserves and its required reserves is its **excess reserves:**

$$\text{Excess reserves} = \text{Reserves} - \text{Required reserves}$$

For example, if the bank's (total) reserves are $5 million and its required reserves are $4 million, then it holds excess reserves of $1 million.

The important point to remember about excess reserves is that banks use them to make loans. In fact, banks have a monetary incentive to use their excess reserves to make loans: If the bank uses the $1 million excess reserves to make loans, it earns interest income. If it does not make any loans, it does not earn interest income.

Fractional Reserve Banking
A banking arrangement that allows banks to hold reserves equal to only a fraction of their deposit liabilities.

Federal Reserve System (the Fed)
The central bank of the United States.

Reserves
The sum of bank deposits at the Fed and vault cash.

Required Reserve Ratio (r)
A percentage of each dollar deposited that must be held on reserve (at the Fed or in the bank's vault).

Required Reserves
The minimum amount of reserves a bank must hold against its checkable deposits as mandated by the Fed.

Excess Reserves
Any reserves held beyond the required amount. The difference between (total) reserves and required reserves.

The Banking System and the Money Expansion Process

The banks in the banking system are prohibited from printing their own currency. Nevertheless, the banking system can create money by increasing checkable deposits. (Remember, checkable deposits are a component of the money supply.)

The process starts with the Fed. For now, suppose the Fed prints $1,000 in new paper money and gives it to Bill. Bill takes the newly created $1,000 and deposits it in bank *A*. We can see this transaction in the following T-account. A **T-account** is a simplified balance sheet that records the *changes* in the bank's assets and liabilities.

<table>
<tr><td colspan="4" align="center">BANK A</td></tr>
<tr><td colspan="2" align="center">Assets</td><td colspan="2" align="center">Liabilities</td></tr>
<tr><td>Reserves</td><td>+$1,000</td><td>Checkable deposits (Bill)</td><td>+$1,000</td></tr>
</table>

Because the deposit initially is added to vault cash, *the bank's reserves have increased by $1,000.* The bank's liabilities also have increased by $1,000 because it owes Bill the $1,000 he deposited in the bank.

Next, the banker divides the $1,000 reserves into two categories: required reserves and excess reserves. The amount of required reserves depends on the required reserve ratio specified by the Fed. We'll set the required reserve ratio at 10 percent. This means the bank holds $100 in required reserves against the deposit and holds $900 in excess reserves. The previous T-account can be modified to show this:

<table>
<tr><td colspan="4" align="center">BANK A</td></tr>
<tr><td colspan="2" align="center">Assets</td><td colspan="2" align="center">Liabilities</td></tr>
<tr><td>Required reserves</td><td>+$100</td><td>Checkable deposits (Bill)</td><td>+$1,000</td></tr>
<tr><td>Excess reserves</td><td>+$900</td><td></td><td></td></tr>
</table>

On the left side of the T-account, the total is $1,000, and on the right side, the total is also $1,000. By dividing total reserves into required reserves and excess reserves, we can see how many dollars the bank is holding above the Fed requirements. These excess reserves can be used to make new loans.

Suppose bank *A* makes a loan of $900 to Jenny. The left (assets) side of the bank's T-account looks like this:

<table>
<tr><td colspan="3" align="center">BANK A</td></tr>
<tr><td colspan="2" align="center">Assets</td><td align="center">Liabilities</td></tr>
<tr><td>Required reserves</td><td>+$100</td><td>See the next T-account.</td></tr>
<tr><td>Excess reserves</td><td>+$900</td><td></td></tr>
<tr><td>Loans</td><td>+$900</td><td></td></tr>
</table>

T-Account
A simplified balance sheet that shows the changes in a bank's assets and liabilities.

Now when bank *A* gives Jenny a $900 loan, it doesn't give her $900 cash. Instead, it opens a checking account for Jenny at the bank, and the balance in the account is $900. This is how things are shown in the T-account:

BANK *A*		
Assets	**Liabilities**	
See the previous T-account.	Checkable deposits (Bill)	+$1,000
	Checkable deposits (Jenny)	+$900

Before we continue, *notice that the money supply has increased.* When Jenny borrowed $900 and the bank put that amount in her checking account, *no one else in the economy had any less money and Jenny had more than before.* Consequently, the money supply has increased. (Think of M1 as equal to currency + checkable deposits + traveler's checks. Through the lending activity of the bank, checkable deposits have increased by $900 and there has been no change in the amount of currency or traveler's checks. It follows that M1 has increased.) In other words, the money supply is $900 more than it was previously.

Now suppose that Jenny spends the $900 on a new computer. She writes a $900 check to the computer retailer, who deposits the full amount of the check in bank *B*. First, what happens to bank *A*? It uses its excess reserves to honor Jenny's check when it is presented by bank *B* and simultaneously reduces her checking account balance from $900 to zero. Bank *A*'s situation is shown here:

BANK *A*			
Assets		**Liabilities**	
Required reserves	+$100	Checkable deposits (Bill)	+$1,000
Excess reserves	$0		
Loans	+$900	Checkable deposits (Jenny)	$0

The situation for bank *B* is different. Because of the computer retailer's deposit, bank *B* now has $900 that it didn't have previously. This increases bank *B*'s reserves and liabilities by $900:

BANK *B*			
Assets		**Liabilities**	
Reserves	+$900	Checkable deposits (Computer Retailer)	+$900

Note that the computer purchase has not changed the overall money supply. Dollars have simply moved from Jenny's checking account to the computer retailer's checking account.

exhibit **1**

The Banking System Creates Checkable Deposits (Money)

In this exhibit, the required reserve ratio is 10 percent. We have assumed that there is no cash leakage and that excess reserves are fully lent out; that is, banks hold zero excess reserves.

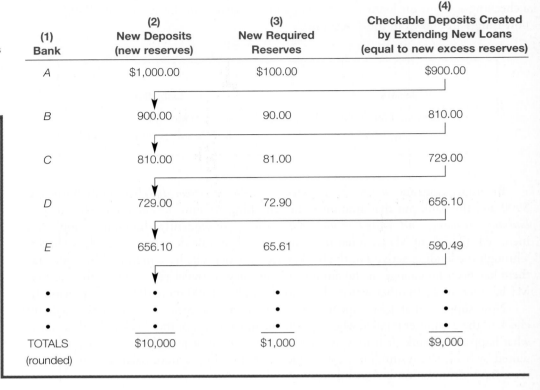

(1) Bank	(2) New Deposits (new reserves)	(3) New Required Reserves	(4) Checkable Deposits Created by Extending New Loans (equal to new excess reserves)
A	$1,000.00	$100.00	$900.00
B	900.00	90.00	810.00
C	810.00	81.00	729.00
D	729.00	72.90	656.10
E	656.10	65.61	590.49
•	•	•	•
•	•	•	•
•	•	•	•
TOTALS (rounded)	$10,000	$1,000	$9,000

The process continues in much the same way for bank *B* as it did earlier for bank *A*. Only a fraction (10 percent) of the computer retailer's $900 has to be kept on reserve (required reserves on $900 = $90). The remainder ($810) constitutes excess reserves that can be lent to still another borrower. That loan will create $810 in new checkable deposits and thus expand the money supply by that amount. The process continues with banks *C, D, E,* and so on until the dollar figures become so small that the process comes to a halt. Exhibit 1 summarizes what happens as the $1,000 originally created by the Fed works its way through the banking system.

Looking back over the entire process, this is what has happened:

- The Fed created $1,000 worth of new money and gave it to Bill, who then deposited it in bank *A*.
- The reserves of bank *A* increased. The reserves of no other bank decreased.
- The banking system, with the newly created $1,000 in hand, made loans and, in the process, created checkable deposits for the people who received the loans.
- Remember, checkable deposits are part of the money supply. So, in effect, by extending loans and, in the process, creating checkable deposits, the banking system has increased the money supply.

The $1,000 in new funds deposited in bank *A* was the basis of several thousand dollars worth of new bank loans and new checkable deposits. In this instance, the $1,000 initially injected into the economy ultimately caused bankers to create $9,000 in new checkable deposits. When this amount is added to the newly created $1,000 the Fed gave to Bill, the money supply has expanded by $10,000. A formula that shows this result is

$$\text{Maximum change in checkable deposits} = (1/r) \times \Delta R$$

where r = the required reserve ratio and ΔR = the change in reserves resulting from the original injection of funds.[1] In the equation, the reciprocal of the required reserve ratio $(1/r)$ is known as the **simple deposit multiplier.** The arithmetic for this example is

$$\text{Maximum change in checkable deposits} = (1/0.10) \times \$1,000$$
$$= 10 \times \$1,000$$
$$= \$10,000$$

Simple Deposit Multiplier
The reciprocal of the required reserve ratio, $1/r$.

Why Maximum? Answer: No Cash Leakages and Zero Excess Reserves

We made two important assumptions in our discussion of the money expansion process.

First, we assumed that all monies were deposited in bank checking accounts. For example, when Jenny wrote a check to the computer retailer, the retailer endorsed the check and deposited the full amount in bank *B*. In reality, the retailer might have deposited less than the full amount and kept a few dollars in cash. This is referred to as a **cash leakage.** If there had been a cash leakage of $300, then bank *B* would have received only $600, not $900. This would change the second number in column 2 in Exhibit 1 to $600 and the second number in column 4 to $540. Therefore, the total in column 2 of Exhibit 1 would be much smaller. A cash leakage that reduces the flow of dollars into banks means that banks have fewer dollars to lend. Fewer loans mean banks put less into borrowers' accounts, so less money is created than when cash leakages equal zero.

Cash Leakage
Occurs when funds are held as currency instead of being deposited into a checking account.

Second, we assumed that every bank lent all its excess reserves, leaving every bank with zero excess reserves. After Bill's $1,000 deposit, for example, bank *A* had excess reserves of $900 and made a new loan for the full amount. Banks generally want to lend all of their excess reserves to earn additional interest income, but there is no law, natural or legislated, that says every bank has to lend every penny of excess reserves. If banks do not lend all their excess reserves, then checkable deposits and the money supply will increase by less than in the original situation (where banks did lend all their excess reserves).

If we had not made our two assumptions, the change in checkable deposits would have been much smaller. Because we assumed no cash leakages and zero excess reserves, the change in checkable deposits is the *maximum* possible change.

Who Created What?

The money expansion process described had two major players: (1) the Fed, which created the new $1,000, and (2) the banking system. Together they created or expanded the money supply by $10,000. The Fed directly created $1,000 and thus made it possible for banks to create $9,000 in new checkable deposits as a by-product of extending new loans.

An easy formula for finding the maximum change in checkable deposits brought about by the banking system (and *only* the banking system) is

$$\text{Maximum change in checkable deposits (brought about by the banking system)} = (1/r) \times \Delta ER$$

---

1. Because only checkable deposits, and no other components of the money supply, change in this example, we could write "Maximum change in checkable deposits = $(1/r) \times \Delta R$" as "Maximum $\Delta M = (1/r) \times \Delta R$" where ΔM = the change in the money supply. In this chapter, the only component of the money supply that we allow to change is checkable deposits. For this reason, we can talk about changes in checkable deposits and the money supply as if they are the same—which they are, given our specification.

where r = the required reserve ratio and ΔER = the change in excess reserves of the first bank to receive the new injection of funds. The arithmetic for our example is

$$
\begin{aligned}
\text{Maximum change in checkable deposits} \\
\text{(brought about by the banking system)} &= (1/0.10) \times \$900 \\
&= 10 \times \$900 \\
&= \$9,000
\end{aligned}
$$

It Works in Reverse: The "Money Destruction" Process

In the preceding example, the Fed created $1,000 of new money and gave it to Bill, who then deposited it in bank A. This simple act created a multiple increase in checkable deposits and the money supply. The process also works in reverse. Suppose Bill withdraws the $1,000 and gives it back to the Fed. The Fed then destroys the $1,000. As a result, bank reserves decline. The multiple deposit contraction process is symmetrical to the multiple deposit expansion process.

Again, we set the required reserve ratio at 10 percent. The situation for bank A looks like this:

BANK A			
Assets		**Liabilities**	
Reserves	−$1,000	Checkable deposits (Bill)	−$1,000

Losing $1,000 in reserves places bank A in a *reserve deficiency position*. Specifically, it is $900 short. Remember, bank A held $100 reserves against the initial $1,000 deposit, so it loses $900 in reserves that backed other deposits ($1,000 × $100 = $900). If this is not immediately obvious, consider the following example.

Suppose the checkable deposits in a bank total $10,000 and the required reserve ratio is 10 percent. This means the bank must hold $1,000 in reserve form. Now let's suppose this is exactly what the bank holds in reserves, $1,000. (We'll assume that the $1,000 is being held as vault cash.) Is the bank reserve deficient at this point? No, it is holding exactly the right amount of reserves given its checkable deposits. Not one penny more, not one penny less.

Now one day a customer of the bank asks to withdraw $1,000. The bank teller goes to the vault, collects $1,000, and hands it to the customer. Two things have happened: (1) reserves of the bank have fallen by $1,000 and (2) checkable deposits in the bank have fallen by the same amount. In other words, checkable deposits go from $10,000 to $9,000.

Does the bank currently have reserves? The answer is no. The bank's reserves of $1,000 were given to the customer, so the bank has $0 in reserves. If the required reserve ratio is 10 percent, how much does the bank need in reserves given that checkable deposits are now $9,000? The answer is $900. In other words, the bank is $900 reserve deficient.

When a bank is reserve deficient, it must take immediate action to correct this situation. What can it do? One thing it can do is to reduce its outstanding loans. Funds from loan repayments can be applied to the reserve deficiency rather than being used to extend new loans. As borrowers repay $900 worth of loans, they reduce their checking account balances by that amount, causing the money supply to decline by $900.

Let's assume that the $900 loan repayment to bank *A* is written on a check issued by bank *B*. After the check has cleared, reserves and customer deposits at bank *B* fall by $900. This situation is reflected in bank *B*'s T-account:

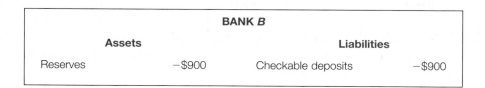

BANK *B*			
Assets		**Liabilities**	
Reserves	−$900	Checkable deposits	−$900

Bank *B* now faces a situation similar to bank *A*'s earlier situation. Losing $900 in reserves places bank *B* in reserve deficiency. It is $810 short. Remember, bank *B* held $90 in reserve form against the $900 deposit, so it loses $810 that backed other deposits ($900 − $90 = $810). Bank *B* seeks to recoup $810 by reducing its outstanding loans by an equal amount. If a customer is asked to pay off an $810 loan and does so by writing a check on his account at bank *C*, that bank's reserves and deposits both decline by $810. As a result, bank *C* is now in reserve deficiency; it is $729 short. Remember, bank *C* held $81 in reserve form against the $810 deposit, so it is short $729 that backed other deposits ($810 − $81 = $729).

As you can see, the figures are the same ones given in Exhibit 1, with the exception that each change is negative rather than positive. When Bill withdrew $1,000 from his account and returned it to the Fed (which then destroyed the $1,000), the money supply declined by $10,000.

Exhibit 2 shows the money supply expansion and contraction processes in brief.

SELF-TEST

1. If a bank's deposits equal $579 million and the required reserve ratio is 9.5 percent, what dollar amount must the bank hold in reserve form?
2. If the Fed creates $600 million in new reserves, what is the maximum change in checkable deposits that can occur if the required reserve ratio is 10 percent?
3. Bank *A* has $1.2 million in reserves and $10 million in deposits. The required reserve ratio is 10 percent. If bank *A* loses $200,000 in reserves, by what dollar amount is it reserve deficient?

exhibit 2

The Money Supply Expansion and Contraction Processes
The money supply expands if reserves enter the banking system; the money supply contracts if reserves exit the banking system. In expansion, reserves rise; thus, excess reserves rise, more loans are made, and checkable deposits rise. Because checkable deposits are part of the money supply, the money supply rises. In contraction, reserves fall; thus, excess reserves fall, fewer loans are made, and checkable deposits fall. Because checkable deposits are part of the money supply, the money supply falls.

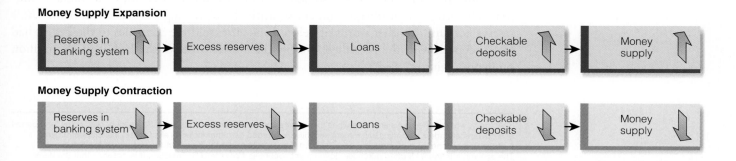

Money Supply Expansion

Reserves in banking system → Excess reserves → Loans → Checkable deposits → Money supply

Money Supply Contraction

Reserves in banking system → Excess reserves → Loans → Checkable deposits → Money supply

THE FEDERAL RESERVE SYSTEM

The Federal Reserve System came into existence with the Federal Reserve Act of 1913 and began operations in November 1914. The act divided the country into 12 Federal Reserve Districts.

Within the Fed, a seven-member **Board of Governors** coordinates and controls the activities of the Federal Reserve System. The Board members serve 14-year terms and are appointed by the president with Senate approval. To limit political influence on Fed policy, the terms of the governors are staggered—with one new appointment every other year—so a president cannot "pack" the Board. The president also designates one member as chairman of the Board for a four-year term.

The major policymaking group within the Fed is the **Federal Open Market Committee (FOMC).** Authority to conduct **open market operations**—the buying and selling of government securities—rests with the FOMC (more on open market operations later). The FOMC has 12 members: the 7-member Board of Governors and 5 Federal Reserve District Bank presidents. The president of the Federal Reserve Bank of New York holds a permanent seat on the FOMC because a large amount of financial activity takes place in New York City and because the New York Fed is responsible for executing open market operations. The other four positions are rotated among the Federal Reserve District Bank presidents.

The most important responsibility of the Fed is to control the nation's money supply. The Fed has three tools at its disposal that it can use to change (or control) the money supply: (1) open market operations, (2) the required reserve ratio, and (3) the discount rate. This section explains how the Fed uses these tools to control the money supply.

Open Market Operations

When the Fed either buys or sells U.S. government securities in the financial markets, it is said to be engaged in *open market operations*.[3] Specifically, when it buys securities, it is engaged in an **open market purchase;** when it sells securities, it is engaged in an **open market sale.** The following paragraphs explain how an open market purchase or sale affects the money supply.

Open Market Purchases

When the Fed buys securities, someone has to sell securities. Suppose bank *ABC* in Denver is the seller. In other words, suppose the Fed buys $5 million worth of government securities from bank *ABC*.[4] When this happens, the securities leave the possession of bank *ABC* and go to the Fed.

Bank *ABC,* of course, wants something in return for the securities—it wants $5 million. The Fed pays for the government securities by increasing the balance in bank *ABC*'s reserve account. In other words, if before bank *ABC* sold the securities to the Fed, it had $0 on deposit with the Fed, then after it sells the securities to the Fed, it has $5 million on deposit with the Fed.

Board of Governors
The governing body of the Federal Reserve System.

Federal Open Market Committee (FOMC)
The 12-member policymaking group within the Fed. The committee has the authority to conduct open market operations.

Open Market Operations
The buying and selling of government securities by the Fed.

Open Market Purchase
The buying of government securities by the Fed.

Open Market Sale
The selling of government securities by the Fed.

---

3. Actually, what the Fed buys and sells when it conducts open market operations are U.S. Treasury bills, notes, and bonds and government agency bonds. Government securities is a broad term that includes all of these financial instruments.
4. If the Fed purchases a government security from a bank, where did the bank get the security in the first place? The answer is that banks often purchase government securities from the U.S. Treasury. It is possible that the bank purchased the government security from the U.S. Treasury months ago.

Now at this point someone will ask, Where did the Fed get the $5 million to put into bank *ABC*'s reserve account? The answer, as odd as it seems, is: *Out of thin air.* This simply means that the Fed has the legal authority to create money. In other words, what the Fed is effectively doing is deleting the "$0" balance in bank *ABC*'s account and, with a few keystrokes, replacing it with the number five and six zeroes— $5,000,000.

As earlier in this chapter, we use T-accounts to show the changes to the accounts affected by the transaction. After the open market purchase, the Fed's T-account looks like this:

THE FED	
Assets	**Liabilities**
Government securities +$5 million	Reserves on deposit in bank *ABC*'s account +$5 million

In other words, the Fed now has assets of $5 million more in government securities, and it is holding (as liabilities) $5 million more for bank *ABC*.

After the open market purchase, bank *ABC*'s T-account looks like this:

BANK *ABC*	
Assets	**Liabilities**
Government securities −$5 million	No change
Reserves on deposit at the Fed +$5 million	

Bank *ABC* has $5 million less in securities and $5 million more in reserves.

Recall that as the reserves of one bank increase with no offsetting decline in reserves for other banks, the money supply expands through a process of increased loans and checkable deposits. In summary, an open market purchase by the Fed ultimately increases the money supply.

Open Market Sales

Sometimes the Fed sells government securities to banks and others. Suppose the Fed sells $5 million worth of government securities to bank *XYZ* in Atlanta. The Fed surrenders the securities to bank *XYZ* and is paid with $5 million previously deposited in bank *XYZ*'s reserve account at the Fed. In other words, the Fed simply reduces the balance in bank *XYZ*'s reserve account by $5 million.

After the open market sale, the Fed's T-account looks like this:

THE FED	
Assets	**Liabilities**
Government securities −$5 million	Reserves on deposit in bank *XYZ*'s account −$5 million

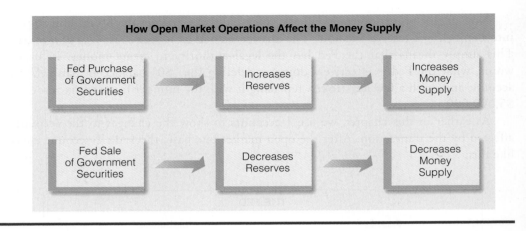

Open Market Operations

An open market purchase increases reserves, which leads to an increase in the money supply. An open market sale decreases reserves, which leads to a decrease in the money supply. (Note: We have assumed here that the Fed purchases government securities from and sells government securities to commercial banks.)

Bank *XYZ*'s T-account looks like this:

BANK *XYZ*	
Assets	**Liabilities**
Government securities +$5 million	No change
Reserves on deposit at the Fed −$5 million	

Now that bank *XYZ*'s reserves have declined by $5 million, it is reserve deficient. As bank *XYZ* and other banks adjust to the lower level of reserves, they reduce their total loans outstanding, which reduces the total volume of checkable deposits and money in the economy.

A nagging question remains: What happened to the $5 million the Fed got from bank *XYZ*'s account? The answer is that it disappears from the face of the earth; it no longer exists. This is simply the other side of the "Fed can create money out of thin air" coin. The Fed can also destroy money too; it can cause money to disappear into thin air.

Exhibit 3 summarizes how open market operations affect the money supply.

The Required Reserve Ratio

The Fed can influence the money supply by changing the required reserve ratio. Recall that we can find the maximum change in checkable deposits (for a given change in reserves) by using the following formula:

$$\text{Maximum change in checkable deposits} = (1/r) \times \Delta R$$

For example, if reserves (*R*) increase by $1,000, and the required reserve ratio (*r*) is 10 percent, then the maximum change in checkable deposits is $10,000:

$$
\begin{aligned}
\text{Maximum change in checkable deposits} &= (1/0.10) \times \$1,000 \\
&= 10 \times \$1,000 \\
&= \$10,000
\end{aligned}
$$

Now suppose Fed officials increase the required reserve ratio from 10 percent to 20 percent. How will this change the amount of checkable deposits? The amount of checkable deposits will decline:

$$\text{Maximum change in checkable deposits} = (1/0.20) \times \$1,000$$
$$= 5 \times \$1,000$$
$$= \$5,000$$

If, instead, the Fed lowers the required reserve ratio to 5 percent, the maximum change in checkable deposits will increase:

$$\text{Maximum change in checkable deposits} = (1/0.05) \times \$1,000$$
$$= 20 \times \$1,000$$
$$= \$20,000$$

We conclude that an increase in the required reserve ratio leads to a decrease in the money supply, and a decrease in the required reserve ratio leads to an increase in the money supply. In other words, there is an inverse relationship between the required reserve ratio and the money supply. As r goes up, the money supply goes down; as r goes down, the money supply goes up.

The Discount Rate

In addition to providing loans to customers, banks themselves borrow funds when they need them. Consider bank *ABC* that currently has zero excess reserves. Then either of the following two events occurs:

- **Case 1:** Mike Smith applies for a loan to buy new equipment for his horse ranch. The bank loan officer believes he is a good credit risk and that the bank could profit by granting him the loan. But the bank has no funds to lend.
- **Case 2:** Lisa Lyndon closes her checking account. As a result, the bank loses reserves and now is reserve deficient.

In Case 1, the bank wants funds so that it can make a loan to Mike Smith and increase its profits. In Case 2, the bank needs funds to meet its **reserve requirement.** In either case, there are two major places the bank can go to acquire a loan: (1) the **federal funds market,** which basically means the bank goes to another bank for a loan, or (2) the Fed (the bank's Federal Reserve District Bank). At both places, the bank will pay an interest rate. The rate it pays for a loan in the federal funds market is called the **federal funds rate.** The rate it pays for a loan from the Fed is called the **discount rate.** Bank *ABC* will try to minimize its costs by borrowing where the interest rate is lower, *ceteris paribus.* Suppose the discount rate is much lower than the federal funds rate; then bank *ABC* will go to the Fed for funds. If the Fed grants the bank a loan, the Fed's T-account looks like this:

Reserve Requirement
The rule that specifies the amount of reserves a bank must hold to back up deposits.

Federal Funds Market
A market where banks lend reserves to one another, usually for short periods.

Federal Funds Rate
The interest rate in the federal funds market; the interest rate banks charge one another to borrow reserves.

Discount Rate
The interest rate the Fed charges depository institutions that borrow reserves from it.

THE FED	
Assets	**Liabilities**
Loan to bank *ABC* +$1 million	Reserves on deposit in bank *ABC*'s account +$1 million

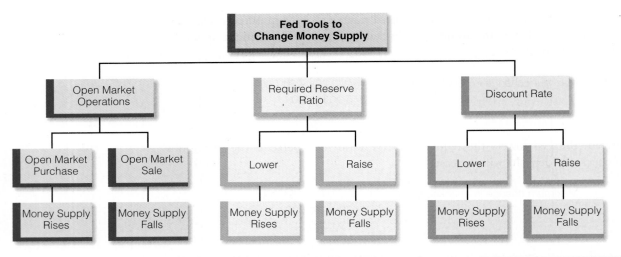

Fed Monetary Tools and Their Effects on the Money Supply
The following Fed actions increase the money supply: purchasing government securities on the open market, lowering the required reserve ratio, and lowering the discount rate relative to the federal funds rate. The following Fed actions decrease the money supply: selling government securities on the open market, raising the required reserve ratio, and raising the discount rate relative to the federal funds rate.

Bank *ABC*'s T-account reflects the same transaction from its perspective:

BANK *ABC*	
Assets	**Liabilities**
Reserves on deposit at the Fed +$1 million	Loan from the Fed +$1 million

Notice that when bank *ABC* borrows from the Fed, its reserves increase while the reserves of no other bank decrease. The result is increased reserves for the banking system as a whole, so the money supply increases. In summary: When a bank borrows at the Fed's discount window, the money supply increases.

A summary of the effects of the Fed's different monetary tools is shown in Exhibit 4.

SELF-TEST

1. How does the money supply change as a result of (a) an increase in the discount rate, (b) an open market purchase, (c) an increase in the required reserve ratio?
2. What is the difference between the federal funds rate and the discount rate?
3. If bank *A* borrows $10 million from bank *B,* what happens to the reserves in bank *A?* in the banking system?
4. If bank *A* borrows $10 million from the Fed, what happens to the reserves in bank *A?* in the banking system?

 ANALYZING THE SCENE

Question from Setting the Scene: How does the Fed expand or contract the money supply?
The 12 members of the FOMC decide the Fed's stance with respect to open market operations. This is one of the tools the Fed can use to increase or decrease the money supply. As discussed in this chapter, the Board of Governors of the Fed has two other tools—the discount rate and reserve requirements—that it can use to control the money supply. In all, the Fed has three principal tools that it can use to expand or contract the money supply.

I'm a junior in college, majoring in economics. Are there any career opportunities at the Fed that I might apply for while I'm still a student?

The Fed operates both summer internships and a Cooperative Education Program for college students. The Fed's summer internship program is "designed to provide valuable work experience for undergraduate and graduate students considering careers in economics, finance, and computer science." The following three divisions at the Federal Reserve Board in Washington, D.C., regularly offer internships:

- Banking Supervision and Regulation
- Information Technology
- Research and Statistics

Summer internships are usually available to college sophomores, juniors, and seniors. The internships are usually unpaid and run from June 1 to September 1.

As an economics major, you may be interested in applying for an internship in the Division of Research and Statistics. This division collects economic and financial information and develops economic analyses that are used by the Board of Governors, the Federal Open Market Committee, and other Fed officials in formulating monetary and regulatory policies.

The Fed's Cooperative Education Program provides paid and unpaid professional work experience to undergraduate and graduate students in economics, finance and accounting, information systems, and law. Here are the assignments in three of these areas:

- Economics: Students have the opportunity to apply their quantitative skills on projects in financial and nonfinancial areas, bank structure and competition, international trade, and foreign and exchange markets.
- Finance and Accounting: Students analyze the financial condition of domestic and foreign banking organizations and process applications filed by these financial institutions.

- Information Systems: Student assignments include creating public and intranet Web pages and assisting application developers in program maintenance, design, and coding.

Generally, employment in the Cooperative Education Program is for a summer or a year, although other assignment lengths are considered. Candidates are selected on the basis of scholastic achievement, recommendations, and completed course work in relevant areas of study.

To obtain more information about the summer internships and the Cooperative Education Program, go to the Federal Reserve Web site at **http://www.federalreserve.gov/**, and click on "Career Opportunities." You can also call the Fed's 24-hour job vacancy line at 1-800-448-4894.

Chapter Summary

What Money Is
> Money is any good that is widely accepted for purposes of exchange and in the repayment of debts.
> Money serves as a medium of exchange, a unit of account, and a store of value.
> Money evolved out of a barter economy as traders attempted to make exchange easier. A few goods that have been used as money include gold, silver, copper, cattle, rocks, and shells.

The Money Supply
> M1 includes currency held outside banks, checkable deposits, and traveler's checks.

> M2 includes M1, savings deposits (including money market deposit accounts), small-denomination time deposits, and money market mutual funds (noninstitutional).
> Credit cards are not money. When a credit card is used to make a purchase, a liability is incurred. This is not the case when money is used to make a purchase.

The Money Creation Process
> Banks in the United States operate under a fractional reserve system in which they must maintain only a fraction of their deposits in the form of reserves (that is, in the form of deposits at the Fed and vault cash). Excess reserves are typically used to extend loans

to customers. When banks make these loans, they credit borrowers' checking accounts and thereby increase the money supply. When banks reduce the volume of loans outstanding, they reduce checkable deposits and reduce the money supply.

> A change in the composition of the money supply can change the size of the money supply. For example, suppose M1 = $1,000 billion, where the breakdown is $300 billion currency outside banks and $700 billion in checkable deposits. Now suppose the $300 billion in currency is put in a checking account in a bank. Initially, this changes the composition of the money supply but not its size. M1 is still $1,000 billion but now includes $0 in currency and $1,000 billion in checkable deposits. Later, when the banks have had time to create new loans (checkable deposits) with the new reserves provided by the $300 billion deposit, the money supply expands.

The Federal Reserve System

> There are 12 Federal Reserve Districts. The Board of Governors controls and coordinates the activities of the Federal Reserve System. The Board is made up of 7 members, each appointed to a 14-year term. The major policymaking group within the Fed is the Federal Open Market Committee (FOMC). It is a 12-member group, made up of the 7 members of the Board of Governors and 5 Federal Reserve District Bank presidents.

Controlling the Money Supply

> The following Fed actions increase the money supply: lowering the required reserve ratio, purchasing government securities on the open market, and lowering the discount rate relative to the federal funds rate. The following Fed actions decrease the money supply: raising the required reserve ratio, selling government securities on the open market, and raising the discount rate relative to the federal funds rate.

Open Market Operations

> An open market purchase by the Fed increases the money supply. An open market sale by the Fed decreases the money supply.

The Required Reserve Ratio

> An increase in the required reserve ratio leads to a decrease in the money supply. A decrease in the required reserve ratio leads to an increase in the money supply.

The Discount Rate

> An increase in the discount rate relative to the federal funds rate leads to a decrease in the money supply. A decrease in the discount rate relative to the federal funds rate leads to an increase in the money supply.

Key Terms and Concepts

Money
Barter
Medium of Exchange
Unit of Account
Store of Value
Double Coincidence of Wants
M1
Currency
Federal Reserve Notes
Checkable Deposits
M2
Savings Deposit

Money Market Deposit Account
Time Deposit
Money Market Mutual Fund
Fractional Reserve Banking
Federal Reserve System (the Fed)
Reserves
Required Reserve Ratio (r)
Required Reserves
Excess Reserves
T-Account
Simple Deposit Multiplier
Cash Leakage

Board of Governors
Federal Open Market Committee
   (FOMC)
Open Market Operations
Open Market Purchase
Open Market Sale
Reserve Requirement
Federal Funds Market
Federal Funds Rate
Discount Rate

Questions and Problems

1. Does inflation, which is an increase in the price level, affect the three functions of money? If so, how?
2. Money makes trade easier. Would having a money supply twice as large as it is currently make trade twice as easy? Would having a money supply half its current size make trade half as easy?

3. "Money is a means of lowering the transaction costs of making exchanges." Do you agree or disagree? Explain your answer.
4. If you were on an island with 10 other people and there was no money, do you think money would emerge on the scene? Why or why not?

5. Can M1 fall as M2 rises? Can M1 rise without M2 rising too? Explain your answers.
6. Why isn't a credit card money?
7. If Smith, who has a checking account at bank *A*, withdraws his money and deposits all of it into bank *B*, do reserves in the banking system change? Explain your answer.
8. If Jones, who has a checking account at bank *A*, withdraws her money, deposits half of it into bank *B*, and keeps the other half in currency, do reserves in the banking system change?
9. Give an example that illustrates a change in the composition of the money supply.
10. Describe the money supply expansion process.
11. Describe the money supply contraction process.
12. Does a cash leakage affect the change in checkable deposits and the money supply expansion process? Explain your answer.
13. Explain how an open market purchase increases the money supply.

14. Explain how an open market sale decreases the money supply.
15. Suppose the Fed raises the required reserve ratio, a move that is normally thought to reduce the money supply. However, banks find themselves with a reserve deficiency after the required reserve ratio is increased and are likely to react by requesting a loan from the Fed. Does this action prevent the money supply from contracting as predicted?
16. Suppose bank A borrows reserves from bank B. Now that bank A has more reserves than previously, will the money supply increase?
17. Explain how a decrease in the required reserve ratio increases the money supply.
18. Suppose you read in the newspaper that all last week the Fed conducted open market purchases and that on Tuesday of last week it lowered the discount rate. What would you say the Fed was trying to do?

Working With Numbers and Graphs

1. Suppose that $10,000 in new dollar bills (never seen before) falls magically from the sky into the hands of Joanna Ferris. What are the minimum increase and the maximum increase in the money supply that may result? Assume the required reserve ratio is 10 percent.
2. Suppose Joanna Ferris receives $10,000 from her friend Ethel and deposits the money in a checking account. Ethel gave Joanna the money by writing a check on her checking account. Would the maximum increase in the money supply still be what you found it to be in Question 1 where Joanna received the money from the sky? Explain your answer.
3. Suppose $r = 10$ percent and the Fed creates $20,000 in new money that is deposited in someone's checking account in a bank. What is the maximum change in the money supply as a result?
4. Suppose $r = 10$ percent and John walks into his bank, withdraws $2,000 in cash, and burns the money. What is the maximum change in the money supply as a result?
5. The Fed creates $100,000 in new money that is deposited in someone's checking account in a bank. What is the maximum

change in the money supply if the required reserve ratio is 5 percent? 10 percent? 20 percent?
6. Use the table below to answer the questions that follow.

Bank	New Deposits (new reserves)	New Required Reserves	Checkable Deposits Created by Extending New Loans (equal to new excess reserves)
A	(1)	$500	$1,400
B	(2)	$342	(3)

a. What dollar amount goes in blank (1)?
b. What does the required reserve ratio equal?
c. What does the cash leakage between bank *A* and bank *B* equal?
d. What dollar amount goes in blank (2)?
e. What dollar amount goes in blank (3)

7. If reserves increase by $2 million and the required reserve ratio is 8 percent, then what is the maximum change in checkable deposits?

8. If reserves increase by $2 million and the required reserves ratio is 10 percent, then what is the maximum change in checkable deposits?

9. If the federal funds rate is 6 percent and the discount rate is 5.1 percent, to whom will a bank be more likely to go for a loan—another bank or the Fed? Explain your answer.

10. Complete the following table:

Federal Reserve Action	Effect on the Money Supply (up or down?)
Lower the discount rate	A
Conduct open market purchase	B
Lower required reserve ratio	C
Raise the discount rate	D
Conduct open market sale	E
Raise the required reserve ratio	F

© Michael Newman/PhotoEdit

chapter 9

MONEY, THE PRICE LEVEL,
AND INTEREST RATES

Setting the Scene

An increase or decrease in the money supply can have far-reaching effects in an economy. It can change Real GDP, the price level, the unemployment rate, and the interest rate. In an economics text, we see the effect of a change in the money supply in a diagram; in real life, we see it in the words and actions of everyday people. The following events occurred on different days not long ago.

March 13

Oliver and Roberta are thinking about buying a house. Mortgage rates are relatively low right now.

"I heard someone say that the Fed is meeting next week and that they might lower interest rates more," Oliver says.

Roberta asks, "Are you saying we should wait to buy a house?"

"Well, maybe," Oliver answers.

June 21

Jim has been out of a job for four months. He's in the kitchen talking to his brother, Sebastian.

"I think someone has got to do something about the job situation," Jim says. "There are simply not that many jobs. I've been looking."

"I was watching the news and read a news blurb at the bottom of the TV screen. It said the Fed chairman was worried about the economy and that

the Fed was likely to stimulate the economy soon," Sebastian says. "Maybe that will help."

"What does the Fed have in mind?" asks Jim.

"I'm not really sure," Sebastian answers.

How would an economist look at these events? Later in the chapter, discussions based on the following questions will help you analyze the scene the way an economist would.

- If the Fed wants to lower interest rates, are interest rates destined to go down? In short, can the Fed do what it wants to do?

- If the Fed does what Sebastian thinks it will do, will his brother, Jim, have a better chance of finding a job?

MONEY AND THE PRICE LEVEL

Do changes in the money supply affect the price level in the economy? Classical economists believed so. Their position was based on the equation of exchange and the simple quantity theory of money.

The Equation of Exchange

Equation of Exchange
An identity stating that the money supply times velocity must be equal to the price level times Real GDP.

The **equation of exchange** is an identity that states that the money supply (M) multiplied by velocity (V) must be equal to the price level (P) times Real GDP (Q).

$$MV \equiv PQ$$

The sign $\equiv$ means "must be equal to"; this is an identity. An identity is valid for all values of the variables.

Velocity
The average number of times a dollar is spent to buy final goods and services in a year.

You are familiar with the money supply, the price level, and Real GDP, but not velocity. **Velocity** is the average number of times a dollar is spent to buy final goods and services in a year. For example, assume an economy has only five one-dollar bills. In January, the first of the one-dollar bills moves from Smith's hands to Jones's hands to buy good X. Then in June, it goes from Jones's hands to Brown's hands to buy good Y. And in December, it goes from Brown's hands to Peterson's hands to buy good Z. Over the course of the year, this dollar bill has changed hands 3 times.

The other dollar bills also change hands during the year. The second dollar bill changes hands 5 times; the third, 6 times; the fourth, 2 times; and the fifth, 7 times. Given this information, we can calculate the number of times a dollar changes hands on average in making a purchase. In this case, the number is 4.6. This number (4.6) is velocity.

In a large economy such as ours, it is impossible to simply count how many times each dollar changes hands; therefore, it is impossible to calculate velocity as in our example. Instead, a different method is used.

First, we calculate GDP; next, we calculate the average money supply; finally, we divide GDP by the average money supply to obtain velocity. For example, if $4,800 billion worth of transactions occur in a year and the average money supply during the year is $800 billion, a dollar must have been used on average 6 times during the year to purchase goods and services. In symbols, we have

$$V \equiv GDP/M$$

GDP is equal to $P \times Q$, so this identity can be written

$$V \equiv (P \times Q)/M$$

Multiplying both sides by M, we get

$$MV \equiv PQ$$

which is the equation of exchange shown at the beginning of this section. Thus, the equation of exchange is derived from the definition of velocity.

The equation of exchange can be interpreted in different ways:

1. The money supply multiplied by velocity must equal the price level times Real GDP: $M \times V \equiv P \times Q$.
2. The money supply multiplied by velocity must equal GDP: $M \times V \equiv GDP$ (because $P \times Q = GDP$).
3. Total spending or expenditures (measured by MV) must equal the total sales revenues of business firms (measured by PQ): $MV \equiv PQ$.

The third way of interpreting the equation of exchange is perhaps the most intuitively easy to understand. It simply says that the total expenditures (of buyers) must equal the total sales (of sellers). Consider a simple economy where there is only one buyer and one seller. If the buyer buys a book for $20, then the seller receives $20. Stated differently, the money supply in the example, or $20, times velocity, 1, is equal to the price of the book, $20, times the quantity of the book.

Notice how velocity in the equation of exchange affects GDP. For example, suppose the money supply is $1,200 billion. Can a money supply of $1,200 billion support a GDP (or PQ) of $11 trillion? The answer is yes; in fact, this money supply can support a GDP level that is either higher or lower than $11 trillion. It all depends on velocity.

From the Equation of Exchange to the Simple Quantity Theory of Money

The equation of exchange is an identity, not an economic theory. To turn it into a theory, we make some assumptions about the variables in the equation. Many eighteenth-century classical economists, as well as the American economist Irving Fisher (1867–1947) and the English economist Alfred Marshall (1842–1924), assumed (1) changes in velocity are so small that for all practical purposes velocity can be assumed to be constant (especially over short periods of time) and (2) Real GDP, or Q, is fixed in the short run. Hence, they turned the equation of exchange, which is simply true by definition, into a theory by assuming that both V and Q are fixed, or constant. With these two assumptions, we have the **simple quantity theory of money:** If V and Q are constant, we would predict that changes in M will bring about *strictly proportional* changes in P. In other words, the simple quantity theory of money predicts that changes in the money supply will bring about strictly proportional changes in the price level.

Exhibit 1 shows the assumptions and predictions of the simple quantity theory. On the left side of the exhibit, the key assumptions of the simple quantity theory are noted: V and Q are constant. Also, $M \times V = P \times Q$ is noted. We use the equal sign (=) instead of the identity sign (≡) because we are speaking about the simple quantity theory and not the equation of exchange. (The = sign here represents "is predicted to be equal"; that is, given our assumptions, $M \times V$, or MV, is predicted to be equal to $P \times Q$, or PQ.)

Starting with the first row, the money supply is $500, velocity is 4, Real GDP (Q) is 1,000 units, and the price level, or price index, is $2.[1] Therefore GDP equals $2,000. In the second row, the money supply increases by 100 percent, from $500 to $1,000, and both V and Q are constant, at 4 and 1,000, respectively. The price level moves from $2 to $4. On the right side of the exhibit, we see that a 100 percent increase in M predicts a 100 percent increase in P. Changes in P are predicted to be strictly proportional to changes in M.

Simple Quantity Theory of Money
The theory that assumes that velocity (V) and Real GDP (Q) are constant and predicts that changes in the money supply (M) lead to strictly proportional changes in the price level (P).

exhibit 1

Assumptions and Predictions of the Simple Quantity Theory of Money
The simple quantity theory of money assumes that both V and Q are constant. (A bar over each indicates this in the exhibit.) The prediction is that changes in M lead to strictly proportional changes in P. (Note: For purposes of this example, think of Q as "so many units of goods" and of P as the "average price paid per unit of these goods.")

		Assumptions of Simple Quantity Theory				Predictions of Simple Quantity Theory	
M	$\times$	$\bar{V}$	$=$	P	$\times$	$\bar{Q}$	% Change in M	% Change in P
$ 500		4		$2		1,000		
1,000		4		4		1,000	+ 100%	+ 100%
1,500		4		6		1,000	+ 50	+ 50
1,200		4		4.80		1,000	− 20	− 20

1. You are used to seeing Real GDP expressed as a dollar figure and a price index as a number without a dollar sign in front of it. We have switched things for the purposes of this example because it is easier to think of Q as "so many units of goods" and P as "the average price paid per unit of these goods."

In the third row, M increases by 50 percent, and P is predicted to increase by 50 percent. In the fourth row, M decreases by 20 percent, and P is predicted to decrease by 20 percent.

In summary, the simple quantity theory assumes that both V and Q are constant in the short run, and therefore predicts that changes in M lead to strictly proportional changes in P.

How well does the simple quantity theory of money predict? In other words, do changes in the money supply lead to *strictly proportional* changes in the price level? For example, if the money supply goes up by 7 percent, does the price level go up by 7 percent? If the money supply goes down by 4 percent, does the price level go down by 4 percent? The answer is that the strict proportionality between changes in the money supply and the price level does not show up in the data (at least not very often). Generally, though, evidence supports the spirit (or essence) of the simple quantity theory of money—the higher the growth rate in the money supply, the greater the growth rate in the price level.

To illustrate, we would expect that a growth rate in the money supply of, say, 40 percent, would generate a greater increase in the price level than, say, a growth rate in the money supply of 4 percent. (Although we wouldn't expect the higher money supply growth rate to generate a 40 percent rise in the price level and the lower money supply growth rate to generate a 4 percent rise in the price level.) And generally, this is what we see. For example, countries with more rapid increases in their money supplies often witness more rapid increases in their price levels than do countries that witness less rapid increases in their money supplies.

The Simple Quantity Theory of Money in an *AD-AS* Framework

You are familiar with the *AD-AS* framework from earlier chapters. In this section, we analyze the simple quantity theory of money in this framework.

The *AD* Curve in the Simple Quantity Theory of Money

The simple quantity theory of money builds on the equation of exchange. Recall that one way of interpreting the equation of exchange is that the total expenditures of buyers (measured by MV) must equal the total sales of sellers (measured by PQ). Thus, we are saying that MV is the total expenditures of buyers and PQ is the total sales of sellers. For now, we concentrate on MV as the total expenditures of buyers:

$$MV = \text{Total expenditures}$$

In an earlier chapter, total expenditures (TE) is defined as the sum of the expenditures made by the four sectors of the economy. In other words,

$$TE = C + I + G + (EX - IM)$$

Because $MV = TE$,

$$MV = C + I + G + (EX - IM)$$

Now recall that at a given price level, anything that changes C, I, G, EX, or IM changes aggregate demand and thus shifts the aggregate demand (AD) curve. But MV equals $C + I + G + (EX - IM)$, so it follows that *a change in the money supply (M) or a change in velocity (V) will change aggregate demand and therefore lead to a shift in the AD curve.* Another way to say this is that aggregate demand depends on *both* the money supply and velocity.

Specifically, an increase in the money supply will increase aggregate demand and shift the *AD* curve to the right. A decrease in the money supply will decrease aggregate demand and shift the *AD* curve to the left. An increase in velocity will increase aggregate demand and shift the *AD* curve to the right. A decrease in velocity will decrease aggregate demand and shift the *AD* curve to the left. But, *in the simple quantity theory*

Economics In

Popular Culture · Technology · Everyday Life · The World

Money and Inflation

The simple quantity theory of money predicts that the larger the percentage increase in the money supply, the larger the percentage increase in the price level. There is some evidence that confirms this theory.

Exhibit 2a shows the average annual growth rate in the money supply and the average annual inflation rate for the period

1980–1990 in Switzerland, Italy, Germany, the United States, Israel, Peru, and Argentina. It is easy to see that the countries with the higher money supply growth rates are also the countries with the higher inflation rates.

Exhibit 2b shows the average annual growth rate in the money supply and the average annual inflation rate for the period

exhibit 2

Money and Inflation

Parts (a) and (b) show that the higher the average annual money supply growth rate in a country, the higher the average annual inflation rate in the country. Part (c) shows annual money supply growth rates and inflation rates in four countries. Usually, countries with higher money supply growth rates have higher inflation rates.

Source: Financial international statistics Yearbook and Handbook of International Economic Statistics, 1993 and 1996.

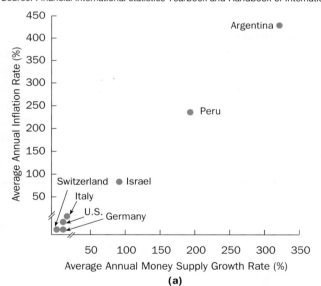

(a)

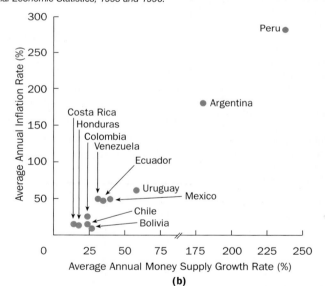

(b)

	Brazil			India			Mexico			South Korea	
Year	Money Supply Growth Rate (%)	Inflation Rate (%)	Year	Money Supply Growth Rate (%)	Inflation Rate (%)	Year	Money Supply Growth Rate (%)	Inflation Rate (%)	Year	Money Supply Growth Rate (%)	Inflation Rate (%)
1990	2,350.8	1,795.0	1990	14.3	9.0	1990	62.6	26.7	1990	21.2	8.6
1991	325.6	478.5	1991	22.5	13.9	1991	119.8	22.7	1991	18.6	9.7
1992	881.6	1,158.0	1992	12.3	11.7	1992	17.0	15.5	1992	18.4	6.2
1993	2,082.1	2,708.6	1993	16.9	6.4	1993	15.8	9.8	1993	17.4	5.8

(c)

(Continued)

1986–1996 for several Latin American countries. Again, the relationship predicted by the simple quantity theory of money holds: the higher the money supply growth rate, the higher the growth rate in prices.

In Exhibit 2c, we look at annual changes (not average annual changes) in both the money supply and prices for four countries: Brazil, India, Mexico, and South Korea. Notice, for example, that the growth rate in the money supply in 1993 in Brazil was 2,082.1 percent. The percentage increase in prices (the inflation rate) in that year in Brazil was 2,708.6 percent. In contrast, the growth rate in the money supply in 1993 in Mexico was 15.8 percent, and the percentage increase in prices was 9.8 percent.

If we were to average the data in Exhibit 2c and compare the average annual growth rates in the money supply to the average annual increases in prices, we'd find that during the period 1990–1993, the money supply in Brazil grew by an average annual rate of 1,410 percent and prices increased by an average annual rate of 1,535 percent, In India, the money supply grew by an average annual rate of 16.5 percent and prices increased by an average annual rate of 10.25 percent. In Mexico, the respective figures were 53.8 percent (money supply) and 18.67 percent (prices). Finally, in South Korea, the respective figures were 18.9 percent (money supply) and 7.57 percent (prices). Again, the relationship between money and prices predicted by the simple quantity theory of money holds: this higher the growth rate of the money supply, the higher the growth rate in prices.

of money, velocity is assumed to be constant. Thus, we are left with only changes in the money supply being able to shift the AD curve.

The AD curve for the simple quantity theory of money is shown in Exhibit 3a. The (M, V) in parentheses next to the curve is a reminder of what factors can shift the AD curve. The bar over V (for velocity) indicates that velocity is assumed to be constant.

The AS Curve in the Simple Quantity Theory of Money
In the simple quantity theory of money, the level of Real GDP is assumed to be constant in the short run. Exhibit 3b shows Real GDP fixed at Q_1. The AS curve is vertical at this level of Real GDP.

AD and AS in the Simple Quantity Theory of Money
Exhibit 3c shows both the AD and AS curves in the simple quantity theory of money. Suppose that AD_1 is initially operational. In the exhibit, AD_1 is based on a money supply of $800 billion and a velocity of 2. The price level is P_1.

Now suppose we increase the money supply to $820 billion. Velocity remains constant at 2. According to the simple quantity theory of money, the price level will increase. We see that it does. The increase in the money supply shifts the AD curve from AD_1 to AD_2 and pushes up the price level from P_1 to P_2.

exhibit **3**

The Simple Quantity Theory of Money in the AD-AS Framework
(a) In the simple quantity theory of money, the AD curve is downward sloping. Velocity is assumed to be constant, so changes in the money supply will change aggregate demand. (b) In the simple quantity theory of money, Real GDP is fixed in the short run. Thus, the AS curve is vertical. (c) In the simple quantity theory of money, an increase in the money supply will shift the AD curve rightward and increase the price level. A decrease in the money supply will shift the AD curve leftward and decrease the price level.

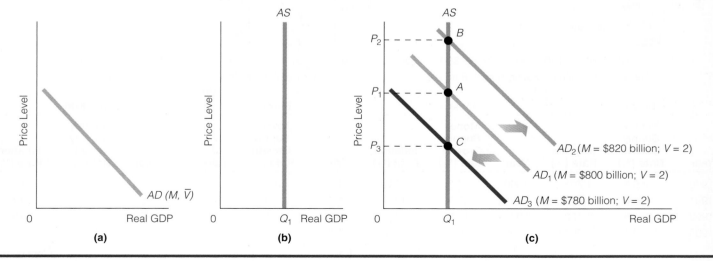

(a)

(b)

(c)

Economics In

Popular Culture | Technology | Everyday Life

© Bettmann/CORBIS

The California Gold Rush, or an Apple for $72

Soon there was too much money in California and too little of everything else.
—J. S. Holiday, author of *The World Rushed In*

The only peacetime rise [in prices] comparable in total magnitude [to the 40 to 50 percent in prices from 1897 to 1914] followed the California gold discoveries in the early 1850s . . .
—Milton Friedman and Anna Schwartz, *A Monetary History of the United States, 1867–1960*

John Sutter was a Swiss immigrant who arrived in California in 1839. James Marshall, a carpenter, was building a sawmill for Sutter. On the chilly morning of January 24, 1848, Marshall was busy at work when something glistening caught his eye. He reached down and picked up the object. Marshall said to the workers he had hired, "Boys, by God I believe I have found a gold mine." Marshall later wrote, "I reached my hand down and picked it up; it made my heart thump, for I was certain it was gold. The piece was about half the size and shape of a pea. Then I saw another."

In time, Marshall and his workers came across more gold, and before long, people from all across the United States, and many other countries, headed to California. The California gold rush had begun.

The California gold rush, which resulted in an increase in the amount of money in circulation, provides an illustration of how a fairly dramatic increase in the money supply can affect prices. As more gold was mined and the supply of money increased, prices began to rise. There was a general rise in prices across the country, but the earliest and most dramatic increases in prices occurred in and near the areas in which gold was discovered. Near the gold mines, the prices of food and clothing sharply increased. For example, while a loaf of bread sold for 4 cents in New York (equivalent to 72 cents today), near the mines, the price was 75 cents (the equivalent of $13.50 today). Eggs sold for about $2 each (the equivalent of $36 today), apples for $4 (the equivalent of $72 today), a butcher's knife for $30 (the equivalent of $540 today), and boots went for $100 a pair (the equivalent of $1,800 today).

In San Francisco, land prices rose dramatically because of the city's relative closeness to the mines. Real estate that cost $16 (the equivalent of $288 today) before gold was discovered jumped to $45,000 (the equivalent of $810,000 today) in 18 months.

The sharp rise in prices that followed the California gold discoveries followed other gold discoveries too. For example, the gold stock of the world is estimated to have doubled from 1890 to 1914, due both to discoveries (in South Africa, Alaska, and Colorado) and to improved methods of mining and refining gold. During this period, world prices increased too.

Suppose that instead of increasing the money supply, we decrease it to $780 billion. Again, velocity remains constant at 2. According to the simple quantity theory of money, the price level will decrease. We see that it does. The decrease in the money supply shifts the AD curve from AD_1 to AD_3 and pushes down the price level from P_1 to P_3.

Dropping the Assumptions That *V* and *Q* Are Constant

If we drop the assumptions that velocity (V) and Real GDP (Q) are constant, we have a more general theory of the factors that cause changes in the price level. Stated differently, changes in the price level depend on three variables: the money supply, velocity, and Real GDP. To see this, let's again start with the equation of exchange.

$$M \times V \equiv P \times Q \tag{1}$$

If the equation of exchange holds, then it follows that:

$$P \equiv (M \times V)/Q \tag{2}$$

By looking at equation 2, we can see that the money supply, velocity, and Real GDP determine the price level. In other words, the price level depends on the money supply, velocity, and Real GDP.

What kinds of changes in *M, V,* and *Q* will bring about inflation (an increase in the price level)? Obviously, *ceteris paribus,* an increase in *M* or *V* or a decrease in *Q* will cause the price level to rise. For example, if velocity rises, *ceteris paribus,* the price level will rise. In other words, an increase in velocity is inflationary, *ceteris paribus.*

Inflationary Tendencies: $M\uparrow$, $V\uparrow$, $Q\downarrow$

What will bring about deflation (a decrease in the price level)? Obviously, *ceteris paribus,* a decrease in *M* or *V* or an increase in *Q* will cause the price level to fall. For example, if the money supply declines, *ceteris paribus,* the price level will drop. In other words, a decrease in the money supply is deflationary, *ceteris paribus.*

Deflationary Tendencies: $M\downarrow$, $V\downarrow$, $Q\uparrow$

SELF-TEST *(Answers to Self-Test questions are in the Self-Test Appendix.)*

1. If *M* times *V* increases, why does *P* times *Q* have to rise?
2. What is the difference between the equation of exchange and the simple quantity theory of money?
3. Predict what will happen to the *AD* curve as a result of each of the following:
   a. The money supply rises.
   b. Velocity falls.
   c. The money supply rises by a greater percentage than velocity falls.
   d. The money supply falls.

MONETARISM

Economists who call themselves monetarists have not been content to rely on the simple quantity theory of money. They do not hold that velocity is constant, nor do they hold that output is constant. Monetarist views on the money supply, velocity, aggregate demand, and aggregate supply are discussed in this section.

Monetarist Views

We begin with a brief explanation of the four positions held by monetarists. Then, we discuss how, based on these positions, monetarists view the economy.

Velocity Changes in a Predictable Way

In the simple quantity theory of money, velocity is assumed to be constant. It follows from this that any changes in aggregate demand are brought about by changes in the money supply only.

Monetarists do not assume velocity is constant. Instead, they assume that velocity can and does change. It is important to note, however, that monetarists believe velocity changes in a predictable way. In other words, it does not change randomly, but rather it changes in a way that can be understood and predicted. Monetarists hold that velocity is a function of certain variables—the interest rate, the expected inflation rate, the frequency with which employees receive paychecks, and more—and that changes in it can be predicted.

Aggregate Demand Depends on the Money Supply and on Velocity

Earlier we showed that total expenditures in the economy (*TE*) equal *MV.* To better understand the economy, some economists—such as Keynesians—focus on the spending components of *TE* (*C, I, G, EX,* and *IM*). Other economists—such as monetarists—focus on the money supply (*M*) and velocity (*V*). For example, while Keynesians often argue that changes in *C, I, G, EX,* or *IM* can change aggregate demand, monetarists often argue that *M* and *V* can change aggregate demand.

The *SRAS* Curve Is Upward-Sloping

In the simple quantity theory of money, the level of Real GDP (*Q*) is assumed to be constant in the short run. So, the aggregate supply curve is vertical, as shown in Exhibit 3. According to monetarists, Real GDP may change in the short run. It follows that monetarists believe that the *SRAS* curve is upward-sloping.

The Economy Is Self-Regulating (Prices and Wages Are Flexible)

Monetarists believe that prices and wages are flexible. It follows that monetarists believe the economy is self-regulating—it can move itself out of a recessionary or an inflationary gap and into long-run equilibrium producing Natural Real GDP.

Monetarism and AD-AS

As we mentioned, monetarists tend to stress velocity and the money supply when discussing how the economy works. We describe the monetarist view using the *AD-AS*

exhibit 4

Monetarism in an *AD-AS* Framework
According to monetarists, changes in the money supply and velocity can change aggregate demand. In (a), an increase in the money supply shifts the *AD* curve to the right and raises Real GDP and the price level. Monetarists believe the economy is self-regulating; in time it moves back to its Natural Real GDP level at a higher price level. The same self-regulating properties are present in (b)–(d).

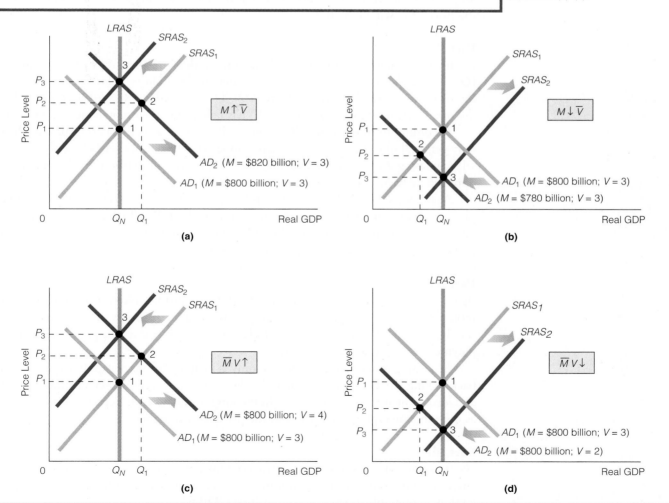

framework. Exhibit 4 helps to explain some of the highlights of monetarism. Each of the four parts (a)–(d) is considered separately.

Part (a)

In (a), the economy is initially in long-run equilibrium producing Natural Real GDP (Q_N) at price level P_1. Monetarists believe that changes in the money supply will change aggregate demand. For example, suppose the money supply rises from $800 billion to $820 billion. If velocity is constant, the AD curve shifts to the right, from AD_1 to AD_2 in the exhibit. As a result, Real GDP rises to Q_1 and the price level rises to P_2. And, of course, if Real GDP rises, the unemployment rate falls, *ceteris paribus*.

According to monetarists, the economy is an inflationary gap at Q_1. Monetarists believe in a self-regulating economy. Thus, because the unemployment rate is less than the natural unemployment rate in an inflationary gap, soon wages will be bid up. This will cause the $SRAS$ curve to shift leftward, from $SRAS_1$ to $SRAS_2$. The economy will return to long-run equilibrium, producing the same level of Real GDP as it did originally (Q_N), but at a higher price level.

We can separate what monetarists predict will happen to the economy in the short run due to an increase in the money supply from what they predict will happen in the long run. In the short run, Real GDP will rise and the unemployment rate will fall. In the long run, Real GDP will return to its natural level, as will the unemployment rate, and the price level will be higher.

Part (b)

In (b), the economy is initially in long-run equilibrium producing Natural Real GDP (Q_N) at price level P_1. A decrease in the money supply, holding velocity constant, will shift the AD curve to the left, from AD_1 to AD_2. This will reduce Real GDP to Q_1 and reduce the price level to P_2. Because Real GDP has fallen, the unemployment rate will rise.

According to monetarists, the economy in (b) is in a recessionary gap. Can the economy get itself out of a recessionary gap? Monetarists think so; they believe the economy is self-regulating. In time, wages will fall, the $SRAS$ curve will shift to the right, and the economy will be back in long-run equilibrium producing Q_N—albeit at a lower price level.

Again, we separate the short-run and long-run effects of a decrease in the money supply according to monetarists. In the short run, Real GDP will fall and the unemployment rate will rise. In the long run, Real GDP will return to its natural level, as will the unemployment rate, and the price level will be lower.

Part (c)

Again, we start with the economy in long-run equilibrium. Now, instead of changing the money supply, we change velocity. An increase in velocity causes the AD curve to shift to the right, from AD_1 to AD_2. As a result, Real GDP rises, as does the price level. The unemployment rate falls as Real GDP rises.

According to monetarists, the economy is in an inflationary gap. In time, it will move back to long-run equilibrium. So, in the short run, an increase in velocity raises Real GDP and lowers the unemployment rate. In the long run, Real GDP returns to its natural level, as does the unemployment rate, and the price level is higher.

Part (d)

We start with the economy in long-run equilibrium. A decrease in velocity causes the AD curve to shift to the left, from AD_1 to AD_2. As a result, Real GDP falls, as does the price level. The unemployment rate rises as Real GDP falls.

According to monetarists, the economy is in a recessionary gap. In time, it will move back to long-run equilibrium. So, in the short run, a decrease in velocity lowers Real GDP and increases the unemployment rate. In the long run, Real GDP returns to its natural level, as does the unemployment rate, and the price level is lower.

The Monetarist View of the Economy

Based on our diagrammatic exposition of monetarism so far, we know the following about monetarists:

1. Monetarists believe the economy is self-regulating.
2. Monetarists believe changes in velocity and the money supply can change aggregate demand.
3. Monetarists believe changes in velocity and the money supply will change the price level and Real GDP in the short run, but only the price level in the long run.

We need to make one other important point with respect to monetarists. But first, consider this question: Can a change in velocity offset a change in the money supply? To illustrate, suppose velocity falls and the money supply rises. By itself, a decrease in velocity will shift the *AD* curve to the left. And by itself, an increase in the money supply will shift the *AD* curve to the right. Can the decline in velocity shift the *AD* curve to the left by the same amount as the increase in the money supply shifts the *AD* curve to the right? This is, of course, possible. If it happens, then a change in the money supply would have no effect on Real GDP and the price level (in the short run) and on the price level (in the long run). In other words, we would have to conclude that changes in monetary policy may be ineffective at changing Real GDP and the price level.

Does this condition—a change in velocity completely offsetting a change in the money supply—occur often? Monetarists generally think not because they believe: (1) Velocity does not change very much from one period to the next, that is, it is relatively stable. (2) Changes in velocity are predictable, as mentioned earlier. In other words, monetarists believe velocity is relatively stable and predictable.

So, in the monetarist view of the economy, changes in velocity are not likely to offset changes in the money supply. This means that changes in the money supply will largely determine changes in aggregate demand and, therefore, changes in Real GDP and the price level. For all practical purposes, an increase in the money supply will raise aggregate demand, increase both Real GDP and the price level in the short run, and increase the price level in the long run. A decrease in the money supply will lower aggregate demand, decrease both Real GDP and the price level in the short run, and decrease the price level in the long run.

SELF-TEST

1. What do monetarists predict will happen in the short run and in the long run as a result of each of the following (in each case, assume the economy is currently in long-run equilibrium)?
   a. Velocity rises.
   b. Velocity falls.
   c. The money supply rises.
   d. The money supply falls.
2. Can a change in velocity offset a change in the money supply (on aggregate demand)? Explain your answer.

Question from Setting the Scene: If the Fed does what Sebastian thinks it will do, will his brother, Jim, have a better chance of finding a job?

Sebastian thinks that if the Fed "stimulates the economy," Jim might have a better chance of finding a job. Is he right?

The answer depends on a number of things. Stimulating the economy often refers to increasing the money supply (or the rate of growth of the money supply) so that the economy's *AD* curve shifts rightward. If the economy's *AS* curve is upward-sloping (at least in the short run, as monetarists believe) and there is no change in velocity to offset the money supply-induced shift in the *AD* curve, then Real GDP in the economy is likely to rise. With more goods and services being produced, Jim's chances of finding work will be better.

But suppose the *AS* curve is vertical (as classical economists assumed). Then a rise in the money supply will lead to higher prices and no change in Real GDP. In this case, Jim's chances of getting a job might not be any better than before the Fed acted.

Our point is that the conditions in the economy determine the outcomes in the economy. If the *AS* curve is upward-sloping, then a shift rightward in the *AD* curve leads to higher Real GDP. But if the *AS* curve is vertical, then a shift rightward in the *AD* curve leaves Real GDP unchanged.

MONEY AND INTEREST RATES

Before we discuss how a change in the money supply affects interest rates, we review some of the ways changes in the money supply affect different economic variables.

What Economic Variables Are Affected by a Change in the Money Supply?

Throughout this text, we have talked about money and have shown how changes in the money supply affect different economic variables. Let's review some of these effects.

1. **Money and the supply of loans.** The last chapter discusses the actions of the Fed that change the money supply. For example, when the Fed undertakes an open market purchase, the money supply increases and reserves in the banking system increase. With greater reserves, banks can extend more loans. In other words, as a result of the Fed conducting an open market purchase, the supply of loans rises. Similarly, when the Fed conducts an open market sale, the supply of loans decreases.

2. **Money and Real GDP.** This chapter shows how a change in the money supply can change aggregate demand and, therefore, change the price level and Real GDP in the short run. For example, look back at Exhibit 4a. The economy starts at point 1, producing Q_N. An increase in the money supply shifts the *AD* curve rightward, from AD_1 to AD_2. In the short run, the economy moves to point 2, and produces a higher level of Real GDP (Q_1). Similarly, in the short run, a decrease in the money supply produces a lower level of Real GDP. (See Exhibit 4b.)

3. **Money and the price level.** This chapter also shows how a change in the money supply can change the price level. Again, look back at Exhibit 4a. Initially, at point 1, the price level is P_1. An increase in the money supply shifts the *AD* curve rightward, from AD_1 to AD_2. In the short run, the price level in the economy moves from P_1 to P_2. In the long run, the economy is at point 3, and the price level is P_3. Exhibit 4b shows how a decrease in the money supply affects the price level.

Thus, we know that changes in the money supply affect (1) the supply of loans, (2) Real GDP, and (3) the price level. Is there anything else the money supply can affect?

Many economists say that because the money supply affects the price level, it also affects the *expected inflation rate*.

The expected inflation rate is the inflation rate that you expect. For example, your expected inflation rate—the inflation rate you expect will be realized over the next year—may be 5 percent, 6 percent, or a different rate. Changes in the money supply affect the expected inflation rate—either directly or indirectly. We know from working with the equation of exchange that the greater the increase in the money supply, the greater the rise in the price level. And, we would expect that the greater the rise in the price level, the higher the expected inflation rate, *ceteris paribus*. For example, we would predict that a money supply growth rate of, say, 10 percent a year generates a greater actual inflation rate, and a larger expected inflation rate, than a money supply growth rate of 2 percent a year.

To summarize: Changes in the money supply (or changes in the rate of growth of the money supply) can affect (1) the supply of loans, (2) Real GDP, (3) the price level, and (4) the expected inflation rate.

The Money Supply, the Loanable Funds Market, and Interest Rates

The loanable funds market is shown in Exhibit 5a. The demand for loanable funds is downward-sloping, indicating that borrowers will borrow more funds as the interest rate declines. The supply of loanable funds is upward-sloping, indicating that lenders will lend more funds as the interest rate rises. The equilibrium interest rate, i_1 percent in the exhibit, is determined through the forces of supply and demand. If there is a surplus of loanable funds, the interest rate falls; if there is a shortage of loanable funds, the interest rate rises.

Anything that affects either the supply of loanable funds or the demand for loanable funds will obviously affect the interest rate. All four of the factors that are affected by changes in the money supply—the supply of loans, Real GDP, the price level, and the expected inflation rate—affect either the supply of or demand for loanable funds.

The Supply of Loans

A Fed open market purchase increases reserves in the banking system and therefore increases the supply of loanable funds. As a result, the interest rate declines. See Exhibit 5b. This change in the interest rate due to a change in the supply of loanable funds is called the **liquidity effect.**

Liquidity Effect
The change in the interest rate due to a change in the supply of loanable funds.

Real GDP

A change in Real GDP affects both the supply of and demand for loanable funds. To understand this, you need to realize that there is (1) a link between supplying bonds and demanding loanable funds and (2) a link between demanding bonds and supplying loanable funds. In other words,

> To *supply bonds* is to *demand loanable funds*.
> To *demand bonds* is to *supply loanable funds*.

To explain, let's suppose that corporations are the only economic actors that supply (sell) bonds and that people (like you) are the only economic actors that demand (buy) bonds. Now when a corporation supplies a bond, it is effectively seeking to borrow funds from you. It is saying, "If you will buy this bond from the corporation for, say, $10,000, the corporation promises to repay you $11,000 at some specified date in the future."

In other words, when the corporation supplies bonds for sale, it (the corporation) demands loanable funds (from you) and you, if you buy or demand the bonds, supply loanable funds to the corporation.

exhibit 5

The Interest Rate and the Loanable Funds Market

The loanable funds market is shown in part (a). The demand for loanable funds is downward-sloping; the supply of loanable funds is upward-sloping. Part (b) shows the liquidity effect, part (c) shows the income effect, part (d) shows the price-level effect, and part (e) shows the expectations effect.

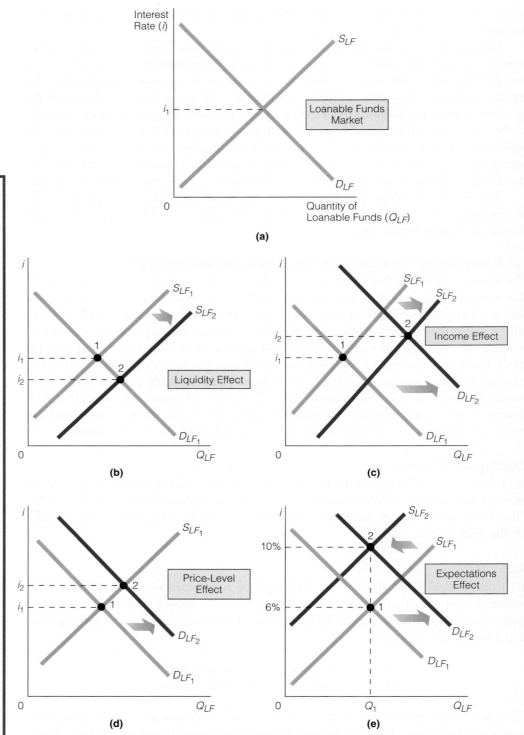

(a)

(b)

(c)

(d)

(e)

Think of a simpler transaction to understand how it is possible that when you supply one thing, you demand something else. When you *supply* the desk for sale that you produced, aren't you effectively *demanding* money? And isn't the person who buys or *demands* the desk from you effectively *supplying* money to you?

With this as background, let's now ask two questions. First, how does Real GDP affect the supply of loanable funds? When Real GDP rises, people's wealth is greater. (Real GDP consists of goods, and goods are one component of wealth.) When people became wealthier, they often demand more bonds (in much the same way that they may demand more houses, cars, and jewelry). But as we have just learned, to demand more bonds is to supply more loanable funds. So, when Real GDP rises, people (demand more bonds and thereby) supply more loanable funds.

Second, how does Real GDP affect the demand for loanable funds? When Real GDP rises, profitable business opportunities usually abound. Businesses decide to issue or supply more bonds to take advantage of these profitable opportunities. But, again, we know that to supply more bonds is to demand more loanable funds. So, when Real GDP rises, corporations (issue or supply more bonds and thereby) demand more loanable funds.

In summary, then, when Real GDP increases, both the supply of and demand for loanable funds increase. What is the overall effect on the interest rate? Usually, the demand for loanable funds increases by more than the supply of loanable funds, so that the interest rate rises. The change in the interest rate due to a change in Real GDP is called the **income effect.** See Exhibit 5c.

The Price Level

When the price level increases, the purchasing power of money falls. In other words, one dollar doesn't buy as much as it did before the price level increased. As a result of the purchasing power of money falling, people may increase their demand for credit or loanable funds in order to borrow the funds necessary to buy a fixed bundle of goods. As a result of the change in the demand for credit or loanable funds, the interest rate changes. This change in the interest rate due to a change in the price level is called the **price-level effect.** See Exhibit 5d.

The Expected Inflation Rate

A change in the expected inflation rate affects both the supply of and demand for loanable funds. To see how, let's suppose the expected inflation rate is currently zero. Let's also assume that when the expected inflation rate is zero, the equilibrium interest rate is 6 percent, as in Exhibit 5e. Now suppose the expected inflation rate rises from 0 percent to 4 percent. What will this rise in the expected inflation rate do to the demand for and supply of loanable funds? Borrowers (demanders of loanable funds) will be willing to pay 4 percent more interest for their loans because they expect to be paying back the loans with dollars that have 4 percent less buying power than the dollars they are being lent. (Another way to look at this: If they wait to buy goods, the prices of the goods they want will have risen by 4 percent. To beat the price rise, they are willing to pay up to 4 percent more to borrow and purchase the goods now.) In effect, the demand for loanable funds curve shifts rightward, so that at Q_1 borrowers are willing to pay a 4 percent higher interest rate. See Exhibit 5e.

On the other side of the loanable funds market, the lenders (the suppliers of loanable funds) require a 4 percent higher interest rate to compensate them for the 4 percent less valuable dollars in which the loan will be repaid. In effect, the supply of loanable funds curve shifts leftward, so that at Q_1 lenders will receive an interest rate of 10 percent. See Exhibit 5e.

Thus, an expected inflation rate of 4 percent increases the demand for loanable funds and decreases the supply of loanable funds, so that the interest rate is 4 percent higher than it was when there was a zero expected inflation rate. A change in the interest rate due to a change in the expected inflation rate is referred to as the **expectations effect** (or *Fisher effect,* after economist Irving Fisher).

Exhibit 6 summarizes how a change in the money supply directly and indirectly affects the interest rate.

Income Effect
The change in the interest rate due to a change in Real GDP.

Price-Level Effect
The change in the interest rate due to a change in the price level.

Expectations Effect
The change in the interest rate due to a change in the expected inflation rate.

exhibit **6**

How the Fed Affects the Interest Rate

This exhibit summarizes the way the Fed (through its monetary policy) affects the interest rate. For example, an open market operation (OMO) directly affects the supply of loanable funds and affects the interest rate. An OMO also affects Real GDP, the price level, and the expected inflation rate, and therefore indirectly affects either the supply of or demand for loanable funds, which in turn affects the interest rate.

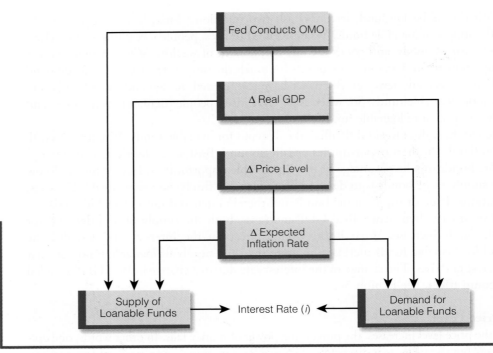

The Difference Between the Price-Level Effect and the Expectations Effect

To many people, the price price-level effect sounds the same as the expectations effect. After all, both have something to do with the price level. So what is the difference?

To illustrate the difference, consider a one-shot change in the money supply that ultimately moves the price level from a price index of 120 to a price index of 135. The price-level effect refers to the change in the interest rate that is related to the fact that the actual price level is rising. Think of the demand for loanable funds creeping up steadily as the price index rises from 120 to 121 to 122 to 123 and so on to 135. Once the price index has hit 135, there is no further reason for the demand for loanable funds to rise. After all, the price level isn't rising anymore. Now as the price level is rising, people's expected inflation rate is rising. In other words, they may see (in their mind's eye) where the price level is headed (from 120 to 135) and adjust accordingly. Once the price level hits 135 (and given that we are talking about a one-shot change in the money supply), the expected inflation rate falls to zero. In other words, any change in the interest rate due to a rise in the expected inflation rate is now over, and therefore the expected inflation rate no longer has an effect on the interest rate. But certainly the price level still has an effect on the interest rate because the price level is higher than it was originally. In the end, the effect on the interest rate due to a rise in the price level remains and the effect on the interest rate due to a rise in the expected inflation rate disappears.

So, What Happens to the Interest Rate as the Money Supply Changes?

Suppose the Fed decides to raise the rate of growth of the money supply, say, from 3 percent to 5 percent a year. What effect will this have on the interest rate? Some people will quickly say, "It will lower the interest rate." They may be thinking that the only effect on the interest rate is the liquidity effect. In other words, as the Fed increases the rate of growth of the money supply, more reserves enter the banking system, more loans are extended, and the interest rate falls.

That would be the right answer if the only thing that an increase in the money supply growth rate did was to affect the supply of loanable funds. But as we have discussed, this isn't the only thing that happens. Real GDP changes, the price level changes, and the expected inflation rate changes, and changes in these factors affect the loanable funds market just as the Fed action did. Figuring out what happens to the interest rate is a matter of trying to figure out when each effect (liquidity, income, price-level, and expectations) occurs and how strong each effect is.

To illustrate, suppose everyone expects the Fed to continue to increase the money supply at a growth rate of 2 percent a year. Then, on January 1, the Fed announces that it will increase the rate of growth in the money supply to 4 percent and will begin open market purchases to effect this outcome immediately. It's possible that one second after the announcement, people's expected inflation rate rises. In other words, the expectations effect begins immediately and affects interest rates accordingly. On January 2, the interest rate is higher than it was one day earlier. At this point, someone could say, "See, an increase in the rate of growth in the money supply raises the interest rate." The problem with saying this, though, is that not all the effects (liquidity, income, and so on) have occurred yet. In time, the liquidity effect puts downward pressure on the interest rate. Suppose this begins to happen on January 15, and the interest rate begins to fall from what it was on January 2. Then, someone on January 15 could say, "It is obvious that an increase in the rate of growth of the money supply lowers interest rates."

Our point is: A change in the money supply affects the economy in many ways—changing the supply of loanable funds directly, changing Real GDP and therefore changing the demand for and supply of loanable funds, changing the expected inflation rate, and so on. The timing and magnitude of these effects determine changes in the interest rate.

ANALYZING THE SCENE

Question from Setting the Scene: If the Fed wants to lower interest rates, are interest rates destined to go down? In short, can the Fed do what it wants to do?
Oliver and Roberta are thinking about buying a house and Oliver has recently heard that the Fed might lower interest rates. If the Fed wants to lower interest rates, will it be able to do so? The answer is, not always. There is little doubt that the Fed can conduct an open market purchase and increase reserves in the banking system. In turn, this is likely to lead to an increased supply of loanable funds. If nothing else happens, the interest rate will go down. This is the liquidity effect.

But the liquidity effect isn't the only effect of a change in the money supply. For example, suppose the market views the recent Fed action of increasing reserves in the banking system as inflationary. In short, the market's expected inflation rate rises. This will push the interest rate up.

The best we can say is: It's possible that the Fed, by increasing the supply of loanable funds, will lower (short-term) interest rates—but this depends on both the *timing* and *magnitude* of the liquidity and expectations effects.

The Nominal and Real Interest Rates

If you were to call a bank and ask what it charges for a given type of loan, the bank would quote some interest rate. The interest rate that it quotes is the interest rate we have been discussing. It is the interest rate that comes about through the interaction of the demand for and supply of loanable funds. Sometimes this interest rate is called the **nominal interest rate** or market interest rate.

The nominal interest rate may not be the true cost of borrowing because part of the nominal interest rate is a reflection of the expected inflation rate. To illustrate, let's

Nominal Interest Rate
The interest rate actually charged (or paid) in the market; the market interest rate. The nominal interest rate = Real interest rate + Expected inflation rate.

suppose the nominal interest rate is 9 percent and the expected inflation rate is 2 percent. If you take out a loan for $10,000 at 9 percent, you will have to pay back the loan amount ($10,000) plus $900 in interest at the end of the year. In other words, for a $10,000 loan, you will have to repay $10,900.

Now let's suppose that the expected inflation rate turns out to be the actual inflation rate. In other words, people expected the inflation rate to be 2 percent and it turns out to be 2 percent. In this case, the dollars you pay back will be worth less than the dollars you borrowed—by 2 percent. In other words, you borrowed dollars that were worth 2 percent more in purchasing power than the dollars you repaid.

This fact should be taken into account in determining your real cost of borrowing. Was the real cost of borrowing 9 percent or 7 percent? Economists would say it was 7 percent. The real cost of borrowing is sometimes called the **real interest rate.** It is equal to the nominal interest rate minus the expected inflation rate.[2]

Real Interest Rate
The nominal interest rate minus the expected inflation rate. When the expected inflation rate is zero, the real interest rate equals the nominal interest rate.

$$\text{Real interest rate} = \text{Nominal interest rate} - \text{Expected inflation rate}$$

Based on this equation, it follows that the nominal interest rate is equal to the real interest rate plus the expected inflation rate.

$$\text{Nominal interest rate} = \text{Real interest rate} + \text{Expected inflation rate}$$

SELF-TEST

1. If the expected inflation rate is 4 percent and the nominal interest rate is 7 percent, what is the real interest rate?
2. Is it possible for the nominal interest rate to immediately rise following an increase in the money supply? Explain your answer.
3. "The Fed only affects the interest rate via the liquidity effect." Do you agree or disagree? Explain your answer.

A READER ASKS   *How Do We Know What the Expected Inflation Rate Equals?*

Is there some way to figure out what the expected inflation rate equals at any given time?

One way to find out what the expected inflation rate equals is to look at the spread—the difference—between the yield on conventional bonds and the yield on indexed bonds with the same maturity. For example, we can look at the spread between the yield on a 10-year Treasury bond (Treasury bond that matures in 10 years) and the yield on an inflation-indexed Treasury bond (inflation-indexed Treasury bond that matures in 10 years).

Before we do this, let's look at the difference between a conventional bond and an inflation-indexed bond. An inflation-indexed bond guarantees the purchaser a certain real rate of return, but a

conventional, or non-indexed, bond does not. For example, suppose you purchase an inflation-indexed, 10-year, $1,000 security that pays 4 percent interest. If there is no inflation, the annual interest payment is $40. But, if the inflation rate is 3 percent, the bond issuer "marks up" the value of your security by 3 percent—from $1,000 to $1,030. Furthermore, your annual interest payment is 4 percent of this new higher amount—that is, it is 4 percent of $1,030, or $41.20.

Investors are willing to accept a lower yield on inflation-indexed bonds because they are receiving something with them that they are not receiving on conventional bonds—protection against

---

2. A broader definition is "Real interest rate = Nominal interest rate − Expected rate of change in the price level." This definition is useful because we will not always be dealing with an expected inflation rate; we could be dealing with an expected deflation rate.

inflation. So while a conventional bond may yield, say, 6 percent, an inflation-indexed bond may yield 4 percent.

What does the difference, or spread, signify? It is a measure of the inflation rate that investors expect will exist over the life of the bond.

To illustrate with some real numbers, we went to bloomberg.com and checked the yield on securities. An inflation-indexed 10-year Treasury bond had a yield of 1.72 percent. A conventional 10-year Treasury bond had a yield of 4.02. The difference, or spread, was 2.3 percent. This means that on this day, investors (or "the market") expected that the inflation rate was going to be 2.3 percent.

So, by checking the spread between yields on conventional and inflation-indexed bonds of the same maturity, you can see what the market expects the inflation rate will be. As the spread widens, the market expects a higher inflation rate; as the spread narrows, the market expects a lower inflation rate.

Once again, here is the process to follow:

1. Go to http://www.bloomberg.com.
2. Click on "U.S. Treasuries."
3. Write down the yield on conventional 10-year Treasury bonds.
4. Write down the yield on inflation-indexed 10-year Treasury bonds.
5. Find the spread between the yields. The spread is the market's expected inflation rate.
6. By doing this daily, you can see if the market's perception of inflation is changing. For example, if the spread is widening, the market believes inflation will be increasing. If the spread is narrowing, the market believes inflation will be decreasing.

Chapter Summary

The Equation of Exchange

> The equation of exchange is an identity: $MV = PQ$. The equation of exchange can be interpreted in different ways: (1) The money supply multiplied by velocity must equal the price level times Real GDP: $M \times V = P \times Q$. (2) The money supply multiplied by velocity must equal GDP: $M \times V = \text{GDP}$. (3) Total expenditures (measured by MV) must equal the total sales revenues of business firms (measured by PQ): $MV = PQ$.

> The equation of exchange is not a theory of the economy. However, the equation of exchange can be turned into a theory by making assumptions about some of the variables in the equation. For example, if we assume that both V and Q are constant, then we have the simple quantity theory of money, which predicts that changes in the money supply cause *strictly proportional* changes in the price level.

> A change in the money supply or a change in velocity will change aggregate demand and therefore lead to a shift in the AD curve. Specifically, either an increase in the money supply or an increase in velocity will increase aggregate demand and therefore shift the AD curve to the right. A decrease in the money supply or a decrease in velocity will decrease aggregate demand and therefore shift the AD curve to the left.

> In the simple quantity theory of money, Real GDP is assumed to be constant in the short run. This means the AS curve is vertical. Also, velocity is assumed to be constant. This means the only thing that can change aggregate demand is a change in the money supply. In the face of a vertical AS curve, any change in the money supply shifts the AD curve and changes only the price level, not Real GDP.

Monetarism

> According to monetarists, if the economy is initially in long-run equilibrium, (1) an increase in the money supply will raise the price level and Real GDP in the short run and will raise only the price level in the long run; (2) a decrease in the money supply will lower the price level and Real GDP in the short run and will lower only the price level in the long run; (3) an increase in velocity will raise the price level and Real GDP in the short run and will raise only the price level in the long run; (4) a decrease in velocity will lower the price level and Real GDP in the short run and will lower only the price level in the long run.

The Money Supply and Interest Rates

> Changes in the money supply can affect the interest rate via the liquidity, income, price level, and expectations effects.

> The change in the interest rate due to a change in the supply of loanable funds is called the liquidity effect. The change in the interest rate due to a change in Real GDP is called the income effect. The change in the interest rate due to a change in the price level is called the price-level effect. The change in the interest rate due to a change in the expected inflation rate is called the expectations effect (or Fisher effect).

Nominal and Real Interest Rates

> Real interest rate = Nominal interest rate − Expected inflation rate

> Nominal interest rate = Real interest rate + Expected inflation rate

Key Terms and Concepts

Equation of Exchange
Velocity
Simple Quantity Theory of Money

Liquidity Effect
Income Effect
Price-Level Effect

Expectations Effect
Nominal Interest Rate
Real Interest Rate

Questions and Problems

1. What are the assumptions and predictions of the simple quantity theory of money? Does the simple quantity theory of money predict well?
2. In the simple quantity theory of money, the *AS* curve is vertical. Explain why.
3. In the simple quantity theory of money, what will lead to an increase in aggregate demand? In monetarism, what will lead to an increase in aggregate demand?
4. Using the simple quantity theory of money, explain the causes of (a) inflation and (b) deflation.
5. In monetarism, how will each of the following affect the price level in the short run?
   a. An increase in velocity
   b. A decrease in velocity
   c. An increase in the money supply
   d. A decrease in the money supply
6. Suppose the objective of the Fed is to increase Real GDP. To this end, it increases the money supply. Is there anything that can offset the increase in the money supply so that Real GDP does not rise? Explain your answer.

7. In recent years, economists have argued about what the true value of the real interest rate is at any one time and over time. Given that the Nominal interest rate = Real interest rate + Expected inflation rate, it follows that the Real interest rate = Nominal interest rate − Expected inflation rate. Why do you think there is so much disagreement over the true value of the real interest rate?
8. To a potential borrower, which would be more important—the nominal interest rate or the real interest rate? Explain your answer.
9. The money supply rises on Tuesday and by Thursday the interest rate has risen. Is this more likely to be the result of the income effect or the expectations effect? Explain your answer.
10. Suppose the money supply increased 30 days ago. Whether the nominal interest rate is higher, lower, or the same today as it was 30 days ago depends upon what? Explain your answer.
11. How does the price-level effect differ from the expectations effect?

Working With Numbers and Graphs

1. How will things change in the *AD-AS* framework if a change in the money supply is completely offset by a change in velocity?

2. Using the loanable funds market, diagrammatically represent (a) the liquidity effect and (b) the expectations effect.

chapter 10

FISCAL POLICY AND
MONETARY POLICY

© Michael Newman/PhotoEdit

Setting the Scene

The following conversations occurred recently.

9:42 A.M.

Georgia Dickens is sitting with a friend at a coffee shop. Georgia and her friend are talking about the new tax bill. Georgia thinks it would be wrong to cut tax rates at this time, "because lower tax rates," she says, "will lead to a larger budget deficit—and the budget deficit is already plenty big."

3:14 P.M.

The economics class will end in 10 minutes. A student asks, "So, expansionary *fiscal policy* stabilizes the economy?"

"Not always," replies the economics professor.

"I don't understand," says the student.

5:00 P.M.

The economics class will end in 15 minutes. A student asks, "So, expansionary *monetary policy* increases Real GDP in the short run?"

"Not always," replies the economics professor.

"I don't understand," says the student.

6:14 P.M.

The Mason family is eating dinner. Frank Mason says, "I think the President is being shortsighted. Bigger deficits are bound to raise interest rates and that will make it much harder for a person to buy a house."

Alice Mason replies, "But aren't budget deficits pretty big right now, and aren't interest rates fairly low?"

"I think you're right," responds Frank. "But just wait. Interest rates are bound to go up."

How would an economist look at these conversations? Later in the chapter, discussions based on the following questions will help you analyze the scene the way an economist would.

- Do lower tax rates mean a larger deficit?
- How can expansionary fiscal policy *not* stabilize the economy?

- How can expansionary monetary policy *not* increase Real GDP in the short run?
- Do bigger budget deficits cause higher interest rates?

GOVERNMENT POLICIES AND THE ECONOMY

As an earlier chapter explains, some economists believe the economy is inherently unstable. These economists argue that government should play a role in managing the economy because the economy can get stuck in a recessionary gap. They believe government should try to move the economy out of the recessionary gap and toward Natural Real GDP.

One of the major ways government can influence the economy is through its *fiscal policy*. Another way is through *monetary policy*. In this chapter, we discuss both of these ways the government can influence the economy.

FISCAL POLICY

Fiscal policy refers to changes in government expenditures and/or taxes to achieve particular economic goals, such as low unemployment, price stability, and economic growth. We begin the discussion of fiscal policy by defining some relevant terms and describing two points that are important to the discussion.

Some Relevant Fiscal Policy Terms

Expansionary fiscal policy refers to increases in government expenditures and/or decreases in taxes to achieve macroeconomic goals. **Contractionary fiscal policy** refers to decreases in government expenditures and/or increases in taxes to achieve these goals.

> Expansionary fiscal policy: Government expenditures up and/or taxes down
> Contractionary fiscal policy: Government expenditures down and/or taxes up

When changes in government expenditures and taxes are brought about deliberately through government actions, fiscal policy is said to be *discretionary.* For example, if Congress decides to increase government spending by, say, $10 billion in an attempt to lower the unemployment rate, this is an act of **discretionary fiscal policy.** In contrast, a change in either government expenditures or taxes that occurs automatically in response to economic events is referred to as **automatic fiscal policy.** To illustrate, suppose Real GDP in the economy turns down, causing more people to become unemployed. As a result, more people automatically receive unemployment benefits. These added unemployment benefits automatically boost government spending.

Two Important Notes

In your study of fiscal policy in this chapter, keep in mind the following two important points:

1. In our discussion of fiscal policy in this chapter, we deal only with *discretionary fiscal policy.* In other words, we consider deliberate actions on the part of policymakers to affect the economy through changes in government spending and/or taxes.
2. We assume that any change in government spending is due to a change in government purchases and not to a change in transfer payments. Stated differently, we assume that transfer payments are constant so that changes in government spending are a reflection of changes in government purchases only.

DEMAND-SIDE FISCAL POLICY

Fiscal policy can affect the demand side of the economy—that is, it can affect aggregate demand. This section focuses on how government spending and taxes can affect aggregate demand.

Fiscal Policy
Changes in government expenditures and/or taxes to achieve particular economic goals, such as low unemployment, stable prices, and economic growth.

Expansionary Fiscal Policy
Increases in government expenditures and/or decreases in taxes to achieve particular economic goals.

Contractionary Fiscal Policy
Decreases in government expenditures and/or increases in taxes to achieve particular economic goals.

Discretionary Fiscal Policy
Deliberate changes of government expenditures and/or taxes to achieve particular economic goals.

Automatic Fiscal Policy
Changes in government expenditures and/or taxes that occur automatically without (additional) congressional action.

Shifting the Aggregate Demand Curve

How do changes in government purchases (*G*) and taxes (*T*) affect aggregate demand? Recall from an earlier chapter that a change in consumption, investment, government purchases, or net exports can change aggregate demand and therefore shift the *AD* curve. For example, an increase in government purchases (*G*) increases aggregate demand and shifts the *AD* curve to the right. A decrease in *G* decreases aggregate demand and shifts the *AD* curve to the left.[1]

A change in taxes (*T*) can affect consumption or investment or both and therefore can affect aggregate demand. For example, a decrease in income taxes increases disposable (after-tax) income, which permits individuals to increase their consumption. As consumption rises, the *AD* curve shifts to the right. An increase in taxes decreases disposable income, lowers consumption, and shifts the *AD* curve to the left.

Fiscal Policy: A Keynesian Perspective

The model of the economy in Exhibit 1a shows a downward-sloping *AD* curve and an upward-sloping *SRAS* curve. As you can see, the economy is initially in a recessionary gap at point 1. Aggregate demand is too low to move the economy to equilibrium at the Natural Real GDP level. The Keynesian prescription is to enact expansionary fiscal policy measures (an increase in government purchases or a decrease in taxes) in order to shift the aggregate demand curve rightward from AD_1 to AD_2 and move the economy to the Natural Real GDP level at point 2.

At this point someone might ask, Why not simply wait for the short-run aggregate supply curve to shift rightward and intersect the aggregate demand curve at point 2'? The Keynesians usually respond that (1) the economy is stuck at point 1 and won't move naturally to point 2'—perhaps the economy is stuck because wage rates won't fall; or (2) the short-run aggregate supply curve takes too long to shift rightward, and in the interim, we must deal with the high cost of unemployment and a lower level of Real GDP.

In Exhibit 1b, the economy is initially in an inflationary gap at point 1. In this situation, Keynesians are likely to propose a contractionary fiscal measure (a decrease in

exhibit 1

Fiscal Policy in Keynesian Theory: Ridding the Economy of Recessionary and Inflationary Gaps
(a) In Keynesian theory, expansionary fiscal policy eliminates a recessionary gap. Increased government purchases, decreased taxes, or both lead to a rightward shift in the aggregate demand curve from AD_1 to AD_2, restoring the economy to the natural level of Real GDP, Q_N. (b) Contractionary fiscal policy is used to eliminate an inflationary gap. Decreased government purchases, increased taxes, or both lead to a leftward shift in the aggregate demand curve from AD_1 to AD_2, restoring the economy to the natural level of Real GDP, Q_N.

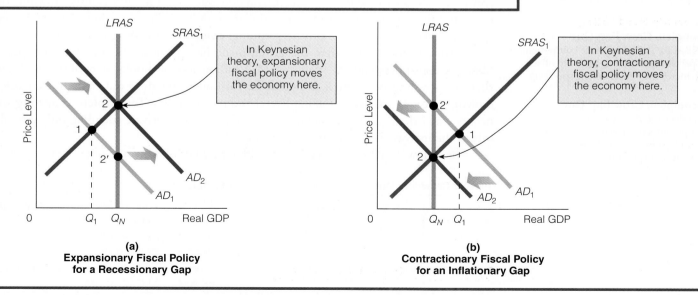

(a)
Expansionary Fiscal Policy for a Recessionary Gap

(b)
Contractionary Fiscal Policy for an Inflationary Gap

---

1. Later in this chapter, when we discuss crowding out, we question the effect of an increase in government purchases on aggregate demand.

government purchases or an increase in taxes) in order to shift the aggregate demand curve leftward from AD_1 to AD_2 and move the economy to point 2.

In Exhibit 1, fiscal policy has worked as intended. In (a), the economy was in a recessionary gap and expansionary fiscal policy eliminated the recessionary gap. In (b), the economy was in an inflationary gap and contractionary fiscal policy eliminated the inflationary gap. In (a) and (b), fiscal policy is at its best: working as intended.

Crowding Out: Questioning Expansionary Fiscal Policy

Not all economists believe that fiscal policy works the way we have just described. Some economists bring up the subject of *crowding out*. **Crowding out** refers to a decrease in private expenditures (consumption, investment, and so on) that occurs as a consequence of increased government spending or the financing needs of a budget deficit.

Crowding out can be direct or indirect as described in these two examples:

1. **Direct effect.** The government spends more on public libraries, and individuals buy fewer books at bookstores.[2]
2. **Indirect effect.** The government spends more on social programs and defense without increasing taxes; as a result, the size of the budget deficit increases. Consequently, the government must borrow more funds to finance the larger deficit. This increase in borrowing causes the demand for credit (or demand for loanable funds) to rise, which, in turn, causes the interest rate to rise. As a result, investment drops. More government spending indirectly leads to less investment spending.

Types of Crowding Out

Let's consider our first example in which the government spends more on public libraries. To be specific, let's say that the government spends $2 billion more on public libraries. Suppose that after the government has spent $2 billion more on public libraries, consumers choose to spend not one dollar less on books at bookstores. Obviously, then, there is no crowding out, or *zero crowding out*.

Now, suppose that after the government has spent $2 billion more on public libraries, consumers choose to spend $2 billion less on books at bookstores. Obviously, crowding out exists and the degree of crowding out is dollar for dollar. When one dollar of government spending offsets one dollar of private spending, **complete crowding out** is said to exist.

Finally, suppose that after the government has spent $2 billion more on public libraries, consumers end up spending $1.2 billion less on books at bookstores. Again, there is crowding out, but it is not dollar-for-dollar crowding out; it is not complete crowding out. In this case, incomplete crowding out exists. **Incomplete crowding out** occurs when the decrease in one or more components of private spending only partially offsets the increase in government spending.

The following table summarizes the different types of crowding out.

Type of Crowding Out	Example
Zero crowding out (sometimes called "no crowding out")	Government spends $2 billion more, and private sector spending stays constant.
Complete crowding out	Government spends $2 billion more, and private sector spends $2 billion less.
Incomplete crowding out	Government spends $2 billion more, and private sector spends $1.2 billion less.

Crowding Out
The decrease in private expenditures that occurs as a consequence of increased government spending or the financing needs of a budget deficit.

Complete Crowding Out
A decrease in one or more components of private spending completely offsets the increase in government spending.

Incomplete Crowding Out
The decrease in one or more components of private spending only partially offsets the increase in government spending.

2. We are not saying that if the government spends more on public libraries, individuals will necessarily buy fewer books at bookstores; rather, if they do, this would be an example of crowding out. The same holds for example 2.

Graphical Representation of Crowding Out

If *complete* or *incomplete crowding out* occurs, it follows that expansionary fiscal policy will have less impact on aggregate demand and Real GDP than Keynesian theory predicts. Let's look at the graphical representation of crowding out.

Exhibit 2 illustrates the consequences of complete and incomplete crowding out. For comparison, the exhibit also includes the case in Keynesian theory where there is zero crowding out.

As we discuss Exhibit 2, keep in mind the three possibilities concerning crowding out:

- Zero crowding out (no crowding out)
- Incomplete crowding out
- Complete crowding out

In Exhibit 2, the economy is initially at point 1, with Real GDP at Q_1. In Keynesian theory, expansionary fiscal policy shifts the aggregate demand curve to AD_2 and moves the economy to point 2. Among other things, this implicitly assumes there is zero crowding out (or no crowding out). Notice that Real GDP has increased from Q_1 to Q_N. It follows that the unemployment rate will fall from its level at Q_1 to a lower level at Q_N. Summary: If there is no crowding out, expansionary fiscal policy increases Real GDP and lowers the unemployment rate.

With incomplete crowding out, the aggregate demand curve only shifts (on net) to AD'_2 because the initial stimulus in aggregate demand due to increased government spending is *partially offset* by a fall in private expenditures. The economy moves to point 2'. Notice that Real GDP has increased from Q_1 to Q'_2. It follows that the unemployment rate will fall from what it was at Q_1 to what it is at Q'_2. But also notice that the changes in both Real GDP and the unemployment rate are smaller with incomplete crowding out than they are with zero crowding out. Summary: If there is incomplete crowding out, expansionary fiscal policy increases Real GDP and lowers the unemployment rate, but not as much as if there is zero crowding out.

In the case of complete crowding out, the initial stimulus in aggregate demand due to increased government spending is *completely offset* by a fall in private expenditures and the aggregate demand curve does not move (on net) at all. Notice that Real GDP does not change, and neither does the unemployment rate. Summary: If there is complete crowding out, expansionary fiscal policy has no effect on the economy. The economy remains at point 1.

See Exhibit 3 for a summary flow chart of the different types of crowding out.

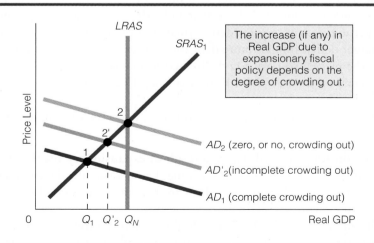

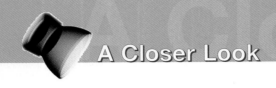

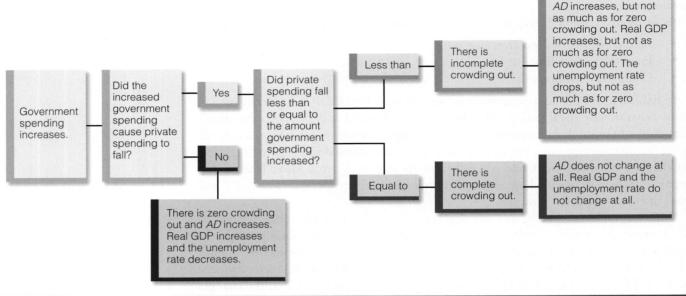

Government spending increases. → **Did the increased government spending cause private spending to fall?** → **Yes** → **Did private spending fall less than or equal to the amount government spending increased?**

No → **There is zero crowding out and *AD* increases. Real GDP increases and the unemployment rate decreases.**

Less than → **There is incomplete crowding out.** → ***AD* increases, but not as much as for zero crowding out. Real GDP increases, but not as much as for zero crowding out. The unemployment rate drops, but not as much as for zero crowding out.**

Equal to → **There is complete crowding out.** → ***AD* does not change at all. Real GDP and the unemployment rate do not change at all.**

---

exhibit 3

Expansionary Fiscal Policy (Government Spending Increases), Crowding Out, and Changes in Real GDP and the Unemployment Rate

The New Classical View of Fiscal Policy

Our examples of crowding out consider both direct and indirect effects. In the direct effect, crowding out is a result of individuals thinking along this line: "Government has increased its spending on books for public libraries, so I'll decrease my private spending on books because I can get them from the library."

In the indirect effect, business owners and managers are thinking this way: "The interest rate has gone up (as a result of increased financing needs related to the deficit), so we'll reduce investment."

The new classical school of economics proposes another way of looking at what people may do. These economists believe that individuals respond to expansionary fiscal policy, a larger deficit, and greater deficit-financing requirements by thinking the following: "A larger deficit implies more debt this year and higher future taxes. I'll simply save more in the present so I can pay the higher future taxes required to pay interest and to repay principal on the new debt. But, of course, if I'm going to save more, I have to consume less."

Based on their belief that people think this way, new classical economists offer a few predictions:

1. **Current consumption will fall as a result of expansionary fiscal policy.** How so? Again, an increase in government spending that increases the deficit and the amount of debt financing will cause individuals to save more (consume less) to prepare for higher future taxes.
2. **Deficits do not necessarily bring higher interest rates.** The reason is simple: A deficit simply means less tax to pay today and more tax to pay in the future.

Knowing this, individuals save more to pay their higher future taxes. The increased saving increases the supply of credit (or supply of loanable funds) and offsets the increased demand for credit that is a consequence of the need to finance the deficit.

Analysis of the New Classical Predictions

The two new classical predictions are illustrated in Exhibit 4. In part (a), the economy is initially at point 1. If individuals do not anticipate higher future taxes as a result of expansionary fiscal policy, the aggregate demand curve will shift rightward from AD_1 to AD_2.

However, new classical economists believe that individuals will anticipate higher future taxes and will therefore reduce their consumption (and increase their saving) to pay those taxes. In this case, the aggregate demand curve does not shift at all. What is the conclusion? Given the condition of anticipated higher future taxes, expansionary fiscal policy leaves Real GDP, unemployment, and the price level unchanged. Expansionary fiscal policy is not stimulative—it is not effective at increasing Real GDP and lowering the unemployment rate. Notice that this analysis of expansionary fiscal policy by new classical economists results in the same conclusion as in complete crowding out: the AD curve does not shift at all.

In Exhibit 4b, the credit market is initially in equilibrium at point 1 and the interest rate is i_1. The result of the government implementing an expansionary fiscal policy measure is a deficit. The deficit requires financing, so the demand for loanable funds shifts rightward from D_1 to D_2. At the same time, individuals perceive the deficit in terms of higher future taxes and increase their saving by enough to offset those taxes. This action shifts the supply of loanable funds from S_1 to S_2. What is the conclusion? The interest rate does not change.

The new classical position on expansionary fiscal policy may be summarized as follows: As long as expansionary fiscal policy is translated into higher future taxes (which new classical economists think is likely), there will be no change in Real GDP, unemployment, the price level, or interest rates. The analysis also holds for contractionary fiscal policy.

ANALYZING THE SCENE

Question from Setting the Scene: Do bigger budget deficits cause higher interest rates?
Whether or not a bigger budget deficit raises the interest rate depends on what happens in the loanable funds market when government seeks to borrow more funds to finance the bigger deficit. All other things constant, a bigger deficit will lead to a greater demand for loanable funds. If nothing else changes, the interest rate in the loanable funds market will rise. Frank is right. But suppose that, to some degree, individuals do translate "bigger deficits" into "higher future taxes" and begin to save more to be able to pay the higher future taxes. If this happens, the new classical position (on deficits) has some merit. The supply of loanable funds will rise and offset, to some degree, the upward pressure on the interest rate brought about by a greater demand for loanable funds. In the end, what happens to the interest rate (rise, fall, remain unchanged) depends on the change in the demand for loanable funds relative to the supply of loanable funds.

Why Would Taxpayers Save More to Pay Higher Future Taxes?

New classical economists believe taxpayers translate a bigger budget deficit into higher future taxes. Taxpayers save more now so that they can pay the higher future taxes. Some have asked, "But why don't the taxpayers today simply let the taxpayers of the future pay off the higher future taxes?"

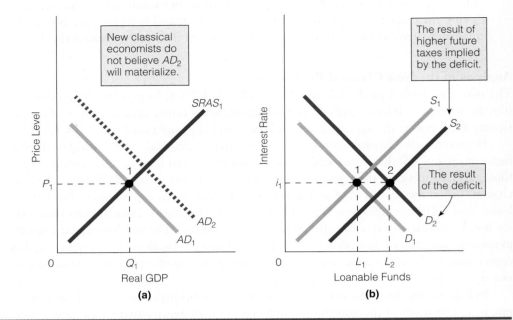

exhibit **4**

The New Classical View of Expansionary Fiscal Policy
New classical economists argue that individuals will link expansionary fiscal policy to higher future taxes and decrease their current consumption and increase their saving as a result. (a) The decreased consumption prevents the aggregate demand curve from shifting rightward from AD_1 to AD_2. (b) The increased saving causes the supply of credit (or supply of loanable funds) to shift rightward from S_1 to S_2, thus offsetting the increased demand for credit (or demand for loanable funds) and maintaining the existing level of interest rates. The new classical position on both (anticipated) expansionary and contractionary fiscal policy is that neither affects Real GDP, unemployment, the price level, or interest rates.

One answer is that the taxpayer today may end up being the taxpayer of the future. But even if this isn't likely (some taxpayers will die before the higher future taxes need to be paid), still taxpayers today might have sons and daughters who will be the taxpayers of the future. The economist Robert Barro has made the point that individuals leave bequests to their children, implying that they care about their children's welfare and, indirectly, about the tax burden their children will one day face. He argues that today's taxpayers will react to an increased budget deficit by increasing their saving in order to leave more to their children, who will pay higher future taxes.

Lags and Fiscal Policy
Suppose we proved, beyond a shadow of a doubt, that there is no, or zero, crowding out. Would it then hold that fiscal policy should be used to solve the problems of inflationary and recessionary gaps? Many economists would answer "not necessarily." The reason is that *lags* exist. There are five types of lags:

1. **The data lag.** Policymakers are not aware of changes in the economy as soon as they happen. For example, if the economy turns down in January, the decline may not be apparent for two to three months.
2. **The wait-and-see lag.** After policymakers are aware of a downturn in economic activity, they rarely enact counteractive measures immediately. Instead, they usually adopt a more cautious, wait-and-see attitude. They want to be sure that the observed events are not just a short-run phenomenon.
3. **The legislative lag.** After policymakers decide that some type of fiscal policy measure is required, Congress or the President will have to propose the measure, build political support for it, and get it passed. This can take many months.
4. **The transmission lag.** After enacted, a fiscal policy measure takes time to be put into effect. For example, a discretionary expansionary fiscal policy measure

mandating increased spending for public works projects will require construction companies to submit bids for the work, prepare designs, negotiate contracts, and so on.

5. **The effectiveness lag.** After a policy measure is actually implemented, it takes time to affect the economy. If government spending is increased on Monday, the aggregate demand curve does not shift rightward on Tuesday.

Taking these five lags together, some economists argue that discretionary fiscal policy is not likely to have the impact on the economy that policymakers hope. By the time the full impact of the policy is felt, the economic problem it was designed to solve (1) may no longer exist, (2) may not exist to the degree it once did, or (3) may have changed altogether.

Exhibit 5 illustrates the effect of lags. Suppose the economy is currently in a recessionary gap at point 1. The recession is under way before government officials recognize it. After it is recognized, however, Congress and the president consider enacting expansionary fiscal policy in the hope of shifting the AD curve from AD_1 to AD_2 so it will intersect the $SRAS$ curve at point 1', at Natural Real GDP.

But in the interim, unknown to everybody, the economy is "healing" or regulating itself: The $SRAS$ curve is shifting to the right. Government officials don't see this change because it takes time to collect and analyze data about the economy.

Thinking that the economy is not healing itself or not healing itself quickly enough, the government enacts expansionary fiscal policy. In time, the AD curve shifts rightward. But by the time the increased demand is felt in the goods and services market, the AD curve intersects the $SRAS$ curve at point 2. In short, the government has moved the economy from point 1 to point 2, and not, as it had hoped, from point 1 to point 1'. The government has moved the economy into an inflationary gap. Instead of stabilizing and moderating the ups and downs in economic activity (the business cycle), the government has intensified the fluctuations.

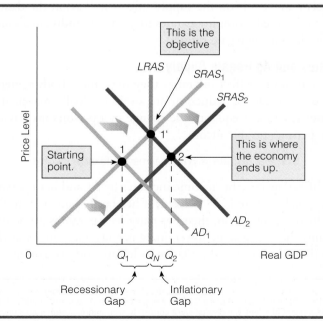

exhibit 5

Fiscal Policy May Destabilize the Economy

In this scenario, the $SRAS$ curve is shifting rightward (healing the economy of its recessionary gap), but this information is unknown to policymakers. Policymakers implement expansionary fiscal policy, and the AD curve ends up intersecting $SRAS_2$ at point 2 instead of intersecting $SRAS_1$ at point 1'. Policymakers thereby move the economy into an inflationary gap, thus destabilizing the economy.

Question from Setting the Scene: How can fiscal policy not stabilize the economy?
As just discussed, fiscal policy comes with lags and sometimes those lags and the "healing properties of the economy" are not timed in such a way to stabilize the economy. For example, if an increase in government spending raises aggregate demand at just the time the economy is coming out a recessionary gap, then the government spending may push the economy into an inflationary gap instead of settling it down in its long-run equilibrium position.

Crowding Out, Lags, and the Effectiveness of Fiscal Policy

Those economists who believe there is zero crowding out and that lags are insignificant conclude that fiscal policy is effective at moving the economy out of a recessionary gap. Those economists who believe crowding out is complete and/or that lags are significant conclude that fiscal policy is ineffective at moving the economy out of a recessionary gap. Keynesians usually view fiscal policy as effective, and monetarists and new classical economists usually view it as ineffective.

SELF-TEST *(Answers to Self-Test questions are in the Self-Test Appendix.)*

1. How does crowding out question the effectiveness of expansionary demand-side fiscal policy?
2. According to new classical economists, how do individuals respond to larger deficits? What changes do they anticipate in the credit or loanable funds market as a result of a larger deficit?
3. How might lags reduce the effectiveness of fiscal policy?

SUPPLY-SIDE FISCAL POLICY

Fiscal policy effects may be felt on the supply side as well as on the demand side of the economy. For example, a reduction in tax rates may alter an individual's incentive to work and produce, thus altering aggregate supply.

Marginal Tax Rates and Aggregate Supply

When fiscal policy measures affect tax rates, they may affect both aggregate supply and aggregate demand. Consider a reduction in an individual's marginal tax rate. The **marginal (income) tax rate** is equal to the change in a person's tax payment divided by the change in the person's taxable income.

Marginal (Income) Tax Rate
The change in a person's tax payment divided by the change in the person's taxable income: ΔTax payment/ΔTaxable income.

$$\text{Marginal tax rate} = \Delta\text{Tax payment}/\Delta\text{Taxable income}$$

For example, if Serena's taxable income increases by $1 and her tax payment increases by $0.28, her marginal tax rate is 28 percent; if her taxable income increases by $1 and her tax payment increases by $0.36, then her marginal tax rate is 36 percent.

All other things held constant, lower marginal tax rates increase the incentive to engage in productive activities (work) relative to leisure and tax-avoidance activities.[3] As

---

3. When marginal tax rates are lowered, two things will happen: (1) individuals will have more disposable income, (2) the amount of money that individuals can earn (and keep) by working increases. As a result of effect 1, individuals will choose to work less. As a result of effect 2, individuals will choose to work more. Whether an individual works less or more on net depends on whether effect 1 is stronger than or weaker than effect 2. We have assumed that effect 2 is stronger than effect 1, so that as marginal tax rates decline, the net effect is that individuals work more.

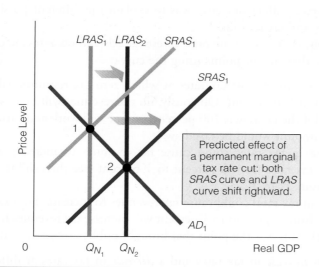

exhibit **6**

The Predicted Effect of a Permanent Marginal Tax Rate Cut on Aggregate Supply
A cut in marginal tax rates increases the attractiveness of productive activity relative to leisure and tax-avoidance activities and shifts resources from the latter to the former, thus shifting rightward both the short-run and the long-run aggregate supply curves.

Predicted effect of a permanent marginal tax rate cut: both SRAS curve and LRAS curve shift rightward.

resources shift from leisure to work, short-run aggregate supply increases. If the lower marginal tax rates are permanent and not simply a one-shot affair, most economists predict that not only will the short-run aggregate supply curve shift rightward but the long-run aggregate supply curve will shift rightward too. Exhibit 6 illustrates the predicted effect of a permanent marginal tax rate cut on aggregate supply.

The Laffer Curve: Tax Rates and Tax Revenues

High tax rates are followed by attempts of ingenious men to beat them as surely as snow is followed by little boys on sleds.

—Arthur Okun, economist, 1928–1980

If (marginal) income tax rates are reduced, will income tax revenues increase or decrease? Most people think the answer is obvious—lower tax rates mean lower tax revenues. The economist Arthur Laffer explained why this may not be the case.

As the story is told, Laffer, while dining with a journalist at a restaurant in Washington, D.C., drew the curve in Exhibit 7 on a napkin. The curve came to be known

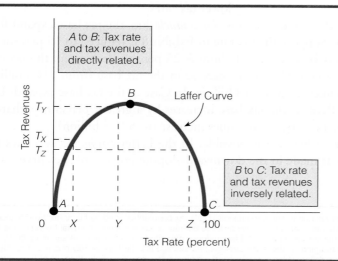

A to B: Tax rate and tax revenues directly related.

B to C: Tax rate and tax revenues inversely related.

exhibit **7**

The Laffer Curve
When the tax rate is either 0 or 100 percent, tax revenues are zero. Starting from a zero tax rate, increases in tax rates first increase (region A to B) and then decrease (region B to C) tax revenues. Starting from a 100 percent tax rate, decreases in tax rates first increase tax revenues (region C to B) and then decrease tax revenues (region B to A). This suggests there is some tax rate that maximizes tax revenues.

Laffer Curve
The curve, named after Arthur Laffer, that shows the relationship between tax rates and tax revenues. According to the Laffer curve, as tax rates rise from zero, tax revenues rise, reach a maximum at some point, and then fall with further increases in tax rates.

as the **Laffer curve.** Laffer's objective was to explain the different possible relationships between tax rates and tax revenues.

In the exhibit, tax revenues are on the vertical axis and tax rates are on the horizontal axis. Laffer made three major points using the curve:

1. There are two (marginal) tax rates at which zero tax revenues will be collected—0 percent and 100 percent. Obviously, no tax revenues will be raised if the tax rate is zero; and if the tax rate is 100 percent, no one will work and earn income because the entire amount would be taxed away.

2. An increase in tax rates could cause tax revenues to increase. For example, an increase in tax rates from X percent to Y percent (see the exhibit) will increase tax revenues from T_X to T_Y.

3. A decrease in tax rates could cause tax revenues to increase. For example, a decrease in tax rates from Z percent to Y percent will increase tax revenues from T_Z to T_Y (see the exhibit). This was the point that brought public attention to the Laffer curve.

How can an *increase* in tax rates and a *decrease* in tax rates at different times both increase tax revenues? This can happen because of the interrelationship of tax rates, the **tax base,** and tax revenues.

Tax revenues equal the tax base times the (average) tax rate:[4]

$$\text{Tax revenues} = \text{Tax base} \times \text{(average) Tax rate}$$

Tax Base
When referring to income taxes, the total amount of taxable income. Tax revenue = Tax base × (average) Tax rate.

Contrast the way economist Laffer thinks about a tax cut with the way the layperson thinks about it. The layperson probably believes that a reduction in tax rates will reduce tax revenues. The layperson focuses on the "arithmetic" of the situation. Laffer, however, focuses on the economic incentives. He asks: What does a lower tax rate imply in terms of a person's incentive to engage in productive activity? How does a lower tax rate affect one's tradeoff between work and leisure? The layperson likely sees only the "arithmetic" effect of a tax cut; the economist sees the incentive effect.

For example, a tax rate of 20 percent multiplied by a tax base of $100 billion generates $20 billion of tax revenues.

Now, obviously, tax revenues are a function of two variables: (1) the tax rate and (2) the tax base. Whether tax revenues increase or decrease as the average tax rate is lowered depends on whether the tax base expands by a greater or lesser percentage than the percentage reduction in the tax rate. Exhibit 8 illustrates the point.

We start with a tax rate of 20 percent, a tax base of $100 billion, and tax revenues of $20 billion. We assume that as the tax rate is reduced, the tax base expands: The rationale is that individuals work more, invest more, enter into more trades, and shelter less income from taxes at lower tax rates.

However, the real question is: *How much* does the tax base expand following the tax rate reduction? Suppose the tax rate in Exhibit 8 is reduced to 15 percent. In Case 1, this increases the tax base to $120 billion: A 25 percent decrease in the tax rate (from 20 to 15 percent) causes a 20 percent increase in the tax base (from $100 billion to $120 billion). Tax revenues drop to $18 billion. In Case 2, the tax base expands by 50 percent to $150 billion. Because the tax base increases by a greater percentage than the percentage decrease in the tax rate, tax revenues increase (to $22.5 billion).

Of course, either case is possible. In the Laffer curve, tax revenues increase if a tax rate reduction is made in the downward-sloping portion of the curve (between points B

---

4. First, the average tax rate is equal to an individual's tax payment divided by his or her taxable income (tax payment/taxable income). Second, a lower average tax rate requires a lower marginal tax rate. This follows from the average-marginal rule, which states that if the marginal magnitude is below the average magnitude, then the average is pulled down; if the marginal is above the average, the average is pulled up. Simply put, if an individual pays less tax on an additional taxable dollar (which is evidence of a marginal tax rate reduction), then his or her average tax naturally falls.

	(1) Tax Rate	(2) Tax Base	(3) Tax Revenues (1) × (2)	Summary	
Start with:	20%	$100	$20	—	
Case 1:	15	120	18	↓Tax rate	↓Tax revenues
Case 2:	15	150	22.5	↓Tax rate	↑Tax revenues

exhibit 8

Tax Rates, the Tax Base, and Tax Revenues

Tax revenues equal the tax base times the (average) tax rate. If the percentage reduction in the tax rate is greater than the percentage increase in the tax base, tax revenues decrease (Case 1). If the percentage reduction in the tax rate is less than the percentage increase in the tax base, tax revenues increase (Case 2). All numbers are in billions of dollars.

and C in Exhibit 7); tax revenues decrease following a tax rate reduction in the upward-sloping portion of the curve (between points A and B).

ANALYZING THE SCENE

Question from Setting the Scene: Do lower tax rates mean a larger deficit?

Could Georgia be right that lower taxes will increase the size of the budget deficit? She could be. It is certainly possible for a decrease in tax rates to lead to a decrease in tax revenues and a larger budget deficit. But this is not necessarily what will happen. Lower tax rates could lead to higher tax revenues and actually lead to a smaller budget deficit. What matters is whether the percentage cut in tax rates is larger or smaller than the percentage rise in the tax base.

SELF-TEST

1. Give an arithmetical example to illustrate the difference between the marginal and average tax rates.

2. If income tax rates rise, will income tax revenues rise too?

MONETARY POLICY

The first part of this chapter explains how expansionary and contractionary fiscal policies might be used to rid the economy of recessionary and inflationary gaps, respectively. We now turn our attention to monetary policy and its role in eliminating recessionary and inflationary gaps. **Monetary policy** refers to changes in the money supply, or in the rate of change of the money supply, to achieve particular macroeconomic goals.

MONETARY POLICY AND THE PROBLEM OF INFLATIONARY AND RECESSIONARY GAPS

In Exhibit 9a, the economy is in a recessionary gap at point 1; aggregate demand is too low to bring the economy into equilibrium at its natural level of Real GDP. Economist A argues that, in time, the short-run aggregate supply curve will shift rightward to point 2 (see Exhibit 9b), so it is best to leave things alone.

Economist B says that the economy will take too long to get to point 2 on its own, and in the interim the economy is suffering the high cost of unemployment and a lower level of output.

Economist C maintains that the economy is stuck in the recessionary gap. Economists B and C propose **expansionary monetary policy** to move the economy to its Natural Real GDP level. An appropriate increase in the money supply will shift the aggregate demand curve rightward to AD_2, and the economy will be in long-run equilibrium at

Monetary Policy
Changes in the money supply, or in the rate of change of the money supply, to achieve particular macroeconomic goals.

Expansionary Monetary Policy
The Fed increases the money supply.

© Bettmann/CORBIS

JFK and the 1964 Tax Cut

In 1962, John F. Kennedy was President of the United States and Walter Heller was one of Kennedy's economic advisers. Heller told the President that the economy needed a tax cut (a form of expansionary fiscal policy) to keep it from sputtering. In December, in a speech before the Economic Club of New York, President Kennedy said, "An economy hampered by restrictive tax rates will never produce enough revenue to balance our budget just as it will never produce enough jobs or enough profits."

Then in January 1963, he said, "It has become increasingly clear that the largest single barrier to full employment . . . and to a higher rate of economic growth is the unrealistically heavy drag of federal income taxes on private purchasing power, initiative and incentive."

Kennedy proposed expansionary fiscal policy—in the form of a tax cut—to raise economic growth and lower the unemployment

rate. He proposed lowering the top individual income tax rate, the bottom individual income tax rate, the corporate income tax, and the capital gains tax. He was assassinated in Dallas before Congress passed his tax program, but Congress did pass it. What was the result?

When the tax bill passed in 1964, the unemployment rate was 5.2 percent; in 1965, it was down to 4.5 percent; in 1966, it was down further, to 3.8 percent. The tax cut is widely credited with bringing the unemployment rate down.

As for economic growth, when the tax cut was passed in 1964, it was 5.8 percent; one year later, in 1965, the growth rate was up to 6.4 percent; and in 1966, the growth rate was even higher, at 6.6 percent. Again, the tax cut received much of the credit for stimulating economic growth.

---

exhibit **9**

Monetary Policy and a Recessionary Gap

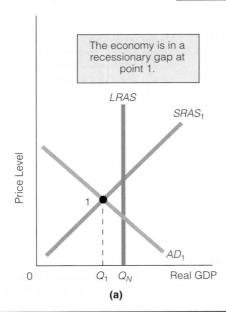

The economy is in a recessionary gap at point 1.

(a)

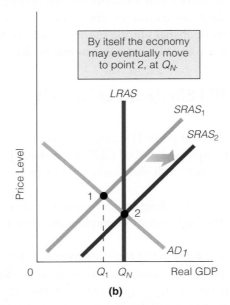

By itself the economy may eventually move to point 2, at Q_N.

(b)

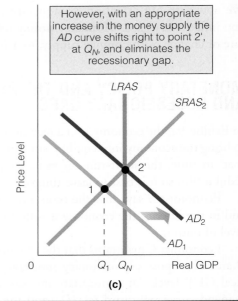

However, with an appropriate increase in the money supply the AD curve shifts right to point 2', at Q_N, and eliminates the recessionary gap.

(c)

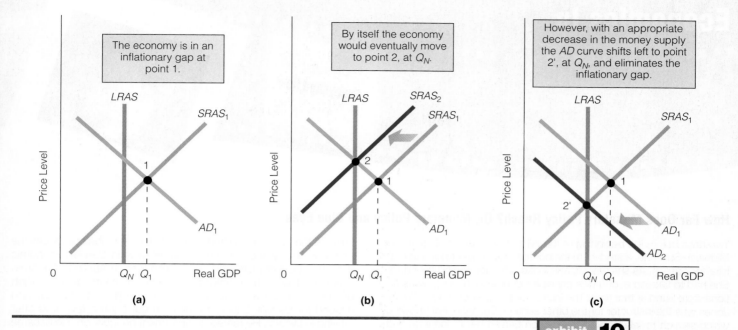

exhibit **10**

**Monetary Policy and
an Inflationary Gap**

point 2' (see Exhibit 9c). The recessionary gap is eliminated through the use of expansionary monetary policy.[5]

In Exhibit 10a, the economy is in an inflationary gap at point 1. Economist A argues that, in time, the economy will move to point 2 (see Exhibit 10b), so it is best to leave things alone.

Economist B argues that it would be better to decrease the money supply (**contractionary monetary policy**) so that aggregate demand shifts leftward to AD_2, and the economy moves to point 2' (see Exhibit 10c).

Economist C agrees with economist B and points out that the price level is lower at point 2' than at point 2 although Real GDP is the same at both points.

Most Keynesians believe that the natural forces of the market economy work much faster and more assuredly in eliminating an inflationary gap than in eliminating a recessionary gap. In terms of Exhibits 9 and 10, they argue that it is much more likely that the short-run aggregate supply curve in Exhibit 10b will shift leftward to point 2, eliminating the inflationary gap, than that the short-run aggregate supply curve in Exhibit 9b will shift rightward to point 2, eliminating the recessionary gap. The reason is that wages and prices rise more quickly than they fall. (Recall that many Keynesians believe wages are inflexible in a downward direction.) Consequently, Keynesians are more likely to advocate expansionary monetary policy to eliminate a stubborn recessionary gap than contractionary monetary policy to eliminate a not-so-stubborn inflationary gap.

Contractionary Monetary Policy
The Fed decreases the money supply.

MONETARY POLICY AND THE ACTIVIST-NONACTIVIST DEBATE

As an earlier section of this chapter points out, some economists argue that fiscal policy is ineffective (owing to crowding out) or works in unintended and undesirable ways (owing to lags). Other economists, notably Keynesians, believe that neither is the case and that

---

5. In a static framework, expansionary monetary policy refers to an increase in the money supply and contractionary monetary policy refers to a decrease in the money supply. In a dynamic framework, expansionary monetary policy refers to an increase in the rate of growth of the money supply, while contractionary monetary policy refers to a decrease in the growth rate of the money supply. In the real world, where things are constantly changing, the growth rate of the money supply is more indicative of the direction of monetary policy.

How Far Does Monetary Policy Reach? Or, Monetary Policy and Blue Eyes

Two days before the beginning of the fall semester at a college in the Midwest, Suzanne, a student at the college, was waiting in line to register for classes. As she waited, she looked through the fall schedule. She had to take an economics principles course at 10 A.M.; two sections were listed at that time. The instructor in one section was Smith; Jones was the instructor for the other section. Suzanne, not knowing which section to take, asked the person behind her in line if he had ever taken a course from either instructor. The person said that he had taken a course with Smith and that he (Smith) was very good. That was enough for Suzanne; she signed up for Smith's class.

While a student in Smith's class, Suzanne met the person whom she ended up marrying. His name is Bob. Suzanne often says to Bob, "You know, if that guy behind me in line that day had said that Smith wasn't a good teacher, or hadn't said anything at all, I might never have taken Professor Smith's class. I might have taken Jones's class instead, and I would never have met you. I'd probably be married to someone else right now."

While this story is untrue, still, it is representative of the many little things that happen every day. Little things can make big differences.

With this in mind, consider monetary policy (which is not really a little thing). Here is another story that is also not true but is still representative of something that, if it hasn't happened, certainly can.

A few years ago, Real GDP was far below its natural level. The Fed decided to increase the money supply. As a result, the *AD* curve in the economy shifted to the right. One of the first places the new demand in the economy was felt was in Denver. Economic activity in Denver increased. Jake, who lived in Austin at the time, was out of work and looking for a job. He heard about the job prospects in Denver, and so one day, he got into his car and headed for Denver. Luckily for him, he got a job a few days after arriving in Denver. He rented an apartment near his job. He became a friend of Nick, who lived in the apartment across the hall.

Nick, knowing that Jake was new in town, asked Jake if he wanted a date with his girlfriend's friend Melanie. Jake said yes. Jake and Melanie ended up dating for two years; they've been married now for ten years. They have three children, all of whom have blue eyes.

One day the youngest child asked her mother why she had blue eyes. Her mother told her it's because both she and her daddy have blue eyes. And that's not an incorrect explanation, as far as it goes.

But we can't help wondering if the youngest child has blue eyes because of an event that took place years ago, an event that has to do with the Fed and the money supply. After all, if the Fed hadn't increased the money supply when it did, maybe Denver's job prospects wouldn't have been so healthy, and maybe Jake wouldn't have left Austin. But, then, if Jake had not left Austin, he wouldn't have married Melanie and had three children, each with blue eyes. We're just speculating, of course.

Activists
Persons who argue that monetary and fiscal policies should be deliberately used to smooth out the business cycle.

Fine-tuning
The (usually frequent) use of monetary and fiscal policies to counteract even small undesirable movements in economic activity.

Nonactivists
Persons who argue against the deliberate use of discretionary fiscal and monetary policies. They believe in a permanent, stable, rule-oriented monetary and fiscal framework.

fiscal policy not only can but also should be used to smooth out the business cycle. This argument is part of the activist-nonactivist debate, which encompasses both fiscal and monetary policy. Here, we examine the activist-nonactivist debate as it relates to monetary policy.

Activists argue that monetary policy should be deliberately used to smooth out the business cycle. They are in favor of economic **fine-tuning,** which is the (usually frequent) use of monetary policy to counteract even small undesirable movements in economic activity. Sometimes the monetary policy they advocate is called either *activist* or *discretionary monetary policy.*

Nonactivists argue *against* the use of activist or discretionary monetary policy. Instead, they propose a rules-based monetary policy. Sometimes the monetary policy they propose is called either *nonactivist* or *rules-based monetary policy.* An example of a rules-based monetary policy is a policy that is based on a predetermined steady growth rate in the money supply, such as allowing the money supply to grow 3 percent a year, no matter what is happening in the economy.

The Case for Activist (or Discretionary) Monetary Policy

The case for activist (or discretionary) monetary policy rests on three major claims:

1. **The economy does not always equilibrate quickly enough at Natural Real GDP.** Consider the economy at point 1 in Exhibit 9a. Some economists maintain that, left to its own workings, the economy will eventually move to point 2 in part (b). Activists often argue that the economy takes too long to move from point 1 to point 2 and that too much lost output and too high an unemployment rate must be tolerated in the interim. They believe that an activist monetary policy speeds things along so that higher output and a lower unemployment rate can be achieved more quickly.

2. **Activist monetary policy works; it is effective at smoothing out the business cycle.** Activists are quick to point to the undesirable consequences of the constant monetary policy of the mid-1970s. In 1973, 1974, and 1975, the money supply growth rates were 5.5 percent, 4.3 percent, and 4.7 percent, respectively. These percentages represent a near constant growth rate in the money supply. The economy, however, went through a recession during this time (Real GDP fell between 1973 and 1974 and between 1974 and 1975). Activists argue that an activist and flexible monetary policy would have reduced the high cost the economy had to pay in terms of lost output and high unemployment.

3. **Activist monetary policy is flexible; nonactivist (rules-based) monetary policy is not.** Activists argue that flexibility is a desirable quality in monetary policy; inflexibility is not. The implicit judgment of activists is that the more closely monetary policy can be designed to meet the particulars of a given economic environment, the better. For example, at certain times the economy requires a sharp increase in the money supply; at other times, a sharp decrease; at still other times, only a slight increase or decrease. Activists argue that activist (discretionary) monetary policy can change as the monetary needs of the economy change; nonactivist, rules-based, or "the-same-for-all-seasons" monetary policy cannot.

The Case for Nonactivist (or Rules-Based) Monetary Policy

The case for nonactivist (or rules-based) monetary policy also rests on three major claims:

1. **In modern economies, wages and prices are sufficiently flexible to allow the economy to equilibrate at reasonable speed at Natural Real GDP.** For example, nonactivists point to the sharp drop in union wages in 1982 in response to high unemployment. In addition, they argue that government policies largely determine the flexibility of wages and prices. For example, when government decides to cushion people's unemployment (such as through unemployment compensation), wages will not fall as quickly as when government does nothing. Nonactivists believe that a laissez-faire, hands-off approach by government promotes speedy wage and price adjustments and therefore a quick return to Natural Real GDP.

2. **Activist monetary policies may not work.** Some economists argue that there are really two types of monetary policy: (1) monetary policy that is anticipated by the public and (2) monetary policy that is unanticipated. Anticipated monetary policy may not be effective at changing Real GDP or the unemployment rate. We discuss this subject in detail in the next chapter, but here is a brief explanation.

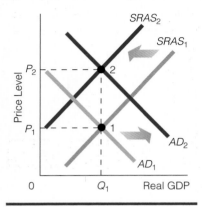

exhibit 11

Expansionary Monetary Policy and No Change in Real GDP
If expansionary monetary policy is anticipated (thus, a higher price level is anticipated), workers may bargain for and receive higher wage rates. It is possible that the SRAS curve will shift leftward to the same degree that expansionary monetary policy shifts the AD curve rightward. Result: no change in Real GDP.

Suppose the public correctly anticipates that the Fed will soon increase the money supply by 10 percent. Consequently, the public reasons that aggregate demand will increase from AD_1 to AD_2 as shown in Exhibit 11, and prices will rise.

Workers are particularly concerned about the expected higher price level because they know higher prices decrease the buying power of their wages. In an attempt to maintain their real wages, workers bargain for and receive higher money wage rates—which shifts the short-run aggregate supply curve from $SRAS_1$ to $SRAS_2$ in Exhibit 11.

Now if the SRAS curve shifts leftward (owing to higher wage rates) to the same degree as the AD curve shifts rightward (owing to the increased money supply), Real GDP does not change. It stays constant at Q_1. Thus, *a correctly anticipated increase in the money supply will be ineffective at raising Real GDP.*

3. **Activist monetary policies are likely to be destabilizing rather than stabilizing; they are likely to make matters worse rather than better.** Nonactivists point to *lags* as the main reason that activist (or discretionary) monetary policies are likely to be destabilizing. For example, economist Robert Gordon has estimated that the total lag in monetary policy is 19.3 months. (The total lag consists of the data, wait-and-see, legislative, transmission, and effectiveness lags discussed earlier.) Nonactivists argue that such a long lag makes it almost impossible to conduct effective activist monetary policy. They maintain that by the time the Fed's monetary stimulus arrives on the scene, the economy may not need any stimulus, and thus it will likely destabilize the economy. In this instance, the stimulus makes things worse rather than better.

Exhibit 12 illustrates the last point. Suppose the economy is currently in a recessionary gap at point 1. The recession is under way before Fed officials recognize it. After they are aware of the recession, however, the officials consider expanding the money supply in the hopes of shifting the AD curve from AD_1 to AD_2 so it will intersect the SRAS curve at point 1', at Natural Real GDP.

exhibit 12

Monetary Policy May Destabilize the Economy
In this scenario, the SRAS curve is shifting rightward (ridding the economy of its recessionary gap), but Fed officials do not realize this is happening. They implement expansionary monetary policy, and the AD curve ends up intersecting $SRAS_2$ at point 2 instead of intersecting $SRAS_1$ at point 1'. Fed officials end up moving the economy into an inflationary gap and thus destabilizing the economy.

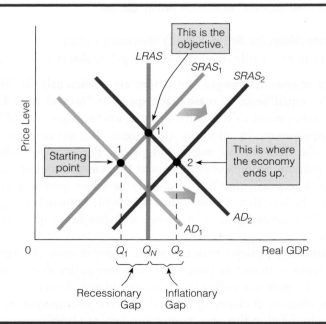

In the interim, however, unknown to everybody, the economy is regulating itself: The *SRAS* curve is shifting to the right. Fed officials don't realize this shift is occurring because it takes time to collect and analyze data about the economy.

Thinking that the economy is not regulating itself, or not regulating itself quickly enough, Fed officials implement expansionary monetary policy. The *AD* curve shifts rightward. By the time the increased money supply is felt in the goods and services market, the *AD* curve intersects the *SRAS* curve at point 2. In short, the Fed has moved the economy from point 1 to point 2, and not, as it had hoped, from point 1 to point 1'. The Fed has moved the economy into an inflationary gap. Instead of stabilizing and moderating the business cycle, the Fed has intensified it.

THINKING LIKE AN
ECONOMIST

Ask an economist a question and you are likely to get a conditional answer. For example, if you ask an economist whether monetary policy stabilizes or destabilizes the economy, she may answer that it can do either—depending on conditions. For instance, starting in a recessionary gap, if expansionary monetary policy shifts the AD curve rightward by just the right amount to intersect the SRAS curve and the LRAS curve at Natural Real GDP, then monetary policy stabilizes the economy. But if the monetary policy shifts the AD curve rightward by more than this amount, it may move the economy into an inflationary gap, thereby destabilizing the economy. If-then thinking is common in economics, as are if-then statements.

ANALYZING THE SCENE

Question from Setting the Scene: How can expansionary monetary policy not increase Real GDP in the short run?

You are accustomed to thinking that an increase in the money supply will shift the *AD* curve rightward. If the *SRAS* curve is upward-sloping, it follows that Real GDP will rise (at least in the short run).

- But now you learn that whether or not this outcome materializes depends on people's expectations. As shown in Exhibit 11, if people think expansionary monetary policy will lead to higher prices (because it shifts the *AD* curve rightward) and thus bargain for and receive higher wages, then the *SRAS* curve might shift leftward at the same time that the *AD* curve shifts to the right. If the *AD* curve shifts to the right to the same degree as the *SRAS* curve shifts to the left, then there will be no change in Real GDP. In other words, expansionary monetary policy might not "expand" Real GDP.

SELF-TEST

1. Why are Keynesians more likely to advocate expansionary monetary policy to eliminate a recessionary gap than contractionary monetary policy to eliminate an inflationary gap?
2. How might monetary policy destabilize the economy?
3. If the economy is stuck in a recessionary gap, does this make the case for activist (expansionary) monetary policy stronger or weaker? Explain your answer.

NONACTIVIST MONETARY PROPOSALS

In this section, we outline three nonactivist (or rules-based) monetary proposals.

A Constant-Money-Growth-Rate Rule

Many nonactivists argue that the sole objective of monetary policy is to stabilize the price level. To this end, they propose a *constant-money-growth-rate rule.* One version of the rule is:

The annual money supply growth rate will be constant at the average annual growth rate of Real GDP.

For example, if the average annual Real GDP growth rate is approximately 3.3 percent, the money supply will be put on automatic pilot and will be permitted to grow at an annual rate of 3.3 percent. The money supply will grow at this rate regardless of the state of the economy.

Some economists predict that a constant-money-growth-rate rule will bring about a stable price level over time. This prediction is based on the equation of exchange ($MV \equiv PQ$). If the average annual growth rate in Real GDP (Q) is 3.3 percent and the money supply (M) grows at 3.3 percent, the price level should remain stable over time. Advocates of this rule argue that in some years the growth rate in Real GDP will be below its average rate, causing an increase in the price level, and in other years the growth rate in Real GDP will be above its average rate, causing a fall in the price level, but over time the price level will be stable.

A Predetermined-Money-Growth-Rate Rule

Critics of the constant-money-growth-rate rule point out that it makes two assumptions: (1) Velocity is constant. (2) The money supply is defined correctly. These critics argue that there have been periods when velocity has not been constant. And it is not yet clear which definition of the money supply (M1, M2, or some broader monetary measure) is the proper one and therefore which money supply growth rate ought to be fixed.

Largely in response to the charge that velocity is not always constant, some nonactivists prefer the following rule:

The annual growth rate in the money supply will be equal to the average annual growth rate in Real GDP minus the growth rate in velocity.

In other words,

$$\%\Delta M = \%\Delta Q - \%\Delta V$$

With this rule, the growth rate of the money supply is not fixed. It can vary from year to year, yet it is predetermined in that it is dependent on the growth rates of Real GDP and velocity. For this reason, we call it the *predetermined-money-growth-rate rule.* To illustrate the workings of this rule, consider the following extended version of the equation of exchange:

$$\%\Delta M + \%\Delta V = \%\Delta P + \%\Delta Q$$

Suppose $\%\Delta Q = 3$ percent and $\%\Delta V$ is 1 percent. The rule would specify that the growth rate in the money supply should be 2 percent. This would keep the price level stable; there would be a zero percent change in P:

$$\%\Delta M + \%\Delta V = \%\Delta P + \%\Delta Q$$
$$2\% + 1\% = 0\% + 3\%$$

The Fed and the Taylor Rule

The economist John Taylor has argued that there may be a middle ground, of sorts, between activist and nonactivist monetary policy. He has proposed that monetary authorities use a rule to guide them in making their discretionary decisions. There is some evidence that recent members of the Fed would agree. Laurence Meyer, a former member of the Board of Governors, said:

Even if we cannot imagine policymakers turning over the conduct of policy to a rule, research on rules might provide guidance to policymakers that could improve their judgmental adjustments to policy. I strongly believe this is the case. No one would argue,

Asset-Price Inflation

During the years 1999–2004, the price level in the United States grew at a fairly modest annual average rate of 2.4 percent. But during those same years, asset prices (especially house prices) grew rapidly. In some cities, house prices increased by 25 to 40 percent. If the rapid rise in house prices had occurred in consumer prices instead, no doubt the Fed would have acted quickly to cool down the rise in consumer prices. In short, the Fed would have likely reduced the money supply.

So why doesn't the Fed act the same way when the rise in prices is in assets? Some economists have argued that it should. They argue that the Fed should target a broadly defined price level that includes both consumer prices and asset prices (such as house and stock prices). A few central banks—namely the European Central Bank, the Bank of England, and the Reserve Bank of Australia (Australia's central bank)—have recently given some support to the view that monetary policy should sometimes consider the growth in asset prices (even when consumer price inflation is low). For example, in 2004, both the Bank of England and the Reserve Bank of Australia began to adjust their respective

monetary policy based on the rapid rise in asset prices in Great Britain and Australia.

In an article in the *Wall Street Journal* on February 18, 2004, Otmar Issing, the chief economist for the European Central Bank (ECB), discussed the role of a central bank in a world where consumer-price inflation is low but asset-price inflation is high. He states, "Just as consumer-price inflation is often described as a situation of 'too much money chasing too few goods,' asset-price inflation could similarly be characterized as 'too much money chasing too few assets.'" He goes on to say that central banks—all central banks—face a challenge in the future: how to deal with asset-price inflation in a way that is not harmful to the overall economy. He states, "As societies accumulate wealth, asset prices will have a growing influence on economic developments. The problem of how to design monetary policy under such circumstances is probably the biggest challenge for central banks in our times."[6]

---

6. Otmar Issing, "Money and Credit," *Wall Street Journal,* 18 February 2004.

---

after all, that good policy is whimsical. On the contrary, good policy should be systematic. Good discretionary policy therefore should be, in some meaningful way, rule-like, though it might be impossible to write down in a simple or even complicated equation all the complex considerations that underpin the conduct of such a systematic monetary policy.[7]

The rule that John Taylor has proposed has come to be known as the *Taylor Rule.* The Taylor Rule specifies how policymakers should set the target for the (nominal) federal funds rate. (Recall from an earlier chapter that the federal funds rate is the interest rate banks charge one another for reserves.) The "economic thinking" implicit in the Taylor Rule is as follows: There is some federal funds rate target that is consistent with (1) stabilizing inflation around a rather low inflation rate and (2) stabilizing Real GDP around its full-employment level. Find this federal funds rate target, and then use the tools of the Fed to hit the target.

The Taylor Rule, which, according to John Taylor, will find the right federal funds rate target, is:

$$\text{Federal funds rate target} =$$
$$\text{Inflation} + \text{Equilibrium real federal funds rate} + \tfrac{1}{2}\,(\text{Inflation gap}) + \tfrac{1}{2}\,(\text{Output gap})$$

---

7. Remarks by Governor Laurence H. Meyer at the Owen Graduate School of Management, Vanderbilt University, Nashville, Tennessee, 16 January 2002.

Let's briefly discuss the four components of the rule:

- **Inflation.** This is the current inflation rate.
- **Equilibrium real federal funds rate.** The real federal funds rate is simply the nominal federal funds rate adjusted for inflation. Taylor assumes the equilibrium real federal funds rate is 2 percent.
- **$\frac{1}{2}$ inflation gap.** The inflation gap is the difference between the actual inflation rate and the target for inflation. Taylor assumes that an appropriate target for inflation is about 2 percent. If this target were accepted by policymakers, they would effectively be saying that they would not want an inflation rate higher than 2 percent.
- **$\frac{1}{2}$ output gap.** The output gap is the percentage difference between actual Real GDP and its full-employment or natural level.

For example, suppose the current inflation rate is 1 percent, the equilibrium real federal funds rate is 2 percent, the inflation gap is 1 percent, and the output gap is 2 percent. What is the federal funds rate target?

$$
\begin{aligned}
\text{Federal funds rate target} &= \text{Inflation} + \text{Equilibrium real federal funds rate} \\
&\quad + \tfrac{1}{2}\,(\text{Inflation gap}) + \tfrac{1}{2}\,(\text{Output gap}) \\
&= 1\% + 2\% + \tfrac{1}{2}\,(1\%) + \tfrac{1}{2}\,(2\%) \\
&= 4.5\%
\end{aligned}
$$

A | READER ASKS

Are Americans Overtaxed?

On a television news program I was watching the other day, a person said that Americans are overtaxed. He went on to back this up by saying that Americans work from January 1 to around the end of April just to pay their taxes. If this is true, then perhaps Americans are overtaxed. What do the economists say, though? Do they say Americans are overtaxed?

Most economists do not usually comment on whether Americans are overtaxed, undertaxed, or taxed just the right amount. Instead, they mainly report on what taxes people pay, how much taxes people pay, and so on.

For example, what you heard on your television news program about how many days Americans work each year to pay their taxes is essentially correct. In 2004, the "average American taxpayer" worked from January 1 to April 17 to pay all her taxes (federal, state, and local). That is a total of 106 days out of a 365-day year. Is that too much? Some people, speaking for themselves, would say yes. After all, they might say, working almost one-third of the year just to pay your taxes is too much.

But consider a different measure of the tax burden: the ratio of tax revenues to GDP. This tax ratio for the United States was about 29 percent in 1998. The same ratio was 51 percent for Sweden, 43 percent for Austria, and 44 percent for France. In fact, of 29 countries studied, the United States had a lower tax-revenue-to-GDP ratio than 24 countries. The same people who said Americans were overtaxed might change their minds when they learn that the United States has a relatively lower tax burden than many other countries have.

Another issue to consider is how the tax burden is distributed among American workers. For example, in 2001, the top 1 percent of income earners in the United States paid 33.71 percent of all federal income taxes while the bottom 50 percent of all income earners paid 3.5 percent of all federal income taxes. Were the top 1 percent of income earners overtaxed and the bottom 50 percent undertaxed?

Finally, there is the issue of who benefits from the taxes. For example, suppose Smith pays $400 in taxes and Jones pays $200 in taxes. Is Smith overtaxed relative to Jones? Maybe not. Smith could receive $500 worth of benefits for the $400 he pays in taxes, whereas Jones could receive $100 worth of benefits for the $200 he pays in taxes. Even though Smith pays twice the taxes that Jones pays, Smith may consider himself much better off than Jones. And Jones may agree.

Chapter Summary

Fiscal Policy: General Remarks

> Fiscal policy refers to changes in government expenditures and/or taxes to achieve particular economic goals. Expansionary fiscal policy refers to increases in government expenditures and/or decreases in taxes. Contractionary fiscal policy refers to decreases in government expenditures and/or increases in taxes.

Demand-Side Fiscal Policy: A Keynesian Perspective

> In Keynesian theory, demand-side fiscal policy can be used to rid the economy of a recessionary gap or an inflationary gap. A recessionary gap calls for expansionary fiscal policy and an inflationary gap calls for contractionary fiscal policy. Ideally, fiscal policy changes aggregate demand by enough to rid the economy of either a recessionary gap or an inflationary gap.

Crowding Out

> Crowding out refers to the decrease in private expenditures that occurs as a consequence of increased government spending and/or the greater financing needs of a budget deficit. The crowding-out effect suggests that expansionary fiscal policy does not work to the degree that Keynesian theory predicts.

> Complete (incomplete) crowding out occurs when the decrease in one or more components of private spending completely (partially) offsets the increase in government spending.

New Classical View of Fiscal Policy

> New classical economists argue that individuals will decrease consumption spending and increase saving to pay the higher future taxes brought on by debt financing of the deficit. This will lead to the same conclusion as for complete crowding out: The AD curve will not shift.

> Deficits do not necessarily bring higher interest rates.

Reasons Why Demand-Side Fiscal Policy May Be Ineffective

> Demand-side fiscal policy may be ineffective at achieving certain macroeconomic goals because of (1) crowding out, and (2) lags.

Supply-Side Fiscal Policy

> When fiscal policy measures affect tax rates, they may affect both aggregate supply and aggregate demand. It is generally accepted that a marginal tax rate reduction increases the attractiveness of work relative to leisure and tax-avoidance activities and thus leads to an increase in aggregate supply.

> Tax revenues equal the tax base multiplied by the (average) tax rate. Whether tax revenues decrease or increase as a result of a tax rate reduction depends on whether the percentage increase in the tax base is greater or less than the percentage reduction in the tax rate. If the percentage increase in the tax base is greater than the percentage reduction in the tax rate, then tax revenues will increase. If the percentage increase in the tax base is less than the percentage reduction in the tax rate, then tax revenues will decrease.

Monetary Policy

> Monetary policy, which refers to changes in the money supply or in the rate of change of the money supply, can be used to rid the economy of a recessionary gap or an inflationary gap. A recessionary gap calls for expansionary monetary policy and an inflationary gap calls for contractionary monetary policy.

The Activist-Nonactivist Debate

> Activists argue that monetary policy should be deliberately used to smooth out the business cycle; they are in favor of using activist, or discretionary, monetary policy to fine-tune the economy. Nonactivists argue against the use of discretionary monetary policy; they propose nonactivist, or rules-based, monetary policy.

> The case for discretionary monetary policy rests on three major claims: (1) The economy does not always equilibrate quickly enough at Natural Real GDP. (2) Activist monetary policy works. (3) Activist monetary policy is flexible, and flexibility is a desirable quality in monetary policy.

> The case for nonactivist monetary policy rests on three major claims: (1) There is sufficient flexibility in wages and prices in modern economies to allow the economy to equilibrate at reasonable speed at Natural Real GDP. (2) Activist monetary policies may not work. (3) Activist monetary policies are likely to make matters worse rather than better.

Nonactivist (or Rules-Based) Monetary Proposals

> The constant-money-growth-rate rule states that the annual money supply growth rate will be constant at the average annual growth rate of Real GDP.

> The predetermined-money-growth-rate rule states that the annual growth rate in the money supply will be equal to the average annual growth rate in Real GDP minus the growth rate in velocity.

> The Taylor Rule holds that the federal funds rate should be targeted according to the following: Federal funds rate target = Inflation + Equilibrium real federal funds rate + $\frac{1}{2}$ (Inflation gap) + $\frac{1}{2}$ (Output gap).

Key Terms and Concepts

Fiscal Policy
Expansionary Fiscal Policy
Contractionary Fiscal Policy
Discretionary Fiscal Policy
Automatic Fiscal Policy
Crowding Out

Complete Crowding Out
Incomplete Crowding Out
Marginal (Income) Tax Rate
Laffer Curve
Tax Base
Monetary Policy

Expansionary Monetary Policy
Contractionary Monetary Policy
Activists
Fine-tuning
Nonactivists

Questions and Problems

1. According to Keynesian economists, how can fiscal policy be used to remove an economy from a recessionary gap? an inflationary gap?
2. What is the new classical view of fiscal policy?
3. Explain two ways crowding out may occur.
4. Why is crowding out an important issue in the debate over the use of fiscal policy?
5. Some economists argue for the use of fiscal policy to solve economic problems; some argue against its use. What are some of the arguments on both sides?
6. The debate over using government spending and taxing powers to stabilize the economy involves more than technical economic issues. Do you agree or disagree? Explain your answer.
7. Explain why a tax rate reduction can raise tax revenues or lower tax revenues.
8. Is crowding out equally likely under all economic conditions? Explain your answer.
9. Tax cuts will likely affect aggregate demand and aggregate supply. Does it matter which is affected more? Explain in terms of the *AD-AS* framework.
10. Explain how expansionary fiscal policy can, under certain conditions, destabilize the economy.
11. The economy is in a recessionary gap and both Smith and Jones advocate expansionary fiscal policy. Does it follow that both Smith and Jones favor "big government"?

12. Will tax cuts that are perceived to be temporary affect the *SRAS* and *LRAS* curves differently than tax cuts that are perceived to be permanent? Explain your answer.
13. How can monetary policy be used to remove the economy from a recessionary gap? an inflationary gap?
14. It has been suggested that nonactivists are not concerned with the level of Real GDP and unemployment because most (if not all) nonactivist monetary proposals set as their immediate objective the stabilization of the price level. Discuss.
15. Suppose the combination of more accurate data and better forecasting techniques made it easy for the Fed to predict a recession 10 to 16 months in advance. Would this strengthen the case for activism or nonactivism? Explain your answer.
16. According to the Taylor Rule, if inflation is 3 percent, the inflation gap is 5 percent, and the output gap is 2 percent, what does the federal funds rate target equal?
17. Suppose the annual average percentage change in Real GDP is 2.3 percent, and the annual average percentage change in velocity is 1.1 percent. Using the monetary rule discussed in the text, what percentage change in the money supply will keep prices stable (on average)?

Working With Numbers and Graphs

1. Graphically show how fiscal policy works in the ideal case.
2. Graphically illustrate how government can use supply-side fiscal policy to get an economy out of a recessionary gap.
3. Graphically illustrate the following:
   a. Fiscal policy destabilizes the economy
   b. Fiscal policy eliminates an inflationary gap
   c. Fiscal policy only partly eliminates a recessionary gap

4. Which panel in the figure below best describes the situation in each of (a)–(d)?
   a. Expansionary monetary policy that effectively removes the economy from a recessionary gap
   b. Expansionary monetary policy that is destabilizing
   c. Contractionary monetary policy that effectively removes the economy from an inflationary gap
   d. Monetary policy that is ineffective at changing Real GDP

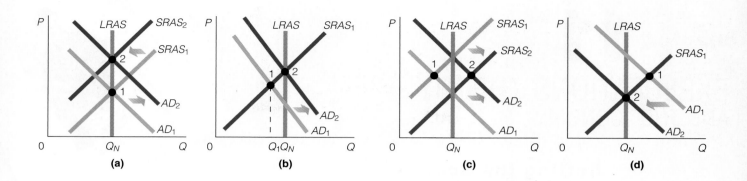

EXPECTATIONS THEORY
AND THE ECONOMY

© DigitalVision/Getty Images

Setting the Scene

The following events occurred not long ago.

10:45 P.M., Steven Wilson's house, Evanston, Illinois.

Steven has had a full day. It's almost time to go to bed, but before he does, Steven goes online to check the weather forecast for tomorrow. "Seventy percent chance of rain by midafternoon," the forecast reads. I'd better put my umbrella out so I don't forget it tomorrow, Steven thinks to himself.

4:15 P.M., the State Fair, Witchita, Kansas.

The fortune teller's sign reads: "The Crystal Ball Never Lies. Your Fortune Told for $10." Three people wait in line to have their fortunes told. Robin, 16 years old, is the third person in line. I'm just here for fun, Robin thinks to himself. Still, I might as well ask the fortune teller—just for fun—whether or not Stephanie will accept my invitation to the Friday night dance.

7:13 P.M., Nick and Michael, brothers, are playing chess in their home in Canyon Country, California.

Nick thinks, If I move from e4 to e5, he'll probably move from f3 to c6, after which I'll move from b5 to c5. But it's the next step that worries me. What is the chance he'll then move from c3 to d6? Nick then moves from e4 to e5. Michael thinks, Nick probably thinks I'm going to move from f3 to c6, after which he'll probably move from b5 to c5. Maybe I should move from d3 to c7.

10:32 P.M., George is watching one of his favorite movies, *The Godfather*, on television. It's the scene where Don Corleone warns Michael about Barzini.

Don Corleone: Barzini will move against you first.

Michael: How?

Don Corleone: He will get in touch with you through someone you absolutely trust. That person will arrange a meeting, guarantee your safety . . .

He rises and looks at Michael . . .

Don Corleone: . . . and at that meeting you will be assassinated.

How would an economist look at these events? Later in the chapter, a discussion based on the following question will help you analyze the scene the way an economist would.

- What do each of the events have to do with rational expectations?

PHILLIPS CURVE ANALYSIS

The *Phillips curve* is used to analyze the relationship between inflation and unemployment. After introducing the Phillips curve, we bring expectations into the discussion and see how they affect the results of our analysis.

We begin the discussion of the Phillips curve by focusing on the work of three economists, A. W. Phillips, Paul Samuelson, and Robert Solow.

The Phillips Curve

In 1958, A. W. Phillips of the London School of Economics published a paper in the economics journal *Economica*. The paper was titled "The Relation between Unemployment and the Rate of Change of Money Wages in the United Kingdom, 1861–1957." As the title suggests, Phillips collected data about the rate of change in money wages, sometimes referred to as wage inflation, and unemployment rates in the United Kingdom over a period of time. He then plotted the rate of change in money wages against the unemployment rate for each year. Finally, he fit a curve to the data points (Exhibit 1).

An Inverse Relationship

The curve came to be known as the **Phillips curve.** Notice that the curve is downward-sloping, suggesting that the rate of change of money wage rates (wage inflation) and unemployment rates are *inversely related*. This inverse relationship suggests a tradeoff between wage inflation and unemployment. Higher wage inflation means lower unemployment; lower wage inflation means higher unemployment.

Policymakers concluded from the Phillips curve that it was impossible to lower both wage inflation and unemployment; one could do one or the other. So, the combination of low wage inflation and low unemployment was unlikely. This was the bad news.

The good news was that rising unemployment and rising wage inflation did not go together either. Thus, the combination of high unemployment and high wage inflation was unlikely.

The Theoretical Explanation for the Phillips Curve

What is the reason for the inverse relationship between wage inflation and unemployment? Early explanations focused on the state of the labor market given changes in aggregate demand. When aggregate demand is increasing, businesses expand production and hire more employees. As the unemployment rate falls, the labor market becomes tighter and employers find it increasingly difficult to hire workers at old wages. Businesses must

Phillips Curve
A curve that originally showed the relationship between wage inflation and unemployment. Now it more often shows the relationship between price inflation and unemployment.

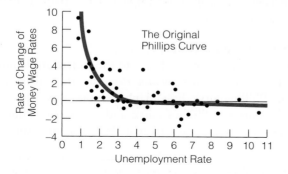

exhibit 1

The Original Phillips Curve
This curve was constructed by A. W. Phillips, using data for the United Kingdom from 1861 to 1913. (The relationship here is also representative of the experience of the United Kingdom through 1957.) The original Phillips curve suggests an inverse relationship between wage inflation and unemployment; it represents a wage inflation–unemployment tradeoff. (Note: Each dot represents a single year.)

exhibit **2**

The Phillips Curve and a Menu of Choices
Samuelson and Solow's early work using American data showed that the Phillips curve was downward-sloping. Economists reasoned that stagflation was extremely unlikely and that the Phillips curve presented policymakers with a menu of choices—point *A*, *B, C,* or *D.*

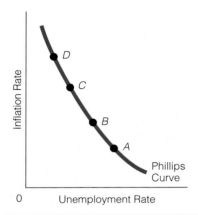

Stagflation
The simultaneous occurrence of high rates of inflation and unemployment.

© Ed Kashi/CORBIS

offer higher wages to obtain additional workers. Unemployment and money wage rates move in opposite directions.

Samuelson and Solow: The Phillips Curve Is Americanized

In 1960, two American economists, Paul Samuelson and Robert Solow, published an article in the *American Economic Review* in which they fit a Phillips curve to the U.S. economy from 1935 to 1959. Besides using American data instead of British data, they measured price inflation rates (instead of wage inflation rates) against unemployment rates. They found an inverse relationship between (price) inflation and unemployment (see Exhibit 2).[1]

Economists concluded from the Phillips curve that **stagflation,** or high inflation together with high unemployment, was extremely unlikely. The economy could register (a) high unemployment and low inflation or (b) low unemployment and high inflation. Also, economists noticed that the Phillips curve presented policymakers with a *menu of choices.* For example, policymakers could choose to move the economy to any of the points on the Phillips curve in Exhibit 2. If they decided that a point like *A,* with high unemployment and low inflation, was preferable to a point like *D,* with low unemployment and high inflation, then so be it. It was simply a matter of reaching the right level of aggregate demand. To Keynesian economists, who were gaining a reputation for advocating fine-tuning the economy, that is, using small-scale measures to counterbalance undesirable economic trends, this conclusion seemed to be consistent with their theories and policy proposals.

THE CONTROVERSY BEGINS: ARE THERE REALLY TWO PHILLIPS CURVES?

This section discusses the work of Milton Friedman and the hypothesis that there are two, not one, Phillips curves.

Things Aren't Always as We Thought

In the 1970s and early 1980s, economists began to question many of the conclusions about the Phillips curve. Their questions were largely prompted by events after 1969. Consider Exhibit 3, which shows U.S. inflation and unemployment rates for the years 1961–2003. The 1961–1969 period, which is shaded, depicts the original Phillips curve tradeoff between inflation and unemployment. The remaining period, 1970–2003, as a whole does not, although some subperiods, such as 1976–1979, do.

Focusing on the period 1970–2003, we note that stagflation—high unemployment and high inflation—is possible. For example, 1975, 1981, and 1982 are definitely years of stagflation. The existence of stagflation implies that a tradeoff between inflation and unemployment may not always exist.

Friedman and the Natural Rate Theory

Milton Friedman, in his presidential address to the American Economic Association in 1967 (published in the *American Economic Review*), attacked the idea of a permanent downward-sloping Phillips curve. Friedman's key point was that there are two, not one, Phillips curves: a short-run Phillips curve and a long-run Phillips curve. Friedman said, "There is always a temporary tradeoff between inflation and unemployment;

---

1. Today, when economists speak of the Phillips curve, they are usually referring to the relationship between price inflation rates and unemployment rates, instead of wage inflation rates and unemployment rates.

exhibit 3

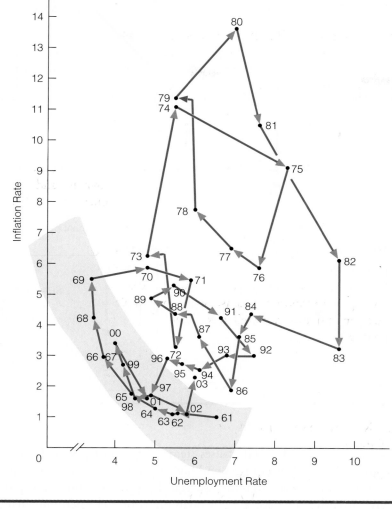

**The Diagram That Raises
Questions: Inflation and
Unemployment, 1961–2003**
The period 1961–1969 clearly depicts
the original Phillips curve tradeoff
between inflation and unemployment.
The later period, 1970–2003, as a whole,
does not. However, some subperiods do,
such as 1976–1979. The diagram
presents empirical evidence that
stagflation may exist; an inflation-
unemployment tradeoff may not
always hold.

there is no permanent tradeoff." In other words, *there is a tradeoff in the short run but not
in the long run.* Friedman's discussion not only introduced two types of Phillips curves to
the analysis but also opened the macroeconomics door wide, once and for all, to expectations theory, that is, to the idea that people's expectations about economic events affect economic outcomes.

Exhibit 4 illustrates both the short-run and long-run Phillips curves. We start with
the economy in long-run equilibrium, operating at Q_1, which is equal to Q_N. This is
shown in Window 1. In the main diagram, the economy is at point 1 at the natural rate
of unemployment. Further, and most important, *we assume that the expected inflation rate
and the actual inflation rate are the same,* both are 2 percent.

Now suppose government *unexpectedly* increases aggregate demand from AD_1 to AD_2,
as shown in Window 2. As a result, the *actual* inflation rate increases (say, to 4 percent), but
in the short run (immediately after the increase in aggregate demand), individual decision
makers do not know this. Consequently, the *expected* inflation rate remains at 2 percent. In
short, aggregate demand increases at the same time that people's expected inflation rate
remains constant. Because of this combination of events, certain things happen.

exhibit **4**

Short-Run and Long-Run Phillips Curves

Starting at point 1 in the main diagram, and assuming that the expected inflation rate stays constant as aggregate demand increases, the economy moves to point 2. As the expected inflation rate changes and comes to equal the actual inflation rate, the economy moves to point 3. Points 1 and 2 lie on a short-run Phillips curve. Points 1 and 3 lie on a long-run Phillips curve. (Note: The percentages in parentheses following the *SRAS* curves in the windows refer to the expected inflation rates.)

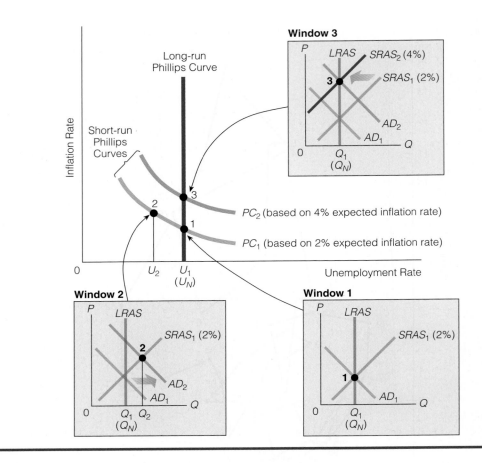

The higher aggregate demand causes temporary shortages and higher prices. Businesses then respond to higher prices and higher profits by increasing output. Higher output requires more employees, so businesses start hiring more workers. As job vacancies increase, many currently unemployed individuals find work. Furthermore, many of these newly employed persons accept the prevailing wage rate because they think the wages will have greater purchasing power (recall that they expect the inflation rate to be 2 percent) than, in fact, those wages will turn out to have.

So far, the results of an increase in aggregate demand with no change in the expected inflation rate are (1) an increase in Real GDP from Q_1 to Q_2 (see Window 2) and (2) a corresponding decrease in the unemployment rate from U_1 to U_2 (see the main diagram). Thus, the economy has moved from point 1 to point 2 in the main diagram.

This raises the question: Is point 2 a stable equilibrium? Friedman answered that it is not. He argued that *as long as the expected inflation rate is not equal to the actual inflation rate, the economy is not in long-run equilibrium.*

For Friedman, as for most economists today, the movement from point 1 to point 2 on PC_1 is a short-run movement. Economists refer to PC_1, along which short-run movements occur, as a short-run Phillips curve.

In time, inflation expectations begin to change. As prices continue to climb, wage earners realize that their real (inflation-adjusted) wages have fallen. In hindsight, they realize that they accepted nominal (money) wages based on an expected inflation rate (2 percent) that was too low. They revise their inflation expectations upward.

At the same time, some wage earners quit their jobs because they choose not to continue working at such low *real wages*. Eventually, the combination of some workers quitting their jobs and most (if not all) workers revising their inflation expectations upward causes wage rates to move upward.

Higher wage rates shift the short-run aggregate supply curve from $SRAS_1$ to $SRAS_2$ (see Window 3), ultimately moving the economy back to Natural Real GDP and to the natural rate of unemployment at point 3 (see the main diagram). The curve that connects point 1, where the economy started, and point 3, where it ended, is called the *long-run Phillips curve*.

Thus, the short-run Phillips curve exhibits a tradeoff between inflation and unemployment, whereas the long-run Phillips curve does not. This is the idea implicit in what has come to be called the **Friedman natural rate theory** (or the *Friedman "fooling" theory*). According to this theory, in the long run, the economy returns to its natural rate of unemployment, and the only reason it moved away from the natural unemployment rate in the first place was because workers were "fooled" (in the short run) into thinking the inflation rate was lower than it was.

How, specifically, do people's expectations relate to the discussion of the short- and long-run Phillips curves? To see how, again look at Exhibit 4. The economy starts out at point 1 in the main diagram. Then something happens in the economy: aggregate demand increases. This raises the inflation rate, *but it takes some time before workers realize the change in the inflation rate*. In the interim, their expected inflation rate is "too low." And because their expected inflation rate is "too low," workers are willing to work at jobs (and produce output) that they wouldn't work at if they perceived the inflation rate realistically.

But in time, workers do perceive the inflation rate realistically. In other words, the expected inflation rate is no longer "too low"—it has risen to equal the actual inflation rate. There is a predicted response in the unemployment rate and output as a result: the unemployment rate rises and output falls.

In short: Because workers' expectations (of inflation) are, in the short run, inconsistent with reality, workers produce more output than they would have produced if those expectations were consistent with reality. Do you see how people's expectations can affect such real economic variables as Real GDP and the unemployment rate?

Exhibit 5 may also help explain the Friedman natural rate theory.

Friedman Natural Rate Theory
The idea that in the long run, unemployment is at its natural rate. Within the Phillips curve framework, the natural rate theory specifies that there is a long-run Phillips curve, which is vertical at the natural rate of unemployment.

How Do People Form Their Expectations?

Implicit in the Friedman natural rate theory is a theory about how individuals form their expectations. Essentially, the theory holds that individuals form their expected inflation rate by looking at past inflation rates. To illustrate, let's suppose that the actual inflation rates in years 1–4 are 5 percent, 3 percent, 2 percent, and 2 percent, respectively. What do you think the inflation rate will be next year, year 5? Friedman assumes that people weight past inflation rates to come up with their expected inflation rate. For example, John may assign the following weights to the inflation rates in the past four years.

Year	Inflation Rate	Weight
1	5 percent	10%
2	3 percent	20%
3	2 percent	30%
4	2 percent	40%

The Friedman Natural Rate Theory

1. Wages and prices are flexible.
2. Expectations are formed adaptively.

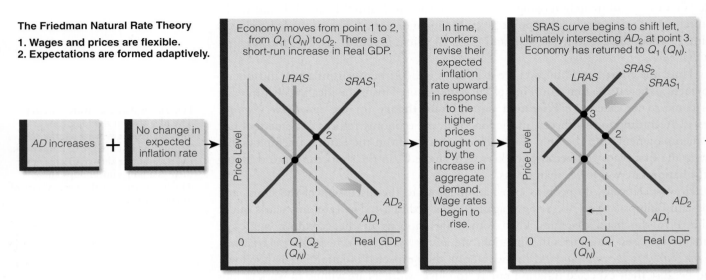

AD increases **+** No change in expected inflation rate →

Economy moves from point 1 to 2, from Q_1 (Q_N) to Q_2. There is a short-run increase in Real GDP.

In time, workers revise their expected inflation rate upward in response to the higher prices brought on by the increase in aggregate demand. Wage rates begin to rise.

SRAS curve begins to shift left, ultimately intersecting AD_2 at point 3. Economy has returned to Q_1 (Q_N).

exhibit 5

Mechanics of the Friedman Natural Rate Theory

In other words, as the upcoming year approaches, the weight assigned to the present year's inflation rate rises. Based on these weights, John forms his expected inflation rate (his "best guess" of the inflation rate in the upcoming year), by finding the weighted average of the inflation rates in the past four years.

Expected inflation rate = 0.10(5 percent) + 0.20(3 percent) + 0.30(2 percent) + 0.40(2 percent)
= 2.5 percent

John's expected inflation rate is 2.5 percent.

Notice that in forming an expected inflation rate this way, the person is always looking to the past. He is, in a sense, looking over his shoulder to see what has happened, and then based on what has happened, "figuring out" what he thinks will happen. In economics, a person who forms an expected inflation rate this way is said to hold **adaptive expectations.** In short, the Friedman natural rate theory implicitly assumes that people hold adaptive expectations.

Some economists have argued this point. They believe that people do not form their expected inflation rate using adaptive expectations. Instead, they believe people hold *rational expectations.* We discuss this in the next section.

Adaptive Expectations
Expectations that individuals form from past experience and modify slowly as the present and the future become the past (as time passes).

SELF-TEST   *(Answers to Self-Test questions are in the Self-Test Appendix.)*

1. What condition must exist for the Phillips curve to present policymakers with a permanent menu of choices (between inflation and unemployment)?
2. Is there a tradeoff between inflation and unemployment? Explain your answer.
3. The Friedman natural rate theory is sometimes called the "fooling" theory. Who is being fooled and what are they being fooled about?

RATIONAL EXPECTATIONS AND NEW CLASSICAL THEORY

Rational expectations has played a major role in the Phillips curve controversy. The work of economists Robert Lucas, Robert Barro, Thomas Sargent, and Neil Wallace is relevant in this discussion.

Rational Expectations

In the early 1970s, a few economists, including Robert Lucas of the University of Chicago (winner of the 1995 Nobel Prize in Economics), began to question the short-run tradeoff between inflation and unemployment. Essentially, Lucas combined the natural rate theory with rational expectations.[2] (In this text, the natural rate theory built on adaptive expectations is called the *Friedman natural rate theory;* the natural rate theory built on rational expectations is called the *new classical theory.*)

Before presenting the new classical theory, we define and discuss **rational expectations.** Rational expectations holds that individuals form the expected inflation rate not only on the basis of their past experience with inflation (looking over their shoulders) but also on their predictions about the effects of present and future policy actions and events. In short, the expected inflation rate is formed by looking at the past, present, and future. To illustrate, suppose the inflation rate has been 5 percent for the past seven years. Then, the chairman of the Fed's Board of Governors speaks about "sharply stimulating the economy." Rational expectationists argue that the expected inflation rate might immediately jump upward, based on the current words of the chairman.

A major difference between adaptive and rational expectations is the *speed* at which the expected inflation rate changes. If the expected inflation rate is formed adaptively, then it is slow to change. It is based only on the past, so individuals will wait until the present and the future become the past before they change their expectations. If the expected inflation rate is formed rationally, it changes quickly because it is based on the past, present, and future. One implication of rational expectations is that people anticipate policy.

Do People Anticipate Policy?

Suppose you chose people at random on the street and asked them this question: What do you think the Fed will do in the next few months? Do you think you would be more likely to receive (1) an intelligent answer or (2) the response, "What is the Fed"?

Most readers of this text will probably choose answer (2). There is a general feeling that the person on the street knows little about economics or economic institutions. The answer to our question "Do people anticipate policy?" seems to be no.

But suppose you chose people at random on Wall Street and asked the same question. This time you would likely receive an informed answer. In this case, the answer to our larger question "Do people anticipate policy?" is likely to be yes.

We suggest that not all persons need to anticipate policy. As long as some do, the consequences may be the same *as if* all persons do. For example, Juanita Estevez is anticipating policy if she decides to buy 100 shares of SKA because her best friend, Tammy Higgins, heard from her friend, Kenny Urich, that his broker, Roberta Gunter, told him that SKA's stock is expected to go up. Juanita is anticipating policy because it is likely that Roberta Gunter obtained her information from a researcher in the brokerage firm who makes it his business to "watch the Fed" and to anticipate its next move.

Rational Expectations
Expectations that individuals form based on past experience and also on their predictions about the effects of present and future policy actions and events.

---

2. Rational expectations appeared on the economic scene in 1961 when John Muth published "Rational Expectations and the Theory of Price Movements" in the journal *Econometrica.* For about 10 years, the article received little attention from the economics profession. Then, in the early 1970s, with the work of Robert Lucas, Thomas Sargent, Neil Wallace, Robert Barro, and others, the article began to be noticed.

Of course, anticipating policy is not done just for the purpose of buying and selling stocks. Labor unions hire professional forecasters to predict future inflation rates, which is important information to have during wage contract negotiations. Banks hire professional forecasters to predict inflation rates, which they incorporate into the interest rate they charge. Export businesses hire professional forecasters to predict the future exchange-rate value of the dollar. The average investor may subscribe to a business or investment newsletter in order to predict interest rates, the price of gold, or next year's inflation rate more accurately. The person thinking of refinancing his or her mortgage watches one of the many financial news shows on television to find out about the government's most recent move and how it will affect interest rates in the next three months.

New Classical Theory: The Effects of Unanticipated and Anticipated Policy

New classical theory makes two major assumptions: (1) expectations are formed rationally; (2) wages and prices are flexible. With these in mind, we discuss new classical theory in two settings: where policy is unanticipated and where policy is anticipated.

Unanticipated Policy

Consider Exhibit 6a. The economy starts at point 1, where $Q_1 = Q_N$. Unexpectedly, the Fed begins to buy government securities, and the money supply and aggregate demand increase. The aggregate demand curve shifts rightward from AD_1 to AD_2. Because the policy action was unanticipated, individuals are caught off guard, so the anticipated price level (P_1), on which the short-run aggregate supply curve is based, is not likely to change immediately. (This is similar to saying, as we did in the discussion of the Friedman natural rate theory, that individuals' expected inflation rate is less than the actual inflation rate.)

In the short run, the economy moves from point 1 to point 2, from Q_1 to Q_2. (In Phillips-curve terms, the economy has moved up the short-run Phillips curve to a higher inflation rate and lower unemployment rate.) In the long run, workers correctly anticipate

---

exhibit **6**

Rational Expectations in an AD-AS Framework
The economy is in long-run equilibrium at point 1 in both (a) and (b). In (a), there is an unanticipated increase in aggregate demand. In the short run, the economy moves to point 2. In the long run, it moves to point 3. In (b), the increase in aggregate demand is correctly anticipated. Because the increase is anticipated, the short-run aggregate supply curve shifts from $SRAS_1$ to $SRAS_2$ at the same time the aggregate demand curves shifts from AD_1 to AD_2. The economy moves directly to point 2, which is comparable to point 3 in (a).

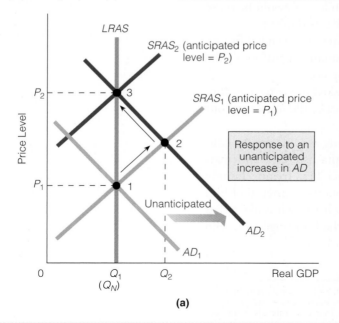

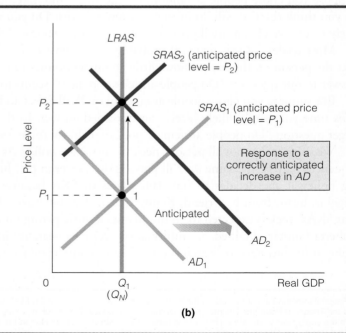

(a)   (b)

Turning the Unanticipated into the Anticipated

If workers have adaptive expectations, they can be fooled into working more than they want to work. (See Friedman's natural rate theory.) Even if they have rational expectations, they will be fooled into working more than they want to work if policy changes are unanticipated. In other words, with either adaptive expectations or rational expectations and unanticipated policy, mistakes can be made.

Is there a way to reduce the number of mistakes? Within the rational expectations framework, people will make fewer mistakes if they can somehow turn unanticipated policies or events into correctly anticipated policies or events.

To illustrate, let's delve into the area of science fiction for a moment. Let's say that during your lifetime, you will correctly anticipate 10 economic policies, you will incorrectly anticipate 9 policies, and you will not anticipate 25 policies (they will take you by surprise).

Now suppose a machine could turn a policy that you do not anticipate into one that you anticipate correctly. It might work like this: You put your hand into the machine. It notices that you do not anticipate policy Z, which the machine knows is looming on the horizon. It then prints the details of this upcoming policy on a computer screen in front of you. When you see the details on the screen, you correctly anticipate a policy that minutes before was unanticipated.

Thus, using the information provided by the machine, you behave accordingly, and you end up anticipating more policies and making fewer mistakes.

Of course, no such machine exists for economic policies. No machine can turn unanticipated policies into correctly anticipated policies and therefore save you from making mistakes. But such a machine may exist in another scientific area.

In the medical field, genetic testing for certain diseases is now possible (to some degree). This technology will no doubt become even more widely developed and widespread in the future. Through genetic testing, people can learn at an early age if they are predisposed to get certain illnesses later in life. For example, women can learn if they are predisposed to get breast cancer. If they are, then many of the women who have this predisposition can take certain drugs to reduce the chances of their getting this disease. Recent clinical trials have revealed that two estrogen-like drugs, tamoxifen and raloxifene, reduce the chances of breast cancer in high-risk women by 50 percent. In other words, genetic testing is a "machine" that can turn the unanticipated into the anticipated. Once anticipated, behavior can change, mistakes that would have been made may not be, and undesirable outcomes that might have arisen may not arise.

---

the higher price level and increase their wage demands accordingly. The short-run aggregate supply curve shifts leftward from $SRAS_1$ to $SRAS_2$ and the economy moves to point 3.

Anticipated Policy

Now consider what happens when policy is anticipated, in particular, when it is *correctly anticipated*. When individuals anticipate that the Fed will buy government securities and that the money supply, aggregate demand, and prices will increase, they will adjust their present actions accordingly. For example, workers will bargain for higher wages so that their real wages will not fall when the price level rises. As a result, the short-run aggregate supply curve will shift leftward from $SRAS_1$ to $SRAS_2$ at the same time that the aggregate demand curve shifts rightward from AD_1 to AD_2. (See Exhibit 6b.) The economy moves directly from point 1 to point 2. Real GDP does not change; throughout the adjustment period, it remains at its natural level. It follows that the unemployment rate does not change either. There is no short-run tradeoff between inflation and unemployment. The short-run Phillips curve and the long-run Phillips curve are the same; the curve is vertical.

Policy Ineffectiveness Proposition (PIP)

Using rational expectations, we showed (see Exhibit 6) *that if the rise in aggregate demand is unanticipated, there is a short-run increase in Real GDP, but if the rise in aggregate demand is correctly anticipated, there is no change in Real GDP.* What are the implications of this result?

Let's consider the two types of macroeconomic policies—fiscal and monetary—that you have studied. Both of these policies can theoretically increase aggregate demand. For example, assuming there is no crowding out or incomplete crowding out, expansionary fiscal policy shifts the *AD* curve rightward. Expansionary monetary policy does the same. In both cases, expansionary policy is effective at increasing Real GDP and lowering the unemployment rate in the short run.

New classical economists question this scenario. They argue that if (1) the expansionary policy change is correctly anticipated, (2) individuals form their expectations rationally, and (3) wages and prices are flexible, then neither expansionary fiscal policy nor expansionary monetary policy will be able to increase Real GDP and lower the unemployment rate in the short run. This argument is called the **policy ineffectiveness proposition (PIP).**

Think what this means. If, under certain conditions, expansionary monetary and fiscal policy are not effective at increasing Real GDP and lowering the unemployment rate, the case for government fine-tuning the economy is questionable.

Keep in mind that new classical economists are not saying that monetary and fiscal policies are never effective. Instead, they are saying that monetary and fiscal policies are not effective under certain conditions—specifically, when (1) policy is correctly anticipated, (2) people form their expectations rationally, and (3) wages and prices are flexible.

Rational Expectations and Incorrectly Anticipated Policy

Suppose that wages and prices are flexible, people form their expectations rationally, and they anticipate policy—but this time they anticipate policy *incorrectly*. What happens?

To illustrate, consider Exhibit 7. The economy is in long-run equilibrium at point 1 where $Q_1 = Q_N$. People believe the Fed will increase aggregate demand by increasing the

Policy Ineffectiveness Proposition (PIP)
If (1) a policy change is correctly anticipated, (2) individuals form their expectations rationally, and (3) wages and prices are flexible, then neither fiscal policy nor monetary policy is effective at meeting macroeconomic goals.

exhibit **7**

The Short-Run Response to an Aggregate Demand-Increasing Policy That Is Less Expansionary Than Anticipated (in the New Classical Theory)
Starting at point 1, people anticipate an increase in aggregate demand from AD_1 to AD_2. Based on this, the short-run aggregate supply curve shifts leftward from $SRAS_1$ to $SRAS_2$. It turns out, however, that the aggregate demand curve only shifts rightward to AD'_2 (less than anticipated). As a result, the economy moves to point 2', to a lower Real GDP and a higher unemployment rate.

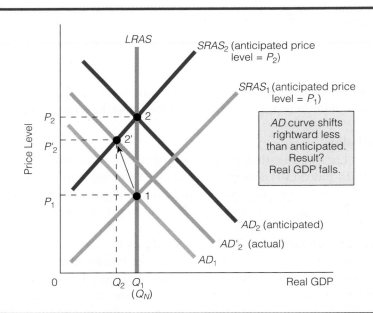

money supply, but they *incorrectly anticipate* the degree to which aggregate demand will be increased. Thinking aggregate demand will increase from AD_1 to AD_2, they immediately revise their anticipated price level to P_2 (the long-run equilibrium position of the AD_2 curve and the *LRAS* curve). As a result, the short-run aggregate supply curve shifts leftward from $SRAS_1$ to $SRAS_2$.

However, the actual increase in aggregate demand is less than anticipated, and the aggregate demand curve only shifts rightward from AD_1 to AD_2'. As a result, the economy moves to point 2', to a lower Real GDP and a higher unemployment rate. We conclude that a policy designed to increase Real GDP and lower unemployment can do just the opposite if the policy is less expansionary than anticipated.

In the example just given, people incorrectly anticipated policy in a particular direction, that is, they mistakenly believed that the aggregate demand curve was going to shift to the right more than it actually did. In other words, they *overestimated the increase in aggregate demand.* If people can overestimate the increase in aggregate demand, then it is likely that they can underestimate the increase in aggregate demand too. In short, when discussing rational expectations, we get different outcomes in the short run depending on whether policy is (1) unanticipated, (2) anticipated correctly, (3) anticipated incorrectly in one direction, or (4) anticipated incorrectly in the other direction.

ANALYZING THE SCENE

Question from Setting the Scene: What do each of the events have to do with economics?
In each of the events, someone is thinking about the future. What will the weather be like tomorrow? What will the fortune teller tell me about my chances of hearing a yes from Stephanie? What will my brother's next move be? How will someone move against Michael?

Also, in each case, the person's "best guess" of what the future holds likely will affect his current behavior. If Steven expects rain tomorrow, he will put out his umbrella today. If the fortune teller tells Robin that Stephanie will not accept his invitation to the dance, he might be less likely to ask her. If one of the two brothers thinks the other brother will move to a certain square, then this will affect how he moves. If Michael believes that Barzini will come against him and that the person who arranges the meeting is working for Barzini, then he'll be more likely to move against both Barzini and the person (it's Tessio) who arranges the meeting.

An important part of rational expectations theory is looking to the future and anticipating what will happen. What one thinks "will happen" largely influences the actions one takes. This is what each of the four events has to do with economics.

The individual who goes from (1) expecting the Fed to raise the money supply, to (2) realizing that a greater money supply means higher prices, and who then (3) bargains for higher wages at work, really isn't thinking much differently than Don Corleone when he tells Michael to prepare for Barzini. In both cases, something "bad" is headed one's way. In both cases, preparing for what's ahead can make all the difference. For the individual faced with higher prices on the horizon, preparing means bargaining for a higher money (or nominal) wage so that her real wage doesn't decline. For Michael, faced with Barzini in his future, preparing means saving his life.

How To Fall Into a Recession Without Really Trying

Suppose the public witnesses the following series of events three times in three years. The federal government runs a budget deficit. It finances the deficit by borrowing from the public (issuing Treasury bills, notes, and bonds). The Fed conducts open market operations and buys many of the government securities. Aggregate demand increases and the price level rises. At the same time all this is going on, Congress says it will do whatever is necessary to bring inflation under control. The chairman of the Fed says the Fed will soon move against inflation. Congress, the President, and the Fed do *not* move against inflation.

According to some economists, if the government says it will do X but continues to do Y instead, then people will see through the charade. They will equate "saying X" with "doing Y." In other words, the equation in their heads will read "Say X = Do Y." They will also always base their behavior on what they expect the government to do, not what it says it will do.[3]

Now, suppose the government changes; it says it will do X and actually does X. People will not know the government is telling the truth this time, and they will continue to think that saying X really means doing Y.

Some new classical economists say this is what happened in the early 1980s and that it goes a long way to explaining the 1981–1982 recession. They tell this story:

1. President Reagan proposed, and Congress approved, tax cuts in 1981.
2. Although some economists insisted that the tax cuts would stimulate so much economic activity that tax revenues would increase, the public believed that the tax cuts would decrease tax revenues and increase the size of the budget deficit (that existed at the time).
3. People translated larger budget deficits into more government borrowing.
4. They anticipated greater money supply growth connected with the larger deficits because they had seen this happen before.
5. Greater money supply growth would mean an increase in aggregate demand and in the price level.
6. The Fed said it would not finance the deficits (buy government bonds), but it had said this before and it had acted contrarily, so few people believed the Fed this time.
7. The Fed actually did not increase the money supply as much as individuals thought it would.
8. This meant the monetary policy was not as expansionary as individuals had anticipated.
9. As a result, the economy moved to a point like 2' in Exhibit 7. Real GDP fell and unemployment increased; a recession ensued.

The moral of the story, according to new classical economists, is that if the Fed says it is going to do X, then it had better do X because if it doesn't, then the next time it says it is going to do X, no one will believe it and the economy may fall into a recession as a consequence. The recession will be an unintended effect of the Fed saying one thing and doing another in the past.

SELF-TEST

1. Does the policy ineffectiveness proposition (PIP) always hold?
2. When policy is unanticipated, what difference is there between the natural rate theory built on adaptive expectations and the natural rate theory built on rational expectations?
3. If expectations are formed rationally, does it matter whether policy is unanticipated, anticipated correctly, or anticipated incorrectly? Explain your answer.

---

3. Rational expectations has sometimes been reduced to the adage, "Fool me once, shame on you; fool me twice, shame on me."

Popular Culture   Technology   Everyday Life   The World

Rational Expectations in the College Classroom

If people hold rational expectations, the outcome of a policy will be different if the policy is unanticipated than if it is anticipated. Specifically, unanticipated policy changes can move the economy away from the natural unemployment rate, but (correctly) anticipated policy changes cannot. Does something similar happen in a college classroom?

Suppose Ana's history class starts at 9:00 A.M. and it is "natural" for her to arrive one minute before class starts. In other words, her "natural waiting time" is one minute.

The first day of class, Ana arrives at 8:59, her instructor arrives at 8:59:30, and she starts class promptly at 9:00 A.M.

The second day of class, Ana arrives at 8:59, her instructor arrives at 9:01:30, and she starts class at 9:02 A.M. On this day, Ana has waited three minutes, which is above her natural waiting time of one minute.

The third, fourth, and fifth days of class are the same as the second. So, for the second through fifth days, Ana is operating at above her natural waiting time.

Rational expectations hold that people will not continue to make the same mistake. In this case, Ana will take her professor's recent arrival time into account and adjust accordingly. On the sixth day of class, instead of arriving at 8:59, Ana arrives at 9:01. This day, the instructor again arrives at 9:01:30 and begins class at 9:02 A.M. Ana has moved back to her natural waiting time of one minute.

Let's summarize our story so far: Ana has a natural waiting time which was met on the first day of class. On the second through fifth days of class, the professor obviously had a "change of policy" as to her arrival time. This change of policy was unanticipated by Ana, so she was fooled into waiting more than her natural waiting time. But Ana did not continue to make the same mistake. She adjusted to her professor's "policy change" and went back to her one-minute natural waiting time.

Now let's change things a bit. Suppose at the end of the first day of class the professor says, "I know I arrived to class at 8:59:30 today, but I won't do this again. From now on, I will arrive at 9:01:30."

In this situation, the professor has announced her policy change. Ana hears the announcement and therefore (correctly) anticipates what the professor will do from now on. With this information, she adjusts her behavior. Instead of arriving to class at 8:59, she arrives at 9:01. Thus, she has correctly anticipated her professor's policy change, and she will remain at her natural waiting time (she will not move from it, even temporarily).

NEW KEYNESIANS AND RATIONAL EXPECTATIONS

The new classical theory assumes complete flexibility of wages and prices. In this theory, an increase in the anticipated price level results in an immediate and equal rise in wages and prices, and the aggregate supply curve immediately shifts to the long-run equilibrium position.

In response to the assumption of flexible wages and prices, a few economists began to develop what has come to be known as the *New Keynesian rational expectations theory.* This theory assumes that rational expectations is a reasonable characterization of how expectations are formed, but drops the new classical assumption of complete wage and price flexibility. Economists who work with this theory argue that long-term labor contracts often prevent wages and prices from fully adjusting to changes in the anticipated price level. (Prices and wages are somewhat sticky, rigid, or inflexible.)

Consider the possible situation at the end of the first year of a three-year wage contract. Workers may realize that the anticipated price level is higher than they expected when they negotiated the contract, but will be unable to do much about it because their

exhibit **8**

The Short-Run Response to Aggregate Demand-Increasing Policy (in the New Keynesian Theory)

Starting at point 1, an increase in aggregate demand is anticipated. As a result, the short-run aggregate supply curve shifts leftward, but not all the way to $SRAS_2$ (as would be the case in the new classical model). Instead it shifts only to $SRAS'_2$ because of some wage and price rigidities; the economy moves to point 2' (in the short run), and Real GDP increases from Q_N to Q_A. If the policy had been unanticipated, Real GDP would have increased from Q_N to Q_{UA}.

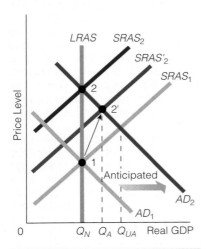

wages are locked in for the next two years. Price rigidity might also arise because firms often engage in fixed-price contracts with their suppliers. As discussed in an earlier chapter, Keynesian economists today put forth microeconomic-based reasons why long-term labor contracts and above-market wages are sometimes in the best interest of both employers and employees (efficiency wage theory).

To see what the theory predicts, look at Exhibit 8. The economy is initially in long-run equilibrium at point 1. The public anticipates an increase in aggregate demand from AD_1 to AD_2. As a result, the anticipated price level changes. Because of some wage and price rigidities, however, the short-run aggregate supply curve does not shift all the way from $SRAS_1$ to $SRAS_2$, and the economy does not move from point 1 to point 2 (as in new classical theory). The short-run aggregate supply curve shifts instead to $SRAS'_2$ because rigidities prevent complete wage and price adjustments. In the short run, the economy moves from point 1 to point 2', from Q_N to Q_A. Note that had the policy been unanticipated, Real GDP would have increased from Q_N to Q_{UA} in the short run.

LOOKING AT THINGS FROM THE SUPPLY SIDE: REAL BUSINESS CYCLE THEORISTS

Throughout this chapter, changes in Real GDP have originated on the demand side of the economy. When discussing the Friedman natural rate theory, the new classical theory, and the New Keynesian theory, we begin our analysis by shifting the AD curve to the right. Then we explain what happens in the economy as a result.

From the discussions in this chapter, it is possible to believe that all changes in Real GDP (and unemployment) originate on the demand side of the economy. In fact, some economists believe this to be true. However, other economists do not. One group of such economists—called *real business cycle theorists*—believe that changes on the supply side of the economy can lead to changes in Real GDP and unemployment.

Real business cycle theorists argue that a decrease in Real GDP (which refers to the recessionary or contractionary part of a business cycle) can be brought about by a major supply-side change that reduces the capacity of the economy to produce. Moreover, they argue that what looks like a contraction in Real GDP originating on the demand side of the economy can be, in essence, the effect of what has happened on the supply side. Exhibit 9 helps explain the process.

We start with an adverse supply shock that reduces the capacity of the economy to produce. This is represented by a shift inward in the economy's production possibilities frontier or a leftward shift in the long-run aggregate supply curve from $LRAS_1$ to $LRAS_2$, which moves the economy from point A to point B. As shown in Exhibit 9, a leftward shift in the long-run aggregate supply curve means that Natural Real GDP has fallen.

As a result of the leftward shift in the $LRAS$ curve and the decline in Real GDP, firms reduce their demand for labor and scale back employment. Due to the lower demand for labor (which puts downward pressure on money wages) and the higher price level, real wages fall.

As real wages fall, workers choose to work less and unemployed persons choose to extend the length of their unemployment. Due to less work and lower real wages, workers have less income. Lower incomes soon lead workers to reduce consumption.

Because consumption has fallen, or businesses have become pessimistic (prompted by the decline in the productive potential of the economy), or both, businesses have less reason to invest. As a result, firms borrow less from banks, the volume of outstanding loans

The Boy Who Cried Wolf (And the Townspeople With Rational Expectations)

You may know the fable about the boy and the wolf: There was a young boy who liked to play tricks on people. One day, the boy's father (a shepherd) had to go out of town. He asked his son to take care of the sheep while he was gone. While the boy was watching the sheep, he suddenly began yelling, "Wolf, wolf, wolf." The townspeople came running because they thought the boy needed help protecting the sheep from the wolf. When they arrived, they found the boy laughing at the trick he had played on them. The same thing happened two or three more times. Finally, one day, a real wolf appeared. The boy called, "Wolf, wolf, wolf," but no one came. The townspeople were not going to be fooled again. And so the wolf ate the sheep.

The fable about the boy and the wolf has something in common with a concept we discuss in this chapter—the unintended consequences of saying one thing and doing another.

In the new classical economic story of the 1981–1982 recession, the public incorrectly anticipated Fed policy and, as a result,

the economy fell into a recession. But the reason the public incorrectly anticipated Fed policy was because, in the past, the Fed had said one thing and done another. It had said X but done Y.

It's the same with the boy and the wolf. The first few times the boy cried wolf, the townspeople found that there was no wolf and the boy was simply playing a trick on them. In their minds, "Crying Wolf" came to equal "No Wolf." So, when the boy cried wolf the last time and actually meant it, no one from the town came to help him. And the wolf ate the sheep.

Just as the Fed might have learned that saying one thing and doing another can result in a recession, the boy learned that saying one thing and meaning another can result in sheep being killed. The moral of our story is that if you tell a lie again and again, people will no longer believe you when you tell the truth.

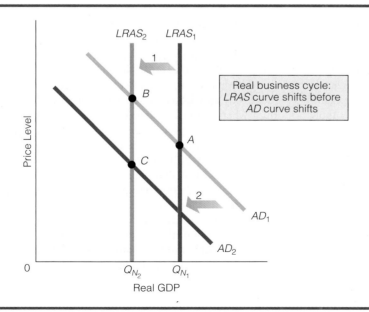

Real business cycle:
LRAS curve shifts before
AD curve shifts

exhibit 9

Real Business Cycle Theory
We start with a supply-side change capable of reducing the capacity of the economy to produce. This is manifested by a leftward shift of the long-run aggregate supply curve from $LRAS_1$ to $LRAS_2$ and a fall in the Natural Real GDP level from Q_{N1} to Q_{N2}. A reduction in the productive capacity of the economy filters to the demand side of the economy and, in our example, reduces consumption, investment, and the money supply. The aggregate demand curve shifts leftward from AD_1 to AD_2.

falls, and therefore the money supply falls. A decrease in the money supply causes the aggregate demand curve to shift leftward, from AD_1 to AD_2 in Exhibit 9, and the economy moves to point C.

Real business cycle theorists sometimes point out how easy it is to confuse a demand-induced decline in Real GDP with a supply-induced decline in Real GDP. In our example, both the aggregate supply side and the aggregate demand side of the economy change, but the aggregate supply side changes first. If the change in aggregate supply is overlooked, and only the changes in aggregate demand are observed (or, specifically, a change in one of the variables that can change aggregate demand, such as the money supply), then the contraction in Real GDP will appear to be demand-induced. In terms of Exhibit 9, the leftward shift in the $LRAS$ curve would be overlooked, but the leftward shift in the AD curve would be observed, giving the impression that the contraction is demand-induced.

If real business cycle theorists are correct, the cause-effect analysis of a contraction in Real GDP would be turned upside down. To take but one example, changes in the money supply may be an effect of a contraction in Real GDP (which originates on the supply side of the economy) and not its cause.

SELF-TEST

1. The *Wall Street Journal* reports that the money supply has recently declined. Is this consistent with a demand-induced or supply-induced business cycle, or both? Explain your answer.
2. How are New Keynesians who believe people hold rational expectations different from new classical economists who believe people hold rational expectations?

A READER ASKS *Do Expectations Matter?*

What insights, if any, does the introduction of expectations into macroeconomics provide?

Think about your study of macroeconomics in earlier chapters. You learned that changes in such things as taxes, government purchases, interest rates, the money supply, and more could change Real GDP, the price level, and the unemployment rate. For example, starting at long-run equilibrium, a rise in the money supply will raise Real GDP and lower the unemployment rate in the short run and raise the price level in the long run. Or, consider that an increase in productivity can shift the $SRAS$ curve to the right and thus bring about a change in Real GDP and the price level. In short, most of this text discusses how changes in real variables can affect the economy.

With the introduction of expectations theory, we move to a different level of analysis. Now we learn that what people think can also affect the economy. In other words, not only can a change in the world's oil supply affect the economy—almost everyone would

expect that—but so can whether or not someone believes that the Fed will increase the money supply.

Think back to our discussion of rational expectations and incorrectly anticipated policy. The economy is in long-run equilibrium when the Fed undertakes an expansionary monetary policy move. The Fed expects to increase the money supply by, say, $100 billion, but somehow economic agents believe the increase in the money supply will be closer to $200 billion. In other words, economic agents think that the money supply will rise by more than it will rise. Does it matter that their thoughts are wrong? Expectations theory says that it does. As shown in Exhibit 7, wrong thoughts can lead to lower Real GDP and higher prices.

In conclusion, the insight that expectations theory provides is that what people think can affect Real GDP, unemployment, and prices. Who would have thought it?

Chapter Summary

The Phillips Curve

> A. W. Phillips plotted a curve to a set of data points that exhibited an inverse relationship between wage inflation and unemployment. This curve came to be known as the Phillips curve. From the Phillips curve relationship, economists concluded that neither the combination of low inflation and low unemployment nor the combination of high inflation and high unemployment was likely.

> Economists Samuelson and Solow fit a Phillips curve to the U.S. economy. Instead of measuring wage inflation against unemployment rates (as Phillips did), they measured price inflation against unemployment rates. They found an inverse relationship between inflation and unemployment rates.

> Based on the findings of Phillips and Samuelson and Solow, economists concluded the following: (1) Stagflation, or high inflation and high unemployment, is extremely unlikely. (2) The Phillips curve presents policymakers with a menu of choices between different combinations of inflation and unemployment rates.

Friedman Natural Rate Theory

> Milton Friedman pointed out that there are two types of Phillips curves: a short-run Phillips curve and a long-run Phillips curve. The short-run Phillips curve exhibits the inflation-unemployment tradeoff; the long-run Phillips curve does not. Consideration of both short-run and long-run Phillips curves opened macroeconomics to expectations theory.

> The Friedman natural rate theory holds that in the short run, a decrease (increase) in inflation is linked to an increase (decrease) in unemployment, but that in the long run, the economy returns to its natural rate of unemployment. In other words, there is a tradeoff between inflation and unemployment in the short run, but not in the long run.

> The Friedman natural rate theory was expressed in terms of adaptive expectations. Individuals formed their inflation expectations by considering past inflation rates. Later, some economists expressed the theory in terms of rational expectations. Rational expectations theory holds that individuals form their expected inflation rate by considering present and past inflation rates, as well as all other available and relevant information—in particular, the effects of present and future policy actions.

New Classical Theory

> Implicit in the new classical theory are two assumptions: (1) Individuals form their expectations rationally. (2) Wages and prices are completely flexible.

> In the new classical theory, policy has different effects (1) when it is unanticipated and (2) when it is anticipated. For example, if the public correctly anticipates an increase in aggregate demand, the short-run aggregate supply curve will likely shift leftward at the same time the aggregate demand curve shifts

rightward. If the public does not anticipate an increase in aggregate demand (but one occurs), then the short-run aggregate supply curve will not shift leftward at the same time the aggregate demand curve shifts rightward; it will shift leftward sometime later. If policy is correctly anticipated, expectations are formed rationally, and wages and prices are completely flexible, then an increase or decrease in aggregate demand will change only the price level, not Real GDP or the unemployment rate. The new classical theory casts doubt on the belief that the short-run Phillips curve is always downward-sloping. Under certain conditions, it may be vertical (as is the long-run Phillips curve).

> If policies are anticipated, but not credible, and rational expectations is a reasonable characterization of how individuals form their expectations, then certain policies may have unintended effects. For example, if the public believes that aggregate demand will increase by more than it (actually) increases (because policymakers have not done in the past what they said they would do), then anticipated inflation will be higher than it would have been, the short-run aggregate supply curve will shift leftward by more than it would have, and the (short-run) outcomes of a policy that increases aggregate demand will be lower Real GDP and higher unemployment.

New Keynesian Theory

> Implicit in the New Keynesian theory are two assumptions: (1) Individuals form their expectations rationally. (2) Wages and prices are not completely flexible (in the short run).

> If policy is anticipated, the economic effects predicted by the new classical theory and the New Keynesian theory are not the same (in the short run). Because the New Keynesian theory assumes that wages and prices are not completely flexible in the short run, given an anticipated change in aggregate demand, the short-run aggregate supply curve cannot immediately shift to its long-run equilibrium position. The New Keynesian theory predicts that there is a short-run tradeoff between inflation and unemployment (in the Phillips curve framework).

Real Business Cycle Theory

> Real business cycle contractions (in Real GDP) originate on the supply side of the economy. A contraction in Real GDP might follow this pattern: (1) An adverse supply shock reduces the economy's ability to produce. (2) The *LRAS* curve shifts leftward. (3) As a result, Real GDP declines and the price level rises. (4) The number of persons employed falls, as do real wages, owing to a decrease in the demand for labor (which lowers money wages) and a higher price level. (5) Incomes decline. (6) Consumption and investment decline. (7) The volume of outstanding loans declines. (8) The money supply falls. (9) The *AD* curve shifts leftward.

Key Terms and Concepts

Phillips Curve   Friedman Natural Rate Theory   Rational Expectations
Stagflation   Adaptive Expectations   Policy Ineffectiveness Proposition (PIP)

Questions and Problems

1. What is a major difference between adaptive and rational expectations? Give an example.
2. It has been said that the policy ineffectiveness proposition (connected with new classical theory) does not eliminate policymakers' ability to reduce unemployment through aggregate demand-increasing policies because they can always increase aggregate demand by more than the public expects. What might be the weak point in this argument?
3. Why does the new classical theory have the word classical associated with it? Also, why has it been said that the classical theory failed where the new classical theory succeeds, as the former could not explain the business cycle ("the ups and downs of the economy"), but the latter can?
4. Suppose a permanent downward-sloping Phillips curve existed and offered a menu of choices of different combinations of inflation and unemployment rates to policymakers. How do you think society would go about deciding which point on the Phillips curve it wanted to occupy?
5. Suppose a short-run tradeoff between inflation and unemployment currently exists. How would you expect this tradeoff to be affected by a change in technology that permits the wider dispersion of economic policy news? Explain your answer.
6. New Keynesian theory holds that wages are not completely flexible because of such things as long-term labor contracts.

New classical economists often respond that experience teaches labor leaders to develop and bargain for contracts that allow for wage adjustments. Do you think the new classical economists have a good point? Why or why not?

7. What evidence can you point to that suggests individuals form their expectations adaptively? What evidence can you point to that suggests individuals form their expectations rationally?
8. Explain both the short-run and long-run movements of the Friedman natural rate theory, assuming expectations are formed adaptively.
9. Explain both the short-run and long-run movements of the new classical theory, assuming expectations are formed rationally and policy is unanticipated.
10. "Even if some people do not form their expectations rationally, this does not necessarily mean that the new classical theory is of no value." Discuss.
11. In the real business cycle theory, why can't the change in the money supply prompted by a series of events catalyzed by an adverse supply shock be considered the "cause" of the business cycle?
12. The expected inflation rate is 5 percent and the actual inflation rate is 7 percent. According to Friedman, is the economy in long-run equilibrium? Explain your answer.

Working With Numbers and Graphs

1. Illustrate graphically what would happen in the short run and in the long run if individuals hold rational expectations, prices and wages are flexible, and individuals underestimate the decrease in aggregate demand.
2. In each of the following figures, the starting point is point 1. Which part illustrates each of the following?
   a. Friedman natural rate theory (short run)
   b. New classical theory (unanticipated policy, short run)
   c. Real business cycle theory
   d. New classical theory (incorrectly anticipated policy, overestimating increase in aggregate demand, short run)
   e. Policy ineffectiveness proposition (PIP)
3. Illustrate graphically what would happen in the short run and in the long run if individuals hold adaptive expectations, prices and wages are flexible, and there is decrease in aggregate demand.

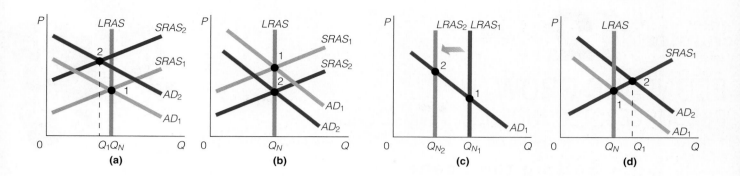

chapter 12

ECONOMIC GROWTH
RESOURCES, TECHNOLOGY, AND IDEAS

© Taxi/Getty Images

Setting the Scene

The following facts are related to your life.

Fact 1

If you had lived during the 1200s in Western Europe, your standard of living would not have been much different than it would have been had you lived in the year 1000. In other words, in 200 years, people's lives had not changed much. Of course, if you had lived during the 1400s in Western Europe, your standard of living would not have been much different than it would have been had you lived in the year 1000. Fact is, had you lived during the 1700s in Western Europe, your standard of living would not have been much different than it would have been had you lived in the year 1000. Most people living at these times did not live long enough to notice any economic growth. The world they were born into and died in was much the same, decade after decade. Their parents, grandparents, and great grandparents lived much the same lives.

Fact 2

In 2004, the per capita Real GDP in North Korea grew 1 percent. Per capita real income in North Korea that year was $1,400. In contrast, the per capita real income in the United States was $40,100. So, the average American was 28.6 times richer (in terms of material goods) than the average North Korean was.

If North Korea maintains its 1 percent growth rate in the future, per capita Real GDP will rise to $2,800 in the year 2078, which is slightly lower than the living standard of the average Cuban in 2004. But if North Korea can increase its growth rate to, say, 3 percent, then per capita Real GDP will rise to $2,800 in 2041, 37 years earlier.

Fact 3

In 2004, the per capita Real GDP in the United States was $40,100, and the economic growth rate was 4.4

percent. If the United States maintains its 4.4 percent growth rate in the future, then in 16 years, the per capita Real GDP will be *twice as large* as it was in 2004. But if the economic growth rate in the United States falls to, say, 3.0 percent, it will take 24 years for per capita Real GDP to double. In other words, 8 years longer.

Fact 4

About 24,000 people die every day from hunger or hunger-related causes. This is down from 35,000 ten years ago, and 41,000 twenty years ago. Three-fourths of the deaths are children under the age of five. The vast majority of people who die of hunger live in countries of the world that have experienced relatively little economic growth.

? **How would an economist look at these facts? Later in the chapter, a discussion based on the following questions will help you analyze the scene the way an economist would.**

- How is your life today different from the lives of your great grandparents?
- Does it matter to the average North Korean what the economic growth rate is in North Korea?
- Does it matter to the average American what the economic growth rate is in the United States?
- Might economic growth matter to hungry people?

A FEW BASICS ABOUT ECONOMIC GROWTH

The term *economic growth* refers either to absolute real economic growth or to per capita real economic growth. **Absolute real economic growth** is an increase in Real GDP from one period to the next. Exhibit 1 shows absolute real economic growth (or the percentage change in Real GDP) for the United States for the period 1990–2004.

Per capita real economic growth is an increase from one period to the next in per capita Real GDP, which is Real GDP divided by population.

Per capita Real GDP = Real GDP/Population

Absolute Real Economic Growth
An increase in Real GDP from one period to the next.

Per Capita Real Economic Growth
An increase from one period to the next in per capita Real GDP, which is Real GDP divided by population.

Do Economic Growth Rates Matter?

Suppose the (absolute) real economic growth rate is 4 percent in one country and 3 percent in another country. The difference in these growth rates may not seem very significant. But if these growth rates are sustained over a long period of time, the people who live in each country will see a real difference in their standard of living.

If a country's economic growth rate is 4 percent each year, its Real GDP will double in 18 years. If a country has a 3 percent annual growth rate, its Real GDP will double in 24 years. In other words, a country with a 4 percent growth rate can double its Real GDP in 6 fewer years than a country with a 3 percent growth rate. (As an aside, to calculate the time required for any variable to double, simply divide its percentage growth rate into 72. This is called the *Rule of 72.*)

Let's look at economic growth rates in another way. Suppose two countries have the same population. Real GDP is $300 billion in country *A* and $100 billion in country *B*. Relatively speaking, country *A* is three times richer than country *B*. Now suppose the annual economic growth rate is 3 percent in country *A* and 6 percent in country *B*. In just 15 years, country *B* will be the richer country.

Growth Rates in Selected Countries

Suppose in a given year, country *A* has an economic growth rate (rate of growth in Real GDP) of 7 percent and country *B* has an economic growth rate of 1 percent. Does it follow that the material standard of living in country *A* is higher than the material standard of living in country *B?* Not at all. A snapshot (in time) of the growth rate in two countries doesn't tell us anything about growth rates in previous years, nor does it speak to per capita Real GDP. For example, did country *A* have the same 7 percent growth rate last year and the year before? Does country *A* have a higher per capita Real GDP?

exhibit 1

Absolute Real Economic Growth Rates for the United States, 1990–2004
The exhibit shows the absolute real economic growth rates (or percentage change in Real GDP) in the United States for the period 1990–2004.
Source: Economic Report of the President, 2005.

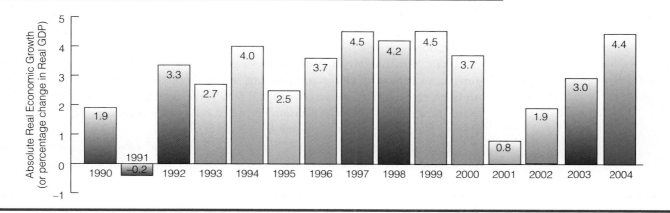

Now suppose the per capita Real GDP in country *C* is $30,000 and the per capita Real GDP in country *D* is $2,000. Does it follow that the material standard of living in country *C* is higher than the material standard of living in country *D?* Probably so, but not necessarily. We say not necessarily because we do not know the *income distribution* in either country. All a per capita Real GDP figure tells us is that *if* we were to divide a country's entire Real GDP equally among all the people in the country, each person would have a certain dollar amount of Real GDP at his or her disposal. In reality, 2 percent of the population may have, say, 70 percent of the country's Real GDP as income, while the remaining 98 percent of the population shares only 30 percent of Real GDP as income.

With these qualifications specified, here are the economic growth rates and per capita Real GDP for selected countries in 2004.[1]

Country	Percentage Growth Rate in Real GDP	Per Capita Real GDP
Argentina	8.3	$12,400
Australia	3.5	30,700
Bangladesh	4.9	2,000
Belgium	2.6	30,600
Canada	2.4	31,500
Cuba	3.0	3,000
Egypt	4.5	4,200
Germany	1.7	28,700
Iran	6.3	7,700
Israel	3.9	20,800
Turkey	8.2	7,400
United States	4.4	40,100

Two Types of Economic Growth

Economic growth can be shown in two of the frameworks of analysis used so far in this book: the production possibilities frontier (PPF) framework and the *AD-AS* framework. Within these two frameworks, we consider two types of economic growth: (1) economic growth that occurs from an inefficient level of production and (2) economic growth that occurs from an efficient level of production.

Economic Growth From an Inefficient Level of Production

A production possibilities frontier is shown in Exhibit 2a. Suppose the economy is currently operating at point *A,* below the PPF. Obviously, the economy is not operating at its Natural Real GDP level. If it were, the economy would be located on the PPF instead of below it. Instead, the economy is at an inefficient point or at an inefficient level of production.

Point *A* in Exhibit 2a corresponds to point *A'* in Exhibit 2b. At point *A'*, the economy is in a recessionary gap, operating below Natural Real GDP. Now suppose that through expansionary monetary or fiscal policy, the aggregate demand curve shifts rightward from AD_1 to AD_2. The economy is pulled out of its recessionary gap and is now producing Natural Real GDP at point *B'* in Exhibit 2b.

What does the situation look like now in Exhibit 2a? Obviously, if the economy is producing at its Natural Real GDP level, it is operating at full employment or at the

---

1. The source of these data is the *CIA World Factbook,* 2005.

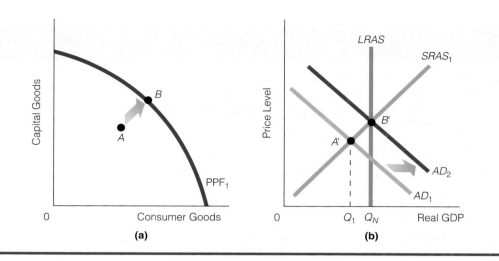

exhibit 2

Economic Growth From an Inefficient Level of Production
The economy is at Point *A* in (a) and at point *A'* in (b). Currently, the economy is at an inefficient point, or below Natural Real GDP. Economic growth is evidenced as a movement from point *A* to *B* in (a), and as a movement from *A'* to *B'* in (b).

natural unemployment rate. This means the economy has moved from point *A* (below the PPF) to point *B* (on the PPF). The economy has moved from operating at an inefficient level of production to operating at an efficient level.

Economic Growth From an Efficient Level of Production

How can the economy grow if it is on the PPF in Exhibit 2a—exhibiting efficiency—or producing at the Natural Real GDP level in Exhibit 2b? The answer is that the PPF must shift to the right (or outward) in (a), or the *LRAS* curve must shift to the right in (b). In other words, if the economy is at point *B* in Exhibit 3a, it can grow if the PPF shifts rightward from PPF_1 to PPF_2. Similarly, if the economy is at point *B'* in Exhibit 3b, the only way Real GDP can be raised beyond Q_{N1} on a permanent basis is if the *LRAS* curve shifts to the right from $LRAS_1$ to $LRAS_2$.

Although we have described economic growth from both an inefficient and efficient level of production, usually when economists speak of economic growth they are speaking about it from an efficient level of production. In other words, they are talking about a shift rightward in the PPF or in the *LRAS* curve.

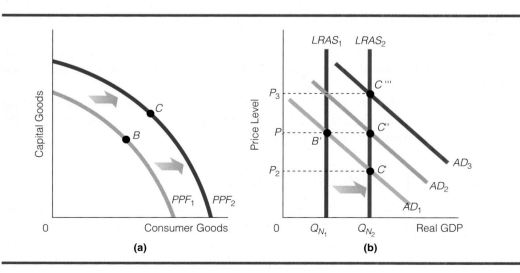

exhibit 3

Economic Growth From an Efficient Level of Production
The economy is at point *B* in (a) and at point *B'* in (b). Economic growth can only occur in (a) if the PPF shifts rightward from PPF_1 to PPF_2. It can only occur in (b) if the *LRAS* curve shifts from $LRAS_1$ to $LRAS_2$.

Questions from Setting the Scene: How is your life today different from the lives of your great grandparents? Does it matter to the average North Korean what the economic growth rate is in North Korea? Does it matter to the average American what the economic growth rate is in the United States? Might economic growth matter to hungry people?

If you have always lived in a country that has experienced many years of economic growth, you might not realize how economic growth affects your life. Some have said that economic growth is one of those things you don't notice until you are without it. In other words, you don't recognize the benefits of economic growth until the benefits are no longer there. In this regard, economic growth is like many of the things that make us better off but that we take for granted.

For example, how many of us think of the importance of antibiotics to our lives? Before Alexander Fleming discovered penicillin in 1928, there were no antibiotics. In a world without antibiotics, individuals regularly died from simple bacterial infections. David Ricardo, the famous nineteenth century economist, died of an ear infection at the age of 51—an ear infection that could have been cured easily with a few doses of antibiotics.

Those of us alive today often take economic growth for granted, perhaps because we were born at a time and in a country that has experienced quite a bit of economic growth. Think back to the year 1865, the last year of the American Civil War. Suppose there had been no economic growth in the United States in any year since 1865. What would your life be like today? How different would your life be?

In addition, economic growth often occurs slowly over time, and perhaps that's why we don't take much notice of it. But like antibiotics, it would be sorely missed if it weren't here. In short, economic growth makes a huge difference to the way we live.

Economic Growth and the Price Level

Economic growth can occur with a falling price level, rising price level, or stable price level. To see this, look again at Exhibit 3b. The $LRAS$ curve shifts from $LRAS_1$ to $LRAS_2$. Three possible aggregate demand curves may be consistent with this new $LRAS$ curve: AD_1, AD_2, or AD_3.

If AD_1 is the relevant AD curve, economic growth occurs with a declining price level. Before the $LRAS$ curve shifted to the right, the price level was P_1; after the shift, it was lower, at P_2.

If AD_2 is the relevant AD curve, economic growth occurs with a stable price level. Before the $LRAS$ curve shifted to the right, the price level was P_1; after the shift, it was the same, at P_1.

If AD_3 is the relevant AD curve, economic growth occurs with a rising price level. Before the $LRAS$ curve shifted to the right, the price level was P_1; after the shift, it was higher, at P_3.

In recent decades, the U.S. economy has witnessed economic growth with a rising price level. This means the AD curve has been shifting to the right at a faster rate than the $LRAS$ curve has been shifting to the right.

WHAT CAUSES ECONOMIC GROWTH?

This section looks at some of the determinants of economic growth, that is, the factors that can shift the PPF or the $LRAS$ curve to the right. These factors include natural resources, labor, capital, technological advances, the property rights structure, and economic freedom. We then discuss some of the policies that promote economic growth.

Natural Resources

People often think that countries that have a plentiful supply of natural resources experience economic growth, whereas countries that are short of natural resources do not. In fact, some countries with an abundant supply of natural resources have experienced rapid growth in the past (such as the United States), and some have experienced no growth or only slow growth. Also, some countries that are short of natural resources, such as Singapore, have grown very fast. It appears that natural resources are neither a sufficient nor a necessary factor for growth: Countries rich in natural resources are not guaranteed economic growth, and countries poor in natural resources may grow. Having said all this, it is still more likely for a nation rich in natural resources to experience growth, *ceteris paribus*. For example, if a place such as Hong Kong, which has few natural resources, had been blessed with much fertile soil, instead of only a little, and many raw materials, instead of almost none, it might have experienced more economic growth than it has.

Labor

With more labor, it is possible to produce more output (more Real GDP), but whether the average productivity of labor rises, falls, or stays constant (as additional workers are added to the production process) depends on how productive the additional workers are relative to existing workers. If the additional workers are less productive than existing workers, labor productivity will decline. If they are more productive, labor productivity will rise. And if they are equally as productive, labor productivity will stay the same. (Note: average labor productivity is total output divided by total labor hours. For example, if $6 trillion of output is produced in 200 billion labor hours, then average labor productivity is $30 per hour.)

Both an increase in the labor force and an increase in labor productivity lead to increases in Real GDP, but only an increase in labor productivity tends to lead to an increase in per capita Real GDP.

How then do we achieve an increase in labor productivity? One way is through increased education, training, and experience. These are increases in what economists call *human capital*. Another way is through (physical) capital investment. Combining workers with more capital goods tends to increase the productivity of the workers. For example, a farmer with a tractor is more productive than a farmer without one.

Capital

As just mentioned, capital investment can lead to increases in labor productivity and, therefore, not only to increases in Real GDP but also to increases in per capita Real GDP. But more capital goods do not fall from the sky. Recall that getting more of one thing often means forfeiting something else. To produce more capital goods, which are not directly consumable, present consumption must be reduced. Robinson Crusoe, alone on an island and fishing with a spear, must give up some of his present fish to weave a net (a physical capital good) with which he hopes to catch more fish.

If Crusoe gives up some of his present consumption—if he chooses not to consume now—he is, in fact, saving. There is a link between nonconsumption, or saving, and capital formation. As the saving rate increases, capital formation increases and so does economic growth.

Exhibit 4 shows that for the period 1970–1990, those countries with higher investment rates largely tended to have higher per capita Real GDP growth rates. For example, investment was a higher percentage of GDP in Austria, Norway, and Japan than it was in the United States. And these countries experienced a higher per capita Real GDP growth rate than the United States did.

exhibit 4

Investment and Per Capita Real Economic Growth for Selected Countries, 1970–1990

Generally, but not always, those countries in which investment is a larger percentage of GDP have higher per capita Real GDP growth rates.
Source: Council of Economic Advisors, *Economic Report of the President,* 1997 (Washington, D.C.: U.S. Government Printing Office, 1997)

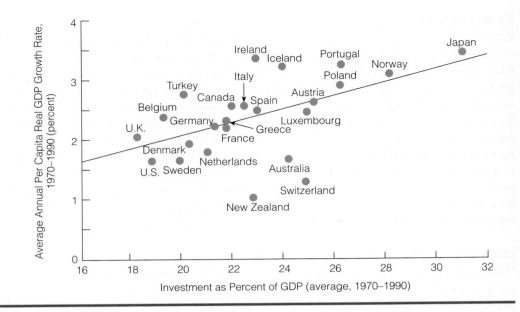

Technological Advances

Technological advances make it possible to obtain more output from the same amount of resources. Compare the amount of work that can be done by a business that uses computers with the amount accomplished by a business that does not use computers.

Technological advances may be the result of new capital goods or of new ways of producing goods. The use of computers is an example of a technological advance that is the result of a new capital good. New and improved management techniques are an example of a new way of producing goods.

Technological advances usually come as the result of companies, and a country, investing in research and development (R&D). Research and development is a general term that encompasses such things as scientists working in a lab to develop a new product and managers figuring out, through experience, how to motivate workers to work to their potential.

Free Trade as Technology

Suppose someone in the United States has invented a machine that can turn wheat into cars.[2] The only problem with the machine is that it works only in Japan. So, people in the United States grow wheat and ship it to Japan. There, the machine turns the wheat into cars. The cars are then loaded on ships and brought to the United States.

Many economists say there is really no difference between a machine that can turn wheat into cars and free trade between countries. When there is free trade, people in the United States grow wheat and ship it to Japan. After awhile the ships come back loaded with cars. This is exactly what happens with our mythical machine. There is really no discernible difference between a machine turning wheat into cars and trading wheat for cars. In both cases, wheat is given up to get cars.

If the machine is a technological advancement, then so is free trade, as many economists point out. In that technological advancements can promote economic growth, so can free trade.

---

2. The essence of this example comes from David Friedman, *Hidden Order* (New York: Harper Collins, 1996), 70.

How Economizing on Time Can Promote Economic Growth

If a society obtains more resources, its PPF will shift to the right, and economic growth is therefore possible. One way to obtain "more resources" is through a technological change or innovation that makes it possible to use fewer resources to produce a particular good. To illustrate, suppose there are 100 units of a given resource. Currently, 10 units of the resource are needed to produce 20 units of good X and 90 units of the resource are used to produce 900 units of other goods.

Now suppose a technological change or innovation makes it possible to produce 20 units of good X with only 5 units of the resource. This means 95 units of the resource can be used to produce other goods. With more resources going to produce other goods, more "other goods" can be produced. Perhaps with 95 units of the resource going to produce other goods, 950 units of other goods can be produced. In short, a technological advance or innovation that saves resources in the production of one good makes growth possible.

With this in mind, consider the resource *time*. Usually, when people think of resources, they think of labor, capital, and natural resources. But *time* is a resource because it takes time (in much the same way that it takes labor or capital) to produce goods. Any technological advance that economizes on time frees up some time that can be used to produce other goods.

To illustrate, consider a simple, everyday example. With today's computers, people can make calculations, write books, key reports, design buildings, and much more in less time than was necessary in the past. Thus, there is more time available to do other things. Having more time to produce other things promotes economic growth.

Let's consider something that is discussed in an earlier chapter—money. Does money economize on time? Before there was money, people made barter trades. In a barter economy, finding people to trade with takes time. Money economizes on this time. Because everyone accepts money, it is easier for people to acquire the goods and services they want. Money makes trading easier. It also makes trading quicker. In other words, it saves time. Money is a "technology" that saves time and promotes economic growth.

Property Rights Structure

Some economists have argued that per capita real economic growth first appeared in areas that had developed a system of institutions and property rights that encouraged individuals to direct their energies to effective economic projects. Here property rights refers to the range of laws, rules, and regulations that define rights for the use and transfer of resources.

Consider two property rights structures. In one structure, people are allowed to keep the full monetary rewards of their labor. In the other, people are allowed to keep only half. Many economists would predict that the first property rights structure would stimulate more economic activity than the second, *ceteris paribus*. Individuals will invest more, take more risks, and work harder when the property rights structure allows them to keep more of the monetary rewards of their investing, risk taking, and labor.

Economic Freedom

Some economists believe that economic freedom leads to economic growth. Countries in which people enjoy a large degree of economic freedom develop and grow more quickly than countries in which people have little economic freedom. The Heritage Foundation and the *Wall Street Journal* have joined together to produce an "index of economic freedom."

This index is based on 50 independent variables divided into 10 broad categories of economic freedom, such as trade policy, monetary policy, property rights structure, regulation, fiscal burden of government, and so on. For example, a country with few tariffs and quotas (trade policy) is considered to have more economic freedom than a country with many tariffs and quotas.

The index is a number between 1 and 5. A country with a great deal of economic freedom has a low index, and a country with little economic freedom has a high index. Thus, free countries have an index between 1.00 and 1.95; mostly free countries, between 2.00 and 2.95; mostly unfree countries, between 3.00 and 3.95; and repressed countries, between 4.00 and 5.00.

The data show that economic freedom and Real GDP per capita are correlated. For the most part, the more economic freedom the people of a country experience, the higher the Real GDP per capita. Some economists believe there is a "cause and effect" relationship: greater economic freedom causes greater economic wealth.

When looking at the causes of economic growth, economists think in terms of both tangibles and intangibles. The tangibles include natural resources, labor, capital, and technological advances. The intangibles include the property rights structure, which directly affects individuals' incentives to apply the tangibles to the production of goods and services. No amount of natural resources, labor, capital, and technological advances can do it alone. People must be motivated to put them all together. In addition, the degree of motivation affects the result. In a world where it is easy to think that only those things that occupy physical space matter, the economist is there to remind us that we often need to look further.

Policies to Promote Economic Growth

Recall from earlier in this chapter that economic growth can occur from either (1) an inefficient level of production or (2) an efficient level of production. When the economy is situated below its PPF, demand-inducing expansionary monetary or fiscal policy is often advocated. Its objective is to increase aggregate demand enough to raise Real GDP (and lower the unemployment rate). We refer to such policies as *demand-side policies.*

There are *supply-side policies* too. These policies are designed to shift the PPF and the *LRAS* curve to the right. The best way to understand the intent of these policies is to first recall the factors that cause economic growth. These factors include natural resources, labor, increases in human capital, increases in (physical) capital investment, technological advances, property rights structure, and economic freedom. Any policies that promote these factors tend to promote economic growth. Two supply-side policies that do this are lowering taxes and reducing regulation.

Tax Policy

Some economists propose cutting taxes on such activities as working and saving in order to increase the productive capacity of the economy. For example, some economists say that if the marginal income tax rate is cut, workers will work more. As they work more, output will increase.

Other economists argue that if the tax is lowered on income placed in saving accounts, the return from saving will increase and thus the amount of saving will rise. In turn, this will make more funds available for investment, which will lead to greater capital goods growth and higher labor productivity. Ultimately, per capita Real GDP will increase.

Regulatory Policy

Some economists say that some government regulations increase the cost of production for business and, consequently, reduce output. These economists are mainly referring to the costs of regulation, which may take the form of spending hours on required paperwork, adding safety features to a factory, or buying expensive equipment to reduce pollution emissions. On net, the benefits of these policies may be greater than, less than, or equal to the costs, but certainly, sometimes the costs are evidenced in the form of less output.

Economists who believe the benefits do not warrant the costs often argue for some form of deregulation. In addition, some economists are trying to make the costs of regulation more visible to policymakers so that regulatory policy will take into account all the benefits and all the costs.

What About Industrial Policy?

Industrial policy is a deliberate government policy of "watering the green spots," or aiding those industries that are most likely to be successful in the world marketplace.

The proponents of industrial policy argue that government needs to work with business firms in the private sector to help them compete in the world marketplace. In particular, they argue that government needs to identify the industries of the future—microelectronics, biotechnology, telecommunications, robotics, and computers and software—and help these industries to grow and develop now. The United States will be disadvantaged in a relative sense, they argue, if governments of other countries aid some of their industries and the United States does not.

Critics maintain that however good the intentions, industrial policy does not always turn out the way its proponents would like for three reasons. First, in deciding which industries to help, government may favor the industries with the most political influence, not the industries that it makes economic sense to help. Critics argue that elected government officials are not beyond rewarding people who have helped them win elections. Thus, industrial policy may turn out to be a way to reward friends and injure enemies rather than good economic policy.

Second, critics argue that the government officials who design and implement industrial policy aren't really smart enough to know which industries will be the industries of the future. Thus, they shouldn't try to impose their uninformed guesses about the future on the economy.

Finally, critics argue that government officials who design and implement industrial policy are likely to hamper economic growth if they provide protection to some industries. For example, suppose the United States institutes an industrial policy. U.S. government officials decide that the U.S. computer industry needs to be protected from foreign competition. In their effort to aid the computer industry, they impose tariffs and quotas on foreign competitors. This action might prompt foreign nations to retaliate by placing tariffs and quotas on U.S. computers. In the end, we might simply have less free trade in the world. This would hurt consumers because they would have to pay higher prices. It would hurt the people who work for export companies because many of them would lose their jobs. And, the reduction in trade would prevent the U.S. computer industry from selling in the world marketplace. The end result would be the opposite of what the policy wants to accomplish.

Economic Growth and Special Interest Groups

While certain economic policies can promote economic growth, will these policies necessarily be chosen? Or will non-growth-promoting policies be more likely to be chosen?

To illustrate, consider two types of economic policies: growth-promoting policies and transfer-promoting policies. A growth-promoting policy increases Real GDP—it enlarges the size of the eco nomic pie. A transfer-promoting policy leaves the size of the economic pie unchanged, but it increases the size of the slice of the pie that one group gets relative to another group.

For example, suppose group A, a special interest group, currently gets 1/1,000 of the economic pie and the economic pie is $1,000. It follows that the group gets a $1 slice of

Popular Culture   Technology   Everyday Life   The World

Religious Beliefs and Economic Growth

For given religious beliefs, increases in church attendance tend to reduce economic growth. In contrast, for given church attendance, increases in some religious beliefs—notably heaven, hell, and an afterlife—tend to increase economic growth.[3]

—Barro and McCleary

Economists have been studying economic growth for more than 200 years. Some of the questions they have asked and tried to answer include: Why are some nations rich and others poor? What causes economic growth? Why do some nations grow faster than other nations?

In our discussion of economic growth in this chapter, we identify and discuss a few of the causes of economic growth. We do not include any cultural determinants of economic growth. Some economic researchers argue that explanations for economic growth should be broadened to include cultural determinants. They argue that culture may influence personal traits, which may in turn affect economic growth. For example, personal traits such as honesty, thriftiness, willingness to work hard, and openness to strangers may be related to economic growth.

Two Harvard economists, Robert Barro and Rachel McCleary, have analyzed one such cultural determinant—the role that religion

plays in economic growth. Their work was based partly on the World Values Survey, which looked at a representative sample of people in 66 countries in all six inhabited continents between 1981 and 1997. The Survey asked at least 1,000 people in each country about their basic values and beliefs: What is their religious affiliation? How often do they attend a religious service? Were they raised religiously or not?

Barro and McCleary found that economic growth responds negatively to church attendance (nations with a high rate of attendance at religious services grow more slowly than those with lower rates of attendance) but positively with religious beliefs in heaven, hell, and afterlife. Specifically, in countries where the belief in heaven, hell, and afterlife is strong, growth of gross domestic product runs about 0.5 percent higher than average. (This result takes into account other factors, such as education, that influence growth rates.) Perhaps more telling, the belief in hell matters more to economic growth than the belief in heaven. Barro and McCleary suggest that the religious beliefs stimulate growth because they help to sustain aspects of individual behavior that enhance productivity.

---

3. Robert Barro and Rachel McCleary, "Religion and Economic Growth" (NBER Working Paper No. 9682).

---

the economic pie. Group *A* wants is to get more than a $1 slice. It can do this in one of two ways. The first way is to lobby for a policy that increases the size of its slice of the given economic pie. In other words, group *A* gets a larger slice (say, a $2 slice) at the expense of someone else getting a smaller slice. Alternatively, group *A* can lobby for a policy that increases the size of the pie—say, from $1,000 to $1,500. (Will group *A* get the full increase of $500? Not at all. It only gets 1/1,000 of the increase, or 50 cents.) So, group *A* has to decide whether it is better for it to lobby for a growth-promoting policy (where it gets 1/1,000 of any increase in Real GDP) or if it is better for it to lobby for a transfer-promoting policy (where it gets 100 percent of any transfer).

According to Mancur Olson, in his *The Rise and Decline of Nations*, special interest groups are more likely to argue for transfer-promoting policies than growth-promoting policies. The cost-benefit calculation of each policy makes it so.[4]

---

4. Mancur Olson, *The Rise and Decline of Nations* (New Haven and London: Yale University Press, 1982).

How does this behavior by special interest groups affect economic growth? Simply that the more special interest groups in a country, the more likely that transfer-promoting policies will be lobbied for instead of growth-promoting policies because individuals will try to get a larger slice of a constant-size economic pie rather than trying to increase the size of the pie. In short, numerous and politically strong special interest groups are detrimental to economic growth.

SELF-TEST *(Answers to Self-Test questions are in the Self-Test Appendix.)*

1. "Economic growth refers to an increase in GDP." Comment.
2. Country *A* has witnessed both economic growth and a rising price level during the past two decades. What does this imply about the *LRAS* and *AD* curves?
3. How can capital investment promote economic growth?

NEW GROWTH THEORY

Beginning in the 1980s, economists began discussing economic growth in ways different from the way it was discussed in previous decades. More attention was placed on technology, ideas, and education. The discussion takes place under the rubric, "new growth theory."

What Was Wrong With the Old Theory? Or, What's New With New Growth Theory?

To talk about *new growth theory* assumes there was a theory of economic growth that came before it. Before new growth theory, there was *neoclassical growth theory.* Some economists believe that new growth theory came to exist to answer some of the questions that neoclassical growth theory could not, in much the same way that a new medical theory may arise to answer questions that an old medical theory can't answer.

Neoclassical growth theory emphasized two resources—labor and capital. Within neoclassical growth theory, technology was discussed, but only in a very shallow way. Technology, it was said, was exogenous; that is, it came from outside the economic system. Stated differently, technology was something that "fell out of the sky," that was outside of our control, that we simply accepted as a given.

New growth theory holds that technology is endogenous; it is a central part of the economic system. More importantly, the technology that is developed—both the amount and the quality—depends on the amount of resources we devote to it: The more resources that go to develop technology, the more and better technology that is developed.

Paul Romer, whose name is synonymous with new growth theory, asks us to think about technology the way we think about prospecting for gold. For one individual, the chances of finding gold are so small that if one did find gold, it would simply be viewed as good luck. However, if there are 10,000 individuals mining for gold across a wide geographical area, the chances of finding gold would greatly improve. As with gold, so with technological advances. If one person is trying to advance technology, his or her chances of success are much smaller than if hundreds or thousands of persons are trying.

New growth theory also places emphasis on the process of discovering and formulating ideas. According to Romer, discovering and implementing new ideas is what causes economic growth.

To explain, we consider the difference between *objects* and *ideas.* Objects are material, tangible things—such as natural resources and capital goods. One of the arguments often made as to why some countries are poor is that they lack objects (natural resources and capital goods). The retort to this argument is that some countries that have had very few objects have been able to grow economically. For example, in the 1950s, Japan had few natural resources and capital goods (it still doesn't have an abundance of natural resources), but still it grew economically. Some economists believe that Japan grew because it had access to ideas or knowledge.

Discovery, Ideas, and Institutions

If the process of discovering ideas is important to economic growth, then it behooves us to figure out ways to promote the discovery process. One way is for business firms not to get locked into doing things one way and one way only. They must let their employees—from the inventor in the lab to the worker on the assembly line—try new ways of doing things. Some might carry this further: Businesses need to create an environment that is receptive to new ideas. They need to encourage their employees to try new ways of doing things.

Employee flexibility, which is a part of the discovery process, is becoming a larger part of the U.S. economy. To some degree, this is seen in the amount of time and effort firms devote to discovery in contrast to the amount of time they devote to actually manufacturing goods. Consider the computer software business. Millions of dollars and hundreds of thousands of work hours are devoted to coming up with new and useful software, whereas only a tiny fraction of the work effort and hours go into making, copying, and shipping the disks or CDs that contain the software.

Expanding Our Horizons

Let's return to Paul Romer. Romer has said that "economic growth occurs whenever people take resources and rearrange them in ways that are more valuable."[5] Let's focus on the word "rearrange." We can think of rearranging as in "rearranging the pieces of a puzzle," or as in "changing the ingredients in a recipe," or as in "rearranging the way a worker goes about his or her daily work." When we rearrange anything, we do that "thing" differently. Sometimes differently is better, and sometimes it is worse.

Think of the way you study for a test. Perhaps you read the book first, then go back and underline, then study the book, and then finally study your lecture notes. Would it be better to study differently? Often you won't know until you try.

As with studying for a test, so it is with producing a car, computer software, or a shopping mall. We do not find the better ways of doing things unless we experiment. And with repeated experiments, we often discover new and better ideas, ideas that ultimately lead to economic growth.

Consider the research and development of new medicines. Sometimes what makes a mildly effective medicine into a strongly effective medicine is a change in one or two molecules of a certain chemical. In other words, small changes—changes perhaps no one would ever think would matter—can make a large difference. There is a policy prescription that follows from this knowledge: We ought to think of ways to make the process of discovering ideas, experimenting with different ways of doing things, and developing new technology more likely. Without this, we are likely to diminish our growth potential.

Stated differently, if we believe ideas are important to economic growth, then we need to have ideas as to how to generate more ideas. Paul Romer calls these meta-ideas: Ideas about how to support the production and transmission of other ideas.

Some ways have been proposed. Perhaps we need to invest more funds in education or research and development; or perhaps we need to find ways to better protect peoples' ideas (few people will invest the time, money, and effort to discover better ideas if those ideas can easily be stolen); and so on.

---

5. Paul Romer, "Economic Growth," in *The Encyclopedia of Economics*, ed. David R. Henderson (New York: Warner Books, 1993), 184.

Popular Culture Technology Everyday Life The

© Annie Knudsen

Professors, Students, and Ideas

Paul Romer, the founder of new growth theory, emphasizes ideas and knowledge as catalysts of economic growth. Ideas and knowledge don't fall from the sky, though; they need to be produced. According to Romer, one way to produce more ideas and knowledge is by investing in research and development (R&D).

But R&D can proceed in different ways. One way, the way Romer believes is currently in operation, is what he calls the linear model of science and discovery. In a business firm, this model is applied the following way: The firm has an R&D department that is responsible for coming up with new ideas and new knowledge. After the R&D department has done its job, the rest of the firm is responsible for turning the knowledge or idea into a product that will sell. In short, the process begins with an idea, gets turned into a product (or service), and is then marketed and distributed.

According to Romer, the linear model is the wrong way to proceed. Scientists and engineers (and others) can come up with new ideas and new knowledge, but it is not just new knowledge for knowledge's sake that is needed. We need new knowledge to solve the problems that we already have. Romer advocates the use of market-like mechanisms to focus research efforts.

Romer believes that one of the problems with the present system is that universities are not producing the kinds of scientists and engineers that the private sector needs. Universities are training and producing scientists and engineers who are copies of their professors and are not necessarily the scientists and engineers who are needed in the marketplace. He believes there are many areas in the private sector where the demand for scientists is not being met.

Why are colleges and universities producing the "wrong" kinds of scientists and engineers? One reason, Romer argues, is that the federal government gives research monies to professors (including monies for research assistants) and then the professors hire the assistants to do what the professors want them to do. In other words, people are trained in areas that professors want them to be trained in, areas that interest the professors. But what interests professors? They are interested in research grants, many of which are given out by the federal government. Thus, professors have an incentive to respond to the research priorities of the federal government. So the federal government indirectly controls much of the research.

Romer proposes a change: Give students and businesses some control over research funds. He says, "The approach I prefer is one where you give students more control over their own funds. Instead of giving the money for student fellowship positions to the research professor in the department, why not give it to the student? That way a student could take the fellowship and say, 'I've seen the numbers. I know I can't get a job if I get a math Ph.D., but if I go into bio-informatics, there is a huge demand for people right now.' If the students could control the funds, the universities would start to cater to their demands, which would be in line with the market and the private sector's needs."[6]

The same outcome, Romer believes, would be forthcoming if businesses had some control over (federal) research monies that go to universities. Businesses would direct the monies into financing research that could help answer questions and solve problems in the private sector.

---

6. See the interview with Paul Romer by Joel Kurtzman in *Strategy and Business* (first quarter 1997):11.

In the twenty-first century, those countries with the most natural resources and capital goods aren't likely to be the ones to grow the fastest. If new growth theory is correct, it will be those countries that have discovered how to encourage and develop the most and best ideas.

SELF-TEST

1. If technology is endogenous, what are the implications for economic growth?
2. According to new growth theory, what countries will be the countries that grow the fastest in this century?

> This chapter explains that economic growth is largely a function of, or dependent upon, such things as the amount of labor and capital an economy employs, technological advancements, the property rights structure, and so on. Are these factors translatable into personal income growth? For example, if my objective is to "grow" my income over time, will knowing how economies grow provide me with any information on how to cultivate the growth of my income?

Let's recall the factors that are important to economic growth: (1) natural resources, (2) labor, (3) capital, (4) technological advances, (5) the property rights structure, and (6) economic freedom. In terms of personal income growth, counterparts exist for some of these factors. For example, an individual's natural talent might be the counterpart of a country's natural resources. Just as a country might be "lucky" to have plentiful natural resources, so might an individual be lucky to be born with a natural talent, especially a talent that others value highly.

Two factors directly relevant to your income growth are labor and (human) capital. We know that more labor and greater labor productivity promote economic growth. Similarly, for an individual, more labor expended and greater labor productivity often lead to income growth. How can you "expend more labor"? The answer is by working more hours. How can you increase your labor productivity? As we said earlier in the chapter, "one way is through increased education, training, and experience." In other words, acquire more *human capital*. Simply put, one way to increase your income is to work more; another way is to work better.

Finally, consider the role the property rights structure and economic freedom play in income growth. We often observe people migrating to places where the property rights structure and level of economic freedom are conducive to their personal income growth. For example, very few people in the world migrate to North Korea, but many people migrate to the United States.

Chapter Summary

Economic Growth

> Absolute real economic growth refers to an increase in Real GDP from one period to the next.
> Per capita real economic growth refers to an increase from one period to the next in per capita Real GDP, which is Real GDP divided by population.
> Economic growth can occur starting from an inefficient level of production or from an efficient level of production.

Economic Growth and the Price Level

> Usually, economists talk about economic growth as a result of a shift rightward in the PPF or in the *LRAS* curve.
> Economic growth can occur along with (1) an increase in the price level, (2) a decrease in the price level, or (3) no change in the price level.

Causes of Economic Growth

> Factors related to economic growth include natural resources, labor, capital, technological advances, the property rights structure, and economic freedom.
> Countries rich in natural resources are not guaranteed economic growth, and countries poor in natural resources may grow. Nevertheless, a country with more natural resources can evidence more economic growth, *ceteris paribus*.

> An increase in the amount of labor or in the quality of labor (as measured by increases in labor productivity) can lead to economic growth.
> More capital goods can lead to increases in economic growth. Capital formation, however, is related to saving: as the saving rate increases, capital formation increases.
> Technological advances may be the result of new capital goods or of new ways of producing goods. In either case, technological advances lead to economic growth.
> Economic growth is not unrelated to the property rights structure in the country. Individuals will invest more, take more risks, and work harder—thus there is likely to be greater economic growth—when the property rights structure allows them to keep more of the fruits of their investing, risk taking, and labor, *ceteris paribus*.
> For the most part, the more economic freedom the people of a country experience, the higher the Real GDP per capita.

Policies to Promote Economic Growth

> Both demand-side and supply-side policies can be used to promote economic growth. Demand-side policies focus on shifting the AD curve to the right. Supply-side policies focus on shifting the LRAS curve to the right.
> Some economists propose cutting taxes on such activities as saving and working in order to increase the productive capacity of

the economy. Other economists argue that regulations on business should be relaxed in order to increase the productive capacity of the economy.

> Industrial policy is a deliberate government policy of "watering the green spots," or aiding those industries that are most likely to be successful in the world marketplace.

> Industrial policy has both proponents and opponents. The proponents argue that the government needs to identify the industries of the future and help these industries to grow and develop now. The United States will fall behind, they argue, if it does not adopt an industrial policy while some other countries do. The opponents of industrial policy argue that the government doesn't know which industries it makes economic sense to help and that industrial policy is likely to become protectionist and politically motivated.

Economic Growth and Special Interest Groups

> According to Mancur Olson, the more special interest groups in a country, the more likely that transfer-promoting policies will

be lobbied for instead of growth-promoting policies because individuals will try to get a larger slice of a constant-size economic pie rather than trying to increase the size of the pie.

New Growth Theory

> New growth theory holds that technology is endogenous as opposed to neoclassical growth theory that holds technology to be exogenous. When something is endogenous, it is part of the economic system, under our control or influence. When something is exogenous, it is not part of the system; it is assumed to be given to us, often mysteriously through a process that we do not understand.

> According to Paul Romer, discovering and implementing new ideas is what causes economic growth.

> Certain institutions can promote the discovery of new ideas, and therefore promote economic growth.

Key Terms and Concepts

Absolute Real Economic Growth   Per Capita Real Economic Growth   Industrial Policy

Questions and Problems

1. Why might per capita real economic growth be a more useful measurement than absolute real economic growth?
2. What does it mean to say "natural resources are neither a sufficient nor a necessary factor for growth"?
3. How do we compute (average) labor productivity?
4. Is it possible to have more workers working, producing a higher Real GDP, at the same time that labor productivity is declining? Explain your answer.
5. How does an increased saving rate relate to increased labor productivity?
6. Economic growth doesn't simply depend on having more natural resources, more or higher-quality labor, more capital, and so on; it depends on people's incentives to put these resources

together to produce goods and services. Do you agree or disagree? Explain your answer.
7. It is possible to promote economic growth from either the demand side or the supply side. Do you agree or disagree? Explain your answer.
8. What is new about new growth theory?
9. How does discovering and implementing new ideas cause economic growth?
10. Explain how each of the following relates to economic growth: (a) technological advance, (b) labor productivity, (c) natural resources, (d) education, (e) special interest groups.
11. Explain how free trade is a form of technology.

Working With Numbers and Graphs

1. The economy of country X is currently growing at 2 percent a year. How many years will it take to double the Real GDP of country X?

2. Diagrammatically represent each of the following: (a) economic growth from an inefficient level of production and (b) economic growth from an efficient level of production.

3. Diagrammatically represent each of the following: (a) economic growth with a stable price level, (b) economic growth with a rising price level, and (c) economic growth with a falling price level.

© Photodisc/Getty Images

Setting the Scene

The following events happened on a day in February.

9:33 A.M.

Daisy Castle, a reporter for a local newspaper, is in the office of Duncan Carlyle, president of a nearby steel company. Daisy is interviewing the president about his company's future.

"Your company has had some problems recently," comments Daisy. "You've had to lay off some workers because your sales have been down. Do things look better for the months ahead?"

"Much depends on what Congress does in the next few weeks," replies Duncan. "We would be greatly helped—and so would this community—if Congress imposes a tariff on steel imports. That would give us the breathing room we need right now."

"Steel imports have risen dramatically the last six months," says Daisy. "Can U.S. companies compete with foreign producers?"

"Not without the tariff," Duncan answers. "We need to level the playing field."

11:54 A.M.

Jack and Harry, engineers for a large telecommunications company, are sitting at lunch, passing the time.

"What do you think about the President's newest plan on immigration?" Jack asks.

"I think the President should be cutting back on the number of immigrants instead of increasing the numbers," Harry replies. "More immigrants in the country simply lead to lower wages for Americans."

"I guess that's true," comments Jack.

"Of course it's true. It's basic supply and demand," Harry says. "An increased supply of people means more people applying for jobs, and wages have to go down."

2:43 P.M.

A student in a college economics class asks her professor if economics is really nothing more than "good ol' common sense"? In response, the professor begins to talk about comparative advantage.

5:01 P.M.

Karen Sullivan is packing for a trip. Tomorrow, at 7:05 A.M., she'll be on a plane headed for London. She'll spend five days in London, then go to Oxford, where she'll spend two days. Then she'll board a train for Scotland and spend four days in Edinburgh. After Edinburgh, she'll head back down to England and spend a day in Harrogate, two days in Birmingham, and finally two days in Cambridge. She's been saving for this trip for three years, and even though the dollar has been falling relative to the pound, she's still going on the trip.

? **How would an economist look at these events? Later in the chapter, discussions based on the following questions will help you analyze the scene the way an economist would.**

- How will a tariff help the domestic steel company?
- Do increased numbers of immigrants lower wages?
- Is economics nothing more than "good ol' common sense"?
- What does the value of the dollar have to do with Karen's trip?

INTERNATIONAL TRADE THEORY

International trade exists for the same reasons that trade at any level exists. Individuals trade to make themselves better off. Pat and Zach, both of whom live in Cincinnati, Ohio, trade because they both value something the other has more than they value some of their own possessions. On an international scale, Elaine in the United States trades with Cho in China because Cho has something that Elaine wants and Elaine has something that Cho wants.

Obviously, different countries have different terrains, climates, resources, worker skills, and so on. It follows that some countries will be able to produce some goods that other countries cannot produce or can produce only at extremely high costs.

For example, Hong Kong has no oil, and Saudi Arabia has a large supply. Bananas do not grow easily in the United States, but they flourish in Honduras. Americans could grow bananas if they used hothouses, but it is cheaper for Americans to buy bananas from Hondurans than to produce bananas themselves.

Major U.S. exports include automobiles, computers, aircraft, corn, wheat, soybeans, scientific instruments, coal, and plastic materials. Major imports include petroleum, automobiles, clothing, iron and steel, office machines, footwear, fish, coffee, and diamonds. Some of the countries of the world that are major exporters are the United States, Germany, Japan, France, and the United Kingdom. These same countries are some of the major importers in the world too.

How Do Countries Know What to Trade?

To explain how countries know what to trade, we need to review the concept of *comparative advantage,* an economic concept first discussed in Chapter 2. In this section, we discuss comparative advantage in terms of countries rather than in terms of individuals.

Comparative Advantage

Assume a two country–two good world. The countries are the United States and Japan, and the goods are food and clothing. Both countries can produce the two goods in the four different combinations listed in Exhibit 1. For example, the United States can produce 90 units of food and 0 units of clothing, or 60 units of food and 10 units of clothing, or another combination. Japan can produce 15 units of food and 0 units of clothing, or 10 units of food and 5 units of clothing, or another combination.

Suppose the United States is producing and consuming the two goods in the combination represented by point *B* on its production possibilities frontier, and Japan is producing and consuming the combination of the two goods represented by point *B'* on its production possibilities frontier. In other words, in this case, neither of the two countries is specializing in the production of one of the two goods, nor are the two countries trading with each other. We call this the *no specialization–no trade (NS-NT) case.* (See column 1 in Exhibit 2.)

Now suppose the United States and Japan decide to specialize in the production of a specific good and to trade with each other, called the *specialization–trade (S-T) case.* Will the two countries be made better off through specialization and trade? A numerical example will help answer this question. But, first, we need to find the answers to two other questions: What good should the United States specialize in producing? What good should Japan specialize in producing?

The general answer to both these questions is the same: *Countries specialize in the production of the good in which they have a comparative advantage.* A country has a **comparative advantage** in the production of a good when it can produce the good at lower opportunity cost than another country can.

Comparative Advantage
The situation where a country can produce a good at lower opportunity cost than another country can.

exhibit 1

United States		
Points on Production Possibilities Frontier	Food	Clothing
A	90	0
B	60	10
C	30	20
D	0	30

Japan		
Points on Production Possibilities Frontier	Food	Clothing
A′	15	0
B′	10	5
C′	5	10
D′	0	15

(a)

Production Possibilities in Two Countries

The United States and Japan can produce the two goods in the combinations shown. Initially, the United States is at point B on its PPF and Japan is at point B' on its PPF. Both countries can be made better off by specializing in and trading the good in which each has a comparative advantage.

(b)

For example, in the United States, the opportunity cost of producing 1 unit of clothing is 3 units of food (for every 10 units of clothing it produces, it forfeits 30 units of food). So the opportunity cost of producing 1 unit of food is 1/3 unit of clothing. In Japan, the opportunity cost of producing 1 unit of clothing is 1 unit of food (for every 5 units of clothing it produces, it forfeits 5 units of food). To recap, in the United States, the situation is $1C = 3F$, or $1F = 1/3C$; in Japan the situation is $1C = 1F$, or $1F = 1C$.

The United States can produce food at a lower opportunity cost ($1/3C$ as opposed to $1C$ in Japan), whereas Japan can produce clothing at a lower opportunity cost ($1F$ as opposed to $3F$ in the United States). Thus, the United States has a comparative advantage in food, and Japan has a comparative advantage in clothing.

Suppose the two countries specialize in the production of the good in which they have a comparative advantage. In other words, the United States specializes in the production of food (producing 90 units), and Japan specializes in the production of clothing (producing 15 units). In Exhibit 1, the United States locates at point A on its PPF, and Japan locates at point D' on its PPF. (See column 2 in Exhibit 2.)

Settling on the Terms of Trade

After they have determined which good to specialize in producing, the two countries must settle on the terms of trade, that is, how much food to trade for how much clothing. The United States faces the following situation: For every 30 units of food it does not produce, it can produce 10 units of clothing, as shown in Exhibit 1. Thus, 3 units of food have an opportunity cost of 1 unit of clothing ($3F = 1C$), or 1 unit of food has a cost of 1/3 unit of clothing ($1F = 1/3C$). Meanwhile, Japan faces the following situation: For every 5 units of food it does not produce, it can produce 5 units of clothing. Thus, 1 unit of food

Country	No Specialization–No Trade (NS-NT) Case		Specialization–Trade (S-T) Case			
	(1) Production and Consumption in the NS-NT Case	(2) Production in the S-T Case	(3) Exports (−) Imports (+) Terms of Trade Are $2F = 1C$	(4) Consumption in the S-T Case (2) + (3)	(5) Gains from Specialization and Trade (4) − (1)
United States					
Food	60 } Point B in	90 } Point A in	−20	70	10
Clothing	10 } Exhibit 1	0 } Exhibit 1	+10	10	0
Japan					
Food	10 } Point B′ in	0 } Point D′ in	+20	20	10
Clothing	5 } Exhibit 1	15 } Exhibit 1	−10	5	0

exhibit **2**

Both Countries Gain From Specialization and Trade

Column 1: Both the United States and Japan operate independently of each other. The United States produces and consumes 60 units of food and 10 units of clothing. Japan produces and consumes 10 units of food and 5 units of clothing. Column 2: The United States specializes in the production of food; Japan specializes in the production of clothing. Column 3: The United States and Japan agree to the terms of trade of 2 units of food for 1 unit of clothing. They actually trade 20 units of food for 10 units of clothing. Column 4: Overall, the United States consumes 70 units of food and 10 units of clothing. Japan consumes 20 units of food and 5 units of clothing. Column 5: Consumption levels are higher for both the United States and Japan in the S-T case than in the NS-NT case.

has an opportunity cost of 1 unit of clothing ($1F = 1C$). Recapping, for the United States, $3F = 1C$, and for Japan, $1F = 1C$.

With these cost ratios, it would seem likely that both countries could agree on terms of trade that specify $2F = 1C$. The United States would benefit by giving up 2 units of food instead of 3 units for 1 unit of clothing, whereas Japan would benefit by getting 2 units of food instead of only 1 unit for 1 unit of clothing. Suppose the two countries agree to the terms of trade of $2F = 1C$ and trade, in absolute amounts, 20 units of food for 10 units of clothing. (See column 3 in Exhibit 2.)

Results of the Specialization–Trade (S-T) Case

Now the United States produces 90 units of food and trades 20 units to Japan, receiving 10 units of clothing in exchange. It consumes 70 units of food and 10 units of clothing. Japan produces 15 units of clothing and trades 10 to the United States, receiving 20 units of food in exchange. It consumes 5 units of clothing and 20 units of food. (See column 4 in Exhibit 2.)

Comparing the consumption levels in both countries in the two cases, the United States and Japan each consume 10 more units of food and no less clothing in the specialization–trade case than in the no specialization–no trade case (column 5 in Exhibit 2). We conclude that a country gains by specializing in producing and trading the good in which it has a comparative advantage.

ANALYZING THE SCENE

Question from Setting the Scene: Is economics nothing more than "good ol' common sense"?

Many people think economics requires only common sense. But common sense often leads us to accept what sounds reasonable and sensible, and much in economics is counterintuitive—that is, it is different than we might expect. Consider the discussion of comparative advantage. One country—the United States—is better than another country—Japan—at producing both food and clothing. Common sense might lead us to conclude that because the United States is better than Japan at producing both food and clothing, the United States could not gain by producing and trading with Japan. But our analysis shows differently. For many people, that conclusion is counterintuitive; it goes against what intuition or good ol' common sense indicates.

How Do Countries Know When They Have a Comparative Advantage?

Government officials of a country do not analyze pages of cost data to determine what their country should specialize in producing and then trade. Countries do not plot production possibilities frontiers on graph paper or calculate opportunity costs. Instead, it is individuals' desire to earn a dollar, a peso, or a euro that determines the pattern of international trade. The desire to earn a profit determines what a country specializes in and trades.

To illustrate, consider Henri, an enterprising Frenchman who visits the United States. Henri observes that beef is relatively cheap in the United States (compared with the price in France) and perfume is relatively expensive. Noticing the price differences for beef and perfume between his country and the United States, he decides to buy some perfume in France, bring it to the United States, and sell it for the relatively higher U.S. price. With his profits from the perfume transaction, he buys beef in the United States, ships it to France, and sells it for the relatively higher French price. Obviously, Henri is buying low and selling high. He buys a good in the country where it is cheap and sells it in the country where the good is expensive.

What are the consequences of Henri's activities? First, he is earning a profit. The larger the price differences in the two goods between the two countries and the more he shuffles goods between countries, the more profit Henri earns.

Second, Henri's activities are moving each country toward its comparative advantage. The United States ends up exporting beef to France, and France ends up exporting perfume to the United States. Just as the pure theory predicts, individuals in the two countries specialize in and trade the good in which they have a comparative advantage. The outcome is brought about spontaneously through the actions of individuals trying to make themselves better off; they are simply trying to gain through trade.

SELF-TEST (Answers to Self-Test questions are in the Self-Test Appendix.)

1. Suppose the United States can produce 120 units of X at an opportunity cost of 20 units of Y, and Great Britain can produce 40 units of X at an opportunity cost of 80 units of Y. Identify favorable terms of trade for the two countries.
2. If a country can produce more of all goods than any other country, would it benefit from specializing and trading? Explain your answer.
3. Do government officials analyze data to determine what their country can produce at a comparative advantage?

TRADE RESTRICTIONS

International trade theory shows that countries gain from free international trade, that is, from specializing in the production of the goods in which they have a comparative advantage and trading these goods for other goods. In the real world, however, there are numerous types of trade restrictions, which raises the question: If countries gain from international trade, why are there trade restrictions?

The answer to this question requires an analysis of costs and benefits; specifically, we need to determine who benefits and who loses when trade is restricted. But first, we need to discuss some pertinent background information.

The Distributional Effects of International Trade

The previous section explains that specialization and international trade benefit individuals in different countries. But this benefit occurs on net. Every individual person may not gain.

Popular Culture

Technology

Everyday Life

The World

EVERYDAY LIFE

EVERYDAY LIFE

EVERYDAY LIFE

EVERYDAY LIFE

Dividing Up the Work

John and Veronica, husband and wife, have divided up their household tasks the following way: John usually does all the lawn work, fixes the cars, and does the dinner dishes, while Veronica cleans the house, cooks the meals, and does the laundry. Why have John and Veronica divided up the household tasks the way they have? Some sociologists might suggest that John and Veronica have divided up the tasks along gender lines—men have for years done the lawn work, fixed the cars, and so on, and women have for years cleaned the house, cooked the meals, and so on. In other words, John is doing "man's work," and Veronica is doing "woman's work."

Well, maybe, but that leaves unanswered the question of why certain work became "man's work" and other work became "woman's work." Moreover, it doesn't explain why John and Veronica don't split every task evenly. In other words, why doesn't John clean half the house and Veronica clean half the house? Why doesn't Veronica mow the lawn on the second and fourth week of every month and John mow the lawn every first and third week of the month?

The law of comparative advantage may be the answer to all our questions. To illustrate, suppose we consider two tasks, cleaning the house and mowing the lawn. The following table shows how long John and Veronica take to complete the two tasks individually.

	Time to Clean the House	Time to Mow the Lawn
John	120 minutes	50 minutes
Veronica	60 minutes	100 minutes

Here is the opportunity cost of each task for each person.

	Opportunity Cost of Cleaning the House	Opportunity Cost of Mowing the Lawn
John	2.40 mowed lawns	0.42 clean houses
Veronica	0.60 mowed lawns	1.67 clean houses

In other words, John has a comparative advantage in mowing the lawn and Veronica has a comparative advantage in cleaning the house.

Now let's compare two settings. In setting 1, John and Veronica each do half of each task. In setting 2, John only mows the lawn and Veronica only cleans the house.

In setting 1, John spends 60 minutes cleaning half of the house and 25 minutes mowing half of the lawn for a total of 85 minutes; Veronica spends 30 minutes cleaning half of the house and 50 minutes mowing half of the lawn for a total of 80 minutes. The total time spent by Veronica and John cleaning the house and mowing the lawn is 165 minutes.

In setting 2, John spends 50 minutes mowing the lawn and Veronica spends 60 minutes cleaning the house. The total time spent by Veronica and John cleaning the house and mowing the lawn is 110 minutes.

In which setting, 1 or 2, are Veronica and John better off? John works 85 minutes in setting 1 and 50 minutes in setting 2, so he is better off in setting 2. Veronica works 80 minutes in setting 1 and 60 minutes in setting 2, so Veronica is better off in setting 2. Together, John and Veronica spend 55 fewer minutes in setting 2 than in setting 1. Getting the job done in 55 fewer minutes is the benefit of specializing in various duties around the house. Given our numbers, we would expect that John will mow the lawn (and nothing else) and Veronica will clean the house (and nothing else).

To illustrate, suppose Pam Dickson lives and works in the United States making clock radios. She produces and sells 12,000 clock radios per year at a price of $40 each. As the situation stands, there is no international trade. Individuals in other countries who make clock radios do not sell their clock radios in the United States.

Then one day, the U.S. market is opened to clock radios from Japan. It appears that the Japanese manufacturers have a comparative advantage in the production of clock radios. They sell their clock radios in the United States for $25 each. Pam realizes that she cannot compete at this price. Her sales drop to such a degree that she goes out of business. Thus, the introduction of international trade in this instance has harmed Pam personally.

The example of Pam Dickson raises the issue of the distributional effects of free trade. In other words, the benefits of international trade are not equally distributed to all individuals in the population. The topics of consumers' and producers' surplus are relevant to our analysis.

Consumers' and Producers' Surplus

The concepts of consumers' and producers' surplus are first discussed in Chapter 3. We review them briefly in this section.

Consumers' surplus is the difference between the maximum price a buyer is willing and able to pay for a good or service and the price actually paid.

Consumers' surplus = Maximum buying price − Price paid

Consumers' surplus is a dollar measure of the benefit gained by being able to purchase a unit of a good for less than one is willing to pay for it. For example, if Yakov would have paid $10 to see the movie at the Cinemax but paid only $4, his consumer surplus is $6. Consumers' surplus is the consumers' net gain from trade.

Producers' surplus (or sellers' surplus) is the difference between the price sellers receive for a good and the minimum or lowest price for which they would have sold the good.

Producers' surplus = Price received − Minimum selling price

Producers' surplus is a dollar measure of the benefit gained by being able to sell a unit of output for more than one is willing to sell it. For example, if Joan sold her knit sweaters for $24 each but would have sold them for as low as (but no lower than) $14 each, her producer surplus is $10 per sweater. Producers' surplus is the producers' net gain from trade.

Both consumers' and producers' surplus are represented in Exhibit 3. In part (a), consumers' surplus is represented by the shaded triangle. This triangle includes the area under the demand curve and above the equilibrium price. In part (b), producers' surplus is represented by the shaded triangle. This triangle includes the area above the supply curve and under the equilibrium price.

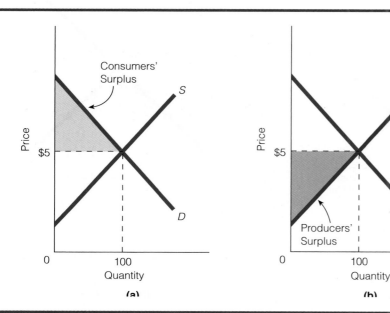

exhibit 3

Consumers' and Producers' Surplus

(a) Consumers' surplus. As the shaded area indicates, the difference between the maximum or highest amount consumers would be willing to pay and the price they actually pay is consumers' surplus. (b) Producers' surplus. As the shaded area indicates, the difference between the price sellers receive for the good and the minimum or lowest price they would be willing to sell the good for is producers' surplus.

The Benefits and Costs of Trade Restrictions

There are numerous ways to restrict international trade. Tariffs and quotas are two of the more commonly used methods. We discuss these two methods using the tools of supply and demand. We concentrate on two groups: U.S. consumers and U.S. producers.

Tariffs

Tariff
A tax on imports.

A **tariff** is a tax on imports. The primary effect of a tariff is to raise the price of the imported good for the domestic consumer. Exhibit 4 illustrates the effects of a tariff on cars imported into the United States.

The world price for cars is P_W, as shown in Exhibit 4a. At this price in the domestic (U.S.) market, U.S. consumers buy Q_2 cars, as shown in part (b). They buy Q_1 from U.S. producers and the difference between Q_2 and Q_1 ($Q_2 - Q_1$) from foreign producers. In other words, U.S. imports at P_W are $Q_2 - Q_1$.

What are consumers' and producers' surplus in this situation? Consumers' surplus is the area under the demand curve and above the world price, P_W. This is areas $1 + 2 + 3 + 4 + 5 + 6$. Producers' surplus is the area above the supply curve and below the world price, P_W. This is area 7. (See Exhibit 4b.)

---

exhibit **4**			
	Consumers' Surplus	**Producers' Surplus**	**Government Tariff Revenue**

The Effects of a Tariff
A tariff raises the price of cars from P_W to $P_W + T$, decreases consumers' surplus, increases producers' surplus, and generates tariff revenue. Because consumers lose more than producers and government gain, there is a net loss due to the tariff.

	Consumers' Surplus	**Producers' Surplus**	**Government Tariff Revenue**
Free trade (No tariff)	$1 + 2 + 3 + 4 + 5 + 6$	7	None
Tariff	$1 + 2$	$3 + 7$	5
Loss or Gain	$-(3 + 4 + 5 + 6)$	$+3$	$+5$

Result of Tariff	= Loss to consumers + Gain to producers + Tariff revenue
	= $-(3 + 4 + 5 + 6)$ + 3 + 5
	= $-(4 + 6)$

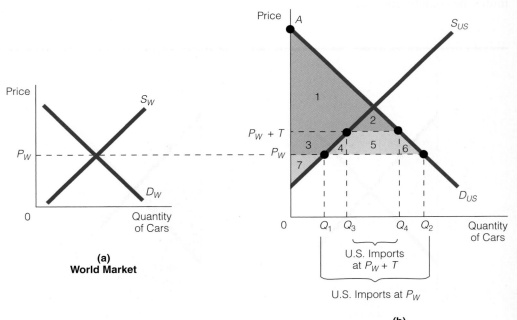

**(a)
World Market**

**(b)
Domestic (U.S.) Market**

Now suppose a tariff is imposed. The price for imported cars in the U.S. market rises to $P_W + T$ (the world price plus the tariff). At this price, U.S. consumers buy Q_4 cars: Q_3 from U.S. producers and $Q_4 - Q_3$ from foreign producers. U.S. imports are $Q_4 - Q_3$, which is a smaller number of imports than at the pretariff price. An effect of tariffs, then, is to reduce imports. What are consumers' and producers' surplus equal to after the tariff has been imposed? At price $P_W + T$, consumers' surplus is areas 1 + 2 and producers' surplus is areas 3 + 7.

Notice that consumers receive more consumers' surplus when tariffs do not exist and less when they do exist. In our example, consumers received areas 1 + 2 + 3 + 4 + 5 + 6 in consumers' surplus when the tariff did not exist but only areas 1 + 2 when the tariff did exist. Because of the tariff, consumers' surplus was reduced by an amount equal to areas 3 + 4 + 5 + 6.

Producers, though, receive less producers' surplus when tariffs do not exist, and more when they do exist. In our example, producers received producers' surplus equal to area 7 when the tariff did not exist, but they received producers' surplus equal to areas 3 + 7 with the tariff. Because of the tariff, producers' surplus increased by an amount equal to area 3.

The government collects tariff revenue equal to area 5. This area is obtained by multiplying the number of imports $(Q_4 - Q_3)$ times the tariff, which is the difference between $P_W + T$ and P_W.[1]

In conclusion, the effects of the tariff are a decrease in consumers' surplus, an increase in producers' surplus, and tariff revenue for government. Because the loss to consumers (areas 3 + 4 + 5 + 6) is greater than the gain to producers (area 3) plus the gain to government (area 5), it follows that *a tariff results in a net loss.* The net loss is areas 4 + 6.

ANALYZING THE SCENE

Question from Setting the Scene: How will a tariff help the domestic steel company?
As just discussed, the domestic steel company gains from a tariff, government gains tariff revenue, and consumers lose. More important, consumers lose more than producers and government gain. It is sometimes thought that private producers are always pro-market. Not so. A domestic company is often better off operating in an environment where its foreign competition has been stifled (as is the case through tariffs).

Quotas

A **quota** is a legal limit on the amount of a good that may be imported. For example, the government may decide to allow no more than 100,000 foreign cars to be imported, or 10 million barrels of OPEC oil, or 30,000 Japanese television sets. A quota reduces the supply of a good and raises the price of imported goods for domestic consumers (Exhibit 5).

Once again, we consider the situation in the U.S. car market. At a price of P_W (established in the world market for cars), U.S. consumers buy Q_1 cars from U.S. producers and $Q_2 - Q_1$ cars from foreign producers. Consumers' surplus is equal to areas 1 + 2 + 3 + 4 + 5 + 6. Producers' surplus is equal to area 7.

Suppose now that the U.S. government sets a quota equal to $Q_4 - Q_3$. Because this is the number of foreign cars U.S. consumers imported when the tariff was

Quota
A legal limit on the amount of a good that may be imported.

---

1. For example, if the tariff is $100 and the number of imports is 50,000, then the tariff revenue is $5 million.

exhibit **5**

The Effects of a Quota

A quota that sets the legal limit of imports at $Q_4 - Q_3$ causes the price of cars to increase from P_W to P_Q. A quota raises price, decreases consumers' surplus, increases producers' surplus, and increases the total revenue importers earn. Because consumers lose more than producers and importers gain, there is a net loss due to the quota.

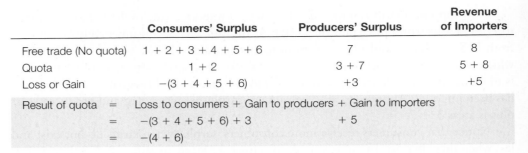

	Consumers' Surplus	Producers' Surplus	Revenue of Importers
Free trade (No quota)	1 + 2 + 3 + 4 + 5 + 6	7	8
Quota	1 + 2	3 + 7	5 + 8
Loss or Gain	−(3 + 4 + 5 + 6)	+3	+5

Result of quota	=	Loss to consumers + Gain to producers + Gain to importers
	=	−(3 + 4 + 5 + 6) + 3 + 5
	=	−(4 + 6)

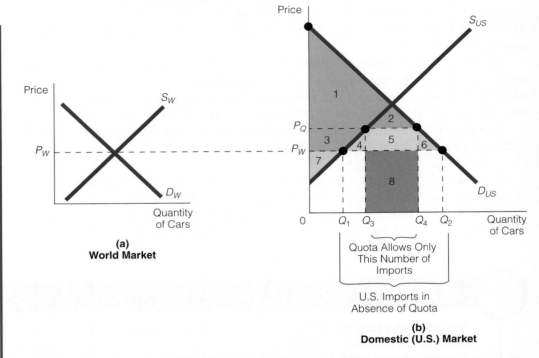

(a)
World Market

Quota Allows Only This Number of Imports

U.S. Imports in Absence of Quota

(b)
Domestic (U.S.) Market

imposed (see Exhibit 4), the price of cars rises to P_Q in Exhibit 5 (which is equal to $P_W + T$ in Exhibit 4). At P_Q, consumers' surplus is equal to areas 1 + 2 and producers' surplus is areas 3 + 7. The decrease in consumers' surplus due to the quota is equal to areas 3 + 4 + 5 + 6; the increase in producers' surplus is equal to area 3.

But what about area 5? Is this area transferred to government, as was the case when a tariff was imposed? No, it isn't. This area represents the additional revenue earned by the importers (and sellers) of $Q_4 - Q_3$. Look at it this way: Before the quota, importers were importing $Q_2 - Q_1$, but only part of this total amount, or $Q_4 - Q_3$, is relevant here. The reason only $Q_4 - Q_3$ is relevant is because this is the amount of imports now that the quota has been established. So, what dollar amount did the importers receive for $Q_4 - Q_3$ before the quota was established? The answer is $P_W \times (Q_4 - Q_3)$ or area 8. Because of the quota, the price rises to P_Q and they now receive $P_Q \times (Q_4 - Q_3)$ or areas 5 + 8. The difference between the total revenues on $Q_4 - Q_3$ with a quota and without a quota is area 5.

In conclusion, the effects of a quota are a decrease in consumers' surplus, an increase in producers' surplus, and an increase in total revenue for the importers who sell the allowed number of imported units. Because the loss to consumers (areas 3 + 4 + 5 + 6)

Offshore Outsourcing or Offshoring

Outsourcing is the term used to describe work done for a company by another company or by people other than the original company's employees. It entails purchasing a product or process from an outside supplier rather than producing this product or process in-house. To illustrate, suppose company X has, in the past, hired employees for personnel, accounting, and payroll services within the company. Currently, though, it has these duties performed by a company in another state. Company X, then, has outsourced certain work activities.

When a company outsources certain work activities to individuals in another country, it is said to be engaged in offshore outsourcing or *offshoring*. Consider a few examples. A New York securities firm replaces 800 software engineering employees with a team of software engineers in India. A computer company replaces 200 on-call technicians in its headquarters in Texas with 150 on-call technicians in India.

The benefits of offshoring for a U.S. firm are obvious—it pays lower wages to individuals in other countries for the same work that U.S. employees do for higher wages. Benefits also flow to the employees hired in the foreign countries. The costs of offshoring are said to fall on those persons who lose their jobs as a result, such as the software engineer in New York or the on-call computer technician in Texas. Some have argued that offshoring will soon become a major political issue and that it could bring with it a wave of protectionism.

There is no doubt that there will be both proponents of and opponents to offshoring. But what are the effects of offshoring on net? Are there more benefits than costs, or more costs than benefits? Consider a U.S. company that currently employs Jones as a software engineer, paying her $\$X$ a year. Then, one day, the company tells Jones that it has to let her go; it is replacing her with a software engineer in India who will work for $\$Z$ a year (where $\$Z$ is less than $\$X$).

Now some have asked why Jones doesn't simply say that she will work for $\$Z$. In other words, why doesn't she offer to work for the same wage as that agreed to by the Indian software engineer? The obvious answer is because Jones can work elsewhere for some wage between $\$X$ and $\$Z$. Assume this wage is $\$Y$. In other words, while offshoring has moved Jones from earning $\$X$ to earning $\$Y$, $\$Y$ is still more than $\$Z$.

In short, the U.S. company is able to lower its costs from $\$X$ to $\$Z$, and Jones's income falls from $\$X$ to $\$Y$. Notice that the U.S. company lowers its costs more than Jones's income falls. That's because the difference between $\$X$ and $\$Z$ is greater than the difference between $\$X$ and $\$Y$.

If the U.S. company operates within a competitive environment, its lower costs will shift its supply curve to the right and end up lowering prices. In other words, offshoring can end up reducing prices for U.S. consumers. The political fallout from offshoring might, in the end, depend on how visible to the average American the employment effects of offshoring are relative to the price reduction effects.

---

is greater than the increase in producers' surplus (area 3) plus the gain to importers (area 5), there is a *net loss as a result of the quota.* The net loss is equal to areas 4 + 6.[2]

If Free Trade Results in Net Gain, Why Do Nations Sometimes Restrict Trade?

Based on the analysis in this chapter so far, the case for free trade (no tariffs or quotas) appears to be a strong one. The case for free trade has not gone unchallenged, however. Some persons maintain that at certain times, free trade should be restricted or suspended. In almost all cases, they argue that it is in the best interest of the public or country as a whole

---

2. It is perhaps incorrect to imply that government receives nothing from a quota. Although it receives nothing directly, it may gain indirectly. Economists generally argue that because government officials are likely to be the persons who will decide which importers will get to satisfy the quota, they will naturally be lobbied by importers. Thus, government officials will likely receive something, if only dinner at an expensive restaurant while the lobbyist makes his or her pitch. In short, in the course of the lobbying, resources will be spent by lobbyists as they curry favor with those government officials or politicians who have the power to decide who gets to sell the limited number of imported goods. In economics, lobbyists' activities geared toward obtaining a special privilege are referred to as rent seeking.

International trade often becomes a battle-ground between economics and politics. The simple tools of supply and demand and consumers' and producers' surplus show that there are net gains from free trade. On the whole, tariffs and quotas make living standards lower than they would be if free trade were permitted.

On the other side, though, are the realities of business and politics. Domestic producers may advocate quotas and tariffs to make themselves better off, giving little thought to the negative effects felt by foreign producers or domestic consumers.

Perhaps the battle over international trade comes down to this: Policies are largely advocated, argued, and lobbied for based more on their distributional effects than on their aggregate or overall effects. On an aggregate level, free trade produces a net gain for society, whereas restricted trade produces a net loss. But economists understand that just because free trade in the aggregate produces a net gain, it does not necessarily follow that every single person benefits more from free trade than from restricted trade. We have just shown how a subset of the population (producers) gains more, in a particular instance, from restricted trade than from free trade. In short, economists realize that the crucial question in determining real-world policies is more often "How does it affect me?" than "How does it affect us?"

to do so. In short, they advance a public interest argument. Other persons contend that the public interest argument is only superficial; down deep, they say, it is a special interest argument clothed in pretty words. As you might guess, the debate between the two groups is often heated.

The following paragraphs describe some arguments that have been advanced for trade restrictions.

The National-Defense Argument

It is often stated that certain industries—such as aircraft, petroleum, chemicals, and weapons—are necessary to the national defense. Suppose the United States has a comparative advantage in the production of wheat and country X has a comparative advantage in the production of weapons. Should the United States specialize in the production of wheat and then trade wheat to country X in exchange for weapons? Many Americans would answer no. It is too dangerous, they maintain, to leave weapons production to another country.

The national-defense argument may have some validity. But even valid arguments may be abused. Industries that are not really necessary to the national defense may maintain otherwise. In the past, the national-defense argument has been used by some firms in the following industries: pens, pottery, peanuts, papers, candles, thumbtacks, tuna fishing, and pencils.

The Infant-Industry Argument

Alexander Hamilton, the first U.S. Secretary of the Treasury, argued that "infant" or new industries often need to be protected from older, established foreign competitors until they are mature enough to compete on an equal basis. Today, some persons voice the same argument. The infant-industry argument is clearly an argument for temporary protection. Critics charge, however, that after an industry is protected from foreign competition, removing the protection is almost impossible. The once infant industry will continue to maintain that it isn't old enough to go it alone. Critics of the infant-industry argument say that political realities make it unlikely that a benefit once bestowed will be removed.

Finally, the infant-industry argument, like the national-defense argument, may be abused. It may well be that all new industries, whether they could currently compete successfully with foreign producers or not, would argue for protection on infant-industry grounds.

The Antidumping Argument

Dumping is the sale of goods abroad at a price below their cost and below the price charged in the domestic market. If a French firm sells wine in the United States for a price below the cost of producing the wine and below the price charged in France, it is said to be dumping wine in the United States. Critics of dumping maintain that it is an unfair trade practice that puts domestic producers of substitute goods at a disadvantage.

In addition, critics charge that dumpers seek only to penetrate a market and drive out domestic competitors; then they will raise prices. However, some economists point to the infeasibility of this strategy. After the dumpers have driven out their competition and raised prices, their competition is likely to return. The dumpers, in turn, would have obtained only a string of losses (owing to their selling below cost) for their efforts.

Dumping
The sale of goods abroad at a price below their cost and below the price charged in the domestic market.

Opponents of the antidumping argument also point out that domestic consumers benefit from dumping because they pay lower prices.

The Foreign-Export-Subsidies Argument

Some governments subsidize the firms that export goods. If a country offers a below-market (interest rate) loan to a company, it is often argued that the government subsidizes the production of the good the firm produces. If, in turn, the firm exports the good to a foreign country, that country's producers of substitute goods call foul. They complain that the foreign firm has been given an unfair advantage that they should be protected against.[3]

Others say that one should not turn one's back on a gift (in the form of lower prices). If foreign governments want to subsidize their exports, and thus give a gift to foreign consumers at the expense of their own taxpayers, then the recipients should not complain. Of course, the recipients are usually not the ones who are complaining. Usually, the ones complaining are the domestic producers who can't sell their goods at as high a price because of the gift domestic consumers are receiving from foreign governments.

The Low-Foreign-Wages Argument

It is sometimes argued that American producers can't compete with foreign producers because American producers pay high wages to their workers and foreign producers pay low wages to their workers. The American producers insist that international trade must be restricted or they will be ruined. However, the argument overlooks the reason American wages are high and foreign wages are low in the first place: productivity. High productivity and high wages are usually linked, as are low productivity and low wages. If an American worker, who receives $20 per hour, can produce (on average) 100 units of X per hour, working with numerous capital goods, then the cost per unit may be lower than when a foreign worker, who receives $2 per hour, produces (on average) 5 units of X per hour, working by hand. In short, a country's high-wage disadvantage may be offset by its productivity advantage; a country's low-wage advantage may be offset by its productivity disadvantage. High wages do not necessarily mean high costs when productivity (and the costs of nonlabor resources) is included.

The Saving-Domestic-Jobs Argument

Sometimes the argument against completely free trade is made in terms of saving domestic jobs. Actually, we have already discussed this argument in its different guises. For example, the low-foreign-wages argument is one form of it. That argument continues along this line: If domestic producers cannot compete with foreign producers because foreign producers pay low wages and domestic producers pay high wages, domestic producers will go out of business and domestic jobs will be lost. The foreign-export-subsidies argument is another form of this argument. Its proponents generally state that if foreign-government subsidies give a competitive edge to foreign producers, not only will domestic producers fail but as a result of their failure, domestic jobs will be lost. Critics of the saving-domestic-jobs argument (in all its guises) often argue that if a domestic producer is being outcompeted by foreign producers and domestic jobs in a particular industry are being lost as a result, the world market is signaling that those labor resources could be put to better use in an industry in which the country holds a comparative advantage.

---

3. Words are important in this debate. For example, domestic producers who claim that foreign governments have subsidized foreign firms say that they are not asking for *economic protectionism*, but only for *retaliation*, or *reciprocity*, or simply *tit-for-tat*—words that have less negative connotation than the words their opponents use.

Question from Setting the Scene: Do increased numbers of immigrants lower wages?

Some residents of the United States argue that increased immigration will cause wages in the United States to decline. Their argument is based on simple supply and demand analysis: increased immigration leads to a greater supply of workers and lower wages.

There is little doubt that increased immigration will affect the supply of labor in the country. But it will affect the demand for labor too. The demand for labor is a derived demand—derived from the demand for the product that labor produces. With increased immigration, there will be more people living in the United States. A larger population translates into higher demand for food, housing, clothes, entertainment services, and so on. A higher demand for these goods translates into a higher demand for the workers who produce these goods.

In summary, increased immigration will affect both the supply of and demand for labor. What will be the effect on wages? It depends on whether the increase in demand is greater than, less than, or equal to the increase in supply. If demand increases by more than supply, wages will rise; if supply increases by more than demand, wages will fall; if demand rises by the same amount as supply rises, wages will not change.

SELF-TEST

1. Who benefits and who loses from tariffs? Explain your answer.
2. Identify the directional change in consumers' surplus and producers' surplus when we move from free trade to tariffs. Is the change in consumers' surplus greater than, less than, or equal to the change in producers' surplus?
3. What is a major difference between the effects of a quota and the effects of a tariff?
4. Outline the details of the infant-industry argument for trade restriction.

THE FOREIGN EXCHANGE MARKET

Foreign Exchange Market
The market in which currencies of different countries are exchanged.

Exchange Rate
The price of one currency in terms of another currency.

If a U.S. buyer wants to purchase a good from a U.S. seller, the buyer simply gives the required number of U.S. dollars to the seller. If, however, a U.S. buyer wants to purchase a good from a seller in Mexico, the U.S. buyer must first exchange her U.S. dollars for Mexican pesos. Then, with the pesos, she buys the good from the Mexican seller.

The market in which currencies of different countries are exchanged is the **foreign exchange market.** In the foreign exchange market, currencies are bought and sold for a price; an **exchange rate** exists. For instance, it might take 96 cents to buy a euro, 10 cents to buy a Mexican peso, and 13 cents to buy a Danish krone.

In this section, we explain why currencies are demanded and supplied in the foreign exchange market. Then we discuss how the exchange rate expresses the relationship between the demand for and supply of currencies.

The Demand for Goods

To simplify our analysis, we assume that there are only two countries in the world, the United States and Mexico. This, then, means there are only two currencies in the world, the U.S. dollar (USD) and the Mexican peso (MXP).[4] We want to answer the following two questions:

1. What creates the demand for and supply of dollars on the foreign exchange market?
2. What creates the demand for and supply of pesos on the foreign exchange market?

© Photodisc Green/Getty Images

---

4. Sometimes the abbreviation MXN instead of MXP is used for the Mexican peso.

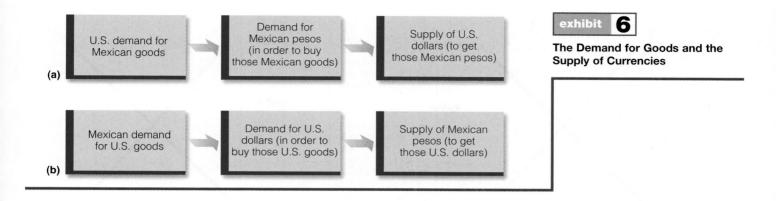

exhibit 6

The Demand for Goods and the Supply of Currencies

(a) U.S. demand for Mexican goods → Demand for Mexican pesos (in order to buy those Mexican goods) → Supply of U.S. dollars (to get those Mexican pesos)

(b) Mexican demand for U.S. goods → Demand for U.S. dollars (in order to buy those U.S. goods) → Supply of Mexican pesos (to get those U.S. dollars)

Suppose an American wants to buy a couch from a Mexican producer. Before he can purchase the couch, the American must buy Mexican pesos—hence, Mexican pesos are demanded. But the American buys Mexican pesos with U.S. dollars; that is, he supplies U.S. dollars to the foreign exchange market in order to demand Mexican pesos. We conclude that *the U.S. demand for Mexican goods leads to (1) a demand for Mexican pesos and (2) a supply of U.S. dollars on the foreign exchange market* (see Exhibit 6a). Thus, the demand for pesos and the supply of dollars are linked:

Demand for pesos ↔ Supply of dollars

The result is similar for a Mexican who wants to buy a computer from a U.S. producer. Before she can purchase the computer, the Mexican must buy U.S. dollars—hence, U.S. dollars are demanded. The Mexican buys the U.S. dollars with Mexican pesos. We conclude that *the Mexican demand for U.S. goods leads to (1) a demand for U.S. dollars and (2) a supply of Mexican pesos on the foreign exchange market* (see Exhibit 6b). Thus, the demand for dollars and the supply of pesos are linked:

Demand for dollars ↔ Supply of pesos

The Demand for and Supply of Currencies

Now let's look at Exhibit 7, which shows the markets for pesos and dollars. Part (a) shows the market for Mexican pesos. The quantity of pesos is on the horizontal axis, and the exchange rate—stated in terms of the dollar price per peso—is on the vertical axis. Exhibit 7b shows the market for U.S. dollars, which mirrors what is happening in the market for Mexican pesos. Notice that the exchange rates in (a) and (b) are reciprocals of each other. If 0.10 USD = 1 MXP, then 10 MXP = 1 USD.

In Exhibit 7a, the demand curve for pesos is downward-sloping, indicating that as the dollar price per peso increases, Americans buy fewer pesos, and as the dollar price per peso decreases, Americans buy more pesos.

Dollar price per peso↑   Americans buy fewer pesos
Dollar price per peso↓   Americans buy more pesos

For example, if it takes 0.10 dollars to buy a peso, Americans will buy more pesos than they would if it takes 0.20 dollars to buy a peso. (It is analogous to buyers purchasing more soft drinks at 3 dollars a six-pack than at 5 dollars a six-pack.) Simply put, the higher the dollar price per peso, the more expensive Mexican goods are for Americans and

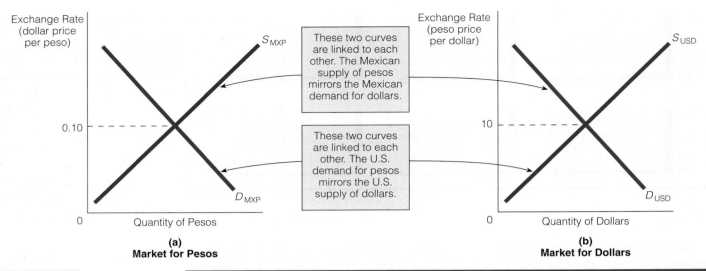

(a)
Market for Pesos

(b)
Market for Dollars

the fewer Mexican goods Americans will buy. Thus, a smaller quantity of pesos are demanded.

The supply curve for pesos in Exhibit 7a is upward-sloping. It is easy to understand why when we recall that the supply of Mexican pesos is linked to the Mexican demand for U.S. goods and U.S. dollars. Consider a price of 0.20 dollars for 1 peso compared with a price of 0.10 dollars for 1 peso. At 0.10 USD = 1 MXP, a Mexican buyer gives up 1 peso and receives 10 cents in return. But at 0.20 USD = 1 MXP, a Mexican buyer gives up 1 peso and receives 20 cents in return. At which exchange rate are U.S. goods cheaper for Mexicans? The answer is at the exchange rate of 0.20 USD = 1 MXP.

To illustrate, suppose a U.S. computer has a price tag of 1,000 dollars. At an exchange rate of 0.20 USD = 1 MXP, a Mexican will have to pay 5,000 pesos to buy the American computer; but at an exchange rate of 0.10 USD = 1 MXP, a Mexican will have to pay 10,000 pesos for the computer:

0.20 USD	= 1 MXP		0.10 USD	= 1 MXP
1 USD	= (1/0.20) MXP		1 USD	= (1/0.10) MXP
1,000 USD	= (1,000/0.20) MXP		1,000 USD	= (1,000/0.10) MXP
	= 5,000 MXP			= 10,000 MXP

To a Mexican buyer, the American computer is cheaper at the exchange rate of 0.20 dollars per peso than at 0.10 dollars per peso.

Exchange Rate	Dollar Price	Peso Price
0.20 USD = 1 MXP	1,000 USD	5,000 MXP [(1,000/0.20) MXP]
0.10 USD = 1 MXP	1,000 USD	10,000 MXP [(1,000/0.10) MXP]

It follows, then, that the higher the dollar price per peso, the greater the quantity demanded of dollars by Mexicans (because U.S. goods will be cheaper), and therefore the greater the quantity supplied of pesos to the foreign exchange market. The upward-sloping supply curve for pesos illustrates this.

FLEXIBLE EXCHANGE RATES

In this section, we discuss how exchange rates are determined in the foreign exchange market when the forces of supply and demand are allowed to rule. Economists refer to this as a **flexible exchange rate system.** In the next section, we discuss how exchange rates are determined under a fixed exchange rate system.

The Equilibrium Exchange Rate

In a completely flexible exchange rate system, the exchange rate is determined by the forces of supply and demand. Suppose in our two country–two currency world that the equilibrium exchange rate (dollar price per peso) is 0.10 USD = 1 MXP, as shown in Exhibit 8. At this dollar price per peso, the quantity demanded of pesos equals the quantity supplied of pesos. There are no shortages or surpluses of pesos. At any other exchange rate, however, either an excess demand for pesos or an excess supply of pesos exists.

At the exchange rate of 0.12 USD = 1 MXP, a surplus of pesos exists. As a result, downward pressure will be placed on the dollar price of a peso (just as downward pressure will be placed on the dollar price of an apple if there is a surplus of apples). At the exchange rate of 0.08 USD = 1 MXP, there is a shortage of pesos, and upward pressure will be placed on the dollar price of a peso.

Changes in the Equilibrium Exchange Rate

Chapter 3 explains that a change in the demand for a good, or in the supply of a good, or in both will change the equilibrium price of the good. The same holds true for the price of currencies. A change in the demand for pesos, or in the supply of pesos, or in both will change the equilibrium dollar price per peso. If the dollar price per peso rises—say, from 0.10 USD = 1 MXP to 0.12 USD = 1 MXP—the peso is said to have **appreciated** and the dollar to have **depreciated.**

A currency has appreciated in value if it takes more of a foreign currency to buy it. A currency has depreciated in value if it takes more of it to buy a foreign currency. For example, a movement in the exchange rate from 0.10 USD = 1 MXP to 0.12 USD = 1 MXP

THINKING LIKE AN ECONOMIST

The demand for dollars is linked to the supply of pesos and the demand for pesos is linked to the supply of dollars. Economists often think in terms of one activity being linked to another because economics, after all, is about exchange. In an exchange, one gives (supply) and gets (demand): John "supplies" $25 in order to demand the new book from the shopkeeper; the shopkeeper supplies the new book in order that he may "demand" the $25. In such a transaction, we usually diagrammatically represent the demand for and supply of the new book—but we could also diagrammatically represent the demand for and supply of money. Of course, in international exchange, where monies are bought and sold before goods are bought and sold, this is exactly what we do.

Flexible Exchange Rate System
The system whereby exchange rates are determined by the forces of supply and demand for a currency.

Appreciation
An increase in the value of one currency relative to other currencies.

Depreciation
A decrease in the value of one currency relative to other currencies.

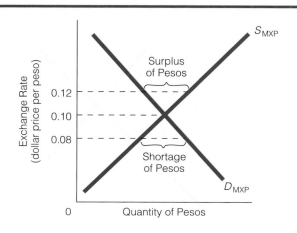

exhibit 8

A Flexible Exchange Rate System
The demand curve for pesos is downward-sloping. The higher the dollar price for pesos, the fewer pesos will be demanded; the lower the dollar price for pesos, the more pesos will be demanded. At 0.12 USD = 1 MXP, there is a surplus of pesos, placing downward pressure on the exchange rate. At 0.08 USD = 1 MXP, there is a shortage of pesos, placing upward pressure on the exchange rate. At the equilibrium exchange rate, 0.10 USD = 1 MXP, the quantity demanded of pesos equals the quantity supplied of pesos.

means that it now takes 12 cents instead of 10 cents to buy a peso, so the dollar has depreciated. The other side of the "coin," so to speak, is that it takes fewer pesos to buy a dollar, so the peso has appreciated. That is, at an exchange rate of 0.10 USD = 1 MXP it takes 10 pesos to buy 1 dollar, but at an exchange rate of 0.12 USD = 1 MXP, it takes only 8.33 pesos to buy 1 dollar.

Factors That Affect the Equilibrium Exchange Rate

If the equilibrium exchange rate can change owing to a change in the demand for and supply of a currency, then it is important to understand what factors can change the demand for and supply of a currency. Three are presented in this section.

A Difference in Income Growth Rates

An increase in a nation's income will usually cause the nation's residents to buy more of both domestic and foreign goods. The increased demand for imports will result in an increased demand for foreign currency.

Suppose U.S. residents experience an increase in income, but Mexican residents do not. As a result, the demand curve for pesos shifts rightward, as illustrated in Exhibit 9. This causes the equilibrium exchange rate to rise from 0.10 USD = 1 MXP to 0.12 USD = 1 MXP. *Ceteris paribus,* if one nation's income grows and another's lags behind, the currency of the higher-growth-rate country *depreciates* and the currency of the lower-growth-rate country *appreciates*. To many persons this seems paradoxical; nevertheless, it is true.

Differences in Relative Inflation Rates

Suppose the U.S. price level rises 10 percent at a time when Mexico experiences stable prices. An increase in the U.S. price level will make Mexican goods relatively less expensive for Americans and U.S. goods relatively more expensive for Mexicans. As a result, the U.S. demand for Mexican goods will increase and the Mexican demand for U.S. goods will decrease.

How will this affect the demand for and supply of Mexican pesos? As shown in Exhibit 10, the demand for Mexican pesos will increase (Mexican goods are relatively cheaper than they were before the U.S. price level rose), and the supply of Mexican pesos will decrease (American goods are relatively more expensive, so Mexicans will buy fewer American goods; thus, they demand fewer U.S. dollars and supply fewer Mexican pesos).

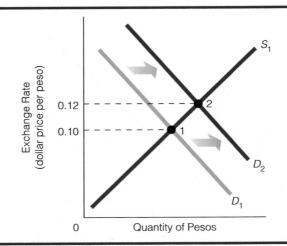

exhibit 9

The Growth Rate of Income and the Exchange Rate
If U.S. residents experience a growth in income but Mexican residents do not, U.S. demand for Mexican goods will increase, and with it, the demand for pesos. As a result, the exchange rate will change; the dollar price of pesos will rise. The dollar depreciates, the peso appreciates.

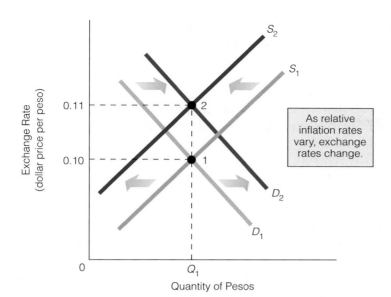

exhibit **10**

Inflation, Exchange Rates, and Purchasing Power Parity (PPP)
If the price level in the United States increases by 10 percent while the price level in Mexico remains constant, then the U.S. demand for Mexican goods (and therefore pesos) will increase and the supply of pesos will decrease. As a result, the exchange rate will change; the dollar price of pesos will rise. The dollar depreciates, and the peso appreciates. PPP theory predicts that the dollar will depreciate in the foreign exchange market until the original price (in pesos) of American goods to Mexican customers is restored. In this example, this requires the dollar to depreciate 10 percent.

As Exhibit 10 shows, the result of an increase in the demand for Mexican pesos and a decrease in the supply of Mexican pesos is an *appreciation* in the peso and a *depreciation* in the dollar. It takes 11 cents instead of 10 cents to buy 1 peso (dollar depreciation); it takes 9.09 pesos instead of 10 pesos to buy 1 dollar (peso appreciation).

An important question is: How much will the U.S. dollar depreciate as a result of the rise in the U.S. price level? (Recall that there is no change in Mexico's price level.) The **purchasing power parity (PPP) theory** predicts that the U.S. dollar will depreciate by 10 percent as a result of the 10 percent rise in the U.S. price level. This requires the dollar price of a peso to rise to 11 cents (10 percent of 10 cents is 1 cent, and 10 cents + 1 cent = 11 cents). A 10 percent depreciation in the dollar restores the *original relative prices of American goods to Mexican customers.*

Consider a U.S. car with a price tag of 20,000 dollars. If the exchange rate is 0.10 USD = 1 MXP, a Mexican buyer of the car will pay 200,000 pesos. If the car price increases by 10 percent to 22,000 dollars and the dollar depreciates 10 percent (to 0.11 USD = 1 MXP), the Mexican buyer of the car will still pay only 200,000 pesos.

Purchasing Power Parity (PPP) Theory
States that exchange rates between any two currencies will adjust to reflect changes in the relative price levels of the two countries.

Exchange Rate	Dollar Price	Peso Price
0.10 USD = 1 MXP	20,000 USD	200,000 MXP [(20,000/0.10) MXP]
0.11 USD = 1 MXP	22,000 USD	200,000 MXP [(22,000/0.11) MXP]

In short, the PPP theory predicts that changes in the relative price levels of two countries will affect the exchange rate in such a way that one unit of a country's currency will continue to buy the same amount of foreign goods as it did before the change in the relative price levels. In our example, the higher U.S. inflation rate causes a change in the equilibrium exchange rate and leads to a depreciated dollar, but one peso continues to have the same purchasing power it previously did.

On some occasions, the PPP theory of exchange rates has predicted accurately, but on others, it has not. Many economists suggest that the theory does not always predict accurately because the demand for and supply of a currency are affected by more than the difference in inflation rates between countries. For example, we have already noted that different income growth rates affect the demand for a currency and therefore the exchange rate. In the long run, however, and in particular, when there is a large difference in inflation rates across countries, the PPP theory does predict exchange rates accurately.

Changes in Real Interest Rates

More than goods flow between countries. Financial capital also moves between countries. The flow of financial capital depends on different countries' *real interest rates*—interest rates adjusted for inflation.

To illustrate, suppose, initially, that the real interest rate is 3 percent in both the United States and Mexico. Then the real interest rate in the United States increases to 4.5 percent. What will happen? Mexicans will want to purchase financial assets in the United States that pay a higher real interest rate than financial assets in Mexico. The Mexican demand for dollars will increase, and therefore Mexicans will supply more pesos. As the supply of pesos increases on the foreign exchange market, the exchange rate (dollar price per peso) will change; fewer dollars will be needed to buy pesos. In short, the dollar will appreciate and the peso will depreciate.

SELF-TEST

1. In the foreign exchange market, how is the demand for dollars linked to the supply of pesos?
2. What could cause the U.S. dollar to appreciate against the Mexican peso on the foreign exchange market?
3. Suppose the U.S. economy grows while the Swiss economy does not. How will this affect the exchange rate between the dollar and the Swiss franc? Why?
4. What does the purchasing power parity theory say? Give an example to illustrate your answer.

FIXED EXCHANGE RATES

Fixed Exchange Rate System
The system where a nation's currency is set at a fixed rate relative to all other currencies, and central banks intervene in the foreign exchange market to maintain the fixed rate.

The major alternative to the flexible exchange rate system is the **fixed exchange rate system**. This system works the way it sounds. Exchange rates are fixed; they are not allowed to fluctuate freely in response to the forces of supply and demand. Central banks buy and sell currencies to maintain agreed-on exchange rates. The workings of the fixed exchange rate system are described in this section.

Fixed Exchange Rates and Overvalued/Undervalued Currency

Once again, we assume a two country–two currency world. Suppose this time, the United States and Mexico agree to fix the exchange rate of their currencies. Instead of letting the

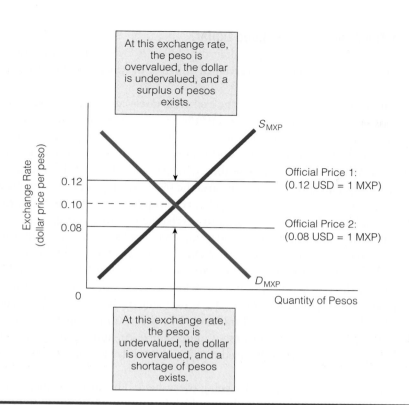

At this exchange rate, the peso is overvalued, the dollar is undervalued, and a surplus of pesos exists.

S_{MXP}

Official Price 1:
(0.12 USD = 1 MXP)

Official Price 2:
(0.08 USD = 1 MXP)

D_{MXP}

Quantity of Pesos

At this exchange rate, the peso is undervalued, the dollar is overvalued, and a shortage of pesos exists.

A Fixed Exchange Rate System
In a fixed exchange rate system, the exchange rate is fixed—and it may not be fixed at the equilibrium exchange rate. The exhibit shows two cases. (1) If the exchange rate is fixed at official price 1, the peso is overvalued, the dollar is undervalued, and a surplus of pesos exists. (2) If the exchange rate is fixed at official price 2, the peso is undervalued, the dollar is overvalued, and a shortage of pesos exists.

dollar depreciate or appreciate relative to the peso, the two countries agree to set the price of 1 peso at 0.12 dollars; that is, they agree to the exchange rate of 0.12 USD = 1 MXP. Generally, we call this the fixed exchange rate or the *official price* of a peso.[5] We will deal with more than one official price in our discussion, so we refer to 0.12 USD = 1 MXP as official price 1 (Exhibit 11).

If the dollar price of pesos is above its equilibrium level (which is the case at official price 1), a surplus of pesos exists. Also, the peso is said to be **overvalued**. This means that the peso is fetching more dollars than it would at equilibrium. For example, if in equilibrium, 1 peso trades for 0.10 dollars but at the official exchange rate, 1 peso trades for 0.12 dollars, then the peso is said to be overvalued.

It follows that if the peso is overvalued, the dollar is undervalued, which means it is fetching fewer pesos than it would at equilibrium. For example if in equilibrium, 1 dollar trades for 10 pesos but at the official exchange rate, 1 dollar trades for 8.33 pesos, then the dollar is undervalued.

Similarly, if the dollar price of pesos is below its equilibrium level (which is the case at official price 2 in Exhibit 11), a shortage of pesos exists. Also, the peso is **undervalued**. This means that the peso is not fetching as many dollars as it would at equilibrium. It follows that if the peso is undervalued, the dollar must be overvalued.

Overvalued peso ↔ Undervalued dollar
Undervalued peso ↔ Overvalued dollar

Overvaluation
A currency is overvalued if its price in terms of other currencies is above the equilibrium price.

Undervaluation
A currency is undervalued if its price in terms of other currencies is below the equilibrium price.

---

5. If the price of 1 peso is 0.12 dollars, it follows that the price of 1 dollar is approximately 8.33 pesos. Thus, setting the official price of a peso in terms of dollars automatically sets the official price of a dollar in terms of pesos.

What Is So Bad About an Overvalued Dollar?

Suppose you read in the newspaper that the dollar is overvalued. You also read that economists are concerned about the overvalued dollar. "But why are economists concerned?" you ask.

Economists are concerned because the exchange rate—and hence the value of the dollar in terms of other currencies—affects the amount of U.S. exports and imports.

To illustrate, suppose the demand for and supply of pesos are represented by D_1 and S_1 in Exhibit 12. With this demand curve and supply curve, the equilibrium exchange rate is 0.10 USD = 1 MXP. Let's also suppose the exchange rate is fixed at this exchange rate. In other words, the equilibrium exchange rate and the fixed exchange rate are initially the same.

Time passes and eventually the demand curve for pesos shifts to the right, from D_1 to D_2. Under a flexible exchange rate system, the exchange rate would rise to 0.12 USD = 1 MXP. But a flexible exchange rate is not operating here—a fixed one is. In other words, the exchange rate stays fixed at 0.10 USD = 1 MXP. This means the fixed exchange rate (0.10 USD = 1 MXP) is below the new equilibrium exchange rate (0.12 USD = 1 MXP).

Recall that if the dollar price per peso is below its equilibrium level (which is the case here), the peso is undervalued and the dollar is overvalued. In other words, at equilibrium (point 2 in Exhibit 12), 1 peso would trade for 0.12 dollars, but at its fixed rate (point 1), it trades for only 0.10 dollars—so the peso is undervalued. At equilibrium (point 2), 1 dollar would trade for 8.33 pesos, but at its fixed rate (point 1), it trades for 10 pesos—so the dollar is overvalued.

But what is so bad about the dollar being overvalued? The answer is that it makes U.S. goods more expensive (for foreigners to buy), which in turn can affect the U.S. **merchandise trade balance.**

For example, suppose a U.S. good costs 100 dollars. At the equilibrium exchange rate (0.12 USD = 1 MXP), a Mexican would pay 833 pesos for the good; but at the fixed exchange rate (0.10 USD = 1 MXP), he will pay 1,000 pesos.

Merchandise Trade Balance
The difference between the value of merchandise exports and the value of merchandise imports.

Exchange Rate	Dollar Price	Peso Price
0.12 USD = 1 MXP (equilibrium)	100 USD	833 MXP [(100/0.12) MXP]
0.10 USD = 1 MXP (fixed)	100 USD	1,000 MXP [(100/0.10) MXP]

The higher the prices of U.S. goods (exports), the fewer of those goods Mexicans will buy, and, as just shown, an overvalued dollar makes U.S. export goods higher in price.

---

exhibit **12**

Fixed Exchange Rates and an Overvalued Dollar
Initially, the demand for and supply of pesos are represented by D_1 and S_1, respectively. The equilibrium exchange rate is 0.10 USD = 1 MXP, which also happens to be the official (fixed) exchange rate. In time, the demand for pesos rises to D_2, and the equilibrium exchange rate rises to 0.12 USD = 1 MXP. The official exchange rate is fixed, however, so the dollar will be overvalued. As explained in the text, this can lead to a trade deficit.

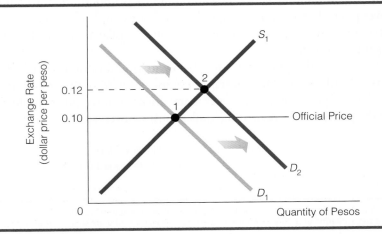

Ultimately, an overvalued dollar can affect the U.S. merchandise trade balance. As U.S. exports become more expensive for Mexicans, they buy fewer U.S. exports. If exports fall below imports, the result is a U.S. **merchandise trade deficit.**[6]

Merchandise Trade Deficit
The situation where the value of merchandise exports is less than the value of merchandise imports.

Government Involvement in a Fixed Exchange Rate System

Look back at Exhibit 11. Suppose the governments of Mexico and the United States agree to fix the exchange rate at 0.12 USD = 1 MXP. At this exchange rate, a surplus of pesos exists. What becomes of the surplus of pesos?

To maintain the exchange rate at 0.12 USD = 1 MXP, the Federal Reserve System (the Fed) could buy the surplus of pesos. But what would it use to buy the pesos? The Fed would buy the surplus of pesos with dollars. Consequently, the demand for pesos will increase and the demand curve will shift to the right, one hopes by enough to raise the equilibrium rate to the current fixed exchange rate.

Alternatively, instead of the Fed buying pesos (to mop up the excess supply of pesos), the Banco de Mexico (the central bank of Mexico) could buy pesos with some of its reserve dollars. (Why doesn't it buy pesos with pesos? Using pesos would not reduce the surplus of pesos on the market.) This action by the Banco de Mexico will also increase the demand for pesos and raise the equilibrium rate.

Finally, the two actions could be combined; that is, both the Fed and the Banco de Mexico could buy pesos.

Options Under a Fixed Exchange Rate System

Suppose there is a surplus of pesos in the foreign exchange market—indicating that the peso is overvalued and the dollar is undervalued. The Fed and the Banco de Mexico each attempt to rectify this situation by buying pesos. But suppose this combined action is not successful. The surplus of pesos persists for weeks, along with an overvalued peso and an undervalued dollar. What is there left to do? There are a few options.

Devaluation and Revaluation

Mexico and the United States could agree to reset the official price of the dollar and the peso. This entails *devaluation* and *revaluation*.

A **devaluation** occurs when the official price of a currency is lowered. A **revaluation** occurs when the official price of a currency is raised. For example, suppose the first official price of a peso is 0.10 USD = 1 MXP. It follows that the first official price of 1 dollar is 10 pesos.

Now suppose Mexico and the U.S. agree to change the official price of their currencies. The second official price is 0.12 USD = 1 MXP. This means, then, that the second official price of 1 dollar is 8.33 pesos.

Moving from the first official price to the second, the peso has been revalued. That's because it takes *more dollars to buy a peso* (12 cents instead of 10 cents). Of course, moving from the first official price to the second means the dollar has been devalued. That's because it takes *fewer pesos to buy a dollar* (8.33 pesos instead of 10 pesos).

Might one country want to devalue its currency but another country not want to revalue its currency? For example, suppose Mexico wants to devalue its currency relative to the U.S. dollar. Would U.S. authorities always willingly comply? Not necessarily.

Devaluation
A government act that changes the exchange rate by lowering the official price of a currency.

Revaluation
A government act that changes the exchange rate by raising the official price of a currency.

---

6. The other side of the coin, so to speak, is that if the dollar is overvalued, the peso must be undervalued. An undervalued peso makes Mexican goods cheaper for Americans. So while the overvalued dollar is causing Mexicans to buy fewer U.S. exports, the undervalued peso is causing Americans to import more goods from Mexico. In conclusion, U.S. exports fall, U.S. imports rise, and we move closer to a trade deficit, or if one already exists, it becomes larger.

To see why, we have to understand that the United States will not sell as many goods to Mexico if the dollar is revalued. That's because, as we stated earlier, revaluing the dollar means Mexicans have to pay more for it—instead of paying, say, 8.33 pesos for 1 dollar, Mexicans might have to pay 10 pesos for 1 dollar. At a revalued dollar (higher peso price for a dollar), Mexicans will find U.S. goods more expensive and not want to buy as many. Americans who produce goods to sell to Mexico may see that a revalued dollar will hurt their pocketbooks and so they will argue against it.

Protectionist Trade Policy (Quotas and Tariffs)

Recall that an overvalued dollar can bring on or widen a trade deficit. How can a country deal with both the trade deficit and the overvalued dollar at once? Some say it can impose quotas and tariffs to reduce domestic consumption of foreign goods. (An earlier section in this chapter explains how both tariffs and quotas meet this objective.) A drop in the domestic consumption of foreign goods goes hand in hand with a decrease in the demand for foreign currencies. In turn, this can affect the value of the country's currency on the foreign exchange market. In this case, it can get rid of an overvalued dollar.

Economists are quick to point out, though, that trade deficits and overvalued currencies are sometimes used as an excuse to promote trade restrictions—many of which simply benefit special interests (such as U.S. producers that compete for sales with foreign producers in the U.S. market).

Changes in Monetary Policy

Sometimes a nation can use monetary policy to support the exchange rate or the official price of its currency. Suppose the United States is continually running a merchandise trade deficit; year after year, imports are outstripping exports. To remedy this, the United States might enact a tight monetary policy to retard inflation and drive up interest rates (at least in the short run). The tight monetary policy will reduce the U.S. rate of inflation and thereby lower U.S. prices relative to prices in other nations. This will make U.S. goods relatively cheaper than they were before (assuming other nations didn't also enact a tight monetary policy) and promote U.S. exports and discourage foreign imports, as well as generate a flow of investment funds into the United States in search of higher real interest rates.

Some economists argue against fixed exchange rates because they think it unwise for a nation to adopt a particular monetary policy simply to maintain an international exchange rate. Instead, they believe domestic monetary policies should be used to meet domestic economic goals—such as price stability, low unemployment, low and stable interest rates, and so forth.

The Gold Standard

If nations adopt the gold standard, they *automatically fix* their exchange rates. Suppose the United States defines a dollar as equal to 1/10 of an ounce of gold and Mexico defines a peso as equal to 1/100 of an ounce of gold. This means that one ounce of gold could be bought with either 10 dollars or 100 pesos. What, then, is the exchange rate between dollars and pesos? It is 10 MXP = 1 USD or 0.10 USD = 1 MXP. This is the fixed exchange rate between dollars and pesos.

To have an international gold standard, countries must do the following:

1. Define their currencies in terms of gold.
2. Stand ready and willing to convert gold into paper money and paper money into gold at the rate specified (for example, the United States would buy and sell gold at 10 dollars an ounce).
3. Link their money supplies to their holdings of gold.

With this last point in mind, consider how a gold standard would work. Let's again look at Mexico and the United States, and initially assume that the gold-standard (fixed) exchange rate of 0.10 USD = 1 MXP is the equilibrium exchange rate. Then, a change occurs: Inflation in Mexico raises prices there by 100 percent. A Mexican table that was priced at 2,000 pesos before the inflation is now priced at 4,000 pesos. At the gold-standard (fixed) exchange rate, Americans now have to pay 400 dollars (4,000 pesos/10 pesos per dollar) to buy the table, whereas before the inflation Americans had to pay only 200 dollars (2,000 pesos/10 pesos per dollar) for the table. As a result, Americans buy fewer Mexican tables; Americans import less from Mexico.

At the same time, Mexicans import more from the United States because American prices are now relatively lower than before inflation hit Mexico. A quick example illustrates our point. Suppose that before inflation hit Mexico, an American pair of shoes cost 200 dollars and, as before, a Mexican table cost 2,000 pesos. At 0.10 USD = 1 MXP, the 200-dollar American shoes cost 2,000 pesos and the 2,000-peso Mexican table cost 200 dollars. In other words, 1 pair of American shoes traded for (or equaled) 1 Mexican table.

Now look at things after inflation has raised the price of the Mexican table to 4,000 pesos, or 400 dollars. Because the American shoes are still 200 dollars (there has been no inflation in the United States) and the exchange rate is still fixed at 0.10 USD = 1 MXP, 1 pair of American shoes no longer equals 1 Mexican table; instead, it equals 1/2 of a Mexican table. In short, the inflation in Mexico has made U.S. goods *relatively cheaper* for Mexicans. As a result, Mexicans buy more U.S. goods; Mexicans import more from the United States.

To summarize: The inflation in Mexico has caused Americans to buy fewer goods from Mexico and Mexicans to buy more goods from the United States. What does this mean in terms of the merchandise trade balance for each country? In the United States, imports decline (Americans are buying less from Mexico) and exports rise (Mexicans are buying more from the United States), so the U.S. trade balance is likely to move into surplus. Contrarily, in Mexico, exports decline (Americans are buying less from Mexico) and imports rise (Mexicans are buying more from the United States), so Mexico's trade balance is likely to move into deficit.

On a gold standard, Mexicans have to pay for the difference between their imports and exports with gold. Gold is therefore shipped to the United States. An increase in the supply of gold in the United States expands the U.S. money supply. A decrease in the supply of gold in Mexico contracts the Mexican money supply. Prices are affected in both countries. In the United States, prices begin to rise; in Mexico, prices begin to fall.

As U.S. prices go up and Mexican prices go down, the earlier situation begins to reverse itself. American goods look more expensive to Mexicans, and they begin to buy less, whereas Mexican goods look cheaper to Americans, and they begin to buy more. Consequently, American imports begin to rise and exports begin to fall; Mexican imports begin to fall and exports begin to rise. Thus, by changing domestic money supplies and price levels, the gold standard begins to correct the initial trade balance disequilibrium.

The change in the money supply that the gold standard sometimes requires has prompted some economists to voice the same argument against the gold standard that is often heard against the fixed exchange rate system; that is, it subjects domestic monetary policy to international instead of domestic considerations. In fact, many economists cite this as part of the reason many nations abandoned the gold standard in the 1930s. At a time when unemployment was unusually high, many nations with trade deficits felt that matters would only get worse if they contracted their money supplies to live by the edicts of the gold standard.

FIXED EXCHANGE RATES VERSUS FLEXIBLE EXCHANGE RATES

As is the case in many economic situations, there are both costs and benefits to any exchange rate system. This section discusses some of the arguments and issues surrounding fixed exchange rates and flexible exchange rates.

Promoting International Trade

Which are better at promoting international trade, fixed or flexible exchange rates? This section presents the case for each.

The Case for Fixed Exchange Rates

Proponents of a fixed exchange rate system often argue that fixed exchange rates promote international trade, whereas flexible exchange rates stifle it. A major advantage of fixed exchange rates is certainty. Individuals in different countries know from day to day the value of their nation's currency. With flexible exchange rates, individuals are less likely to engage in international trade because of the added risk of not knowing from one day to the next how many dollars or euros or yen they will have to trade for other currencies. Certainty is a necessary ingredient in international trade; flexible exchange rates promote uncertainty, which hampers international trade.

Economist Charles Kindleberger, a proponent of fixed exchange rates, believes that having fixed exchange rates is analogous to having a single currency for the entire United States instead of having a different currency for each of the 50 states. One currency in the United States promotes trade, whereas 50 different currencies would hamper it. In Kindleberger's view:

> The main case against flexible exchange rates is that they break up the world market. . . . Imagine trying to conduct interstate trade in the USA if there were fifty different state monies, none of which was dominant. This is akin to barter, the inefficiency of which is explained time and again by textbooks.[7]

The Case for Flexible Exchange Rates

Advocates of flexible exchange rates, as we have noted, maintain that it is better for a nation to adopt policies to meet domestic economic goals than to sacrifice domestic economic goals to maintain an exchange rate. They also say that there is too great a chance that the fixed exchange rate will diverge greatly from the equilibrium exchange rate, creating persistent balance of trade problems. This leads deficit nations to impose trade restrictions (tariffs and quotas) that hinder international trade.

SELF-TEST

1. Under a fixed exchange rate system, if one currency is overvalued, then another currency must be undervalued. Explain why this is true.
2. How does an overvalued dollar affect U.S. exports and imports?
3. In each case, identify whether the U.S. dollar is overvalued or undervalued.
   a. The fixed exchange rate is 2 dollars = 1 pound and the equilibrium exchange rate is 3 dollars = 1 pound.
   b. The fixed exchange rate is 1.25 dollars = 1 euro and the equilibrium exchange rate is 1.10 dollars = 1 euro.
   c. The fixed exchange rate is 1 dollar = 10 pesos and the equilibrium exchange rate is 1 dollar = 14 pesos.
4. Under a fixed exchange rate system, why might the United States want to devalue its currency?

---

7. Charles Kindleberger, *International Money* (London: Allen and Unwin, 1981), p.174.

Optimal Currency Areas

As of 2004, the European Union (EU) consists of 25 member states. According to the European Union, its ultimate goal is "an ever close union among the peoples of Europe, in which decisions are taken as closely as possible to the citizen." As part of meeting this goal, the EU established its own currency—the euro—on January 1, 1999.[8] Although euro notes and coins were not issued until January 1, 2002, certain business transactions were made in euros beginning January 1, 1999.

The European Union and the euro are relevant to a discussion of an *optimal currency area*. An **optimal currency area** is a geographic area in which exchange rates can be fixed or a *common currency* used without sacrificing domestic economic goals—such as low unemployment. The concept of an optimal currency area originated in the debate over whether fixed or flexible exchange rates are better. Most of the pioneering work on optimal currency areas was done by Robert Mundell, the winner of the 1999 Nobel Prize in Economics.

Before discussing an optimal currency area, we need to look at the relationships among labor mobility, trade, and exchange rates. Labor mobility means that it is easy for the residents of one country to move to another country.

Optimal Currency Area
A geographic area in which exchange rates can be fixed or a common currency used without sacrificing domestic economic goals—such as low unemployment.

Trade and Labor Mobility

Suppose there are only two countries, the United States and Canada. The United States produces calculators and soft drinks and Canada produces bread and muffins. Currently, the two countries trade with each other and there is complete labor mobility between the two countries.

One day, the residents of both countries reduce their demand for bread and muffins and increase their demand for calculators and soft drinks. In other words, there is a change in relative demand. Demand increases for U.S. goods and falls for Canadian goods. Business firms in Canada lay off employees because their sales have plummeted. Incomes in Canada begin to fall and the unemployment rate begins to rise. In the United States, prices initially rise because of the increased demand for calculators and soft drinks. In response to the higher demand for their products, U.S. business firms begin to hire more workers and increase their production. Their efforts to hire more workers drive wages up and reduce the unemployment rate.

Because labor is mobile, some of the newly unemployed Canadian workers move to the United States to find work. This will ease the economic situation in both countries. It will reduce some of the unemployment problems in Canada, and with more workers in the United States, more output will be produced, thus dampening upward price pressures on calculators and soft drinks. Thus, changes in relative demand pose no major economic problems for either country if labor is mobile.

Trade and Labor Immobility

Now let's change things. Suppose that relative demand has changed but this time labor is not mobile between the United States and Canada (labor immobility). There are either political or cultural barriers to people moving between the two countries. What happens in the economies of the two countries if people cannot move? The answer depends largely on whether exchange rates are fixed or flexible.

If exchange rates are flexible, the value of U.S. currency changes vis-à-vis Canadian currency. If Canadians want to buy more U.S. goods, they will have to exchange their domestic currency for U.S. currency. This increases the demand for U.S. currency on the foreign exchange market at the same time that it increases the supply of Canadian

---

8. So far, 12 of the 25 member states have adopted the euro as their official currency.

currency. Consequently, U.S. currency appreciates and Canadian currency depreciates. Because Canadian currency depreciates, U.S. goods become relatively more expensive for Canadians, so they buy fewer. And because U.S. currency appreciates, Canadian goods become relatively cheaper for Americans, so they buy more. Canadian business firms begin to sell more goods, so they hire more workers, the unemployment rate drops, and the bad economic times in Canada begin to disappear.

If exchange rates are fixed, however, U.S. goods will not become relatively more expensive for Canadians and Canadian goods will not become relatively cheaper for Americans. Consequently, the bad economic times in Canada (high unemployment) might last for a long time indeed instead of beginning to reverse. Thus, if labor is immobile, changes in relative demand may pose major economic problems when exchange rates are fixed but not when they are flexible.

Costs, Benefits, and Optimal Currency Areas

There are both costs and benefits to flexible exchange rates. The benefits we have just discussed. The costs include the cost of exchanging one currency for another (there is a charge to exchange, say, U.S. dollars for Canadian dollars or U.S. dollars for Japanese yen) and the added risk of not knowing what the value of one's currency will be on the foreign exchange market on any given day. For many countries, the benefits outweigh the costs, and so they have flexible exchange rate regimes.

Suppose some of the costs of flexible exchange rates could be eliminated, while the benefits were maintained. Under what conditions could two countries have a fixed exchange rate or adopt a common currency and retain the benefits of flexible exchange rates? The answer is when labor is mobile between the two countries. Then, there is no reason to have separate currencies that float against each other because resources (labor) can move easily and quickly in response to changes in relative demand. There is no reason why the two countries cannot fix exchange rates or adopt the same currency.

When labor in countries within a certain geographic area is mobile enough to move easily and quickly in response to changes in relative demand, the countries are said to constitute an *optimal currency area.* Countries in an optimal currency area can either fix their currencies or adopt the same currency and thus keep all the benefits of flexible exchange rates without any of the costs.

It is commonly argued that the states within the United States constitute an optimal currency area. Labor can move easily and quickly between, say, North Carolina and South Carolina in response to relative demand changes. Some economists argue that the countries that compose the European Union are within an optimal currency area and that adopting a common currency—the euro—will benefit these countries. Other economists disagree. They argue that while labor is somewhat more mobile in Europe today than in the past, there are still certain language and cultural differences that make labor mobility less than sufficient to truly constitute an optimal currency area.

SELF-TEST

1. What is an optimal currency area?
2. Country 1 produces good X and country 2 produces good Y. People in both countries begin to demand more of good X and less of good Y. Assume there is no labor mobility between the two countries and that a flexible exchange rate system exists. What will happen to the unemployment rate in country 2? Explain your answer.
3. How important is labor mobility in determining whether or not an area is an optimal currency area?

If tariffs and quotas result in higher prices for U.S. consumers, then why does the government impose them?

The answer is that government is sometimes more responsive to producer interests than to consumer interests. But, then, we have to wonder why. To try to explain why, consider the following example.

Suppose there are 100 U.S. producers of good X and 20 million U.S. consumers of good X. The producers want to protect themselves from foreign competition, so they lobby for and receive a quota on foreign goods that compete with good X. As a result, consumers must pay higher prices. For simplicity's sake, let's say that consumers must pay $40 million more. Thus, producers receive $40 million more for good X than they would have if the quota had not been imposed.

If the $40 million received is divided equally among the 100 producers, each producer receives $400,000 more as a result of the quota. If the additional $40 million paid is divided equally among the 20 million consumers, each customer pays $2 more as a result of the quota.

A producer is likely to think, "I should lobby for the quota because if I'm effective, I'll receive $400,000." A consumer is likely to think, "Why should I lobby against the quota? If I'm effective, I'll only save $2. Saving $2 isn't worth the time and trouble my lobbying would take."

In short, the benefits of quotas are concentrated on relatively few producers, and the costs of quotas are spread out over relatively many consumers. This makes each producer's gain relatively large compared with each consumer's loss. We predict that producers will lobby government to obtain the relatively large gains from quotas but that consumers will not lobby government to keep from paying the small additional cost due to quotas.

Politicians are in the awkward position of hearing from those people who want the quotas but not hearing from those people who are against them. It is likely the politicians will respond to the vocal interests. Politicians may mistakenly assume that consumers' silence means that the consumers accept the quota policy, when in fact they may not. Consumers may simply not find it worthwhile to do anything to fight the policy.

Chapter Summary

Specialization and Trade

> A country has a comparative advantage in the production of a good if it can produce the good at a lower opportunity cost than another country can.

> Individuals in countries that specialize and trade have a higher standard of living than would be the case if their countries did not specialize and trade.

> Government officials do not analyze cost data to determine what their country should specialize in and trade. Instead, the desire to earn a dollar, peso, or euro guides individuals' actions and produces the unintended consequence that countries specialize in and trade the good(s) in which they have a comparative advantage. However, trade restrictions can change this outcome.

Tariffs and Quotas

> A tariff is a tax on imports. A quota is a legal limit on the amount of a good that may be imported.

> Both tariffs and quotas raise the price of imports.

> Tariffs lead to a decrease in consumers' surplus, an increase in producers' surplus, and tariff revenue for the government. Consumers lose more through tariffs than producers and government (together) gain.

> Quotas lead to a decrease in consumers' surplus, an increase in producers' surplus, and additional revenue for the importers who sell the amount specified by the quota. Consumers lose more through quotas than producers and importers (together) gain.

Arguments for Trade Restrictions

> The national-defense argument states that certain goods—such as aircraft, petroleum, chemicals, and weapons—are necessary to the national defense and should be produced domestically whether the country has a comparative advantage in their production or not.

> The infant-industry argument states that "infant" or new industries should be protected from free (foreign) trade so that they may have time to develop and compete on an equal basis with older, more established foreign industries.

> The antidumping argument states that domestic producers should not have to compete (on an unequal basis) with foreign producers that sell products below cost and below the prices they charge in their domestic markets.

- The foreign-export-subsidies argument states that domestic producers should not have to compete (on an unequal basis) with foreign producers that have been subsidized by their governments.
- The low-foreign-wages argument states that domestic producers cannot compete with foreign producers that pay low wages to their employees when domestic producers pay high wages to their employees. For high-paying domestic firms to survive, limits on free trade are proposed.
- The saving-domestic-jobs argument states that through low foreign wages or government subsidies (or dumping, and so forth), foreign producers will be able to outcompete domestic producers, and therefore domestic jobs will be lost. For domestic firms to survive and domestic jobs not be lost, limits on free trade are proposed.
- Everyone does not accept the arguments for trade restrictions as valid. Critics often maintain that the arguments can be and are abused and, in most cases, are motivated by self-interest.

The Foreign Exchange Market

- The market in which currencies of different countries are exchanged is called the foreign exchange market. In this market, currencies are bought and sold for a price; an exchange rate exists.
- If Americans demand Mexican goods, they also demand Mexican pesos and supply U.S. dollars. If Mexicans demand American goods, they also demand U.S. dollars and supply Mexican pesos. When the residents of a nation demand a foreign currency, they must supply their own currency.

Flexible Exchange Rates

- Under flexible exchange rates, the foreign exchange market will equilibrate at the exchange rate where the quantity demanded of a currency equals the quantity supplied of the currency; for example, the quantity demanded of U.S. dollars equals the quantity supplied of U.S. dollars.

- If the price of a nation's currency increases relative to a foreign currency, the nation's currency is said to have appreciated. For example, if the price of a peso rises from 0.10 USD = 1 MXP to 0.15 USD = 1 MXP, the peso has appreciated. If the price of a nation's currency decreases relative to a foreign currency, the nation's currency is said to have depreciated. For example, if the price of a dollar falls from 10 MXP = 1 USD to 8 MXP = 1 USD, the dollar has depreciated.
- Under a flexible exchange rate system, the equilibrium exchange rate is affected by a difference in income growth rates between countries, a difference in inflation rates between countries, and a change in (real) interest rates between countries.

Fixed Exchange Rates

- Under a fixed exchange rate system, countries agree to fix the price of their currencies. The central banks of the countries must then buy and sell currencies to maintain the agreed-on exchange rate.
- If a persistent deficit or surplus exists at a fixed exchange rate, the nation has a few options to deal with the problem: devalue or revalue its currency, enact protectionist trade policies (in the case of a deficit), or change its monetary policy.
- A gold standard automatically fixes exchange rates. To have an international gold standard, nations must do the following: (1) define their currencies in terms of gold; (2) stand ready and willing to convert gold into paper money and paper money into gold at a specified rate; and (3) link their money supplies to their holdings of gold. The change in the money supply that the gold standard sometimes requires has prompted some economists to voice the same argument against the gold standard that is often heard against the fixed exchange rate system: It subjects domestic monetary policy to international instead of domestic considerations.

Key Terms and Concepts

Comparative Advantage	Exchange Rate	Purchasing Power Parity (PPP) Theory	Merchandise Trade Balance
Tariff	Flexible Exchange Rate System	Fixed Exchange Rate System	Merchandise Trade Deficit
Quota	Appreciation	Overvaluation	Devaluation
Dumping	Depreciation	Undervaluation	Revaluation
Foreign Exchange Market			Optimal Currency Area

Questions and Problems

1. Although a production possibilities frontier is usually drawn for a country, one could be drawn for the world. Picture the world's production possibilities frontier. Is the world positioned at a point on the PPF or below it? Give a reason for your answer.

2. "Whatever can be done by a tariff can be done by a quota." Discuss.

3. Consider two groups of domestic producers: those that compete with imports and those that export goods. Suppose the domestic producers that compete with imports convince the legislature to impose a high tariff on imports, so high, in fact, that almost all imports are eliminated. Does this policy in any way adversely affect domestic producers that export goods? How?

4. Suppose the U.S. government wants to curtail imports; would it be likely to favor a tariff or a quota to accomplish its objective? Why?

5. Suppose the landmass known to you as the United States of America had been composed, since the nation's founding, of separate countries instead of separate states. Would you expect the standard of living of the people who inhabit this landmass to be higher, lower, or equal to what it is today? Why?

6. Even though Jeremy is a better gardener and novelist than Bill is, Jeremy still hires Bill as his gardener. Why?

7. Suppose that tomorrow, a constitutional convention were called and you were chosen as one of the delegates from your state. You and the other delegates must decide whether it will be constitutional or unconstitutional for the federal government to impose tariffs and quotas or restrict international trade in any way. What would be your position?

8. Some economists have argued that because domestic consumers gain more from free trade than domestic producers gain from (import) tariffs and quotas, consumers should buy out domestic producers and rid themselves of costly tariffs and quotas. For example, if consumers save $400 million from free trade (through paying lower prices) and producers gain $100 million from tariffs and quotas, consumers can pay producers something more than $100 million but less than $400 million and get producers to favor free trade too. Assuming this scheme were feasible, what do you think of it?

9. If there is a net loss to society from tariffs, why do tariffs exist?

10. Explain how a flexible exchange rate system works.

11. Suppose the only two countries in the world are Mexico and the United States. Explain why the demand for dollars in the foreign exchange market is related to the supply of pesos and the demand for pesos is related to the supply of dollars.

12. Suppose the United States and Japan have a flexible exchange rate system. Explain whether each of the following events will lead to an appreciation or depreciation in the U.S. dollar and Japanese yen. (a) U.S. real interest rates rise above Japanese real interest rates. (b) The Japanese inflation rate rises relative to the U.S. inflation rate. (c) Japan imposes a quota on imports of American radios.

13. Give an example that illustrates how a change in the exchange rate changes the relative price of domestic goods in terms of foreign goods.

14. What are the strong and weak points of the flexible exchange rate system? What are the strong and weak points of the fixed exchange rate system?

Working With Numbers and Graphs

1. Using the data in the table, answer the following questions: (a) For which good does Canada have a comparative advantage? (b) For which good does Italy have a comparative advantage? (c) What might be a set of favorable terms of trade for the two countries? (d) Prove that both countries would be better off in the specialization–trade case than in the no specialization–no trade case.

Points on Production Possibilities Frontier	Canada		Italy	
	Good X	Good Y	Good X	Good Y
A	150	0	90	0
B	100	25	60	60
C	50	50	30	120
D	0	75	0	180

2. In the following figure, P_W is the world price and $P_W + T$ is the world price plus a tariff. Identify the following:

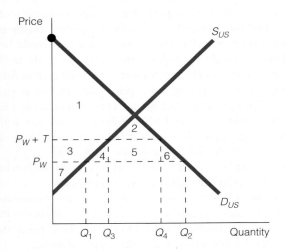

a. The level of imports at P_W

b. The level of imports at $P_W + T$

c. The loss in consumers' surplus as a result of a tariff

d. The gain in producers' surplus as a result of a tariff

e. The tariff revenue as the result of a tariff

f. The net loss to society as a result of a tariff

g. The net benefit to society of moving from a tariff situation to a no-tariff situation

3. The following foreign exchange information appeared in a newspaper:

	U.S. Dollar Equivalent		Currency per U.S. Dollar	
	THURS.	FRI.	THURS.	FRI.
Russia (ruble)	0.0318	0.0317	31.4190	31.5290
Brazil (real)	0.3569	0.3623	2.8020	2.7601
India (rupee)	0.0204	0.0208	48.9100	47.8521

a. Between Thursday and Friday, did the U.S. dollar appreciate or depreciate against the Russian ruble?

b. Between Thursday and Friday, did the U.S. dollar appreciate or depreciate against the Brazilian real?

c. Between Thursday and Friday, did the U.S. dollar appreciate or depreciate against the Indian rupee?

4. If 1 dollar equals 0.0093 yen, then what does 1 yen equal?

5. If 1 dollar equals 7.7 krone (Danish), then what does 1 krone equal?

6. If 1 dollar equals 31 rubles, then what does 1 ruble equal?

Self-Test Appendix

CHAPTER 1

Chapter 1, page 4

1. False. It takes two things for scarcity to exist: finite resources and infinite wants. If peoples' wants were equal to or less than the finite resources available to satisfy their wants, there would be no scarcity. Scarcity exists only because peoples' wants are greater than the resources available to satisfy their wants. Scarcity is the condition of infinite wants clashing with finite resources.
2. Both define economics as having to do with ends and means, which implicitly brings up the concept of scarcity. In short, both Friedman and Robbins emphasize the concept of scarcity in their definitions.
3. Positive economics deals with what is; normative economics, with what should be. Macroeconomics deals with human behavior and choices as they relate to an entire economy. Microeconomics deals with human behavior and choices as they relate to relatively small units—an individual, a firm, an industry, a single market.

Chapter 1, page 13

1. Because of scarcity, there is a need for a rationing device. People will compete for the rationing device. For example, if dollar price is the rationing device, people will compete for dollars.
2. Every time a person is late to history class, the instructor subtracts one-tenth of a point from the person's final grade. If the instructor raised the opportunity cost of being late to class—by subtracting one point from the person's final grade—economists predict there would be fewer persons late to class. In summary, the higher the opportunity cost of being late to class, the less likely people will be late to class.
3. An example is a politician who says: "My opponent has been in office for the past two years and during this time, interest rates have gone up and bankruptcies have gone up. We don't need any more bad economics. Don't cast your vote for my opponent. Vote for me." The politician implies that his opponent caused the dismal economic record when this is probably not the case.
4. Unless stated otherwise, when economics instructors identify the relationship between two variables, they implicitly make the *ceteris paribus* assumption. In other words, the instructor is really saying, "If the price of going to the movies goes down, people will go to the movies more often—assuming that nothing else changes, such as the quality of movies, etc." Instructors don't always state *"ceteris paribus"* because if they did, they would be using the term every minute of a lecture. So the instructor is right, although a student new to economics might not know what the instructor is assuming but not saying.

Chapter 1, page 16

1. The purpose of building a theory is to explain something that is not obvious. For example, the cause of changes in the unemployment rate is not obvious, and so the economist would build a theory to explain changes in the unemployment rate.
2. A theory of the economy would seek to explain why certain things in the economy happen. For example, a theory of the economy might try to explain why prices rise or why output falls.

A description of the economy is simply a statement of what exists in the economy. For example, we could say the economy is growing, or the economy is contracting, or more jobs are available this month than last month. A description doesn't answer questions; it simply tells us what is. A theory tries to answer a "why" question, such as: Why are more jobs available this month than last month?

3. If you do not test a theory, you will never know if you have accomplished your objective in building the theory in the first place. That is, you will not know if you have accurately explained or predicted something. We do not simply accept a theory if it "sounds right" because what sounds right may actually be wrong. For example, no doubt during the time of Columbus, the theory that the earth was flat sounded right to many people and the theory that the earth was round sounded ridiculous. The right-sounding theory turned out to be wrong, though, and the ridiculous-sounding theory turned out to be right.

CHAPTER 2

Chapter 2, page 46

1. A straight-line PPF represents constant opportunity costs between two goods. For example, for every unit of *X* produced, one unit of *Y* is forfeited. A bowed-outward PPF represents increasing opportunity costs. For example, we may have to forfeit one unit of *X* to produce the eleventh unit of *Y,* but we have to forfeit two units of *X* to produce the one hundredth unit of *Y.*
2. A bowed-outward PPF is representative of increasing costs. In short, the PPF would not be bowed outward if increasing costs did not exist. To prove this, look back at Exhibits 1 and 2. In Exhibit 1, costs are constant (not increasing) and the PPF is a straight line. In Exhibit 2, costs are increasing and the PPF is bowed outward.
3. The first condition is that the economy is currently operating *below* its PPF. It is possible to move from a point below the PPF to a point on the PPF and get more of all goods. The second condition is that the economy's PPF shifts outward.
4. False. Take a look at Exhibit 4. There are numerous productive efficient points, all of which lie on the PPF.

Chapter 2, page 50

1. Transaction costs are the costs associated with the time and effort needed to search out, negotiate, and consummate a trade. The transaction costs are likely to be higher for buying a house than for buying a car because buying a house is a more detailed and complex process.
2. Under certain conditions, Smith will buy good *X* from Jones. For example, suppose Smith and Jones agree on a price of, say, $260, and neither person incurs transaction costs greater than $40. If transaction costs are zero for each person, then each person benefits $40 from the trade. Specifically, Smith buys the good for $40 less than his maximum price and Jones sells the good for $40 more than his minimum price. But suppose each person incurs a transaction cost of, say, $50. Smith would be unwilling to pay $260 to Jones and $50 in transaction costs (for a total of $310) when he is only willing to pay a maximum price of $300 for good *X.*

Similarly, Jones would be unwilling to sell good X for $260 and incur $50 in transaction costs (leaving him with only $210, or $10 less than his minimum selling price).

Chapter 2, page 55

1. If George goes from producing $5X$ to $10X$, he gives up $5Y$. This means the opportunity cost of 5 more X is 5 fewer Y. It follows that the opportunity cost of $1X$ is $1Y$. Conclusion: the opportunity cost of $1X$ is $1Y$.

2. If Harriet produces 10 more X, she gives up $15Y$. It follows that the opportunity cost of $1X$ is $1.5Y$ and the opportunity cost of $1Y$ is $0.67X$. If Bill produces 10 more X, he gives up $20Y$. It follows that the opportunity cost of $1X$ is $2Y$ and the opportunity cost of $1Y$ is $0.5X$. Harriet is the lower-cost producer of X, and Bill is the lower-cost producer of Y. In short, Harriet has the comparative advantage in the production of X; Bill has the comparative advantage in the production of Y.

Chapter 2, page 60

1. What goods will be produced? How will the goods be produced? For whom will the goods be produced?

2. Trade benefits the traders. If George buys a book for $40, both George and the bookseller have been made better off. George would not have traded $40 for the book unless he expected to be made better off. Similarly, the seller would not have sold the book unless she expected to be made better off.

3. One of the questions every society must answer is *What goods will be produced?* In a way, this is no different than *Where on its PPF will an economy operate?* In other words, what combination of goods will be produced? Under capitalism, where on its PPF the economy operates is largely decided by the market (buyers and sellers). Under socialism, where on its PPF the economy operates is largely decided by government.

4. A price control implies a different set of property rights than exist in the absence of a price control. Specifically, a price control implies that individuals can sell their property for only a certain price or less. The absence of a price control implies individuals can sell their property for any price that is agreed upon by them and buyers.

CHAPTER 3

Chapter 3, page 73

1. Popcorn is a normal good for Sandi. Prepaid telephone cards are an inferior good for Mark.

2. Asking why demand curves are downward-sloping is the same as asking why price and quantity demanded are inversely related (as one rises, the other falls). There are two reasons mentioned in this section: (1) As price rises, people substitute lower-priced goods for higher-priced goods. (2) Because individuals receive less utility from an additional unit of a good they consume, they are only willing to pay less for the additional unit. The second reason is a reflection of the law of diminishing marginal utility.

3. Suppose only two people, Bob and Alice, have a demand for good X. At a price of $7, Bob buys 10 units and Alice buys 3 units; at a price of $6, Bob buys 12 units and Alice buys 5 units. One point on the market demand curve represents a price of $7 and a quantity demanded of 13 units; another point represents $6 and 17

units. A market demand curve is derived by adding the quantities demanded at each price.

4. A change in income, preferences, prices of related goods, number of buyers, and expectations of future price can change demand. A change in the price of the good changes the quantity demanded of the good. For example, a change in *income* can change the *demand* for oranges, but only a change in the *price* of oranges can directly change the *quantity demanded* of oranges.

Chapter 3, page 78

1. It would be difficult to increase the quantity supplied of houses over the next 10 hours, so the supply curve in (a) is vertical, as in Exhibit 7. It is possible to increase the quantity supplied of houses over the next 3 months, however, so the supply curve in (b) is upward-sloping.

2. **a.** The supply curve shifts to the left.
   b. The supply curve shifts to the left.
   c. The supply curve shifts to the right.

3. False. If the price of apples rises, the *quantity supplied* of apples will rise—not the *supply* of apples. We are talking about a *movement* from one point on a supply curve to a point higher up on the supply curve and not about a shift in the supply curve.

Chapter 3, page 85

1. Disagree. In the text, we plainly saw how supply and demand work at an auction. Supply and demand are at work in the grocery store, too, although no auctioneer is present. The essence of the auction example is the auctioneer raising the price when there was a shortage and lowering the price when there was a surplus. The same thing happens at the grocery store. For example, if there is a surplus of corn flakes, the manager of the store is likely to have a sale (lower prices) on corn flakes. Many markets without auctioneers act *as if* there are auctioneers raising and lowering prices in response to shortages and surpluses.

2. No. It could be the result of a higher supply of computers. Either a decrease in demand or an increase in supply will lower price.

3. **a.** Lower price and quantity
   b. Lower price and higher quantity
   c. Higher price and lower quantity
   d. Lower price and quantity

4. At equilibrium quantity, the maximum buying price and the minimum selling price are the same. For example, in Exhibit 14, both prices are $40 at the equilibrium quantity 4. Equilibrium quantity is the only quantity at which the maximum buying price and the minimum selling price are the same.

5. $46; $34

Chapter 3, page 90

1. Yes, if nothing else changes—that is, yes, *ceteris paribus.* If some other things change, though, they may not. For example, if the government imposes an effective price ceiling on gasoline, Jamie may pay lower gas prices at the pump but have to wait in line to buy the gas (due to first-come-first-served trying to ration the shortage). It is not clear if Jamie is better off paying a higher price and not waiting in line or paying a lower price and having to wait in line. The point, however, is that buyers don't necessarily prefer lower prices to higher prices unless everything else (quality, wait, service, and so on) stays the same.

2. Disagree. Both long-lasting shortages and long lines are caused by price ceilings. First the price ceiling is imposed, creating the shortage; then the rationing device first-come-first-served (FCFS) emerges because price isn't permitted to fully ration the good. There are shortages every day that don't cause long lines to form. Instead, buyers bid up price, output and price move to equilibrium, and there is no shortage.

3. Buyers might argue for price ceilings on the goods they buy—especially if they don't know that price ceilings have some effects they may not like (such as fewer exchanges, FCFS used as a rationing device, and so on.) Sellers might argue for price floors on the goods they sell—especially if they expect their profits to rise. Employees might argue for a wage floor on the labor services they sell—especially if they don't know that they may lose their jobs or have their hours cut back as a result.

CHAPTER 4

Chapter 4, page 100

1. The CPI is calculated as follows: (1) Define a market basket. (2) Determine how much it would cost to purchase the market basket in the current year and in the base year. (3) Divide the dollar cost of purchasing the market basket in the current year by the dollar cost of purchasing the market basket in the base year. (4) Multiply the quotient times 100. For a review of this process, see Exhibit 1.

2. Approximately 8.08 percent.

3. Annual (nominal) income has risen by 13.85 percent while prices have risen by 4.94 percent. We conclude that because (nominal) income has risen more than prices, real income has increased. Alternatively, you can look at it this way: Real income in year 1 is $31,337 and real income in year 2 is $33,996.

Chapter 4, page 105

1. The frictionally unemployed person has readily transferable skills and the structurally unemployed person does not.

2. It implies that the (actual, measured) unemployment rate in the economy is greater than the natural unemployment rate. For example, if the unemployment rate is 8 percent and the natural unemployment rate is 6 percent, the cyclical unemployment rate is 2 percent.

Chapter 4, page 109

1. Transfer payments aren't included in GDP because they do not represent payment to individuals for current production.

2. No. GDP doesn't account for all productive activity (e.g., it omits the production of nonmarket goods and services). Even if GDP is $0, it doesn't necessarily follow that there was no production in the country.

Chapter 4, page 111

1. In the expenditure approach, GDP is computed by finding the sum of consumption, investment, government purchases, and net exports. (Net exports is equal to exports minus imports.)

2. Yes. To illustrate, suppose consumption is $200, investment is $80, and government purchases are $70. The sum of these three spending components of GDP is $350. Now suppose exports are $0 but imports are $100, which means that net exports are -

$100. Since GDP $= C + I + G + (EX - IM)$, it follows that GDP is $250.

3. No. Each individual would have $40,000 worth of goods and services only if the entire GDP were equally distributed across the country. There is no indication that this is the case. The $40,000 (per capita GDP) says that the "average" person in the country has access to $40,000 worth of goods and services, but in reality there may not be any "average" person. Example: If Smith earns $10,000, and Jones earns $20,000, then the average person earns $15,000. But neither Smith nor Jones earns $15,000, so neither is average.

Chapter 4, page 115

1. We can't know for sure; we can say what might have caused the rise in GDP. It could be: (a) a rise in prices, no change in output, or (b) a rise in output, no change in prices, or (c) rises in both prices and output, or (d) a percentage increase in prices that is greater than the percentage decrease in output, or some other situation.

2. More output was produced in year 2 than in year 1.

3. Yes. Business cycles—ups and downs in Real GDP—don't prevent Real GDP from growing over time. Exhibit 5 shows Real GDP higher at the second peak than at the first peak even though there is a business cycle between the peaks.

CHAPTER 5

Chapter 5, page 130

1. Real balance effect: a rise (fall) in the price level causes purchasing power to fall (rise), which decreases (increases) a person's monetary wealth. As people become less (more) wealthy, the quantity demanded of Real GDP falls (rises).

2. If the dollar appreciates, it takes more foreign currency to buy a dollar and fewer dollars to buy foreign currency. This makes U.S. goods (denominated in dollars) more expensive for foreigners and foreign goods cheaper for Americans. In turn, foreigners buy fewer U.S. exports and Americans buy more foreign imports. As exports fall and imports rise, net exports fall. If net exports fall, total expenditures fall, *ceteris paribus*. As total expenditures fall, the *AD* curve shifts to the left.

3. If personal income taxes decline, disposable incomes rise. As disposable incomes rise, consumption rises. As consumption rises, total expenditures rise, *ceteris paribus*. As total expenditures rise, the *AD* curve shifts to the right.

4. If the budget deficit becomes smaller, the federal government will need to borrow less and the demand for loanable funds will shift leftward. As a result, the interest rate will fall, *ceteris paribus*.

Chapter 5, page 134

1. As wage rates decline, the cost per unit of production falls. In the short run (assuming that prices are constant), profit per unit rises. Higher profit causes producers to produce more units of their goods and services. In short, the *SRAS* curve shifts to the right.

2. Last year, ten workers produced 100 units of good X in one hour. This year, ten workers produced 120 units of good X in one hour.

Chapter 5, page 139

1. **a.** Real GDP rises, price level falls
    b. Real GDP falls, price level rises
    c. Real GDP rises, price level rises
    d. Real GDP falls, price level falls
    e. Real GDP rises, price level rises
    f. Real GDP falls, price level rises
2. To identify the change in short-run equilibrium, first identify the factor that has changed. Next determine whether the factor affects *AD, SRAS,* or neither. If it affects *AD* or *SRAS,* decide whether the factor causes *AD* or *SRAS* to rise or fall. Then note how the price level, Real GDP, and the unemployment rate are affected. For example, suppose there is an increase in the money supply. This affects *AD.* Specifically, it causes *AD* to increase and the *AD* curve to shift to the right. As a result, Real GDP and the price level rise and the unemployment rate falls in the short run.

Chapter 5, page 140

1. In long-run equilibrium, the economy is producing Natural Real GDP. In short-run equilibrium, the economy is not producing Natural Real GDP, although the quantity demanded of Real GDP equals the quantity supplied of Real GDP.
2. The diagram should show the price level in the economy at P_1 and Real GDP at Q_1, but the intersection of the *AD* curve and the *SRAS* curve at some point other than (P_1, Q_1). In addition, the *LRAS* curve should not be at Q_1 or at the intersection of the *AD* and *SRAS* curves.

CHAPTER 6

Chapter 6, page 149

1. Say's Law states that supply creates its own demand. In a barter economy, Jones supplies good *X* only so that he can use it to demand some other good, say good *Y.* The act of supplying is motivated by the desire to demand. Supply and demand are opposite sides of the same coin.
2. No, total spending will not decrease. For classical economists, an increase in saving (reflected in a decrease in consumption) will lower the interest rate and stimulate investment spending. So, one spending component goes down (consumption) and another spending component goes up (investment). Moreover, according to classical economists, the decrease in one spending component will be completely offset by an increase in another spending component so that overall spending does not change.
3. They are flexible; they move up and down in response to market conditions.

Chapter 6, page 154

1. A recessionary gap exists if the economy is producing a Real GDP level that is less than Natural Real GDP. An inflationary gap exists if the economy is producing a Real GDP level that is more than Natural Real GDP.
2. There is a surplus in the labor market when the economy is in a recessionary gap. There is a shortage in the labor market when the economy is in an inflationary gap.
3. The economy is somewhere above the institutional PPF and below the physical PPF.

Chapter 6, page 160

1. In a recessionary gap, the existing unemployment rate is greater than the natural unemployment rate. This implies that unemployment is relatively high. When old wage contracts expire, business firms negotiate contracts that pay workers lower wage rates. As a result, the *SRAS* curve shifts rightward. As this happens, the price level begins to fall. The economy moves down the *AD* curve—eventually moving to the point where it intersects the *LRAS* curve. At this point, the economy is in long-run equilibrium.
2. In an inflationary gap, the existing unemployment rate is less than the natural unemployment rate. This implies that unemployment is relatively low. When old wage contracts expire, business firms negotiate contracts that pay workers higher wage rates. As a result, the *SRAS* curve shifts leftward. As this happens, the price level begins to rise. The economy moves up the *AD* curve—eventually moving to the point where it intersects the *LRAS* curve. At this point, the economy is in long-run equilibrium.
3. Any changes in aggregate demand will affect—in the long run—only the price level and not the Real GDP level or the unemployment rate. Stated differently, changes in *AD* in an economy will have no long-run effect on the Real GDP that a country produces or on its unemployment rate; changes in *AD* will only change the price level in the long run.

CHAPTER 7

Chapter 7, page 170

1. They mean that an economy may not self-regulate at Natural Real GDP (Q_N). Instead, an economy can get stuck in a recessionary gap.
2. To say that the economy is self-regulating is the same as saying that prices and wages are flexible and adjust quickly. This is just two ways of describing the same thing.
3. The main reason is because Say's law may not hold in a money economy. This raises the question, Why *doesn't* Say's law hold in a money economy? Keynes argued that an increase in saving (which leads to a decline in demand) does not necessarily bring about an equal amount of additional investment (which would lead to an increase in demand) because neither saving nor investment is exclusively affected by changes in the interest rate. See Exhibit 1 for the way Keynes might have used numbers to explain his position.

Chapter 7, page 175

1. Autonomous consumption is one of the components of overall consumption. To illustrate, look at the consumption function: $C = C_0 + (MPC)(Y_d)$. The part of overall consumption (*C*) that is autonomous is C_0. This part of consumption does not depend on disposable income. The part of consumption that does depend on disposable income (that is, changes as disposable income changes) is the "$(MPC)(Y_d)$" part. For example, assume the *MPC* = 0.8. If Y_d rises by $1,000, then consumption goes up by $800.
2. $1/(1 - 0.70) = 1/0.30 = 3.33$

Chapter 7, page 179

1. Keynes believed that the economy may not always self-regulate itself at Natural Real GDP. In other words, households and businesses (the private sector of the economy) were not always capable of generating enough aggregate demand in the economy so that the economy equilibrated at Natural Real GDP.

2. The increase in autonomous spending will lead to a greater increase in total spending and to a shift rightward the *AD* curve. If the economy is operating in the horizontal section of the Keynesian *AS* curve, Real GDP will rise and there will be no change in prices.

3. Agree. The economist who believes the economy is inherently unstable sees a role for government. Government is supposed to stabilize the economy at Natural Real GDP. The economist who believes the economy is self-regulating (capable of moving itself to Natural Real GDP) sees little if any role for government in the economy because the economy is already doing the job government would supposedly do.

Chapter 7, page 185

1. When *TP* > *TE*, firms are producing and offering for sale more units of goods and services than households and government want to buy. As a result, business inventories rise above optimal levels. In reaction, firms cut back on their production of goods and services. This leads to a decline in Real GDP. Real GDP stops falling when *TP* = *TE*.

2. When *TE* > *TP*, households and businesses want to buy more than firms are producing and offering for sale. As a result, business inventories fall below optimal levels. In reaction, firms increase the production of goods and services. This leads in a rise in Real GDP. Real GDP stops rising when *TP* = *TE*.

CHAPTER 8

Chapter 8, page 196

1. Money evolved because individuals wanted to make trading easier (less time-consuming). It was this that motivated individuals to accept that good (in a barter economy) that had relatively greater acceptability than all other goods. In time, the effect snowballed and finally the good that (initially) had relatively greater acceptability emerged into a good that was widely accepted for purposes of exchange. At this point, the good became money.

2. No. M1 will fall, but M2 will not rise—it will remain constant. To illustrate, suppose M1 = $400 and M2 = $600. If people remove $100 from checkable deposits, M1 will decline to $300. For purposes of illustration, think of M2 as equal to M1 + money market accounts. The M1 component of M2 falls by $100, but the money market accounts component rises by $100, so there is no net effect on M2. In conclusion, M1 falls and M2 remains constant.

3. In a barter (moneyless) economy, a double coincidence of wants will not occur for every transaction. When it does not occur, the cost of the transaction increases because more time must be spent to complete the trade. In a money economy, money is acceptable for every transaction, so a double coincidence of wants is not necessary. All buyers offer money for what they want to buy and all sellers accept money for what they want to sell.

Chapter 8, page 203

1. $55 million
2. $6 billion
3. $0. Bank *A* was required to hold only $1 million in reserves, but held $1.2 million instead. Therefore, its loss of $200,000 in reserves does not cause it to be reserve deficient.

Chapter 8, page 208

1. **a.** Money supply falls
    b. Money supply rises
    c. Money supply falls

2. The federal funds rate is the interest rate one bank charges another bank for a loan. The discount rate is the interest rate the Fed charges a bank for a loan.

3. Reserves in bank *A* rise; reserves in the banking system remain the same (bank *B* lost the reserves that bank *A* borrowed).

4. Reserves in bank *A* rise; reserves in the banking system rise because there is no offset in reserves for any other bank.

CHAPTER 9

Chapter 9, page 220

1. If *M* times *V* increases, total expenditures increase. In other words, people spend more. For example, instead of spending $3 billion on goods and services, they spend $4 billion on goods and services. But if there is more spending (greater total expenditures), it follows that there must be greater total sales. *P* times *Q* represents this total dollar value of sales.

2. The equation of exchange is a truism: *MV* necessarily equals *PQ*. This is similar to saying that 2 + 2 necessarily equals 4. It cannot be otherwise. The simple quantity theory of money, which is built on the equation of exchange, can be tested against real-world events. That is, the simple quantity theory of money assumes that both velocity and Real GDP are constant and then, based on these assumptions, predicts that changes in the money supply will be strictly proportional to changes in the price level. This prediction can be measured against real-world data, so the simple quantity theory of money may offer insights into the way the economy works. The equation of exchange does not do this.

3. **a.** *AD* curve shifts rightward
    b. *AD* curve shifts leftward
    c. *AD* curve shifts rightward
    d. *AD* curve shifts leftward

Chapter 9, page 223

1. **a.** As velocity rises, the *AD* curve shifts to the right. In the short run, *P* rises and *Q* rises. In the long run, *Q* will return to its original level and *P* will be higher than it was in the short run.
    b. As velocity falls, the *AD* curve shifts to the left. In the short run, *P* falls and *Q* falls. In the long run, *Q* will return to its original level and *P* will be lower than it was in the short run.
    c. As the money supply rises, the *AD* curve shifts to the right. In the short run, *P* rises and *Q* rises. In the long run, *Q* will return to its original level and *P* will be higher than it was in the short run.
    d. As the money supply falls, the *AD* curve shifts to the left. In the short run, *P* falls and *Q* falls. In the long run, *Q* will return to its original level and *P* will be lower than it was in the short run.

2. Yes, a change in velocity can offset a change in the money supply (on aggregate demand). Suppose that the money supply rises and velocity falls. A rise in the money supply shifts the *AD* curve to the right and a fall in velocity shifts the *AD* curve to the left. If the strength of each change is the same, there is no change in *AD*.

Chapter 9, page 230

1. 3 percent.
2. Yes, it is possible. This would occur if the expectations effect immediately set in and outweighed the liquidity effect.
3. Certainly the Fed directly affects the supply of loanable funds and the interest rate through an open market operation. But it works as a catalyst to indirectly affect the loanable funds market and the interest rate via the changes in Real GDP, the price level, and the expected inflation rate. We can say this: The Fed directly affects the interest rate via the liquidity effect, and it indirectly affects the interest rate via the income, price-level, and expectations effects.

CHAPTER 10

Chapter 10, page 242

1. If there is no crowding out, expansionary fiscal policy is predicted to increase aggregate demand and, if the economy is in a recessionary gap, either reduce or eliminate the gap. However, if there is, say, complete crowding out, expansionary fiscal policy will not meet its objective. The following example illustrates complete crowding out: If government purchases rise by $100 million, private spending will decrease by $100 million so that there is no net effect on aggregate demand.
2. Individuals translate larger deficits today into higher taxes in the future. As a result, they begin to save more today in order to pay the higher taxes in the future. As to the credit or loanable funds market, a larger deficit increases the demand for loanable funds, and the higher anticipated taxes that result from the larger deficit increase the supply of loanable funds. In the end, it is possible that the increase in demand will be offset by the increase in supply so that interest rates do not change.
3. Suppose the economy is currently in a recessionary gap at time period 1. Expansionary fiscal policy is needed to remove the economy from its recessionary gap, but the fiscal policy lags (data lag, wait-and-see lag, and so on) may be so long that by the time the fiscal policy is implemented, the economy has moved itself out of the recessionary gap, making the expansionary fiscal policy not only unnecessary but potentially capable of moving the economy into an inflationary gap. Exhibit 5 describes the process.

Chapter 10, page 245

1. Let's suppose that a person's taxable income rises by $1,000 to $45,000 and that her taxes rise from $10,000 to $10,390 as a result. Her marginal tax rate—the percentage of her additional taxable income she pays in taxes—is 39 percent. Her average tax rate—the percentage of her (total) income she pays in taxes—is 23 percent.
2. Not necessarily. It depends on whether the percentage rise in tax rates is greater than or less than the percentage fall in the tax base. Here's a simple example: Suppose the average tax rate is 10 percent and the tax base is $100. Tax revenues then equal $10. If the tax rate rises to 12 percent (a 20 percent rise) and the tax base falls to $90 (a 10 percent fall), tax revenues rise to $10.80. In other words, if the tax rate rises by a greater percentage than the tax base falls, tax revenues rise. But, then, let's suppose that the tax base falls to $70 (a 30 percent fall) instead of to $90. Now tax revenues are $8.40. In other words, if the tax rate rises by a smaller percentage than the tax base falls, tax revenues fall.

Chapter 10, page 251

1. Because they believe that prices and wages are inflexible downward, but not upward. They believe it is more likely that natural forces will move an economy out of an inflationary gap than out of a recessionary gap.
2. Suppose the economy is regulating itself out of a recessionary gap, but this is not known to Fed officials. Thinking that the economy is stuck in a recessionary gap, the Fed increases the money supply. When the money supply is felt in the goods and services market, the *AD* curve intersects the *SRAS* curve (that has been moving rightward, unbeknownst to officials) at a point that represents an inflationary gap. In other words, the Fed has moved the economy from a recessionary gap to an inflationary gap instead of from a recessionary gap to long-run equilibrium at the Natural Real GDP level.
3. It makes it stronger, *ceteris paribus.* If the economy can't get itself out of a recessionary gap, then the case is stronger that the Fed should. This does not mean to imply that expansionary monetary policy will work ideally. There may still be problems with the correct implementation of the policy.

CHAPTER 11

Chapter 11, page 264

1. A given Phillips curve identifies different combinations of inflation and unemployment; for example, 4 percent inflation with 5 percent unemployment and 2 percent inflation with 7 percent unemployment. For these combinations of inflation and unemployment to be permanent, there must be only one (downward-sloping) Phillips curve that never changes.
2. Sometimes there is and sometimes there isn't. Look at Exhibit 3. Unemployment is higher and inflation is lower in 1964 than in 1965, so there is a tradeoff between these two years. But both unemployment and inflation are higher in 1980 than in 1979—that is, between these two years there is not a tradeoff between inflation and unemployment.
3. Workers are fooled into thinking that the inflation rate is lower than it is. In other words, they underestimate the inflation rate and, therefore, overestimate the purchasing power of their wages.

Chapter 11, page 270

1. No. PIP says that, under certain conditions, neither expansionary fiscal policy nor expansionary monetary policy will be able to increase Real GDP and lower the unemployment rate in the short run. The conditions are that the policy change is anticipated correctly, individuals form their expectations rationally, and wages and prices are flexible.
2. None. When there is an unanticipated increase in aggregate demand, the economy moves from point 1 to 2 (in Exhibit 6a) in the short run, and then to point 3. This occurs whether people are holding rational or adaptive expectations.
3. Yes. To illustrate, suppose the economy is initially in long-run equilibrium at point 1 in Exhibit 6a. As a result of an unanticipated rise in aggregate demand, the economy will move from point 1 to point 2, and then, to point 3. If there is a correctly anticipated rise in aggregate demand, the economy will simply move from point 1 to point 2, as in Exhibit 6b. If there is an incorrectly anticipated rise in aggregate demand—and furthermore, the anticipated rise overestimates the actual rise—then the economy will move from point 1 to point 2' in Exhibit 7. In con-

clusion, Real GDP may initially increase, may remain constant, or may decline depending on whether the rise in aggregate demand is unanticipated, anticipated correctly or anticipated incorrectly (overestimated in our example), respectively.

Chapter 11, page 274

1. Both. The relevant question is, Was the decline in the money supply caused by a change on the supply side of the economy? If the answer is no, then the decline in the money supply is consistent with a demand-induced business cycle. If the answer is yes, then it is consistent with a supply-induced (real) business cycle.

2. New Keynesians believe that prices and wages are somewhat inflexible; new classical economists believe that prices and wages are flexible.

CHAPTER 12

Chapter 12, page 289

1. An increase in GDP does not constitute economic growth because GDP can rise from one year to the next if prices rise and output stays constant. Economic growth refers to an increase either in Real GDP or in per capita Real GDP. The emphasis here is on "real" as opposed to nominal (or money) GDP.

2. If the *AD* curve remains constant, a shift rightward in the *LRAS* curve (which is indicative of economic growth) will bring about falling prices. If the *AD* curve shifts to the right by the same amount that the *LRAS* curve shifts rightward, prices will remain stable. Only if the *AD* curve shifts to the right by more than the *LRAS* curve shifts to the right could we witness economic growth and rising prices.

3. Labor is more productive when there are more capital goods. Furthermore, a rise in labor productivity promotes economic growth (an increase in labor productivity is defined as an increase in output relative to total labor hours). So, increases in capital investment can lead to increases in labor productivity and, therefore, to economic growth.

Chapter 12, page 291

1. If technology is endogenous, then we can promote advances in technology. Technology does not simply "fall out of the sky"; we can promote technology, not simply wait for it to "rain down" on us. This means we can actively promote economic growth (because advances in technology can promote economic growth).

2. In new growth theory, ideas are important to economic growth. Those countries that discover how to encourage and develop new and better ideas will likely grow faster than those that do not. New growth theory, in essence, places greater emphasis on the intangibles (such as ideas) in the growth process than on the tangibles (natural resources, capital, and so on).

CHAPTER 13

Chapter 13, page 297

1. For the United States, $1X = 1/6Y$ or $1Y = 6X$. For England, $1X = 2Y$ or $1Y = 1/2X$. Let's focus on the opportunity cost of $1X$ in each country. In the United States, $1X = 1/6Y$, and in Great Britain, $1X = 2Y$. Terms of trade that are between these two endpoints would be favorable for the two countries. For example, suppose we choose $1X = 1Y$. This is good for the United States because it

would prefer to give up $1X$ and get $1Y$ in trade than to give up $1X$ and only get $1/6Y$ (without trade). Similarly, Great Britain would prefer to give up $1Y$ and get $1X$ in trade than to give up $1Y$ and get only $1/2X$ (without trade). Any terms of trade between $1X = 1/6Y$ and $1X = 2Y$ will be favorable to the two countries.

2. Yes; this is what the theory of comparative advantage shows. Exhibit 1 shows that the United States could produce more of both food and clothing than Japan. Still, the United States benefits from specialization and trade, as shown in Exhibit 2. In column 5 of this exhibit, the United States can consume 10 more units of food by specializing and trading.

3. No. It is the desire to buy low and sell high (earn a profit) that pushes countries into producing and trading at a comparative advantage. Government officials do not collect cost data and then issue orders to firms in the country to produce X, Y, or Z. We have not drawn the PPFs in this chapter and identified the cost differences between countries to show what countries actually do in the real world. We described things technically to simply show how countries benefit from specialization and trade.

Chapter 13, page 301

1. Domestic producers benefit because producers' surplus rises; domestic consumers lose because consumers' surplus falls. Also, government benefits in that it receives the tariff revenue. Moreover, consumers lose more than producers and government gain, so that there is a net loss resulting from tariffs.

2. Consumers' surplus falls by more than producers' surplus rises.

3. With a tariff, the government receives tariff revenue. With a quota, it does not. In the latter case, the revenue that would have gone to government goes, instead, to the importers who get to satisfy the quota.

4. Infant or new domestic industries need to be protected from older, more established competitors until they are mature enough to compete on an equal basis. Tariffs and quotas provide these infant industries the time they need.

Chapter 13, page 305

1. As the demand for dollars increases, the supply of pesos increases. For example, suppose someone in Mexico wants to buy something produced in the United States. The American wants to be paid in dollars, but the Mexican doesn't have any dollars—she has pesos. So, she has to buy dollars with pesos; in other words, she has to supply pesos to buy dollars. Thus, as she demands more dollars, she will necessarily have to supply more pesos.

2. The dollar is said to have appreciated (against the peso) when it takes more pesos to buy a dollar and fewer dollars to buy a peso. For this to occur, either the demand for dollars must increase (which means the supply of pesos increases) or the supply of dollars must decrease (which means the demand for pesos decreases). To see this graphically, look at Exhibit 7b. The only way for the peso price per dollar to rise (on the vertical axis) is for either the demand curve for dollars to shift to the right or the supply curve of dollars to shift to the left. Each of these occurrences is mirrored in the market for pesos in part (a) of the exhibit.

3. *Ceteris paribus,* the dollar will depreciate relative to the franc. As incomes for Americans rise, the demand for Swiss goods rises. This increases the demand for francs and the supply of dollars on the foreign exchange market. In turn, this leads to a depreciated dollar and an appreciated franc.

4. The theory states that the exchange rate between any two currencies will adjust to reflect changes in the relative price levels of the two countries. For example, suppose the U.S. price level rises 5 percent and Mexico's price level remains constant. According to the PPP theory, the U.S. dollar will depreciate 5 percent relative to the Mexican peso.

Chapter 13, page 308

1. The terms *overvalued* and *undervalued* refer to the equilibrium exchange rate: the exchange rate at which the quantity demanded and quantity supplied of a currency are the same in the foreign exchange market. Let's suppose the equilibrium exchange rate is 0.10 USD = 1 MXP. This is the same as saying that 10 pesos = 1 dollar. If the exchange rate is fixed at 0.12 USD = 1 MXP (which is the same as 8.33 pesos = 1 dollar), the peso is overvalued and the dollar is undervalued. Specifically, a currency is overvalued if 1 unit of it fetches more of another currency than it would in equilibrium; a currency is undervalued if 1 unit of it fetches less of another currency than it would in equilibrium. In equilibrium, 1 peso would fetch 0.10 dollars and at the current exchange rate it fetches 0.12 dollars—so the peso is overvalued. In equilibrium, 1 dollar would fetch 10 pesos and at the current exchange rate it fetches only 8.33 pesos—so the dollar is undervalued.

2. An overvalued dollar means some other currency is undervalued—let's say it is the Japanese yen. An overvalued dollar makes U.S. goods more expensive for the Japanese, so they buy fewer U.S. goods. This reduces U.S. exports. On the other hand, an undervalued yen makes Japanese goods cheaper for Americans, so they buy more Japanese goods; the United States imports more.

Thus, an overvalued dollar reduces U.S. exports and raises U.S. imports.

3. a. Dollar is overvalued.
  b. Dollar is undervalued
  c. Dollar is undervalued.

4. When a country devalues its currency, it makes it cheaper for foreigners to buy its products.

Chapter 13, page 322

1. An optimal currency area is a geographic area in which exchange rates can be fixed or a common currency used without sacrificing any domestic economic goals.

2. As the demand for good Y falls, the unemployment rate in country 2 will rise. This increase in the unemployment rate is likely to be temporary, though. The increased demand for good X (produced by country 1) will increase the demand for country 1's currency, leading to an appreciation in country 1's currency and a depreciation in country 2's currency. Country 1's good (good X) will become more expensive for the residents of country 2, and they will buy less. Country 2's good (good Y) will become less expensive for the residents of country 1, and they will buy more. As a result of the additional purchases of good Y, country 2's unemployment rate will begin to decline.

3. Labor mobility is very important to determining whether or not an area is an optimal currency area. If there is little or no labor mobility, an area is not likely to be an optimal currency area. If there is labor mobility, an area is likely to be an optimal currency area.

Glossary

Absolute (Money) Price   The price of a good in money terms. (Chapter 3)

Absolute Real Economic Growth   An increase in Real GDP from one period to the next. (Chapter 12)

Abstract   The process (used in building a theory) of focusing on a limited number of variables to explain or predict an event. (Chapter 1)

Activists   Persons who argue that monetary and fiscal policies should be deliberately used to smooth out the business cycle. (Chapter 10)

Adaptive Expectations   Expectations that individuals form from past experience and modify slowly as the present and the future become the past (as time passes). (Chapter 11)

Aggregate Demand   The quantity demanded of all goods and services (Real GDP) at different price levels, ceteris paribus. (Chapter 5)

Aggregate Demand (AD) Curve   A curve that shows the quantity demanded of all goods and services (Real GDP) at different price levels, *ceteris paribus*. (Chapter 5)

Aggregate Supply   The quantity supplied of all goods and services (Real GDP) at different price levels, *ceteris paribus*. (Chapter 5)

Appreciation   An increase in the value of one currency relative to other currencies. (Chapter 5, 13)

Automatic Fiscal Policy   Changes in government expenditures and/or taxes that occur automatically without (additional) congressional action. (Chapter 10)

Autonomous Consumption   The part of consumption that is independent of disposable income. (Chapter 7)

Bad   Anything from which individuals receive disutility or dissatisfaction. (Chapter 1)

Barter   Exchanging goods and services for other goods and services without the use of money. (Chapter 8)

Base Year   The year chosen as a point of reference or basis of comparison for prices in other years; a benchmark year. (Chapter 4)

Board of Governors   The governing body of the Federal Reserve System. (Chapter 8)

Business Cycle   Recurrent swings (up and down) in Real GDP. (Chapter 4)

Capital   Produced goods that can be used as inputs for further production, such as factories, machinery, tools, computers, and buildings. (Chapter 1)

Cash Leakage   Occurs when funds are held as currency instead of being deposited into a checking account. (Chapter 8)

Ceteris Paribus   A Latin term meaning "all other things constant," or "nothing else changes." (Chapter 1)

Checkable Deposits   Deposits on which checks can be written. (Chapter 8)

Comparative Advantage   The situation where an individual or country can produce a good at lower opportunity cost than another individual or country can. (Chapter 2, 13)

Complements   Two goods that are used jointly in consumption. If two goods are complements, the demand for one rises as the price of the other falls (or the demand for one falls as the price of the other rises). (Chapter 3)

Complete Crowding Out   A decrease in one or more components of private spending completely offsets the increase in government spending. (Chapter 10)

Consumer Price Index (CPI)   A widely cited index number for the price level; the weighted average of prices of a specific set of goods and services purchased by a typical household. (Chapter 4)

Consumers' Surplus (CS)   The difference between the maximum price a buyer is willing and able to pay for a good or service and the price actually paid. CS = Maximum buying price − Price paid. (Chapter 3)

Consumption   The sum of spending on durable goods, nondurable goods, and services. (Chapter 4)

Consumption Function   The relationship between consumption and disposable income. In the consumption function used here, consumption is directly related to disposable income and is positive even at zero disposable income: $C = C_0 + (MPC)(Y_d)$. (Chapter 7)

Contractionary Fiscal Policy   Decreases in government expenditures and/or increases in taxes to achieve particular economic goals. (Chapter 10)

Contractionary Monetary Policy   The Fed decreases the money supply. (Chapter 10)

Crowding Out   The decrease in private expenditures that occurs as a consequence of increased government spending or the financing needs of a budget deficit. (Chapter 10)

Currency   Coins and paper money. (Chapter 8)

Cyclical Unemployment Rate   The difference between the unemployment rate and the natural unemployment rate. (Chapter 4)

Decisions at the Margin   Decision making characterized by weighing the additional (marginal) benefits of a change against the additional (marginal) costs of a change with respect to current conditions. (Chapter 1)

Demand   The willingness and ability of buyers to purchase different quantities of a good at different prices during a specific time period. (Chapter 3)

Demand Schedule   The numerical tabulation of the quantity demanded of a good at different prices. A demand schedule is the numerical representation of the law of demand. (Chapter 3)

Depreciation   A decrease in the value of one currency relative to other currencies. (Chapter 5, 13)

Devaluation   A government act that changes the exchange rate by lowering the official price of a currency. (Chapter 13)

Discount Rate   The interest rate the Fed charges depository institutions that borrow reserves from it. (Chapter 8)

Discretionary Fiscal Policy   Deliberate changes of government expenditures and/or taxes to achieve particular economic goals. (Chapter 10)

Disequilibrium   A state of either surplus or shortage in a market. (Chapter 3)

Disequilibrium Price   A price other than equilibrium price. A price at which quantity demanded does not equal quantity supplied. (Chapter 3)

Disutility   The dissatisfaction one receives from a bad. (Chapter 1)

Double Coincidence of Wants   In a barter economy, a requirement that must be met before a trade can be made. It specifies that a trader must find another trader who is willing to trade what the first trader wants and at the same time wants what the first trader has. (Chapter 8)

Double Counting   Counting a good more than once when computing GDP. (Chapter 4)

(Downward-sloping) Demand Curve The graphical representation of the law of demand. (Chapter 3)

Dumping The sale of goods abroad at a price below their cost and below the price charged in the domestic market. (Chapter 13)

Economic Growth Increases in Real GDP. (Chapter 4)

Economics The science of scarcity; the science of how individuals and societies deal with the fact that wants are greater than the limited resources available to satisfy those wants. (Chapter 1)

Efficiency Exists when marginal benefits equal marginal costs. (Chapter 1)

Efficiency Wage Models These models hold that it is sometimes in the best interest of business firms to pay their employees higher-than-equilibrium wage rates. (Chapter 7)

Employment Rate The percentage of the civilian noninstitutional population that is employed: Employment rate = Number of employed persons/Civilian noninstitutional population. (Chapter 4)

Entrepreneurship The particular talent that some people have for organizing the resources of land, labor, and capital to produce goods, seek new business opportunities, and develop new ways of doing things. (Chapter 1)

Equation of Exchange An identity stating that the money supply times velocity must be equal to the price level times Real GDP. (Chapter 9)

Equilibrium Equilibrium means "at rest"; it is descriptive of a natural resting place. Equilibrium in a market is the price-quantity combination from which there is no tendency for buyers or sellers to move away. Graphically, equilibrium is the intersection point of the supply and demand curves. (Chapter 1, 3)

Equilibrium Price (Market-Clearing Price) The price at which quantity demanded of the good equals quantity supplied. (Chapter 3)

Equilibrium Quantity The quantity that corresponds to equilibrium price. The quantity at which the amount of the good that buyers are willing and able to buy equals the amount that sellers are willing and able to sell, and both equal the amount actually bought and sold. (Chapter 3)

Ex Ante Phrase that means "before," as in before a trade. (Chapter 2)

Ex Post Phrase that means "after," as in after a trade. (Chapter 2)

Excess Reserves Any reserves held beyond the required amount. The difference between (total) reserves and required reserves. (Chapter 8)

Exchange Rate The price of one currency in terms of another currency. (Chapter 5, 13)

Expansionary Fiscal Policy Increases in government expenditures and/or decreases in taxes to achieve particular economic goals. (Chapter 10)

Expansionary Monetary Policy The Fed increases the money supply. (Chapter 10)

Expectations Effect The change in the interest rate due to a change in the expected inflation rate. (Chapter 9)

Exports Total foreign spending on domestic (U.S.) goods. (Chapter 4)

Fallacy of Composition The erroneous view that what is good or true for the individual is necessarily good or true for the group. (Chapter 1)

Federal Funds Market A market where banks lend reserves to one another, usually for short periods. (Chapter 8)

Federal Funds Rate The interest rate in the federal funds market; the interest rate banks charge one another to borrow reserves. (Chapter 8)

Federal Open Market Committee (FOMC) The 12-member policymaking group within the Fed. The committee has the authority to conduct open market operations. (Chapter 8)

Federal Reserve Notes Paper money issued by the Fed. (Chapter 8)

Federal Reserve System (the Fed) The central bank of the United States. (Chapter 8)

Final Good A good in the hands of its final user. (Chapter 4)

Fine-tuning The (usually frequent) use of monetary and fiscal policies to counteract even small undesirable movements in economic activity. (Chapter 10)

Fiscal Policy Changes in government expenditures and/or taxes to achieve particular economic goals, such as low unemployment, stable prices, and economic growth. (Chapter 10)

Fixed Exchange Rate System The system where a nation's currency is set at a fixed rate relative to all other currencies, and central banks intervene in the foreign exchange market to maintain the fixed rate. (Chapter 13)

Fixed Investment Business purchases of capital goods, such as machinery and factories, and purchases of new residential housing. (Chapter 4)

Flexible Exchange Rate System The system whereby exchange rates are determined by the forces of supply and demand for a currency. (Chapter 13)

Foreign Exchange Market The market in which currencies of different countries are exchanged. (Chapter 13)

Fractional Reserve Banking A banking arrangement that allows banks to hold reserves equal to only a fraction of their deposit liabilities. (Chapter 8)

Frictional Unemployment Unemployment due to the natural "frictions" of the economy, which is caused by changing market conditions and is represented by qualified individuals with transferable skills who change jobs. (Chapter 4)

Friedman Natural Rate Theory The idea that in the long run, unemployment is at its natural rate. Within the Phillips curve framework, the natural rate theory specifies that there is a long-run Phillips curve, which is vertical at the natural rate of unemployment. (Chapter 11)

Full Employment The condition that exists when the unemployment rate is equal to the natural unemployment rate. (Chapter 4)

Good Anything from which individuals receive utility or satisfaction. (Chapter 1)

Government Purchases Federal, state, and local government purchases of goods and services and gross investment in highways, bridges, and so on. (Chapter 4)

Government Transfer Payments Payments to persons that are not made in return for goods and services currently supplied. (Chapter 4)

Gross Domestic Product (GDP) The total market value of all final goods and services produced annually within a country's borders. (Chapter 4)

Imports Total domestic (U.S.) spending on foreign goods. (Chapter 4)

Income Effect The change in the interest rate due to a change in Real GDP. (Chapter 9)

Incomplete Crowding Out The decrease in one or more components of private spending only partially offsets the increase in government spending. (Chapter 10)

Industrial Policy A deliberate policy by which government "waters the green spots," or aids those industries that are most likely to be successful in the world marketplace. (Chapter 12)

Inferior Good A good the demand for which falls (rises) as income rises (falls). (Chapter 3)

Inflation An increase in the price level. (Chapter 4)

Inflationary Gap   The condition where the Real GDP the economy is producing is greater than the Natural Real GDP and the unemployment rate is less than the natural unemployment rate. (Chapter 6)

Intermediate Good   A good that is an input in the production of a final good. (Chapter 4)

Inventory Investment   Changes in the stock of unsold goods. (Chapter 4)

Investment   The sum of all purchases of newly produced capital goods, changes in business inventories, and purchases of new residential housing. (Chapter 4)

Labor   The physical and mental talents people contribute to the production process. (Chapter 1)

Labor Force Participation Rate   The percentage of the civilian noninstitutional population that is in the civilian labor force. Labor force participation rate = Civilian labor force/Civilian noninstitutional population. (Chapter 4)

Laffer Curve   The curve, named after Arthur Laffer, that shows the relationship between tax rates and tax revenues. According to the Laffer curve, as tax rates rise from zero, tax revenues rise, reach a maximum at some point, and then fall with further increases in tax rates. (Chapter 10)

Laissez-faire   A public policy of not interfering with market activities in the economy. (Chapter 6)

Land   All natural resources, such as minerals, forests, water, and unimproved land. (Chapter 1)

Law of Demand   As the price of a good rises, the quantity demanded of the good falls, and as the price of a good falls, the quantity demanded of the good rises, *ceteris paribus*. (Chapter 3)

Law of Diminishing Marginal Utility   For a given time period, the marginal (additional) utility or satisfaction gained by consuming equal successive units of a good will decline as the amount consumed increases. (Chapter 3)

Law of Increasing Opportunity Costs   As more of a good is produced, the opportunity costs of producing that good increase. (Chapter 2)

Law of Supply   As the price of a good rises, the quantity supplied of the good rises, and as the price of a good falls, the quantity supplied of the good falls, *ceteris paribus*. (Chapter 3)

Liquidity Effect   The change in the interest rate due to a change in the supply of loanable funds. (Chapter 9)

Long-Run Aggregate Supply (LRAS) Curve
The *LRAS* curve is a vertical line at the level of Natural Real GDP. It represents the output the economy produces when wages have adjusted to their (final) equilibrium levels and workers do not have any relevant misperceptions. (Chapter 5)

Long-Run Equilibrium   The condition that exists in the economy when wages have adjusted to their (final) equilibrium levels and workers do not have any relevant misperceptions. Graphically, long-run equilibrium occurs at the intersection of the *AD* and *LRAS* curves. (Chapter 5)

M1   Includes currency held outside banks + checkable deposits + traveler's checks. (Chapter 8)

M2   Includes M1 + savings deposits (including money market deposit accounts) + small-denomination time deposits + money market mutual funds (noninstitutional). (Chapter 8)

Macroeconomics   The branch of economics that deals with human behavior and choices as they relate to highly aggregate markets (such as the goods and services market) or the entire economy. (Chapter 1)

Marginal (Income) Tax Rate   The change in a person's tax payment divided by the change in the person's taxable income: ΔTax payment/ΔTaxable income. (Chapter 10)

Marginal Benefits   Additional benefits. The benefits connected to consuming an additional unit of a good or undertaking one more unit of an activity. (Chapter 1)

Marginal Costs   Additional costs. The costs connected to consuming an additional unit of a good or undertaking one more unit of an activity. (Chapter 1)

Marginal Propensity to Consume (MPC)
The ratio of the change in consumption to the change in disposable income: $MPC = \Delta C/\Delta Y_d$. (Chapter 7)

Marginal Propensity to Save (MPS)   The ratio of the change in saving to the change in disposable income: $MPS = \Delta S/\Delta Y_d$. (Chapter 7)

Medium of Exchange   Anything that is generally acceptable in exchange for goods and services. A function of money. (Chapter 8)

Merchandise Trade Balance   The difference between the value of merchandise exports and the value of merchandise imports. (Chapter 13)

Merchandise Trade Deficit   The situation where the value of merchandise exports is less than the value of merchandise imports. (Chapter 13)

Microeconomics   The branch of economics that deals with human behavior and choices as they relate to relatively small units—an individual, a firm, an industry, a single market. (Chapter 1)

Monetary Policy   Changes in the money supply, or in the rate of change of the money supply, to achieve particular macroeconomic goals. (Chapter 10)

Monetary Wealth   The value of a person's monetary assets. Wealth, as distinguished from

monetary wealth, refers to the value of all assets owned, both monetary and nonmonetary. In short, a person's wealth equals his or her monetary wealth (such as $1,000 cash) plus nonmonetary wealth (a car or a house). (Chapter 5)

Money   Any good that is widely accepted for purposes of exchange and in the repayment of debt. (Chapter 8)

Money Market Deposit Account   An interest-earning account at a bank or thrift institution. Usually a minimum balance is required for an MMDA. Most MMDAs offer limited check-writing privileges. (Chapter 8)

Money Market Mutual Fund   An interest-earning account at a mutual fund company. Usually a minimum balance is required for an MMMF account. Most MMMF accounts offer limited check-writing privileges. Only noninstitutional MMMFs are part of M2. (Chapter 8)

Multiplier   The number that is multiplied by the change in autonomous spending to obtain the overall change in total spending. The multiplier (*m*) is equal to $1/(1 - MPC)$. If the economy is operating below Natural Real GDP, then the multiplier turns out to be the number that is multiplied by the change in autonomous spending to obtain the change in Real GDP. (Chapter 7)

Natural Real GDP   The Real GDP that is produced at the natural unemployment rate. The Real GDP that is produced when the economy is in long-run equilibrium. (Chapter 5)

Natural Unemployment   Unemployment caused by frictional and structural factors in the economy. Natural unemployment rate = Frictional unemployment rate + Structural unemployment rate. (Chapter 4)

Net Exports   Exports minus imports. (Chapter 4)

Neutral Good   A good the demand for which does not change as income rises or falls. new residential housing. (Chapter 3)

Nominal Income   The current-dollar amount of a person's income. (Chapter 4)

Nominal Interest Rate   The interest rate actually charged (or paid) in the market; the market interest rate. The nominal interest rate = Real interest rate + Expected inflation rate. (Chapter 9)

Nonactivists   Persons who argue against the deliberate use of discretionary fiscal and monetary policies. They believe in a permanent, stable, rule-oriented monetary and fiscal framework. (Chapter 10)

Normal Good   A good the demand for which rises (falls) as income rises (falls). (Chapter 3)

Normative Economics   The study of "what should be" in economic matters. (Chapter 1)

Open Market Operations   The buying and selling of government securities by the Fed. (Chapter 8)

Open Market Purchase   The buying of government securities by the Fed. (Chapter 8)

Open Market Sale   The selling of government securities by the Fed. (Chapter 8)

Opportunity Cost   The most highly valued opportunity or alternative forfeited when a choice is made. (Chapter 1)

Overvaluation   A currency is overvalued if its price in terms of other currencies is above the equilibrium price. (Chapter 13)

Own Price   The price of a good. For example, if the price of oranges is $1, this is (its) own price. (Chapter 3)

Per Capita Real Economic Growth   An increase from one period to the next in per capita Real GDP, which is Real GDP divided by population. (Chapter 12)

Phillips Curve   A curve that originally showed the relationship between wage inflation and unemployment. Now it more often shows the relationship between price inflation and unemployment. (Chapter 11)

Policy Ineffectiveness Proposition (PIP)   If (1) a policy change is correctly anticipated, (2) individuals form their expectations rationally, and (3) wages and prices are flexible, then neither fiscal policy nor monetary policy is effective at meeting macroeconomic goals. (Chapter 11)

Positive Economics   The study of "what is" in economic matters. (Chapter 1)

Price Ceiling   A government-mandated maximum price above which legal trades cannot be made. (Chapter 3)

Price Floor   A government-mandated minimum price below which legal trades cannot be made. (Chapter 3)

Price Index   A measure of the price level. (Chapter 4)

Price Level   A weighted average of the prices of all good and services. (Chapter 4)

Price-Level Effect   The change in the interest rate due to a change in the price level. (Chapter 9)

Producers' (Sellers') Surplus (PS)   The difference between the price sellers receive for a good and the minimum or lowest price for which they would have sold the good. PS = Price received − Minimum selling price. (Chapter 3)

Production Possibilities Frontier (PPF)   Represents the possible combinations of the two goods that can be produced in a certain period of time, under the conditions of a given state of technology and fully employed resources. (Chapter 2)

(Production) Subsidy   A monetary payment by government to a producer of a good or service. (Chapter 3)

Productive Efficiency   The condition where the maximum output is produced with given resources and technology. (Chapter 2)

Productive Inefficiency   The condition where less than the maximum output is produced with given resources and technology. Productive inefficiency implies that more of one good can be produced without any less of another good being produced. (Chapter 2)

Purchasing Power   The quantity of goods and services that can be purchased with a unit of money. Purchasing power and the price level are inversely related: As the price level goes up (down), purchasing power goes down (up). (Chapter 5)

Purchasing Power Parity (PPP) Theory   States that exchange rates between any two currencies will adjust to reflect changes in the relative price levels of the two countries. (Chapter 13)

Quota   A legal limit on the amount of a good that may be imported. (Chapter 13)

Rational Expectations   Expectations that individuals form based on past experience and also on their predictions about the effects of present and future policy actions and events. (Chapter 11)

Rationing Device   A means for deciding who gets what of available resources and goods. (Chapter 1)

Real Balance Effect   The change in the purchasing power of dollar-denominated assets that results from a change in the price level. (Chapter 5)

Real GDP   The value of the entire output produced annually within a country's borders, adjusted for price changes. (Chapter 4)

Real Income   Nominal income adjusted for price changes. (Chapter 4)

Real Interest Rate   The nominal interest rate minus the expected inflation rate. When the expected inflation rate is zero, the real interest rate equals the nominal interest rate. (Chapter 9)

Recessionary Gap   The condition where the Real GDP the economy is producing is less than the Natural Real GDP and the unemployment rate is greater than the natural unemployment rate. (Chapter 6)

Relative Price   The price of a good in terms of another good. (Chapter 3)

Required Reserve Ratio (r)   A percentage of each dollar deposited that must be held on reserve (at the Fed or in the bank's vault). (Chapter 8)

Required Reserves   The minimum amount of reserves a bank must hold against its checkable deposits as mandated by the Fed. (Chapter 8)

Reserve Requirement   The rule that specifies the amount of reserves a bank must hold to back up deposits. (Chapter 8)

Reserves   The sum of bank deposits at the Fed and vault cash. (Chapter 8)

Revaluation   A government act that changes the exchange rate by raising the official price of a currency. (Chapter 13)

Savings Deposit   An interest-earning account at a commercial bank or thrift institution. Normally, checks cannot be written on savings deposits and the funds in a savings deposit can be withdrawn (at any time) without a penalty payment. (Chapter 8)

Say's Law   Supply creates its own demand. Production creates demand sufficient to purchase all goods and services produced. (Chapter 6)

Scarcity   The condition in which our wants are greater than the limited resources available to satisfy those wants. (Chapter 1)

Shortage (Excess Demand)   A condition in which quantity demanded is greater than quantity supplied. Shortages occur only at prices below equilibrium price. (Chapter 3)

Short-Run Aggregate Supply (SRAS) Curve   A curve that shows the quantity supplied of all goods and services (Real GDP) at different price levels, *ceteris paribus*. (Chapter 5)

Short-Run Equilibrium   The condition that exists in the economy when the quantity demanded of Real GDP equals the (short-run) quantity supplied of Real GDP. This condition is met where the aggregate demand curve intersects the short-run aggregate supply curve. (Chapter 5)

Simple Deposit Multiplier   The reciprocal of the required reserve ratio, $1/r$. (Chapter 8)

Simple Quantity Theory of Money   The theory that assumes that velocity (V) and Real GDP (Q) are constant and predicts that changes in the money supply (M) lead to strictly proportional changes in the price level (P). (Chapter 9)

Stagflation   The simultaneous occurrence of high rates of inflation and unemployment. (Chapter 11)

Store of Value   The ability of an item to hold value over time. A function of money. (Chapter 8)

Structural Unemployment   Unemployment due to structural changes in the economy that eliminate some jobs and create others for which the unemployed are unqualified. (Chapter 4)

Substitutes   Two goods that satisfy similar needs or desires. If two goods are substitutes, the demand for one rises as the price of the other rises (or the demand for one falls as the price of the other falls). (Chapter 3)

Supply   The willingness and ability of sellers to produce and offer to sell different quantities of a good at different prices during a specific time period. (Chapter 3)

Supply Schedule   The numerical tabulation of the quantity supplied of a good at different prices. A supply schedule is the numerical representation of the law of supply. (Chapter 3)

Surplus (Excess Supply)   A condition in which quantity supplied is greater than quantity demanded. Surpluses occur only at prices above equililbrium price. (Chapter 3)

T-Account   A simplified balance sheet that shows the changes in a bank's assets and liabilities. (Chapter 8)

Tariff   A tax on imports. (Chapter 13)

Tax Base   When referring to income taxes, the total amount of taxable income. Tax revenue = Tax base × (average) Tax rate. (Chapter 10)

Technology   The body of skills and knowledge concerning the use of resources in production. An advance in technology commonly refers to the ability to produce more output with a fixed amount of resources or the ability to produce the same output with fewer resources. (Chapter 2)

Terms of Trade   How much of one thing is given up for how much of something else. (Chapter 2)

Theory   An abstract representation of the real world designed with the intent to better understand that world. (Chapter 1)

Tie-in Sale   A sale whereby one good can be purchased only if another good is also purchased. (Chapter 3)

Time Deposit   An interest-earning deposit with a specified maturity date. Time deposits are subject to penalties for early withdrawal. Small-denomination time deposits are deposits of less than $100,000. (Chapter 8)

Total Surplus *(TS)*   The sum of consumers' surplus and producers' surplus. $TS = CS + PS$. (Chapter 3)

Trade (Exchange)   The process of giving up one thing for something else. (Chapter 2)

Transaction Costs   The costs associated with the time and effort needed to search out, negotiate, and consummate an exchange. (Chapter 2)

Transfer Payment   A payment to a person that is not made in return for goods and services currently supplied. (Chapter 4)

Undervaluation   A currency is undervalued if its price in terms of other currencies is below the equilibrium price. (Chapter 13)

Unemployment Rate   The percentage of the civilian force that is unemployed: Unemployment rate = Number of unemployed persons/Civilian labor force. (Chapter 4)

Unit of Account   A common measure in which relative values are expressed. A function of money. (Chapter 8)

(Upward-sloping) Supply Curve   The graphical representation of the law of supply. (Chapter 3)

Utility   The satisfaction one receives from a good. (Chapter 1)

Value Added   The dollar value contributed to a final good at each stage of production. (Chapter 4)

Velocity   The average number of times a dollar is spent to buy final goods and services in a year. (Chapter 9)

Wealth   The value of all assets owned, both monetary and nonmonetary. (Chapter 5)

Index

Page numbers in italics indicate exhibits.